Computer Graphics 1987

Proceedings of CG International '87

Edited by Tosiyasu L. Kunii

With 310 Figures
67 of them in Color

Springer-Verlag
Tokyo Berlin Heidelberg New York
London Paris

Dr. Tosiyasu L. Kunii
Professor and Director
Kunii Laboratory of Computer Science
Department of Information Science
Faculty of Science
The University of Tokyo

Cover Design: Textile pattern.
© Kunii Laboratory of Computer Science, The University of Tokyo and
Software Research Center, Ricoh Co., Ltd.

ISBN-13:987-4-431-68059-8   e-ISBN-13:987-4-431-68057-4
DOI: 10.1007/987-4-431-68057-4

Preface

This volume presents the proceedings of the 5th International Conference on Computer Graphics in Japan. This series of conferences has attracted increasing numbers of high-quality research papers on computer graphics from all countries. Following the decision to hold future conferences in different parts of the world, the new name "CG International" has been adopted.

Recent developments in computer graphics have largely involved the following: Integration of computer graphics and image analysis through computer data structure; integration of CAD/CAM as computer-integrated manufacturing (CIM) through the design and simulation of manufacturing processes using computer graphics; progress in basic research on the modeling of complex and mathematical graphic objects, such as computational geometry, graphic databases, hierarchical windows, and texture; use of computer graphics as an improved human interface to present information visually and multidimensionally; and advancement of industrial technology and computer art based on developments in the areas listed above. These trends are strongly reflected in the contents of the present volume either as papers dealing with one particular aspect of research or as multifaceted studies involving several different areas. The proceedings comprise thirty selected, previously unpublished original papers presented in nine chapters.

The first chapter aims to present a survey of recent developments in four contributions invited by the editor. The remaining chapters consist of twenty five papers submitted to CG International '87 that were selected following the recommendations of expert reviewers in the respective fields.

In computer graphics, various methods have now been devised to produce static images which are astonishingly life like. Other areas of recent research concern the real-time production of a series of high-quality images. To achieve this, significant improvement of algorithms is taking place this work is presented in Chap. 2.

Chapter 3 deals with advanced rendering techniques. These techniques integrate conventional methods and concepts from other fields, e.g., image processing and projective geometry.

The speeding-up of graphics operations ultimately leads to the hardware implementation of algorithms. New approaches to three practical applications in this area are presented in Chap. 4.

Computational geometry, as dealt with in Chap. 5, constitutes basic computer graphics and its applications, notably CAD/CAM.

Ray tracing is the best rendering technique known today. Chapter 6 explores the full capability of this technique both theoretically and in terms of algorithms. In addition to a representation of reality, various visual effects are often required; Chap. 7 introduces the reader to the whole new world of image-generation methods.

The use of computer graphics as a human interface is discussed in Chap. 8 from three aspects — graphics interfaces, languages, and databases. With respect to the modeling of complex graphic objects, a hierarchical approach is commonly taken; this facilitates both a high space/time efficiency and human recognition. The final chapter presents two novel hierarchical approaches applicable to computer graphics.

Among the papers are ten from the USA, seven from Japan, six from Europe, and three from Canada. The contents of this volume should apprise the reader of the developments that are currently taking place and the state of the art in computer graphics.

Tosiyasu L. Kunii

Table of Contents

List of Contributors

The page numbers given below refer to the page on which contribution begins.

Binay K. Bhattacharya   89
Tim Brown   315
Jichun Bu   181
M. Burgess   45
Sudeb Chattopadhyay   335
Yong C. Chen   347, 443
Hiroaki Chiyokura   249
Ed F. Deprettere   181
Bernard Dimsdale   25
Rae A. Earnshaw   11
L. Forest   45
Akira Fujimoto   335
Issei Fujishiro   461
Koichi Harada   367
Roger D. Hersch   207
Sener Ilgen   145
Masa Inakage   381
Alfred Inselberg   25
Kazufumi Kaneda   367
Marja-Riitta Koivunen   393
Hideko S. Kunii   427
Tosiyasu L. Kunii   461
Geoff Levner   285
Hong Lip Lim   75
Richard J. Lobb   107
Mamoru Maekawa   303
Nadia Magnenat-Thalmann   45
Ranjit Makkuni   407
Xiaoyang Mao   461
Daniele Marini   285
Martti Mäntylä   393
Craig McPheeters   129
Syunsuke Minami   427
Catherine M. Murphy   443
Naomasa Nakajima   427
Eihachiro Nakamae   367

Tsukasa Noma   461
Masataka Ohta   303
Son Pham   221
Steven P. Punte   159
Hitoshi Saji   427
Akinao G. Sato   367
Isaac D. Scherson   145, 159
Paolo Tassinari   285
Daniel Thalmann   45
Godfried T. Toussaint   89
Alistair Ward   315
Tony C. Woo   269
Charles D. Woodward   197
Michael J. Wozny   3
Brian Wyvill   129
Geoff Wyvill   129, 315
Mineo Yasuda   367
Qiuming Zhu   59

Chapter 1

Current Status of
Computer Graphics

Beyond Computer Graphics and CAD/CAM

Michael J. Wozny

ABSTRACT

Computer graphics and geometry research in the 1960's and 1970's paved the way for the rapid commercial development of CAD/CAM systems in the 1970's and early 1980's. For the last few years the commercial field has been in a steady state mode, involving primarily incremental improvements. Current signs indicate that the field is poised to move again. However, the ultimate direction is unclear.

This paper will review various NSF sponsored research activities in the broad area of mechanical CAD/CAM, in an effort to focus on possible future directions of the field.

Keywords: computer graphics, geometry, CAD/CAM, design, computer integrated electronics

1.0 INTRODUCTION

Computer graphics and computer geometry research in the 1960's and 1970's paved the way for the rapid commercial market penetration of mechanical CAD/CAM systems in the 1970's and early 1980's. However, there has been no significant increase in market penetration in the past few years. Recent research results indicate that the field is poised to move again.

Commercial CAD/CAM vendors lost markets for a variety of reasons. Perhaps the most notable is that existing systems could not meet the evolving automation needs, such as providing for downstream manufacturing requirements. Other reasons include the emergence of new computing platforms such as the personal computer, and the realization that better tools were needed to aid the decisions being made early in the design cycle which committed the majority of downstream manufacturing funds.

The past growth of this field was based on incremental improvements in technology and not necessarily on fundamental principles. Although this will continue, significant future progress will require a more fundamental understanding of the field.

My division at the National Science Foundation is committed to supporting university research needed to create this fundamental scientific base for both design and manufacturing.

This paper will characterize the emerging technical trends in computer graphics and CAD/CAM, and examine several promising research areas which are adding to the scientific base of this field.

2.0   COMPUTING PLATFORMS

Most of the commercial growth in CAD/CAM over the past few years is due to the rapid change in the computing platforms. This has resulted in more cost effective systems, but not necessarily increased technical functionality. Although the market has continued to grow, one can characterize this period as a time for consolidation and standardization of both hardware and software.

Five years ago the IBM PC had just been introduced but was not considered seriously as a platform for CAD/CAM. The workstation concept was just emerging.

Today the PC is the platform of choice for the low-end CAD/CAM market while the workstation is rapidly becoming the dominant platform for CAD/CAM. Almost all major CAD/CAM packages now run on workstations. It is interesting to note that the hardware offered by every major turnkey vendor of five years ago is now obsolete.

What will happen in the next five years? First of all, we will witness the full emergence of the standalone workstations. Workstations are evolving so rapidly that their current life is about 18 months. Typical workstation performance 18 months ago was about 1 to 2 MIPS. Today this level is 4 to 5 MIPS, and conservative projections for the next 18 months is about 10 MIPS. This spectacular growth is due, in part, to the research results in electronic CAD in the late 1970's and early 1980's.

Today, VLSI CAD/CAM technology is mature and cost-effective, and chips are being produced to handle many specialized functions in high-end graphics workstations. Typical examples are the geometry engine in the Silicon Graphics systems, and the superb antialiasing capabilities on the recently introduced Evans and Sutherland PS390 system. It is clear that the poor line quality of raster displays is no longer an issue. The new chips for shading and rendering being demonstrated in the laboratory at places like Adage and Raster Technologies, for example, will add dynamics to the high quality color shaded images in the near future.

In addition to graphics, new VLSI chips are also penetrating engineering applications. The rapidly increasing capability of floating point chips is providing, for example, cost-effective specialized engineering analysis processors such as the new Trancept Inc. board. There are also laboratory attempts to develop CSG solid modeler chips. These next generation machines will also exhibit

parallel and other new architectures, yielding new levels of performance and functionality. One precursor of this class of machines is the multi-transputer ray tracing engine.

RISC architectures, currently exploited by IBM and HP, are paving the way for very powerful future workstations in the 20 MIP range by companies like Dana, and Stellar. New architectures for symbolic computation are also expected.

Engineering workstations will solidify distributed networked environments, thus establishing a different relationship to the host computer. However, the host will not disappear, but will become even more important as the needs for storage and organization, as well as release of engineering data, increase. Supercomputers will become more important as the needs for storage and organization, as well as release of engineering data, increase. Supercomputers will become more important in engineering analysis and simulation as described later.

Software issues will predominate in the next five years. Most workstations vendors have moved to UNIX(tm). However, current research in abstract data types, object-oriented programming environments, knowledge-base structures, and expert systems will force changes in current operating system paradigms.

PHIGS (Programmers Hierarchical Interactive Graphics System) represents the first step in organizing graphics languages along object and hierarchical lines. Object-oriented environments for handling complex geometry and databases are somewhat limited in performance, but this will change in the next five years.

3.0 SOLID MODELING

The majority of today's solid modelers are based on research from the late 1960's and 1970's. This research provided the constructive solid geometry and boundary representations, the regularized boolean operators, and other basic results. Contrary to expectations, however, solids did not create the wave of the future, and gained acceptance primarily for visualization. The overall utilization in industry was disappointingly small.

The main bottlenecks were the lack of application knowledge and engineering methodologies required to take advantage of the cross-functional value of solids, and the bounded commercial market potential (not like drafting).

However, recent research results in new methodologies for automated finite element modeling, assembly, numerical control, process planning, and tolerancing have opened up new opportunities for industry acceptance. In addition, sophisticated geometric representations, such as rational tricubic solid primitives, and progress toward the exact solution to the surface-surface intersection problem will allow exact solid modeling of complex shapes with just a few complex primitives. Precise solid modelers are essential for product/process automation.

Feature-based geometry is emerging not only as a conceptual design language but also as a means for linking design to manufacturing processes.

Research in tolerancing has made much progress. A recent PhD thesis [Turner 87] in the RPI Center for Interactive Computer Graphics, for example, has developed methods for tolerance analysis and synthesis in which all necessary geometric relationships are automatically derived from the assembly solid model without designer guidance. This work has also developed methods that are effective in solving three-dimensional tolerancing problems as well as a general framework that applies across the range of possible design constraints. Finally, the framework supports both worst-case and statistical methods as well as the capability of supporting both geometric tolerances and traditional plus-minus dimensional tolerances. The fundamental research contribution is a theory which provides an unambiguous mathematical interpretation for given tolerance specifications. This work has also lead to a general architecture for modeling assemblies and part assembly relationships, and for constructive variational geometry.

The analysis of engineering problems based on solid geometric models has been hampered by the requirements that all geometric entities must have a finite volume. Engineering analysis has many abstract situations where, for example, a line in space may have air flow volumes associated with it, or a plane in space defining a particular cross-section is a key element in the analysis. Another recent PhD thesis by Kevin Weiler [Weiler 86], investigated topological adjacency operators for geometric models has also yielded a data structure framework (radial edge) which handles non-manifold geometry. This data structure handles solids, surfaces, and wireframe geometry in one common data representation.

4.0   USER INTERFACE MANAGEMENT AND VISUALIZATION

The highly sophisticated user interfaces required by modern engineering applications are becoming a serious impediment to user flexibility and productivity. First of all they are very difficult to build. In some cases, up to 70% of the overall development effort goes into creating the interactive user interface. More seriously, however, they cause users to waste valuable time, forcing retraining in some cases, because each application has a unique user interface.

Future user interface management systems must provide a means for easily reconfiguring the interface (layout and interactive sequences) so that a common component exists across all applications of interest with the remaining portions easily tuned to user preferences. In effect, the manager contains a shell of higher level routines (objects), built on top of the graphics software, which handles the reconfiguration functions of the interface. The interface must also provide the ability to access a variety of third party software through the given commercial I/O structure.

A joint GE-RPI research project [Wozny 87] at RPI has demonstrated that this degree of flexibility can be met by inserting in the user interface a new, fast, relational, object-oriented, engineering database whose entities can be very complex. This database provides the necessary link controlling the parameters of the application program I/O structure, and the corresponding desired actions of the interface shell driving the graphics system.

Visualization issues are becoming more important as supercomputers churn out numerical data at higher and higher rates. This problem was identified at a recent NSF panel meeting on visualization as a major impediment to the effective utilization of supercomputers for scientific research.

A typical problem may require the identification of a new phenomenon, like a here-to-fore unknown wing tip vertex, from a database of 3D vector fields generated on a supercomputer "numerical wind tunnel". Thus, one needs tools to explore numerical data for previously unknown physical phenomena.

A specific example is given by Haber's work on the dynamic fracture of brittle materials [Haber 86]. The numerical solutions obtained

for these problems demonstrated an unusual oscillatory behavior in
the crack tip fracture parameters during the fracture process.
Initially it was felt that this may be a numerical solution artifact.
To better understand the entire fracture process, Haber developed an
animation of the fracture process which used color to portray strain
energy content and height of the surface to portray kinetic energy
content. This animation clearly showed how the boundaries reflected
kinetic energy waves back into the domain which then temporarily
retarded the acceleration of the crack front as they passed it, thus
giving the proper physical explanation of the previously unexplained
oscillations.

5.0   INFORMATION FRAMEWORK TO SUPPORT PRODUCT/PROCESS DESIGN

Successful implementation of computer-integrated design and
manufacturing requires the capability of efficiently communicating
product descriptions from one computer-aided or automated application
to another in an error-free manner. Research is needed to support
the concept of exchanging product model data with sufficient
information content so as to be interpretable directly by design and
manufacturing application programs.

Both IGES and PDES represent standardization efforts in this
direction. However, the problem is much broader. At one end of the
spectrum is the mechanical CAE efforts, such as Congnition Inc.,
which has developed a very flexible system for conceptualizing
designs. The system ties together the ability to easily create
geometry, associate design handbook information with the geometry,
and perform analysis directly, displaying explicit mathematical
formulations when possible. At the other extreme are efforts by
companies such as Automated Technology Products which has tied
geometry and features to an advanced engineering database capable of
supporting NC and other CIM functions.

However, there is still a need for being able to evolve a product
design from initial concept through detailed design as well as the
design of associated manufacturing processes without the cumbersome
and continual transformation of data from one representation to
another.

Thus, the search for an overall conceptual framework poses the
question of what consistent software system abstractions serve best
to unify the facilities required of an advanced design engineering
environment. Research is needed into highly extensible environments
and utilities, which includes support for product design activities
(e.g., conceptual design), process design activities (e.g., process
selection, process modeling), project management, and utilities
specific to different classes of products and processes.

6.0   DESIGN AND RAPID PROTOTYPING

Surprisingly little is known about the process of design. Yet it is
the essence of engineering practice. Understanding engineering
design at a fundamental level will allow the development of future
computer-aided systems to be based on scientific principles and not
be bound by specific technologies.

The NSF research program on design theory and methodology focuses on theories and axioms for engineering design using both perspective and descriptive methods. Areas of active research include design grammars, complexity measurement and use, physical and functional hierarchies, task decomposition, synthesis, and relationship between form and function. Research in this area also addresses such issues as design for manufacturability and operability, constraint characterization and negotiation, and methodologies aimed at improving design through design automation and optimization.

Design for manufacturability and functionality is a research area of special interest. Any successful design, whether it be for a mechanical part of a chemical process, must ultimately be produced, used, serviced, and retired with efficiency, reliability, and economy. Hence, at each stage in the design process, all downstream constraints must be accounted for at the appropriate level of specificity and ambiguity. The paradigm of design for manufacture is one element of this overall objective of providing information when and where it is needed. The intellectual challenge of this area is the development of a general theory of constraint representation, propagation, and arbitration in design. Thus, product lead times can be reduced by reducing changes due to conditions that could have been anticipated.

Rapid prototyping of mechanical devices and systems represent the next major frontier for CAD/CAM. In a sense, it embodies the integration of design and manufacturing into a very flexible environment. A major bottleneck in the development of innovative manufacturing systems is the excessive time required to experiment with and fully understand trial production concepts before committing them to the production floor. NSF research goals in this area include the creation of modular, distributed, coherent testbed systems, incorporating a unified user interface and advanced database, in which a product can be designed, simulated, produced, assembled, and tested. The other goals are to increase the level of hardware experimentation and improve the opportunities for building innovative new machines.

7.0 REFERENCES

[Turner 87] Turner, J., "Tolerances in Computer-Aided Geometric Design", PhD Thesis, Rensselaer Polytechnic Institute, (Also RPI Center for Interactive Computer Graphics Technical Report TR-87018), Troy, New York, 1987.

[Haber 86] Haber, R.B. and Koh, H.M., "Eulerian-Lagrangian Dynamic Fracture Analysis", First World Congress in Computational Mechanics, September 1986.

[Wozny 87] Wozny, M., Shephard, M., Spooner, D., and Hardwick, M., "Selected Research in Finite Element Modeling, Databases, and User Interfaces for Mechanical CAD/CAE/CAM - Part 2", Rensselaer Polytechnic Institute, Center for Interactive Computer Graphics, Technical Report TR-87009, March 30, 1987.

[Weiler 86] Weiler, K., "Topological Structures for Geometric Modeling", PhD Thesis, Rensselaer Polytechnic Institute, (Also RPI Center for Interactive Computer Graphics, Technical Report TR-86032), Troy, New York, 1986.

 Michael J. Wozny (S'58–A'62) joined Rensselaer Polytechnic Institute, Troy, NY, in 1977 to establish the Center for Interactive Computer Graphics. He is currently on leave to the National Science Foundation as Division Director for the Design, Manufacturing, and Computer-Integrated Division. His previous appointments include Purdue University, Oakland University, GM Research labs, NASA Electronics Research Center and NSF. Dr. Wozny has served on a number of advisory boards, (OTA, CAD/CAM ALERT, WORKSTATION ALERT, Who's Who in Computer Graphics), was Chairman of a National Academy of Sciences panel which prepared a briefing document "Research Opportunities for Design and Manufacturing" was a member of the IEEE Computer Society Publications Board, and a former Director of NCGA. He was the first Editor-in-Chief of IEEE Computer Graphics and Applications, and presently serves on the Editorial Boards or Visual Computer and IEEE Proceedings. He is a Director of the Computer Graphics Society and a Director of two companies.

Address: National Science Foundation, Division of Design, Manufacturing and Computer-Integrated Engineering, 1800 G Street, NW, Washington, DC, 20550.

The Mathematics of Computer Graphics

Rae A. Earnshaw

ABSTRACT

Until relatively recently, researchers in computer graphics paid scant
attention to the numerics of their computations. Computation was used
as a simple tool to evaluate algorithms or transform data into some
appropriate pictoral representation. Thus standard computer graphics
texts have little to say about numerical methods, just as earlier
numerical analysis textbooks had little to say about computer graphics.
This is now changing, for the important reasons outlined in this paper.

Keywords: numerical methods, Euclidean geometry, picture generation,
computer graphics, image processing, interpolation, fractal mathematics

1. COMPUTER GRAPHICS AND NUMERICAL METHODS

1.1 Introduction

To date there has been relatively little interaction between computer
graphics and numerical methods, except in standard 'mathematical'
areas. A number of important considerations are currently reversing
this trend. Geometric computations must be performed more accurately
(in some sense) since the power of rendering and presentation now
enables model construction to be more clearly seen. Computer-aided
animation and image synthesis can consume large amounts of compute
power - such computations need to be more carefully constructed.
Computer graphics and image processing techniques are drawing
closer together as a result of the developments in parallel processing
architectures, silicon-compilation and execution, transputers, and
other engines. Thus traditional aspects of image processing such as
sampling, aliasing, Fourier transforms, convolution and basic systems
theory are developing their correlates in the computer graphics field.
And finally, further areas of overlap and intersection are in the
areas of differential and algebraic geometry, fractal mathematics,
curve definition, dynamics, and shape deformation, for reasons to do
with the exploitation of these techniques (often originating in more
'classical' fields) in specialised areas of computer graphics.

This synergism will produce an added rigour to the definition and
execution of graphics processes - whether in hardware or software -
and enable the coupling of numerics and pictures to take place to
their mutual benefit. This in turn will enable the next generation
of graphics processors to be designed on a rigorous and consistent
basis. When this is coupled with the application of formal methods
to algorithm specification and execution, pipeline transformations,
graphics language and interface design, and parallelism, our
understanding of the processes of picture production will be greatly
enhanced.

This paper reviews the aspects of mathematics and numerical analysis of relevance to computer graphics and the anticipated developments in the future.

1.2 Survey and Background

Historically there has always been an overlap between computer graphics and numerical methods and geometry due to requirements in areas such as the following:-

- (i) Manipulation of matrices representing points, lines etc
- (ii) Calculation of Euclidean distances e.g. unit normals and perpendiculars from points on to lines
- (iii) Calculation of line intersections and lines with planes
- (iv) Calculation of points on curves and surfaces in order to represent them on some display device
- (v) Mapping pictures on to display screens that are effectively approximate, e.g. discrete grid or raster
- (vi) Prevention of the accumulation of round-off error when approximating pictures on incremental devices

In addition, a knowledge of numerical properties and methods has been essential in the following areas:-

- (i) Choice of the type of curve or surface to best represent the physical properties of the system or object being represented
- (ii) Choice of curve or surface that is invariant when the defining points are transformed or rotated (essential for the preservation of shape)
- (iii) Methods for calculating expressions and functions so that intermediate values do not cause overflow or underflow on the particular hardware being used
- (iv) Reformulation of algorithms to produce faster execution speeds
- (v) Producing reliable, and accurate geometric computations to ensure consistency under all circumstances

Further interesting areas are those concerned with artefacts (e.g. jaggies or staircasing) and are often due to a combination of factors. Well-established techniques exist for smoothing out such anomalies.

Standard mathematical techniques for representing points, lines, curves and surfaces, and manipulating them, are not the province of this paper. They are well covered in standard text books such as "Mathematical Elements for Computer Graphics" (Rogers 1976).

The following is a convenient summary of the operations that must be performed for basic modelling and picture production given by Blinn (1984):-

Representation: The exact form and use of the numerical parameters which define the object must be specified.

Modelling: It must be possible to generate the appropriate mathematical parameters from some conceptualisation of the desired shape in the mind of the designer.

Transformation: These are the basic geometrical transformations (scaling, rotation, translation and perspective) which are represented by the homogeneous 4 by 4 matrix. This operation is usually performed by deriving new mathematical parameters for the transformed surface from those of the old surface and the contents of the transformation matrix.

Boundary Checking: A surface defined solely by functions may potentially
stretch to infinity. Real objects are typically modelled as pieces of
such surfaces sliced off at various boundaries. These boundaries then
form space curves. Determination of whether a point is inside or
outside the boundary must be performable.

Intersections: It must be possible to find the intersection of the
surface with other surfaces, lines, and planes.

Surface Normals: It must be possible to calculate the surface normal
vector at any desired point. This is useful in two contexts: it serves
to define the silhouette edge of the surface, and it is also a prime
constituent of the intensity calculation when shaded pictures are to
be drawn.

2. MATHEMATICAL MODELS AND REPRESENTATIONS

As a branch of mathematics dealing with shape and spatial relations,
geometry has been the focus of attention with regard to the handling
of 3D objects in a computer. However, one of the basic problems in 3D
graphics is the representation of objects in a way which makes the
analysis and rendering of them feasible in a finite time. In addition,
it would be particularly useful to have some generalised model into
which different shapes and components could be fitted, since these
would be more tractable to elegant mathematical representation and
manipulation. Informationally complete representations would enable
any well-defined geometrical property of any represented object, or
set of objects, to be calculated automatically. Requicha and Tilove
(1978), Requicha (1980), and Requicha and Voelcker (1982, 1983)
summarise some of the early approaches to solid modelling. Aspects
of modelling and computational geometry of current interest are domain
extensions for modellers; handling dimensioning, tolerances, and
geometrical constraints; algorithms for rapid editing; null object and
interference detection; conversion from one representation into
another; analysing the complexity of geometric algorithms; and handling
precision problems in numerical geometry.

Representing objects in the form of hierarchical structures is surveyed
by Tilove (1981, 1984), Meagher (1982), Kedem and Ellis (1984), and
Samet (1984). Further advances are noted in Samet (1985), Samet and
Tamminen (1985), Nelson and Samet (1986), and Muuss (1987). Hybrid
models are needed to effectively cater for all the requirements of
modelling and representation. In addition, as the hardware of display
architecture evolves, data structures and algorithms have to be mapped
in such a way as to fully exploit the capabilities of the new
developments.

A related approach to the modelling and representation of shape is
presented by Brady (1981, 1984) from the standpoint of computer vision.
This applies more to vision recognition problems than to computer
graphics, but automated robots and assembly plants need to know how
to deal with shape as part of the process of recognition and
manipulation.

As an example of the interdependency of representation, model, and
picture, van Overveld (1987) considers the following example. When a
3D object is rendered into pixel space, the method chosen depends on the
mathematical representation of the object to be rendered. If this is a
list of polygons, then processing consists of raster scan conversion
for each polygon in order to locate all the pixels of interest. If it
is represented as a CSG tree, then this is interpreted and the

appropriate CSG primitives rendered. However, a boundary representation
of the same object (to highlight joints for example) involves a
different strategy requiring the calculation of the intersection of the
CSG primitives and utilising a line or curve drawing algorithm to
select the pixels to be highlighted. But there is no guarantee that
these pixels coincide with the locations of the joins as they appear in
the picture generated initially. Franklin (1986) notes the same
problem when different algorithms are being used in the same picture -
producing missing and spurious pixels, the tell-tale signs of anomalous
behaviour. What is needed is a more consistent and unified approach
based on a rigorous model, with uniform operations.

A further example given by Forrest (1985) highlights the complex
scenario in evaluating the seemingly simple case of the intersection of
two lines. Careful attention to numerical detail is required and also a
a consistent ordering of geometric operations within practical systems.
Mixing of different types of coordinate system can also be a non-trivial
situation; mapping from one into the other requires detailed
consideration. For example, the intersection between two line segments
whose end points are on an integer grid may not be representable in the
floating point number system, since the rounding or truncation to a
unique floating point number has to be done consistently.

Some possible solutions are standardised floating point arithmetic;
algebraic and symbolic manipulation; interval arithmetic (e.g. Mudur
and Koparker 1984); and the use of rational arithmetic. However,
the latter cannot cater for a general set of points.

Considerations in the areas of production automation and manufacturing
have made it clear that it is no longer sufficient to use exact models
to represent objects. Tolerance needs to be formulated and represented
in some way. Process planning - the automation of robots and machine
tools - needs more than just a description of stationary objects -
we need to know how these objects move in space, and where they are at
any given point in time (Cameron 1984). This involves spatial updating
processes. In specialised application areas (e.g. sheep shearing
machines and robots), flexible models have to be represented.

Some further problems of interest are handling the complexity
introduced by assemblies of objects; the representation and
interpretation of object properties such as mass, surface texture,
and appearance; and handling the processes of motion, machining, and
assembly of parts. One of the ultimate goals is to be able to
automate the creation, analysis, transmission and management of all
product definitions, process definitions, and associated business
data.

3. EUCLIDEAN GEOMETRY

More general considerations of numerical computations in a graphical
or geometrical context are given by Duff (1984), including order of
convergence, designing look-up tables, function evaluation, intersection
calculations, and spline interpolation and approximation. An
interesting example in calculating Euclidean distance is cited from
Moler and Morrison (1983). An algorithm for calculating sqrt(a*a + b*b)
is needed which is fast, robust, and does not cause overflow or
underflow when calculating the intermediate values of a*a or b*b.
The method by Moler and Morrison does not suffer from these problems,
provided the result is in range. It has cubic convergence and may
even be faster than sqrt(a*a + b*b). The following is a C
implementation:-

```
double hypot (p,q)
double p,q;
(
    double r,s;
    if (p<0) p = -p
    if (q<0) q = -q
    if (p<q) (r = p; p = q; q = r;)
    if (p==0) return 0;
    for (;;) (
            r = q/p
            r*= r;
            s = r + 4
            if (s==4) return p;
            r/= s;
            p+= 2*r*p;
            q*= r;
            )

)
```

The result is accurate to 6.5 digits after two iterations, to 20 digits
after three, and 62 digits after four. Thus normal use would specify
the extent of the iteration and omit the test. Dubrelle (1983) analyses
the algorithm geometrically and outlines a set of generalisations with
arbitrarily large order of convergence. Duff (1984) estimates that
calculating Euclidean distance accounts for 90% of the square roots in
computer graphics applications. In addition, most illumination models
need the unit normal to each visible surface to be computed at each
pixel.

A further example, the CORDIC rotation algorithm from Volder (1959) and
described in Turkowski (1982), can be used to calculate rotations in 2D,
rectangular to polar and polar to rectangular conversion, Euclidean
point-point, point-line and point-line segment distance, circular and
hyperbolic trigonometric functions, exponentials, logarithms, and
square roots.

Locating the zeros of non-liner equations is required for producing
the ray-traced rendering of a 3D surface. Blinn (1982) developed a
hybrid Newton-Raphson/false position iterative method to locate the
right root, with quadratic convergence whenever Newton-Raphson would
give the right root.

Hanrahan (1983) uses multivariate polynomial functions for ray-tracing
algebraic surfaces, including planes, quadric surfaces and tori.

An introduction to curve interpolation and approximation with particular
reference to computer graphics is given in Brodlie (1985) and Earnshaw
(1985). There are many survey works on the uses and applications of
the different kinds of splines (Bartels, Beatty and Barsky 1984;
Barnhill and Riesenfeld 1974; Barsky 1987).

4. SAMPLING, CONVOLUTION AND FOURIER TRANSFORMS

Methods and techniques from image processing have increasing relevance
for computer graphics as the two areas draw closer together through
the use of analogous procedures in the areas of sampling, parallel
processing, real-time image production, recognition of graphics and
text, interactive CAD and robotics, AI and computer vision, and
theoretical foundations.

Aliasing arises from inadequate sampling of the continuous environment
(the picture) with the discrete raster grid (the display). This

causes jaggedness along lines (also known as 'staircasing') Similarly
in the time domain, temporal aliasing arises from objects moving
quickly with respect to the camera causing strobing in animated
sequences of objects (Porter 1984).   The basic problem in the former
is scanline to scanline changes, and in the second frame to frame
changes.

Two theorems relating to convolution and multiplication in the time
and frequency domain elaborate on the problem of aliasing (Kajiya 1984).
When an input signal is sampled, its values at an equally spaced set
of points are taken as representative of the complete signal. Sampling
an input signal s(t) at discrete intervals can be represented as a
multiplication by a train of delta signals:-

$$s(t) = \sum_{n=-\infty}^{\infty} \delta(t - nT_s)$$

where T_s is the sampling interval.

The Fourier trasnform of a train of delta signals is a similar sequence
with different spacing:-

$$S(w) = \sum_{n=-\infty}^{\infty} \delta(w - n\Omega_s)$$

where Ω_s is the sampling rate.

Thus sampling an input signal can be modelled as a convolution in the
time domain.   The convolution is a sequence of delta signals separated
by Ω_s, and results in copies of the input spectrum being inserted into
the frequency domain, each bein centred at the position of the
corresponding delta signal.   This may give rise to regions where these
copies overlap, producing aliasing.   In the spatial domain this
produces jaggies; in the frequency domain it produces a set of
frequencies which wrap around to produce different frequencies.   For
no aliasing to occur the original spectrum should have no frequencies
beyond a small range around zero (Shannon sampling theorem).

This if x(t) has Fourier transform X(w) such that X(w)=0 for $|w| > \Omega_s/2$,
then x(t) can be determined by

$$x = x(nT)$$

where T is the sampling interval.   This uses the convolution and
Fourier transform properties.   To recover the original signal, all
extra copies are suppressed by convolving the output with the kernel:-

$$h(t) = \sin(\Omega_s t/2)/(\Omega_s/2)$$

This has as its Fourier transform a rectangle function which is non-
zero only in the region about the original spectrum.

$$H(w) = \begin{cases} 1 & \text{if } |w| < \Omega_s/2 \\ 0 & \text{otherwise} \end{cases}$$

Further material is contained in Kajiya (1984), Oppenheim and Shafer
(1975) and Pratt (1978).

5. FURTHER TOPICS

5.1 Deformation of Primitives

Barr (1981, 1984) outlines hierarchical solid modelling operations for twisting, bending, tapering, compression, and expansion of geometric objects. The position vectors and normal vectors in the simpler objects are used to calculate the position and normal vectors in the more complex forms. Each level in the deformation hierarchy requires an additional matrix multiply for the normal vector calculation. In addition to simulating the bending of bars or sheet metal, deformations can also be utilised for flexible objects such as plastic, fabric, or rubber.

5.2 Einstein Summation Notation

Barr (1984) introduces the use of the Einstein summation notation for a short-hand method of expressing multi-dimensional cartesian equations. The advantages of this representation include ease of manipulation of long expressions, particularly for cross products, determinants, rotations, and matrix inverses. Further references to this convention can be found in the texts describing tensor analysis and 3D mechanics (Segel 1977; Solkolnikoff 1956).

5.3 Differential and Algebraic Geometry

The aspects of differential geometry of relevance to computer graphics are those concerned with manifolds, differential forms, and connections. Algebraic geometry contributes homogeneous polynomials, factorisation, elimination, and the theory of plane curves (Spivak 1965, 1974; Kajiya 1984; Hartshorne 1977).

5.4 Dynamics and Motion

Classical Newtonian mechanics can provide the basis for the animation of objects. There are many texts which summarise these aspects of computational physics (Courant and Hilbert 1962; Arnold 1975; Goldstein 1980).

5.5 Human Interface Modelling

Graphics is often an integral part of the interface between man and machine. Effective utilisation of computers will rely increasingly on amore rigorous and quantitative assessment of human-computer interface characteristics (Newman 1987). This in turn will benefit from a modelling of the processes at the interface; a study of the appropriateness of the choice of input tools for particular applications; and the construction of methodologies for specifying the design of the interface (Preece, Davies, Woodman and Ince 1987; Pfaff 1985).

5.6 Fractal Mathematics

Uncovering orderliness within the framework of apparent chaos is one of the purposes of the investigation of nature, and its representation by means of models, theories, and mathematical constructions. Interestingly, there appears to be a symmetry between the micro analysis of nature and its macro appearance and representation in the large. This may be coincidental but it is more likely to reflect the deep structure of nature and the laws that govern the relationship of its constituent parts. Examples of macro structure and appearnce are trees, clouds, coastlines, rivers, mountain ranges, and landscapes - all apparently random - but in fact encapsulating an underlying

principle of order which can be expressed in terms of simple mathematics
However, Euclidean geometry is inadequate for this purpose; fractal
geometry (Mandelbrot 1977, 1983) provides the basis for a framework
for representing shapes in nature and also entities in mathematics.
Fractal geometries exhibit the property of self-similarity, i.e. the
whole replicates the part, and also has a dimensionality. Earlier
geometric forms such as dragon curves, the von Koch snowflake curve,
and the Sierpinski curve, all display exact self-similarity, whereas
objects in nature display statistical self-similarity. For example,
a coastline drawn at different scales (equivalent to zooming into or
out of a given region) produces a set of pictures that are fundamentally
similar. In fact, they are so similar that they could be taken for
different sections of the same coastline all at a constant scale. In
physical terms this appears like regularity within irregularity. In
mathematical terms it represents a high degree of invariance under
changes of scale.

The combination of Mandelbrot sets, computers, and computer graphics
has provided a powerful toolset for exploring the complex plane and the
behaviour of dynamical systems: "Imagining the formerly unimaginable"
(Salinger 1987). This has contributed greatly to our understanding of
both mathematics and complex systems, and has been well documented
(e.g. Pietgen and Richter 1985). This phenomenon is illustrative of
an important point: computer graphics has provided a powerful tool to
uncover mathematical and physical behaviour, and in turn the mathematics
has provided the basis for developments in computer modelling and
representation of natural scenes. The former is a very interesting
analogue of the latter, and vice-versa. There has been some discussion
on the extent to which the methods used by computer graphicists (e.g.
Fournier, Fussel and Carpenter 1982) embody the mathematical purity of
the Mandelbrot fractals (Mandelbrot 1982), but the pictures produced
continue to be impressively realistic, whether for natural terrain,
flakes, or clouds. Voss (1985) summarises some of the principal
mathematical constructs and relations underlying the definition of
fractals.

5.7 Space-Filling Curves

Some recent developments in space-filling curves and Peano curves
embody a different strategy for generating pixel images giving greater
speed. These are described in Peano (1890), Witten and Wyvill (1983),
and Cole (1987).

5.8 The Mathematics of Parallelism

Designing algorithms for parallel architectures and their exploitation
for the manipulation and display of objects is an area of current
interest. Moore, McCabe and Urquhart (1987), Dew (1985, 1986),
Handler et al (1986), and May and Shepherd (1986) provide a summary
of the current work, including systolic arrays and their implications.
Fuchs (1987) gives a summary of current VLSI work

Techniques for mapping synchronous, data-independent calculations
such as convolutions and transformations are well understood.
However, extensions to the synchronous and data-dependent cases are
much more difficult - currently there is no formal and comprehensive
treatment. Mapping algorithms on to transputers requires a
partitioning which minimises the need to communicate with the overall
model.

Exploiting parallelism is the subject of some recent investigations
(e.g. Theoharis 1986). Occam provides a parallel processing
environment. Goldfeather, Hultquist and Fuchs (1986) describe a
method of exploiting spatial parallelism by using a central control
and a logical processor at each node to evaluate the polynomial.
For quadratic primitives the results have been impressive in terms of
executing the processes required by the CSG trees. However, in order
to develop automated methods for implementing algorithms on parallel
processors, some form of general model representation for parallelism
is needed.

5.9 Methodology of Design

Recent studies have focussed on the area of design with a view to
obtaining greater understanding and elaboration of the design
process (Lansdown 1985, 1987; Lawson 1983, 1987; King 1987).
A number of models have been postulated: firstly, those based on
gradual iteration towards the final design in a well-defined way (so
called 'robust' designs), and secondly those that represent progress
in a more discontinuous way - related to the generation of new ideas
(so called 'lean' designs). Models in Catastrophe Theory have been
used to illustrate that these two approaches can be represented by an
overall unified model. Modification of existing designs can be aided
by the provision of 'standard' options for the designer to choose
from. Where a chosen sequence of these options is interrelated (e.g.
in designing a building the doors and windows cannot be larger than
the walls) it should be possible to incorporate knowledge-based
approaches into the design process. However, dealing with the
incompleteness which is the essence of the process is a non-trivial
task.

6. CONCLUSIONS

6.1 Algorithm Formulation and Complexity

Students of algorithms have demonstrated the inherent complexity in
even the seemingly simplest of algorithms. Computer graphics algorithms
concerned with hideen-line and hidden-surface removal have received
considerable attention with a view to optimisation and improvement.
Bresenham's algorithm (1965) has been the subject of much investigation
and refinement - even involving program transformations (Sproull 1982).
However, formal and mathematical analysis of anything other than the
simplest of algorithms (e.g. sorting and searching) has proved
inordinately difficult (Tucker 1985).

6.2 Handling Geometric and Algorithmic Complexity

Assemblies of objects or aggregations of components are surprisingly
difficult to represent in an informationally complete sense, such that
all the requirements of the model can be satisfied unambiguously.
In addition, the complexity of computations arising from even the
simplest operation is such that greater optimisation or more powerful
hardware is needed for the task to be performed in a reasonable time.
Shamos (1975) has noted the complexity arising in geometric operations.
Mapping algorithms on to parallel architectures is a non-trivial task.
Forrest (1987) argues for the application of rigorous software
engineering techniques when constructing large and complex geometric
systems, such that computations can be performed reliably, accurately,
and consistently.

6.3 Notation and Conceptualisation

Appropriate notation and representation of abstraction will enable
a better understanding of the processes and problems involved.
In addition, a mental model that is able to represent a mass of
complexity often suggest new ways of thinking about problems. This is
often the way forward.

6.4 Integration of Computer Graphics and Computer Vision

Computers are rapidly moving from information processing machines to
vision processing machines. The input process corresponds to the
transformation of an object scene into an object representation in
the computer for anaylsis and manipulation. The output process
corresponds to the transformation of object data into picture data.
If all this has to be performed in real-time, then the processes
have to be efficiently represented and executed. A model of a vision
processing machine is needed into which these components will fit
as integral parts.

6.5 Mathematics, Models and Computer Graphics

Some recent studies in the area of models have demonstrated the power,
capability and advantages of a rigorous conceptualisation framework.
Examples are Kunii (1987) in CAD and graphics communication networks,
Wooodwark and Quarendon (1987) in graphics, and Hall (1987) in
colour reproduction and illumination models. Future work should build
on this rigorous and systematic approach. Computer graphics is rapidly
moving from a discipline based largely on pragmatics and trial and
error solutions to one based on rigorous analysis and formal methods.
The unifying tools in this transition are models, metrics and
mathematics.

REFERENCES

Arnold V. I. (1975) "Mathematical Methods of Classical Mechanics",
   Springer-Verlag
Barnhill R. E. and Riesenfeld R. F. (1974) "Computer-Aided Geometric
   Design", Academic Press, 1974
Barr A. H. (1984) "Global and Local Deformations of Solid Primitives",
   SIGGRAPH Tutorial Notes
Barr A. H. (1981) "Superquadrics and Angle-Preserving Transformations",
   IEEE CG & A, Vol 1, No 1, pp 11-23
Barr A. H. (1984) "Introduction to the Einstein Summation Notation",
   SIGGRAPH Tutorial Notes
Barr A. H. (1986) "Ray Tracing Deformed Surfaces", ACM SIGGRAPH,
   Vol 20, No 4, pp 287-296
Barsky B. A. (1987) Computer Graphics and Geometric Modelling using
   Beta-Splines", Springer-Verlag
Bartels R. H., Beatty J. C. and Barsky B. A. (1984) "An Introduction
   to the Use of Splines in Computer Graphics", University of Waterloo
   TR CS-83-09, UC Berkeley TR UCB/CSD 83-136

Blinn J. F. (1982) "A Generalization of Algebraic Surface Drawing",
   ACM Transactions on Graphics, Vol 1, No 3, pp 235-256
Blinn J. F. (1984) "The Algebraic Properties of Homogeneous Second
   Order Surfaces", SIGGRAPH Tutorial Notes
Brady M. (1981) "Computer Vision", North-Holland, Amsterdam
Brady M. (1984) "Representing Shape", Report, MIT AI Laboratory
Brady M. (1984) "Criteria for Representations of Shape" In:
   Rosenfeld and Beck (Eds) "Human and Machine Vision", Academic Press
Bresenham J. E. (1965) "Algorithm for Computer Control of a Digital
   Plotter", IBM Systems Journal, Vol 4, No 1, pp 25-30
Brodlie K. W. (1985) "Methods for Drawing Curves", In: Earnshaw R. A.
   (Ed) "Fundamental Algorithms for Computer Graphics", Springer-
   Verlag, pp 304-323
Cameron S. A. (1984) "Modelling Solids in Motion", PhD Thesis,
   University of Edinburgh
Carpenter L. (1980) "Computer Rendering of Fractal Curves and Surfaces",
   ACM SIGGRAPH, Vol 14, No 3, p 109 (Abstract)
Chazelle B. and Dobkin D. P. (1980) "Detection is Easier than
   Computation", Proc 12th Annual ACM Symposium on the Theory of
   Computing, pp 146-152
Cohen E. (1983) "Some Mathematical Tools for a Modeller's
   Workbench", IEEE CG & A, Vol 3, No 7, pp 63-66
Cole A. J. (1987) "Compaction Techniques for Raster Scan Graphics
   Using Space-Filling Curves", Computer Journal, Vol 30, No 1, pp 87-92
Courant R. and Hilbert D. (1962) "Methods of Mathematical Physics",
   Wiley
Dew P. M., Dodsworth J. and Morris D. T. (1985) "Systolic Array
   Architectures for High Performance CAD/CAM Workstations", In:
   Earnshaw R. A. (Ed) "Fundamental Algorithms for Computer Graphics",
   Springer-Verlag, pp 659-694
Dew P. M., Manning L. J. and McEvoy K. (1986) "A Tutorial on
   Systolic Array Architectures for High Performance Processors",
   Report No 205, Dept of Computer Studies, University of Leeds, UK
Dubrulle A. A. (1983) "A Class of Numerical Methods for the
   Computation of Pythagorean Sums", IBM Journal of Research and
   Development, Vol 27, No 6, pp 582-589
Duff T. (1984) "Numerical Methods for Computer Graphics", SIGGRAPH
   Tutorial Notes
Earnshaw R. A. (1985) "A Review of Curve Drawing Algorithms", In:
   Earnshaw R. A. (Ed) "Fundamental Algorithms for Computer Graphics",
   Springer-Verlag, pp 289-301
Pfaff G. E. (Ed) (1985) "User Interface Management Systems",
   Springer-Verlag
Forrest A. R. (1985) "Computational Geometry in Practice". In:
   Earnshaw R. A. (Ed) "Fundamental Algorithms for Computer Graphics",
   Springer-Verlag, pp 707-724
Forrest A. R. (1987) "Computational Geometry and Software Engineering",
   In: Rogers D. F. and Earnshaw R. A. (Eds) "Techniques in Computer
   Graphics", Springer-Verlag, to be published
Fournier A., Fussel D. and Carpenter L. (1982) "Computer Rendering
   of Stochastic Models", CACM, Vol 25, pp 371-384
Franklin W. R. and Barr A. H. (1981) "Faster Calculation of
   Superquadric Surfaces", IEEE CG & A, Vol 1, No 3, pp 41-47
Franklin W. R. (1986) "Problems with Raster Graphics Algorithms".
   In: Kessener L. R. A., Peters F. J. and van Lierop M. L. P. (Eds)
   "Data Structures for Raster Graphics", Springer-Verlag
Fuchs H. (1987) "VLSI for Graphics" In: Rogers D. F. and
   Earnshaw R. A. (Eds) "Techniques in Computer Graphics",
   Springer-Verlag, to be published
Goldfeather J. and Fuchs H. (1986) "Quadratic Surface Rendering on a
   Logic-Enhanced Frame-Buffer Memory", IEEE CG & A, Vol 6, No 1,
   pp 48-59

Goldfeather J., Hultquist J. P. M. and Fuchs H. (1986) "Fast
  Constructive Solid Geometry Display in the Pixel-Powers Graphics
  System", ACM SIGGRAPH, Vol 20, No 4, pp 107-116
Goldstein H. (1980) "Classical Mechanics", Addison-Wesley
Guillemin V. and Pollack A. (1974) "Differential Topology",
  Prentice-Hall
Hall R. (1987) "Color Reproduction and Illumination Models" In:
  Rogers D. F. and Earnshaw R. A. (Eds) "Techniques in Computer
  Graphics", Springer-Verlag, to be published
Händler W., Haupt D., Jeltsch R., Juling W. and Lange O. (Eds) (1986)
  CONPAR86. Proceedings of the Conference on Algorithms and Hardware
  for Parallel Processing, Aachen, September 1986, Springer-Verlag,
  Lecture Notes in Computer Science 237
Hanrahan P. (1983) "Ray Tracing Algebraic Surfaces", ACM SIGGRAPH,
  pp 83-90
Hartshorne R. (1977) "Algebraic Geometry", Springer-Verlag
Kajiya J. T. (1984) "Transform Theory", SIGGRAPH Tutorial Notes
Kajiya J. T. (1984) "Differential and Algebraic Geometry",
  SIGGRAPH Tutorial Notes
Kedem G. and Ellis J. L. (1984) "Computer Structures for Curve-Solid
  Classification in Geometric Modelling", TR84-37, Microelectronic
  Center of North Carolina
King M. (1987) "Towards an Integrated Computer Art System", In:
  Earnshaw R. A. and Lansdown R. J. (Eds) "Computer Graphics in Art,
  Animation and Design", Springer-Verlag, to be published
Kunii T. L. (1987) "A Model-Driven approach to CAD and Graphics
  Communication Networks" In: Rogers D. F. and Earnshaw R. A. (Eds)
  "Techniques in Computer Graphics", Springer-Verlag, to be published
Lansdown R. J. (1987) "Computer Graphics in Design", In: Rogers D. F.
  and Earnshaw R. A. (Eds) "Techniques in Computer Graphics",
  Springer-Verlag, to be published
Lansdown R. J. (1987) "A Theory of Computer-Aided Design", In:
  Earnshaw R. A. and Lansdown R. J. (Eds) "Computer Graphics in Art,
  Animation and Design", Springer-Verlag, to be published
Lansdown R. J. (1987) "Some Notes on Fractals". In: Earnshaw R. A.
  Parslow R. D. and Woodwark J. R. (Eds) "Geometric Modelling and
  Computer Graphics Applications and Techniques", Technical Press, 1987
Lawson B. (1983) "How Designers Think", Architectural Press, London
Lawson B. (1987) "Intelligent Building Systems and Coordinated
  Drafting Systems", In: Earnshaw R. A. and Lansdown R. J. (Eds),
  "Computer Graphics in Art, Animation and Design", Springer-Verlag,
  to be published
Mandelbrot B. B. (1977) "Fractals: Form, Chance and Dimension",
  Freeman, San Francisco
Mandelbrot B. B. (1983) "The Fractal Geometry of Nature", Freeman,
  San Francisco
Mandelbrot B. B. (1982) "Comment on Computer Rendering of Fractal
  Stochastic Models", CACM, Vol 25, pp 581-584
May D. and Shepherd R. (1986) "Communicating Process Computers",
  Conference on Communicating Parallel Architectures, Esprit
  Summer School on Future Parallel Computers, 1986
Meagher D. J. R. (1982) "The Octree Encoding Method for Efficient
  Solid Modelling", IPL-TR-032, Image Processing Lab, RPI
Moler C. and Morrison D. (1983) "Replacing Square Roots by
  Pythagorean Sums", IBM Journal of Research and Development, Vol 27,
  No 6, pp 577-581
Moore W., McCabe A. and Urquhart R. (Eds) (1987) "Systolic Arrays",
  Proceedings of the First International Workshop on Systolic Arrays,
  2-4 July 1986, Oxford, England, Adam Hilger, Bristol & Boston
Mudur S. P. and Koparker P. A. (1984) "Interval Methods for Processing
  Geometric Objects", IEEE CG & A, Vol 4, No 2, pp 7-17

Mudur S. P. (1986) "Mathematical Elements for Computer Graphics".
  In: Enderle G., Grave M. and Lillehagen F. (Eds) "Advances in
  Computer Graphics I", Springer-Verlag
Muuss M. J. (1987) "Understanding the Preparation and Analysis of
  Solid Models" In: Rogers D. F. and Earnshaw R. A. (Eds) "Fundamental
  Techniques for Computer Graphics", Springer-Verlag, to be published
Nelson R. C. and Samet H. (1986) "A Consistent Hierarchical
  Representation for Vector Data", ACM SIGGRAPH, Vol 20, No 4,
  pp 197-206
Newman W. M. (1987) "Designing Integrated Systems for the Office
  Environment", McGraw-Hill, pp 421-422
Oppenheim A. V. and Shafer R. W. (1975) "Digital Signal Processing",
  Prentice-Hall, Englewood Cliffs, New Jersey
van Overveld C. W. A. M. (1987) "A Family of Algorithms for Generating
  Discrete Embeddings of Continuous Objects". In: "Theoretical
  Foundations of Computer Graphics and CAD", Springer-Verlag, to
  appear
Pavlidis T. J. (1982) "Algorithms for Graphics and Image Processing",
  Springer-Verlag
Peano G. (1890) "Sur une courbe, qui remplit toute une aire plaine",
  Mathematische Annalen, Vol 36, pp 157-160
Pietgen H-O and Richter P. H. (1985) "The Beauty of Fractals: Images
  of Complex Dynamical Systems", Springer-Verlag
Pietgen H-O and Saupe D. (1983) "Julia - a Scheme for the Generation
  of Self-Similar Images", Proceedings CG83, Online, pp 731-741
Porter T. (1984) "Motion Blur", SIGGRAPH Tutorial Notes
Pratt W. K. (1978) "Digital Image Processing", Wiley
Preece J., Davies G., Woodman M. and Ince D. C. (1987) "A Coherent
  Specification Method for the User Interface of Documentation
  Systems" In: Earnshaw R. A. (Ed) "Workstations and Publication
  Systems", Springer-Verlag, to be published, 1987
Preparata F. P. and Shamos M. I. (1985) "Computational Geometry",
  Springer-Verlag
Requicha A. A. G. and Tilove R. B. (1978) "Mathematical Foundations
  of Constructive Solid Geometry - General Topology of Closed Regular
  Sets", TM-27a, Production Automation Project, University of Rochester
Requicha A. A. G. (1980) "Representations of Rigid Solids: Theory,
  Methods and Systems", ACM Computing Surveys, Vol 12, No 4,
  pp 437-464
Requicha A. A. G. and Voelcker H. (1982) "Solid Modelling: A
  Historical Summary and Contemporary Assessment", IEEE CG & A,
  Vol 2, No 2, pp 9-24
Requicha A. A. G. and Voelcker H. (1983) "Solid Modelling: Current
  Status and Research Directions", IEEE CG & A, Vol 3, No 7, pp 25-37
Rogers D. F. and Adams J. A. (1976) "Mathematical Elements for Computer
  Graphics", McGraw Hill, New York
Salinger D. L. (1987) Private Communication
Samet H. (1984) "The Quadtree and Related Hierarchical Structures",
  ACM Computing Surveys, Vol 16, No 2, pp 187-260
Samet H. (1985) "Approximating CSG Trees of Moving Objects",
  TR-1472, Computer Science, University of Maryland
Samet H. and Tamminen M. (1985) "Bintrees, CSG Trees and Time",
  ACM SIGGRAPH, Vol 19, No 3, pp 121-130
Segel L. A. (1977) "Mathematics Applied to Continuum Mechanics",
  Macmillan
Shamos M. I. (1975) "Geometric Complexity", Seventh ACM Annual Symp
  on Theory of Computing, pp 224-233
Solkolnikoff (1956) "Mathematical Theory of Elasticity", McGraw Hill
Spivak M. (1965) "Calculus on Manifolds", Benjamin
Spivak M. (1975) "A Comprehensive Introduction to Differential
  Geometry", 5 vols, Berkeley

Sproull R. F. (1982) "Using Program Transformations to Derive Line-Drawing Algorithms", ACM Transactions on Graphics, Vol 1, No 4, pp 259-273

Theoharis T. A. (1986) "Exploiting Parallelism in the Graphics Pipeline", MSc Thesis, Oxford University Programming Research Group, PRG-54

Tilove R. B. (1981) "Exploiting Spatial and Structural Locality in Geometric Modelling", PhD Thesis, University of Rochester

Tucker J. V. (1985) "Theoretical Considerations in Algorithm Design", In: Earnshaw R. A. (Ed) "Fundamental Algorithms for Computer Graphics", Springer-Verlag, pp 855-878

Turkowski K. (1982) "Antialiasing using Coordinate Rotations", ACM Transactions on Graphics, Vol 1, No 3, pp 215-234

Volder J. E. (1959) "The CORDIC Trigonometric Technique", IRE Trans. Electronic Comput. EC-8, 3, pp 330-334

Voss R. F. (1985) "Random Fractal Forgeries" In: Earnshaw R. A. (Ed) "Fundamental Algorithms for Computer Graphics", Springer-Verlag, pp 805-835

Witten I. H. and Wyvill B. (1983) "On the Generation and Use of Space Filling Curves", Software - Practice and Experience", Vol 6, pp 519-525

Woodwark J. R. and Quarendon P. (1987) "The Model for Graphics", In: Rogers D. F. and Earnshaw R. A. (Eds) "Techniques in Computer Graphics", Springer-Verlag, to be published

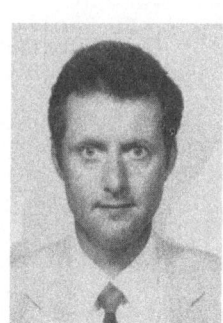
Rae A. Earnshaw is Head of the Graphics Team at the University of Leeds, with interests in graphics algorithms, integrated graphics and text, display technology, CAD/CAM, and human-computer interface issues. He has been a Visiting Professor at Illinois Institute of Technology, George Washington University, and Northwestern Polytechnical University, China. He has acted as a consultant to US companies and the College CAD/CAM Consortium and given seminars at a variety of UK and US institutions and research laboratories. He is a Fellow of the British Computer Society and Chairman of the Computer Graphics and Displays Group. He was a Director of the 1985 ASI "Fundamental Algorithms for Computer Graphics, and Co-Chair of the BCS/ACM International Summer Institute on "State of the Art in Computer Graphics" held in Stirling, Scotland in 1986. Earnshaw received his BSc and PhD in computer science from the University of Leeds.
Address: University of Leeds, Leeds LS2 9JT, United Kingdom.

Parallel Coordinates for Visualizing Multi-Dimensional Geometry

Alfred Inselberg and Bernard Dimsdale

ABSTRACT

By means of parallel coordinates a mapping $R^N \to R^2$, *which is not a projection* is obtained. Relations among N variables, for any positive integer N, are "represented" by their planar images. These planar diagrams have geometrical properties corresponding to certain properties of the relation they represent. Starting from a *point* ← → *line* duality when $N = 2$, the representation of lines in R^N is given and illustrated by an application to Air Traffic Control (i.e. for R^4). It is followed by the representation of hyperplanes, polytopes and more general convex and some nonconvex (i.e. "pretsels" in R^N) hypersurfaces. An algorithm for constructing and *exhibiting any interior point* to such a hypersurface is shown. Such a display shows some *local (i.e. near the point)* properties of the hypersurface and information on the point's *proximity* to the boundary. Graphics from the computer implementation of the representations and algorithms are included.

* KEYWORDS & PHRASES: * Computational Geometry, Parallel Coordinates, Multi-Dimensional Graphics Duality, Multi-dimensional Lines, Hyperplanes and Surfaces, Proximity, Conflict Avoidance, Air Traffic Control.

Definitions and Basic Results in R^2

The fascination with dimensionality and the abundance of important multivariate problems have motivated the development of methodologies for displaying Multi-Dimensional Data and Multivariate Relations. Such methods have come about aided by the developments in Computer Graphics ([1], [2], [4] and the bibliographies in [5] and:[14], for example). The methodology described here is based on a system new system of *Parallel Coordinates*. To accomodate for the constraints of space as well as the rapid continuous development in this field only an anthology of the key results to date is provided at this stage. For some applications of this method the reader is referred to [6], [11], [12], [13] and [15].

On the plane with xy-Cartesian coordinates, and starting on the y-axis, N copies of the real line,

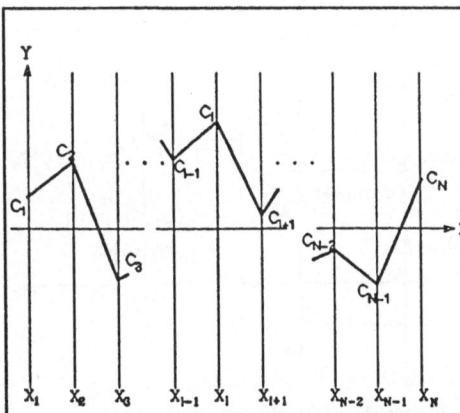

Figure 1: -- Parallel axes for R^N.

The polygonal line shown represents the point $C = (c_1, \ldots, c_{i-1}, c_i, c_{i+1}, \ldots, c_N)$.

labeled x_1, x_2, ..., x_N, are placed equidistant and perpendicular to the x-axis. They are the axes of the *parallel coordinate* system for Euclidean N-Dimensional Space R^N all having the same positive orientation as the y-axis --see Figure 1. A point C with coordinates $(c_1, c_2, ..., c_N)$ is represented by the polygonal line whose N vertices are at $(i-1, c_i)$ on the x_i-axis for $i = 1, ..., N$. In effect, a 1-1 correspondence between points in R^N and planar polygonal lines with vertices on x_1, x_2, ..., x_N is established. A *convex* hypersurface in R^N is represented by the envelope of the family of polygonal lines representing all points on the hypersurface (see [3]). In short, a mapping $R^N \to R^2$ — *which is not a projection* — is established. The key idea is that the description of a higher dimensional object is captured, to a considerable extent, in the *2-dimensional representation* of the envelope of the polygonal lines representing its points.

Points are denoted by capitals and lines (or arcs of curves) by lower-case letters respectively. In parallel coordinates, the corresponding symbols are shown with a bar superscript (i.e. $\bar{l}$ represents the line l, $\bar{P}$ represents the point P etc.).

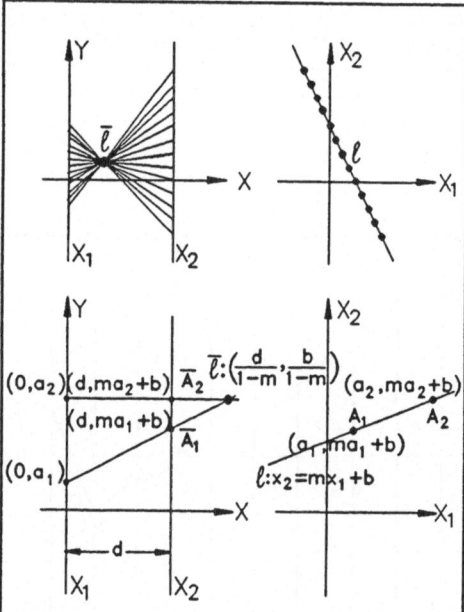

Figure 2: -- **In the plane parallel coordinates induce duality.**

Top part shows the family of segments, representing points on a given line, *intersecting* at a point. Lower part shows the duality line $l \leftrightarrow \bar{l}$ point in general.

The Fundamental Point $\leftrightarrow$ Line Duality & Curves in R^2

Points on the plane are represented by segments between the x_1 and x_2-axis and, in fact, by the *line* containing the segment. In Figure 2, the distance between the x_1 and x_2 axes is "d". The line

$$l: x_2 = mx_1 + b, \quad m < \infty$$

is the collection of points A. They are represented by the infinite collection of lines $\bar{A}$ on the xy-plane which when $m \neq 1$ intersect at the *point*:

$$\bar{l}: (\frac{d}{1-m}, \frac{b}{1-m}),$$

given with respect to the xy-Cartesian coordinates The reason for representing the point P by the *whole* line $\bar{P}$, rather than just the *segment* between the parallel axes, is that $\bar{l}$ may lie outside the strip between the axes. For lines with $m = 1$, we consider xy and x_1x_2 as two copies of the *Projective Plane* [7] so that the line l corresponds to the *ideal point* $\bar{l}$ with tangent direction (i.e. slope) b/d. Conversely, in the x_1x_2-projective plane the *ideal point* with slope m is mapped into the *vertical line* at $x = d/(1-m)$ of the xy-projective plane. Hence, we have a *duality* between points and lines of the Projective Plane. This duality as expressed by means of homogeneous coordinates is a linear transformation a—*correlation*—between the line coordinates $[m, -1, b]$ of l and the point coordinates $(d, b, 1-m)$ of $\bar{l}$. Specifically, the correlation

$$C_A : l \leftrightarrow \bar{l}, \quad k(\bar{l}) = A[l]$$

where $[l]$ and $(\bar{l})$, the line and point (homogeneous) coordinates respectively, are taken as *column vectors*, k is a proportionality constant and

$$A = \begin{bmatrix} 0 & -d & 0 \\ 0 & 0 & 1 \\ -1 & -1 & 0 \end{bmatrix}, A^{-1} = \begin{bmatrix} d^{-1} & 0 & -1 \\ -d^{-1} & 0 & 0 \\ 0 & 1 & 0 \end{bmatrix},$$

maps *lines* of the x_1x_2-plane into *points* of the xy-plane. This shows that the computation involved in going to and from parallel coordinates is minimal.

The practical problem of plotting points $\bar{l}$ representing lines with slope close to 1 can be solved by a simple stratagem. For a line l with positive slope m a reflection about the x_2- axis (i.e. $x_1 \to -x_1$ yields a line l' with negative slope $-m$. Consequently, the point $\bar{l'}$ lies between the x_1 and x_2 parallel axis. For any constructions and computations performed with $\bar{l'}$ the result must again be reflected to obtain the actual value of x_1 for the line l.

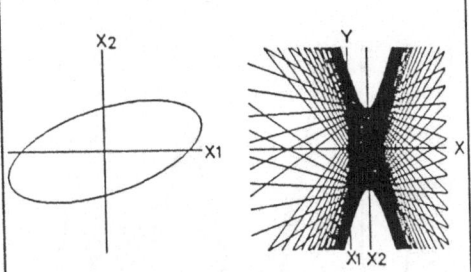

Figure 3: -- A (point) curve is mapped into a (line) curve formed by the tangents at each one of its points.

Here an ellipse is mapped into a hyperbola. In general, conics are always mapped to conics.

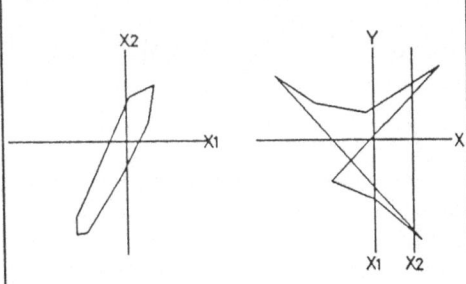

Figure 5: -- Convex polygon to a polygonal hstar

Here the hstar is a section of a pyramid

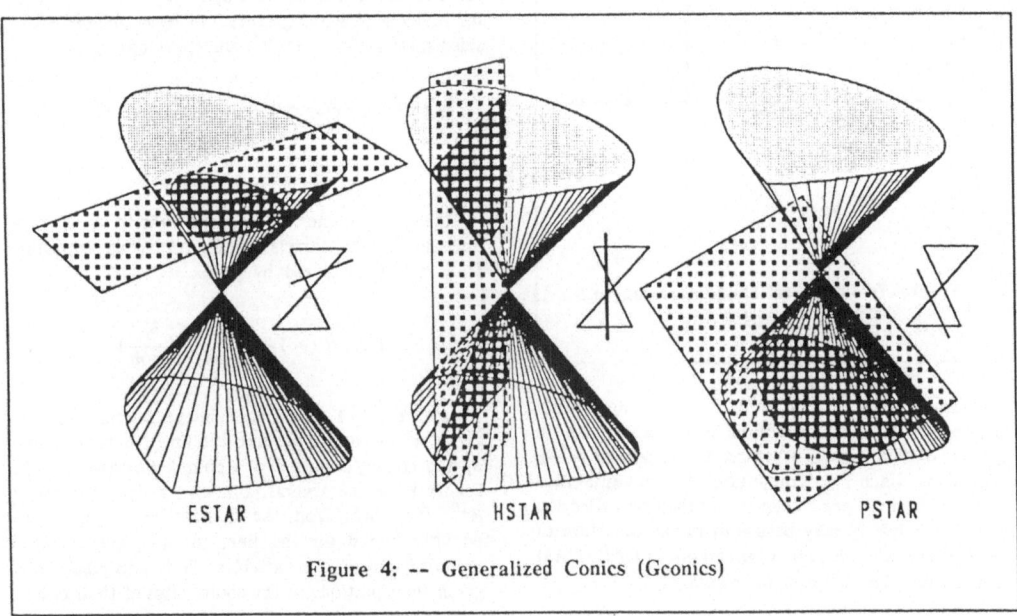

ESTAR HSTAR PSTAR

Figure 4: -- Generalized Conics (Gconics)

By means of the correlation C_A above the collection of points on a curve is mapped into a collection of lines which can be considered as tangents to another curve ("*line curve*"--see Figure 3). On the plane conics map into conics (see [8]). Actually, this property is more general and applies to *generalized conics*. Consider a double cone whose base is *any* bounded convex set as shown in Figure 4. As in the ordinary conics, three kinds of planar sections exist, those having *bounded, unbounded* or *two disjoint unbounded* components. By analogy to the ordinary conics they are called *estars, pstars and hstars* (the "e"

for ellipse, "p" for parabola and "h" for hyperbola) respectively. Collectively, they are referred to as *gconics*. It turns out that gconics map into gconics (see [12]) and in particular estars map into hstars with Figure 3 and Figure 5 showing two instances. This yields a new duality betweem bounded and unbounded convex sets and hstars as well as a duality between Convex Merge (Convex Union) and Intersection. Based on these results efficient new algorithms for Convex Hull construction, and the Convex Merge and Intersection of Convex sets were derived (see [15]).

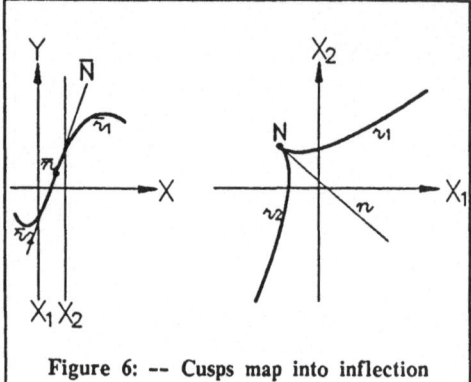

Figure 6: -- Cusps map into inflection
points

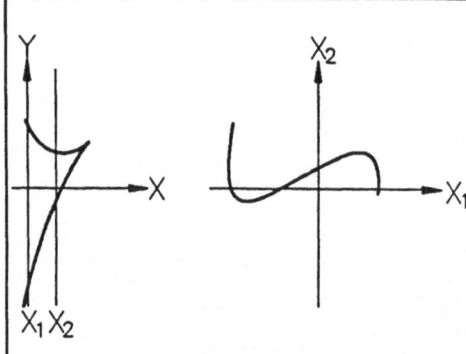

Figure 7: -- Inflection points map into
cusps

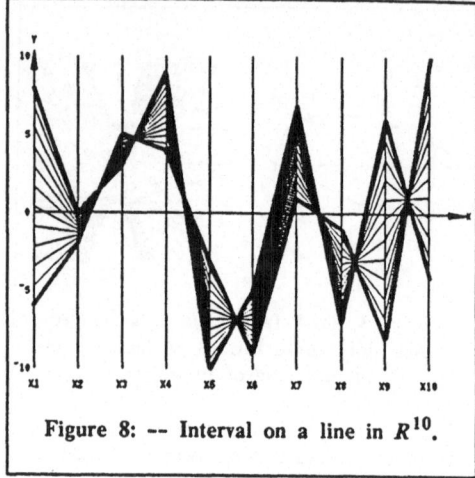

Figure 8: -- Interval on a line in R^{10}.

For non-convex curves there is a striking duality between cusps and inflection points as shown in Figure 6 and Figure 7 which is *independent of the orientation*. Since it is computationally advantageous to test if a curve has a cusp rather than an inflection point, the duality may be useful in the detection of inflection points in such applications as CAD/CAM and Pattern Recognition in general.

Extensions to higher dimensions

Lines in R^N

One of our objectives is to represent multivariate relations *geometrically* so that, for example, pencil and paper construction of points on the line is possible. Other objectives are, for example, calculation of closest points on a pair of lines;

for another example, development of a foundation for investigating the geometry of hyperplanes. Consider now a line ℓ in R^N described by:

$$\ell_{i,i+1} : x_{i+1} = m_i x_i + b_i \quad i = 2, ..., N.$$
$$m_i \neq 0$$

In the $x_i x_{i+1}$-plane the relation labeled $\ell_{i,i+1}$ is a line and by the correlation C_A translated appropriately it is represented by the *point*

$$\bar{\ell}_{i,i+1} : (i - 1 + \frac{1}{1 - m_i} , \frac{b_i}{1 - m_i}).$$

There are $N - 1$ such independent relations in the given set of equations, ergo the line ℓ is represented by the corresponding $N - 1$ points. For example, in Figure 8 we see several points on a line interval in R^{10}. It is clear from the diagram how a point can be constructed on the line, for any given initial value of one of the variables. It is also clear how, given the equations or the coordinates of their equivalent points in parallel coordinates, points on the line can be calculated.

In the given set of equations the constraint $m_i \neq 0$ requires some attention. Note that if some intermediate $m_i = 0$ the implication is that the variable x_{i+1} has a fixed non varying value. There is no reason why a straight line should not have such a property. However there is a deficiency in the procedure outlined above. For, starting with a value of x_1 the values of the variables up through x_{i+1} can be constructed (calculated) without difficulty, but it is not possible to continue. Conversely starting at, for example, x_N it is not possible to construct (compute) values of the x's before x_{i+1}. One solution

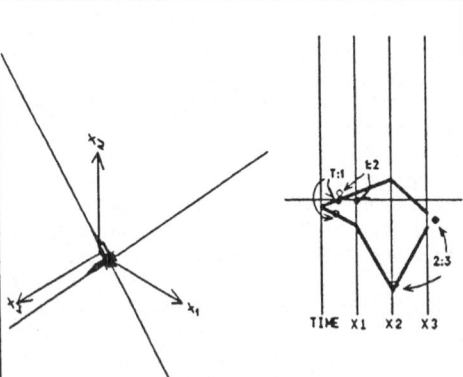

Figure 9: -- Closest approach of two air-craft. The time at which this occurs and their corresponding positions.

On the four parallel axes a polygonal line shows the time, value on the T-axis, when the position (x_1, x_2, x_3) is attained. Even in an accurate 3-D isometric (above left) appearances are deceptive. Though the air-craft look as if they are close to colliding, the information in parallel coordinates shows that this is not the case.

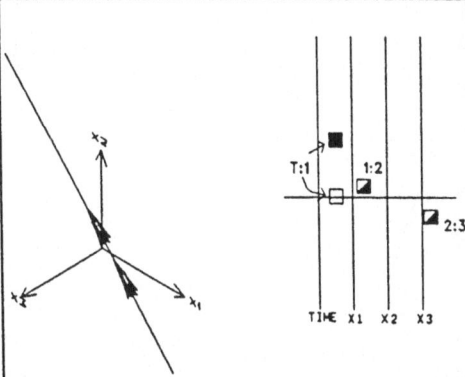

Figure 10: -- Two aircraft flying the same path with the same velocity.

Note that the 1:2 , 2:3 points are shared indicating that the paths in 3-D are the same. When that occurs, the leftmost T:1 corresponds to the greater speed. Here the airplanes have the same velocity since the two T:1 points have the same horizontal position.

to a problem such as this is, for example, to replace the linear relation between x_{i+2} and x_{i+1} by a linear relation between x_{i+2} and x_i, thus bypassing the fixed value x_{i+1}. Note that there are still $N-1$ equations, hence $N-1$ points defining the line in parallel coordinates. Obviously there are many ways to represent a line algebraically by sets of linear equations each equation of which specifies a relation between two variables. Using graph theoretic meth-ods it can be shown [14] that the distinct number of such systems is N^{N-1}, each of which are repre-sented in parallel coordinates by exactly $N-1$ points.

Another difficulty has to do with graphic display of the $N-1$ points which define a line. For any slope $m_i = 1$ the corresponding point becomes an ideal point and can be represented as a direction. For slopes sufficiently near 1 the corresponding point is simply off scale. This problem can be resolved by modifying the definition of the representative point as follows. If $m_i > 0$ replace m_i by $m'_i = -m_i$. It can be shown that if this is done with appropriate attention to detail points on the original line can be constructed (computed) by constructing a pseudopoint with the modified representation and then changing the signs of components in a manner consistent with the order in which the signs of

slopes are changed. It can also be shown that the modified representative points are bounded in a manner greatly simplifying the graphical represen-tation. For example $\bar{l}_{i,i+1}$ becomes $\bar{l}'_{i,i+1}$ whose x-coordinate is bounded by $(i-1,i)$ and whose y coordinate is absolutely bounded by $|b_{i1}|$.

Another procedure for definition of a line in R^N is to select two distinct points P_1, P_2. The set of points on the line is then

$$P = \lambda P_1 + (1-\lambda) P_2.$$

Given two lines, or possibly segments each defined by a pair of end-points, it is not difficult to calculate the shortest distance between the two lines, and the respective points of closest approach on each line. Also it is equally easy to solve this problem with the constraint that some one variable be the same on both lines. In particular the points of closest approach of two timed trajectories require of course that the time be the same for both trajectories. By the same token, if the lines intersect their common point can be found and shown by an easy construc-tion. It turns out that this construction can be used to discover *proximity* when the two lines are nearly intersecting or better yet when their minimun dis-tance is less than some specified bound. This can be computed very efficiently *without need for computing the actual distance*. The construction is shown in Figure 11.

30

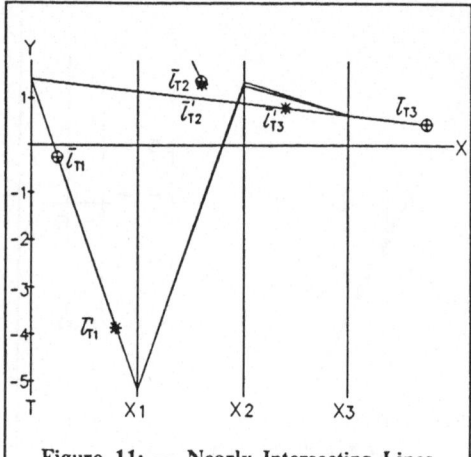

Figure 11: -- Nearly Intersecting Lines

There is a potential application to *Air Traffic Control* based on this representation. The trajectory of an aircraft is a function of four variables, time T and three space variables say x_1, x_2, x_3. A straight line trajectory for constant vector velocity can be represented by three stationary points say $T{:}1$, $1{:}2$, $2{:}3$ as shown in Figure 9, Figure 10. The time axis can be thought of as a "clock". At any given time T, the position of the aircraft is found by selecting the value of T on the T-axis. From this representation lines that are "nearly" intersecting in time and space can be visualized. From this and other properties collision avoidance and trajectory assignment (routing) algorithms are derived as is illustrated in Figure 12. It is planned to experiment with more general collision avoidance strategies for *Robotics* based on this approach.

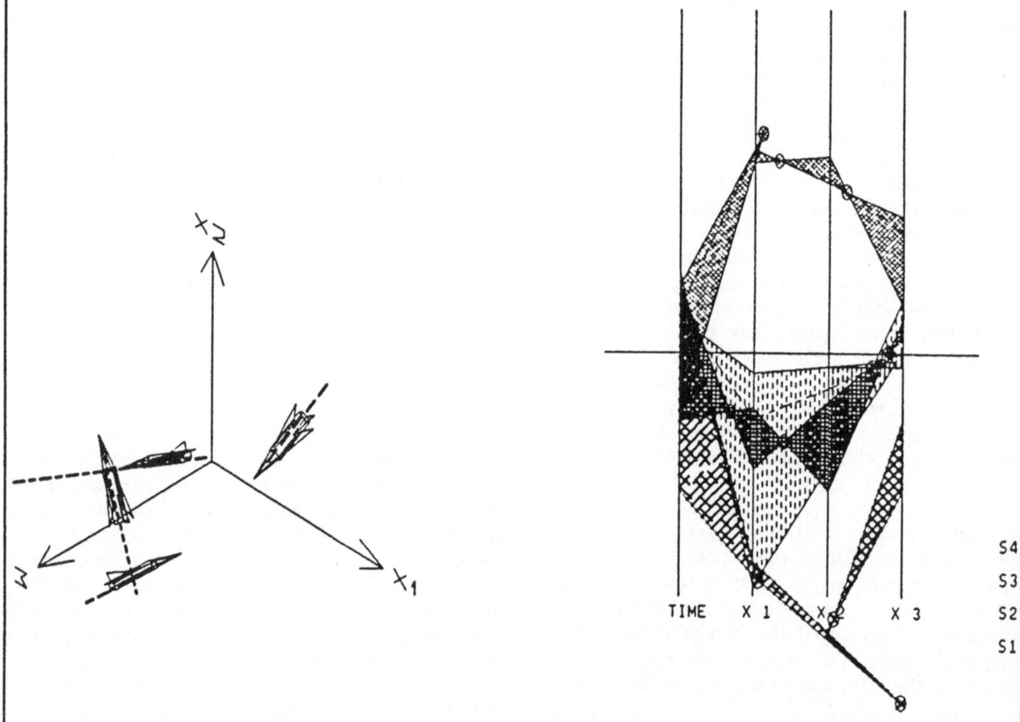

Figure 12: -- Aircraft flying straight line paths for specified time periods (segments).

Here 3 paths intersect yet two aircraft actually collide. Such a situation is impossible to discern in 3-D though it is easily found (both algorithmically and visually) in parallel coordinates.

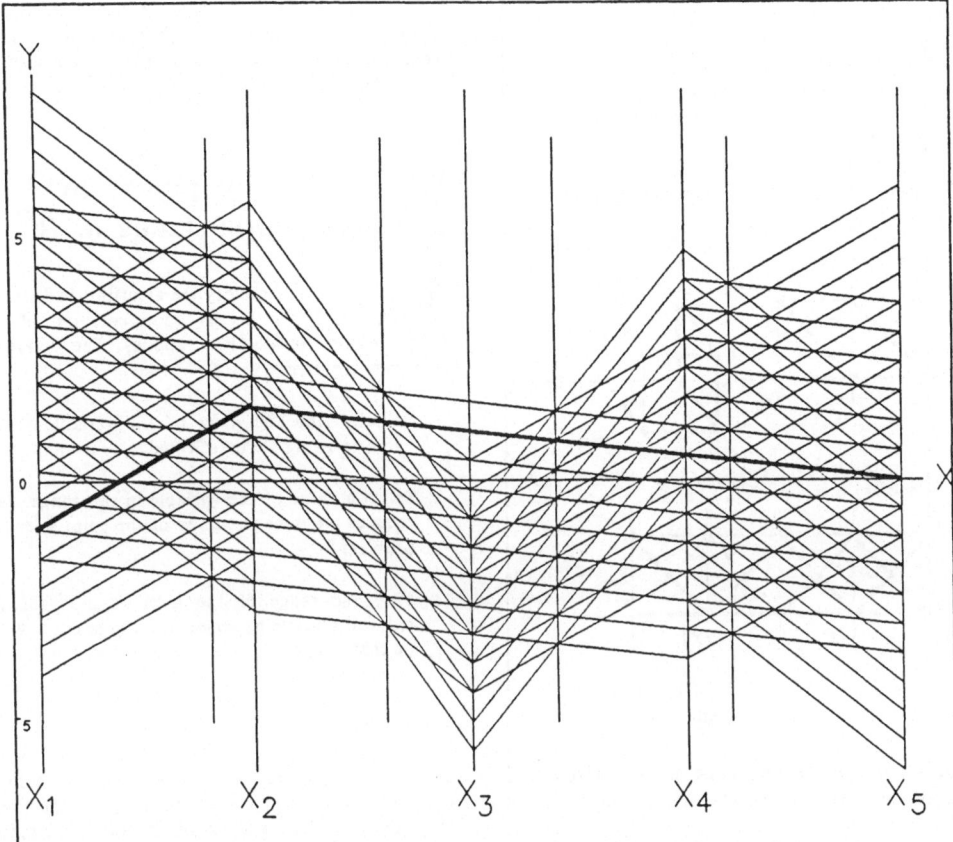

Figure 13: -- A set of points on a 5-Dimensional hyperplane.

Here the plane is represented by the point (-1,1.5,1,.5,0) and the four vertical lines X = .8, X = 1.6, X = 2.4, X=3.2.

Hyperplanes in R^N

U p to this point a very special and useful fact concerning straight lines has not been mentioned. In two dimensions a line in Euclidean space transforms into a point in parallel coordinates. Every line parallel to such a line also transforms into a point in parallel coordinates. The x-coordinate of every such line is the same as the x-coordinate of every other such line, namely $1/(1-m)$. That is to say, the set of parallel lines in Euclidean coordinates transforms into a vertical line in parallel coordinates. In N-dimensions a set of parallel lines transforms into $N-1$ vertical lines. This is the basis for the representation of hyperplanes.

For convenience of exposition, assume that the hyperplane intersects all $N-1$ coordinate planes x_i, x_{i+1}, defining at each intersection an N-

dimensional line. Each one of these lines is represented by $N-1$ points, and each family of parallel lines is represented by $N-1$ vertical lines. Thus it would appear $(N-1)^2$ lines are required. However not all the lines of these parallel families belong to a single hyperplane. The sets of families of lines in fact lie on a family of parallel hyperplanes. In order to specify a single hyperplane it is necessary to specify one point on the hyperplane. It is then possible to represent the hyperplane in terms of this point and just one of the $N-1$ vertical lines per family (see [11]). Effectively this process defines an $N-1$ dimensional coordinate system on the hyperplane. As with any such coordinate system, it can easily be transformed into another coordinate system by a non-singular transformation.

Figure 13 exhibits a set of points on the plane

$$X_1 + X_2 + X_3 + X_4 + X_5 = 2.$$

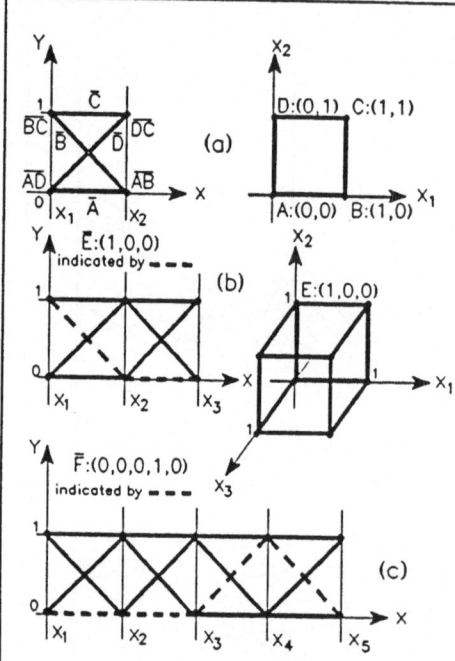

Figure 14: -- Hypercube Representation in Parallel Coordinates.

Graph of square (a), cube in 3-D (b) and Cube in 5-D (c) all having unit side.

for a local coordinate system for which twelve of the sixteen lines are at infinity.

Given a point and a hyperplane, it can be easily ascertained — from this kind of representation — whether the point is "above", "below" or on the hyperplane. Normals to a hyperplane can be constructed and hyperplanes so represented can be intersected with lines or other hyperplanes. These, and other properties have important implications for areas like Linear Programming and Convex-Hull construction in R^N.

A feel for the power of the representation can be gained from Figure 14 from which, with a bit of practice, the vertices, edges and faces, and their interrelationship, of the hypercube can be recognized.

There has been considerable interest for this methodology in the area of Statistics known as Exploratory Data Analysis. In Figure 15 a set of about 2000 of 8-dimensional points is shown. They are actual measurements of an industrial process involving a number of variables not of all which are shown here. The pattern in between the R111 and R112-axes resembles one of the vertical lines in the hyperplane

representation. This is confirmed subsequently in Figure 16 and Figure 17. That a linear relation would be found in industrial data by mere inspection was surprising to us.

Finding interior points to certain hypersurfaces in R^N

In the interest of brevity the algorithm is discussed concurrently with the representation of the hypersurfaces to which it applies. The following steps are required:

1. Initially find the *range* of the variable whose value is going to be selected.

2. Select a value of the variable in this range. This reduces the dimensionality of the point selection problem.

3. Find the range of the next variable for the reduced convex hypersurface and select a value in that range.

4. Repeat the previous step until the last variable is selected.

The convexity and boundedness of the convex hypersurface guarantee that in each case the range is an interval. The success of the algorithm hinges on finding the intervals efficiently.

As we will see, for bounded convex hypersurfaces the intervals are found by taking the projections of sections of the hypersurface. The boundary of these sections is transformed into the parallel coordinates resulting in the stepwise display of the point selection process. Ideally, one would like to have a display where the *relation between any pair of variables, say* x_i *and* x_j is apparent. There $N(N-1)/2$ such pairs for N variables which suggests that $O(N^2)$ displays with different orderings may be needed. Fortunately this is not the case. It turns out, [16], that for $N = 2n$ exactly n "well chosen" displays suffice while for $N = 2n + 1$, $n + 1$ displays suffice. This is due to the fact that a complete graph of N vertices can be obtained as a union of that many "properly chosen" spanning trees. For example, for $N = 6$ the permutations 126354, 231465, 342516 contain every possible pair (independent of the order) of *adjacent* subscripts from 1 to 6. Such a display provides:

1. information on the *local* properties of the hypersurface and
2. *proximity* information for the selected point i.e. a measure of distance of the point from the boundary.

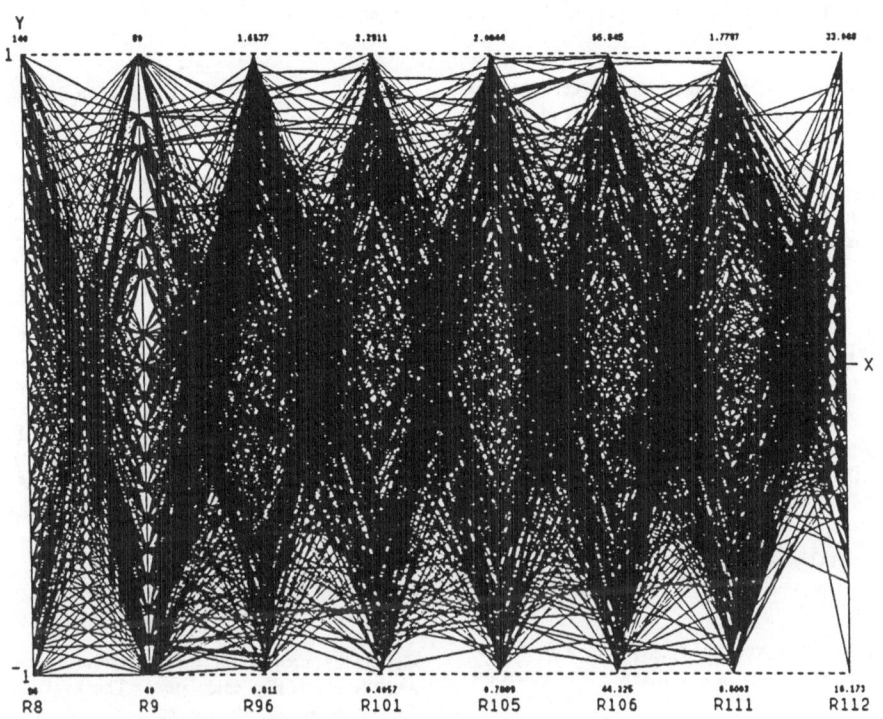

Figure 15: -- Industrial Data where only the measurements of 8 variables are shown.

Note pattern between the variables R111 and R112

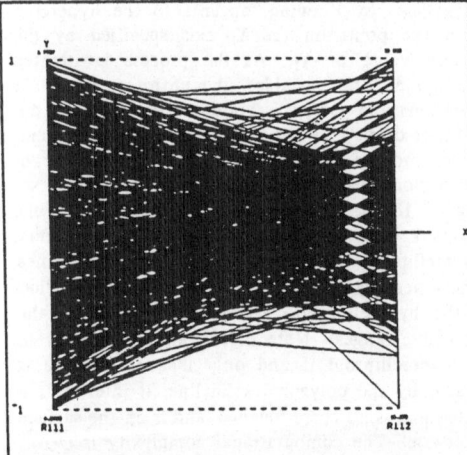

Figure 16: -- Enlarging the R111 - R112 portion of previous plot.

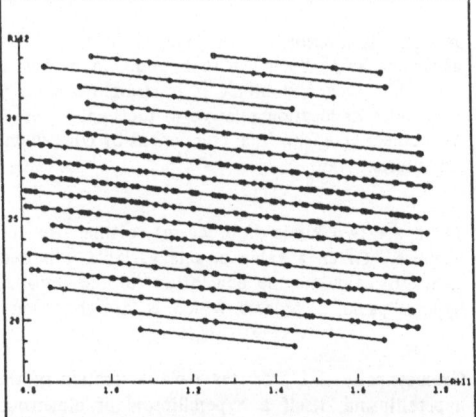

Figure 17: -- R111 vs. R112 in Cartesian Coordinates showing a linear relation between these 2 variables and another parameter.

These points are illustrated subsequently when the algorithm is applied to some specific kinds of hypersurfaces.

A generalization of the algorithm for certain non-convex hypersurfaces where the available ranges are a finite union of intervals at every stage of the point selection process will also be illustrated. Then a specific component (i.e. interval) of the available range is selected first and then a value within that interval is selected as in the convex case.

The Hyperellipsoids

Let A be a positive definite symmetric matrix and consider the function

$$F(X) = (X, 1) \begin{pmatrix} A & e^T \\ e & \alpha \end{pmatrix} \begin{pmatrix} X^T \\ 1 \end{pmatrix}$$

where X is a row vector $(X_1, X_2, ..., X_N)$, e is a row vector, and alpha is a constant. The equation

$$F(X) = 0$$

defines a hyperellipsoid with real points X provided that

$$e A^{-1} e^T - \alpha > 0.$$

A point is interior, on, or exterior to the surface according as $F(X)$ is less than, equal to, or greater than 0. Given a point X it is straightforward to determine its location relative to the hyperellipsoid. The object here is to find, component by component, an interior point.

There are two kinds of processes required for this purpose. Given a value of one variable it is necessary to calculate the new array for the resulting hyperellipsoid, a process which is straightforward.

Geometrically this produces a planar section of the hyperellipsoid, itself a hyperellipsoid of dimension one less than the original. The other requirement is to calculate the available range of the remaining

free variables by taking the projection of the reduced hyperellipsoid on a coordinate plane. Now let

$$A = \begin{pmatrix} A_1 & B^T \\ B & C \end{pmatrix}, \ e = (e_1, e_2)$$

where A_1 consists of the first two by two minor of A, C is A with the first two rows and columns deleted, B and B^T account for the remainder of A, e_1 is the first two elements of e, e_2 is the remainder of e.

Theorem:-- Let $\tilde{X} = (X_1, X_2)$. The projection of $F(X)$ on the X_1, X_2 plane is the ellipse

$$f(\tilde{X}) = 0 = (\tilde{X}, 1) \begin{pmatrix} \bar{A} & \bar{e}^T \\ \bar{e} & \bar{a} \end{pmatrix} \begin{pmatrix} \tilde{X}^T \\ 1 \end{pmatrix}$$

and

$$\bar{A} = A - B^T C^{-1} B$$
$$\bar{e} = e_1 - e_2 C^{-1} B$$
$$\bar{a} = \alpha - e_2 C^{-1} e_2^T$$

Given the projection, the maximum ranges of X_1 and X_2 are easily calculated. The available range for X_2, given X_1, is also easily calculated.

The hyperbola which is the transform of the ellipse into parallel coordinates is essential for display of the selection process. For one thing, the available range of X_1 is the interval on the X_1 axis between the two branches of the hyperbola, and similarly for X_2. Furthermore, the *range* of X_2, once X_1 is selected is *exhibited* by drawing tangents to the hyperbola from the point on the X_1 axis specified by the chosen value of X_1. As the process is iterated through all the variables, the entire sequence of selections and ranges is presented in a parallel coordinate display. Furthermore the hyperbolas themselves provide indications as to the sensitivity of various choices. For an example of the display, see Figure 18. In that picture the outer hyperbolic segments are the transforms of the original hyperellipsoid projections on the coordinate planes. The inner segments come from the successive slices of the hyperellipsoid. The dotted lines show the successive ranges. Note that a point is exterior to the hyperellipsoid if and only if a dotted line is crossed by the polygonal solid line, is interior if a dotted line is nowhere touched, and is on the surface otherwise. The computational complexity is $O(N^3)$ (see [9]).

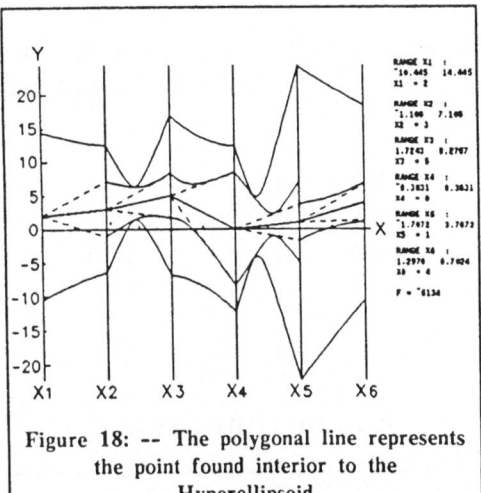

Figure 18: -- The polygonal line represents
the point found interior to the
Hyperellipsoid

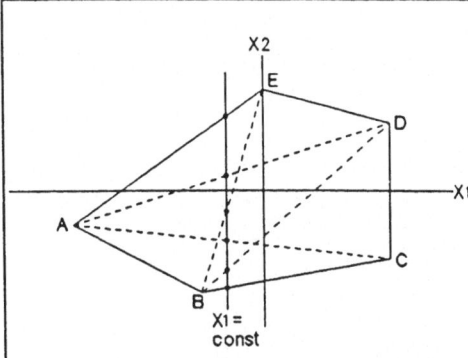

Figure 19: -- Intersection of a 3-D Face
with a Plane

There are six potential points of intersection, of which only two are relevant.

The Convex Polytope

For a convex polytope two input items are required,
vertex data and face data. The vertex data for N
dimensions with M vertices is an M by N array of
coordinate data. The face data is an array each of
whose rows specify the vertices of a face. Clearly
this is not enough to define a face in detail. For
example, in three dimensions the *sequence* of edges
is required to complete the definition. For present
purposes, however, no further detail is required.

A slice of the polytope by a hyperplane $X_1 =$ constant is a convex polytope of dimension $N - 1$. In
order to iterate the process it is required to produce
vertex data and face data of the same kind as the
original data. As for the hyperellipsoid the procedure
involves projecting the polytope on the X_1, X_2 plane
to find bounds for the variables or, given the value
of one variable, to find the range of the other.
Mathematically the projection is the convex hull of
the projection on the coordinate plane of the vertices,
which latter is simply the first two columns of the
vertex data. As for display the ellipse is replaced
by the polygon defined by the convex hull, the
hyperbola by an hstar and tangents by supporting
lines. The various statements regarding range of X_1,
range of X_2, and range of X_2 for specified X_1 are
reinterpreted in terms of the existing hstar.

To clarify subsequent discussion, consider a three
dimensional convex polytope, in particular, one of
its faces. Let the face be intersected by a plane
(e.g. $X_1 =$ constant). This would result in a picture
something like Figure 19 (in which the X_3 axis is
perpendicular to the plane of the paper). If the

sequence of edges is known the relevant points of
intersection with the face are also known. That is
to say, a face of the resultant two dimensional
polytope is known. If, on the other hand, the sequence is not known there are in this example six
points, some two of which define the face of the
reduced polytope. The remaining four points are
interior points of the segment defining the new face.
Of the six points, four of them originate in only
one face, call it F_1, two of them originate in more
than one face, say faces F_1, F_2. In any case the
face associated with points of the first kind is a
subset of the faces associated with points of the
second kind. In N dimensions a more complex situation exists. Now the points produced by
hyperplane intersections with a convex polytope of
dimension N can belong to many faces. The procedure required is to produce the complete list of
points from all faces. To each point is attached
the identification of the faces of origin. Then the
set of *distinct* points is determined and, for each such
point the list identifying the faces of origin. The
point selection rule appropriate to N dimensions
is follows:

Theorem:-- Let P_i be a point of the generated set
and let S_i be the set of face identifiers for the faces
originating this point. Let P_j be another point and
S_j its associated set. Whenever $S_i \subset S_j$ the point P_i
will be an interior point of a generated face.

When the process implied by this theorem is carried
to its conclusion the result is an array of points
which constitute the vertices of the resulting
polytope. Since for each such point it is known
which faces originated it, it is a simple matter to

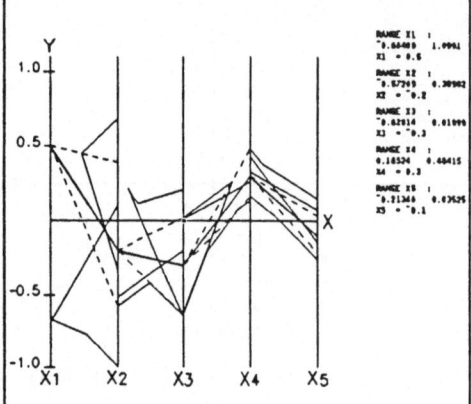

Figure 20: -- Solid polygonal line from x_1 to x_5 represents the point found interior to the polytope.

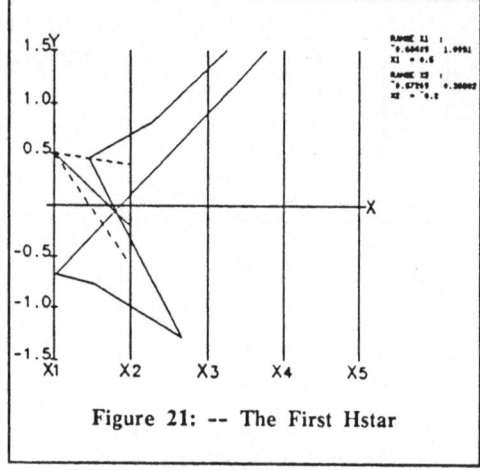

Figure 21: -- The First Hstar

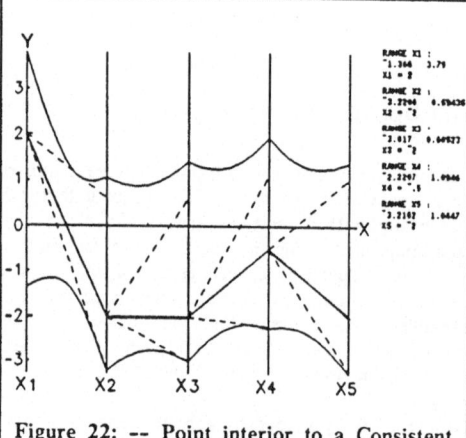

Figure 22: -- Point interior to a Consistent Hyperellipse

produce, for each new face, its defining vertices, thus completing one step of the iteration.

An example of the process is exhibited in Figure 20 Again the dotted lines show the successive ranges and serve to separate interior, exterior, and surface points. Note that for the hyperellipsoid and hyperellipse it was pictorially adequate to exhibit only the segments of the hyperbolas in the interval of interest. This is not true for the polytope. Figure 21 exhibits one step of the process in the preceding picture with its complete hstar. The question of computational complexity is open.

The Hyperellipse

The procedure for hyperellipsoids calls for repeated projections on coordinate planes, at a considerable cost in computational complexity. The obvious suggestion is to define an object whose projections do not change as the iteration proceeds.

Consider a collection of hypercylinders whose projections on coordinate planes are ellipses. The intersection of such a set of hypercylinders, if it exists, is clearly a convex object. With some attention to detail such objects can be defined so that they exist, are bounded, and have a property called *consistency* which, briefly, means that a valid value for *any* variable is consistent with a valid value for *any other* variable. For an example see Figure 22. Note that the hyperbola segments are fixed once for all, and that they are in fact continous across the (parallel) coordinate axes, which is the way the consistency

property appears in the parallel coordinate picture. The dotted lines serve the same purpose as previously. A notable property of this kind of surface is that the computational complexity is $O(N)$, since the surface is defined by $N - 1$ ellipses whence $N - 1$ quadratic equations must be solved. (see [9]).

The Hyperesp

Defining objects as intersections of hypercylinders suggests a generalization. The projection of a hypercylinder on a coordinate plane, for present purposes, may be one or more closed curves. For the example of Figure 23 ellipses, splines, and polygons are used, hence the name hyperesp [10].

37

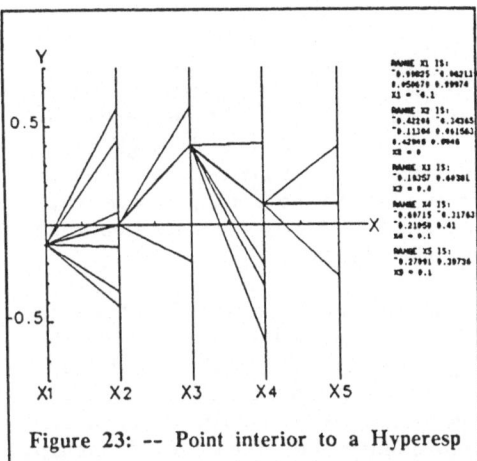

Figure 23: -- Point interior to a Hyperesp

Though necessarily brief, we hope to have conveyed a notion of a new geometrical tool for visualizing and analyzing multivariate processes. Parallel Coordinates have a "built-in mechanism" for generalizing "lower-dimensional" intuition and results without any intrinsic limit on the dimensionality.

ACKNOWLEDGEMENT

It is a pleasure to acknowledge the valuable suggestions and help received from A. Hurwitz, T. Chomut, M. Boz and N. Shavit.

Bibliography

[1] D. Asimov (1985), *The Grand Tour: A Tool For Viewing Multidimensional Data* SIAM J. of Scient. & Stat. Comp. 6:128-143,

[2] V. Barnett Edit. (1981), Interpreting Multivariate Data, Wiley, New York,

[3] V. G. Boltyanskii (1964), Envelopes, Translated from the Russian by R. B. Brown, Pergamon Press, New York,

[4] D. Brissom Edit. (1979), Hypergraphics: Visualizing Complex Relationships in Art, Science and Technology Amer. Assoc. Adv. Sc., Westview Press, Boulder Colorado,

[5] J.M. Chambers, W.S. Cleveland, B. Kleiner & P.A. Tukey (1983) Graphical Methods for Data Analysis Duxbury Press, Boston,

[6] S. Cohan, D. C. Yang (1986) *Mobility Analysis Of Planar Four-Bar Mechanisms Through the Parallel Coordinate System*, Mech. & Mach. Theor. 21:63-71,

[7] H. S. M. Coxeter (1974), Projective Geometry, Univ. of Toronto Press, Toronto,

[8] B. Dimsdale (1981), Conic Transformations, IBM Los Angeles Scientific Center Report # G320-2713,

[9] B. Dimsdale (1981), Operating Point Selection for Multivariate Systems, IBM Los Angeles Scientific Center Report # ZZ20-6249,

[10] B. Dimsdale (1982), The Hyperesp, IBM Los Angeles Scientific Center Report (Unpublished),

[11] A. Inselberg (1981), N-Dimensional Graphics Part I: Lines & Hyperplanes, IBM Los Angeles Scientific Center Report # G320-2711,

[12] A. Inselberg (1985), *The Plane with Parallel Coordinates*, Special Issue on *Computational Geometry* The Visual Computer 1:69-91,

[13] A. Inselberg, B. Dimsdale (1986), *Intelligent Process Control & Integrated Instrumentation*, First Conference on Intelligent and Integrated Manufacturing Anaheim, CA, Dec. 1986, ASME vol.21 341-358,

[14] A. Inselberg, B. Dimsdale (1987) *Representing Multi-dimensional Lines*, to be submitted for publication,

[15] A. Inselberg, M. Reif, T. Chomut (1987) *Convexity Algorithms in Parallel Coordinates*, to appear in J. of ACM,

[16] E. Wegman (1986) Hyperdimensional Data Analysis Using Parallel Coordinates, Tech. Rep. #1, Center for Computational Statistics and Probability, George Mason Univ., Fairfax, VA,

Color Figure Titles

- Fig C0 -- A line interval in 10-D. The polygonal lines represent points on the line. Note that all polygonal lines pass through the 9 points on the XY-plane which represent the line. Four of these points are within the scale of this picture while the remaining 5 are outside. They can be found as the intersection of two segments (between adjacent axes) belonging to two polygonal lines.

- Fig C1 -- On the left the 3-D path of an aircraft is shown in Isometric. By path is meant the collection of **all** points which the aircraft will occupy **during** its flight. On the the right the **trajectory** -- that is the space and time relationship for the aircraft's straight line path with constant velocity -- is shown in Parallel Coordinates. The point labeled *T:1* represents the linear relationship between **Time, T** and the **Space variable X1**. Similarly, the point labeled *1:2* represents the linear relationship between the space variables *X1*, *X2* and so on for the point labeled *2:3*. By specifying the value of the *Time, T* the *Position, i.e. values of X1, X2 and X3* is found as follows:

    1. On the Time Axis, the point with the value of time is joined to the point *T:1*. The intersection of this line with the *X1-axis* yields the corresponding value of *X1*.
    2. That value of *X1* is joined to the point *1:2* and the intersection of that line with the *X2-axis* yields the value of *X2*.
    3. Similarly the value of *X3* is found.
    4. The *Polygonal Line* shown in parallel coordinates represents the specified value of time and the corresponding position.
    5. The small airplane shown in isometric is at the corresponding position on the given path which is parallel coordinates is determined from the *two* points *1:2 and 2:3*.

    In this way the TIME-axis is used a "clock". Also, it is possible to specify the value of any of the space variables and determine in the same way the corresponding values of the remaining space variables and time.

- C2 -- The positions of *several* aircraft at any time can be determined and shown. Note how 3-D appearances can be misleading. The "blue" and "white" aircraft look as if they may be colliding while from parallel coordinates it is clear that they are far apart.f

- C3 -- Here the *Time* and *Positions* at which two aircraft will be the *closest* is shown. This is the "worst case" condition. Again their 3-D appearances are deceptive.

- C4 & C5 -- Here the trajectories for a specified time interval (as indicated on the Time- axis) are shown. The green area specifies the region that the collection of polygonal lines for the the "green" aircraft will occupy and so it represents the time and space segment for the "green" aircraft's trajectory. Similarly for the other colors. Only the 3 *T:1, 1:2, 2:3* light-blue points (on the red region) are shown rather than the whole region. The "light-blue" aircraft is flying during the same time interval as the other airplanes.

  In the isometric a possible intersection between the green and white paths is indicated. By noticing that one green point does not fall on the white region (or that one white point does not fall on the green region) in parallel coordinates that possibility is eliminated. Similarly the possibilities of red & white or light-blue & white intersections are eliminated from the parallel coordinate representation.

  Since the light-blue points all lie on the red region a more elaborate check is required. The *2:3* points of the two colors are joined and the intersection of this line with the *X2-axis* is determined. Continuing, the *1:2* points of the two colors are joined and the intersection of this line with the *X1 and X2* axes is found. Since these two lines intersect the *X2-axis at the SAME POINT* we can conclude that the two paths intersect (in space) and the aircraft will pass through the same point. Proceeding by joining the *T:1* points and noting that this line does not intersect the *X1-axis* where previous line (joining the *1:2*) points did we conclude that the two aircraft do NOT collide. Their separation in time and space can be easily found.

- C6 -- A hyperplane in 4-D the *three vertical lines* representing it are shown in yellow while a collection of points on the hyperplane is shown by the red polygonal lines.

- C7 -- A polyhedron in 3-D and its representation in parallel coordinates. The red and blue portions represent the transparent projection of the object on the X1X2 and X2X3-planes respectively. The green portion represents the additional information needed to reconstruct the object from these two transparent projections. The union of the three portions is the parallel coordinate representation which uniquely and completely represents the polyhedron.

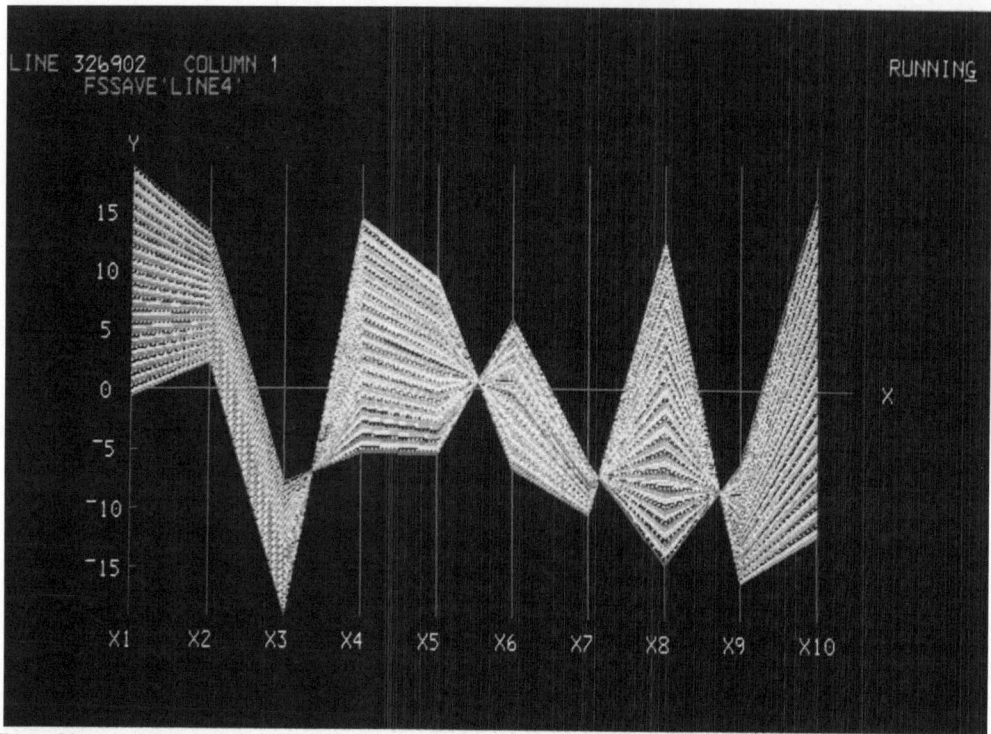

Fig C0

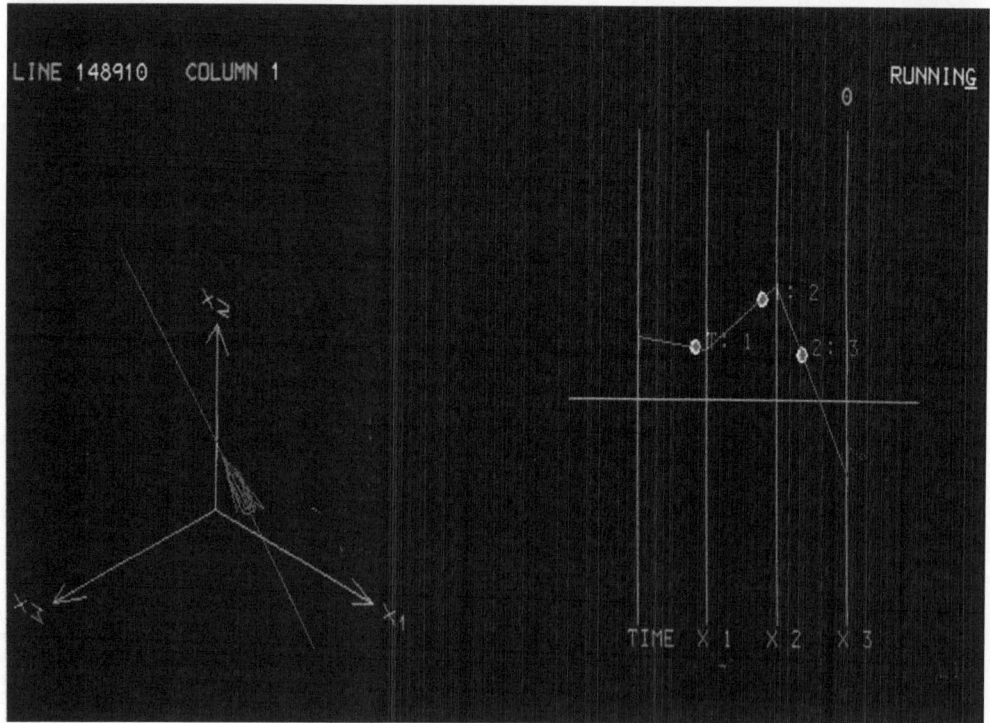

Fig C1

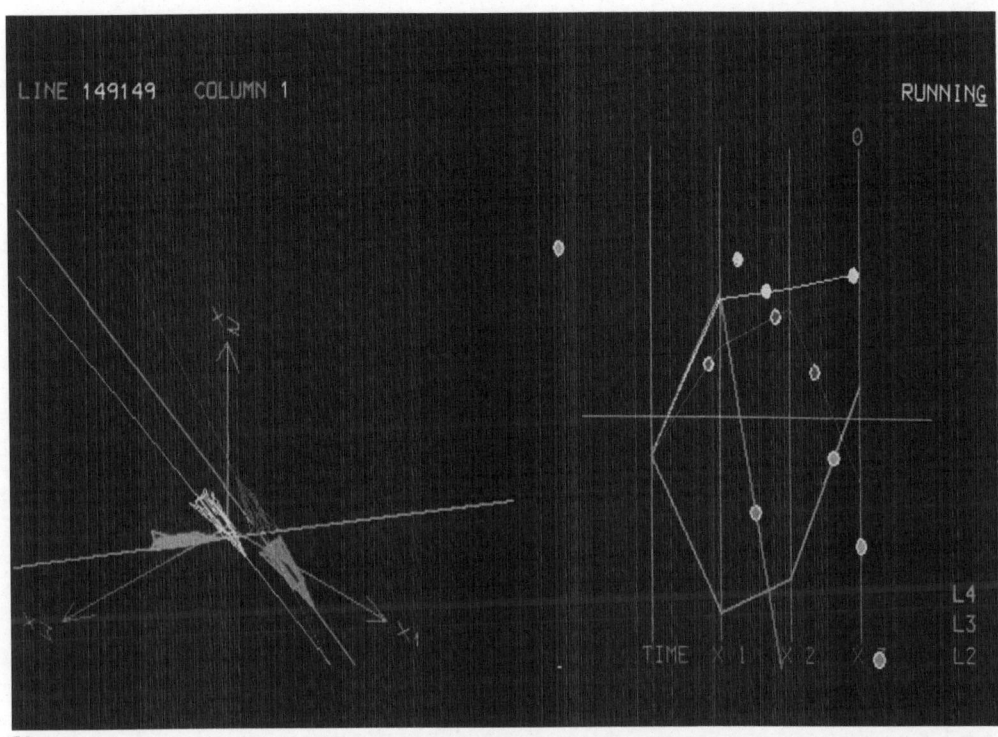

C2

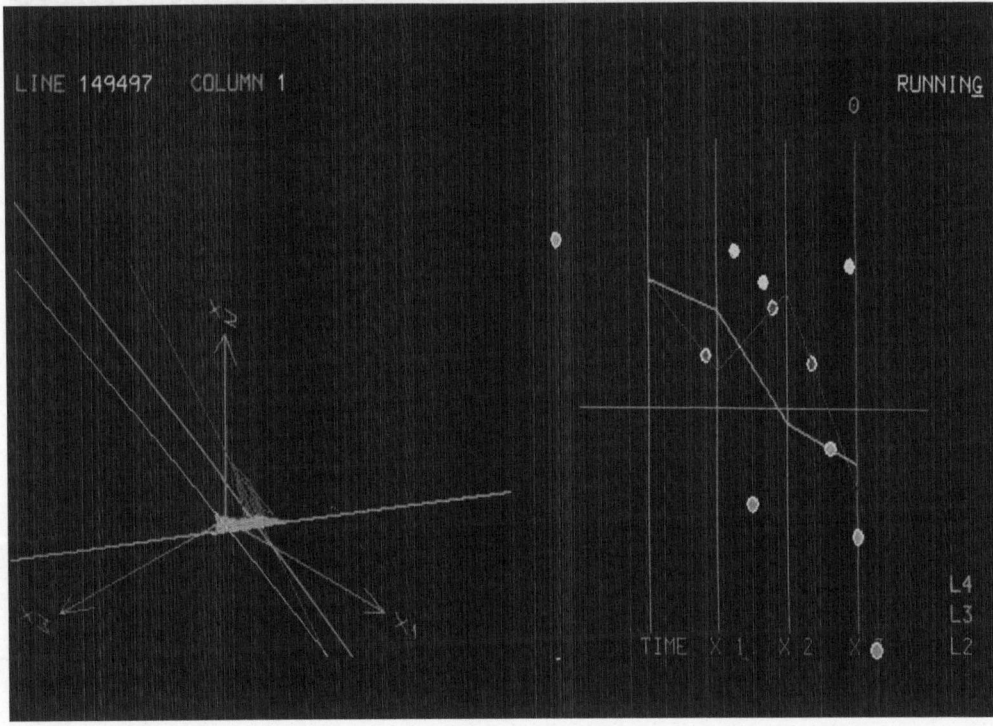

C3

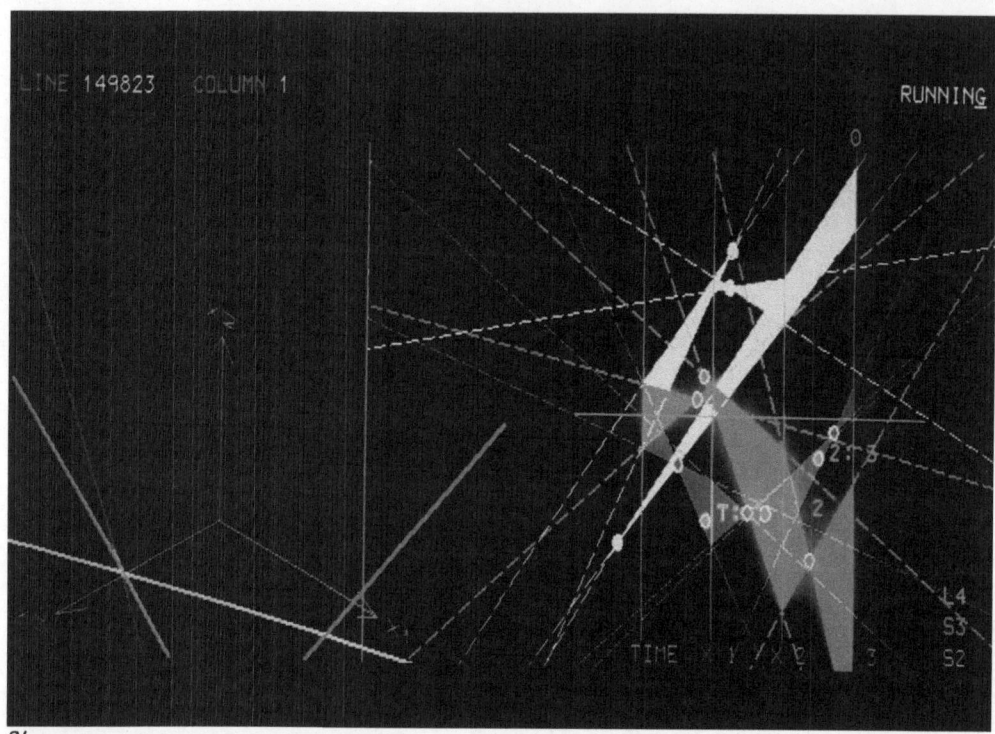

C4

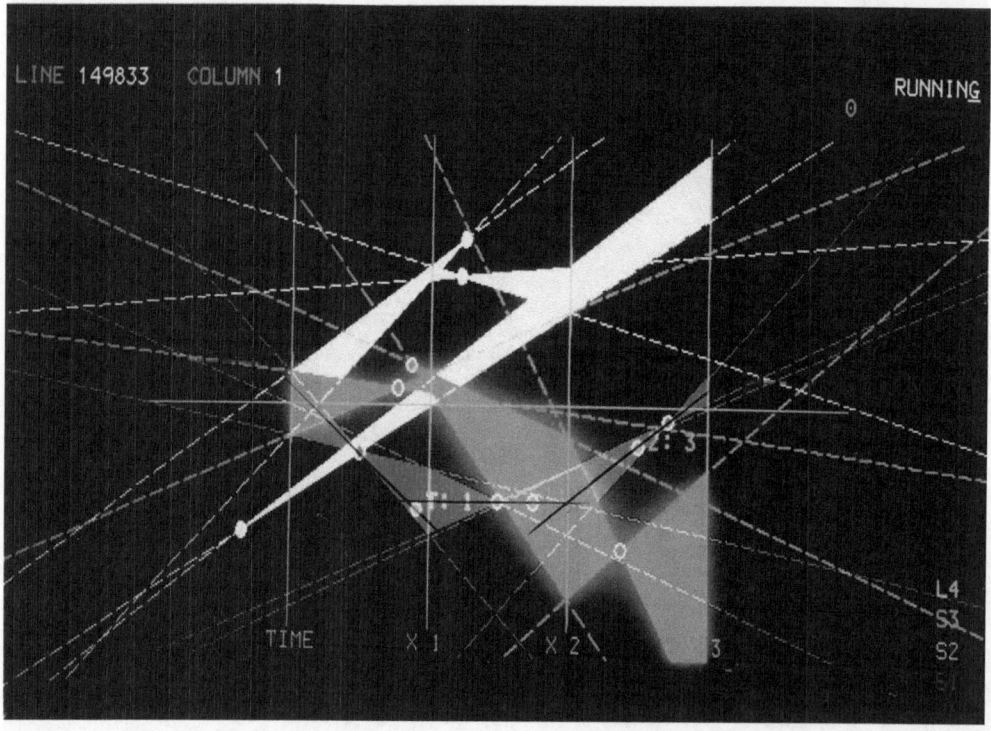

C5

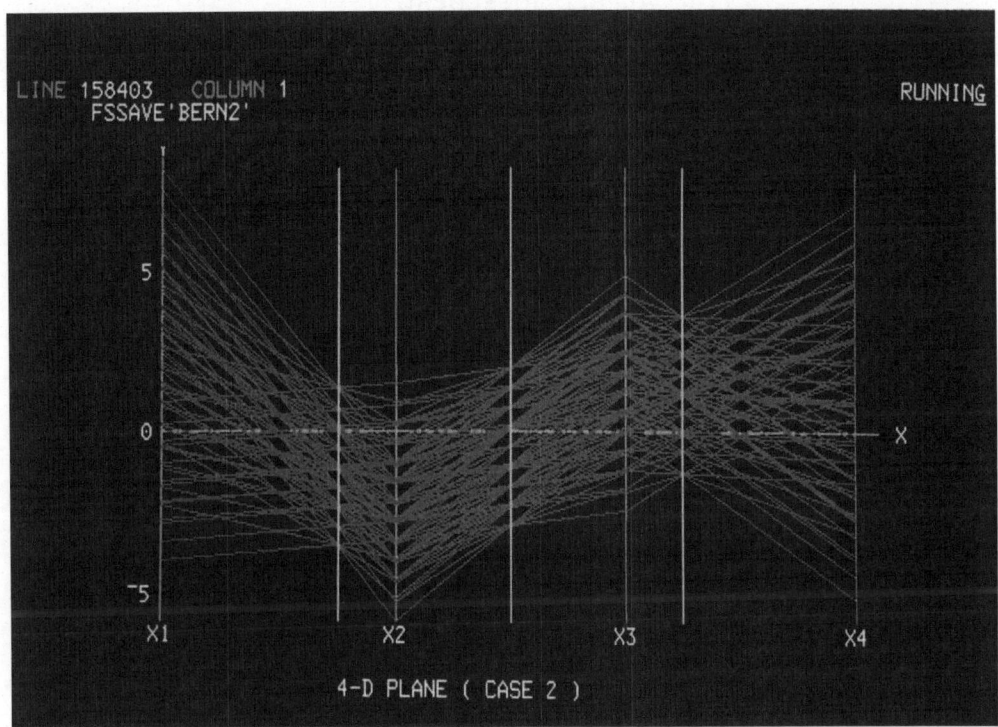

C6

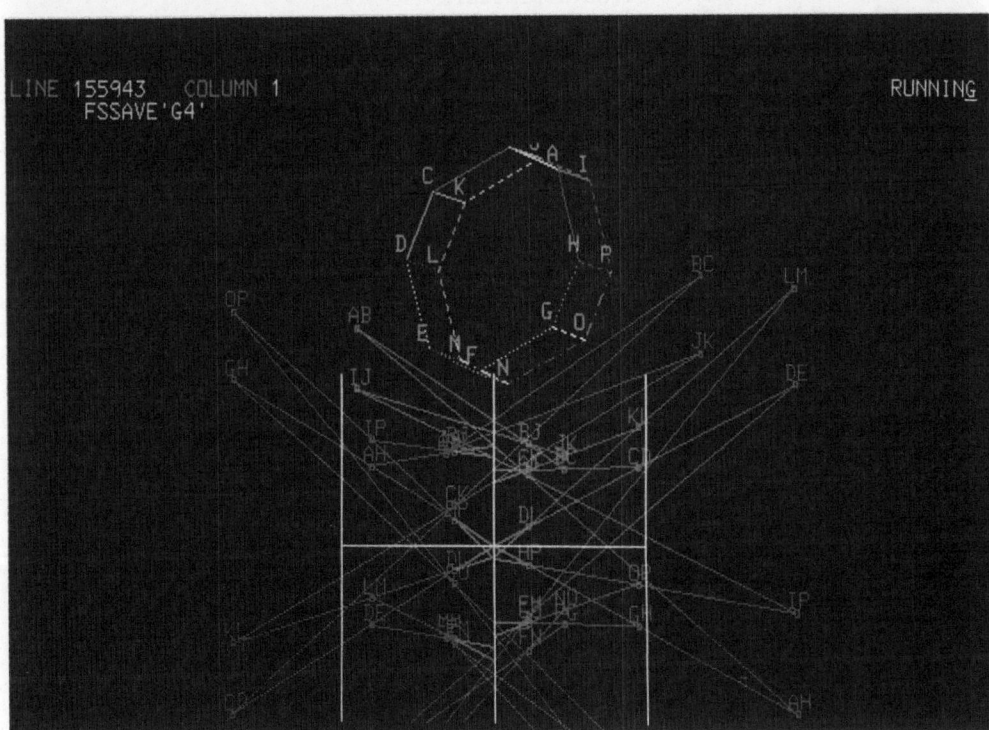

C7

ALFRED INSELBERG

In 1965 Alfred Inselberg received a Ph.D. in Applied Mathematics from the University of Illinois, where he was a member (since 1959) of the Biological Computer Lab (BCL)--a Cybernetics group--in the Electrical Engineering Department. He was Research Assistant Professor at BCL from 6/65 to 9/66. He then joined the IBM Los Angeles Scientific Center where he is to-date. In 1985 he was appointed IBM Corporate Senior Technical Staff Member. He is also Professor at the Computer Science Dept. at the University of California in Los Angeles. He has been Senior Lecturer (1971-73) at the Technion--Dept. of Applied Math. and Associate Professor (1977-83) at the Dept. of Computer Science Ben-Gurion Univ. in Israel. His research has primarily been in the Analysis and Synthesis of Nonlinear systems, Mathematical Models of the Inner Ear and a more recently developed a methodology for Multi-Dimensional Graphics based on Parallel Coordinates. From this methodology an Air Traffic Control system was developed for which a Patent has been applied. He has about 40 publications in the technical literature.

Bernard Dimsdale

The Ph.D. in mathematics was granted at the University of Minnesota in 1940. A term as assistant professor at Purdue University in 1946 followed a military interregnum. From 1947 to 1952 served as chief of research in the computing laboratory of the Ballistics Research Laboratory of Aberdeen Proving Ground. Was principally responsible there for development of algorithmic and programming techniques in order to utilize the Eniac. This was done in close association with John von Neumann. Following this, at Raytheon Manufacturing Company 1953 - 1955 was head of a commercial computing service. Have been associated with IBM since 1956 in various roles, principally with the Los Angeles Scientific Center. Notable activities during this period included development of a Natural Language System for medical applications, creation of the programming system for control of Project Mercury (Americas first man in space), research in geometric design for the aerospace industry (currently called CADCAM), and a high speed nonlinear programming algorithm for optimizing veneer production when cutting logs - in real time. There are about 40 publications in technical journals.

A Geometric Study of Parameters for the Recursive Midpoint Subdivision

N. Magnenat-Thalmann, M. Burgess, L. Forest, and D. Thalmann

ABSTRACT

For producing numerous frames as in computer animation, the direct application of the Mandelbrot theory of fractals is very expensive. The recursive midpoint subdivision is much more efficient although it sacrifices mathematical purity for execution speed. In our implementation, fractal polygons are created using subdivisions of meshes of triangles. But the midpoint is randomly generated inside a revolution volume where the axis is the edge itself. Based on this implementation, we study the impact of three geometric parameters for controlling this algorithm: the edge threshold, the eccentricity of the smallest cylinder surrounding the revolution volume and the displacement of the revolution volume towards the segment center.

Several examples are provided. The subdivision algorithm is also applied to generate textures by perturbation of the normal length.

Keywords: fractals, recursive midpoint subdivision, revolution volumes, stochastic textures

1. INTRODUCTION

Complex natural phenomena such as coastlines, mountains, galaxies or clouds seem beyond rigorous description for scientists. How can one model a jagged and wild mountain using Euclidean-geometry methods? This is not possible, because of the irregular (in the Euclidean meaning of the term) shapes of the real world. However, Mandelbrot [1975, 1977, 1982] has studied the structure of these complex natural objects and succeeded in describing them well introducing a new kind of geometry: **fractal-geometry**. He shows that objects constructed in his geometry, called **fractal objects**, can represent the shape of mountains, the pattern of stars in the sky and fluid networks in the organism. Fractal-geometry has become a new field of mathematics and it seems to provide a clearer look at our universe.

However, for producing numerous frames as in computer animation, the direct application of this theory based on fractional Brownian motion (fBm) is very expensive. For this reason, Fournier et al. [1982] introduce a simplification of the Mandelbrot methods. They propose a **recursive subdivision algorithm** to generate approximations of the sample path of one-dimensional Brownian motion. The method is much more efficient than previous methods; however, as pointed out by Mandelbrot [1982b], it sacrifices mathematical purity for execution speed in its approximation to fBm.

2. REVIEW OF RANDOM MIDPOINT DISPLACEMENT ALGORITHMS

2.1 One-Dimensional Primitives

This algorithm corresponds to the construction of a "fractal polyline" primitive from an initial deterministic line segment. It recursively subdivides the interval, as shown in Fig.1, and generates a scalar value at the midpoint. This value is taken as a displacement of the midpoint at each step in the recursion and is used as an offset from that midpoint along a vector normal to the original segment. This offset d is calculated by the following equation:

$$d = s.GAUSS (sd,tm) \qquad (1)$$

where GAUSS is a function that returns a Gaussian random variable with zero mean and unit variance, sd is the seed, tm is the middle of the interval $(t_1+t_2)/2$, and s is the current standard deviation given by:

$$s = k \, 2^{-iH} \tag{2}$$

where i is the iteration level, k a scale factor and H the fractal dimension.

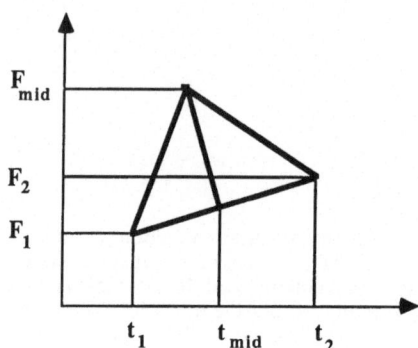

Fig.1 Subdivision of an interval

Fig.2 shows a MIRA-2D implementation of the algorithm which subdivides the interval $[t_1,t_2]$ based on the formulation by Fournier et al [1982].

```
type STOCHASTIC= figure (SEED:INTEGER; EPSI,H,SCALE:REAL);

procedure FRACTAL(T1,T2,EPSI,H,SCALE:REAL; SEED:INTEGER);
var
  F1,F2,RATIO,STD:REAL;

  procedure SUBDIVIDE(F1,F2,T1,T2,STD:REAL);
  var
    FMID,TMID:REAL;
    begin
    if (T2-T1) > EPSI then
      begin
        TMID:=(T1+T2)/2;
        FMID:=(F1+F2)/2+GAUSS(SEED,TMID)*STD;
        STD:=STD*RATIO;
        SUBDIVIDE(F1,FMID,T1,TMID,STD);
        SUBDIVIDE(FMID,F2,TMID,T2,STD)
      end else lineabs <<T2,F2>>
    end;

begin
  F1:=GAUSS(SEED,T1)*SCALE;
  F2:=GAUSS(SEED,T2)*SCALE;
  moveabs <<T1,F1>>;
  RATIO:=2**(-H);
  STD:=SCALE*RATIO;
  SUBDIVIDE(F1,F2,T1,T2,STD)
end;
```

Fig. 2 An implementation of the recursive subdivision algorithm

One-dimensional fractal primitives can be combined in arbitrary ways to represent natural phenomena such as rivers or coastlines. By choosing an appropriate value for H, it is possible to generate realistic shapes.

Fig. 3 shows three differents fractal polylines; the first (Fig.3a) was obtained using a pertirbation in y; the second curve (Fig.3b) was obtained by using the normal to the subsegment as the direction of perturbation; in the last case (Fig.3c), the midpoint perturbation is performed in x and y.

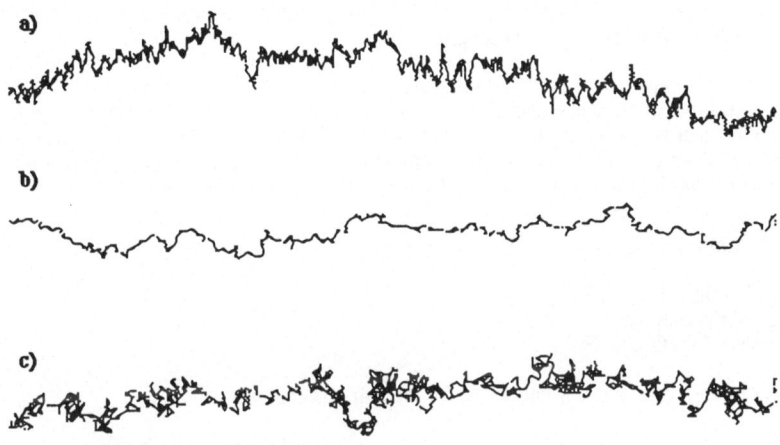

Fig.3 Three fractal polylines. **a** perturbation in y; **b** perturbation in the direction of the normal to the subsegment; **c** perturbation in x and y

2.2 Two-Dimensional Primitives

Fractal polygons can be created similarly to fractal polylines. For example, surfaces consisting of triangles can be easily used to represent stochastic surfaces. Each triangle is subdivided into four by connecting the midpoints of the sides as shown in Fig. 4. The positions of the midpoints are obtained by the same process as for polylines.

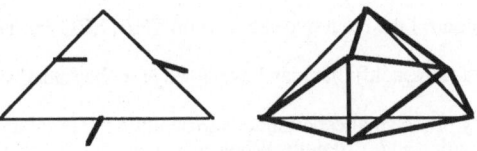

Fig. 4 Principle of fractals using triangles

One of the most important problems to be solved is external coherence: how to move the middle of the edge when it is shared by several triangles? One solution is to store the seed of the random function for the vertices and keep a hashtable to retrieve the midpoints, unperturbed, along the edges of the original polygons.

3. THE MIRALAB IMPLEMENTATION

At MIRALab, fractals have been implemented in the MIRANIM director-oriented animation system [Magnenat-Thalmann et al. 1985] using the recursive midpoint subdivision. Fractal polygons are created using algorithms similar to those previously described. In particular, subdivisions of meshes of triangles and quadrilaterals are widely used.

Before explaining how the technique was implemented, we should define the operation. It consists in receiving an object F_1 and generating a fractal surface F_2 composing of triangles with edges of a length less than a threshold value THR. The fractal surface F_2 is generated from the original object F_1; if this object is not a mesh of triangles, it is first triangulated.

At each step, each triangle has to be subdivided into three smaller triangles, as previously discussed. When triangles are subdivided, it is essential to pay attention to the external consistancy. In this case, this consistancy means that two adjacent triangles which share a same too long edge, will have to share the same new generated vertex. To solve this problem, new vertices are generated using a hashtable of records with a key consisting of the numbers of the two vertices defining an edge.

The general algorithm is as follows:

for each triangle of the original object
    for each edge of the triangle
      if the edge has a length ≥ THR
      then
        if a vertex has not been already generated for the pair of vertices
        then
          Calculate a new vertex between the two vertices and record it into the hashtable

4. CONTROLLING THE CHOICE OF THE MIDPOINT IN THE RECURSIVE SUBDIVISION

When an edge is too long, it is subdivided with a process similar to this previously described. However, a larger way of choosing the midpoint has been developed. The midpoint is randomly generated inside a revolution volume where the axis is the edge itself.

Now, we may completely define our FRACTAL operation by the means of a procedure:

procedure FRACTAL(F1:FIG; THREDGE, ECC, DISP:REAL; **var** F2:FIG)

Three parameters allow to control the recursive subdivision THR, ECC and DISP.

THR is the maximum length (threshold) that may have an edge in the fractal surface.

ECC defines the eccentricity of the smallest cylinder surrounding the revolution volume. It represents the ratio between the cylinder radius and its length. When ECC has a large value, the fractal surface is more irregular.

For ECC=0, all generated points are on the axis, which means that the shape of the figure is not changed, but triangles are smaller. With a small value of ECC, there are only small irregularities. Fig.5 shows the effect of the ECC parameter.

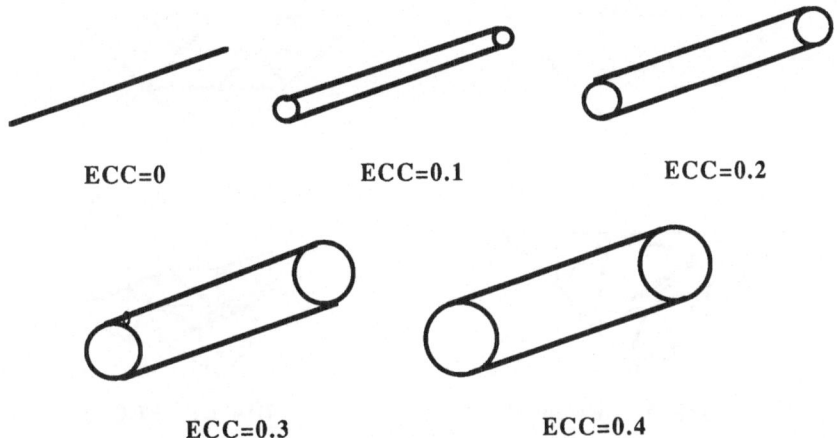

ECC=0   ECC=0.1   ECC=0.2

ECC=0.3   ECC=0.4

Fig.5 Effect of the ECC parameter

DISP is a parameter which specifies the displacement of the revolution volume towards the segment center. Fig.6 shows interesting values of DISP and the corresponding shape of the revolution volume. Interesting combinations of the parameters ECC and DISP are also presented for a single triangle in Fig.7.

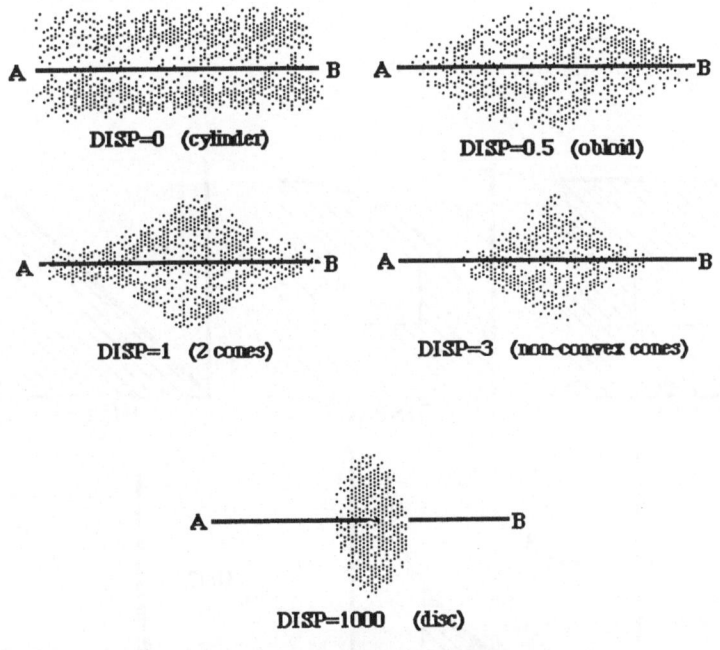

DISP=0 (cylinder)   DISP=0.5 (obloid)

DISP=1 (2 cones)   DISP=3 (non-convex cones)

DISP=1000   (disc)

Fig.6 Effect of the DISP parameter

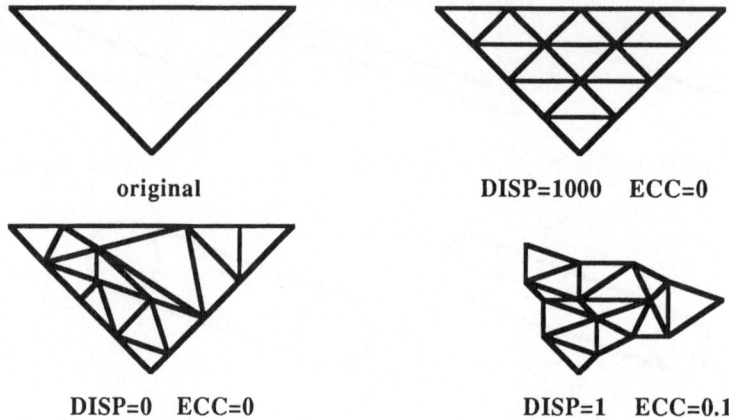

Fig.7 Combinations of the parameter ECC and DISP for a single triangle

5. ALGORITHM TO GENERATE THE MIDPOINT

The revolution volume is determined from the parameters ECC and DISP. When we consider the half volume in the reference system $<0,1> \times <0,1>$, we may use the formula:

$$y = x^{DISP} \tag{3}$$

Fig.8 shows the function for different values of DISP.

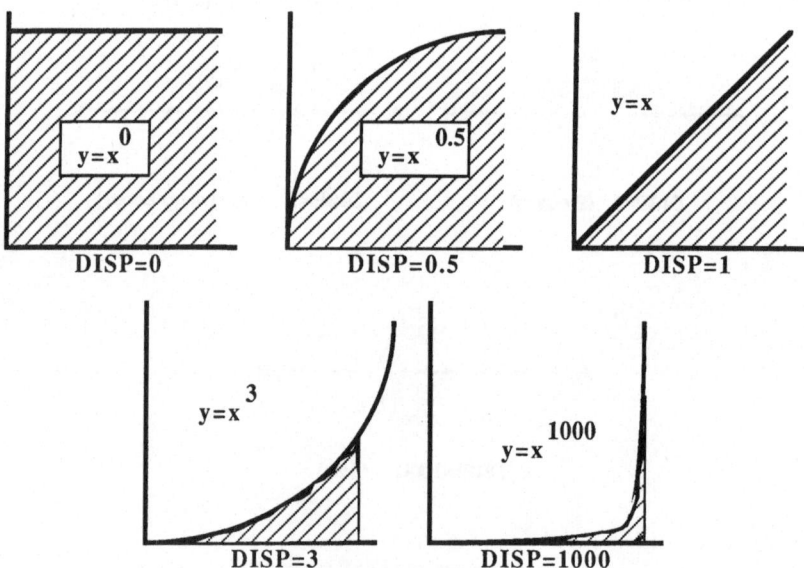

Fig.8 Examples of functions $y = x^{DISP}$

The function may be easily applied to the axis using a reference system transformation with B_1 and B_2, two perpendicular vectors, normalized and perpendicular to the axis as shown in Fig.9. Let B_3 a vector along the axis with a random length. B_3 is calculated using Eq. (3) and a random value H between 0 and 1. The z value, between 0 and 1, is obtained by Eq. (4).

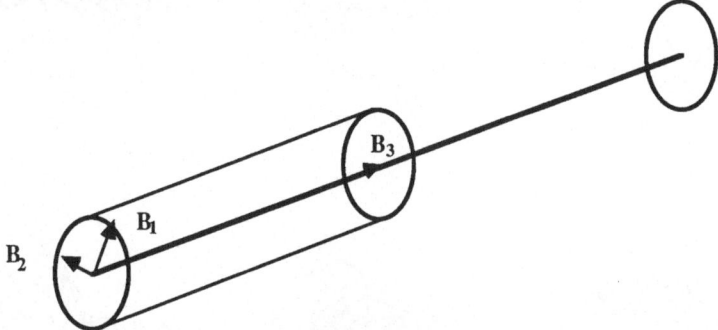

Fig.9 Determination of the midpoint

$$(\int_0^z \pi \, (x^{DISP})^2 \, dx) \, / \, (\int_0^1 \pi \, (x^{DISP})^2 \, dx) = z^{2DISP+1} = H \qquad (4)$$

$$z = H^{1/(2DISP+1)} \qquad (5)$$

6. EXAMPLES

Fig.10-12 shows the impact of the parameters: THR, ECC and DISP using a tetrahedron as basic object.

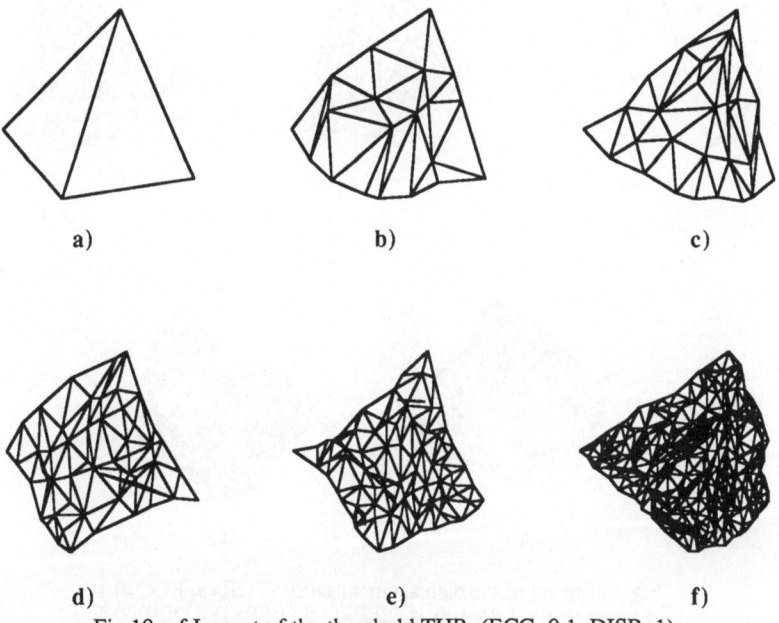

a)   b)   c)

d)   e)   f)

Fig.10 a-f Impact of the threshold THR (ECC=0.1, DISP=1).
a original; b THR=12; c THR=9; d THR=7; e THR=5; f THR=3

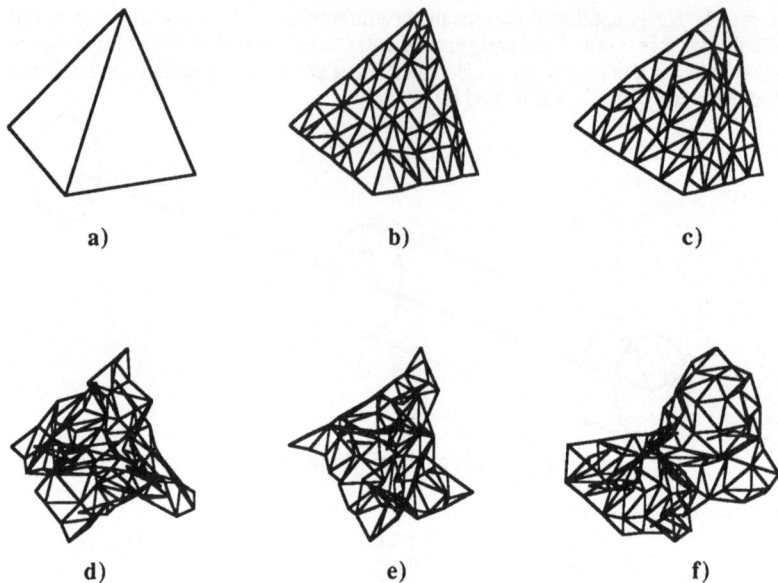

Fig.11 Impact of the eccentricity ECC (THR=6, DISP=2)
a original; b ECC=0; c ECC=0.2; d ECC=1; e ECC=2; f ECC=3

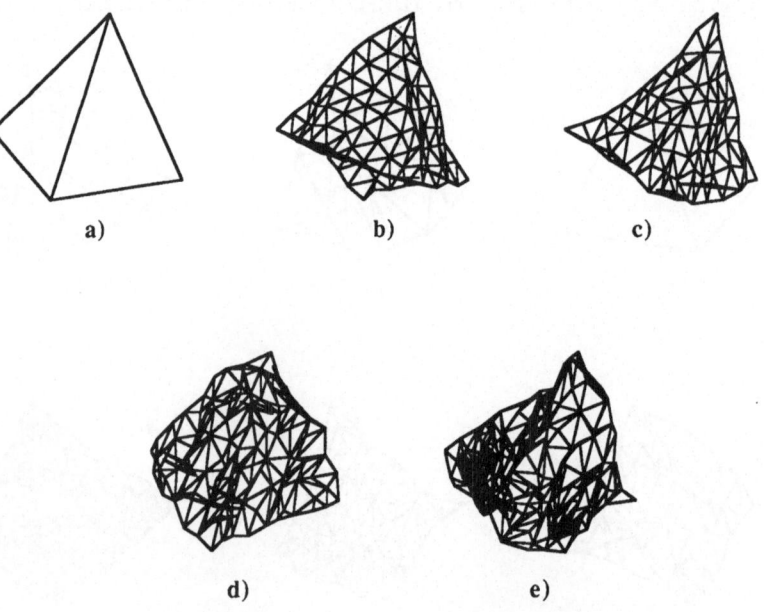

Fig.12 Impact of the displacement DISP (THR=5, ECC=0.1)
a original; b DISP=100; c DISP=5; d DISP=1; e DISP=0.3

Fig.13 shows the process to develop an image of candies based on the previous algorithm.

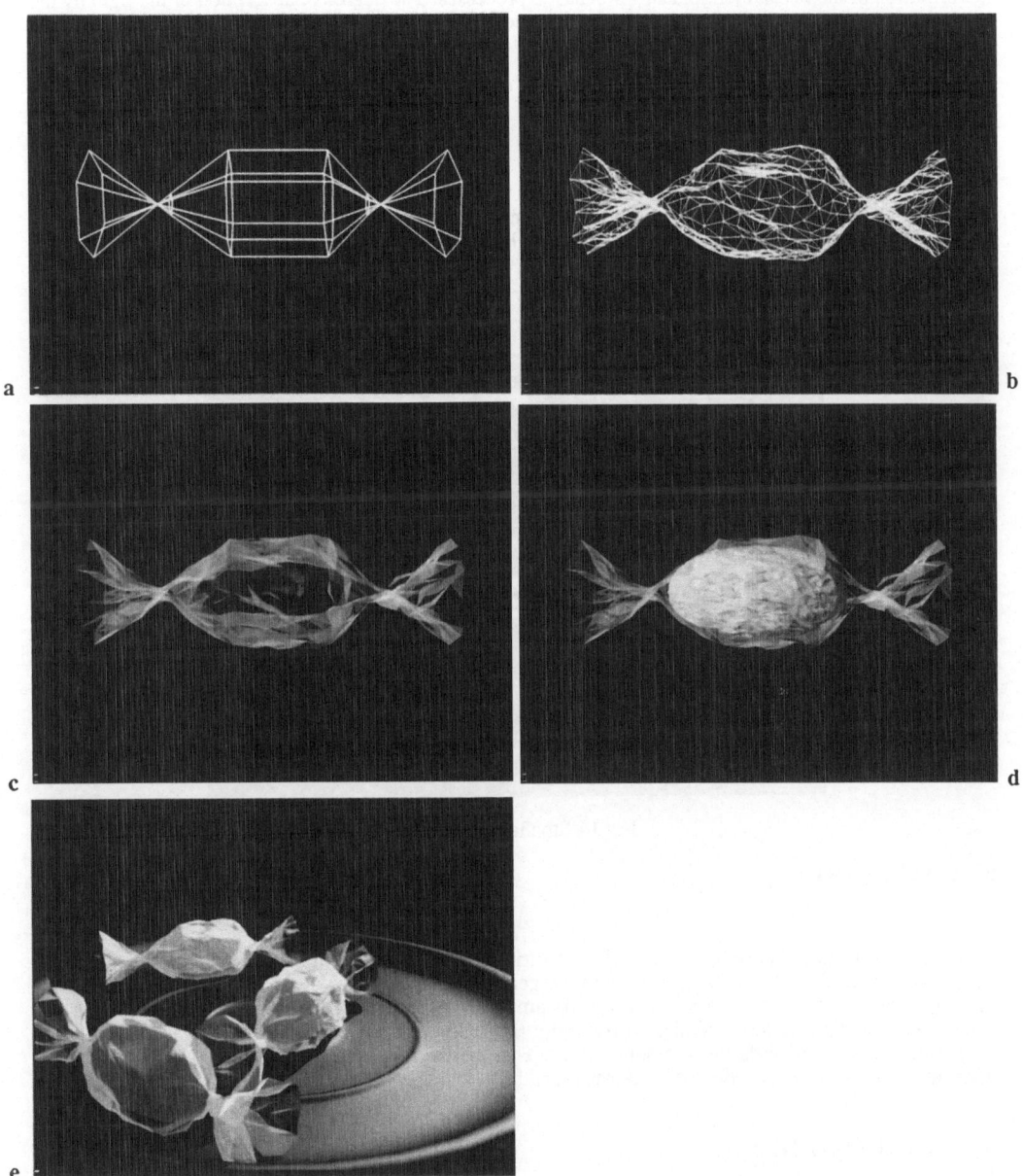

Fig.13 a-e Development of a fractal-based image. **a** original object; **b** wire-frame fractal; **c** transparent fractal; **d** shaded candy; **e** final image

7. STOCHASTIC TEXTURES

Based on work from Blinn [1978] and Haruyama and Barsky [1984], Burgess [1987] proposes a perturbation of the normal length using stochastic processes. The degree of absorption of the light by the surface is changed by modifying the length of the normal at the points corresponding to the pixels of the surface. The equation of the perturbed normal is as follows:

$$N' = d\, N \qquad\qquad (6)$$

with $d = |S|$ if $|S| \le 1$ $d=1$ otherwise

S is the result of a fBm function computed from the values of h and the scale factor as previously explained. The seeds used for the pseudo-random generator of the normal law centered at zero are derived from the initial seed given by the user, with h and the scale factor given by the user at the surface creation.
Fig.14 shows an image of such textures.

Fig.14 Stochastic textures

8. CONCLUSION

In this paper, we have study the impact of geometric parameters for controlling the recursive midpoint subdivision algorithm. The midpoint is randomly generated inside a revolution volume where the axis is the edge itself. Based on examples, three parameters have been studied: the edge threshold, the eccentricity of the smallest cylinder surrounding the revolution volume and the displacement of the revolution volume towards the segment center. The subdivision algorithm has been also applied to generate textures by perturbation of the normal length.

ACKNOWLEDGEMENTS

The authors are grateful to Marie-Andrée Allaire who designed the candy images. They also would like to express their gratitude to the referees for their helpful comments. The research was supported by Natural Sciences and Engineering Research Council of Canada and FCAR Foundation.

REFERENCES

Blinn JF (1978) Simulation of Wrinkled Surfaces, *Proc. SIGGRAPH '78, Computer Graphics*, Vol.12, No3, pp.286-292

Burgess (1987) Introduction of texture in the MIRA-SHADING language (in French), MSc thesis, MIRALab, Université de Montréal.

Fournier A, Fussell D, Carpenter L (1982) Computer Rendering of Stochastic Models, *Comm. ACM*, vol.25, N0 6, pp. 371-384

Haruyama S, Barsky BA (1984) Using Stochastic Modeling for Texture Generation, *IEEE Computer Graphics and Applications*, Vol.4, No3, pp.7-19

Magnenat-Thalmann N, Thalmann D, Fortin M (1985) MIRANIM: An Extensible Director-Oriented System for the Animation of Realistic Images, *IEEE Computer Graphics and Applications*, Vol. 5, No 3, pp. 61-73

Mandelbrot B (1975) Stochastic models for the earth's relief, the shape and fractal dimension of coastlines, and the number area rule for islands, *Proc. National Acad.-Sc USA*, Vol 72, No 10, pp. 2825-2828

Mandelbrot B (1977) *Fractals: Form, Chance and Dimension*, WH Freeman, San Francisco

Mandelbrot B (1982) *The Fractal Geometry of Nature*, WH Freeman, San Francisco

Mandelbrot B (1982b) Comment on Computer Rendering of Fractal Stochastic Models, *Comm. ACM* Vol.25, No3, pp.581-582.

Nadia Magnenat-Thalmann is professor of communication and computer science at the graduate business school of the University of Montreal. She is also codirector of the MIRALab computer graphics laboratory. From 1977 to 1979, she taught computer science at the University Laval in Québec. During the 1983 academic year, she was a visiting professor at the University of Geneva. Her research interests include the design of graphical interfaces, business graphics, computer animation, and knowledge-based graphical systems. She has written and edited several books and research papers in various application areas of computer science, and she was producer and codirector of the computer-generated films *Dream Flight, Eglantine* and *Rendez-vous à Montréal*. She served as general chairperson of the Graphics Interface '85 Conference. A member of the Council of Science and Technology of the Government of Quebec and of the Council of Science and Technology of the Canadian Broadcasting Corporation, she also serves as a director of the Computer Graphics Society in Canada.

Magnenat-Thalmann received a BSc in psychology, an MSC in biochemistry, and a PhD in quantum physics and computer graphics from the University of Geneva.

Michel Burgess received his BSc from the University of Montreal and he is now a student in computer graphics at MIRALab. He will obtain his MSc thesis in 1987. His research interests are textures and fractals.

Luc Forest is currently a master course graduate student of computer science at the University of Montreal. His research interests include image synthesis, computer animation and artificial intelligence. He received the BSc degree in computer science in 1985 from the University of Montreal.

Daniel Thalmann is professor and codirector of the MIRALab computer graphics laboratory at the University of Montreal. He has taught at the Swiss Federal Institute of Technology and at the University of Nebraska and has been a research member of the Computer Graphics Group at CERN. His research interests are computer graphics, computer animation, image synthesis and the design of programming languages. He has published over 50 papers in theses areas and is coauthor of eight books, including Computer Animation: Theory and Practice. He was codirector of the computer-generated films *Dream Flight, Eglantine* and *Rendez-vous à Montréal*. Thalmann served as program chairman of the Graphics Interface '85 Conference and is a member of the editorial board of The Visual Computer. He served as a director of the Canadian Man-Machine Communication Society and is a member of the IEEE Computer Society, ACM, Eurographics, and SIGGRAPH.

Thalmann received his diploma in nuclear physics and hos phD in computer science from the Univeristy of Geneva.

Questions about this article can be directed to Magnenat-Thalmann at HEC, Université de Montréal, 5255 avenue Décelles, Montréal, Québec H3T 1V6 Canada

N.Magnenat-Thalmann and D.Thalmann

Chapter 2

Fast Algorithms

A Two-Phase Fast Hidden Line Removal Algorithm

Qiuming Zhu

ABSTRACT

A computationally fast algorithm for hidden line removal is
presented. It handles the case of objects with curved faces rather
than just polygons. The algorithm spatially sorts the drawing curved
lines into a number of squared grid cells partitioning the drawing
plane to reduce the amount of complex geometric computations for line
intersections. Hidden line segments in the algorithm are separated
into two types and processed in different phases. The algorithm
achieves, on the average, nearly linear time complexity.

Keywords: Hidden lines, Spatial sorting, Cellular partition,
Line intersection

1. INTRODUCTION

A large number of publications have dealt with hidden-line and
hidden-surface removal algorithms (Sutherland 1974, Griffiths 1979,
Wittran 1981, Williamson 1972, Woon 1972). Depending upon the
working environment, the algorithms have been classified into three
categories: object-space algorithms that work on 3D descriptions of
the objects in the environment; image-space algorithms that are
directly orientated to the 2D display of the objects; and algorithms
that use both 2D display and 3D description information. The most
critical problem still remaining in hidden-line removal algorithms,
especially in real-time applications, is the speed of the operation.

Another problem is that most of the previous algorithms tailored
their strategies to a particular data representation model of the
objects. Usually planar-faced objects using a polyhedral
representation were assumed. In cases where objects are
non-planar faced, a planar approximation is used to model the
non-planar faces as a combination of a number of smaller planar
faces. Objects then still use a polyhedral representation. There
is always a trade-off between the precision of the representation and
the speed of the operation. Most of the time, when a high
precision is required, the time response of the operation becomes
intolerable.

In this paper we present a new algorithm for the fast removal of the hidden lines of non-planar faced objects which are not necessarily represented by a specific geometric or solid model. In our approach, the hidden-line segments of the objects are separated into two classes according to the relations between the hidden segments and the hiding objects in the 2D drawing plane.   The process is then developed in two phases corresponding to these two hidden segment classes.   Regularities inherent in each class of these hidden line segments are thus effectively utilized to speed up the process in each phase.   By taking advantage of the area coherence of the objects in the drawing, a 2D spatial sorting and segmentation scheme is employed.   It reduces the amount of complex geometric computations required by the non-planar object representations. Nearly linear performance is achieved in the program.

2. A   2D SPATIAL SORTING SCHEME

Sorting is a fundamental technique for efficiently processing large amount of data in solving many computer application problems.   A general sorting scheme is to sort the data in one dimension, that is, to order the data into a sequence by considering one key entity at a time.   It is observed that when dealing with two or three dimensional data, such as used to represent the positional relations of a number of curved lines arbitrarily distributed, the general one dimensional sorting scheme is not adequate.   Thus to effectively process 2D and 3D geometric data, a more sophisticated sorting scheme is necessary.

A 2D spatial sorting scheme is used in our hidden-line removal algorithm. Applying this scheme, a 2D drawing plane is partitioned into a number of rectangular or squared grids (Franklin 1981). Let G denote this partitioned plane,

$$G = \{g_{11}, g_{12}, \ldots, g_{mn}\}$$

Where g_{ij} represents the grid cell in the partition.   An integer number is further assigned to each of these grid cells, such that

$$g_{ij} = (j - 1)*m + i \quad where \quad j = 1, \ldots, n; \quad i = 1, \ldots, m$$

These grid cells then form a quantity base for the two dimensional spatial sorting to be implemented.

When a line drawing of the objects in the environment is generated in the 2D projection plane, the line segments are allocated in terms of the grid cells and sorted into these grid cells at the same time. It is analogous to covering the 2D line drawing with a grid plane and assigning the line segments to each of these grid cells in terms of their positions.   Each line segment is thus associated with a set of integer numbers which properly represent the relative locations of the line segment in the 2D drawing.   Note that this sorting scheme is independent of the representation of the line segments, thus is applicable to any object model.

Figure 1 shows a 2D drawing partitioned by the grid cells. In the drawing, the straight line AB is sorted into grid cells 18, 26, 34, 42, and 50; arc BC is sorted into 50 and 51; and ellipse AD is sorted into 10, 11, 18, and 19; etc.

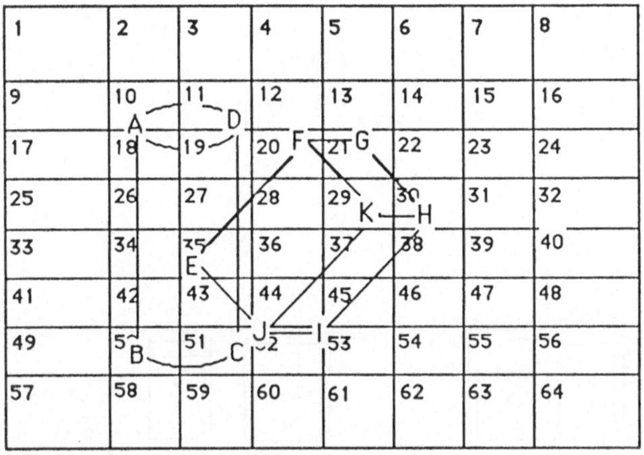

Fig.1 A 2D drawing partitioned by grid celles

The realization of the above sorting scheme is achieved by a special data structure built by the algorithm. From the object list which contains the geometric and topological information in 3D, a 2D drawing line-segment list is generated which is the central part of the data structure in the algorithm. In this list, line segments belonging to the same object are circularly linked together. At the other end of the structure is a list of grid cells to which line segments are sorted. The line-segment list and grid-cell list are circularly connected via two list indices: the line-grid index and the grid-line index. A diagram of the data structure is shown in Fig.2

As for the drawing in Fig.1, the line-grid.index in the data structure will have entries such that

```
Line    AB        18, 26, 34, 42, 50
Arc     BC        50, 51
Ellipse AD        10, 11, 18, 19
Line    EF        35, 27, 28, 20
• • •
```

The grid-line.index will have entries such that

```
Grid 10        AD
Grid 50        AB, BC
Grid 35        CD, EF, JF
• • •
```

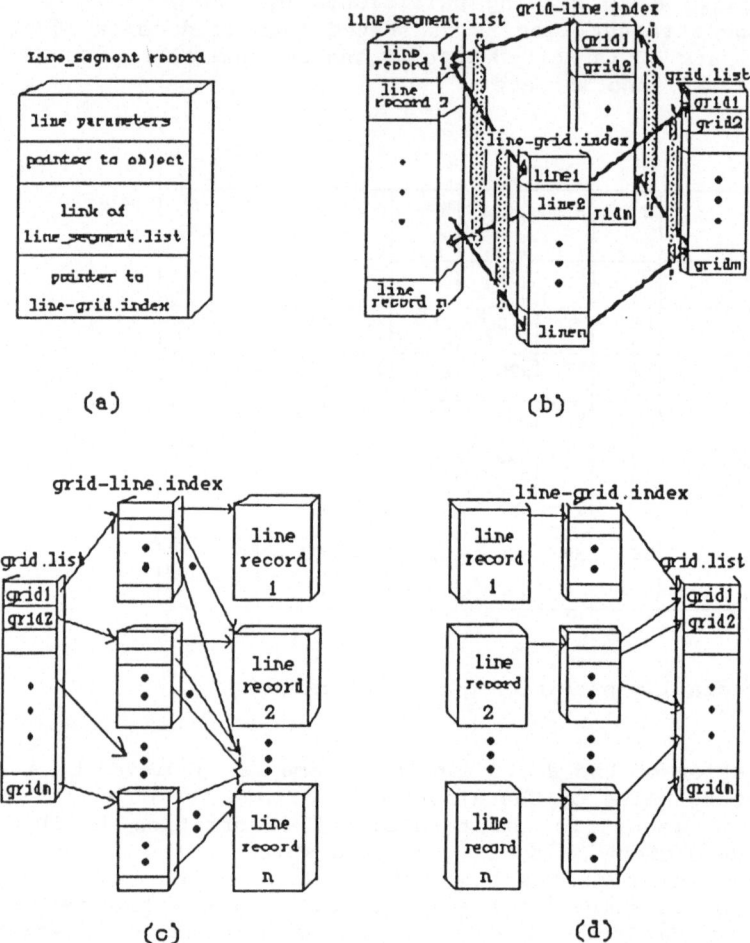

(a)

(b)

(c)

(d)

Fig.2 Diagram of the data structure for implementing the grid sorting. (a) line segment data record; (b) grid sorting data structure; (c) grid-line list index; (d) line-grid list index.

The redundance of these indices is to provide fast retrieving of the demanded data entries for the computations in the hidden line removal process.

The 2D spatial sorting scheme described here has essential differences from the recursive area subdivision algorithm developed by WarnocK (1969). In our algorithm, the size of the grid cells are predetermined and simply fixed in the process rather then dynamically making recursive subdivisions. It is easy and fast to process size fixed grid cells. The line segments in the process are not cut into short pieces according to the edges of grid cells, thus avoiding a large number of small segments being created.

The grid-line index provides an approach for fast searching the
potentially intersecting curved line segments. From this point of
view, the 2D spatial sorting scheme is an extension of the
surrounding rectangle method used for polygon intersection
computations (Ahuja 1980). The underlying concept of the method
lies in that it is sufficient to say that there is no intersection
between two complex polygons if there is no intersection between the
two simple surrounding rectangles which are the approximations of the
original ones. Usually these approximating rectangles are
arbitrarily oriented and the concave property of the approximated
polygon is not reserved. The grid cell sorting for the curved lines
is, in a sense, an approximation of the drawing areas occupied by
the curved line segments. It is able to reserve the non-convaxity of
the curves. Morever, the possibility of numerically coding these
grid cells provides an simpler and quicker means than the
rectangular method for testing the closeness of the curves, therefore
for computing the intersections and visibilities.

3. CLASSIFYING THE HIDDEN LINE SEGMENTS

The fundamental task for the hidden line removal algorithm is to
search for the hidden line segments in the 2D drawing plane. Many
previous algorithms compared each line segment with the object
surfaces to find whether the line segment is visible or not. The
inclusion of curved line segments makes this comparison more complex
than the straight-line case. Instead of working on the relations
between the lines and surfaces, our algorithm is designed to simply
work on the relations between the line segments on the 2D drawing. To
be effective for the processing, we separate the hidden line
segments in the drawing into two types according to their relations
with the drawing lines of the hiding objects:

- H1: The hidden line segment intersects with the drawing
       line segments of the hiding objects.
- H2: The hidden line segment has no intersection with any of
       the drawing line segments of the hiding objects.

Figure 3 illustrates these two types of hidden line segments, where
line segments BC and CD of object 3 is hidden by object 1 in type H1
and line segment AB is in type H2.

The H2 line segments might occur initially in generating the 2D
drawing or be generated by the process of eliminating the H1 line
segments.

To deal with the H1 segments, one way is to find the intersections
of the segments and then test the visibilities for the corresponding
parts of the segments. It is found that the H2 segments can be
solved easily by using the results that come from the solutions for
the H1 segments. A two phase algorithm is then developed in which
each phase removes each type of hidden line segment from the line
drawing.

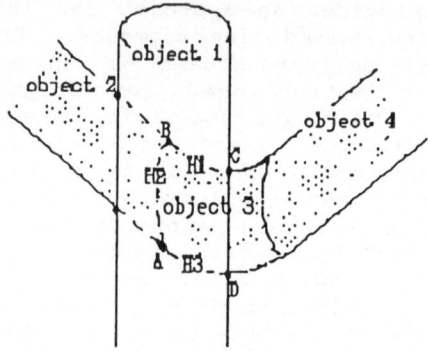

Fig.3 Illustration of hidden line segment types

4. LINE INTERSECTION PROCEDURE

Intersection detection for straight lines with O(nlogn + klogn) time
and O(n + k) space was reported by Bentley and Ottmann (1979), where
n is the number of line segments and k is the number of intersecting
pairs. The algorithm was improved by Brown (1981) to reduce the space
to O(n). Chazelle (1984) reported an algorithm for the same problem
with O(n $\log^2$n/log(log n) + k)   time and O(n + k) space.   The
extension of the previous algorithm to curved lines, however, is not
so straightforward, since the algorithms all base their strategy on
one-dimensional sorting. That is, the lines are sorted in terms of
either the x, or the y coordinate of their terminal points. This
sorting scheme is at a certain level intrinsic to the straight line
segment, but it is unfortunately not applicable to curved line
segments.

The problem of intersection detection for curved line segments is
facilitated by our 2D grid sorting scheme. Since the computation of
the intersections between two curves is more complex and time
consuming than for straight lines, it is important to reduce as
much as possible irrelevant segment pairs is especially important
so as to speed up the computation. The main effect of the grid
sorting is that the integer number associated with each line segment
provides a concise index to the intersected segment pairs, thus
avoiding the search for all possible intersecting pairs among an
enormous number of segments.

The line intersection process proceeds following the order of the
grid cells. The line segments in each grid cell are paired and
computed for the intersection points. In this way, the search for
the potentially intersected pairs is then restricted to the
neighborhood area inside the range of the grid cells. The line
segments without any intersection with other segments are either
totally visible or H2 segments, which are processed in phase 2. An

intersecting point list (INTPL) is established for each line segment in this process which contains the parametric values of the intersecting points and the indices to the intersected segments. This intersecting point list is later to be used by the visibility testing process to further determine the exact hidden part of the segment. A pseudocode description of the procedure is the following:

Procedure LINE_INTERSECTION;

Begin

/* *Partition the drawing plan and sorting the line segments into grid cells.*
line-grid.index contains pointers for each line_segment pointing to the grid.list
grid-line.index contains the indices from the grid cells to the line segments sorted */
LINE_SORTING (line-grid.index, grid-line.index)

/* *intersection computing for each line_segment* */
While line_segment.list not empty **Do**

   /* *retrieve the line_segement parameters from data records in the line_segment.list* */
   GET_PARAMETERS(line_segment)

   /* *loop on each grid cell to which the line_segment were sorted* */
   While line-grid.index(line_segment) not empty **Do**

      current_grid = line-grid.index(line_segment)

      /* *check intersections for every line_segment sorted in current grid cell* */
      While grid-line.index(current_grid) not empty **Do**

         current_line_segment = grid-line.index(current_grid)
         line_segment_pair = (line_segment, current_line_segment)

         If line_segment_pair has not been processed **Then**

            GET_PARAMETERS(current_line_segment)

            /* *solve the parametric equations to get the intersection points* */
            INTERSECTION_POINT(line_segment, current_line_segment,
INTPL)

      next of line_segment in grid-line.index(current_grid);

   next of grid in line-grid.index(line_segment);

next of line_segment in line segment list;

End;

Procedure LINE_SORTING(line-grid.index, grid-line.index)

/*This procedure sorts the line segments into grid cells and generats
the line-grid.list and grid-line.list */
Begin

While line_segment.list not empty **Do**

   From begining_point **To** end_point of line_segment **Step**
   grid_cell_size **Do**

      If NEW_GRID(point) **Then**

        /*request and fill in the entries of the data structure */
        FILL_LIST(NEW_GRID(point), line-grid.index, grid-line.index);

End;

It is easy to derive the execution time for the above intersection
detection process. Assume that the line drawing of the objects are
generated as N line segments, and the drawing plane is partitioned
into D grid cells. To sort N line segments into the grid cells takes
just N times. In the worst case, if we partition the drawing plane
into D constant number of grid cells and use exhaustive search inside
each grid cell, the time complexity will be

$$\frac{\dfrac{N}{D}\left(\dfrac{N}{D}+1\right)}{2}\,D$$

It is quadratic to the number of line segments in the drawing.

In practice we select D being proportional to the density of the line
segments in the drawing plane, such that D = N / c, where c is a
constant. The density of the drawing can be evaluated by the ratio
of the total length of the drawing lines to the area of the drawing
plane. Each grid cell thus has an approximately constant c = N/D
line segments. The process of finding the intersected pairs in
the drawing then takes

$$\frac{c(c+1)}{2}\,D$$

times if exhaustive search is performed inside each grid cell.

Since D = N/c, replace D in the expression gives

$$\frac{c+1}{2}\,N$$

Taking the time of computing the intersection for each pair as a unit, the entire process of finding the intersected line segments is then approximately O(N) times. Since the value c is inter-related with D, O(N) is the best value for the algorithm. The optimal value D usually is not easy to obtain, the performance of the algorithm is therefore worse than O(N) and in the worst case quadratic to N.

Un-uniformly divided grid cells can also be implemented in the above algorithm. A straight forward way is to treat the central part of the drawing as the denser region, so with smaller sizes. It will partially improves the performance of the algorithm.

5. VISIBILITY TESTING

To begin the description of the visibility testing, two assumptions are taken in the algorithm: that there is no hidden relations between the lines belonging to same object; and there are no intersections between these objects in 3D. These conditions are easy to satisfied by a pre-processor to split the objects according to these requirements.

From the intersection point list INTPL established in the intersection detection process, an "Effective Points List (EPTL)" is formed for each line segment at the beginning of the visibility testing process. The EPTL list includes not only the intersecting points, but also the starting and end points of the line segment.

The segments intersected with the current segment are backtracked in the data structure constructed previously to find their parent objects. These objects are denoted as "Relevant Components (RCOM)" of the intersecting points.

We call the line segment being processing the current segment. The visibility of the line segment is decided by the following steps:

1. <u>Point Matching</u> The points in the EPTL of the current segment are inspected pair by pair. If two points in the EPTL refer to a common RCOM, this pair is denoted as a "Point Matching (PMT)". The fact is that the line segment in type H1 may only be hidden in the interval between these two matched points. The PMT is empty in the case where there is no intersecting point on this line segment. In this case the line segment either is totally visible or belongs to H2 type.

2. <u>Hidden Checking</u> When a PMT is found, an interpolating point between these two matched points are checked with the RCOM to determine whether the line segment between these two points are hidden by the object. It is adequate to say that the segment part is hidden by the RCOM as long as the interpolating point between the matched points is hidden. When the line segment part is asserted to be hidden, the matched point pair is put into a "Hidden Segment List (HIDL)".

3. <u>Segment Merging</u>   There   may   be   a number of   adjacent or
   co-incident hidden segment parts in   the   HIDL formed from
   hidden checking.   These parts are then merged together.   It
   gives the final segment parts to be removed from the current
   line segment.

4. <u>Line Splitting</u>   According to the   HIDL, the current line
   segment is split in the segment list to eliminate the invisible
   parts of the line segment.   The corresponding links of the
   segments and the pointers to the beloning objects are
   re-constructed.

Figure 4 illustrates a case for the above process.   Assume line
segment AB is behind object 2 but is in front of object 1.   By the
intersection procedure,   intersection point 1, 2, 3, 4, and 5 will be
recorded in the INTPL of line AB.   At the point matching step, the
point pairs 1-3, 2-4, 2-5, and 4-5 will be reported in PMT.   But only
line segment parts 2-4, 2-5, and 4-5   are   put into the Hidden
Segment List HIDL by the Hidden Checking because the points between 1
and 3 are all visible.   After the Segement Merging, only line segment
2-5 will remain in HIDL.   The splitting process finally divides AB
into two visible segments A-2 and 5-B in the line_segment list and
set segment 2-5 invisible.

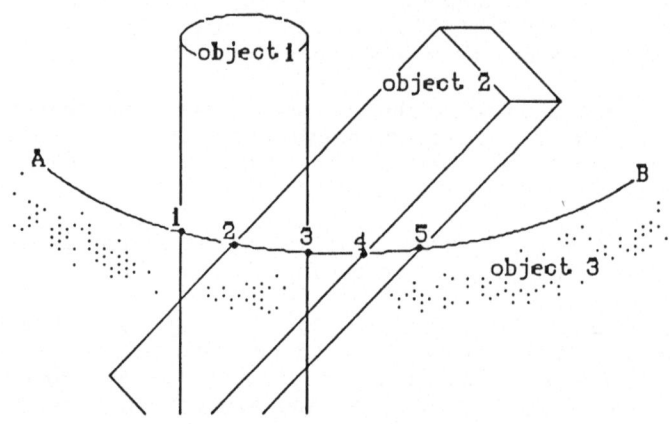

Fig.4   Illustration of line segment visibility testing

For the removal of the H2 line segment,   only visibility testing is
required.   It is performed by simply checking the starting and the
end points of line segments.   It is sufficient to conclude that the
entire line segment is type H2 if the starting and the end points in
invisible after processing the type H1 segments,   thus those line
segments are marked as invisible and eliminated from the drawing.

6.   IMPLEMENTATION AND TIME COMPLEXITY

The algorithm discussed above was implemented in a computer aided
industrial piping design system (Zhu 1985). The algorithm is invoked
in the interactive design process to provide a quick check of the
designed piping structures.   The real time response is considered
critical for this application.   The objects in a piping system are
composed of a number of piping components, such as pipe segments,
elbows, valves, flanges, etc.   Most of the objects are non-planar
faced. The line drawing of these piping components in. our system
consists of straight lines,   circular arcs and elliptic arcs. These
drawing line segments are represented in quadratic form of parametric
equations. Fig. 5 shows an example of the industrial piping system
design with hidden lines removed.

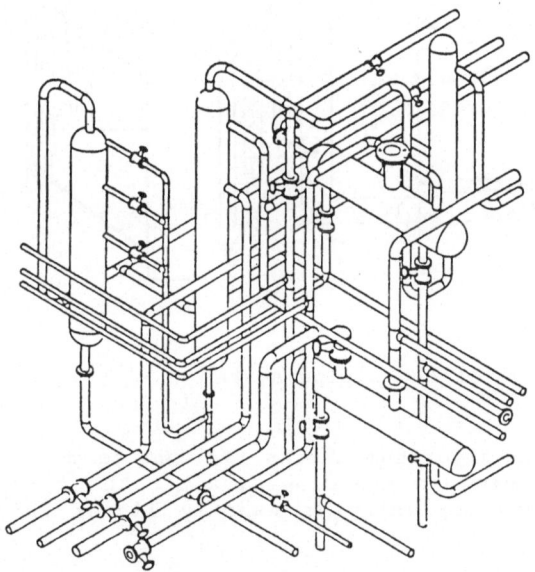

Fig.5 Example of an industrial piping system design

A two-directional interconnected data structure was built for the
representation of the piping design as we described before.   From
each line segment record in the line segment list, there is a pointer
points to the belonging object. This pointer makes fast check for the
visibility of interpolating point between point matching in the
hidden checking step.   Figure 6 shows a diagram of this structure.

As the phase 1 algorithm consists of two processes: (1) the line
intersection detection; and (2) the visibility testing,   the time
complexity is also a combination of them. By the proper selection of
the grid number D, the execution time for the line intersection
detection is, as derived before, no worse than quadratic and nearly
linear in the number of line segments.   In the visibility testing,
the procedure inspects the intersecting points one pair by one pair,
it is theoretically quadratic in the worst case if we pair every

points in the process.   But this is an impossible case.   Since the
the process pairs the intersection points for each line segment, it
is also linear in the best case, if the line segments are uniformaly
distributed in the drawing.   By summing the two parts, we can
conclude that the time complexity of the   hidden line   removal
algorithm for phase 1 is between quadratic and linear, depending on
the distribution of the line segments in the drawing.

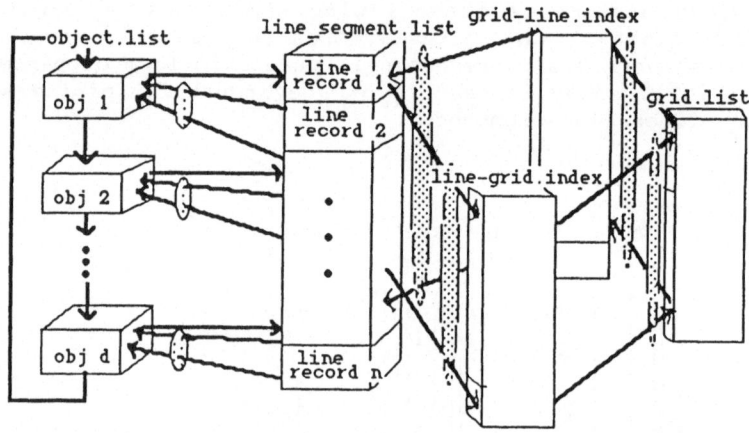

Fig.6 Data structure of the piping system

The phase 2 of the algorithm checks the two terminating points for
all segments remaining in the drawing after the phase 1 operation,
therefore the time complexity is exactly linear in the number of
these line segments.

In the application of hidden line removal algorithm on the CAD
generated drawings, for the readability of the design, the drawings
are usually constructed such that the lines are uniformly
distributed. The above algorithm in these cases can achieve nearly
linear performance proportional to the number of line segments in the
drawing plus the number of intersecting points.

The algorithm is tested using a number of experimental test cases.
Table 1   below shows a set of the test result and Fig. 7 shows the
plot of the data.   The results support the analysis above.

Table 1. CPU execution time for hidden line removal algorithm

# line segments	# intersect. points	CPU time (sec.)
65	16	.163
129	34	.327
199	67	.447

260	82	.770
356	250	1.907
440	374	2.743
526	459	3.293
641	476	3.787
734	586	4.693
807	714	5.793
961	1225	8.034
1090	1303	10.220
1183	1573	12.263
1533	2431	20.677
1682	3470	25.290

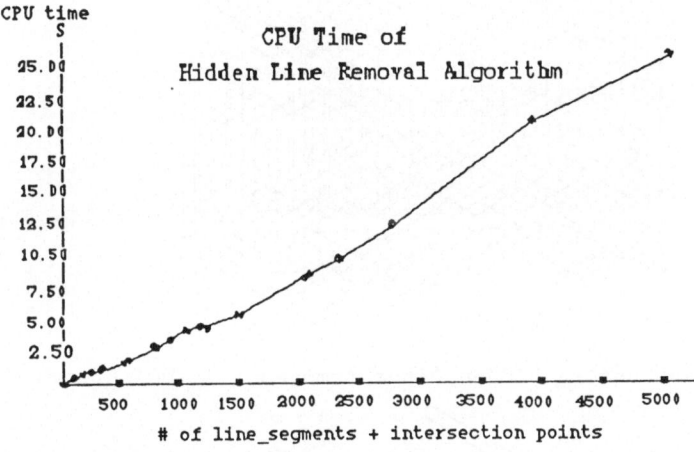

Fig.7 Plot of time complexity for the testing data of the hidden line removal algorithm

The above data has obtained on a Prime-750 computer with an IMLAC graphics terminal run in PRIMOS.

Fig. 8 shows one of the test cases in which hidden lines were not removed and Fig. 9 is the visible-line-only drawing corresponding to Fig. 8.

CONCLUSION

The two phase algorithm presented in this paper is based on the approach that the drawing lines are approximated and spatially sorted by a number of grid cells. These approximation and sorting allow a quick search for the intersecting line segments and reduces the amount of computations, thus speeds up the process. The visibility test of the line segments does not involve the surface information of the object. It then avoids the complexity of the geometric computations caused by the curveness of the surfaces of the objects. The algorithm was applied to the drawings with parametrically represented curves, but is not limited to these cases. The grid sorting scheme and visibility testing approach described in this paper are essentially independent of the representations used for the objects.

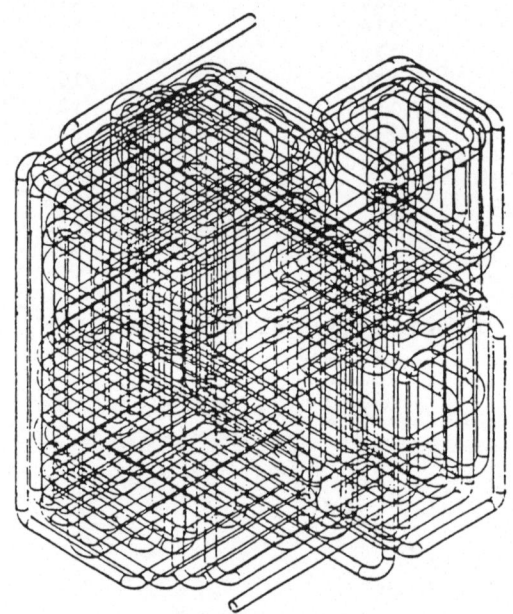

Fig.8 Test case before hidden lines removed

Fig.9 Test case of visible_line_only drawing corresponding to Fig.8

ACKNOWLEDGMENTS

The author thank Dr. Herbert. Freeman, New Jersey professor of computer engineering for his suggestion and encouragement of this research work. The author would also like to thank Dr. Richard Haskell, professor of engineering and computer science at Oakland University for his careful review and valuable comments on this manuscript.

REFERENCES

Sutherland Ivan E., Sproull R. F. and Schumacker R. A. (1974) "A Characterization of Ten Hidden Surface Algorithms", *Computer Surveys*, Vol.6, No. 1, 1974 PP.1-55

Griffiths J. G. (1979) "Eliminating Hidden Edges in Line Drawing", *Computer Aided Design*, Vol.11, No.2, 1979, pp.70-78

Wittran M. (1981) "Hidden Line Algorithm for Scenes of High Complexity", *Computer Aided Design*, Vol.13, No.4, 1981, pp.187

Williamson H. (1972) "Hidden Line Plotting Program", *Communication ACM*, Vol.15, NO.2, 1972, pp.100-103

Woon P. and Freeman H. (1972) "A Procedure for Generating Visible-line Projections of Solids Bounded by Quadric Surfaces", *Information Processing 71*, North-holland publishing Company, 1972

Franklin W. R. (1981) "Efficiently Computing the Haloed Line Effect for Hidden Line Elimination", *Tech. Report, IPL-81-004* RPI, 1981

Warnock, J. E (1969) "A Hidden-Surface Algorithm for Computer-Generated Halftone Pictures", Computer Science Department, University of Utah, TR 4-15, June 1969

Ahuja N., Chien R. T., Yen R., and Bridwell N. (1980) "Interference Detection and Collision Avoidance Among Three Dimensional Objects", *Proc. 1st Annu. National Conference on Artificial Intelligence*, Polo Alto, 1980, pp.44-48

Appel A. (1976) "The Notion of Quantitative Invisibility and the Machine Rending of Solids", *Proc. ACM. National Conference 1976*, pp.387-393

Loutrel P. P. (1970) "A Solution to the Hidden-Line Problem for Computer-drawn Polyhedra", *IEEE Trans. on Computers*, Vol. C-19, NO. 3, 1970, pp.205

Bentley J. L. and Ottmann T. (1979) "Algorithms for Reporting and Counting Ceometric Intersections", *IEEE Trans. Computer*, Vol.C-28, 1979, pp.643-647

Brown K. Q. (1981) "Comments on Algorithms for Reporting and Counting Geometric Intersections", *IEEE Trans. Computer*, Vol. C-30, 1981, pp.147-148

Chazelle B. M. (1984) "intersecting is Easier than Sorting", *Proc. 16th ACM Annu. Symp. Theory Comput.*, 1984, pp.125-134

Zhu Q. (1985) "A New Approach to the Fast Design of Piping Systems", *Tech. Report, IPL TR-85-022* Rensselaer Polytechnic Institute, 1985

 **Qiuming Zhu** is currently an assistant professor of Computer Science and Engineering at Oakland University. He was a postdoctoral research associate in the Center for Computer Aids for Industrial Productvity at Rutgers University, New Jersey, and a faculty member in the Department of Computer Science and Engineering at Nanjing Institute of Technology, China, before came to Oakland University. His research interests include artificial intelligence, computer graphics, CAD/CAM systems, computer vision, and software engineering.

Zhu received his B.E. in computer science and engineering from Nanjing Institute of Technology in 1982, his M.S. and Ph.D. in computer and systems engineering from Rensselaer Polytechnic Institute in 1986.

Address: School of Engineering and Computer Science, Oakland University, Rochester, Michigan, 48063 U.S.A.

Fast Hidden Surface Removal Through Structural Analysis and Representation of Objects and Their Contours

H.L. Lim

ABSTRACT

A vital factor to the efficiency of hidden surface algorithms is how they represent the objects. While the early algorithms simply subdivide the surfaces of objects and represent them by isolated polygons, the more advanced algorithms have analysed the surfaces more thoroughly and represented them as connected polygons bounded by contour edges. In this paper, a hidden surface algorithm which applies a further enhanced surface representation is suggested. In the representation, contour edges are analysed and hierarchically described according to how they are connected and what objects they belong to. The algorithm makes full use of the hierarchical contour structure to determine contour intersections and detect surrounding contours without using elaborate global comparisons. The visibility of contour edges is then evaluated, from which visible surfaces can be determined.

KEYWORDS AND PHRASES: Hidden surface elimination, analysis of algorithms, visible surface algorithms, surface analysis, contours.

I. INTRODUCTION.

The generation of realistic three-dimensional images by computers requires the removal of surfaces which are hidden and should not be displayed. Due to the complicated geometry of objects, hidden surface removal is complicated and requires a lot of calculations. Hidden surface algorithms are techniques developed to reduce these calculations.

The common strategy of hidden surface algorithms is to compare surfaces to determine their occlusion relationship. Because of the complicated geometry of objects, the algorithms have to analyse the geometry of objects in detail and represent these object in data structures before the actual comparisons of surfaces can be carried out. This analysis of surfaces also yields vital information about the existence of surface coherence which can then be used to reduce calculations. Therefore, although the algorithms apply widely different techniques to determine hidden surfaces, their efficiency is closely related to how they analyse and represent the structure of objects.

Almost all algorithms perform some basic surface analysis through the subdivision of complicated surfaces into simpler polygonal patches. Usually these patches are approximated by polygons and the algorithms determine visible surfaces through calculating the visibility of these polygons. The actual strategy, however, differs widely. According to the survey by Sutherland et al [1], the algorithms can be classified into two groups, the image space and the object space algorithms. Object space algorithms got their name because they directly compare the geometric structures of polygonal patches to determine surface visibility. Due to their mode of processing, the importance of structural analysis in them is the most apparent. Therefore, this paper will focus on these algorithms.

In the early object space algorithms [2, 3, 4], the polygon patches are treated as independent entities. The algorithms simply compare each polygon with all the other polygons to determine whether it is overlapped. They further require elaborate comparisons between edges of the polygons. The calculations grow rapidly as the number of polygons increases. Therefore, these algorithms are very slow if the scene is complicated.

Since the drawbacks of the early object space algorithms are due to their simple representation of the objects, improvements on them have been achieved through better surface representations. The first major improvement was the Weiler and Atherton's polygon area sorting algorithm [5]. The algorithm explicitly defines the scene as a set of polygons and make use of the geometry of these polygons to reduce calculations.

More recently, several algorithms such as the Hubschman and Zucker's algorithm [6] or the Hornung's algorithm [7] have further adopted a contour-oriented approach. In these algorithms, each polygon is not treated as an isolated entity but as an integrated part of a surface, using the information about how they are connected. The algorithms analyse these polygons to detect contour edges and use these edges to define regions of surfaces. If the scene consists solely of non-penetrating surfaces, the better surface description can be applied to reduce calculations substantially: since the visibility of these surfaces can only change at areas directly below visible contours, these algorithms only need to evaluate the visibility of polygons in these areas.

The improvements through using more advanced contour and polygon structures have shown the advantages of using better surface representations in hidden surface algorithms. In this paper, the fruitfulness of this approach will be further demonstrated. The paper will describe a new algorithm which could further enhance the efficiency of hidden surface removal through improving the existing surface representations.

II.   A SURVEY OF THE EXISTING OBJECT SPACE ALGORITHMS AND THEIR REPRESENTATION OF SURFACES.

An important prerequisite to the understanding of the suggested algorithm is knowing the mechanism and evolution of the earlier object space algorithms it developed from.   These algorithms can be classified into the following three groups:

1.   The Edge-Intersection Algorithms.

The edge-intersection algorithms are a major group of early object space algorithms. These algorithms determine visible edges by counting the quantitative invisibility of points on the edges.   The quantitative invisibility of a point is defined to be the number of surfaces that occlude the point.

The algorithms process the surfaces in clusters, each cluster is a collection of overlapping polygons and edges. For each cluster, a vertex is selected and its quantitative invisibility is calculated by exhaustively searching all the other polygons that lie on that point.   Edges intersect with each edge emanating from the vertex are determined, and the change in quantitative visibility due to each intersection is evaluated. From the quantitative invisibility of the starting vertex of the edge and the net quantitative invisibility changes that take place along the edge, the quantitative invisibility of one ending vertex is obtained.

The ending vertex now becomes the starting vertex and the quantitative invisibility changes that occur on the remaining edges emanating from the vertex are again calculated. The whole process is repeated until all the overlapping surfaces and edges have been accessed. The next cluster is then processed.

The edge-intersection algorithms have only minor differences. In Appel's algorithm [2], intersecting edges are tested by comparing the orientation of edges with the viewpoint. Loutrel [3] computes edge intersections by projecting the edges onto the image plane. Galimberti and Montanari [4], on the other hand, calculate the set of polygon patches hiding a point instead of computing the number of polygons hiding it. A point is visible if its set of occluding polygons is empty.

As the algorithms are among the earliest algorithms developed, they are characterized by the simple surface definition and limited use of surface properties.   In them, most of the calculations treat edges as unrelated entities without regards to how polygons and surfaces are formed from these edges. The calculations therefore increase quadratically.

2.   The Weiler and Atherton Algorithm [5].

The hidden surface algorithm developed by Weiler and Atherton is an improvement over the edge-intersection algorithms described in previous section. In the algorithm, visible surfaces are determined by the recursive subdivision of polygons.

The algorithm first roughly sorts the polygons by depth. The first polygon of the sorted list of polygons is used to clip each of the rest of the polygons in the list. Through the clipping operations, polygons are divided into two lists of polygons which are inside and outside the clip polygon. Polygons which are inside and behind the clip polygon are invisible and can be deleted from the inside list.

For each polygon which is inside and in front of the clip polygon, the clipping operation is recursively applied. A polygon is further clipped with the rest of the polygons in the inside list. After all the polygons in the inside list have been clipped, the inside list is displayed and further clipping operations are repeated on the polygons in the outside list.

The algorithm has improved the edge-intersection algorithms through using polygons as full geometric entities. In it, edges are no more treated as isolated entities but integral parts of polygons. With the better representation of surfaces, the algorithm could make more effective use of the geometry of polygons so that intersection calculations between edges can be reduced.

3.   The Contour-Oriented Algorithms.

The contour-oriented algorithms are a group of recently developed algorithms. In them, each polygon is not treated as an isolated entity but as an integrated part of a surface. The algorithms first carry out an analysis of surfaces. In this analysis, the connectivity of polygons is first determined. After which, contour edges are detected by checking whether the boundaries of polygons are surface boundaries, where the edges are not shared by two polygons, or internal silhouettes, where the pair of polygons sharing each edge are facing opposite directions with respect to the viewpoint.

The algorithms then determine the visibility of the contour edges by projecting these edges to surfaces they partially cover or being covered. A contour edge is visible if it is not completely covered by the polygons forming these surfaces. Since the contour edges divide the surfaces into regions which are homogeneously visible or invisible, visible surfaces can be easily determined by accessing only the polygons in the homogeneously visible surface regions.

The first contour-oriented object space algorithm was developed by Hubschman and Zucker [6]. The algorithm was specifically designed for dynamic scenes. In addition to using the above technique, it also uses the geometry of contour edges so that frame-to-frame coherence can be effectively applied. On the other hand, Hornung has also applied similar strategy in his hidden-line algorithm [7]. He has however carried out a more formal study of the role of contours in hidden surface removal.

These algorithms are a major improvement over the early object space algorithms. In many situations they can avoid most of the calculations which involve internal edges. Besides, because the display of surfaces ends at the boundaries of visible contour edges, they can also reduce calculations involving invisible surfaces. However, these algorithms still require elaborate calculations which can be further reduced by the algorithm suggested here.

III.   A NEW SURFACE DESCRIPTION USING HIERARCHICAL CONTOUR STRUCTURE.

The proposed algorithm uses comprehensive data structures to describe surfaces. In it, surfaces are described by the polygons and contour edges, just as the existing contour-oriented algorithms would describe them. However, the algorithm interrelates connected contour edges and constructs higher level contour structures out of these edges. The surface description is created through bottom-up processing of the basic polygonal description of objects:

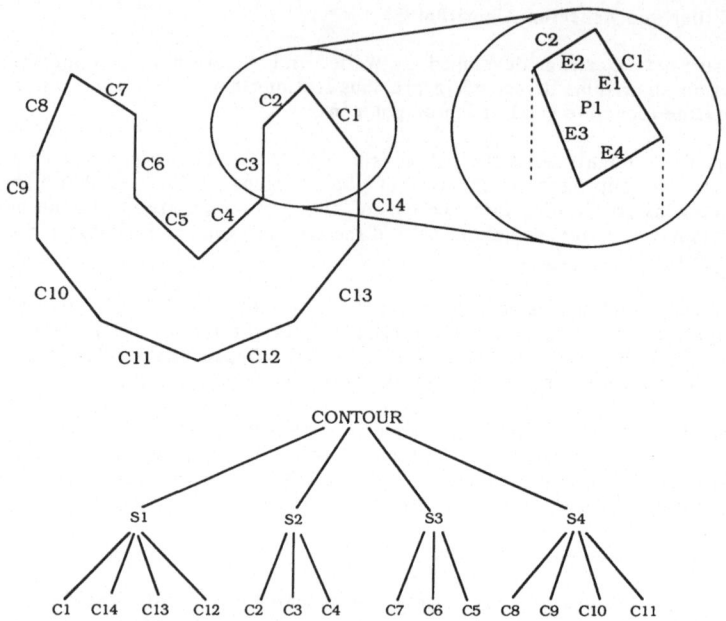

Fig. 1: A Contour & Surface Hierarchy

The object shown here consists of fourteen edges. As the junctions between edges C1 and C2, C4 and C5, C7 and C8, C11 and C12 are local Y minimums and maximums, the contour is divided into segments which have endpoints at these junctions. The inset shows more detailed structure of part of the surface.

1.   Creation of Polygon Records and Edge Records.

Surfaces are subdivided and approximated by polygon meshes. Each polygon is described by a polygon record and a list of edge records. Reflecting how the edges are connected, the edge records are circularly linked together.

2.   Creation of the Connectivity Information of Polygons.

Two connected polygons are interrelated through the common edge they share. By using index searching, the pair of polygons sharing an edge is known. The two edge records which correspond to the common edge are related through a common edge pointer in each of them. Using these pointers, all the polygon records or edge records can be accessed from the record of any edge on the same surface.

3.   Creation of Contour Edge Records.

In this paper, a distinction is made between contour and contour edges. While a contour here refers to a natural surface boundary or a silhouette of an object, a contour edge refers to an edge of a polygon which is part of a contour. Therefore, a contour is represented and approximated by a list or network structure of connected contour edges.

Contour edges are detected by analysing the edges of the polygons. An edge is a surface boundary if it is not shared by two polygons and the record of it has a null common edge pointer. A surface silhouette is detected by checking whether the z components of the normals of the polygons sharing an edge are pointing at opposite directions. In many applications, back-facing polygons can be ignored and only surface boundaries need to be considered.

If an edge is found to be a contour edge, a contour edge record is created to represent it.

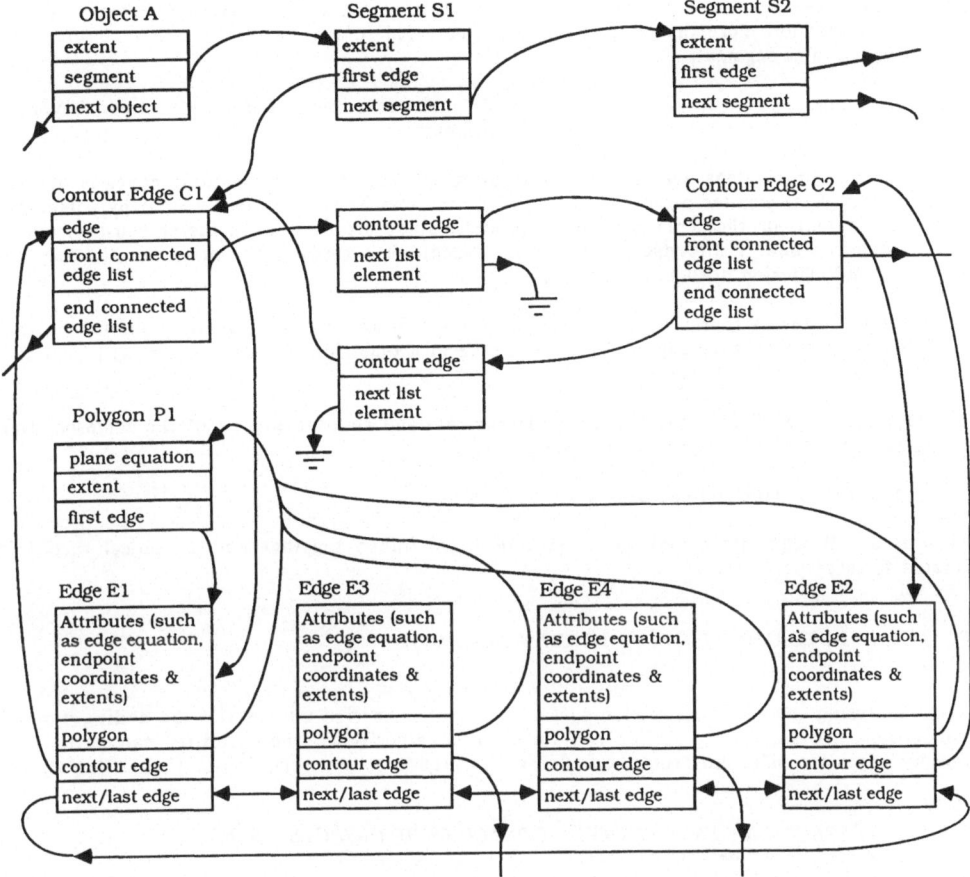

Fig. 2: Data structure for representing the surface and contour structure shown in figure 1. Note that the edges are doubly linked with their associated contour edges and their connected edges.

4.   Linking of contour records:

The contour edges are in turn examined. From information about edges in each polygon and common edges of connected polygons, connected contour edges are detected. Their records are linked together. Note that there could be more than one contour edge linked to one end of a contour edge.

5.   Creation of contour segment records:

Both contours and contour edges have limitations to be used as geometric entities in hidden surface calculations. The former are usually too complicated to be treated as simple entities without the need to be further analysed. On the other hand, contour edge representation is often too elaborate and handling it requires a lot of redundant calculations. Segments of contours, each of which is constructed from a few linearly connected contour edges, are used here as entities whose complexity is between the contours and contour edges.

After the linkage between the contour edges has been computed, a control segment record is created to reference a few connected contour edges which satisfy the following rules:

5.1   The edges are linearly connected, i.e. all edges in the segment are connected in such a way that not more than one of them is connected to one end of the other contour edge in the same segment.

5.2   The contour segment is single valued in x. Hence a segment does not extend beyond a vertex which is a local y maximum or minimum.

5.3   A contour segment which is too long or which has too many contour edges is divided into several smaller pieces. The first situation can be efficiently detected by comparing the extents of the segments with a predetermined size. For even faster construction of segments and if all edges in the environment have roughly the same length, only the second criterion need to be checked.

The contour segments represent geometric entities which are simpler than the contours but not as elaborate as the contour edges. They have several geometric properties which will be useful in calculations in the later stage.

The representation of a contour by contour segments and contour edges and the corresponding data structures are shown in figures 1 and 2.

6.   **Creation of Object Records:**

Records of all segments belonging to an object are linked together and an object record is created to reference them.

IV.   **THE DETERMINATION OF HIDDEN SURFACES.**

After analysing the surfaces, hidden surface removal is carried out. While the ending part of calculations are similar to earlier contour-oriented algorithms, the visibility calculations of contour edges are different from them. Below is a pseudo code description of these calculations:

```
INTERSECTION TESTS BETWEEN CONTOURS OF OBJECTS { to be
discussed in section 1 } :

    FOR each object in the global object list:
        compare extents of segments within the object
        compare extents of segments of the object with
        extents of segments of all the other objects
        IF extents of any two segments overlap THEN
            INTERSECT_EDGE

INTERSECT_EDGE :

    FOR each contour edge of 1st segment, starting from the
        lower end of the segment:
        FOR each contour edge of 2nd segment, starting from
            the lower end of the segment:
            find the intersection between the two contour
            edges, create/update their contour chains
            if they intersect
            IF upper end of the contour edge of 2nd segment
                has larger Y than that of 1st segment THEN
                    exit to the outer loop to access next
                    contour edge on 1st segment, contour edge
                    on 2nd segment remains unchanged.
            ELSE
                    access next contour edge on 2nd segment
```

DETECTION OF SURROUNDING CONTOURS { to be discussed in section 2 } :

> *FOR each chain record in the global chain list:*
> *FOR each object record in the global object list:*
> *IF the chain & object pass the surrounding tests THEN*
> *find the testpoint of the chain*
> *find the contour edges of the object which*
> *are at the left of the testpoint*
> *IF left-facing contour edges more than right-*
> *facing contour edges THEN*
> *FOR each of the left-facing contour edge:*
> *PROPAGATE_POLYGON from polygon*
> *connected to the contour edge*

PROPAGATE_POLYGON :

> *IF polygon not at the left of the testpoint OR polygon*
> *has been accessed THEN   return FAILED*

> *IF testpoint is surrounded by the polygon THEN*
> *add the polygon to list of polygons surrounding*
> *the testpoint, return STOP*

> *FOR each edge of the polygon:*
> *IF edge is not a contour THEN*
> *access the neighbouring polygon from the edge*
> *PROPAGATE_POLYGON from the neighbouring polygon*
> *IF PROPAGATE_POLYGON returns STOP THEN return STOP*
> *IF PROPAGATE_POLYGON returns FAILED THEN*
> *access next edge of the polygon*

> *return FAILED because none of the polygons accessed from*
> *the current polygon can reach the testpoint*

Below is a detail description of the calculations carried out by the algorithm:

1. Intersection tests between contour edges:

Contour edges are compared with each other to determine their intersections. The calculations are reduced by the following top-down comparisons between the entities in the hierarchical contour description:

1.1 Comparisons between objects:

The extents of each pair of objects are compared, if they do not overlap, their contour edges are obviously not overlapped.

1.2 Comparisons between contour segments:

If the extents of objects are overlapped, an extent test is carried out between each contour segment from one object with each contour segment from the other object. In addition, an extent test is also carried out between each contour segment from one object and all the other contour segments from the same object as they also may be overlapped (as indicated in figure 3).

1.3 Comparisons between contour edges:

As the contour segments are single valued in x, they do not curve back and intersect themselves. There is therefore no necessity to determine the intersections between contour edges in each segment. The tests of intersections between contour edges are only needed between each pair of segments which pass the extent tests described in the previous section.

Intersection tests between contour edges can also be reduced by applying the special geometry of contour segments. Since each segment is single valued in x, edges on it are always in increasing or decreasing y order. Therefore, By applying the merge-sort technique, intersection tests between contour edges can be carried out by simultaneously accessing edges from both segments. This technique allows edges in each segment to be sequentially accessed only once. The intersection tests therefore have only linear time complexity.

During the intersection test, extent tests are again used to reject contour edges which clearly do not intersected. The lengthy calculations of the exact locations of edge intersections are carried out only between pairs of contour edges which are not rejected by earlier extent tests.

1.4   Creation of contour chains:

Records of each pair of intersecting contour edges are linked together by pointers. With these pointers and the pointers between connected contour edges, all contour segments connected or intersected in the image plane are effectively linked together to form a contour chain. A contour chain record is created to reference it.

Figure 3 shows several contour chains formed from intersecting contours.

2.   Detection of surrounded contour chains.

If objects do not surround each other, the information about how contour edges are intersected and connected alone will be sufficient to determine the visibility of contour edges and hence the visibility of all surfaces. However, if one object is totally inside another object without any intersection between their contours, it may be totally visible or invisible. Furthermore, its visibility cannot be calculated by the intersection tests described in previous section and has to be determined by elaborate evaluation of surfaces overlapping it. Previous contour-oriented algorithms cannot detect surrounding contours and have to resort to exhaustive global comparisons between polygons and contour edges to find out the actual visibility of contours. The algorithm described here determines the presence of surrounding contours and their occlusion relationship more effectively using the method described below:

2.1   Extent tests between contour chains and objects:

The extent of a contour chain is compared with the extent of each object. If the extent of the former is not totally within the extent of the later, the contour chains are not surrounded by the object it tested with. Note that although the objective here is to determine surrounding objects, the comparisons are instead carried out between contour chains and objects. Contour chains are used to reduce calculations as once an object surrounds a contour, it also surrounds other contours which belong to the same chain. Besides, once the surfaces overlapping a contour of a chain are known, surfaces overlapping other contours which belong to the same chain can be determined by the visibility propagation method to be described in section 3.

There are also reasons behind why the internal contour chains are tested with objects instead of individual contours or contour chains.   Individual contours cannot be used because the surrounding objects may comprise several contours and each of these contours may not fully surround the internal contour chain. Contour chains cannot be used because the rigorous surrounding tests to be described in section 2.3 below require the simultaneous consideration of all contours of each object.

2.2   Selecting a testpoint:

For each contour chain which passes the extent test, a contour testpoint is selected. Usually the left most point on the chain is chosen. Picking such a point instead of an arbitrary one simplifies calculations in sections 2.3 and 2.4 because surfaces originated from the contour chain itself need not be considered.

2.3   Rigorous surrounding tests between contour chains and objects:

A contour chain may not be surrounded by the contours of an object even though the extent of the former is totally within the extent of the later (as shown in figure 4). If they pass the extent test, the following tests are carried out:

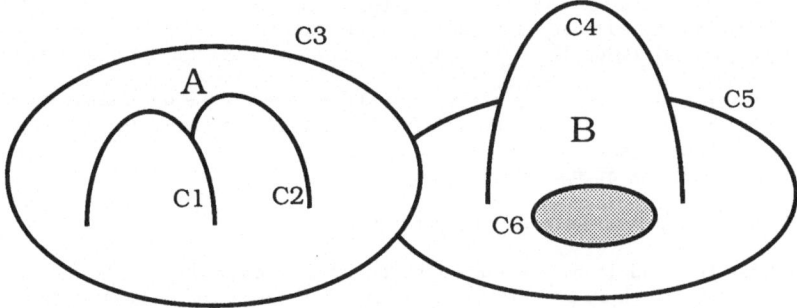

Fig. 3: Contour Chains

Several contour chains are formed from contours from two objects, A and B. Note that the contours may be surface boundaries, such as C3, C5 and C6, or silhouettes, such as C1, C2 and C4. It can also be a hole, such as C6. A chain may be formed from contours belonging to different objects, such as C3, C4 and C5, or the same object, such as C1 and C2. The chain may only consist of one contour, such as C6. Conversely, an object may have one or several chains.

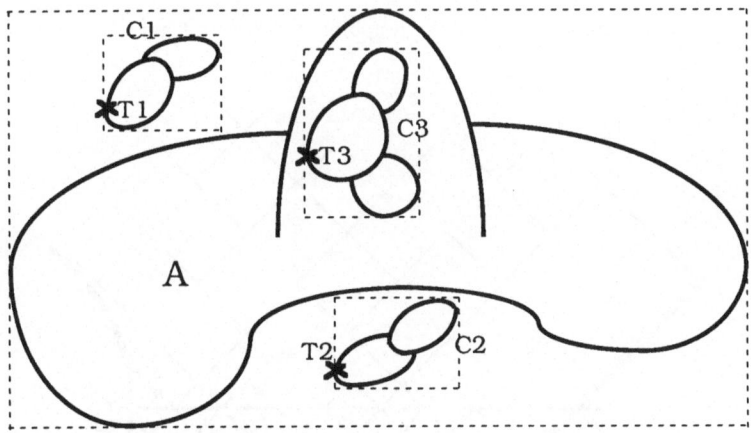

Fig. 4: Test of Surrounded Contour Chains

Several contour chains whose extents are totally within the extent of an object A are shown. Two of these chains, C1 and C2, are not surrounded by the object. This is detected by calculating the number of left facing and right facing contour edges at the left of the testpoints, T1 and T2. In this case, the numbers equal, hence the chains do not fall on the surface of the object.

In the case of contour chain C3, there are two left facing contours and no right facing contours at its left, hence it is inside the object and surrounded by two surfaces.

2.3.1 By top-down searching from contour segments to contour edges, external contour edges which are at the left hand side and whose y extents overlap the y coordinates of the testpoint are calculated. Note that contour edges outside the viewport cannot be ignored.

2.3.2 The number of surfaces which are directly above or below the testpoint is the difference between the number of external left-facing contour edges and the number of right-facing contour edges. Therefore, if the difference of them is greater than one, the contour chain is being surrounded.

2.4   Calculation of polygons surrounding the testpoint.

If the testpoint is found to be surrounded by an object, the occlusion relationship between them, and the surfaces which are directly above or below the testpoint have to be determined. This is done through constraint propagation of polygons on the surfaces. A round of propagation starts from a left facing contour edge calculated in section 2.3. From the polygon connected to the contour edge, other polygons connected to it whose vertical extents also cover the y coordinate of the testpoint are accessed. This access of polygons is repeated until either a right contour edge or the polygon surrounds the testpoint is reached. However, if the testpoint falls on the contour of a hole, it is also likely that the accessed polygon is connected to the testpoint.

The propagation of polygons is repeated for all the left contour edges. Generally this search for the polygons above or below the testpoint is reasonably fast as most of the time only the extent tests are needed.

If concave polygons are present, a polygon may be accessed more than once. The recursion algorithm keeps track of polygons which have been accessed so that if any of them is accessed again, it backtracks to search for the next polygon.

The calculation of polygons surrounding the testpoint is shown in figure 5.

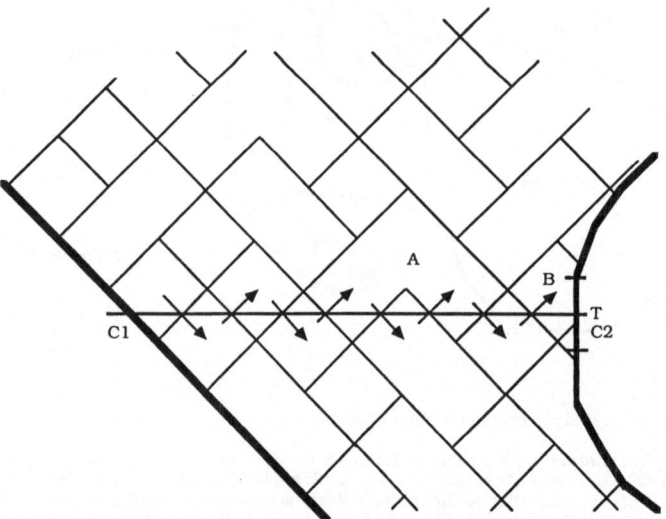

Fig 5:   Constraint Propagation from External Contour to Internal Contour

Surfaces directly below (or above) the testpoint T on the internal contour edge C2
is determined by constraint propagation which starts from the external contour edge
C1. The access of polygons are shown by the arrows. Because polygon A is a
concave polygon, it is accessed twice. A backtracking algorithm is used to avoid an
endless loop. The propagation ends at polygon B which is directly below the testpoint.

2.5 Calculation of multiple surrounding contours.

Occasionally a contour chain may be surrounded by more than one object. Therefore, steps 2.3 and 2.4 have to be repeated for all objects until all surrounding contours are found.

3. Calculation of visibility status of the contour edges.

The determination of visibility status of contour edges begins at the testpoint of each contour chain. From results calculated in section 2, the visibility status of the testpoint and polygons above and beneath it are obtained. Contour edges connected to it are accessed. At the same time, polygons above and beneath these edges are calculated from the information about the previously accessed polygons and the contour intersections. The visibility status of the accessed contour edges are calculated from the polygons overlapping them.

4. Display of visible surfaces.

Visible surfaces are displayed by propagation from the visible contours as described in detail by Hornung [7]. This involves recursive access of visible polygons which have not been accessed before until all the visible polygons have been obtained.

V. DISCUSSION.

Using a modular approach, the proposed algorithm is implemented on top of the basic contour-oriented algorithm which in turn is built on top of the edge-intersection algorithm. It was first written on an IBM PC/AT computer using C language and recently ported to an IBM RT/PC computer. By deliberately not creating and using the higher level contour descriptions, the implemented program could also function as the most basic edge-intersection algorithm or the original contour oriented algorithm. Test results showing the performance difference of the algorithms under this arrangement are shown in figure 6.

The test results have indicated that the proposed algorithm is advantageous as compared with its earlier counterparts especially when the scene consists of many contours. This is achieved through better representation of surfaces which in turn results in the net reduction of calculations in several computation intensive areas. This will be apparent in the qualitative analysis of the algorithms carried out below which uses the following symbols:

OBJ	:	total number of objects in the scene
EDG	:	total number of edges in the scene
PH	:	total number of polygons in the scene
CH	:	total number of contour chains in the scene
CT	:	total number of contour edges in the scene
seg	:	average number of segments per object
ct	:	average number of contours per segment
pgn	:	average number of polygons accessed for each round of constraint propagation of polygons

Most of the hidden surface calculations in the original contour-oriented algorithms are in the contour intersection tests and the calculation of polygons which overlap the contours. The algorithm achieves its first major reduction of calculations through the hierarchical representation of contour edges. While the original contour-oriented algorithms require edge intersection tests between each pair of the contour edges, the extent tests between the higher level geometric entities in the hierarchical contour representation can eliminate many edge intersection tests between contour edges which are obviously not intersected. When the comparisons between contour edges are unavoidable, they are reduced by the geometry of contour segments which allow the edges comprising them to be compared in linear time complexity. The growth rate of the edge intersection calculations is therefore reduced to $O\ (OBJ^2 * seg^2 * ct)$. Since CT is equal to $OBJ * seg * ct$, and since seg is a constant, the time complexity can be simplified to $O\ (CT * OBJ)$. By comparison, the edge intersection tests of the contour-oriented algorithms and the basic edge-intersection algorithms grow in $O\ (CT^2)$ and $O\ (EDG^2)$ respectively.

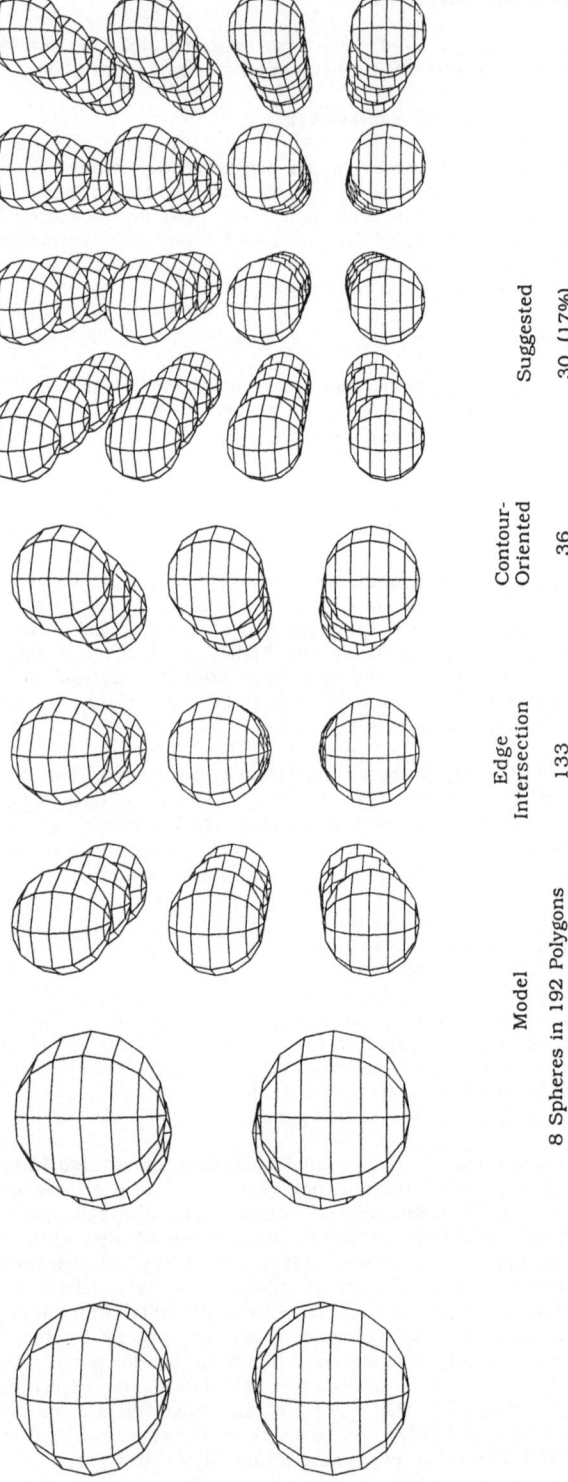

Model	Edge Intersection	Contour-Oriented	Suggested
8 Spheres in 192 Polygons	133	36	30 (17%)
27 Spheres in 648 Polygons	1192	228	167 (27%)
64 Spheres in 1536 Polygons	--	988	575 (42%)

Fig. 6 Performance comparisons between the basic edge intersection, contour-oriented and the suggested algorithm. The time spent on the actual plotting of the images is not included. Figures in brackets are the percentages of time saved by the suggested algorithm over the contour-oriented algorithm.

The fast determination of surrounding contours could also reduce many calculations. The existing contour-oriented algorithms cannot detect the presence of surrounding contours. Therefore, all the polygons in the scene are required to compare with the contour chains to determine the polygons overlapping the later. The calculations as a result run in $O\ (CH * PH)$ complexity. In the new algorithm, such tests are avoided by two methods. First, the comparisons between entities in the contour structure provide a fast and effective way to detect surrounding contours. The growth rate of these calculations is only $O\ (CH * OBJ)$. Second, if surrounding contours do occur, the propagation of polygons from the surrounding contours to the testpoint on each contour chain enables the efficient calculations of surfaces which surround the internal contours. These calculations have $O\ (CH * OBJ * pgn)$ complexity, if the worst case scenario of all objects are one in front of the others without any intersection between their contours is assumed. Since pgn is a constant, it can be dropped and the overall time complexity for the surrounding tests becomes $O\ (CH * OBJ)$, which is clearly less than the growth rates of the equivalent calculations in the earlier contour-oriented algorithms.

In addition to providing an efficient hidden surface algorithm which could be further enhanced in the future, the surface analysis techniques described in this paper have also strengthened the relationship between computer vision and computer graphics. In the former, the detection of contours from images and the evaluation of the contour structure have always been a cornerstone to the model-based image recognition techniques which infer object structures from images. In works done by Marimont [8], Asada and Brady [9], for example, contours are divided into segments according to how their curvature changes. These contour representation schemes are in principle similar to the use of contour segments and contour edges to represent the contour hierarchy described here. Further works based on the techniques suggested in this paper may be able to apply the complicated data structures and contour description techniques used in computer vision. Conversely, developments in computer vision may benefit from the algorithm suggested here which is more elaborate in analysing and manipulating the surface and contour geometry.

VI.   CONCLUSION.

This paper has indicated the importance of structural analysis of objects and their contours in hidden surface algorithms. The close relationship between this analysis and the efficiency of hidden surface algorithms have been shown through a discussion of several object space algorithms and further strengthened by the new algorithm described here. Using elaborate analysis and representation of objects and their contours, the suggested algorithm is able to apply the surface geometry effectively to reduce several computation intensive operations in hidden surface removal. The similarities between the algorithm and many image processing techniques have also indicated the possibility of having cross-disciplinary works between computer graphics and computer vision.

ACKNOWLEDGEMENT:

The author wishes to thank Institute of Systems Science for funding this project. The assistance and encouragement from Dr. Wellington Yu and Dr. K. C. Chu are especially appreciated. Thanks also go to Miss Cindy Chng for helping to prepare the manuscript. The basic ideas expressed in this paper were first conceived while the author was studying at University of Essex and were kindly supported by Mr. H. Farmer and other staff in the computer science department.

REFERENCES:

1.   Sutherland, I.E., Sproull, R. F. and Schumacker, R. A. "A Characterization of Ten Hidden Surface Algorithms," Computing Surveys Vol. 6 No 1, (Mar 1974), pp. 1-55.

2.   A. Appel, "The Notion of Quantitative Invisibility and the Machine Rendering of Solids," Proc. 22nd ACM National Conference (1967), pp. 387-393.

3.   P. P. Loutrel, "A Solution to the Hidden-Line Problem for Computer Drawn Polyhedra," IEEE Trans. Computers, Vol. C-19, No 3, (1970), pp. 205-213.

4.   Galimberti, R., and Montanari, U., "An Algorithm for Hidden-Line Elimination", Comm. ACM, 12, 4, (April 1969), pp. 206-211.

5.   Weiler, K. and P. Atherton, "Hidden Surface Removal Using Polygon Area Sorting", Computer Graphics, pp. 214-222.

6.   Hubschman, H. and S.W.Zucker, "Frame-to-Frame Coherence - Constraints of a Convex Hull," Computer Graphics Vol. 15, No 3, (Aug 1981), pp. 45-54

7.   Hornung, C., "An Approach to a Calculation-Minimised Hidden Surface Algorithm," Computing and Graphics Vol. 16 No 3, (1982), pp. 26-33

8.   Marimont, D., "A Representation for Image Curves," Proceedings of the National Conference on Artificial Intelligence, AAAI, (Aug 1984), pp. 237-242.

9.   Asada, H. and Brady, M., "The Curvature Primal Sketch," IEEE Transactions on Pattern Analysis and Machine Intelligence, Vol. PAM1-8, No 1, (Jan 1986), pp. 8-17.

H. L. Lim is a research assistant at Institute of Systems Science, National University of Singapore. His research interest is computer graphics and computer vision. He received his MSc in computer science from University of Essex and has a BSc in physics from University of Singapore.   His address is: Institute of Systems Science, National University of Singapore, Heng Mui Keng Terrace, Kent Ridge, Singapore 0511

Fast Algorithms for Computing the Diameter of a Finite Planar Set

Binay K. Bhattacharya and Godfried T. Toussaint

Abstract

Three algorithms for computing the diameter of a finite planar set are proposed. Although all three algorithms have $O(n^2)$ worst-case running time, an expected-complexity analysis shows that, under a reasonable probability model, all three algorithms have linear expected running time. Experimental results indicate that two of these algorithms perform very well for some distributions, and are competitive with an existing method. Finally, we exhibit situations where exact algorithms out-perform an approximate algorithm.

Keywords

diameter, convex hull, maximal vectors, expected complexity, algorithms, computational geometry, graphics

1. Introduction

Let $S = \{ p_1, p_2,..., p_n \}$ be a set of n points in the plane. Let each point p_i be identified by the cartesian coordinates x_i and y_i. The diameter of the set S, denoted by DIAM(S), is defined by

$$\text{DIAM(S)} = \max \{d(p_i, p_j)\}$$

where $d(p_i, p_j)$ is the euclidean distance between the points p_i and p_j.

In the clustering problem [15] one often requires to find the pair of points of a set which are farthest apart. This is precisely the diameter of the set. The diameter of a defect in an artillery shell is the crucial feature in an automatic inspection of radiographs of artillery shells [16]. In statistics, the bivariate range of a set is defined as the diameter of the set [10]. The bivariate range is used by applied ballisticians as a rapidly computed measure of the "precision" of small arms fire [10]. Finally, the diameter is used as a measure of the length of bilogical objects in morphology [22].

One obvious way of computing DIAM(S) is by the brute-force method. Here one first computes all the interpoint distances of the set S. Thus we have to compute $O(n^2)$ distances and therefore, the brute force method requires $O(n^2)$ running time.

Shamos [20] presented an algorithm to compute DIAM(S) based on the fact that the pair of points realizing DIAM(S) are convex hull points of S, i.e., DIAM(S) = DIAM(CH(S)) where CH(S) is the convex hull of S. There are many $O(n\log n)$ worst-case algorithms to compute the convex hull of S [1,4,23]. Under some mild conditions, the expected running time of the algorithm in [4] is O(n). Once CH(S) is computed, the diameter of the result-ing convex polygon can be computed in linear time by first recognizing the "antipodal" pairs of points [5,20]. Several linear time algorithms have been proposed to compute the diameter of a convex polygon [9,14,21]. However these algorithms have been shown to be incorrect [2,6]. Shamos proposed another diameter algorithm which uses the "furthest point" Voronoi diagram of S [19]. However, it is shown through a counterexample this algorithm does not always work [8]. Snyder et al. [21] proposed a diameter algorithm which has O(n^2) worst-case running time but, as claimed by the authors, has a fast expected-case running time. Firschein et al. [16] and Fischler [17] presented an O(mn) algorithm to approximate the diameter of S where m is the number of directions con-sidered. The maximum percentage error in estimating the length of the true diameter is $100(1-\cos(\frac{90^o}{m}))\%$. The approximation gets better as m increases.

From the above discussion we see that the diameter of S can be computed by the algo-rithm in [20] in O(nlogn) time in the worst case and in O(n) time in the expected case under some mild conditions.

In this paper, the main emphasis is on designing and comparing algorithms which have fast expected running times. In section 2, we describe three new algorithms after developing the necessary background. The running times, both in the worst case and the expected case, are investigated. Section 3 contains a Monte Carlo simulation to empirically compare the performances of the proposed algorithms, along with the algorithms of Shamos (called here SHAMOS) [20] and Snyder et al. (called here SNYDER) [21].

2. Proposed Algorithms

2.1 Definitions

A point $p_i = (x_i, y_i)$ **dominates** a point $p_j = (x_j, y_j)$ in (s_1, s_2) sense if $s_1 x_i > s_1 x_j$ and $s_2 y_i > s_2 y_j$ where $s_1, s_2 = +,-$. A point of S is **maximal** in (s_1, s_2) sense if and only if it is not dominated in (s_1, s_2) sense by any other point of S. Let $S_m^{(s_1, s_2)}$ be the **maximal subset** of S in (s_1, s_2) sense. Let

$$S_m = S_m^{(+,+)} \cup S_m^{(-,+)} \cup S_m^{(-,-)} \cup S_m^{(+,-)}.$$

It is not difficult to see that the convex hull points of S is contained in S_m.

Let S_e be the extremal subset of S obtained by first finding the eight extreme points of S in X, Y, X+Y and Y-X directions and deleting all points lying in the interior of the result-ing convex polygon. Again S_e contains the convex hull points of S.

We now show by citing counterexamples that S_m and S_e are not subsets of each other.

(a) S_m is not always contained in S_e

Let $p_1, p_2,..., p_8$ be the eight extreme points of S (Fig.1). Let us assume that all the remaining points of S lie inside the convex polygon (Fig.1). Therefore, $S_e = \{p_1, p_2,...,p_8\}$. Let us consider a point q ϵ S and q $\notin S_e$. Clearly, q could be a maximal point if no point lies inside the quadrant shown in Fig.1. Therefore, q may belong to S_m. Hence S_m is not always contained in S_e.

(b) S_e is not always contained in S_m

Let $p_1, p_2,..., p_8$ be the eight extreme points of S. Let q_1 and q_2 be two other points of S belonging to S_e (Fig.2). Clearly, q_1 is dominated by the points of S in all the four senses. Therefore, $q_1 \notin S_m$. Hence S_m does not contain S_e.

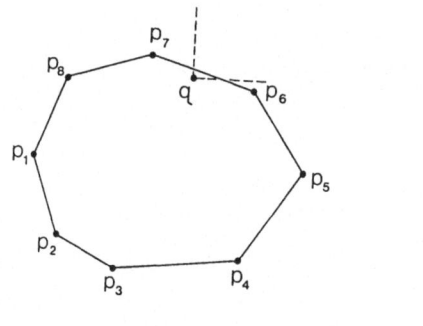

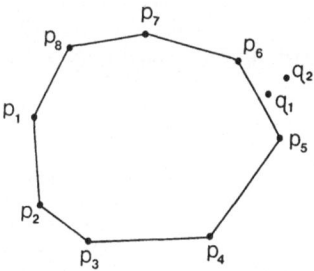

Fig. 1   Fig. 2

2.2 Algorithm DIAM1

We know that the pair of points that realize DIAM(S) are convex hull points of S. Also it is observed that the convex hull points of S are contained in S_m. The algorithm DIAM1, designed on the basis of these observations, is described as follows:

Step 1: Determine the maximal set S_m in S.
Step 2: Compute the distance between all pairs of points of S_m.
Step 3: Determine the maximum of the distances computed in step 2.

2.2.1 Analysis of DIAM1

Each of the algorithms of Bentley et al. [3] and Kung et al. [18] to compute S_m has O(nlogn) worst-case running time complexity. Step 1 is called the throw-away step. In this step all the non-maximal points are identified and these points are rejected from further consideration. Steps 2 and 3 of DIAM1 are dependent on the cardinality of S_m. The size of S_m could be as high as O(n) in the worst case. Therefore, $O(n^2)$ is the worst-case running time of DIAM1.

In practice, it is rarely the case that all the points of S are maximal points. Let us assume that the data points are drawn independently at random from some underlying distribution $\mathbf{f}$. Let N be the cardinality of S_m. Then the complexity C of DIAM1 is given by

$$C = C(S_m) + kN^2$$

where k is a positive constant and $C(S_m)$ denotes the complexity of determining the set S_m. The expected complexity of DIAM1, denoted as E{C}, is by

$$E\{C\} = E\{C(S_m)\} + kE\{N^2\}.$$

The algorithm in [3] to compute S_m has linear expected running time when E{N} is $O(n^p)$, p < 1. This is true whenever the density $\mathbf{f}$ can be written as the product of densities [4]. In other words, $E\{C(S_m)\}$ is O(n) when the coordinates of the points of S are drawn from independent distributions. Under this assumption Devroye [11] has shown that $E\{N^2\}$ is also O(n). Therefore, the expected running time of DIAM1 is linear when the coordinates of the points of S are drawn from independent distributions.

2.3 Algorithm DIAM2

We know that the convex hull of S is contained in S_e. Therefore we can apply the exhaustive approach to the points of S_e, as in DIAM1, to compute DIAM(S).

Step 1: Determine the extremal set S_e.
Step 2: Compute the distance between all pairs of points in S_e.
Step 3: Determine the maximum of the distances computed in Step 2.

2.3.1 Analysis of DIAM2

The extremal set S_e can be obtained from S in a fairly simple manner in linear time. Like DIAM1, Step 1 in DIAM2 is called the throw-away step. The time required to implement steps 2 and 3 are dependent on the cardinality of S_e. If S_e contains N points, DIAM2 takes $O(N^2)$ time to compute steps 2 and 3. Therefore, the worst case complexity of DIAM2 is $O(n^2)$.

Concerning the expected complexity, Devroye and Toussaint [13] have shown that, when the points of S have a density f such that $0 < t \leq T < \infty$ where t and T are constants, for x in a rotated rectangle in 2-dimensional space and zero elsewhere, $E\{N^2\} \leq kn$, k a positive constant. Thus DIAM2 runs in linear expected time when points of S are distributed uniformly in a rectangle. However, it is not linear for normally distributed points.

2.4 Algorithm DIAM3

2.4.1 Theoretical basis

It is noticed from Shamos' algorithm [20], DIAM1 and DIAM2 that each algorithm removes quickly in their throw-away step a subset of points of S which lie in the "center of S". In the case of Shamos' algorithm, any point of S which is not a convex hull point of S can be considered to be lying in the center of'the set. Similar arguments apply for non-maximal points in DIAM1 and non-extremal points in DIAM2. In DIAM3 we consider yet another approach to reduce the search space efficiently.

Let E be the set of (possibly eight) extreme points of S in the X, Y, X+Y and Y-X directions. The DIAM(S) is bounded below by DIAM(E). We enclose all the points of S by a rectangle with corners A_1, A_2, A_3, A_4, determined by the four extreme points in the X and Y direction. Clearly, DIAM(E) is greater than or equal to the length of the greatest side of the rectangle.

Corresponding to each corner A_i, there exists a region R_{i+2} such that for any point x in R_{i+2}, $d(A_i, x) \geq$ DIAM(E), i=1,2,3,4 and $R_5 \equiv R_1$ and $R_6 \equiv R_2$. Let

$$R = \bigcup_{i=0}^{4} R_i,$$

$$Q = \text{rectangle } A_1 A_2 A_3 A_4, \text{ and}$$

$$T = Q\text{-}R.$$

It is readily seen that for a pair of points p_i and p_j belonging to S with at least one of them, say p_i, lying in the interior of T, $d(p_i, p_j) <$ DIAM(E). Thus it follows that the pair of points p_i and p_j of S having $d(p_i, p_j) \geq$ DIAM(E) must belong to the set R. Let S_i be the set of points of S lying in the region R_i. Then, once DIAM(E) is known, we need to consider only S_i, i=1,2,3,4 to compute DIAM(S). All the points of S lying in the interior of T are considered to be lying in the center of the set. Thus we have reduced the search space from S to $\bigcup_{i=0}^{4} S_i$. This search space can still be reduced further as shown in the following theorem.

Theorem 1

The pair of points realizing DIAM(S) is such that one point belongs to S_i and the other belongs to S_{i+2}, i=1,2.

Proof: It is sufficient to show that all the pairs of points in $S_i \bigcup S_{i+1}$, i=1,2,3,4; $S_5 \equiv S_1$ need not be considered. Due to symmetry, we need only consider the case $S_1 \bigcup S_2$.

Let $\bar{S}_{i,j} = S_i \bigcap S_j$. We can then partition S_1 and S_2 as follows:

$$S_2 = \bar{S}_{1,2} \bigcup S'_2 \bigcup \bar{S}_{2,3}.$$

Therefore, (Fig.3)

$$S_1 \bigcup S_2 = \bar{S}_{1,4} \bigcup S'_1 \bigcup \bar{S}_{1,2} \bigcup S'_2 \bigcup \bar{S}_{2,3}.$$

It is quite clear that some of $\bar{S}_{i,j}$ and S'_k could be empty.

(i) Since $\bar{S}_{1,4} = S_1 \bigcap S_4$ and $\bar{S}_{1,2} = S_1 \bigcap S_2$, it is not required here to compute d(p,q) when $p \in \bar{S}_{1,4}$ and $q \in \bar{S}_{1,2}$ because this pair will be considered again in the sets S_2 and S_4. Similar arguments apply for the subsets $\bar{S}_{1,2}$ with $\bar{S}_{2,3}$ and $\bar{S}_{1,4}$ with $\bar{S}_{2,3}$.

(ii) We do not have to compute d(p,q) when $p \in \bar{S}_{1,4}$ and $q \in S'_2$ since this pair will be considered again in the sets S_2 and S_4. Similarly, $\bar{S}_{2,3}$ and S'_1 need not be considered together.

(iii) It also follows from the construction that for any pair of points p and q, both belonging to $\bar{S}_{1,4} \bigcup S'_1$ or $S'_1 \bigcup \bar{S}_{1,2}$ or $\bar{S}_{1,2} \bigcup S'_2$ or $S'_2 \bigcup \bar{S}_{2,3}$, d(p,q) < DIAM(E). Therefore, we can also neglect these cases.

(iv) The only remaining part to be proved is that for any $p \in S'_1$ and $q \in S'_2$, d(p,q) < DIAM(E). In this case it is sufficient to show that for any point p in the line segment $A_3 B_3$ or on the arc $B_3 D_2$ and for any point q on the line segment $A_4 B_4$ or on the arc $B_4 D_1$, d(p,q) < DIAM(E) (Fig.3).

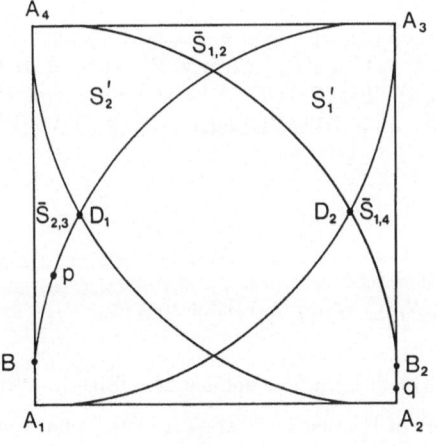

Fig. 3

Without loss of generality, let the distance of p from the line A_3A_4 be more than the distance of the point q from A_3A_4. In this case, angle(pqA_4) > angle (pA_4q) which implies that d(p,q) < d(p,A_4) i.e. d(p,q) < DIAM(E). Q.E.D.

2.4.2 Steps of the algorithm DIAM3

The algorithm DIAM3 to compute the diameter of an arbitrary set S is described below:

Step 1: Compute the set E of extreme points of S in the X, Y, X+Y and Y-X directions.

Step 2: Enclose the set S by the rectangle defined by the extreme points in the X and Y directions.

Step 3: Compute DIAM(E) by the brute force method.

Step 4: Determine the points of S which belong to S_i, i=1,2,3,4.(Throw-away step)

Step 5: Compute the distances between all pairs of points p and q where p ϵ S_i and q ϵ S_{i+2},i=1,2.

Step 6: Select the maximum distance encountered in step 5 as the diameter of S.

2.4.3 Analysis of DIAM3

Worst-case Analysis

It is clear that steps 1 through 4 require O(n) time in the worst case. The running time of step 5 is dependent on the number of points in each of the sets S_i. If the points of S are such that they all lie on a circle, then all the points of S are involved in $\bigcup_{i=1}^{4} S_i$. In this case $O(n^2)$ operations are required to execute step 5. Therefore, the worst-case complexity of DIAM3 is $O(n^2)$.

Expected case analysis

It will be assumed that the underlying distribution of the points of S is uniform in a unit square. We now show that the expected running time of step 5 in DIAM3 is sublinear and therefore, the expected running time of DIAM3 is O(n) when the points are distributed uniformly in a unit square. The proof given below is due to Devroye [12].

Let $A_1A_2A_3A_4$ be the rectangle R which encloses the points of S generated uniformly in the unit square R' :$A'_1A'_2A'_3A'_4$. Clearly, R' encloses R totally. We already know that DIAM(E) $\leq$ DIAM(S). Let R_i (R'_i) be the regions of R (R') such that for any point q in R_i (R'_i), d(A_i,q) $\geq$ DIAM(E) [d(A'_i,q) $\geq$ DIAM(E)]. First we prove the following lemma.

Lemma 1

When DIAM(E) $> \sqrt{\dfrac{5}{4}}$, $R_i \subseteq R'_i$, i=1,2,3,4 always.

Proof: First R' is partitioned into four sub-squares [Fig.4]. When DIAM(E) $> \sqrt{\dfrac{5}{4}}$, it is clear that the four corners of R must lie in the four sub-squares of R' [Fig.4].

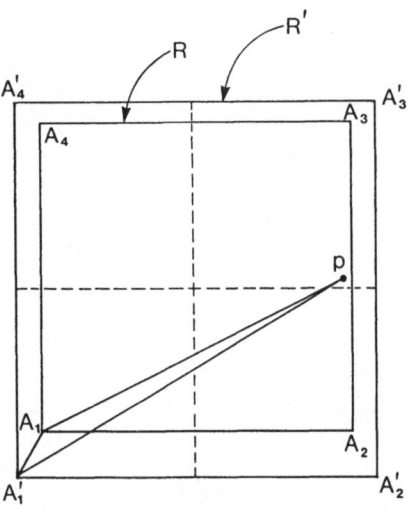

Fig. 4

Let p be a point in R_1. It is now easy to show that when DIAM(E) $> \sqrt{\frac{5}{4}}$, the point p must lie in the region shown in Fig.4. In this case, angle($A'_1 A_1 p$) $\geq 90°$, thereby implying that $d(A'_1, p) \geq d(A_1, p) >$ DIAM(E). Hence, if any point p is in R_1, it is also in R'_1. Therefore, $R_1 \subseteq R'_1$. Similar arguments apply for other regions also. Hence $R_i \subseteq R'_i$, i=1,2,3,4 when DIAM(E) $> \sqrt{\frac{5}{4}}$. Q.E.D.

Let us now consider the square R' [Fig.5]. We construct the triangles $A'_i E'_i C'_i$, i=1,2,3,4 with base at 45° and height $\delta < \frac{1}{2}[\sqrt{2} - \sqrt{\frac{5}{4}}]$. We now construct circles with centers at A'_i, i=1,2,3,4 and radius r = $\sqrt{2} - 2\delta$. Clearly, r $> \sqrt{\frac{5}{4}}$. These circles determine points B'_{i+2} and D'_{i+2}, i=1,2,3,4, (indices taken modulo 4) on the perimeter of the square R'. Let 2θ be the distance between B'_i and D'_i. From the triangle $A'_3 B'_1 A'_2$ (Fig.5), we see that

$$(\sqrt{2} - 2\delta)^2 = 1 + (1 - \sqrt{2}\theta)^2$$
$$\text{i.e. } \delta^2 - \sqrt{2}\,\delta = \frac{\theta^2}{2} - \frac{\theta}{\sqrt{2}}$$

Furthermore, as δ approaches zero, θ also approaches zero (Fig.5). Hence, for small δ, we have

$$\theta = (2 + O(1))\delta \qquad\qquad (1)$$

Let C and C' be the complexities of Step 5 when working with the rectangles R and R', respectively. When DIAM(E) $> \sqrt{\frac{5}{4}}$, it is clear from Lemma 1 that C < C'.

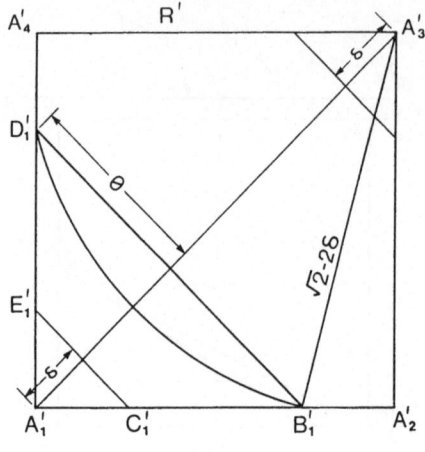

Fig.5

Lemma 2

If N is binomial (n,p), then $E\{N^2\} \leq 2(1+n^2p^2)$.

Proof: We know that

$$E\{N^2\} = n^2p^2 + np(1\text{-}p) \leq n^2p^2 + np.$$

When $np \leq 1$, $E\{N^2\} \leq 2$ and when $np \geq 1$, $E\{N^2\} \leq 2n^2p^2$. Therefore,

$$E\{N^2\} \leq 2(1+n^2p^2). \qquad (2) \quad \text{Q.E.D.}$$

Let N_o be the total number of points of S in $\bigcup_{i=1}^{4} \Delta\, A'_{\,i}\, B'_{\,i}\, D'_{\,i}$. Let $Z=1$ if some of the triangles $A'_{\,i}\, C'_{\,i}\, E'_{\,i}$, i=1,2,3,4, are empty. Otherwise let $Z=0$. Clearly both N_o and Z are random variables. If $Z=1$ then at least one small triangle $A'_{\,i}\, B'_{\,i}\, C'_{\,i}$ is empty and thus DIAM(E) could be smaller than or equal to $\sqrt{2}$ -2δ and thus fewer points would be thrown away (in the worst case, maybe no points), resulting in an $O(n^2)$ complexity. If on the other hand, $Z=0$, then no small triangle is empty and therefore, DIAM(E) would be larger than $\sqrt{2}$ - 2δ. Hence more points would be thrown away.

Theorem 2

$$E\{C'\} \leq kn, \, k > 0.$$

Proof: C', the complexity of executing Step 5 of DIAM3, can be expressed as

$$C' \leq k_1 N_o^2 + k_2 Z n^2 \qquad (3)$$

where k_1 and k_2 are nonnegative constants and let $\delta < \frac{1}{2}[\sqrt{2} - \frac{5}{4}]$. The expected value of C' , $E\{C'\}$, can be expressed as

$$E\{C'\} \leq k_1 E\{N_o^{\,2}\} + k_2 n^2 E\{Z\} \qquad (4)$$

Let p be the probability of a point falling in the triangle $A'_i B'_i D'_i$. Let q be the probability of a point falling in the triangle $A'_i C'_i E'_i$. Clearly, $p=\theta^2$ and $q=\delta^2$. Hence, using (1), we get $p = (4 + O(1))\delta^2$. Thus (4) can be written as [using the equation (2)]

$$EC' \leq 8k_1 + 8k_1 n^2 p^2 + 4k_2 n^2 (1-q)^n$$

$$= 8k_1 + 8k_1 n^2 (16 + O(1))\delta^4 + 4k_2 n^2 (1-\delta^2)^n$$

$$\leq 8k_1 + 8k_1 n^2 (16 + O(1))\delta^4 + 4k_2 n^2 e^{-n\,\delta^2}$$

$$[\text{ since } 1\text{-}x \leq e^{-x}]$$

If we now take $\delta = \sqrt{\dfrac{2logn}{n}}$, for large n, $\delta < \dfrac{1}{2}[\sqrt{2} - \sqrt{\dfrac{5}{4}}]$. Therefore,

$$E\{C'\} \leq k' \ log^2 n, \ k' > 0. \qquad \text{Q.E.D.}$$

3. Experimental results

A Monte Carlo simulation was carried out to compare the performances of DIAM1, DIAM2, DIAM3 with the algorithms SNYDER [21] and SHAMOS [20].

We first discuss the implementation details of these algorithms which were coded in standard FORTRAN. Algorithms DIAM2, DIAM3 and SNYDER were implemented in the straight-forward manner. Implementing DIAM1 and SHAMOS were nontrivial. The maximal set in DIAM1 was computed using the standard divide-and-conquer approach [3]. The convex hull in SHAMOS was computed using the algorithm of Akl and Toussaint [1] as implemented in [7]. This algorithm has O(nlog n) worst case running time [1] and O(n) expected running time [13] under a reasonable probability model. The algorithm in [1] first computes S_e , the extremal set of S, and then the convex hull of S_e . Thus the throw-away step of DIAM2 is identical to the throw-away step of the algorithm in [1]. The antipodal pairs of a convex polygon [19] were computed using the algorithm described in [5].

Space

The storage space requirement of each of DIAM1, DIAM2, DIAM3, SNYDER and SHAMOS is shown in Table 1. Each algorithm requires 2n storage space for the input. The remaining storage space consists of work space. Thus DIAM2, DIAM3 and SNYDER may be the most desirable algorithms to use when the storage space requirement is an important factor.

Table 1: Storage space requirements of the algorithms in terms of n, the input size.

DIAM1	DIAM2	DIAM3	SNYDER	SHAMOS
5n	3n	3n	3n	5n

Time

All the algorithms were run on an IBM 3033 computer running MTS 5.0 using the FOR-TRAN G1 compiler. Several Monte Carlo simulations were carried out varying the number of points. The sample sizes considered for the number of data points were 100, 500, 1000, 3000, 5000, 7000, 10000, 12000 and 15000. Pseudo-random samples were generated for the following distributions:

(a) uniform in a unit square,

(b) normal with covariance matrix $\begin{pmatrix} 1 & 0 \\ 0 & 1 \end{pmatrix}$, and

(c) normal with covariance matrix $\begin{pmatrix} 0.5 & 0.375 \\ 0.375 & 0.5 \end{pmatrix}$.

Tables 2 through 4 show the results of the experiments. Each experiment was repeated 20 times. The running times are given in milliseconds.

It is seen from Table 2 that DIAM3 and SHAMOS are equally efficient when the points are distributed uniformly in a unit square. However, DIAM3 has slightly larger standard deviation. Other algorithms, i.e. DIAM1, DIAM2 and SNYDER, have slower running times for all values of n. From Table 2 we can conclude the following:

(i) DIAM3 throws more points away than DIAM1, DIAM2 and SNYDER. This supports the theoretical claim that the expected running time of Step 5 of DIAM3 is $O(\log^2 n)$.

(ii) DIAM2 is about 15% slower than SHAMOS. This suggests that the size of S_e is large because the difference of the running times of DIAM2 and SHAMOS to compute DIAM(S) is the same as the difference of the running times of the $O(n^2)$ brute force approach and $O(n \log n)$ approach of SHAMOS to compute DIAM(S_e) without any throw-away step.

All the five algorithms have average running times that are linear in n (Fig.6). These results support the theoretical claim that the expected running time of each of DIAM1, DIAM2, DIAM3 and SHAMOS is linear in n when the points are distributed uniformly in a unit square.

Table 2: Average running times (in milliseconds) to find the diameter of data sets generated uniformly in a unit square. Each experiment was repeated 20 times.

# of pts	DIAM1		DIAM2		DIAM3		SNYDER		SHAMOS	
	time	std.dev	time	std.dev	time	std.dev	time	std.dev	time	std.dev
100	6.3	0.10	3.3	0.12	3.0	0.00	3.6	0.11	4.1	0.08
500	28.6	0.16	15.1	0.51	13.5	0.15	16.9	0.28	15.3	0.17
1000	56.4	0.38	29.4	0.53	26.9	0.32	32.3	0.35	28.9	0.18
3000	166.9	1.24	85.3	1.73	82.5	0.77	98.9	0.91	82.0	0.66
5000	276.6	1.51	146.3	3.16	133.5	1.74	165.1	1.98	133.7	0.84
7000	392.7	1.58	210.7	4.49	187.8	2.29	239.3	4.10	188.0	1.36
10000	560.8	2.58	298.4	7.45	272.8	2.77	339.0	4.50	266.8	1.73
12000	672.8	3.78	360.9	11.18	321.7	4.04	403.4	5.93	318.5	1.67
15000	835.4	2.67	455.2	9.76	409.2	4.16	523.0	7.16	393.7	2.43

POINTS ARE DISTRIBUTED UNIFORMLY
IN A UNIT SQUARE

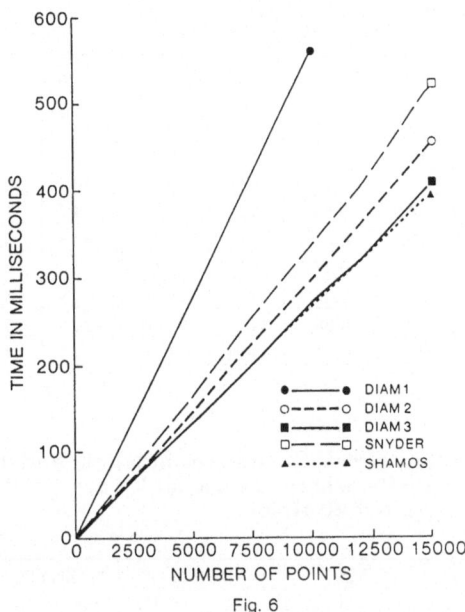

Fig. 6

Tables 3 and 4 give the running times in milliseconds of all the five algorithms when the points of S are distributed normally with covariance matrices $\begin{pmatrix} 1.0 & 0.0 \\ 0.0 & 1.0 \end{pmatrix}$ and $\begin{pmatrix} 0.5 & 0.375 \\ 0.375 & 0.5 \end{pmatrix}$ respectively. When the coordinates of the data points are uncorrelated, DIAM2 is the fastest. SHAMOS is about 10% slower than DIAM2 even though SHAMOS has lower worst-case running time complexity. DIAM3 is quite slow which indicates that not many points get thrown away during the throw-away step. DIAM1 and SNYDER are considerably slower. However, the picture changes significantly when the coordinates of the data points are correlated. In this case DIAM2, DIAM3 and SHAMOS have similar running times. This means that the points being rejected at the throw-away step are very sensitve to the direction in which the data points are oriented. If the general direction of data points is along any coordinate axis, DIAM2 will remove more points than DIAM3 in the throw-away step. However, the general direction of data points makes larger angles with both of the axes, DIAM3 removes considerably more points. The standard deviation of DIAM2 is quite large. This could be attributed to the fact that the size of S_e is very much dependent to the extreme values of the coordinates of the data points as mentioned in [13].

Figs. 7 and 8 show the average running times of theses algorithms when the data points are normally distributed. Each of these algorithms shows a running time linear in n.

We also implemented the algorithm in [16,17] and average running times in milliseconds for m=4, 8 and 16 are shown in table 5. We see from this table that even the **approximate** algorithm, for m > 8, is slower than DIAM3 or SHAMOS when the points are uniformly distributed. This is also true for data points distributed normally. Thus if one is interested in computing the approximate diameter with maximum percentage error within 100(1-cos(90 over 9))%=1.5% of the true diameter, it is better, on an average, to use either DIAM2, DIAM3 or SHAMOS to compute the exact diameter.

Table 3: Average running times (in milliseconds) to find the diameter of data sets generated normally with unit covariance matrix. Each experiment was repeated 20 times.

# of pts	DIAM1		DIAM2		DIAM3		SNYDER		SHAMOS	
	time	std.dev	time	std.dev	time	std.dev	time	std.dev	time	std.dev
100	6.2	0.11	2.5	0.11	2.9	0.11	3.1	0.07	3.3	0.10
500	28.2	0.19	10.8	0.15	14.9	0.34	15.1	0.24	12.4	0.13
1000	56.2	0.36	20.1	0.13	30.0	0.36	30.7	0.47	23.0	0.10
3000	167.5	1.16	58.9	0.35	95.7	3.11	94.7	1.32	65.9	0.27
5000	279.4	1.15	97.9	0.61	146.9	3.04	153.5	2.40	109.1	0.57
7000	391.5	1.98	135.1	0.37	222.3	8.07	217.3	2.99	150.6	0.24
10000	556.1	3.25	191.3	0.43	320.2	10.40	314.8	3.19	213.5	0.34
12000	673.0	2.57	230.1	0.88	396.1	17.20	372.2	5.74	256.0	0.55
15000	830.0	5.55	288.4	0.93	450.1	7.90	474.5	4.35	320.9	0.80

Table 4: Average running times (in milliseconds) to find the diameter of data sets generated normally where the variables are positvely correlated. Each experiment was repeated 20 times.

# of pts	DIAM1		DIAM2		DIAM3		SNYDER		SHAMOS	
	time	std.dev	time	std.dev	time	std.dev	time	std.dev	time	std.dev
100	6.2	0.16	3.0	0.14	2.8	0.08	3.1	0.05	3.8	0.11
500	29.3	0.25	13.5	0.55	12.5	0.19	13.9	0.22	13.9	0.22
1000	55.4	0.41	25.8	1.26	24.3	0.31	28.3	0.29	26.0	0.54
3000	168.9	1.37	71.0	4.03	73.9	0.67	82.9	1.00	72.3	1.63
5000	280.4	1.93	122.8	4.86	117.5	1.75	136.9	1.74	122.9	2.38
7000	393.5	2.47	157.1	5.09	171.9	1.48	194.9	2.46	162.3	1.78
10000	558.9	4.53	228.4	4.56	247.0	1.54	282.5	4.39	236.3	2.80
12000	677.7	4.81	278.0	8.81	296.1	1.85	329.6	4.19	283.8	3.83
15000	837.1	6.88	370.2	19.95	365.2	3.78	411.7	5.24	357.9	5.32

Table 5: Average running times (in milliseconds) of the algorithm in [16,17] to approximate the diameter of data sets generated uniformly in a unit square. Each experiment was repeated 20 times.

# of pts	# of directions					
	4		8		16	
	time	std.dev	time	std.dev	time	std.dev
100	1.0	0.00	3.0	0.00	5.1	0.07
500	6.2	0.08	13.0	0.00	26.0	0.00
1000	13.0	0.00	25.8	0.09	51.0	0.00
3000	38.1	0.07	76.6	0.11	152.5	0.11
5000	64.0	0.00	128.5	0.11	257.4	0.75
7000	90.0	0.00	179.8	0.10	369.2	0.12
10000	128.1	0.05	256.5	0.11	512.6	0.16
12000	153.7	0.10	308.0	0.07	615.1	0.21
15000	192.0	0.00	384.2	0.09	769.1	0.23

POINTS ARE DISTRIBUTED NORMALLY (uncorrelated)

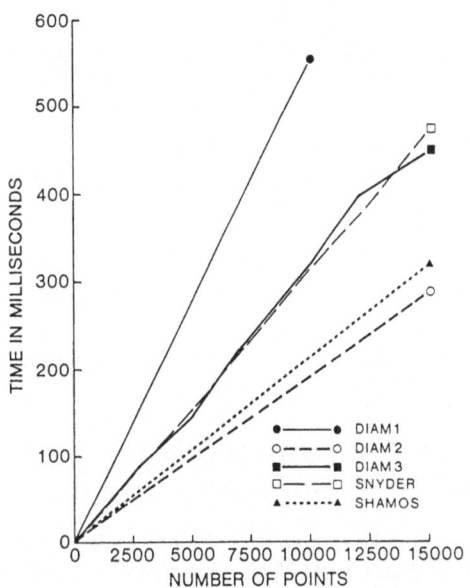

Fig. 7

POINTS ARE DISTRIBUTED NORMALLY (correlated)

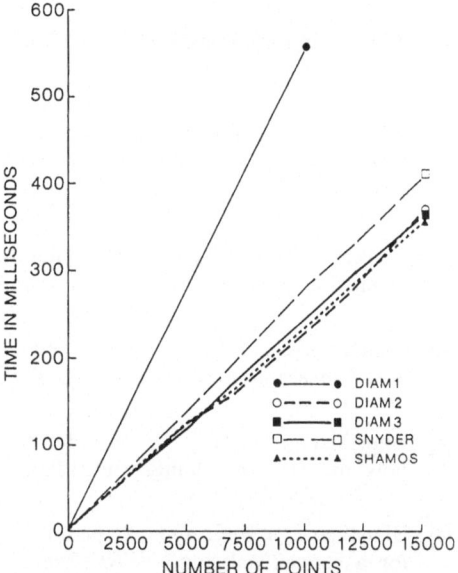

Fig. 8

4. Conclusion

We have proposed three algorithms DIAM1, DIAM2 and DIAM3 to compute the diameter of a planar set of points. Each of these algorithms uses the "throw-away" principle [1] to reduce the search space considerably. Though all three algorithms have $O(n^2)$ running time in the worst case, analysis of the expected complexity shows that under a reasonable probability model, all of these algorithms have linear expected running time. DIAM1, DIAM2 and DIAM3 are experimentally compared with SNYDER [21] and SHAMOS [20]. Experimental results indicate that DIAM3 and SHAMOS perform very well when the points are distributed uniformly in a unit square. When the points are distributed normally, DIAM2 works best for the set of data points whose coordinates are uncorrelated. However, when the coordinates of the data points are correlated, DIAM3 has the similar average running time as that of SHAMOS. DIAM2 and DIAM3 require 3n storage space whereas SHAMOS requires 5n storage space. DIAM2 and DIAM3 are very easy to implement whereas implementing SHAMOS is nontrivial. It is also seen that DIAM2 and DIAM3 compare very well with the approximate algorithm of Firschein et al. [16] and Fischler[17] when one is interested in estimating the true diameter with maximum percentage error within 1.5% of the true diameter. In fact we have exhibited situations where the exact algorithm runs faster than an approximate algorithm. This suggests that care is needed when designing **approximate** algorithms to increase the speed of their execution.

References

[1] Akl S. and Toussaint G.T.,"A fast convex hull algorithm," *Information Processing Letters*, Vol.7, pp.219-222, 1978.

[2] Avis D., Toussaint G.T. and Bhattacharya B.K., "on the multimodality of distances in convex polygons," *Computers and Mathematics with Applications*, Vol.8, pp.153-156, 1982.

[3] Bentley J.L., Kung H.T., Schkolnick M. and Thompson C.D., "On the average number of maxima in a set of vectors and applications," *Journal of ACM*, Vol.25, pp.536-543.

[4] Bentley J.L. and Shamos M.I., "Divide and conquer for linear expected time," *Information Processing Letters*, Vol.7, pp.87-91, 1978.

[5] Bhattacharya B.K., "On the determination of all the antipodal pairs of a convex polygon," *Internal manuscript*, 1982.

[6] Bhattacharya B.K. and Toussaint G.T., "A counterexample to a diameter algorithm for a convex polygon," *IEEE Transactions on Pattern Analysis and Machine Intelligence*, Vol.PAMI-4, pp.306-309, 1982.

[7] Bhattacharya B.K. and Toussaint G.T., "Time-and-storage efficient implementation of an optimal planar convex hull algorithm," *Image and Vision Computing*, Vol.1, pp.140-144, 1983.

[8] Bhattacharya B.K. and Toussaint G.T., "On geometric algorithms that use the furthest-point Voronoi diagram," In *Computational Geometry*, Editor *Toussaint G.T.*, North-Holland, pp.43-61, 1985.

[9] Brown K.Q., *Geometric transformations for fast geometric algorithms*, Ph.D. Thesis, Carnegie-Mellon University, 1979.

[10] Cacoullos T. and De Cicco H., "On the distribution of bivariate range," **Technometrics**, Vol.9, pp.476-480, 1967.

[11] Devroye L.P., "A note on finding convex hulls via maximal vectors," *Information Processing Letters*, Vol.11, pp.53-56, 1980.

[12] Devroye L.P., *Private Communication*, 1982.

[13] Devroye L.P. and Toussaint G.T., "A note on linear expected time algorithms for finding convex hulls," *Computing*, Vol.26, pp.361-366, 1981.

[14] Dobkin D. and Snyder L., "On general method for maximizing and minimizing among certain geometric models," *20th Annual Symposium on Foundation of Computer Science*, pp.9-17, 1979.

[15] Duda R.O. and Hart P.E., *Pattern Classification and Scene Analysis*, John Wiley, New York, 1973.

[16] Firschein O., Eppler W., and Fischler M.A., "A fast defect measurement algorithm and its array processor mechanization," *Proceedings IEEE Computer Society Conference on Pattern recognition and Image Processing*, Chicago, pp.109-113, August 1979.

[17] Fischler M.A., "Fast algorithms for maximal distance problems with applications to image analysis," *Pattern Recognition*, Vol.12, pp.35-40, 1980.

[18] Kung H.T., Luccio F., and Preparata F.P., "On finding the maxima of a set of vectors," *Journal ofACM*, Vol.22, pp469-476, 1975.

[19] Shamos M.I., *Computational Geometry*, Ph.D. Thesis, Yale University, 1978.

[20] Shamos M.I. and Hoey D., "Closest point problems," *Proceedings 16th Annual IEEE Symposium on Foundation of Computer Science* pp.151-162, 1975.

[21] Snyder W.E. and Allan Tang D., "Finding the extrema of a region," *IEEE Transaction on Pattern Analysis and Machine Intelligence*, Vol.PAMI-2, pp.266-269, 1980.

[22] Toussaint G.T., "Computational geometry and morphology," *Proc. First International Symposium on Science of Form*, Tsukuba, Japan, Nov.1985.

[23] Toussaint G.T., "A historical note on convex hull finding algorithms," *Pattern Recognition Letters*, Vol.3, pp.21-28, 1985.

Godfied T. Toussaint received the B.Sc. degree from the University of Tulsa, Tulsa, OK, and the M.A.Sc. and Ph.D. degrees from the University of British Columbia, in 1968, 1970, and 1972, respectively, all in Electrical Engineering. Since 1972 he has been with the School of Computer Science, McGill University, Montreal, working in the areas of information theory, pattern recognition, computational linguistics, and computational geometry. During the summers of 1975 and 1977 he was a visiting scholar at Stanford University. The sabbatical year 1980-81 he spent as a Visiting Scientist at the Applied Mathematics Research Center, University of Montreal. During the spring of 1986 he was a visiting scholar at the Courant Institute of Mathematical Sciences, NYU.

Dr. Toussaint is a past-council-member of the North American Branch of the Classification Society and past Associate Editor of the IEEE Transactions on Information Theory. Presently, he is an Associate Editor of the Pattern Recognition Journal and the Journal of Discrete and Computational Geometry. He is a member of several learned societies including the IEEE, the Pattern Recognition Society, and the New York Academy of Sciences. He recently edited a book titled COMPUTATIONAL GEOMETRY, North Holland, 1986. He was the recipient of the Pattern Recognition Society's 1978 Best Paper of the Year Award, and in 1985 he was awarded a Killam Fellowship by the Canada Council.

B.K. Bhattacharya received his M.Sc. & Ph.D. degrees in computer science from McGill University, Quebec, Canada in 1978 and 1982, respectively.

He joined the School of Computing Science at Simon Fraser University, British Columbia, Canada in January 1982 where he is currently an Assistant Professor. His research interests include design and analysis of algorithms in computational geometry and data structures, pattern recognision and computer graphics.

Chapter 3

Rendering
Techniques

Antialiasing of Polygons with a Weighted Filter

Richard J. Lobb

ABSTRACT

The phenomenon of aliasing in computer graphics is reviewed, and the antialiasing approach of prefiltering before sampling adopted. The theoretical performance of five different types of convolutional filter is studied, and a rotated Hamming filter is selected as the best. The Edge Spread Function, which forms the basis for the antialiasing scheme, is given for the different filters. A decomposition approach reduces the problem of filtering an arbitrary polygon to the problem of filtering acute-angled segments of coordinate space, called *vertex areas*. A scheme for filtering vertex areas is developed and shown to have a maximum error, in a small region around the vertex itself, of about 4% of the intensity of the polygon. The scheme is incorporated into a scan-line algorithm for scan-conversion of two-dimensional polygonal scenes; the algorithm is believed to be simpler and faster than any existing antialiasing schemes that use weighted filters.

Keywords: Rendering, Antialiasing, Sampling, Image filtering, Scan-conversion.

1. ALIASING ARTIFACTS

A fundamental signal-processing theorem, the Sampling Theorem, states that the frequency at which uniformly spaced samples of a continuous one-dimensional signal are taken should be greater than twice the maximum frequency present within the signal. Failure to follow this rule makes it impossible to reconstruct unambiguously the original signal from the samples: those signal frequencies greater than half the sampling frequency cannot be distinguished from lower *alias* frequencies. Figure 1 illustrates this so-called *aliasing* problem: the set of samples from the high-frequency signal is the same as the set from the much lower frequency signal, and we say that the two different signals are aliases of one another.

In computer graphics, aliasing problems occur in both the temporal and the spatial domains. Temporal domain aliasing gives rise to stroboscopic effects in animated sequences, e.g. backward-rotating wagon wheels, while spatial domain aliasing is responsible for the defects in individual frames of 'staircasing' of slanted edges and Moiré patterns. This paper is concerned only with the spatial domain problem, i.e. we will confine our attention to the case of a two-dimensional *picture* being sampled on a regular grid of points to give an array of pixels that we refer to as an *image*.

The extension of the one-dimensional sampling theorem into two dimensions is straightforward: the x and y sampling frequencies should be greater than twice the maximum x and y spatial frequencies present in the picture being sampled (Gonzalez 1977). Pedantically, it

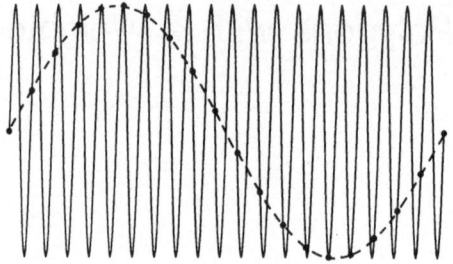

Fig. 1. One-dimensional Aliasing

may be pointed out that no finite-length signal can in fact be band-limited (i.e. contain only frequency components below some upper bound), but for signals of the length involved in computer graphics the finiteness of the record can be safely ignored, except very near the image border.

It is often assumed that if the Sampling Theorem is 'obeyed', the sequence of samples provides a good representation of the original signal, and that no aliasing problems will occur. This is correct only in the sense that the original signal can be mathematically reconstructed from the samples. In computer graphics displays, the 'reconstruction' process is usually just a simple smoothing operation applied by eye (possibly with some help from the restricted bandwidth of the video amplifier), and difficulties can still occur (Pratt 1978). Figure 2 shows what happens when samples are taken at a frequency of f_s from a sinusoid of frequency $(f_s/2) - \Delta$, where Δ is small. Without further processing the sample sequence is subjectively unsatisfactory, and in fact is identical to the sequence obtained by sampling a sinusoid of frequency $(f_s/2) + \Delta$. In both cases, the varying amplitude effect can be regarded as a *beating* of the original frequency, f_o, say, with a new component, introduced by the sampling process (Gonzalez 1977), at a frequency of $f_s - f_o$. We will call this type of aliasing artifact *alias beating*. In principle, alias beating should not normally be relevant to computer graphics, because spatial frequencies as high as $f_s/2$ should be averaged out by the eye at

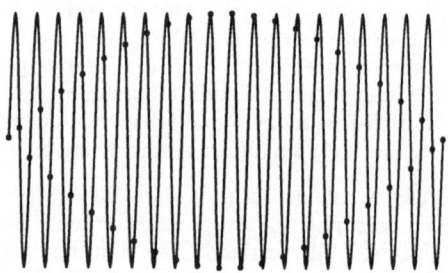

Fig. 2. Alias Beating

normal viewing distances. In practice, however, displays are often not correctly compensated (Catmull 1979), so that the displayed intensity is not linearly proportional to the calculated image intensity; an intensity variation at the beat frequency is then observed.

If alias beating is visible on a display, it can be avoided by ensuring that the highest frequency picture component is somewhat below $f_s/2$, say $f_s/3$. Conversely, if alias beating is invisible, the picture can contain somewhat higher frequency components than $f_s/2$ without visible aliasing artifacts resulting. We return briefly to this issue in section 7; in the meantime, we will assume the usual figure of $f_s/2$ for the maximum permissable signal frequency.

Some authors regard the 'staircase' problem as resulting from failure to filter the signal during reconstruction, rather than from aliasing, and they refer to it as a 'rastering' problem. However, sampling an unfiltered step function causes errors in the estimated position of the step, no matter how much post-filtering is applied. It is precisely those positional errors that cause slanted edges to be jagged. Since the steps are very small, post-filtering (blurring) of the image can greatly alleviate the problem, but it cannot strictly eliminate it. Staircasing and Moiré patterns are both aliasing artifacts, but the former tends to be much easier to deal with. This is because the precise position of a step is determined by very high frequency components, which are adequately filtered by almost any type of filter. Because of the difference in behaviour of the two classes of aliasing artifact, we will sometimes find it convenient to refer to staircasing and Moiré patterns by the rather loose terms *edge aliasing* and *frequency aliasing* respectively.

2. ANTIALIASING METHODS

There are two ways of avoiding aliasing artifacts in computer-generated images.

(1) Take samples at a non-uniform spacing. This approach, called *stochastic sampling*, has been receiving considerable attention recently, particularly for use with ray-tracing (Dippé and Wold 1985; Lee et al 1985). However, it tends to introduce visible noise into the image, and it is not yet clear that it provides a cost-effective antialiasing scheme for other than ray-tracing applications.

(2) Take samples at a regular spacing, but obey the Sampling Theorem. This is the traditional approach, and is the one taken by this paper. It may be noted, however, that the results of the next section, on the choice of filter function, are also relevant to the stochastic-sampling approach.

If the sampling theorem is to be 'obeyed', then either the sampling frequency must be increased to greater than twice the maximum frequency present within the signal (the method of *supersampling*), or the signal must be filtered before sampling to remove frequency components greater than one half the sampling frequency (the method of *prefiltering*). Supersampling does not provide a general solution to aliasing, because most pictures are not even approximately band-limited. The post-filtering operation implicit in supersampling (to reduce the number of samples down to the number of pixels) does, as noted in the previous section, provide an approximate solution to staircasing but not to Moiré patterns. Furthermore, supersampling has been shown to be more expensive than prefiltering (Crow 1981).

Prefiltering is normally done by convolution in the spatial domain, i.e. if $p(x,y)$ denotes the intensity of a picture at the point (x,y), and $i(x,y)$ denotes the intensity of the image after filtering by a filter function $h(x,y)$, then

$$i(x,y) = p(x,y) * h(x,y) = \int_{-\infty}^{\infty} \int_{-\infty}^{\infty} p(x',y') h(x-x',y-y')\, dx'\, dy' \qquad (1)$$

The function $h(x,y)$ is often called the *impulse response* of the filter.

The most common filter (Fiume 1983; Catmull 1978; Carpenter 1984) is a simple 'box' filter, which results in the value at an image point being the average picure intensity over a rectangular area surrounding the point. Weighted circularly-symmetric filters, in which the contribution that a picture point makes to an image point varies with the distance between the two, should give better results than a box filter. This is the issue, addressed from a theoretical viewpoint, of the next section.

3. CHOICE OF FILTER FUNCTION

3.1. The Fourier Transform of a Filter

The convolution of a picture p and a filter function h is represented in the frequency domain by the product of the respective Fourier transforms P and H. Examination of the Fourier transform of a filter thus shows what effect it will have on the spatial frequencies making up a picture. The transform of the ideal filter would have a sharp cut-off at half the sampling frequency, thereby passing the maximum amount of information. Practical (finite-extent) filters can only approximate this ideal, and must always pass some of the 'bad' aliasing components while attentuating some of the 'good' non-aliasing components. Note, too, that if we require that the rendering of an object does not alter if it is rotated, then the presampling filter function and its Fourier transform should be circularly symmetric.

The Fourier transform, or *frequency spectrum*, $G(\mu, v)$ of a function $g(x,y)$ is defined as (Pratt 1978)

$$G(\mu, v) = \int\limits_{-\infty}^{\infty} \int\limits_{-\infty}^{\infty} g(x,y) \exp[-j(\mu x + vy)]\, dx\, dy \tag{2}$$

where μ and v are the x and y angular spatial frequencies[1]. We will now examine the Fourier transforms of some common filters.

3.2. The Box Filter

The common antialiasing method of *area sampling* is equivalent to point sampling after prefiltering with a square 'box' filter. We can define a square box filter function, with a side of length $2a$ and unit volume, as

$$f(x,y) = \begin{cases} 1/4a^2 & |x| < a \text{ and } |y| < a \\ 0 & \text{otherwise} \end{cases}$$

Then (2) gives, for the Fourier transform $F(\mu, v)$,

$$F(\mu, v) = \frac{\sin\mu a}{\mu a} \frac{\sin v a}{v a}$$

---

[1] 'Angular spatial frequency' is simply a term for the product 2π times spatial frequency. The use of this so-called 'angular' measure avoids having to write factors of 2π throughout the equations.

For future comparison with circularly symmetric filters, we define the radius, r, of a box filter as half its diagonal. Figure 3 shows how the magnitude of the Fourier transform of the box filter varies with spatial frequency f along the frequency-space axes (fig. 3a), and along a line at 45° to the axes (fig. 3b). The first of these curves defines the effect of the filter on periodic components with a 'wavefront' aligned along either the x or the y axis, while the second defines the effect on components with a wavefront at 45° to the x and y axes. The difference between the two curves highlights the unsymmetric behaviour of the filter. For example, a picture frequency component of $1/r$ is completely removed if it is at an angle of 45° to the x and y axes, but if it is oriented along either the x or the y axis, it is merely reduced to 22% of its original magnitude.

3.3. Circularly Symmetric Filters

We can define, for any one-dimensional filter $h_1(x)$, a two-dimensional circularly symmetric 'rotated' filter $h_2(x,y) = h_1(\sqrt{x^2 + y^2})$. Huang (1972) has shown that a 'good' $h_1(x)$ should yield a 'good' $h_2(x,y)$.

The Fourier transform $H_2(\mu,v)$ of a rotated filter is given by (Rosenfeld and Kak 1976)

$$H_2(\mu,v) = H_r(\rho) = 2\pi \int_0^\infty l\, h_1(l)\, J_0(\rho l)\, dl \qquad (3)$$

$$\text{where } \rho = \sqrt{\mu^2 + v^2}$$

$$l = \sqrt{x^2 + y^2}$$

and $J_0(x)$ is the zero order Bessel function of the first kind.

For a filter function of limited extent, for which there exists some r such that $h_1(l) = 0$ for all $l \geq r$, the upper limit of the integral becomes r. (3) is then easily integrated numerically to find the radial variation, $H_r(\rho)$, of the Fourier transform. Figure 4 shows this variation for the following filters:

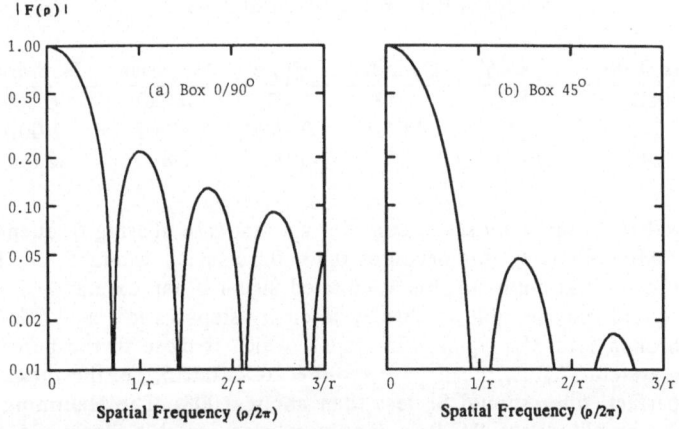

Fig. 3. Magnitude of Fourier Transform of Box Filter

(1) A cylindrical filter:

$$h_1(l) = \begin{cases} k & l < r \\ 0 & l \geq r \end{cases}$$

(4a)

(2) A cone filter:

$$h_1(l) = \begin{cases} k\,(1 - l/r) & l < r \\ 0 & l \geq r \end{cases}$$

(4b)

(3) A limited-extent Gaussian filter:

$$h_1(l) = \begin{cases} k\,\exp[-\tfrac{1}{2}(l/\sigma)^2] & l < r \\ 0 & l \geq r \end{cases}$$

(4c)

Following other workers (Feibush et al 1980), we have used $r = 2\sigma$, although somewhat larger cutoff radii are more common in one-dimensional work.

(4) A Hamming Filter:

$$h_1(l) = \begin{cases} k\,[0.56 + 0.44\cos(\pi l/r)] & l < r \\ 0 & l \geq r \end{cases}$$

(4d)

In each of the above filters, the constant k is chosen to make the volume of the filter unity.

All filters have a spectrum which drops to zero at some *cutoff frequency* and then exhibits a series of bumps, or *sidelobes*, the amplitude of which tends to die out with increasing frequency. The amplitude of the largest sidelobe is a useful figure of merit for an antialiasing filter, since it defines the least attenuation suffered by any frequency that would ideally be totally suppressed by the filter. Table 1 shows the maximum sidelobe amplitude S_{max}, and the cutoff frequency f_{cutoff} for each filter. It also gives the minimum radius r_{min}, measured in pixel spacings, for the filter to satisfy the sampling condition

$$f_{cutoff} \leq \tfrac{1}{2} \times \text{sampling-frequency} = \tfrac{1}{2} \times (1/\text{pixel-spacing})$$

TABLE 1. FILTER RESULTS

	Box 0/90°	Box 45°	Cylinder	Cone	Gaussian	Hamming
S_{max}	0.22	0.047	0.13	0.022	0.020	0.009
f_{cutoff}	0.71/r	1/r	0.61/r	0.94/r	0.88/r	1.00/r
r_{min}	1.4	2.0	1.2	1.9	1.8	2.0

Using a normalized (0-1) intensity scale, consider a worst-case aliasing frequency component $0.5 + 0.5\sin\omega x$. After filtering, this becomes $0.5 + 0.5\alpha\sin\omega x$ where $\alpha \ll 1$. The intensity ratio, maximum to minimum, of this attenuated signal is approximately $1 + 2\alpha$. A high quality imaging system may be able to display intensity steps as low as 1.5% (given a 50/1 dynamic range, broken into 256 equal-ratio steps), which is close to the perceptual limit of the human visual system. Thus, ideally, we require $2\alpha < 0.015$, i.e. the maximum sidelobe amplitude of a 'perfect' filter should be less than about 0.008. The Hamming filter, with a maximum sidelobe amplitude of 0.009, comes very close to this ideal, and the cone and Gaussian filters also offer very good worst-case attenutation factors of around 50. In practice,

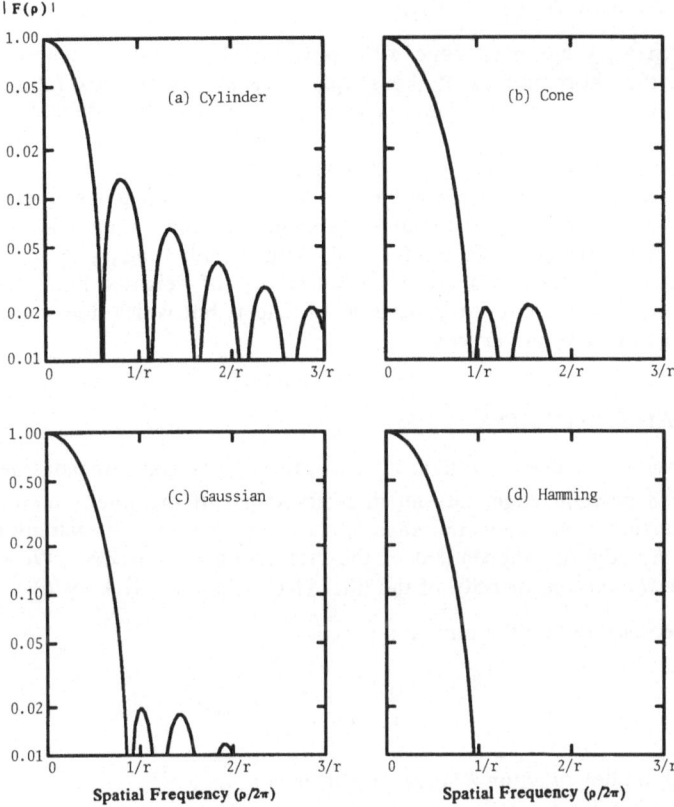

Fig. 4. Magnitude of Fourier Transform - Rotated Filters

all three weighted filters can probably be classified as 'perfect' and will probably produce equivalent results. The cylinder and box filters, with worst-case attentuation factors of about eight and five respectively, are much less satisfactory.

The minimum radius values given in Table 1 are, for the weighted filters, approximately those that should be used in practice. The values given for the two unweighted filters (box and cylinder) are not as meaningful, because the large side lobes of these filters make the very concept of a 'cutoff frequency' rather meaningless. Such filters are really not adequate for frequency antialiasing, though they are apparently reasonably satisfactory for the less demanding task of edge antialiasing. Figure 12 demonstrates the inadequacy of a box filter in a practical context.

The foregoing discussion is concerned with filtering in general; it is applicable to filtering of lines, polygon edges and texture, using both stochastic and uniform sampling schemes. The remainder of this paper is concerned only with the filtering of polygon edges and vertices for use with a uniform sampling scheme. The problem of texture filtering is not addressed.

3.4. Previous Work with Weighted Filters

Very little research work has been done with weighted filters, partly because many workers were unaware of the shortcomings of the simple 'area averaging' box filter approach, and partly because of the high computational cost of existing weighted filter schemes. Feibush, Levoy and Cook (1980) have demonstrated the inadequacy of a box filter, and have described a weighted filter scheme that, being table driven, can be adapted to any type of circularly-symmetric filter. Their scheme handles filtering of both polygon edges and of texture, but is rather expensive computationally. Their method for dealing with polygon vertices has since been incorporated by Catmull (1984) into a full imaging system that includes motion blur. Turkowski (1982) has also discussed the use of weighted filters, using a method that is basically similar to the one introduced in this paper, but which does not offer a general method for filtering of polygon vertices.

4. EDGE SPREAD FUNCTIONS

Before considering the problem of filtering an arbitrary polygon, we consider the case of filtering an isolated polygon edge, i.e. an intensity step[2]. If the filter function is circularly symmetric, its blurring effect upon the edge is such that the intensity variation along a line perpendicular to the edge is independent of the orientation of the edge. We call that variation the *Edge Spread Function*, or ESF, of the filter (Rosenfeld and Kak 1976).

An edge can be represented by the unit step function

$$S(x,y) = \begin{cases} 0 & x < 0 \\ 1 & x \geq 0 \end{cases} \quad \text{for all } y$$

After filtering with a filter function $h(x,y)$ we get, using (1),

$$i(x,y) = \int_{-\infty}^{\infty} \int_{0}^{\infty} h(x-x',y-y') \, dx' dy' = \int_{-\infty}^{\infty} \int_{-\infty}^{x} h(u,v) \, du \, dv$$

The ESF, $e(x)$, for the filter $h(x,y)$ is therefore

$$e(x) = \int_{-\infty}^{\infty} \int_{-\infty}^{x} h(u,v) \, du \, dv \qquad (5)$$

This is just the volume of the filter function $h(u,v)$ to the left of the plane $u = x$. Since $h(x,y)$ is circularly symmetric, we can write

$$h(x,y) = h_r(l) \quad \text{where } l = \sqrt{x^2 + y^2}$$

Using this in (5), and assuming a filter of unit volume, we can show (Turkowski 1982)

---

[2] Throughout this paper we regard intensity as being a scalar, i.e. we consider only black-and-white pictures. The generalization to colour pictures, in which 'intensity' becomes a 3-tuple specifying a point in RGB colour space, is trivial.

$$e(x) = \begin{cases} 2\int\limits_{-\infty}^{x} h_r(l)\cos^{-1} l \, dl & x \leq 0 \\ 1 - e(-x) & x > 0 \end{cases} \qquad (6)$$

The case for $x \leq 0$ in (6) can be integrated analytically for the cylindrical filter, giving

$$e_{cyl}(x) = (1/\pi)[\cos^{-1}\beta + \beta(1 - \beta^2)^{\frac{1}{2}}]$$

$$\text{where} \quad \beta = x/r \quad \text{and} \quad -1 \leq \beta \leq 0$$

and for the cone filter, giving

$$e_{cone}(x) = (3/\pi)\left\{\cos^{-1}\beta + 2\beta(1 - \beta^2)^{\frac{1}{2}} + \beta^3 \log\left[\frac{1 + (1 - \beta^2)^{\frac{1}{2}}}{-\beta}\right]\right\}$$

The other two filters defined in (4) are rather intractable, and (6) must be integrated numerically. Figure 5 shows the results for all four circularly symmetric filters. The box filter ESFs are not plotted: at 45° the box ESF is very close to the Gaussian filter ESF, while at 0/90° the box ESF is a straight line from $(-1/\sqrt{2}, 0)$ to $(1/\sqrt{2}, 1)$. The similarity of the shapes of the ESFs for the three weighted filters lends further weight to the contention that the three weighted filters will produce equivalent results when applied to actual pictures.

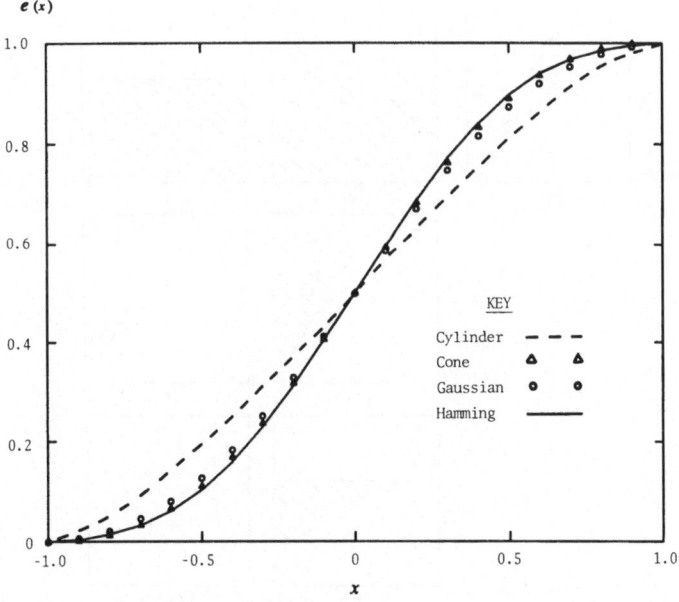

Fig. 5. Edge Spread Functions - Rotated Filters

5. FILTERING OF POLYGONS

5.1. Vertex Areas

We confine our attention to two-dimensional pictures comprised of polygons. For use in a general three-dimensional image-rendering system the tasks of decomposing the scene into polygons, calculating shadings, and performing visibility resolution must already have been done by earlier phases. The last of those phases, visibility resolution, requires that the original set of 3D polygons be reduced to a set of fully-visible 2D polygons; the Weiler-Atherton algorithm (Weiler and Atherton 1977) is the logical choice here. The 2D polygons are assumed to have a uniform intensity, though extension for approximate handling of a uniform intensity gradient should be straightforward.

It is clear from (1) that if we can represent a picture as a sum of polygons, then the filtered image can be represented as the sum of the filtered polygons. To simplify the filtering of a general polygon, we resolve it into a set of fundamental areas we call *vertex areas*. A vertex area is an infinite-area segment of the coordinate plane, having either positive or negative intensity, with its vertex on one of the polygon vertices, and with one of its bounding edges horizontal. Figure 6 illustrates this decomposition: the triangular area (a) is obtained by summing the vertex areas (b) through (g). Note that each edge of a polygon (except for horizontal edges, which can be ignored) contributes two vertex areas, one with a positive intensity and the other with a negative intensity. The decomposition is trivial to implement: no arithmetic is involved.

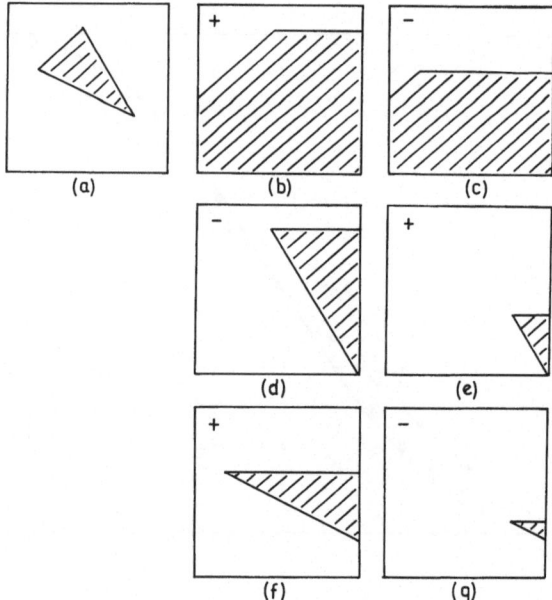

Fig. 6. Decomposition of a Polygon (a) into Vertex Areas (b) - (g)

The problem of filtering an arbitrary polygon is now reduced to the problem of filtering an arbitrary vertex area. We further restrict our attention to acute-angled vertex areas by noting that an obtuse-angled vertex area can be constructed by subtracting an acute-angled vertex area from an isolated edge (intensity step).

5.2. Filtering of Vertex Areas

Figure 7 shows the zones of interest around a vertex area COD, with unit intensity, that is being filtered by a circularly-symmetric filter of radius r. The zones are

(1) All points further than r away from the vertex area. The intensity due to the vertex area is zero in this zone.

(2) All points lying within the vertex area that are further than r away from either edge. The intensity due to the vertex area is unity.

(3) All points within a distance of r of one edge but more than r away from the other. The intensity depends only upon the perpendicular distance to the nearest edge, and is given by the ESF discussed in the previous section. Thus, if we define α and β as the distances from edges OD and OC respectively, measured in units of r in a direction towards zone 2, we have

$$i(x,y) = \begin{cases} e(\alpha) & \text{in zone 3a} \\ e(\beta) & \text{in zone 3b} \end{cases} \tag{7}$$

(4) All points within a distance of r of both edges but further than r from the vertex. In this zone, there are two separate non-intersecting portions of the filter volume lying outside the vertex area, and the intensity is given by

$$i(x,y) = 1 - [1 - e(\alpha)] - [1 - e(\beta)] = e(\alpha) + e(\beta) - 1 \quad \text{in zone 4} \tag{8}$$

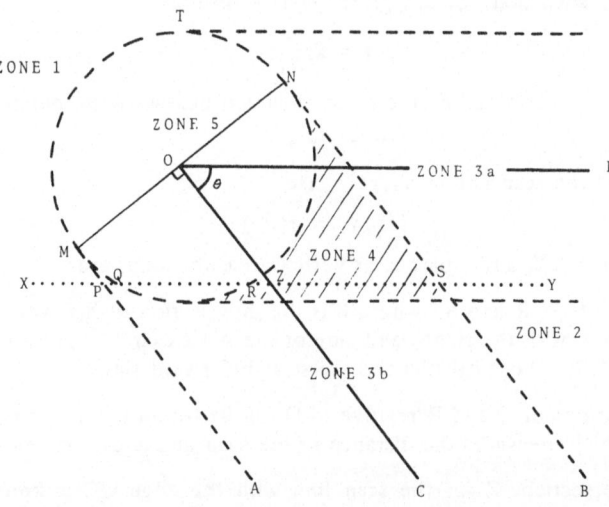

Fig. 7. Zones of a Vertex Area

(5) All points less than a distance r from the vertex. This zone needs special treatment, as described in the following subsection.

Note that equations (7) and (8), together with the trivial cases of

$$i(x,y) = \begin{cases} 0 & \text{in zone 1} \\ 1 & \text{in zone 2} \end{cases} \tag{9}$$

define the result of filtering a vertex area, except within zone 5.

5.3. Approximation within the Vertex Circle

We consider now the calculation of intensity within zone 5, the area bounded by the *vertex circle*. From (7), (8) and (9), the intensity and its gradient are known at all points on the circle itself. The intensity is also known to be exactly $\theta/2\pi$ at the circle centre, where θ is the vertex angle. With all that information, very accurate but time-consuming polynomial surface approximation formulae could be found. Another possibility would be to use the method of Feibush et al (1980), but this involves a considerable amount of geometric calculation and five table lookups. We need to find a faster method than either of those, suitable for use in a scan-line algorithm.

With reference to figure 7, the intensity and its gradient are both zero along the line TMPA, while along the line TNSB the intensity is $e(\alpha)$ and its gradient is zero. For any given scan line, e.g. XY in figure 7, one might identify the points P and S and simply scale the ESF to fit between these two points. This simple method is very accurate for vertex angles of 90°, but the errors increase steadily as the length of the span PS increases and become unacceptably large for vertex angles less than about 10°. To handle such small vertex angles it appears to be necessary to use the exact formula of (8) in zone 4; along the portion PR of the scan line we use a portion of the ESF, with horizontal shifting and scaling such that it fits the exact values at the points P and R. More precisely the procedure is as follows.

Define a parameter γ such that, for any given point V on PS,

$$\gamma = k\frac{PV}{PS} \tag{10a}$$

where k is a constant, determined by the method shown below. Also, define

$$\gamma' = 2\gamma - 1 \tag{10b}$$

Over the range PR of the scan line in figure 7, use

$$i(x,y) = e(\gamma') \tag{10c}$$

For any given scan line XY, and a particular vertex area, the steps are

(1) Identify the points P, R and S, where P is the intersection of XY with the line TMA, R is the intersection with the right-hand side of the vertex circle, and S is the intersection with the line TNB. Those calculations are straightforward since:

    (a) The locations of Q and R relative to O can be found using a lookup table indexed by α, which measures the distance of the scan line above or below O.

    (b) The intersection, Z, of the scan line with the edge OC is known by the usual scan-line method.

(c)　The vertical distance of M and N above and below O is constant for the vertex area.

(d)　The point P *is* the point Q above M, while below M it is a constant offset δ from Z.

(e)　The point S *is* the point R above N, while below N it is δ from Z.

(2)　If S is above N, use $k = 1$. Otherwise,

(a)　Calculate, from (8), the intensity i_R at point R

(b)　Find γ'_R such that $e(\gamma'_R) = i_R$. This involves just a lookup in a table of $\gamma' = e^{-1}(i)$.

(c)　Find k from (10a) and (10b), viz $k = (\gamma'_R + 1).PS/(2.PR)$

Once those calculations have been done, the intensity at any point on the scan line is easily obtained from (7), (8), (9) or (10) as appropriate. It may be noted that, for maximum performance, the parameters resulting from the above procedure could all be precomputed and stored in a two-parameter lookup table, indexed by α and θ; our current implementation, however, does not perform this optimization. Note, too, that since the parameter β, given by $ZV/(r\sin\theta)$, changes by a constant amount at each step along a scan line, the increment could be stored in the vertex area record for efficiency.

The set of equation (7), (8), (9) and (10) define the intensity at all points after filtering a vertex area. Of these, only (10) is not exact, i.e. errors occur only within the vertex circle. The accuracy of this approximation has been thoroughly investigated over all vertex angles. We take as our measure the absolute error in the approximation divided by i_0, the polygon intensity (assumed to be unity in the above equations). Over all vertex angles, the maximum error occurs at an angle of 59°, and is 4.1% of the intensity of the vertex area. At a vertex angle of 90°, the maximum error is less than 1.2%. Figures 8, 9 and 10 show some representative scan lines for vertex angles of 90°, 59° and 30° respectively: the continuous lines are the true values, while the plotted circles are the approximation results. The errors around 60° are certainly visible on such plots, but it is most unlikely that they are large enough to introduce any significant aliasing problems. They occur only within a small region near the vertex, in the middle of a large intensity gradient, and over a fairly small range of vertex angles. The tests described in section 7 certainly do not reveal any aliasing artifacts.

6. THE SCAN CONVERSION ALGORITHM

6.1. Introduction

The algorithm for antialiased scan conversion of a two-dimensional picture consisting of a set of polygons is similar to a traditional non-antialiased scan-line method with the following differences:

(1)　Vertex areas are used instead of edge areas. Thus the y-buckets point to lists of vertex areas, and there is an Active Vertex List (AVL) rather than an Active Edge List.

(2)　A vertex area becomes active when the scan-line y-value is within r of the vertex y-value, rather than when the scan line physically intersects the edge.

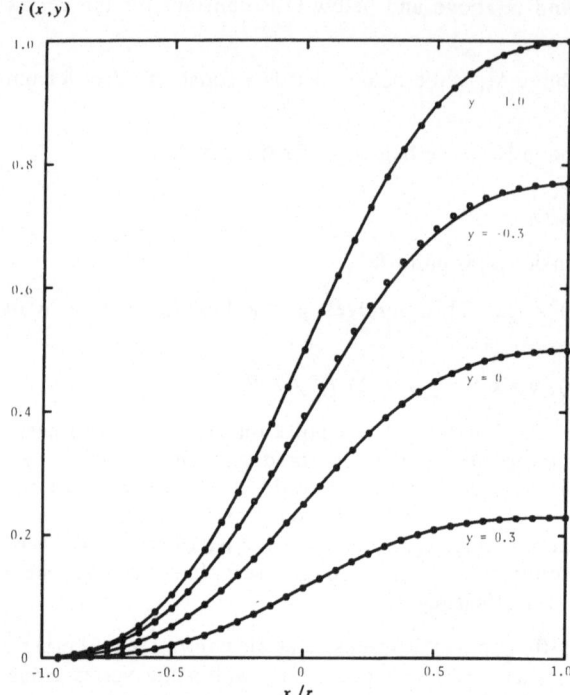

Fig. 8. Representative Scan Lines
for a Vertex Angle of 90°

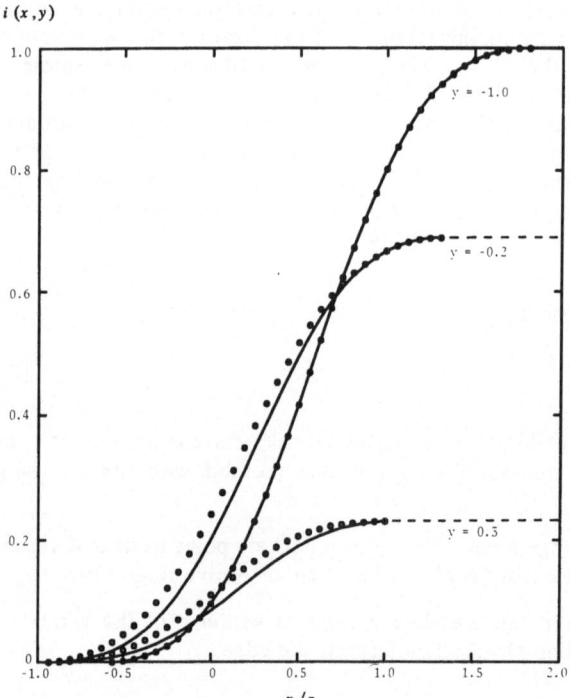

Fig. 9. Representative Scan Lines
for a Vertex Angle of 59°

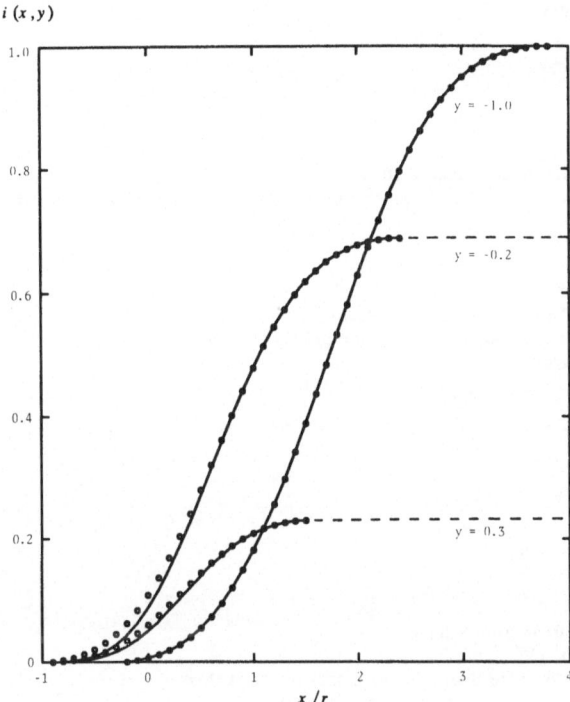

Fig. 10. Representative Scan Lines for a Vertex Angle of 30°

(3) Whereas, with the traditional method, an edge either has no effect on a pixel or contributes the full intensity of the polygon to which it belongs, a vertex area makes a varying contribution over a portion of the scan line. At any point along the scan line we thus have a set of *busy* vertex areas, whose contribution is changing with x. As soon as the contribution of a vertex area has stopped varying it becomes *non-busy*, its contribution is added into the current total for the scan line, and the vertex area does not enter into subsequent calculations for that scan line.

(4) Instead of removing an edge from the 'Active' list when the scan line drops below its bottom end, we must remove (for efficiency, rather than necessity) the pair of vertex areas associated with an edge as soon as the scan line is more than r below the bottom vertex. This necessitates some form of cross-linking between vertex areas in the AVL.

6.2. The Algorithms

Main Program:

```
for each polygon
        for each edge
                Generate edge record (note 1)
                Generate two vertex area records, and link to appropriate y-bucket lists
        end for
end for

for each scan line
        Update_AVL()  (see algorithm below)
        Set current scan line intensity value to background
        for each pixel
                Set_Pixel (Sum_Busy_Vertices())
        end for
        Move edges from TUVL (note 2) into AVL
end for
```

Update_AVL:

```
Add new vertex areas from y-bucket
for each vertex in AVL
        if scan line is more than r below associated edge then
                remove pair of vertex areas from AVL
        else
                Calculate vertex parameters (refer section 5)
        end if
end for
Sort AVL by GhostLeft parameter (note 3)
```

Sum_Busy_Vertices:

```
Set accumulated intensity to current scan line value
for each AVL entry
        if current x < GhostLeft then
                exit for
        end if
        Intensity :=  Polygon intensity * Intensity_factor()
        if associated edge is on right-hand side of polygon then
                Negate intensity
        end if
        Add intensity to accumulated intensity
        if x > GhostRight (note 3) then
                Add intensity to current scan line value
                Move vertex from AVL to TUVL (note 2)
        end if
end for
```

Intensity_Factor: (note 4)

```
if x > GhostRight then
        factor := e(α)   (notes 5,6)
elsif α ≥ 1 then
        factor := e(β)   (note 5)
elsif β ≥ β_cr then   (note 7)
        factor := e(α) + e(β) − 1   (notes 5,6)
else
        Calculate factor from equation (10)
end if
if this vertex is at the top of an edge then
        return (factor)
else
        return (− factor)
end if
```

Notes

(1)   An edge record contains polygon edge data that is the same for the two associated vertex areas (e.g. polygon intensity).

(2)   In order to ensure that, at any time during processing of a scan line, the 'busy' vertices are all at the head of the AVL, vertices that become non-busy are moved onto a *Temporarily Unused Vertex List*, or TUVL.

(3)   The terms *GhostLeft* and *GhostRight* denote the left and right x limits of the 'busy' range for a particular vertex area and a particular scan line.

(4)   The handling of obtuse angled vertex areas is omitted for simplicity.

(5)   ESF values are precomputed and stored in a table.

(6)   The value $e(α)$ is computed by the vertex parameter calculation procedure at the start of processing of a scan line, and is stored in the vertex area record, for efficiency.

(7)   The vertex area parameter, $β_{cr}$, is the value of $β$ at the right-hand intersection point of the vertex circle with the scan-line.

7. RESULTS

Figure 11 shows a two-point perspective projection of a 'paling fence' pattern, rendered without antialiasing on an AED 512 display with a resolution of 512 × 512 pixels. This pattern, also used by Feibush et al (1980), is recommended as a very good test for antialiasing algorithms, because it gives pronounced frequency aliasing (Moiré pattern) as well as the more common edge aliasing (staircasing). Figure 12 shows the same pattern rendered using a single-pixel box filter; the Moiré pattern, while reduced in amplitude, is still very pronounced. Figure 13 shows the pattern rendered using the method described in this paper; the Hamming filter radius was two pixel intervals. The Moiré pattern is totally removed, yet the resolution remains excellent. Although not evident in the small photographs, the removal of staircasing is also more satisfactory; the box filter produces a slightly 'braided' appearance, whereas no such artifact is present with the Hamming filter.

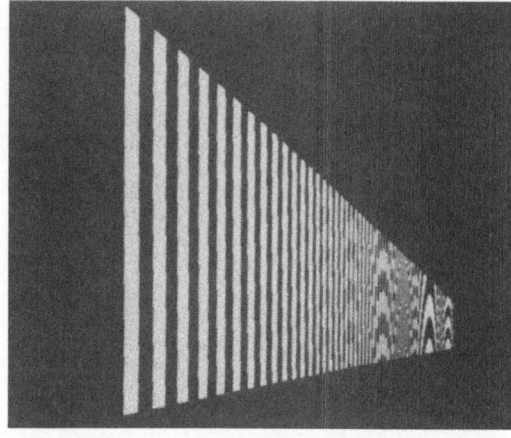

Fig. 11. Fence Test Pattern.
No antialiasing.

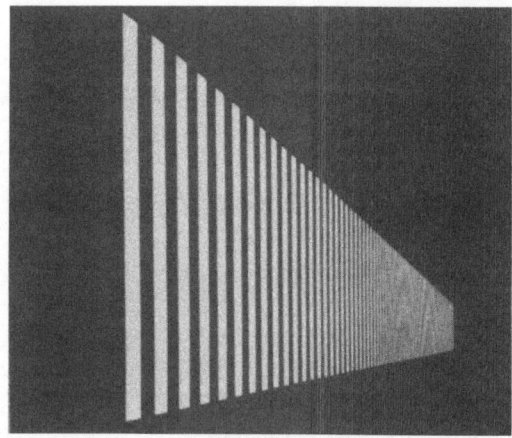

Fig. 12. Fence Test Pattern.
One-pixel Box Filter

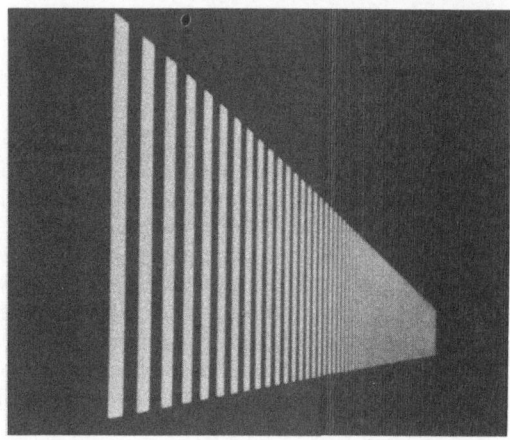

Fig. 13. Fence Test Pattern.
Two-pixel Radius
Hamming Filter

A similar sequence of tests was performed on a picture made from a perspective view of a pattern of hexagons. Figures 14 and 15 show two of the three results. The box filter performed rather better on this test: although very slight deficiencies were visible on the original screen, they could not be seen in the smaller-scale photograph, which was effectively identical to figure 15.

Since the box filter has much better characteristics along the 45° line in frequency space, i.e. is much better at filtering periodicities with 'wavefronts' inclined at 45° to the x and y axes, it is interesting to apply the box filter to the picture of Figure 11 rotated 45°. Using a box filter with a side of length 2.8, which corresponds to a radius of 2.0 as required by Table 1, essentially perfect results were obtained (like Figure 13 rotated). This was certainly not the case with the same size box filter applied to a non-rotated picture, when a Moiré pattern was

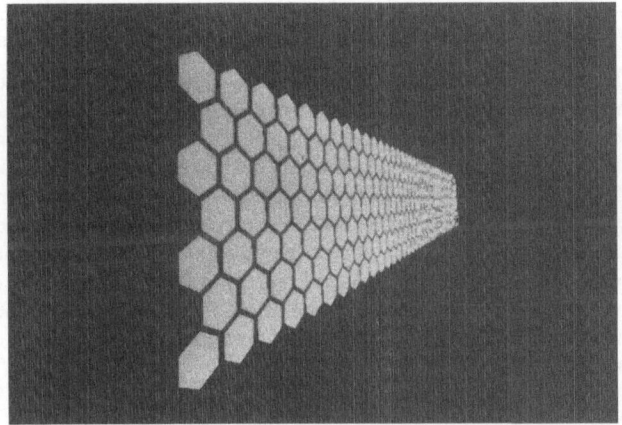

Fig. 14. Hexagonal Test Pattern. No Antialiasing

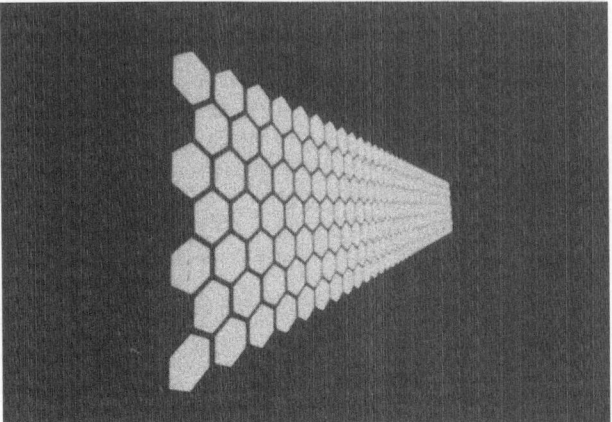

Fig. 15. Hexagonal Test Pattern. Two-pixel Radius Hamming Filter

still obvious. Those results confirm the theoretical predictions, and also show that, at least with our frame buffer and monitor, a stopband[3] attenuation factor of only 20 (that of the first sidelobe of the box filter at 45°) is sufficient. Cone and Gaussian filters should therefore be just as good as a Hamming filter in practice.

Using the fence test pattern, we experimented briefly with different radii Hamming filters. Somewhat surprisingly, the Moiré pattern did not become apparent until the radius was reduced to a low value of around 1.1 pixels. Closer examination, however, showed that 'alias beating' artifacts *were* occurring in the image with larger filter radii (up to about 2.5 pixels), but, because of their high spatial frequency, they were not apparent until the image was magnified. They could also be made apparent without magnification, at filter radii of up to 1.6 pixels, by disabling the 'gamma compensation' (Catmull 1979); this issue was briefly discussed in section 1. Taking all effects into consideration, we felt that a filter radius of around 1.7 pixels was optimum; values of above about 2 pixels start to cause noticeable loss of resolution (with a 512 × 512 display), and below about 1.5 pixels start to introduce aliasing effects when the monitor is imperfectly compensated.

The current implementation of the algorithm uses floating point arithmetic throughout and does not make any of the optimizations mentioned earlier, such as obtaining the vertex parameters by table lookup; it is therefore not a very good indicator of the potential speed of the algorithm. Scan conversion of the hexagonal pattern of Figure 15, which contains 1680 edges, required 125 seconds on a VAX-11/780, of which about 26% was frame-buffer loading time. The *IntensityFactor* procedure consumed only 20% of the total, and the *FindVertex-Parameters* procedure a further 8%. The remainder was spent in list manipulation and other non-arithmetic 'overheads'. The relatively small percentage of the total time (28%) spent on arithmetic operations makes the traditional scheme for estimating the efficiency of a scan-conversion algorithm by counting the number of inner-loop arithmetic operations somewhat questionable in this case.

8. CONCLUSIONS

The behaviour of several different types of antialiasing filters has been investigated from a theoretical viewpoint. The weighted filters are shown to be much superior to the unweighted box and cylinder filters. The best of the weighted filters was a Hamming filter, and this was selected for use within the scan-conversion algorithm, although the distinction between it, the Gaussian filter, and the cone filter is almost certainly negligible in practice.

A scan-line algorithm has been presented for antialiased scan-conversion of a picture comprised of polygons. The algorithm is believed to be simpler and faster than any existing antialiasing schemes that use weighted filters. Although an approximation is involved in the method, the errors are negligible. Experiments with two demanding test-patterns show that the algorithm produces excellent alias-free images. Visible-surface determination is not incorporated into the algorithm but must be done by a previous phase, if it is to be used in a general-purpose three-dimensional rendering system.

Acknowledgements

This work was carried while while I was on leave at the Computer Science Department of the University of Toronto. I would like to thank Allan Borodin for giving me the opportunity to visit the Department, and Alain Fournier of the Computer Science Research Institute for

---

[3] The term *stopband* denotes the region in frequency space over which the filter would ideally have infinite attentuation, in this case all spatial frequencies greater than the cutoff frequency.

providing the research environment and computing funds for this work. I would also like to thank Geoff Wyvill, of the University of Otago, for his encouragement and for his generous offer to present this paper to the conference in my absence.

References

Carpenter L (1984) The A-buffer, an antialiased hidden surface method. Computer Graphics 18 (3): 103-108

Catmull E (1978) A hidden-surface algorithm with anti-aliasing. Computer Graphics 12 (3): 6-11

Catmull E (1979) A tutorial on compensation tables. Computer Graphics 13 (2): 1-7

Catmull E (1984) An analytic visible surface algorithm for independent pixel processing. Computer Graphics 18 (3): 109-115

Crow FC (1981) A comparison of antialiasing techniques. IEEE CG & A 1 (1): 40-48

Dippé MAZ , Wold EH (1985) Antialiasing through stochastic sampling. Computer Graphics 19 (3): 69-78

Feibush EA, Levoy M, Cook RL (1980) Synthetic texturing using digital filters. Computer Graphics 14 (3): 294-301

Fiume E, Fournier A, Rudolph L (1983) A parallel scan conversion algorithm with anti-aliasing for a general purpose ultracomputer. Computer Graphics 17 (3): 141-149

Gonzalez RC (1977) Digital Image Processing. Addison-Wesley, Reading, MA

Huang TS (1972) Two dimensional windows. IEEE Trans. Audio Electroacoust. AU-20 (1): 88-89

Lee ME, Redner RA, Uselton SP (1985) Statistically optimized sampling for distributed ray tracing. Computer Graphics 19 (3): 61-65

Pratt WK (1978) Digital Image Processing. John Wiley and Sons, New York

Rosenfeld A, Kak AC (1976) Digital Picture Processing. Academic Press, New York

Turkowski K (1982) Anti-aliasing through the use of coordinate transformations. ACM Trans. on Graphics 1 (3): 215-234

Weiler K, Atherton P (1977) Hidden surface removal using polygon area sorting. Computer Graphics 11 (2): 214-221

Richard J.Lobb received the BSc and MSc degrees in Physics and the PhD degree in Radio Science from the University of Auckland in 1968, 1970 and 1975 respectively. He has spent two years as a software consultant in Europe, involved in real-time software and data communications. In 1978 he joined the staff of the computer science department at the University of Auckland where he is now a Senior Lecturer. His interest in computer graphics began in 1985, while he was on leave at the University of Toronto.

Address: Department of Computer Science, University of Auckland, Private Bag, Auckland, New Zealand.

Solid Texturing of Soft Objects

Geoff Wyvill, Brian Wyvill, and Craig McPheeters

Abstract

Since the shape of a Soft object changes in response to its surroundings, it is difficult to give a single position in space as the location of the object. Indeed objects can and do break into sub-objects dynamically. This means that you cannot map a solid texture onto such an object simply using a function of the space co-ordinates.

We have taken a different approach. Our soft objects are modelled as the volume enclosed by an iso-surface of a field calculated from a set of key points. We ascribe to each key point a set of values which represent a *position* in an abstract *texture space*. Any point on the surface of an object has a field value due to each key point and this value is used as a weight in finding a weighted vector sum of these *positions*. This vector sum is used to select a surface specification from the *texture space*.

These textures retain their consistency during distortion and metamorphoses of objects. A great variety of animation effects can be achieved with this process.

Keywords: Soft Objects, Texture Mapping, Solid texturing, Animation,
                    In-betweening.

Introduction

The last five years has seen great progress in representing natural objects in computer-generated pictures. Two techniques are of particular significance: texture mapping and soft objects. Texture mapping (Blinn 1976, Blinn 1978 and Peachey 1985) has enabled us to represent rich surface details with otherwise simple models. Soft object modelling (Wyvill 1986b, Blinn 1982, Nishimura 1985) has provided a simple way to represent objects whose shape changes with time.

We want to represent objects which are both soft and textured. A good example is concrete being poured where small stones or grains of sand are visible on the surface of a mass which is changing shape. This task introduces some special problems and seemingly self-contradictory requirements.

To explain these problems we give a brief description of texture mapping and soft object modelling. This is followed by a description of our technique, some examples and a short discussion.

Texture mapping

The fundamental notion behind texture mapping is that we can separate the description of an object into two parts. The first describes the major aspects of the shape and the second describes a refinement in terms of surface detail.

The reasons for the success of this separation are variously physical, perceptual and technical. The physical justification is that many objects are literally constructed in this way. A painted object has its surface appearance uniformly modified by the layer of paint; an otherwise flat water surface is disturbed by surface ripples and so on. The perceptual aspect is connected with the way in which we deduce surface detail from the visual appearance. At a distance, a slightly wavy or bumpy surface is visible only because of the perceived colour or shade differences produced by the bumps. The technical reason is that we already have efficient ways to model and render objects of smooth, simple shapes and texture mapping allows us to extend this range of objects at low computational cost.

The description of surface detail is called a texture map and it can be represented by mathematical functions or tables. In the process of texture mapping we must relate each visible point on the surface of an object to a point in the texture map. A "point" for this purpose, will correspond to a pixel in the final image. The general method of doing this requires that we set up a co-ordinate system on the object's surface. The method used to construct such a co-ordinate system depends on the way the object is defined. If parametric patches have been used then each surface element is already defined as a function of some s, t and the same s, t make convenient co-ordinates for texture mapping. If the surface is defined by polygons, the simplest approach is to divide the polygons into rectangles or triangles and then treat these as a special case of patches. Continuity at patch borders is achieved by careful definition of the texture map, using complementary co-ordinates (1-s, 1-t) in adjacent patches and other methods.

Peachey (1985) introduced the idea of using 3D co-ordinates of surface points for texture mapping. This is equivalent to carving the object out of a non-uniform substance represented by the 3D texture map. This is an excellent approach for modelling materials like wood and marble where the surface is indeed the result of carving from a material patterned in 3D. Where this approach can be used, there are advantages over the 2D method. Consistency of texture is achieved regardless of the topology of the object. For most rendering techniques, the 3D coordinate values which correspond to a particular screen pixel have to be calculated anyway, so the co-ordinates for texture mapping are available at no extra computational cost.

There are, however, cases where 3D texture mapping is unsuitable: surface marks on machined objects, patterns on textiles and applied patterns like paintwork. In these examples the texture of the object we are modelling is not a surface manifestation of a three dimensional structure so we should not expect to be able to model it that way. Soft objects do not lend themselves to solid texturing for different reasons, explained below.

An excellent recent survey of texture mapping can be found in Heckbert (1986).

Soft objects

Our soft objects are represented by surfaces of constant value in a scalar field. Details of this representation and methods of rendering have been described elsewhere (Blinn 1982, Wyvill 1986b, Nishimura 1985). In this paper we give only sufficient background to explain the rather special problems associated with adding texture.

A soft object is defined by a number of key points in space and these key points form a kind of skeleton around which the soft object is drawn. We regard each key point as a source of energy, a hot spot around which the temperature drops off as a function of distance. Every point in space is then considered to possess an energy or *field* value. The field value due to two or more key points is the sum of the values due to the individual key points. The surface of the soft object is a surface whose field value is constant and equal to a special value which we call *magic*.

The field value of an isolated key point at the location of the key point is greater that *magic*. So the soft object due to a single key point is a sphere. A collection of key points produces a shape which is a kind of blending of these spheres. This shape can be very complicated. During animation, the key points can move relative to each other causing a smooth change of shape. Indeed, if the key points move far enough apart, the objects actually break up. A single closed surface can change its topology as holes appear and disappear. This kind of effect is discussed in Wyvill (1986a).

To achieve these smooth changes, the field produced by each key point has to conform to certain rules. In particular, the function, f, which describes the field must vanish to zero at some distance from the key point. For a point at distance r from a key point, the derivative:

$$\frac{df}{dr}$$

must also vanish at this special distance. We call this the 'radius of influence' of a key point: the distance at which the field contribution falls to zero.

This modelling technique is still fairly new and there are many further developments expected. We have already been experimenting with a new formulation in which the key points are replaced by a more complex key with three associated axes (Wyvill 1986c). Some of the figures have been generated using the new technique but the texturing technique is the same and easier to understand in the context of the original method.

Texturing soft objects

It should be clear from the last two sections that soft objects present a special problem for texture mapping. If we use a conventional, two-dimensional map, we have to provide some sort of co-ordinate system on the surface of our object. But this surface not only changes shape, it can change topologically. A torus can change (nearly) smoothly into a sphere and as the hole closes up, we may not want an obvious discontinuity in the texture.

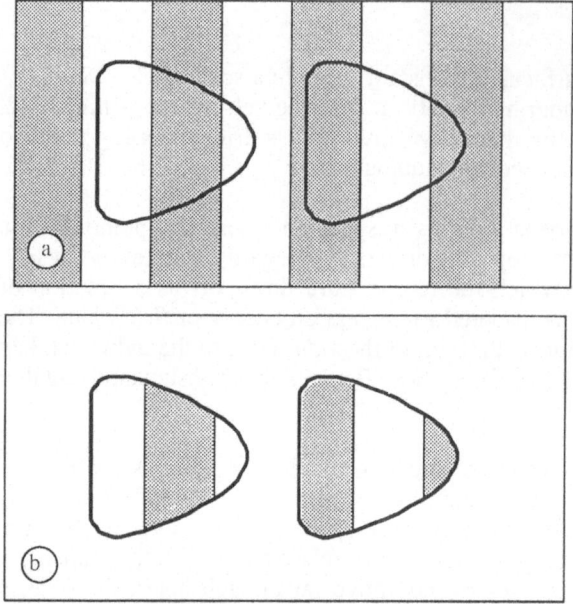

Fig. 1: a) The same object is shown in two different positions relative to a solid texture space.
         b) The result is that the object changes its appearance as it moves.

It would seem that our only choice is to use a three-dimensional (solid) texture, but this, too, is unsatisfactory for the following reason. Suppose we use a three-dimensional texture map which is fixed in world space, then the texture of an object moving through space will change as it moves, Fig. 1. One way to avoid this, is to tie the texture space to the object. That is, we use a co-ordinate system in which the object is defined to be stationary and define our texture map there. During the rendering process, we must translate the co-ordinates of each surface component back into the object's system before we look up the texture. This is a satisfactory solution for rigid objects, but it fails in many cases for soft objects.

Figure 2 shows such a case. A large droplet splits into two smaller ones. If we regard the two droplets as a single object, then the origin of the texture space will be at the centre of gravity of the large droplet. In the final frame, it will be mid-way between two separate objects travelling in opposite directions. Each of these objects will be travelling through a texture space just as if it were tied to the world co-ordinates.

Similar problems arise when we consider the rotation of soft objects. If an object rotates without distortion, then the textures on its surface should not change. This implies that the solid texture space must rotate with the object. But it is an essential feature of the soft object modelling technique that we do not refer to objects as such. We control the position of key points and allow the surface topology to change as it will. It seems that whatever method we choose, we can find an example where we do not get the effect we are seeking.

We need a method of setting up a texture map which refers only to key points and never to objects. Each key point, therefore, is embedded in its own **abstract texture space.** This space is used only as a device for assigning a value to every part of the surface. It need have no geometrical significance. There are many ways in which we can set up this abstract texture space, so let us first demonstrate it by means of a simple example. Suppose a key point is considered to be at the origin of an ordinary co-ordinate system. Then <x, y, z> is the name of a point in space defined with respect to this key point. In creating the coordinate system, we have also given the key point a new property. It is no longer symmetrical. We can assign properties to the space surrounding it and we have given meaning to the idea that the point itself can rotate: Rotation of a key point implies rotation of these local co-ordinates. We define the abstract texture space as follows:

$$f = F(x, y, z)$$
$$h = H(x, y, z)$$
$$c = C(x, y, z)$$

<f, h, c> is the name of a point in abstract texture space and the functions F, H, C can be chosen at will, depending on the application. In most of what follows, we simply set $f = x$, $h = y$, $c = z$ so that <f, h, c> can be regarded as a point in space in a system whose origin is a particular key point.

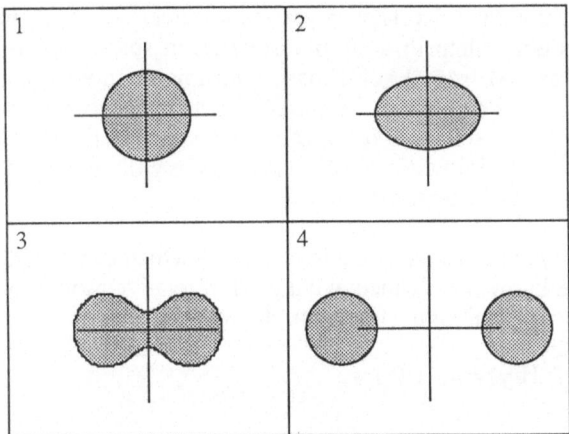

Fig. 2: Four stages of an animation. The texture space co-ordinates are tied to the centre of gravity of the object. By frame 4, we have two objects moving through texture space.

For our purpose, we need to assign an <f, h, c> triplet to every point P, on the surface of a soft object. We do this by means of a simple, weighted sum. Each key point i, contributes an amount Q_i to the field at P. If <f_i, h_i, c_i> are the values of the abstract co-ordinates of P in the system of i, then:

$$f = \Sigma f_i Q_i / \Sigma Q_i$$
$$h = \Sigma h_i Q_i / \Sigma Q_i$$
$$c = \Sigma c_i Q_i / \Sigma Q_i$$

Of course, ΣQ_i is equal to *magic,* the field value at the surface.

Once we have defined <f, h, c> for a point on the surface, we can look up values in tables, cr apply functions to describe the texture and colour at that point. Our textures become functions of the three dimensional f-h-c space and we can perform solid texturing just as we would for a conventional object in world space.

Properties of f-h-c space

Figure 3 shows a classical soft object picture with texturing. In this case, identical F, H, C functions are used for each of two key points, so when they are sufficiently separated, they appear as two identical spheres. As the key points approach each other, parts of the surface acquire <f, h, c> values interpolated by the weighted sum and the texture changes accordingly. Notice that at no stage does the texture exhibit a sudden break. Even at the moment the two objects become one, the texture retains its continuity. This is because the values of f, h and c change continuously both as functions of time and as functions of position on the surface.

There is, of course, distortion. In Fig. 3, the texture is defined as a pattern of coloured slices in f-h-c space. Because we are using $F(x) = x, H(y) = y, C(z) = z$, every <f, h, c> in the region of an isolated key point is equivalent to a simple position in space and the isolated sphere appears to have been carved from a solid mass with this texture. In the region where the droplets begin to merge, <f, h, c> is interpolated between two values. One is characteristic of the top of the lower sphere and the other is characteristic of the bottom of the upper sphere. Thus in a small region of physical space there will be a rapid, continuous change in f-h-c space. This causes the texture to appear stretched.

Such distortion is inevitable when we try to map a texture onto a surface which can stretch and even change its topology, but if we know, in advance, what kind of relative motion of key points to expect, we can take steps to minimise this. For example, we can define:

$$F(x) = x, \quad H(y) = y, \quad C(z) = z$$

as before, for the top key point and:

$$F(x) = x, \quad H(y) = y - R, \quad C(z) = z$$

for the lower point, where R is the radius of influence associated with these key points. The effect of this is that the two spheres appear to have been carved out of different parts of f-h-c space, but when they merge, the parts of the surface most violently affected by the interpolation are not too far apart in f-h-c space. This is illustrated in Fig. 4.

Solid textures as functions

Any solid texture can be regarded as a function in that it maps position in space into values which describe surface properties. Similarly, we express any surface property as a function of f-h-c space. Figures 5 to 7 show the droplets textured with a variety of simple functions. In Fig. 6, we are using the function to describe perturbations of the surface normal, not changes in colour. This produces a bump map and, as before, continuity is maintained during the motion. Figure 7 shows both bumps and colour changes.

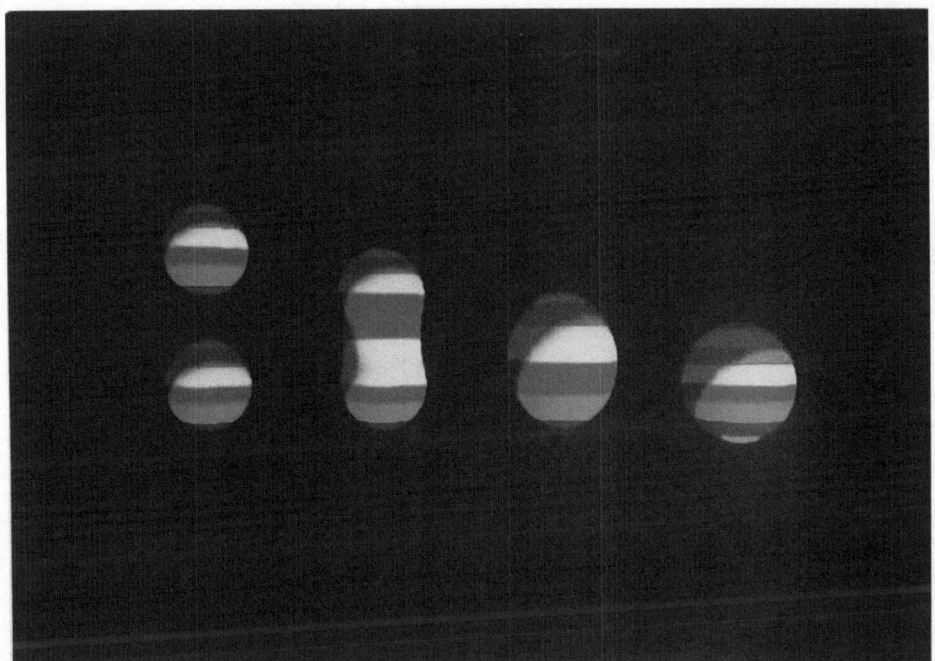

Fig. 3: Textured droplets merging.

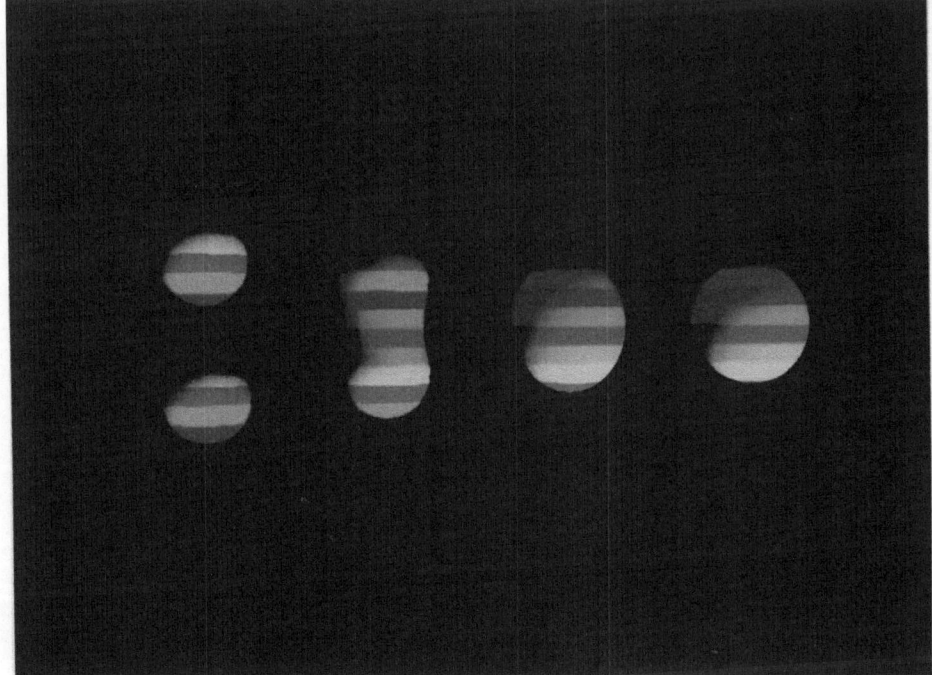

Fig. 4: Shifted f, h, c space to minimise stretching.

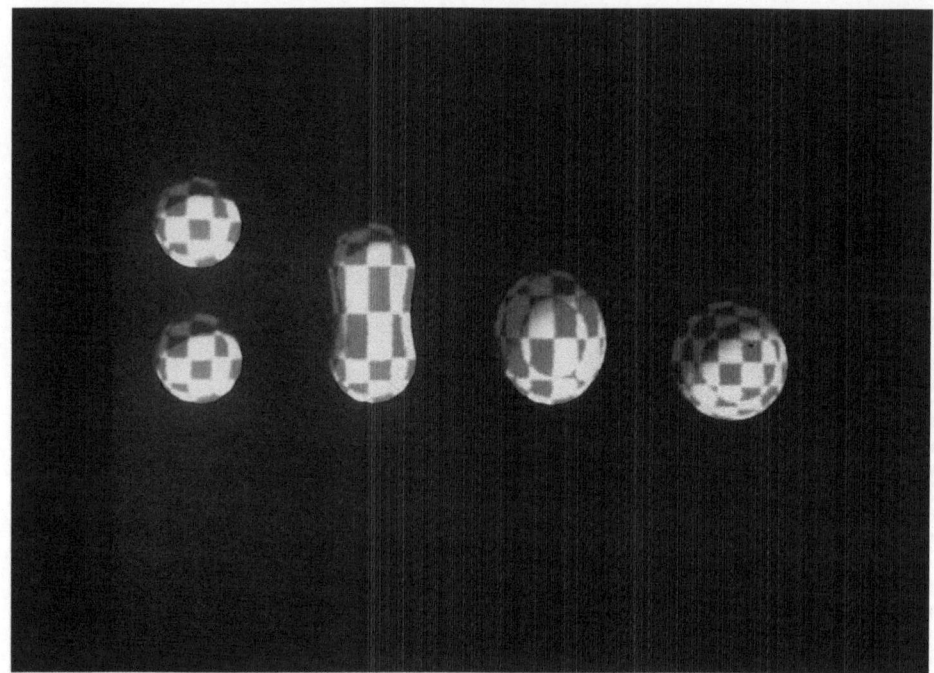

Fig. 5: Droplets with squared pattern.

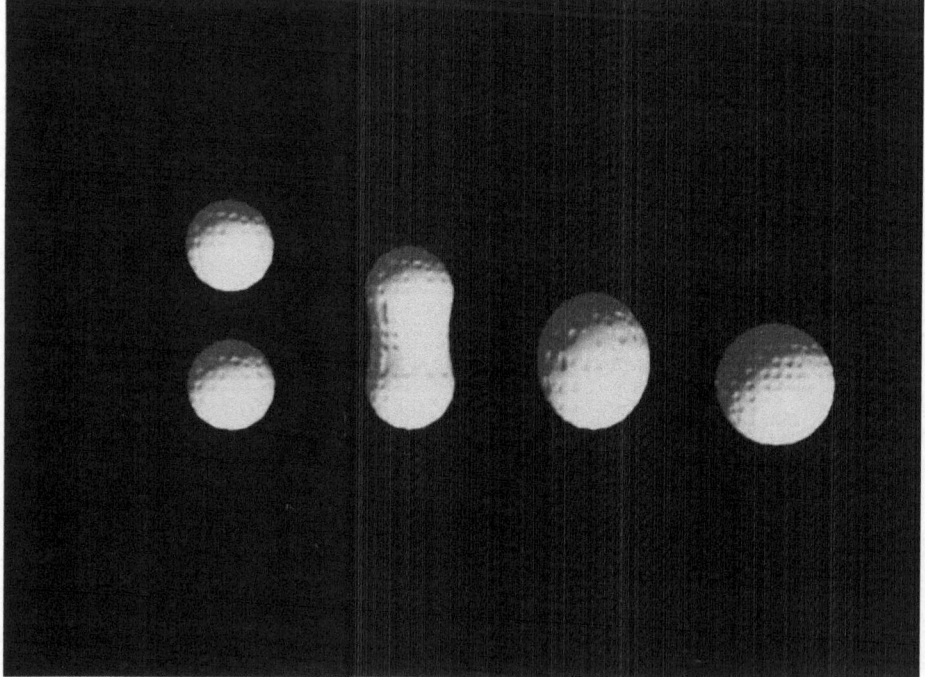

Fig. 6: Bump mapping.

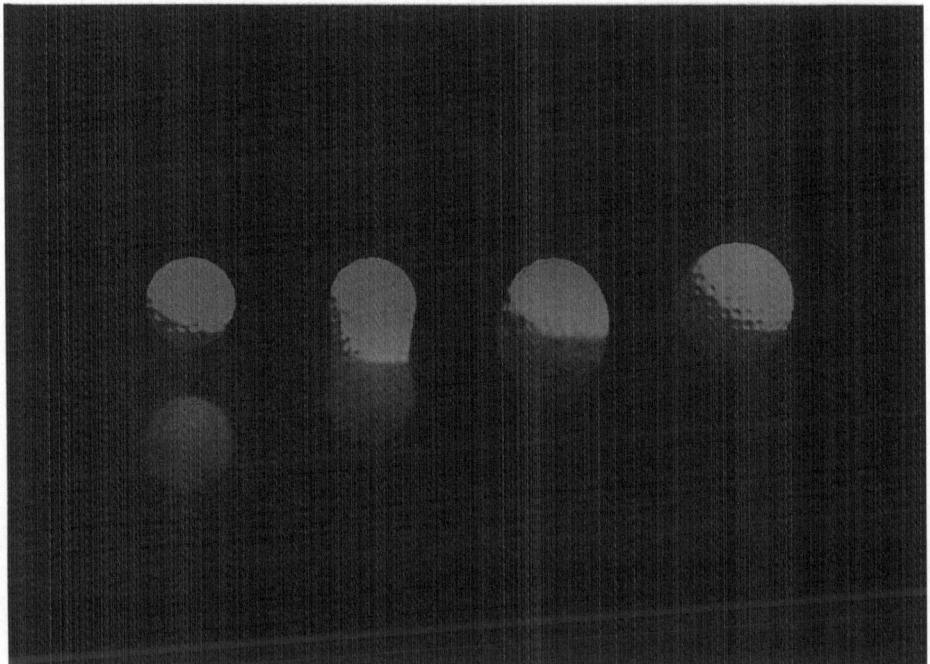

Fig. 7: Droplets textured and coloured.

Smoothing

It is not the purpose of this paper to describe the rendering of textured soft objects. But it is worth noting that the use of an abstract texture space applies equally well to rendering by scan-line techniques or ray tracing. Ray tracing of soft objects has been described (Nishimura et al 1985), but the photographs in this paper were all produced using a modified A-buffer algorithm (Carpenter 1984, Abram 1985). The soft objects are first converted into a fine polygon mesh and colour values are assigned to the polygon vertices as for Gouraud shading (Gouraud 1971). At this stage, each vertex is also associated with an <f, h, c> value and a surface normal direction which is an average of the normals for the polygons which meet at that vertex.

As each polygon is scanned, the colour, surface normal and <f, h, c> values are interpolated independently and stored in a pixel buffer. Different colour and textures can be applied, after rendering, by post processing in this buffer. This technique follows Perlin (1985).

In-betweening

One of the most pleasing features of soft objects is that in-betweening of three dimensional shapes becomes much easier than with other modelling techniques. The surfaces of soft objects are guaranteed to be closed and this enables us to produce consistent in-betweening even when the starting and finishing shapes are topologically different. This is discussed in more detail in Wyvill (1986a). When we add texture, we also add the requirement that sudden breaks should not occur in the texture and this is handled very neatly by the use of the abstract texture space. A further problem occurs if the starting and finishing shapes are required to have different textures. Figure 8 shows a sphere with texture in-betweened into a torus in four stages. The texture change is effected by separately interpolating the features of the two textures. In this example, the textures are simply patterns of colour. The colour at any point is described by red, green and blue values, r,g,b where:

$$
\begin{aligned}
r &= R(f, h, c) \\
g &= G(f, h, c) \\
b &= B(f, h, c)
\end{aligned}
$$

and R, G and B are texture functions. If the in-betweening takes place over n frames of animation, then for frame i we set:

$$
\begin{aligned}
r &= ((n\text{-}i) * R_1(f, h, c) + i * R_2(f, h, c)) / n \\
g &= ((n\text{-}i) * G_1(f, h, c) + i * G_2(f, h, c)) / n \\
b &= ((n\text{-}i) * B_1(f, h, c) + i * B_2(f, h, c)) / n
\end{aligned}
$$

In a similar way, other kinds of texture can be interpolated. Instead of r,g,b, we can interpolate the parameters of a reflectance model or the components of surface normal perturbations. Thus we can in-between a dull object into a reflective one showing highlights, or a smooth surface into a bumpy one.

Discussion

There would appear to be no simple, consistent way to create surface co-ordinates for texture mapping on soft objects, nor can they be treated satisfactorily by the technique of solid texturing. By creating an abstract texture space related to each control point, however, we can successfully map textures onto soft objects which are moving, deforming and even changing topology.

The way the texture behaves in animation, depends on what we suppose the motion means. Figure 9 shows two ways to rotate a complicated object. The original object is on the left. In the centre, the object is shown rotated while the abstract space attached to each key point maintains its orientation. The object on the right has been rotated by the same amount, but this time the abstract space coordinates have been rotated as well. Because the object has not changed its shape, we see this right hand object as the correct one. If we want to regard the motion of a collection of key points as a rotation, then we must rotate the <f, h, c> space. Otherwise the texture behaves as if the object has merely transformed to the new shape by distortion. There is nothing *wrong* with the central object in Fig. 9. The animation represents a blob of soft material whose surface is changing (perhaps because of some internal flow of material). Only if we want to regard the motion as a rotation without distortion need we deliberately rotate the abstract texture space.

We can, indeed, represent objects which both rotate and distort. In doing so, we make a conscious choice about how to handle our abstract space. We are made to specify just how much of the motion of key points is attributable to the rotation. What appeared to be an impasse, turns out to be a need for more detailed specification. The idea of an abstract texture space gives us a simple tool with which to express that specification.

Fig. 8: A sphere in-betweening to a torus in four stages.

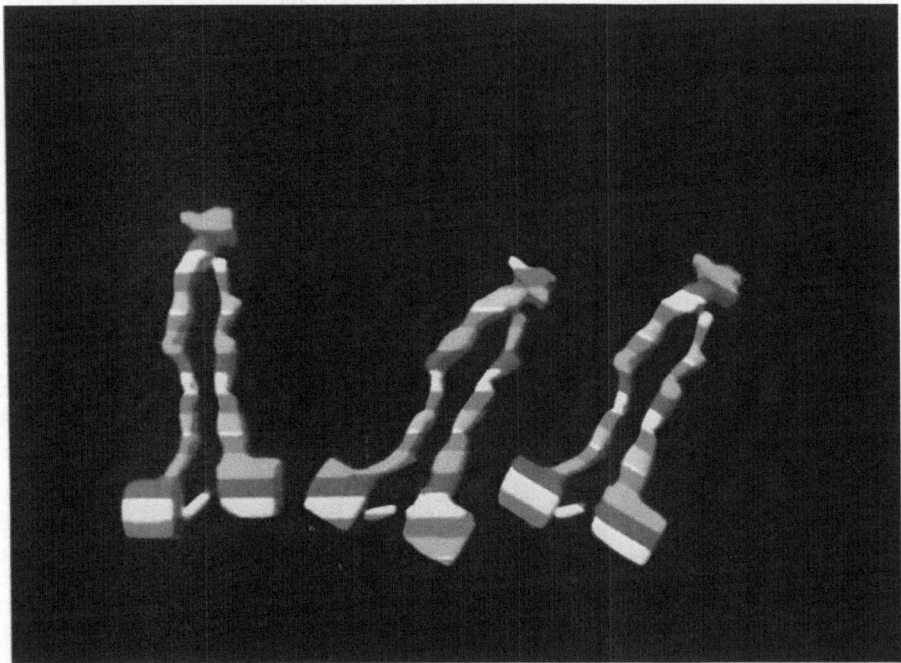

Fig. 9:   Two ways to realise rotation. Left: The object to be rotated.
Right: The abstract space is rotated with the key points.
Centre: The abstract space is not rotated.

Acknowledgments

This project was funded jointly by the University of Otago, the University Grants Committee of New Zealand, the University of Calgary and the Natural Science and Engineering Research Council of Canada.

References

Abram G, Westover L and Whitted T (1985) "Efficient Alias-free Rendering Using Bit-masks and Look-up Tables" *Computer Graphics (Proc. SIGGRAPH '85)* Vol 19 No 3 pp 53-59

Blinn J (1982) "A Generalization of Algebraic Surface Drawing" ACM Transactions on Graphics Vol 1 pp 235

Blinn J and Newell M (1976) "Texture and Reflection in Computer Generated Images" *CACM* Vol 19 No 10 pp 542-547

Blinn J (1978) "Simulation of Wrinkled Surfaces" *Computer Graphics (Proc. SIGGRAPH '78)* Vol 12 No 3 pp 286-292

Carpenter LC (1985) "The A-buffer, an Antialiased Hidden Surface Method" *Computer Graphics (Proc. SIGGRAPH '84)* Vol 18 No 3 pp 103-108

Gouraud H (1971) "Continuous Shading of Curved Surfaces" *IEEE Transactions on Computers* C-20 No 6 pp 623-628

Heckbert P (1986) "Survey of Texture Mapping" *IEEE Computer Graphics & Applications,* Vol 6 No 11 pp 56-67

Nishimura H, Hirai M, Kawai T, Kawata T, Shirakawa I and Omura K (1985) "Object Modeling by Distribution Function and a Method of Image Generation" Journal of papers given at the Electronics Communication Conference '85 Vol. J68-D No 4 (in Japanese)

Peachey, D (1985) "Solid Texturing of Complex Surfaces" *Computer Graphics (Proc. SIGGRAPH '85)* Vol 19 No 3 pp 279-286

Perlin K (1985) "An Image Synthesizer" SIGGRAPH 85 Computer Graphics Vol 19 No 3 pp 287-296

Wyvill BLM, McPheeters C and Wyvill G (1986a) "Animating Soft Objects" *The Visual Computer* Vol 2 No 4 pp 235-242

Wyvill G, McPheeters C and Wyvill BLM (1986b) "Data Structure for Soft Objects" *The Visual Computer* Vol 2 No 4 pp 227-234

Wyvill BLM and Wyvill G (1986c) "Using Soft Objects in Computer Generated Animation" BCS Conference: State of The Art in Computer Animation and Computer Art, Royal College of Art, London, December 1986 (Proceedings to be published by Springer Verlag)

Geoff Wyvill graduated in physics from Jesus College, Oxford, and started working with computers as a research technologist with the British Petroleum Company. He gained MSc and PhD degrees in computer science from the University of Bradford where he lectured in computer science from 1969 until 1978. He is currently senior lecturer in computer science at the University of Otago. He is on the editorial board of The Visual Computer and a member of ACM, SIGGRAPH and NZCS.

Address: Department of Computer Science,University of Otago Box 56, Dunedin, New Zealand

Brian Wyvill received his PhD from the University of Bradford in 1975 and continued his interest in computer animation as a research fellow of the Royal College of Art. Wyvill is now an Associate Professor at the University of Calgary where he leads the *Graphicsland* animation research team. His current interests are in "soft" objects, motion control and recursive data structures for computer animation. He is a member of ACM, CGS and SIGGRAPH and the editorial board of The Visual Computer.

Address: Department of Computer Science, University of Calgary, 2500 University Drive N.W., Calgary, Alberta, Canada, T2N 1N4

Craig McPheeters graduated from the University of Calgary with a degree in computer science in 1984. He worked as a research associate on the Graphicsland animation system until 1987. He is now a PhD student at the Dorset Institute of Technology, in Bournemouth, England.

Address: Dorset Institute of Higher Education, Wallisdown Road, Poole, Dorset BH12 5BR, England

Chapter 4

Graphics Hardware

Real Time Virtual Window Management for Bit Mapped Raster Graphics

Sener Ilgen and Isaac D. Scherson

ABSTRACT

In this paper we present a hardware real time window system which uses a virtual address mapping scheme based on associative memories. Until now, bit block transfer operations were used to update screen contents from main memory window information. Since these operations transfer large blocks of data from main memory to the frame buffer whenever window parameters are changed, the response times of window systems were slow. With the proposed approach, the frame buffer may be completely eliminated and replaced by a large virtual video memory which is capable of holding all the window data in non-overlapping locations. Mapping becomes now a dynamic real-time function which assigns screen addresses to different areas of the virtual video memory at different times.

Keywords: virtual window management, raster grapics, bitblt operation, associative memories

INTRODUCTION

Recent advances in computer graphics applications have resulted in widespread research and development efforts to improve the performance of "windowing systems" for bit-mapped raster-scan displays [Guibas 1982, Ingalls 1981, Pike 1983]. A windowing system allows the creation of logical windows over the data space for display in different areas of the display screen. The data mapped onto the different windows can be either alphanumerical, graphical, or a combination of both.

A number of windowing systems have been proposed and implemented using bit-map transfers from main to display memory. Specialized software keeps track of the windows' priorities and is responsible for the contents of the frame buffer. The latter is a one-to-one mapping of screen pixels to memory locations. Bit block transfer (BitBlt) operations are widely used to update frame buffer contents from main memory window information. The BitBlt operation transfers blocks of data in main memory to the frame buffer memory whenever window parameters are changed. Although BitBlt operation gives a fast response time, this response may not be fast enough at times when the system load is high (especially in multi-user systems) and a large number of overlapping windows are used.

In this paper we present a hardware real time window system which uses a virtual address mapping scheme. The scheme is based on associative memories and constitutes a departure from the old frame buffer concept. With the proposed approach, the frame buffer may be completely eliminated and replaced by a large virtual video memory which is capable of holding all the window data in *non-overlapping* locations. Mapping becomes now a dynamic function which assigns screen addresses to different areas of the virtual video memory at different times.

WINDOWING SYSTEM OVERVIEW

A window is an area of a display screen in which text or graphics information can be displayed. Referring to Fig. 1, we shall assume a screen coordinate system in which the origin (0,0) is at the upper left corner of the screen, X increases to the right and Y increases downwards. A window will be specified by its upper left corner location in screen coordinates (Xw, Yw), its width in the X direction (DX), and its height in the Y direction (DY). In addition, a memory address (MA) will be defined to point to the contents of the window in a virtual video memory space. An alternate way to define a window is through the definition of two diagonally opposed corners. It is clear that the latter definition is equivalent to the one proposed and might be used interchangeably.

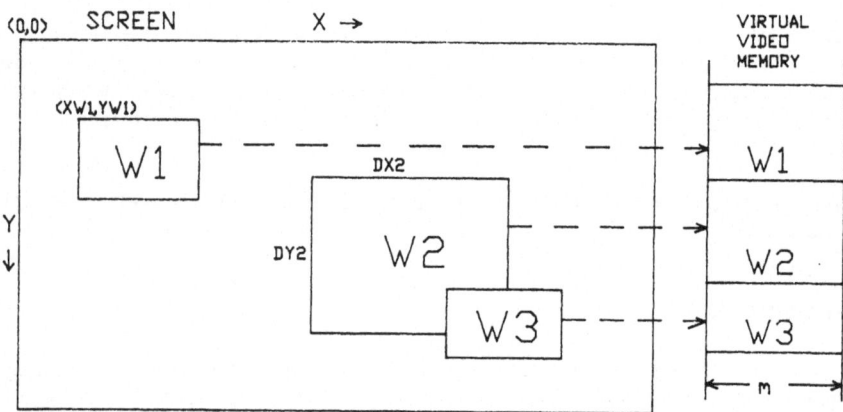

Fig. 1.   WINDOW – MEMORY RELATIONSHIP

The virtual video memory space is a word-oriented storage where each word is a m-bit binary entity. A word can contain graphics information or text information (e.g. in ASCII representation). Windows will be mapped to this storage by the memory address generated by the window processor. The first (DX/m) words of the memory corresponds to the first row of a window. The virtual video memory will hold all windows (alpha or graphics) which may exist at once in the system. It will be seen that memory bandwidth requirements dictate that windows start on word boundaries. This requirement also affects the screen address of a window: a window can be located in the X direction only on a pixel which is a multiple of m. There is no restriction in the Y direction.

A window location operation is a mapping from the display screen location pointed to by the window screen address (Xw, Yw) to the memory pointed to by the window memory address (MA). A window can be shrunk (expanded) by decrementing (incrementing) DX and/or DY. The window contents can be changed by changing the window memory address or by modifying video memory contents.

The windowing system consists of a processing unit, a video generation unit, a CRT controller unit, video memory and the virtual window processor, as shown in Fig. 2.

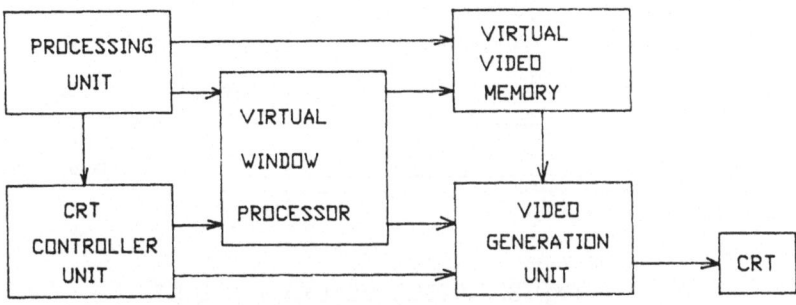

Fig. 2.   WINDOWING SYSTEM

The video generation unit displays the contents of video memory on the CRT screen. The window processor maps a screen address generated by the CRT controller unit into a video memory address - whose contents are displayed by the display unit. The processing unit accomplishes the user interface and controls the video memory and the window processor.

The processing unit (PU) is responsible for the user interface and the control of the windowing processor and the video memory. The PU can be a general purpose computer system, a simple microcomputer system, or even a microprocessor with proper memory and communication hardware. The PU controls the window processor by loading the window parameters (X, Y, DX, DY, MA ...) of any window created by the user. The video memory is loaded by the PU with the graphics information generated by the user that will be displayed in a window.

The video generation unit (VGU) contains the hardware to display text and graphics information on the CRT screen. It has an m bit wide data path to the video memory and a control path to the window processor and the CRT controller. The memory data can be graphics information - in which case the incoming m bits can be loaded into a shift register to be sent to the CRT; or the data can be text information - in which case the incoming m/8 bytes must be fed into m/8 character generators before loading into the m bit shift register. The shift register contents are shifted out at the video rate to the CRT. Fig. 3 shows the VGU organization.

The CRT controller unit (CCU) is responsible for the refresh of the CRT with proper data. It generates the screen address (Xs, Ys) and CRT timing signals (horizontal and vertical blanking, ...). The screen address is generated in the same way the electron beam scans the CRT screen - Xs is incremented first, Ys is incremented when Xs exhausts the scan line.

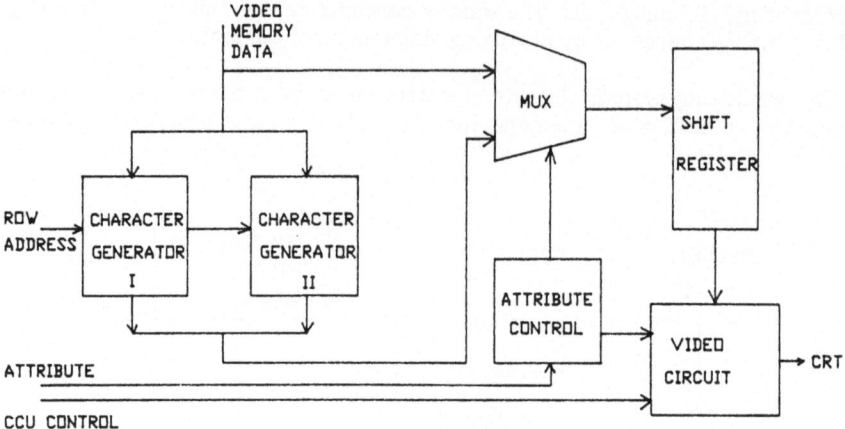

Fig. 3. VIDEO GENERATION UNIT

The video memory can be thought of as any standard memory system with the requirements that there has to be m bits per word and the memory has to be fast enough to allow both the PU and the window processor to access it every operation cycle. It will be later seen that inexpensive MOS dynamic memory chips can be used in the virtual video memory. The size of the video memory is limited by the window processor with the number of memory address lines. Since the window processor will map any screen location into an available video memory address, there is no need for the frame buffer.

VLSI VIRTUAL WINDOW PROCESSOR

The virtual window processor (VWP) will map screen addresses (Xs, Ys) into virtual memory addresses (MA). For this process, the window processor must utilize the window parameters in an efficient way to achieve real time processing speeds. The main operation of the window processor will be to test a screen address for containment in all the windows. This test requires comparison operations (less than, greater than) which would slow down the response of the window processor. In our approach, equality tests are used by dynamically changing window parameters every operation cycle - making the window follow the screen address until the screen address is out of window bounds. The equality tests of the screen address with the window addresses will be accomplished by associative memories.

An associative memory can be defined as a memory system in which stored data words are identified according to their contents [Parhami 1973]. The associative memory will get as an input a comparand value (screen address (Xs, Ys)), compare this comparand to all the selected associative words (window screen addresses (Xw, Yw)), and set or reset a responder flag depending on the outcome of the search.

Referring to Fig. 4, the window processor consists of a number of "processing words" - one word per window entry. These processing words contain a set of registers for storing window parameters which are the window screen address (Xw, Yw), widths in X and Y directions (DX, DY), video memory address of the window (MA), attributes of the window (AT), character generator row address (RA), selection flag (S), responder flag (R), and a word select flag (WS). Some of these registers have increment or decrement capabilities and some have associative capabilities for compare operations. Before going into the definition of the window processor hardware, the window processor operation will be detailed.

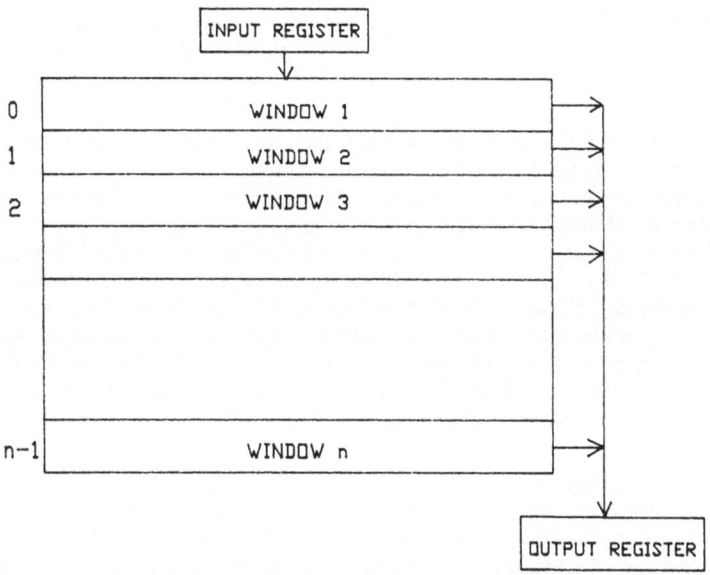

Fig. 4.   WINDOW PROCESSOR

We have three different timing periods available in the screen mapping process: active video time - in which the actual mapping will be done, horizontal blanking time - in which window parameters will be prepared for the next scan line, and vertical blanking time - in which window parameters will be prepared for the next picture frame.

In active video time, a screen address (Xs, Ys) will be generated by the CCU. This address will be compared for equality to all the selected window screen addresses (Xw, Yw). A window will be flagged as selected if it is created by the user. If there is a responder to this associative search, the corresponding memory address (for the virtual video memory), row address (for the character generator), and attributes of the window will be output. If there are more than one window responding to (containing) a screen address, the first window in the window list will be used. This selection is done by a "First Responder Select" operation. Overlapping window conflicts has to be handled by the PU by ordering windows before loading into the window processor. If no window is found that contains a screen address, this fact will be reported to the VGU to generate background color for that screen address.

The equality test is only half of the required processing, though. The window screen addresses should be prepared for the next screen address. This operation will be done on all those list entries which have responded to the previous search. The window X addresses will be incremented, X widths will be decremented and memory addresses will be incremented. A window entry will be denoted as processed if DX becomes zero, indicating that the screen address is out of window bounds.

In horizontal blanking time, all the windows that have been processed during the previous scan line will be prepared for the next scan line. The window Y addresses will be incremented and Y widths will be decremented. Window X addresses and X widths will be restored to their original values to handle the screen addresses of the next scan line. This will require registers to save original X and DX values. A window is completely processed if DY becomes zero.

If a window contains graphics information, no other processing is needed in horizontal blanking time. If we have a text window, however, we must adjust the memory address depending on the value of the character generator row address. The memory address should be restored to its previous character row value if the generation of the character is not complete - if RA is not zero. RA will initially contain the row count of the character, and will be decremented every horizontal blanking time to generate a different row of characters. If RA becomes zero, the character generation is complete and the memory address will not be changed since it will be pointing to the correct character. Also, this address should be saved for pointing to the previous character row value. RA has to be restored from its original value if it becomes zero for the next row of characters.

In vertical blanking time, all the valid window parameters have to be restored to their original values for the next picture frame. After this reinitialization, the PU can use this time to modify existing window parameters or load new window parameters into the window processor. The addressing of words in loading the window processor will be accomplished by the word select flag (WS). The WS flags of adjacent words will be connected to form a shift register and contents of the flag bits can be shifted. The load operation will load the input data to all words which have a one in the WS flag. Clearing all window processor X and Y registers can be accomplished by setting all the WS flags and loading zero. Since the window processor can be loaded by the PU every picture frame, real time window management objective is achieved with the least overhead on the PU.

Due to the incremental nature of our algorithm, all windows must completely be enclosed in the screen area. To handle windows partially seen, we must add the X width of the window to the starting row memory address. This addition poses no timing problems since it will be done in the horizontal blanking time, but will complicate the hardware. Due to this complexity, our current algorithm does not handle overflowing windows.

It should also be noted that all these operations will be applied to all the words (window entries) of the window processor in parallel. Only first select and load data operations will be sequential. An example of the window processor operation is given in Fig. 5.

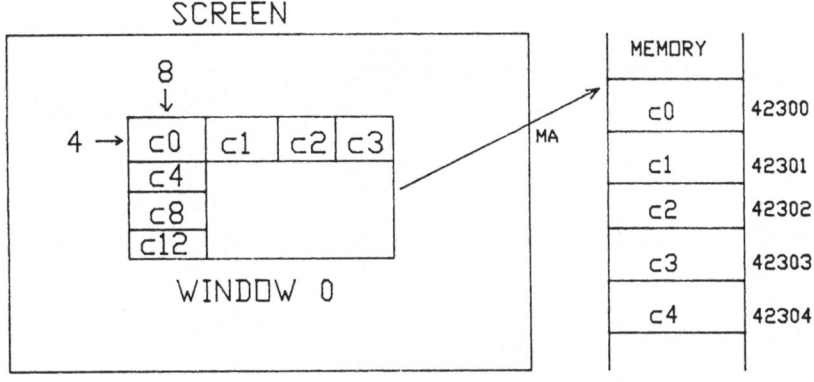

Window 0: $X_w = 8$, $Y_w = 4$, MA = 42300, DX = 4, DY = 4, AT = 0.

		SA		X	Y	MA	DX	DY	AT	RA	S	R	OUT	ACTION
						WINDOW 0								
		7	4	8	4	42300	4	4	0	x	1	0	-	
		8	4	8	4	42300	4	4	0	x	1	1	c0	X++,MA++,DX--.
A		9	4	9	4	42301	3	4	0	x	1	1	c1	X++,MA++,DX--.
		10	4	10	4	42302	2	4	0	x	1	1	c2	X++,MA++,DX--.
		11	4	11	4	42303	1	4	0	x	1	1	c3	X++,MA++,DX--.
		12	4	12	4	42304	0	4	0	x	1	0	-	
H		-	-	8	5	42304	4	3	0	x	1	0	-	Y++, DY--, R(X,DX).
V		-	-	8	4	42300	4	4	0	x	1	0	-	R(X,DX,Y,DY,MA).

SA is SCREEN ADRESS. ++ is increment. -- is decrement. R̄( ) is restore.
A is active time, H is horizontal blanking, V is vertical blanking.

Figure 5.   VWP OPERATION EXAMPLE

The window processor hardware architecture is given in Fig. 6. There is an input register (INREG), an output register (OUTREG), and a number of "processing words". Only the contents of one word are shown in the figure. The other words will contain exactly the same hardware. TREG is the temporary register that will contain the data to be output (MA, AT, and RA register data). This register is loaded at the start of the mapping operation, enabling the window processor to change contents of MA, AT, or RA register any time after the transfer. AREG is the associative register which will contain the window screen addresses (Xw, Yw). DREG , MAREG, ATREG, and RAREG stand for width (DX, DY), memory address, attributes, and row address registers, respectively. OLDAREG, OLDDREG, OLDMAREG, and OLDRAREG stand for the original content registers of the (X,Y), (DX,DY), (MA), and (RA) parameters. Register SMAREG is used to save the MAREG register contents every character row in case of a alpha window. SREG is the select flag, RREG is the result flag, and WS is the word select flag. First select logic ensures only one TREG is enabled to the OUTPUT register bus.

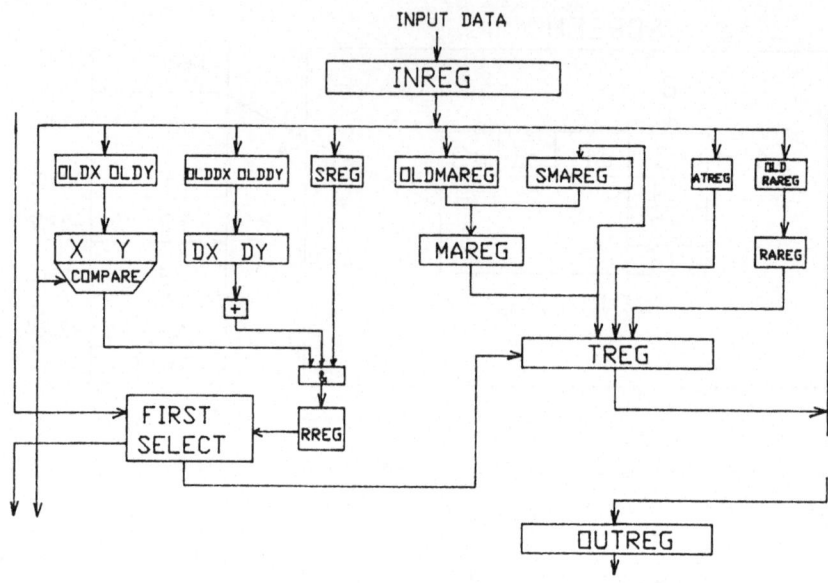

Fig. 6. WINDOW PROCESSOR ARCHITECTURE

This architecture can easily be incorporated into VLSI to execute the following mapping algorithm written in terms of a pseudo register transfer language:

FOR ALL i DO IN PARALLEL:

   ACTIVE DISPLAY PERIOD

• { INREG ← SCREEN ADDRESS ; $TREG_i$ ← ($MAREG_i$ $ATREG_i$ $RAREG_i$) }
• { $RREG_i$ ← (INREG == $AREG_i$) and ($DREG_i$!= 0) and ($SREG_i$ == 1) }
• IF($RREG_i$ == 1) →
        { AX_i ← AX_i + 1 ; DX_i ← DX_i - 1 ; $MAREG_i$ ← $MAREG_i$ + 1 ; SELECT FIRST RESPONDER
}
• {OUTREG ← $TREG_i$ }

   HORIZONTAL BLANKING PERIOD

• { DX_i ← $OLDDX_i$; AX_i ← $OLDX_i$; AY_i ← AY_i + 1 ; DY_i ← DY_i - 1 ; $RAREG_i$ ← $RAREG_i$ - 1 }
• IF((AT == ALPHA) and ($RAREG_i$ == 0)) → { $RAREG_i$ ← $OLDRAREG_i$; $SMAREG_i$ ← $MAREG_i$ }
• IF((AT == ALPHA) and ($RAREG_i$!= 0)) → { $MAREG_i$ ← $SMAREG_i$ }

   VERTICAL BLANKING PERIOD

• { $AREG_i$ ← $OLADREG_i$, $DREG_i$ ← $OLDDREG_i$, $MAREG_i$ ← $OLDMAREG_i$, $RAREG_i$ ← $OLDRAREG_i$ }
• { LOAD WINDOW PROCESSOR }

This algorithm uses simple searches, increment/decrement/assignment operations and simple conditional statements. All these operations can be easily implemented using current VLSI technology, which shows that the window processor architecture is feasible.

The VWP can be implemented with the following minimum instruction set:
0) No operation
1) Load INREG with outside data (SCREEN ADDRESS) and load TREG with (MA, AT, and RA).
2) Compare the associative memory contents to data in input register (INREG).
3) Increment/decrement working register set 1 (AX, DX, MA) and select first responder.
4) Load output register (OUTREG) from chosen temporary register (TREG).
5) Increment/decrement working register set 2 (AY, DY, RA) and restore (AX, DX).
6) Load working registers from the original content registers (A, D, M, R).
7) Load original content register (defined by register select pins) from INREG.
8) Set all bits of WS register.
9) Set first bit of WS register.
10) Shift WS register.

Register select pins select one of four original content registers: OAREG, ODREG, OMREG, ORREG. The result of the First Responder operation will be seen on the Responder pin of the chip: if this bit is ONE, there is a responder.

PERFORMANCE ANALYSIS AND COST EFFECTIVENESS

Assuming that the dot clock cycle is d nanoseconds, we have a word time of md nsec. During this time:
1) a screen address must be generated by the CCU,
2) this screen address must be mapped into a memory address by the VWP,
3) the contents of the memory must be read out,
4) these contents must be either
  a) routed to the shift register
  b) fed into the character generators
5) the shift register must be loaded with appropriate data

This time must also allow for accesses by the PU and the VWP. Therefore, the time allowed to the PU for memory access is at most md/2 nsec, which should be greater than the cycle time of the memory system. In the other md/2 nsec, the memory will be accessed by the VWP address. Although the VWP has md/2 nsec to access the memory, it has md nsec for the whole mapping process. This is accomplished by feeding the next screen address to VWP while the current memory address is valid. This can be seen from the timing diagram of the system which is given in Fig. 7. The next screen address is input as the previous memory address is output. The next memory address will be generated after approximately 5 clock cycles. As for intermediate operations, first clock cycle will be used for latching the input data to INREG, and loading $TREG_i$ with appropriate data. During the second cycle, the associative search will be done. Selecting the first responder will have 3 cycles, after which OUTREG will be loaded with TREG data. And the next memory address will be available in cycle 6. The increment and decrement operations will start in cycle 3, and will operate concurrently with the first select and read out operations.

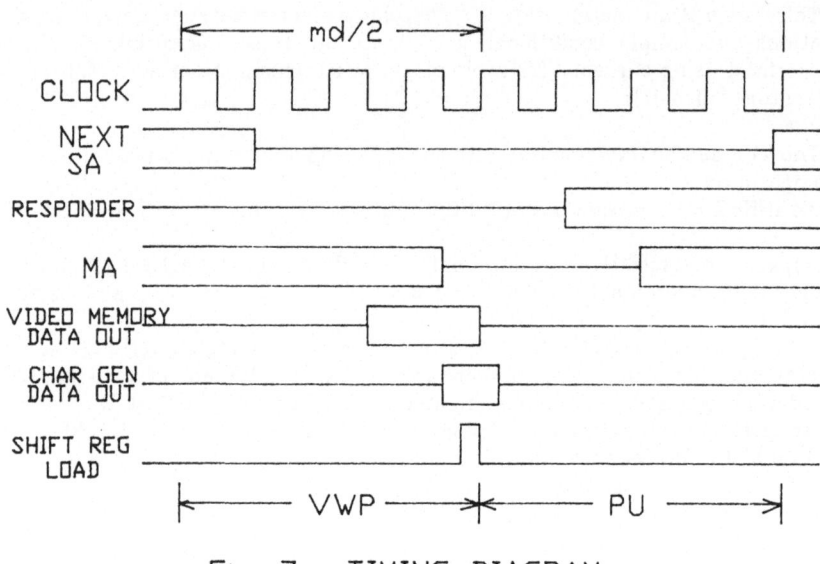

Fig. 7. TIMING DIAGRAM

For some common display formats the dot clock frequency is as follows [Whitton 1984]:

640 * 480	38.73 nsec.
800 * 600	26.31 nsec.
1024 * 768	16.52 nsec.
1024 * 1024	11.42 nsec.
1280 * 960	10.50 nsec.
1280 * 1024	10.06 nsec.

The following table shows the possible combinations of these dot clock frequencies and possible word lengths (md/2) in nanoseconds giving the possible memory cycle times:

	m = 8 bits	m = 16 bits	m = 32 bits	m = 64 bits
640*480	154.92	309.84	619.68	1239.36
800*600	105.24	210.48	420.96	841.92
1024*768	66.08	132.16	264.32	528.64
1024*1024	45.68	91.36	182.72	365.44
1280*960	42.00	84.00	168.00	336.00
1280*1280	40.24	80.48	160.96	321.92

The choice of word lengths will depend on the cycle times of dynamic RAMs. For a cycle time of 200 nsec (commonly available inexpensive 64Kx4 dynamic RAMs with 120 nsec access times), a word size of 8 seems unfeasible even for 640*480 resolution.

For resolutions up to 800*600, a 16 bit word size can be used. A resolution of 1024x768 would require a word length of 32. For higher resolution graphics, there are choices that has to be decided on the cost-performance requirements of the system. The first choice is to use very fast RAMs (with cycle times of 160 nsec) with a word length of 32 bits. Although it gives the highest performance, this option is the most expensive one. Another option is to use a word length of 64 bits with slow RAMs (cycle times of 320 nsec). This option restricts the number of windows and their locations in the X direction. As a last resort, the access of the PU to the video memory can be limited to the retrace intervals. This would permit using slow RAMs (320 nsec cyce time) with a word length of 32 bits. Of course, updating the memory with new data would be much slower than having the PU and the VWP access the memory every cycle. In the worst case, the VWP will have 320 nsec for the whole operation. Referring to the timing diagram again, we see that the cycle time of VWP will be 40 nsec in the highest resolution mode. This will require the registers to be latched in 40 nsec. Also, the associative search must be finished in 40 nsec, and first select in 120 nsec, which is quite reasonable with current technology. Increment/decrement operations will have about 240 nsec for completion.

From the preceding discussion, we have observed that the hardware parameters will depend largely on the display size. So, the VWP should be general enough to be used with different display formats. Nevertheless, upper bounds have to be set to keep the VWP simple. The following specifications will be used for the hardware:

Max display size in X direction	8192
Max display size in Y direction	8192
Min word size	16 bits
Memory address capacity	4 M words
Max Character Generator rows	32
Max window attributes	32

From these specifications, we obtain the following VWP register sizes:

$$
\begin{aligned}
\text{Max AX register size} &= \log(\text{Max display size in X direction/Min word size}) \\
&= \log(8192/16) = \log(512) \\
&= 9 \text{ bits} \\
\text{Max AY register size} &= \log(\text{Max display size in Y direction}) \\
&= \log(8192) \\
&= 13 \text{ bits} \\
\text{Max MA register size} &= \log(\text{Memory address capacity}) \\
&= \log(4194304) \\
&= 22 \text{ bits} \\
\text{Max RA register size} &= \log(\text{Max Character Generator rows}) \\
&= \log(32) \\
&= 5 \text{ bits} \\
\text{Max AT register size} &= \log(\text{Max window attributes}) \\
&= \log(32) \\
&= 5 \text{ bits}
\end{aligned}
$$

The other X (Y) registers, namely DX, OLDAX, OLDDX (DY, OLDAY, OLDDY) will have as many bits as the AX (AY) register has.

These parameters require the VLSI processor chip to have a 22 bit input bus (9 bits for X and 13 bits for Y) and a 32 bit output bus (22 bits for MA, 5 bits for AT, and 5 bits for RA). Also, there are 4 bits for the instruction, 2 bits for register select, 1 bit for responder flag, 1 bit for clock, and 2 bits for power. This makes a total of 64 pins for the VWP chip. Fig. 8 shows the chip pin definition.

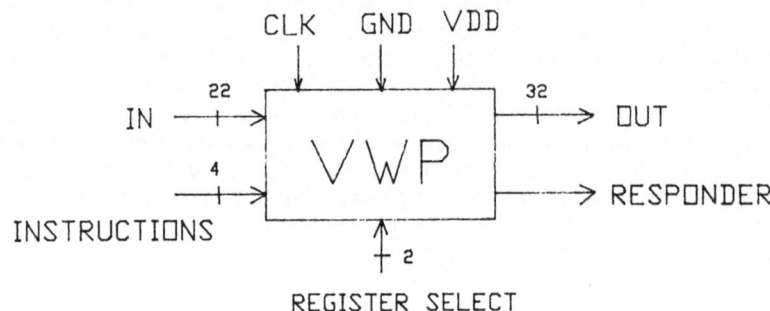

Fig. 8. PINOUT

CONCLUSIONS

A novel hardware virtual window manager architecture is presented. The concept is feasible for VLSI implementation, which would result in a very simple window interface to any graphics system while giving the users real time window managing ability. Judging from the fact that each word of the window manager requires static memory cells of 2 rows of 100 bits each, a VLSI implementation with 64 words (a total of 12800 cells) is not unfeasible. (By comparison, a 2Kx8 static RAM has 16384 memory cells).

We believe that the simplicity of the PU-VWP interface, the freedom of memory location independence for window data, real time response, and the ability to utilize low cost dynamic RAMs in windowing system implementations would make the VWP a definite choice in window manager design. When compared to the usual implementations of windowing systems using BitBlt operations, the VWP shows definite performance improvements. Since there is no need to transfer blocks of graphics information from the video memory to the frame buffer, memory bandwidth is increased considerably. The managing of windows by the VWP (in real time) is far superior to those of BitBlt implementations, which depend on the availability of the CPU time. It should be noted that BitBlt operations can be used in a windowing system in which the window management is done by the VWP, although these operations would mainly be used to create data that will be displayed on the screen. Although there are disadvantages in using the virtual window processor, we think that the advantages outweigh the disadvantages to a degree for the VWP to be considered in windowing system design. We conclude by listing the (dis)advantages of the VWP, letting the reader decide.

Disadvantages of VWP:

    1) Windows can start only on word boundaries in X direction.

    2) Window width in X direction should be a multiple of m.

    3) A window cannot contain both graphics and alphanumeric information.

    4) In alphanumeric mode, individual characters can not have attributes.

    5) Number of windows is limited by hardware.

Advantages of VWP:

    1) Real time window mapping.

    2) Minimum PU overhead in window manipulation.

    3) Virtual video memory: window data is location independent.

    4) Whole windows can have attributes.

    5) Animation can be achieved in real time by changing memory addresses every frame.

REFERENCES

Foley, J. D. and Van Dam, A. "Fundamentals of Interactive Computer Graphics", Addison-Wesley, 1982.

Guibas, L. J. and Stilfi, J. "A Language for Bitmap Manipulation", ACM Transactions on Graphics, July 1982, pp 191-214.

Ingalls, D. H. H. "The Smalltalk Graphics Kernel", BYTE, August 1981, pp 168-194.

Newman, W. M. and Sproull, R. F. "Principles of Interactive Computer Graphics", McGraw Hill, 1979.

Parhami, B. "Associative Memories and Processors: An Overview and Selected Bibliography", Proceedings of IEEE, June 1973, pp 722-730.

Pike, R. "Graphics in Overlapping Bitmap Layers", ACM Transactions on Graphics, April 1983, pp 135-160.

Whitton, M. C. "Memory Design for Raster Graphics Displays", IEEE CG&A, March 1984, pp 48-65.

Sener Ilgen is currently working towards a Ph.D. degree in Computer Engineering at the University of California, Santa Barbara. His research interests include associative parallel processing, computer graphics, and computer aided design. Ilgen received his BS in electrical engineering from Bogazici University, Istanbul, Turkey, and his MS in computer engineering from Syracuce University, Syracuse, NY in 1981 and 1984, respectively.

Isaac D. Scherson is an Assistant Professor in the Department of Electrical and Computer Engineering at the University of California, Santa Barbara. He received a BSEE and a MSEE from the National University of Mexico, and a PhD in Computer Sciences from the Weizmann Institute of Science, Rehovot, Israel. Dr. Scherson's main research interests lie in the general area of parallel processing. He has received considerable support from the National Science Foundation for his reseach in Associative Processing. The introduction of the Orthogonal Access Multiprocessing system led his group to the discovery of novel numerical and non-numerical algorithms for the resulting computational model (e.g. Shear-Sort). Computer Graphics is another area of interest. Dr. Scherson is currently studying parallel processing techniques applied to image generation and rendering.
Isaac Scherson is a member of the ACM and the IEEE.

Address: Department of Electrical and Computer Engineering, University of California, Santa Barbara, CA 93106 USA.

A Characterization of Orthogonal Access Multiprocessing for Graphics Video Buffers

Isaac D. Scherson and Steven P. Punte

ABSTRACT

A parallel processing architecture suitable for fast graphics image generation is presented. Named Orthogonal Access Multiprocessing (OAMP), it allows N processors to access NxN memory banks in either row mode or column mode. The video image is partitioned by least significant bit on both axes, then regrouped into either rows or columns by a dedicated interconnection network. The selected access mode depends upon the currently executed graphics primitive. Potential Speedup is introduced as a figure of merit which measures the "parallelizability" of the graphics task. The analysis holds true for any job divided among several processor for concurrent execution. A second figure of merit, "alpha," characterizes any given algorithm by a single numeric constant which relates Potential Speedup to task size. The OAMP's effectiveness in executing basic graphics primitives, such as vector generation, is discussed in light of the suggested performance measures.

Keywords: Video Buffer, Graphics Multiprocessing, Parallel Graphics Algorithms, Potential Speedup, Multiprocessing Saturation Limits.

1. INTRODUCTION

Images are frequently the best, and sometimes the only, manner to transfer information from the digital computer binary domain to the conceptual human thought domain. Computer generated images can take on a symbolic nature, such as schematics, or they can take on a realistic nature, such as natural scenes. Compared to pure text, images are more palatable to human communication. Thus there is, and will continue to be, a need for faster and more efficient graphics generation systems.

Since the introduction of computers, computer graphics: the process of producing computer generated images, has proven to be a computationally intensive challenge for digital systems. An image is defined as a two-dimensional array of picture elements (pixels) whose integer values define color and intensity. Graphics images are generated by the color assignment of each and every pixel one at a time. The procedure is in essence a translation of the high-level application-dependent scene description to the low level primitive descriptors of the frame buffer projection. In turn, the latter are processed to generate the actual pixel values. Special purpose co-processors which off load the main processing unit from this tedious graphics generation task are currently entering the market (TI 34010, INTEL 82786, NEC 7220, Hitachi HD-63484). These co-processors can produce pixels at peak rates of 5-10

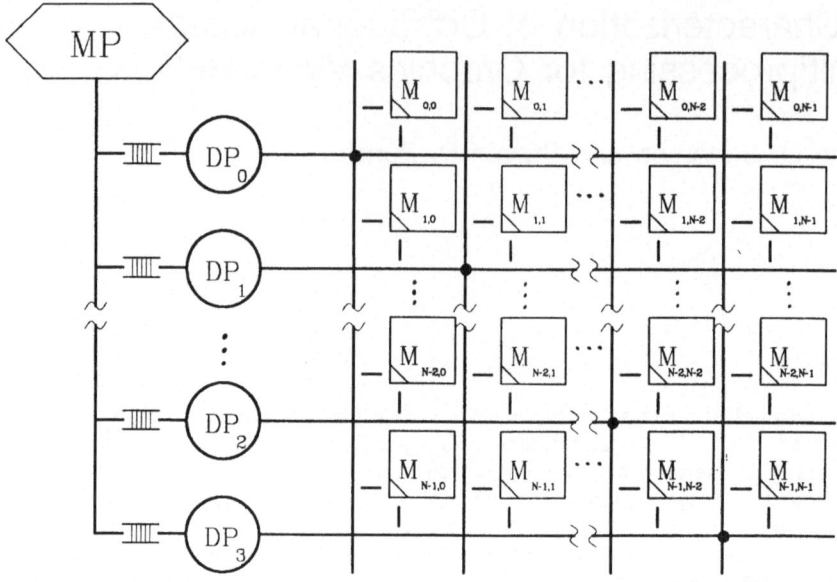

Figure 1: Orthogonal Bus OAMP Topology.

million pixels per second. Although these throughput rates sound impressive, they still are not fast enough for many situations. In particular, those in which small amounts of high-level scene descriptors explode into large number of pixel computations. Such is the case of images which require "painted" polygons: a four sided polygon (described by four points in the cartesian plane) may cover an area of tens of thousands of pixels in the frame buffer.

Further advancement in throughput of the single co-processor approach is limited by the master clock rate: a saturating technology parameter. Parallel processing therefor is the next exploitable frontier to realize faster graphics buffer systems. It provides an independent approach which benefits from other technological advances, such as new high-speed graphics co-processors. Graphics generation seems to be a natural for parallel processing as many independent disjoint tasks are mapped into a large video buffer. The real question is ARCHITECTURE. H. Fuchs [FUCH79] and F. I. Parks [PARK80] pioneered the research in graphics multiprocessing. Their approach to image sectioning (MSB partitioning) and image grid division (LSB partitioning) demonstrates graphics multiprocessing, but at a cost of frequent redundant effort by the display processors. Pixar corporation [PIXA84] has demonstrated a radically different and effective approach. Multiple layers of computer architecture coupled with extremely high speed data busses have produced an impressive graphics and image processing machine.

In this paper we introduce a new tightly coupled multiprocessing architecture which allows the parallel execution of simple graphics primitives such as vector generation and polygon filling. The video buffer is partitioned into $n \times n$ memory banks connected to N processors, also referred here as display processing units, which may access the banks by rows or by columns. Hence the name of the system: Orthogonal Access Multiprocessor (OAMP). The interconnection network allows for a wide variety of memory to processor mappings depending on which bits of the (x,y) pixel address are used to define the pixel-bank storage rule. As will become apparent, the most useful mapping is the orthogonal access to pixel rows or pixel columns which includes the fine image grid partitioning. The interconnect mesh also allows for multiple busses and thus achieves the greater memory bandwidth needed to support high speed graphics generation.

In order to tally the performance of the system in the execution of some basic video buffer primitives, a simulator that uses Motorola's 68000 microprocessor as a cost model was developed. It is not our intent to apply 68000 processors for multiprocessing. Rather the execution time of the various assembly language operations is used as a cost model for our display processing units. Four graphics algorithms: arbitrary line angle, special case line angle, triangle fill, and rectangle fill are described and their performance on the OAMP architecture measured. Our results show that the surface fill algorithms can be easily and effectively "parallelized." However, the parallel processing of line algorithms is limited.

In order to quantify how "good" an algorithm is for parallel processing, the figure of merit "Potential Speedup" is introduced. It is a measure of how much parallelism can be extracted from a given task. This concept applies not only to graphics multiprocessing, but also to multiprocessing of any task in general. The potential speedup of a graphics task is roughly proportional to its size. Larger graphics tasks can be "parallelized" more efficiently. A second figure of merit called "alpha" is also introduced. It is a proportionality constant between potential speedup and task size, and it characterizes a given algorithm with a single numeric value!

Finally, the overall limits of this graphics multiprocessing approach, and graphics multiprocessing using any classical Von Neumann processor are discussed.

2. THE ORTHOGONAL ACCESS MULTIPROCESSING ARCHITECTURE

When first approached, the application of parallel processing to graphics generation seems straight-forward. However, once the journey is begun, the complexity and difficulty of "HOW" emerges. Graphics multiprocessing is a challenge of resource designation and allocation. The idea is to partition the video buffer such that a number of processors (also referred to as Display Processors or DP for short) have concurrent access to disjoint areas of the image. This DP-Memory allocation can be attained by partitioning the image into equal areas, or by interleaving a number of lower resolutions grids, or a combination of the above. In the first case, it is the most significant bits of the memory address that determine the segmentation. In the second case, the least significant bits apply in the resolution interleaving scheme. The main disadvantage of the MSB partition is the poor balancing of the system when dealing with images whose complexity is concentrated in only a few partitions. The LSB partition provides the high granularity required to achieve good load balance. However, assuming each lower resolution grid is allocated to each DP, the classical mapping of algorithms bogs down as the DP to DP communication becomes an unbearable burden.

Consider the fundamental line drawing algorithm (Bresenham [BRE65]) which assumes an incident line angle to the controlling axis of less than 45 degrees. Each DP will approximate the given vector in its own grid. For every step of the independent variable, a number of pixels which depend on the overlap between the grids, will become possible candidates to approximate the line. The selection of the optimal one can then be done via DP to DP communication of by some localized decision variable. Obviously, the speed up of such a scheme is far from N for a N DP system. The solution to this problem is the minimization of grid overlap. By defining irregular grids, formed by horizontal or vertical stripes of pixels, the overlap is eliminated. However, an architecture that favors access in either the horizontal or the vertical direction will exhibit an asymmetrical behavior. We present the OAMP architecture as one possible solution which incorporates both vertical and horizontal grids and provides no grid overlap. The OAMP is both a processor-memory interconnect mesh and a memory allocation scheme.

An N-processor OAMP has $n \times n$ memory modules organized in the way depicted in Figure 1. We shall use the symbol M_{ij} for the memory module on the i-th row, j-th column, and P_i for the i-th processor. There is a master processor for control. It can initiate or mask off any of the processors and provides two memory mapping modes:

RM (Row mapping) : Processor P_i has access to and only to any of the memory modules in the i-th row.

CM (Column mapping) : Processor P_j has access to and only to any of the memory modules in the j-th column.

Let us assume an n by n pixel array $Q = [q_{ij}]$ is stored in the $n \times n$ memory array such that $q_{ij} \varepsilon M_{ij}$. In a RM mode, parallel access to all elements in a column is possible, that is each P_i can fetch a q_{ix}. Similarly, CM allows parallel access to rows of Q. Furthermore, we note that the diagonal of Q can be concurrently fetched in either memory mapping mode. Figure 2 illustrates the pixels accessible by processor P_l in both horizontal and vertical access modes. For a $kn \times kn$ pixel array, the following storage rule, together with the accessing modes defined, allow the conflict-free access to the irregular horizontal or vertical grids introduced previously.

OAMP STORAGE RULE: q_{ij} is stored in memory module $M_{i \bmod n, j \bmod n}$.

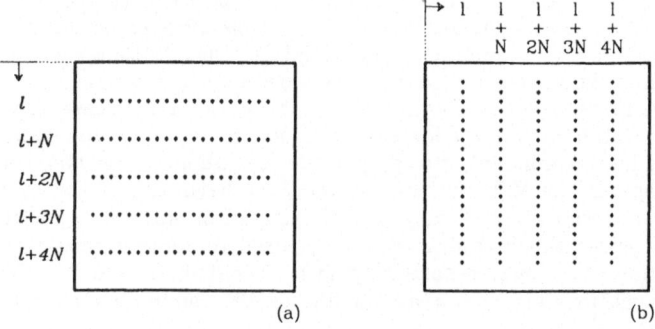

(a) (b)

Figure 2: Pixels are accessible by display processor "l" in (a) row mode, or (b) column mode.

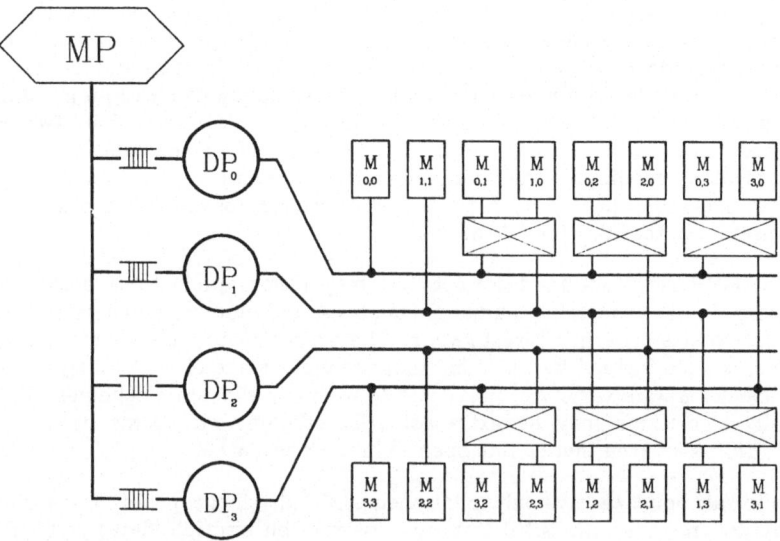

Figure 3: Linear bus OAMP topology for a four processor system.

For an OAMP of order n, there are n horizontal and n vertical busses, each permanently connected along the diagonal intersections as shown in Figure 1. A two way switch is attached to each memory module M_{ij} to allow either processor P_i or P_j access. The architecture can also be laied out in a uni-bus topology as shown in Figure 3. The uniform bus topology uses a fewer number of cross switches between the processor bus and memory modules. The main disadvantage of both topologies is the second order growth of memory modules compared to display processors. The number of memory modules is always the square of the number of display processors. The number of pixels per memory module decreases rapidly with increasing N to densities that do not take advantage of current RAM memory technologies. Table I shows the hardware and memory requirements for various order systems.

Table I			
OAMP ARCHITECTURE COMPLEXITY			
System Order	Number of Memory Modules	Number of Cross Switches(1)	Pixels per Memory Module(2)
2	4	1	256k
4	16	6	64k
8	64	28	16k
16	256	120	4k
32	1024	496	1k

(1) For uni-bus topology only.

(2) For a single 1024 by 1024 pixel image plane.

The OAMP falls under the category of a tightly coupled shared memory architecture. It is a product of both a hardware interconnect mesh concept and an access control mode allocation. Each processor has its own communication bus. An N'th order system has N busses and a peak memory bandwidth N times greater than a single bus system. Since most memory modules can be accessed by two different processors, but not simultaneously, they act as a natural interprocessor communication medium. This communication medium is not exploited in the graphics algorithms presented here, but is effectively used for bit block transfers, and is useful to other OAMP applications.

The OAMP architecture described has may other applications beside graphics processing. Image processing, numerical analysis, and numerical processing are other fields that we are presently investigating. The processor to memory module mapping can be organized instead by the MSB. Independent choice of controlling bits on both axes allow for a wide variety of processor to memory allocation schemes. Extremely unusually algorithms may be extraordinarily efficient with some creative access modes. This is an area that is wide open to further research.

Up to this point we have only mentioned OAMP physical aspects. The architecture can operate in either the MIMD (multiple instruction multiple data) or SIMD (single instruction multiple data) mode. For the purpose of graphics processing, we choose the MIMD mode. In other applications, such as image processing, one would find the SIMD mode more effective.

The processing of a graphics task is subdivided into two sections. First, a graphics task is received from some host system and preprocessed by the MP (Master Processor) into a format more palatable to the DP (Display Processor). The MP also controls the current access mode of the orthogonal architecture. The semi-processed graphic tasks are then placed in a dual port MP/DP communication queue. The DP receives these tasks and performs the actual drawing algorithm: placing colored information in the video image buffer.

Since the DPs are operating in a MIMD mode, one DP can begin a new graphic task while another is completing a previous task. The execution time of each DP unit is roughly the same for large tasks, but can be considerably different for small tasks. As long as the net execution time of the MP is less than the DPs, the communication queues will stay filled with tasks and the DPs will remain busy. Ideally, both the MP and the DPs should remain active at all times. This balance requires a careful choice of algorithm design, and is also very application dependent. Large graphics tasks consume more DP execution time than smaller tasks, but their MP execution time are identical.

Finally, the image is extracted from the video buffer along a separate bus structure by a CRT controller (not shown). The access of the CRT controller is time domain multiplexed with the access of the DP units so no interference is noticed.

3. OAMP GRAPHICS ALGORITHMS

The OAMP architecture is not only a concurrent multiprocessor, but also a two stage pipeline multiprocessor; the second stage is composed of many DP units. Fortunately, graphic algorithms subdivide naturally into this tree type hierarchy. A task received from the host is processed through several software layers before pixels are assigned to the video buffer. Each software layer processes the graphic task to more regular and restricted format which is more easily processed by the next lower level. The three main software levels are: MP pre-processing, DP overhead, and DP draw loop. In this context, "Draw," meaning the assignment of integer values to a set of pixels selected according to some criterion.

The MP first accepts a graphics command from the outside world. The vertices are then organized in a predefined order according to the command type. The access mode is specified, and certain global parameters (such as slope for the line algorithm) are calculated. Identical parameters are passed to all DP units. The second software functional block (DP overhead) reads the parameters from the communication queue and processes the information to calculate the necessary draw loop control constants. Algorithm parameters, such as starting point, are adjusted according to the access mode and the unique memory bank allocation of the particular DP. The third software functional block uses these adjusted parameters to control a tightly written drawing loop that actually places color information in the appropriate video buffer address.

The video buffer memory appears to the DP units as a linear array of address locations. The x and y coordinates of every given pixel must be transformed into such a linear address. To increase the draw loop execution speed, a pixels' location is represented as a single integer, namely its linear address. This eliminates the need to formulate a linear address each time a pixel is targeted thus speeding up the draw loop considerably.

As a standard, we have chosen the Breshenham [BRE65] algorithm for the style of lines to be drawn. The Breshenham algorithm yields a high density of points that are closest to the actual true line.

The objective of our research is not to produce a commercially finished product, rather to investigate graphics multiprocessing. Features such as edge clipping and 'Z' buffering have not been implemented. The algorithms examined and analyzed here are by no means completely finished and optimized. Throughout our research the algorithms seemed to be in a constant state of evolution. In addition, an optimum algorithm seems to depend upon the exact application. Since we desire our research application to be general in nature, the optimal algorithms have been elusive. Nevertheless, the algorithms presented here have given us great insight into the field of graphics multiprocessing and its limitations.

-A- ARBITRARY ANGLE LINE ALGORITHM

For the sake of simplicity, let us assume that the line segment originates at the origin and lies in the first quadrant. Since the direction of maximum change is x in the first octant, x is chosen as the independent variable. This ensures a fairly dense set of points. The access mode of the system is set to column mode. Each processor is responsible for determining a value of y for each independent variable x under its control. The algorithm is iterative in nature. A new (x,y) pair is calculated from a previous pair. However, unlike the classical Bresenham algorithm, the information of the immediate previous drawn pixel is unavailable since it resides in a different display processor. Except for the initial start up period, information from the previous N'th - 1 pixel is used to place the current pixel, see Figure 4. For each iteration the x coordinate is incremented by the number of processors N, and the y coordinate is incremented by a variable *range*. An auxiliary variable called *residual* is also incremented. *residual* represents the fractional height of the location. If residual becomes positive, it is decremented by *delta_residual*, and the y coordinate is incremented by one unit. The appendix contains a 'C' version listing of this algorithm in which the x and y locations are combined into a single variable called address (*address* = $x + kN \times y$). A similar algorithm has been presented by R. Sproull [SPRL82].

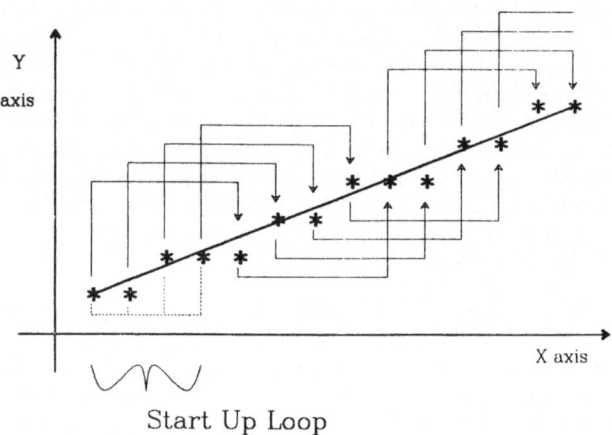

Start Up Loop

Figure 4: Extended Bresenham algorithm iterations.

-B- SPECIAL ANGLE LINE ALGORITHM

A "special angle" line is one that has an angular orientation of a multiple of 45 degrees. Vertical, horizontal, and diagonal lines occur so frequently in graphics that the use of a separate algorithm results in significant improvement. There are of course eight such line orientations, folding into four non-redundant cases. The exact change in linear address from one pixel to the next is uniform over the entire line segment. The algorithm requires no fractional height component as in the general case algorithm. Thus an even more tightly written draw loop can be used for these special angle cases.

The MP line algorithm detects such cases and identifies the appropriate quadrant. This information, along with the end point locations, is passed to the DP units. No *slope*, *range* or *delta_residual* variable calculations are needed. Thus the execution time in the master processor is reduced. The DPs directly calculate the appropriate starting position for the given particular grid. The appendix also includes a 'C' version listing. As can be seen, fewer calculations are required per loop pass. This section of the algorithm is thus faster than its corresponding general case algorithm.

Since all three software sections of this algorithm are smaller than the corresponding arbitrary angle algorithm, it will naturally run faster and yield a greater throughput. The more interesting question is, will it offer better or poorer speedup capabilities compared to its more general partner?

-C- TRIANGLE FILL ALGORITHM

Any large multi-vertex polygon can be divided into simple triangles: "polygon triangularization." We thus choose to implement a simple triangle drawing algorithm instead of the more general polygon algorithm. The challenge of polygon triangularization can be handled at the MP level, or even higher. Several people have recently investigated polygon triangularization algorithms: [CHAZ80] and [GARY78]. We are primarily interested in the throughput capacity of drawing a triangle to the video image buffer.

The vertices of the triangle are received by the MP and reformulated into a highly restricted quadrangle format, see Figure 5. The quadrangle is represented by four vertices: top, right, bottom, and left. The quadrangle is a general format that can represent a triangle in any orientation by collapsing two vertices into one. The master processor identifies the correct vertices. The preferred drawing access mode (row or column) is determined. These parameters are then passed to the DPs by way of the communication queues. The display processors then need only draw from starting edge to ending edge.

The DP algorithm has two temporary linear arrays the size of the screen image: $start[]$, and $end[]$. The same line algorithm as described in section 3.A is used to calculate the leading and trailing edge as seen by the given access mode. This is performed by the subroutine $scan\_line()$. Only edge points accessible to the given DP need be determined. A null line (identical beginning and ending point) is detected and simply represented as a single point.

The main draw loop simply fills in all pixels between the start edge and the end edge for a given row or column. The quadrangle edge calculations appear to be overhead to the actual draw loop, but are actually equally subdivided among the DP units. This is an important distinction as opposed to true overhead code which is reproduced in every additional DP.

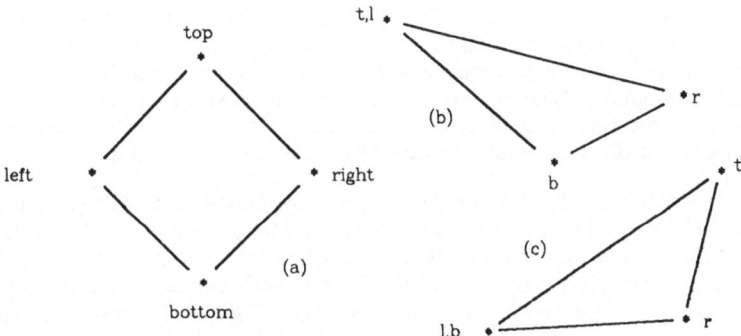

Figure 5: General surface quadrangle format (a). Collapsed quadrangle format to represent triangles (b & c).

-D- RECTANGLE FILL ALGORITHM

The rectangle algorithm is motivated by a similar philosophy as the special case line angle algorithm: the more regular graphics tasks occur frequently and thus deserve their own ad-hoc algorithms.

The MP receives a rectangle command followed by two vertices representing opposing corners. The upper left and lower right corners are determined and passed to the DPs along with the desired access mode. As before, the DP performs some offset calculations according to the DPs grid access. The main draw loop is actually two nested loops: one to draw pixels across the chosen access mode, the other to shift location on the opposing axis.

4. ARCHITECTURE AND ALGORITHMS SIMULATIONS

Without a hardware architecture to operate on, an algorithm accomplishes nothing. Without an algorithm to guide it, an architecture sits idle. To achieve useful work, the two are inseparable. Thus, the architecture and the algorithm must be evaluated as a pair, much as a software compiler and a hardware processor are evaluated as a pair. One can be optimized while holding the other fixed, but neither can be optimized independently. We shall hold the architecture (OAMP) fixed and search for optimum algorithms.

Our objective is maximum speedup: the decrease in overall execution time relative to the uniprocessor case. However, one must be careful not to lose sight of the original goal: to process graphic commands as quickly as possible. An algorithm must be evaluated for speedup after it has been optimized for throughput. There is no point in speeding up a low performance algorithm. It is easy to create algorithms that achieve near perfect speedup on a multiprocessor system but accomplish no useful tasks. An example is a program that simply idles. Certainly a thousand processors will produce a thousand times as much "idling" in the same amount of time. Speedup must be referenced to the production of useful work.

We formally define speedup as the ratio of single processor to multiprocessor execution time. The multiprocessor execution time is usually smaller, thus speedup assumes a value greater than unity. Our uniprocessor model is actually a dual processor system: one MP and one DP. A true single processor system would require different algorithms, compounding the problem of comparison. The increase in speed of this two stage "simulated uniprocessor" system approximately is offset by the extra effort expended to pass parameters between the two processors. Therefore, we shall accept the method of speedup determination as roughly correct even though the architecture is not directly compared to a true uniprocessor system.

We have written a software simulation program called "GAPSIM" (Graphics Array Processor SIMulator). The program simulates the simultaneous parallel operation of several display processing units, a single master processor unit, and keeps track of the passage of time. Only one copy of the DP software exists. The code is executed multiple times for the multiprocessing system. Figure 6 shows the simulator organization.

Each display processor simulation routine has static variables that remain in place. One of these variables is accumulated time. The controller checks each processors' accumulated time index and allows the processor with least accumulated time to execute any pending tasks. If no tasks are pending, the given processor is allowed to idle. In this manner parallel processing is simulated. However the accuracy of the simulation depends upon the granularity of the individual tasks. The larger the tasks, the more likely an interprocessor communication token is not addressed in a timely manner. Fortunately, our architecture passes information only from the MP to the DP. Our simulations show that the MP is idling frequently and thus the DPs are kept routinely active. Therefore, this mechanism of error occurs infrequently.

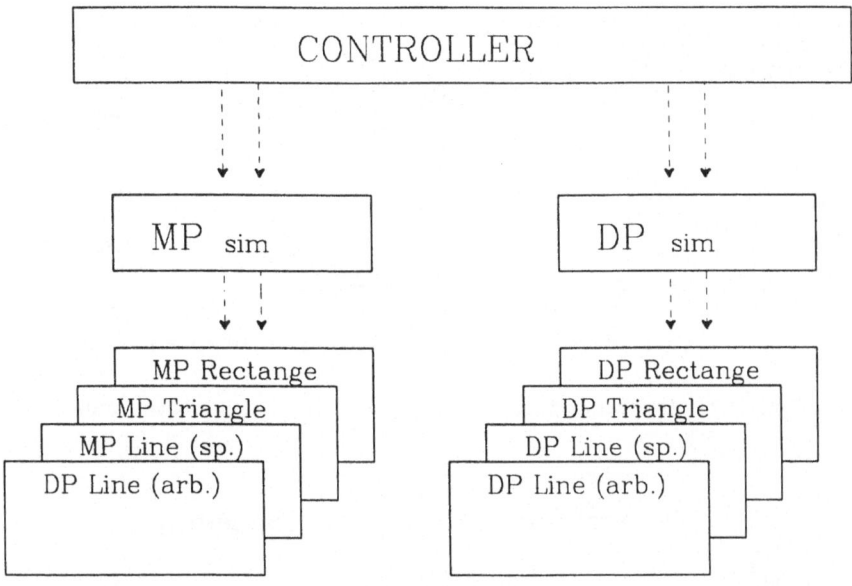

Figure 6: GAPSIM Simulator Organization.

The algorithms are written in a 68000 like assembly code named "PLIS" (Pseudo Language Instruction Set). This language consists of about 12 generic instructions with some addressing variations. Each instruction is actually a 'C' subroutine. The subroutine performs the required operation, and increments the time counted by an amount appropriate to that instruction. We chose the 68000 assembly code as a reasonable cost function to implement the algorithms with. An actual system would be constructed with high speed special purpose graphic generation processors.

A separate host simulating program called "stat-gatherer" was written to gather performance statistics. This program operates in two modes: deterministic or random (stochastic) generated tasks. The absolute placement and the angular orientation is random whenever possible, since these parameters have little effect on algorithm performance. In deterministic mode, performance is measured against the number of DPs and task size. In stochastic mode, performance is measured against the number of DPs and an ensemble of tasks. The task size is modeled using the Rayleigh density function. Line tasks are assigned a peak density at length 64. Surface tasks have the same distribution function, but squared.

Figures 7 through 11 show the more interesting performance measurements of this architecture. All measurements are run under conditions of high load to swamp out filling effects of the two stage processor pipeline, thus, the maximum throughput of the system is measured. Throughput is measured in units of pixels drawn per thousand clock cycles, speedup is in absolute units.

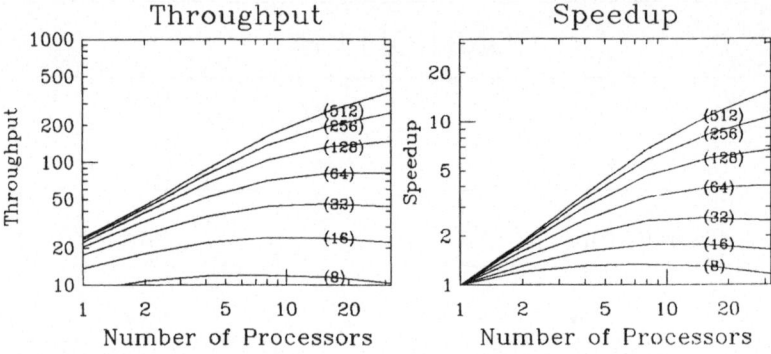

Figure 7: Arbitrary Angle Line Algorithm (Line length values in parentheses).

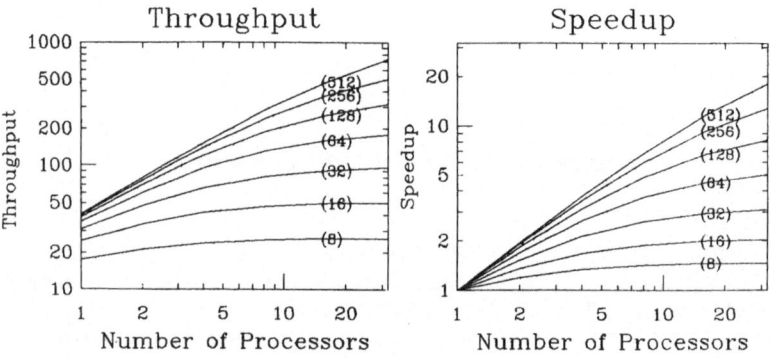

Figure 8: Special Angle Line Algorithm (Line length values in parentheses).

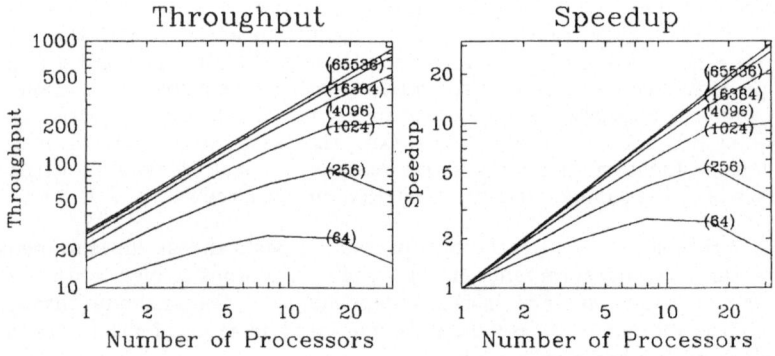

Figure 9: Triangle Fill Algorithm (Surface area values in parentheses).

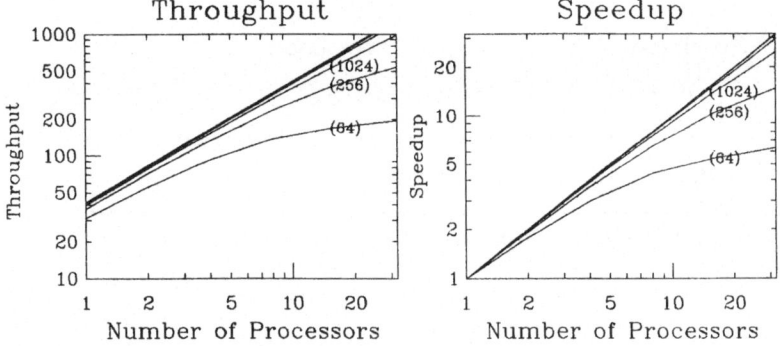

Figure 10: Triangle Fill Algorithm (Surface area values in parentheses).

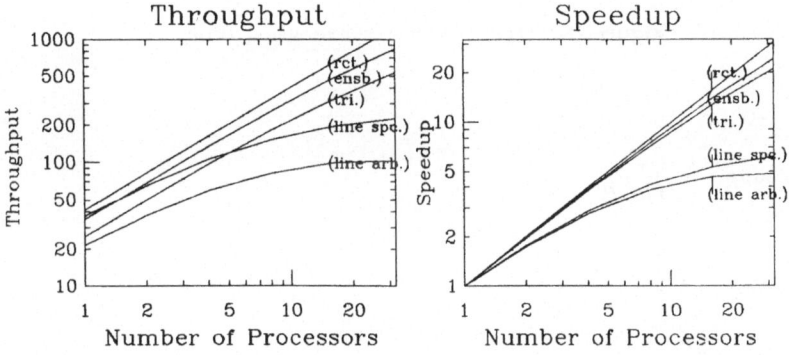

Figure 11: Algorithm Benchmark Performances (Algorithm type in parentheses).

5. ANALYSIS OF RESULTS

For purpose of analysis let us assume that the MP is never the bottleneck of the system. That is, the MP always has ready some tasks pending in the communication queues for the DPs. The throughput and performance are thus completely dependent upon the DPs. This is the preferred state of the architecture, since it is less wasteful to keep one MP idle than many DPs idle. We can model the DP execution code as two parts: Overhead code "O", and draw Loop code "L"; see Figure 12. The execution time of the 'loop code' is inversely proportional to the number of DPs (N). The execution time of the DP overhead code remains constant with the number of processors. The multiprocessor execution time can be expressed as:

$$Execution\ time = O + L/N \tag{1}$$

Speedup is defined as the ratio of uniprocessor execution time to multiprocessor execution time:

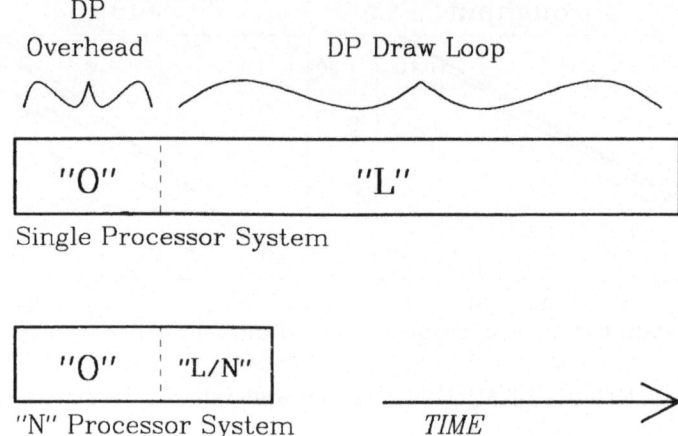

Figure 12: Display Processor Execution Time.

$$Speedup = \frac{O+L}{O+L/N} \tag{2}$$

or,

$$Speedup = N\left[\frac{1+L/O}{N+L/O}\right] \tag{3}$$

The L/O factor is a fundamental parameter that determines the achieved level of speedup. We thus formally define the figure of merit "Potential Speedup" and its relation to actual speedup as:

$$PS\ (Potential Speedup) = L/O, \tag{4}$$

$$Actual\ Speedup = N\left[\frac{1+PS}{N+PS}\right] \tag{5}$$

If the number of processors is allowed to increase without bound:

$$\lim_{N \to \infty} Actual\ Speedup = 1+PS, \tag{6}$$

then "Potential Speedup" is shown to be the best speedup possible that can be extracted from a given task. PS is a figure of merit on how "parallelizable" a task is. This analysis holds true for any task, not just graphics tasks, that are divided among several processors and executed concurrently.

As PS increases without bound:

$$\lim_{PS \to \infty} Actual\ Speedup = N, \tag{7}$$

actual speedup approaches the desired upper limit, the number of display processors, and maximum utilization of the system is realized. Hence, we desire to write algorithms such that this figure of merit PS is maximized!

Each speedup performance curve in figures 7 through 11 can be characterized by a constant PS value. Furthermore, for each algorithm, the PS factor is roughly proportional to the task size. Therefore, we introduce the constant "alpha": a conversion factor from task size to potential speedup:

$$PS = SIZE(task)/\alpha. \tag{8}$$

Each algorithm can now be characterized by the single figure of merit: "alpha!" Alpha takes on the units of length or area per additional unit of speedup. Its meaning is, how large a task must be in order to gain an additional unit of speedup.

Table II is the best calculated alpha constants from the data presented in figures 7 thorough 11. Alpha is a measure of how "parallelizable" the task is. It is independent from absolute uniprocessor throughput performance.

Table II MEASURED ALPHA CONSTANTS		
Algorithm	Alpha	Units
Line (arbitrary angle)	16.	length/speedup
Line (special angle)	13.	length/speedup
Triangle Fill	~52.	area/speedup(3)
Rectangle Fill	10.	area/speedup

The previous described model is simplistic and first order in nature, however this is also its main virtue. Several secondary effects cause the actual speedup to differ. First, under conditions of light DP load, the MP can become the throughput bottleneck. This condition occurs for small graphic tasks sizes and larger order systems. Second, the draw loop of any algorithm is quantum in nature, it can not be arbitrarily divided as depicted in figure 12. Third, some sections of the DP code actually grow with larger order system. An example is the initial grid adjustment for the Bresenham loop. Fourth, the loop code execution time is not always linear with task size. The triangle fill algorithm execution time, for example, is proportional to both its area and its perimeter. Finally, some extra time is needed to fill and empty the two stage processor pipeline. Nevertheless, the alpha figure of merit serves extremely well to characterize the performance of these algorithms.

---

(3) Potential Speedup is a function of both triangle area and triangle perimeter. For most instances, the dependency upon triangle perimeter can be neglected.

$$PS = \frac{area}{\alpha_a} + \frac{perimeter}{\alpha_p}$$

$\alpha_a = 52 \quad pixel-area/speedup$

$\alpha_p = 25 \quad pixel-length/speedup$

The lower the alpha figure of merit, the more parallelism can be extracted from a given algorithm and identical tasks size. The rectangle fill algorithm achieves first place! It has extremely low overhead, and is most efficient at drawing pixels due primarily to its simplicity. The triangle algorithm has the poorest alpha. It requires a large amount of overhead processing to set up the fill loop. The line algorithms appear almost as effective as the rectangle algorithm, but this is deceiving. The number of pixels drawn for an average line is orders of magnitude less that for an average surface task. Thus the average potential speedup for surface tasks will be much larger than for line tasks.

The deterministic approach yields an excellent analysis of graphic multiprocessing fundamentals limits. But how will this architecture and algorithms perform under real conditions? Obviously the speedup achieved is highly task dependent, in particular larger tasks yield better speedup . A suitable benchmark definition of typical graphics applications is needed. Unfortunately, there are no typical graphics applications. For lack of a better benchmark definition, we have chosen a collection of Rayleigh distributed tasks to be our benchmark. For our screen size of 1024 by 1024, we have chosen a Rayleigh peak density of length 64. Line tasks have a distribution as described above. Surface tasks, such as triangle and rectangle, have the same distribution function but squared. We have also defined an overall benchmark condition to be a random and uniform collection of the four algorithms, each under the said stochastic load.

The expected performance of any algorithm under stochastic load can be predicted using the previous model. The potential speedup is just the expected value of the net loop code divided by the overhead code:

$$PS = \mathbf{E}\left[L/O\right] = \mathbf{E}\left[SIZE(task)/\alpha\right] \tag{9}$$

Given that the probability density function is Rayleigh with a maximum density of b (b = 64), the PS can be evaluated to:

$$PS = \int_{x=0}^{x=\infty} \frac{x}{\alpha} \times P_X(x)\,dx \tag{10}$$

$$PS = \frac{1}{\alpha}\int_{x=0}^{x=\infty} x\,\frac{x}{b^2}\,e^{-\frac{x^2}{2b^2}} \tag{11}$$

$$PS = \frac{b}{\alpha}\sqrt{\frac{\pi}{2}}. \tag{12}$$

Similarly, for surface tasks the PS parameter can be calculated:

$$PS = \int_{x=0}^{x=\infty} \frac{x^2}{\alpha} \times P_X(x)\,dx \tag{13}$$

$$PS = \frac{1}{\alpha}\int_{x=0}^{x=\infty} x^2\,\frac{x}{b^2}\,e^{-\frac{x^2}{2b^2}} \tag{14}$$

$$PS = \frac{2b^2}{\alpha} \tag{15}$$

The potential speedup can be calculated in a similar manner for any probability density model. Models which favor larger size tasks will show a greater potential speedup and vice-versa.

Table III is a comparison of the measured stochastic potential speedup from graph 11 and the calculated potential speedup using equations 12 and 15 and table II. A value of 64 is used for the constant "b." We also note that although the two line algorithms have substantially different throughputs, they have roughly the same potential speedup.

Table III POTENTIAL SPEEDUP		
Algorithm	Predicted PS	Measured PS
Line (arbitrary angle)	5.0	4.5-5.6
Line (special angle)	6.2	6.3-6.5
Triangle Fill	77.	52-59
Rectangle Fill	819	660-900
Ensemble	-	95-100

All algorithms that generate surfaces, i.e. the triangle and rectangle algorithm, exhibit adequate speedup. However, the line algorithms, under random realistic use, do not demonstrate great speedup potential. The fundamental drawback is that lines are simply not composed of many pixels! This is why lines are normally fast to draw to begin with. If a medium size line, say of length 64, is processed using say 32 processors, then each processor ends up drawing only 2 pixels! No matter what algorithm is used, the time coloring drawing these two pixels will be significantly less than the overhead time spent setting up the routine. However, an advantage of line algorithms are that they are naturally fast since few pixels are being drawn.

The measured PS factors agree well with the predicted values for the line algorithms, but show more variations for the surface algorithms. This discrepancy is not yet well understood. Never the less, this method and the results serve as a useful guideline for predicting the actual performance of a graphic multiprocessing system.

The data presented here is subjective in nature. As previously stated, the simulations and measurements were performed using a 68000 like cost function. If the simulations and measurements were repeated under a different cost function, probably similar results would occur. The quantification of algorithm performance can never be totally separated from the architecture and hardware it is performed on.

Our final benchmark measurement is called "ensemble." It is an equal and random combination of the four algorithms, each under stochastic load, intended to represent a single performance statistic. The ensemble measurements follow the general trend of being a weighted average of the four algorithm. Since line tasks have few actual pixels, their poor performance contribution does not seriously effect the overall performance. In summary, the architecture has very acceptable and encouraging performance for real life mixed bag random applications.

6. CONCLUSIONS AND SUMMARY

The application of graphics processing to the orthogonal access multiprocessor has been demonstrated and characterized. Four major observations can be drawn from the efforts of this research:

* The OAMP master processor execution time must be kept small. If for any tasks, or ensemble of tasks, the master processor execution time is greater than the DP execution time, the master processor then becomes the bottleneck, and the system effectiveness drops off sharply. If there is a tradeoff, it is much more hardware efficient to allow one MP to be idle rather than multiple DPs.

* Any concurrent multiprocessing task that can be modeled as a fixed portion and a dividable portion, can be assigned a figure of merit called "potential speedup." Potential speedup is the upper limit to how "parallelizable" the given task is. For the graphic benchmark described in this paper, we measure a potential speedup of about 100.

* Graphics algorithms can be characterized by a single figure of merit named "alpha." The graphics task size, in units of length or area, divided by the constant alpha for that algorithm yields its potential speedup.

* Surface graphic algorithms (triangle and rectangle for example) exhibit good speedup on the OAMP. Line graphic algorithms exhibit only fair speedup on the OAMP. It is difficult to achieve good speedup for line algorithms since very few pixels are actually being drawn. However, for the same reason, line algorithms are to begin with inherently fast. Thus their marginal speedup is acceptable.

The efficient and effective multiprocessing of graphic algorithms on the OAMP architecture seems to primarily depend upon the overhead execution in the display processors. The greater the number of DPs, the more often this overhead is repeatedly processed, and the more it consumes processing power of the system. Therefore an effective large OAMP system should have special purpose two-stage-pipeline display processing units. The first stage calculates the controlling draw loop constants from the primitive graphic command, and the second stage executes the draw loop. This addition in pipeline staging hides the DP overhead so that it is less of a limiting factor.

The instruction sequence of graphics algorithms is inherently data dependent. The cost of this data dependency reveals itself as overhead computations which are reproduced, with slight variations, in each processing unit. The efficient parallelization of such tasks demands a multistage-multibranching overall architecture: multistaging to provide maximum software algorithm layering as a task is digested to its most primitive form, multibranching to achieve uniform load balance. Thus, it appears that, the optimum architecture of such data dependent algorithms is very application and algorithm dependent.

7. REFERENCES

[BRES65] J.E. Bresenham, " Algorithm for computer control of a Digital Plotter," IBM Systems Journal, Vol. 4, No. 1. 1965, pp. 25-30.

[CHAZ82] B. Chazelle, "A theorem on polygon cutting with applications," Proc. 23rd Annual Symp. on Foundations of Comput. Sci., pp. 339-349 (1982).

[FUCH79] Henry Fuchs, "An Expandable Multiprocessor Architecture for Video Graphics," Proceedings of the Sixth Annual Symposium on Computer Architecture, 1979, pp 58-67.

[GARE78] M. R. Garey, D. S. Johnson, F. P. Preparata, and R. E. Tarjan, "Triangulating a simple polygon," Inform. Proc. Lett. 7(4), pp. 175-180 (1978).

[PARK80] Fredrick J. Parke, "Simulation and Expected Performance Analysis of Multiple processor Z-Buffer Systems," Proceedings SIGGRAPH '80, 1980, pp. 48-56.

[PIXA84] A. Levinthal, T. Porter, "Chap - A SIMD Graphics Processor," Proceedings SIGGRAPH '84, 1984, pp. 77-82.

[SPRL82] R.F. Sproull, " Using program transformations to derive line- drawing algorithms," ACM Transactions on Graphics, Vol. 4, Oct 1982 pp. 259-273.

APPENDIX - INNER DRAW LOOP OF GRAPHIC ALGORITHMS

-A- ARBITRARY ANGLE LINE ALGORITHM

```
while( count > 0 ) {
    vbm[ address ] = color ;
    address += delta_address;
    resid   += delta_resid;
    if( resid >= 0 ) {
        address += chng_address;
        resid   += chng_resid;
        }
    count--;
    }
}
```

-B- SPECIAL ANGLE LINE ALGORITHM

```
while( count > 0 ) {
    vbm[ address ] = color ;
    address += delta_address;
    count--;
    }
}
```

-C- POLYGON FILL ALGORITHM

Row fill only

```
scan_line( p->vr, p->vt, end_edge);
scan_line( p->vb, p->vr, end_edge);
scan_line( p->vb, p->vl, start_edge);
scan_line( p->vl, p->vt, start_edge);

y_out = y_min << L;
for( y = y_min ; y<= y_max ; y += NPROC ) {
    for( x = start_edge[y] ; x <= end_edge[y] ; x++ ) {
        address = x + y_out;
        vbm[ address ] = color ;
    }
    y_out += NPROC << L;
}
```

-D- RECTANGLE FILL ALGORITHM

```
while( cnt_outer > 0 ) {
    for( i=0 ; i< cnt_inner ; i++ ) {
        vbm[ address ] = color ;
        address += delta_address;
        }
    address += chng_address;
    cnt_outer--;
    }
}
```

Isaac D. Scherson is an Assistant Professor in the Department of Electrical and Computer Engineering at the University of California, Santa Barbara. He received a BSEE and a MSEE from the National University of Mexico, and a PhD in Computer Sciences from the Weizmann Institute of Science, Rehovot, Israel. Dr. Scherson's main research interests lie in the general area of parallel processing. He has received considerable support from the National Science Foundation for his reseach in Associative Processing. The introduction of the Orthogonal Access Multiprocessing system led his group to the discovery of novel numerical and non-numerical algorithms for the resulting computational model (e.g. Shear-Sort). Computer Graphics is another area of interest. Dr. Scherson is currently studying parallel processing techniques applied to image generation and rendering.
Isaac Scherson is a member of the ACM and the IEEE.

Steven P. Punte (IEEE M'81) was born in Syracuse, NY on February 18 1956. He received his B.S. degree in 1983 and his M.S. degree in 1986 both in electrical and computer engineering from the University of California Santa Barbara. He has contributed his services to such companies as Hewlett-Packard, Harris, and Raytheon on various research projects. His expertise span a broad range from analog to digital and microwave to operating systems. He is presently teaching senior levels engineering courses at U.C. Santa Barbara and pursuing research in new data base structures for CAD tools.

A VLSI Algorithm for Computing Form-Factors in Radiative Transfer Computer Image Synthesis*

Jichun Bu and Ed F. Deprettere

ABSTRACT

In this paper we describe a novel algorithm for accelerating the computation of form-factors in the so-called radiosity technique for CAD 3D-image synthesis. The described algorithm is suitable for VLSI multi-processor implementation. Pipelined CORDIC processors are used as processing elements (PE's). Basically, the algorithm implements the hemi-cube approximation technique, where the surface(patch)-to-hemi-cube projections are computed by ray-tracing. Object surfaces are approximated by polygon patches for which constant radiosity is assumed. An algorithm for ray-tracing convex polygons with CORDIC processors is described. Applications of this ray-tracing algorithm are by no means limited to the computation of form-factors as described here.

Keywords: VLSI for Computer graphics, radiosity, form-factors, ray-tracing, (silicon) algorithms, CORDIC processor.

1. INTRODUCTION

Determining global illumination effects accurately plays an important role in three dimensional computer image synthesis. Goral et al, [3] have introduced a method which models the interaction of light between diffusely reflecting surfaces. The "diffuse" and "ambient" terms found in typical image synthesis algorithms are represented accurately. This light model, also referred to as radiosity method, is used to synthesize realistic images of non-existent scenes [4]. It gives a good prediction of global illumination effects.

The light radiosity method calculates object-to-object diffuse reflections of light within a complex environment. The object surfaces are assumed to have "ideal" diffuse, or so called "Lambertian" reflection; i.e., the incident light is reflected from a surface in all directions with equal intensity. Each surface is treated as a secondary light source: after reflection from a surface, the history of rays is lost. Radiosity b of a surface (patch) is defined as the total rate of energy leaving the surface (patch), which is equal to the sum of emitted energy e and reflected energy e_r. (The energy rate has dimension energy per unit time per unit area per unit frequency interval). The reflected energy is equal to the reflection coefficient ρ of the surface times the total incident energy e_{inc}. Clearly, only a fraction $f_{i,j}$ of the energy leaving a surface (patch) P_j will land on another surface P_i. The factor $f_{i,j}$ is called the form-factor between P_j and P_i. The total energy incident on a surface (patch) is the sum of incident energies radiated from all surfaces.

In a closed environment, the object surfaces are subdivided into small areas, or patches. In this paper, a patch is considered to be a convex polygon with constant radiosity. For each patch we can write the energy balance equation

$$b_i = e_i + \rho_i \sum_{j=1}^{N} f_{i,j} b_j, \ 1 \leqslant i \leqslant N,$$

* This work has been supported by the Dutch National Applied Science Foundation under grant STW DEL 44.0643.

where N is the number of patches, b_i is the radiosity of patch P_i, e_i is the rate of emitted light energy, ρ_i is the reflectivity of P_i and $f_{i,j}$ is the form-factor between P_j and P_i. In matrix form, the above equation can be written as:

$$(I - \Lambda F)B = E_{emt.}.$$ (1.1)

where $B = \{b_i\}$, $E_{emt} = \{e_i\}$, $\Lambda = diag(\rho_i)$ and, $F = \{f_{i,j}\}$.

Equation (1.1) describes an equilibrium energy balance within the enclosure. When the form-factors are known, the radiosity B is obtained by solving the set of linear equations (1.1).

Computing the form-factors is a time consuming task. The exact calculation of a form-factor requires the evaluation of a double surface integral [1,2]. An approximating calculation, called the "hemi-cube" projection method, is described in [4]. It approximates a hemispherical projection by projecting a surface onto a hemi-cube. The form-factor is then approximated by the sum of "delta-form-factors". Although this approach considerably reduces the computational complexity, the total time needed to generate an image is still dominated by the form-factor computations.

In this paper, we describe a VLSI algorithm to accelerate the form-factor calculations. It is suitable for VLSI multi-processor implementation, in particular using high throughput pipelined CORDIC processors [6,9]. (A brief description of a CORDIC algorithm and its VLSI implementation is given in appendix B). In our algorithm, the surface (patch) to hemi-cube projections are determined by ray-tracing.

The remainder of the paper is organized as follow. In the next section we discuss the approximative form-factor computation which is based on ray-tracing techniques. In section 3 we give an algorithm to compute ray-patch (polygon) intersections using (pipelined) CORDIC processors. This algorithm can also be used in a more general ray-tracing system. In section 4 we describe a multiprocessor system for computing the form-factors.

2. COMPUTING A FORM-FACTOR BY USING THE RAY-TRACING TECHNIQUE

In this section, we first give a definition of form-factor. Then, we give a brief description of the hemi-cube projection method for an approximative computation of form-factors. A detailed description of this method can be found in [4]. Finally, we show how the ray-tracing technique can be invoked to further simplify and speed up the computation of form-factors.

2.1 The Form-Factors

Within a closed environment, the form-factor $f_{i,j}$ between surfaces A_j and A_i is defined as the average energy leaving surface A_j which lands on surface A_i. That is, [1,4]:

$$f_{i,j} = \frac{1}{A_j} \int_{A_j} \int_{A_i} \frac{\cos\phi_j \cos\phi_i}{\pi r^2} HID(j,i) dA_j dA_i.$$ (2.1)

where the distance r and the angles ϕ_j and ϕ_i are as shown in Figure 1, and

$$HID(j,i) = \begin{cases} 1 \text{ if } dA_j \text{ can "see" } dA_i \\ 0 \text{ if } not \end{cases}$$

Because of the double integral, the computation of the form-factor $f_{i,j}$ is a fairly time consuming task. Different methods to evaluate this integral have been developed [1,4]. In [1], Nusselt introduced a hemisphere projection technique. The idea is illustrated in Figure 2(a) for the 2D case, where the form-factor is the fraction of the x-axis covered by the projection of the surface A onto the unit circle.

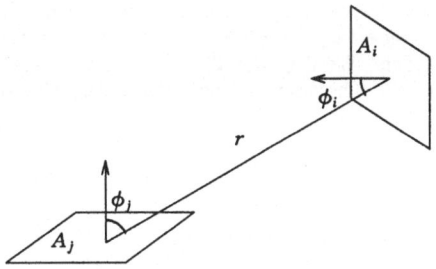

Figure 1. Form-Factor Geometry.

2.2 The Hemi-Cube Method

The hemi-cube projection method described in [4] gives an approximation of the projection of a surface onto a hemisphere. As shown in Figure 2(b), a hemi-cube is constructed around the hemi-sphere. The surface of the hemi-cube is divided into "pixels". The i-th pixel has a delta-form-factor Δf_i. The value of Δf_i is pre-calculated and stored in a table, referred to as F-table. Now, instead of projecting A onto the hemisphere, A is projected onto the hemi-cube and the form-factor is then obtained as $\sum_j \Delta f_j$. This result is correct only if the pixels entering this sum are all completely covered by the projection. (We will explain hereafter how to determine whether a pixel is covered by a projection). When a pixel is covered by more surface projections, then the closest surface is accounted for.

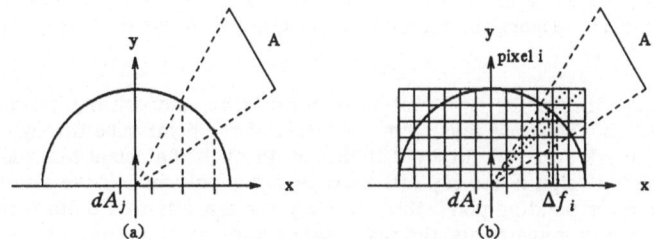

Figure 2. Hemi-Sphere/Hemi-Cube Methods.

2.3 Approximating the Projection by using Ray-Tracing Technique

Here we start out with a known technique to classify the pixels. Then we give an alternative, which is as accurate as the known one but is better suited for our purpose.

Let us look at a typical projection of a polygon on a hemi-cube(see Figure 3). To determine whether or not a pixel is covered by the projection, the projected polygon is approximated firstly by the "closest" pixel contour (line segments connecting pixel vertices). The commonly used algo-rithm is Bresenham's line algorithm [7]. In this algorithm, an edge-grid line intersection is rounded to the closest grid point. In Figure 3, edges of the projected polygon are represented by the solid lines. The result of Bresenham's algorithm is given by the dashed line segments. The area between the edges of the two polygons represents the error introduced by the approximation. In this method, a pixel is said to be inside the projection polygon when its area is inside the Bresenham's approximation for more than 50%.

Now let us look at an alternative approach. Using the same example, we mark a pixel with a dot if the center of the pixel is inside the projected polygon, and we mark a pixel with a "+" if the center of the pixel is on an edge. We consider then the dotted pixels as covered, and the pixels marked with "+" as half covered. The resulting polygon is also shown in Figure 3 by dotted line segments.

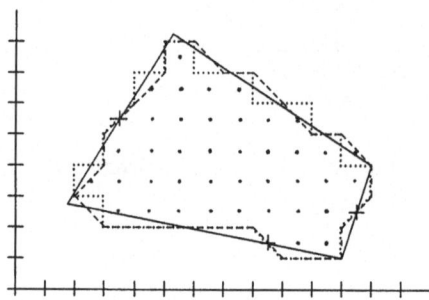

Figure 3. Approximating a polygon.

The results of the above two approaches differ only at the pixels containing edge segments or vertices. Suppose that the area of a pixel is much smaller than the area of the projection such that a pixel can only contain (1) a segment of an edge, or (2) a vertex of the projected polygon. Then it can be shown that both methods make the largest error, greater than $\frac{1}{2}\Delta f$, at the pixel containing a vertex of the projected polygon; and the error in the pixel containing an edge segment is in both cases smaller than $\frac{1}{2}\Delta f$. Hence the second method can also be used for approximating the projected polygon.

The second approach allows the classification of pixels using ray-tracing, without actually performing the projection. We trace rays from the origin of the hemi-cube through the center of the pixels, and (1) we mark a pixel with a dot if the ray through that pixel hits the polygon; (2) we mark the pixel with "+" sign if the ray hits an edge of the polygon. If we assign to each ray the same index as the corresponding pixel, then each ray corresponds to a delta-form-factor as well. So, the hemi-cube can be replaced by the rays passing through the center of the pixels. We will call the rays corresponding to the hemi-cube at the origin $(0,0,0)$, above the y-z plane normalized rays. The computation of ray-polygon intersection is discussed in the next section.

3. COMPUTING A RAY-POLYGON INTERSECTION USING (PIPELINED) CORDIC PROCESSORS

In this section, we give an algorithm which computes ray-polygon patch intersections. The main operations are planar vector rotations, which can be accomplished in CORDIC arithmetic.

A patch P is characterized by an ordered list of vertex points $\bar{P}_i$, which are defined in the normalized device coordinate system [7], and the unit normal $\bar{n}_p = (x_p, y_p, z_p)^t$ of the plane N of the polygon:

$$P : \{ (\bar{n}_p, \bar{P}_i) \mid \bar{P}_i = (x_i, y_i, z_i)^t, i = 1, 2, ... m \}.$$

Recall that all the patches are assumed to be convex polygons. Without loss of generality, we shall assume that the vertices are numbered clockwise.

A ray $\bar{R}$ is characterized by its origin $\bar{P}_r$ and a unit vector $\bar{r} = (x_r, y_r, z_r)^t$ specifying the direction of the ray. A point on the ray is specified by the vector, that is,

$$\bar{R}(t) = \bar{P}_r + t*\bar{r}, t > 0,$$

where t measures the distance from the point from $\bar{P}_r$ along the ray. Without loss of generality, we assume from now on that $\bar{P}_r = \bar{0}$.

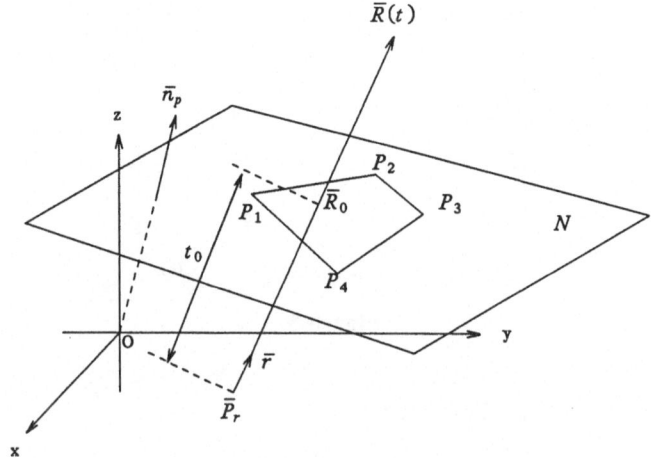

Figure 4. Ray-Tracing Convex Planar Polygon.

The intersection of the ray with the polygon is computed in two steps (see Figure 4). First, the intersection $\bar{R}_0$ of the ray $\bar{R}(t)$ with the plane N of the polygon, if any, is calculated. Note that $\bar{R}_0 = \bar{R}(t_0) = t_0*\bar{r}$. Then, we test whether $\bar{R}_0$ is enclosed by the polygon P. If $\bar{R}_0$ is inside (or on an edge of) the polygon, the ray intersects the polygon at $t_0*\bar{r}$. Otherwise there is no intersection.

3.1 Computing Intersection of the Ray with the Plane of the Polygon

Suppose $\bar{R}(t)$ intersects N at $\bar{R}_0$. $\bar{R}_0$ satisfies the equation

$$\bar{n}_p \cdot (\bar{R}_0 - \bar{P}_i) = 0 \text{ or } \bar{n}_p \cdot (t_0*\bar{r} - \bar{P}_i) = 0, \tag{3.1}$$

where P_i could be any vertex of P. Now if Σ is an orthogonal matrix transformation, i.e., $\Sigma\Sigma^t = I$, then the equation (3.1) is invariant under Σ:

$$(\Sigma\bar{n}_p) \cdot (t_0* \Sigma\bar{r} - \Sigma\bar{P}_i) = 0. \tag{3.2}$$

We can chose Σ in such a way that $\Sigma\bar{n}_p = (1,0,0)^t$. It is easy to show that Σ is then of the form:

$$\Sigma = \Sigma(\theta_2)\Sigma(\theta_1) = \begin{vmatrix} \cos\theta_2 & \sin\theta_2 & 0 \\ -\sin\theta_2 & \sin\theta_2 & 0 \\ 0 & 0 & 1 \end{vmatrix} \begin{vmatrix} \cos\theta_1 & 0 & \sin\theta_1 \\ 0 & 1 & 0 \\ -\sin\theta_1 & 0 & \cos\theta_1 \end{vmatrix}. \tag{3.3}$$

where $\theta_1 = \tan^{-1}(z_p/x_p)$, $\theta_2 = \tan^{-1}(y_p/x_p^{\cdot})$ and $x_p^{\cdot} = x_p\cos\theta_1 + z_p\sin\theta_1$.

Once Σ is known, we compute transformed vectors as follows:

$$(\bar{r}, \bar{P}_1, \bar{P}_2, \cdots, \bar{P}_m) = \Sigma(\theta_2)\Sigma(\theta_1)(\bar{r}, \bar{P}_1, \bar{P}_2, \cdots, \bar{P}_m). \tag{3.4}$$

Since the normal to the plane N' is $(1,0,0)^t$, N' is completely specified by $x'=d$, where $d \geqslant 0$ is the distance between N' and the $z'-y'$ plane. Hence we have $x'_1 = x'_2 = \cdots = x'_m = d$.

Referring to Figure 5(a) for a symbolic representation of a CORDIC processor, a flow–graph representation of the equations (3.3) and (3.4) is shown in Figure 5(b).

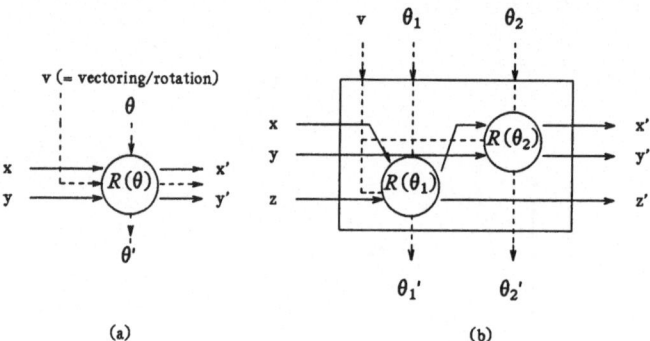

(a)   (b)

Figure 5

Finally, from equation (3.2), t_0 follows from

$$t_0 * x'_r - x'_1 = 0,$$ (3.5)

and the intersection with N' is given by

$$t_0 * \vec{r} = t_0 * (x'_r, y'_r, z'_r) = (x'_1, t_0 * y'_r, t_0 * z'_r).$$ (3.6)

If $x'_r < 0$, then t_0 will be negative, hence the ray $\vec{R}(t)$ will not intersect the plane N', nor the plane N; if $x'_r = 0$, then there are infinitely many intersections; i.e., the ray lies in the plane N. The corresponding pixel does not contribute to the form-factor.

The solution to equations (3.5) and (3.6) can also be obtained in CORDIC arithmetic using vectorization and rotation operations in the linear coordinate system (see appendix B). First we compute t_0 by vectoring the vector $(x'_r, -x'_1)$:

$$\begin{bmatrix} * \\ 0 \end{bmatrix} = \begin{bmatrix} 1 & 0 \\ t_0 & 1 \end{bmatrix} \begin{bmatrix} x'_r \\ -x'_i \end{bmatrix}.$$ (3.7)

Then, the y and z components of the intersection are obtained by rotating the vectors $(y'_r, 0)$ and $(z'_r, 0)$ over t_0:

$$\begin{bmatrix} * \\ y \end{bmatrix} = \begin{bmatrix} 1 & 0 \\ t_0 & 1 \end{bmatrix} \begin{bmatrix} y'_r \\ 0 \end{bmatrix}, \quad \begin{bmatrix} * \\ z \end{bmatrix} = \begin{bmatrix} 1 & 0 \\ t_0 & 1 \end{bmatrix} \begin{bmatrix} z'_r \\ 0 \end{bmatrix}.$$ (3.8)

Note that since we are assuming normalized device coordinates, t_0 will always be bounded $(max(|t|) \leqslant \sqrt{3})$.

In this way, we can compute t_0 and the intersection point $\vec{R}'_0 = t_0 * (x'_r, y'_r, z'_r)$ by using CORDIC operations only. The processor configuration for computing equations (3.7) and (3.8) is shown in Figure 6. When pipelined CORDIC processors are used (see appendix B), high throughputs can be obtained.

3.2 Testing Whether the Intersection Point Is Enclosed by the Polygon

Once the intersection $\overline{R}'_0$ is known, the next step is to test whether this point is inside (or on an edge of) the polygon. It is easy to show that the point $\overline{R}(t_0)$ is inside (or on an edge of) the polygon P, if and only if $\overline{R}'_0$ is inside (or on an edge of) the polygon P', where $P' = \{(1,0,0)^t, \overline{P}'_i \mid i = 1,2,....,m\}$.

We introduce vectors $V_i = \overline{P}'_i - \overline{R}'_0$, and angles $\phi_i \in [-\pi,\pi]$ between the V_i and the positive y' axis, for $i = 1,2,....,m$. Since all the vectors have the same x component, we ignore the x component of the vectors in the computation. Now if $\Sigma(\phi_i)$ is a circular rotation, we compute the vectors V'_{i+1} according to

$$V'_{i+1} = \Sigma(\phi_i)V_{i+1}, i = 1,2,\cdots,m-1, V'_1 = \Sigma(\phi_m)V_1. \tag{3.9}$$

The order in which the vectors are rotated must be as indicated. To determine whether $\overline{R}'_0$ is inside or on an edge of the polygon P' we use the following proposition. The proof of the proposition is given in Appendix A.

Proposition : Suppose that the V_i, ϕ_i, $\Sigma(\phi_i)$ and V'_i, for $i = 1,2,....,m$ are defined as above. Then :

1. $\overline{R}'_0$ is inside P' *iff* the z' components of all the vectors V'_i's are non-zero and have the same sign.

2. If there is one (or more) V'_i with zero z' component, and all the non-zero z' components have the same sign, then $\overline{R}'_0$ is on an edge of P'.

Clearly, computing the angles ϕ_i and signs of the V'_i can be both carried out by a CORDIC operation. The angle ϕ_i is computed by vectoring V_i and the sign of the z' component of V'_{i+1} is determined by rotating the vector V_{i+1} over the angle ϕ_i. These operations are repeated for all the V_i's and V_{i+1}'s, in the order specified in (3.9). In this case, the same CORDIC configuration is used as the one shown in Figure 6, now using the circular coordinate system.

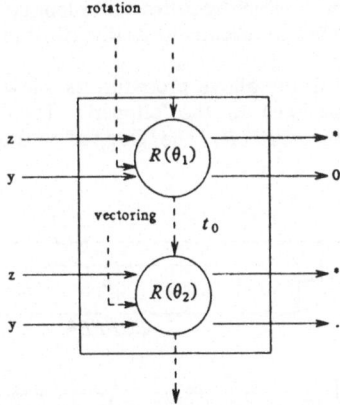

Figure 6. Processor Configuration for Equation 3.7 and 3.8.

4. A SILICON ALGORITHM FOR COMPUTING THE FORM-FACTORS

In the radiosity technique, we have to compute a matrix F of form-factors as required in equation 1.1. In this section, we present a VLSI algorithm for the computation of this matrix by using the ray-tracing method described in the previous sections.

Suppose that there are N surfaces (patches). A procedure for computing the form-factors $f_{i,j}$, $i,j = 1,2,...,N$, is given below. In this procedure, computing the projections of the patches onto a hemi-cube is accomplished by implementing the ray-tracing algorithm described in sections 2 and 3. In addition to the patch specifications given in the previous section, we also assume that the coordinates of the centers $P_{i,c}$ of the patches are available.

For each patch P_i, $i = 1,2,...,N$ {
PartI : transform and clip;
    - Transform the origin of the coordinate system to $P_{i,c}$.
    - Determine $\Sigma = \Sigma(\theta_2)\Sigma(\theta_1)$, such that $\Sigma \bar{n}_{P_i} = (1,0,0)^t$.
    - For each patch P_j, $j = 1,2,...,N$ {
        - Transform P_j to the new origin $P_{i,c}$.
        - Determine $P'_j = \Sigma P_j$.
        - If not all the x-components of P_j have negative sign,
            add P_j to a patch buffer *BUFFER*.
    }
PartII : compute the intersections;
    - Computing the intersections of normalized ray r_i with the patches $P_j \in BUFFER$.
    - If a ray hits one patch, P_k, store the index of the patch in the corresponding pixel.
    If a ray hits more than one patch, P_k
    store the index of the patch which has the smallest t_0 in the corresponding pixel.
PartIII : table lookup;
    - For each patch P_j, $P_j \in BUFFER$ {
        $f_{j,i} = \sum_q f_q$, where the patch number stored in pixel q is equal to j,
        and f_q is the delta-form-factor of the pixel q.
    }
}

Procedure: computing the form-factors in CORDIC arithmetic.

Except for part III of the procedure, which requires table-lookup and addition operations, all the other operations can be done in CORDIC arithmetic as described in the previous sections.

A full-size system architecture for the above procedure is shown in Figure 7. To compute the form-factor $f_{*,i}$, P_i is firstly assigned to the "clipper". Then, other patches are selected by "Clipper" and loaded into the buffer *BUFFER*. The "Clipper" will only select those patches that are

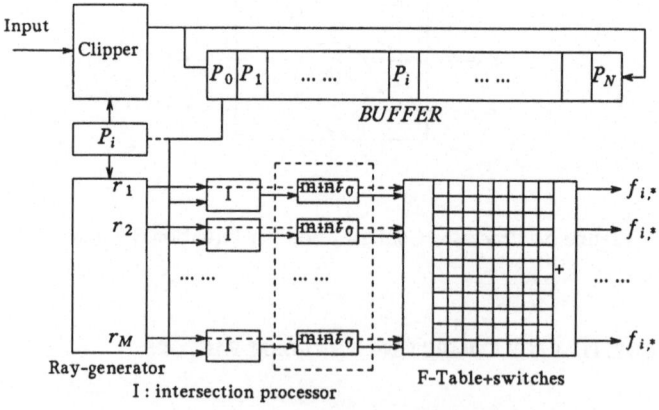

Figure 7. System Architecture.

"above" it; i.e., those patches which have at least one positive x' coordinate. The intersection processors can already be started after the first patch is loaded into the buffer. Intersections of the rays with all the patches in the buffer are computed. For each ray, the index of the patch which has the smallest t_0 is passed to the unit F-table+switches (see Figure 7). After the table lookup, the form-factors are generated.

5. CONCLUDING REMARKS

Computing form-factors is a time consuming task. In this paper we have described a VLSI implementable algorithm for accelerating form-factor calculations. The application is not restricted to computer graphics. Indeed, there are many other applications that involve form-factor computations [1].

It is evident that the ray tracing technique is a powerful approach. This technique is exploited in the algorithm presented in this paper. Since rays can be traced independently, the algorithm is highly parallel. Also, the system can be partitioned in many ways without too much effort. This property makes the trade off between execution time and the amount of hardware flexible.

The algorithm for computing ray-convex polygon intersections with CORDIC processors can also be used in a general ray-tracing system.

In Figure 7 we give a straightforward implementation of the procedure of section 4. The problem of partitioning will be discussed elsewhere. We have not mentioned how the patches are organized within a system. When a more sophisticated database is used for coding patches, e.g. an octree [8], patches can be pre-selected at high rate before they are loaded into the system. Hence less intersection computations will be required.

6. ACKNOWLEDGEMENTS

The authors would like to thank A. de Lange and A. van der Hoeven for providing the CORDIC processor illustrations.

7. APPENDIX A

In this appendix we give a proof of the proposition in section 3.2. Without loss of generality, we assume that the intersection $\overline{R}'_0$ is at the origin, and all the vectors are in the z'-y' plane. So we have $V_i = \overline{P}_i$, for $i = 1,2,....,m$. (see section 3.2). Note that V_i's are assumed being numbered clockwise. Suppose that $\phi_i \in [-\pi,\pi]$ is the angle of V_i with the positive y' axis, for $i = 1,2,....,m$, and $\Sigma(\phi_i)$ is a circular rotation. We compute the new vectors in the given order :

$$V'_{i+1} = \Sigma(\phi_i)V_{i+1}, i = 1,2, \cdots ,m-1, V'_1 = \Sigma(\phi_m)V_1.$$

Proposition : Suppose that the V_i, ϕ_i, $\Sigma(\phi_i)$ and V'_i, for $i = 1,2,....,m$ are defined as above, Then :

1. $\overline{R}'_0$ is inside P' iff the z' components of all the vectors V'_i's are non-zero and they have the same sign.

2. If there is one (or more) V'_i with zero z' component, and all the non-zero z' components have the same sign, then $\overline{R}'_0$ is on an edge of P'.

We shall give a proof of case (1) only. The proof of case (2) is similar and is omitted.

Proof.: In this proof we use the following facts. Suppose that u_i is the unit vector in the direction of V_i', for $i = 1,2,...,m$. If we rotate a unit vector u from u_1 to u_2 ...., from u_{m-1} to u_m and then back to u_1, then, (1) if the origin is enclosed by the convex polygon P', the sum of angles over which u is rotated is equal to 2π and the direction of the rotations are all the same; (2) if the origin is outside the polygon, the sum of angles over which u is rotated is equal to zero and there is at least one rotation direction that is opposite to the others.

In our case, the rotation direction from u_i to u_{i+1}, for $i = 1,2,....m-1$, is indicated by the sign of the z'-component of the vector V_i' and, the rotation direction from u_m to u_1 is indicated by the sign of the z' component of the vector V_1' defined above. Thus, if the z' components of all vectors V_i' are non-zero and have the same sign, then the origin is enclosed by polygon P' and *vice versa*. Hence the proof.

8. APPENDIX B

CORDIC stands for *coordinate rotation digital computer*. It is a rotation algorithm, which was originally proposed by Volder [10]. This algorithm was modified and optimized by the authors [6]. In this appendix we give a quick description of our CORDIC algorithm. A CMOS CORDIC pipeline processor is currently being designed and is described elsewhere [9].

The behavior of our CORDIC algorithm is summarized by the following proposition.

Proposition: Given the "micro-rotations"

$$\begin{bmatrix} x_{i+1}(n+1) \\ y_{i+1}(n+1) \end{bmatrix} = R(\sigma_i(n),m_i(n))\begin{bmatrix} x_i(n) \\ y_i(n) \end{bmatrix} \tag{8.1}$$

where,

- $R(\sigma_i(n),m_i(n)) = \begin{vmatrix} 1 & -m_i(n)\sigma_i(n)(2^{-S_i}+\eta_{m,i}2^{-S_i'}) \\ \sigma_i(n)(2^{-S_i}+\eta_{m,i}2^{-S_i'}) & 1 \end{vmatrix};$

- $m_i(n) = \pm 1$ *and* $m_{i+1}(n+1) = m_i(n)$;

- $i = 1,2,....,p$ *(p=17 in our case as shown in Table 1), $n = ...,-1,0,1,....$;*

- S_i, S_i' *and* $\eta_{m,i}$ *are given in Table 1;*

- $\sigma_i(n) = \pm 1$ *is either given or equal to the sign of* $y_i(n)$, *that is* $\sigma_i(n) = \begin{cases} 1 & \text{if } y_i(n) \geqslant 0 \\ -1 & \text{else} \end{cases}$.

Then, there exist constant numbers K_m, as given in Table 1, such that

$$K_m \cdot R(\sigma_p(n+p),m_p(n+p)) \cdot R(\sigma_{p-1}(n+p-1),m_{p-1}(n+p-1)) \cdots \tag{8.2}$$

$$\cdots R(\sigma_0(n),m_0(n)) = \begin{vmatrix} \cos(m^{\frac{1}{2}}\alpha_m(n)) & -m^{\frac{1}{2}}\sin(m^{\frac{1}{2}}\alpha_m(n)) \\ m^{-\frac{1}{2}}\sin(m^{\frac{1}{2}}\alpha_m(n)) & \cos(m^{\frac{1}{2}}\alpha_m(n)) \end{vmatrix}$$

where,

- $m = m_0(n)$;

- $R(\sigma_0(n),m_0(n)) = \begin{vmatrix} \frac{1}{2}(1-m) & -\frac{1}{2}(1+m)\sigma_0(n) \\ \frac{1}{2}(1+m)\sigma_0(n) & \frac{1}{2}(1-m) \end{vmatrix} \cdot \sigma_0(n) = \pm 1;$

- $\alpha_m(n) = \sum_{i=0}^{p} \sigma_i(n+i)\alpha_{m,i}$ *for all* $|\alpha_m(n)| \leqslant \pi$, $\alpha_{m,0} = \frac{1}{2}(1+m)\frac{1}{2}\pi$;

- $m^{-\frac{1}{2}}\tan(m^{\frac{1}{2}}\alpha_{m,i}) = 2^{-S_i} + \eta_{m,i}2^{-S_i'}.$

The reader can verify the statement by substituting the parameters given in Table 1 in equations (8.1) and (8.2). Using these parameters, the accuracy of $\alpha_m(n)$ is 16-bit.

TABLE 1. Optimal CORDIC parameters

index i	S,S,η_{-1}	S,S,η_1	α_{-1}	α_1
1	0 4 -1	0 3 +1	1.716994	0.844154
2	1 8 -1	1 8 +1	0.544111	0.466768
3	1 6 -1	1 6 +1	0.528685	0.476069
4	2 14 -1	2 14 +1	0.255348	0.245036
5	2 4 -1	2 4 -1	0.189745	0.185348
6	4 6 +1	4 6 +1	0.078285	0.077967
7	4 10 -1	4 10 -1	0.061601	0.061446
8	5	5	0.031260	0.031240
9	6	6	0.015626	0.015624
10	7	7	0.007813	0.007812
11	8	8	0.003906	0.003906
12	9	9	0.001953	0.001953
13	10	10	0.000977	0.000977
14	11	11	0.000488	0.000488
15	12	12	0.000244	0.000244
16	13	13	0.000122	0.000122
17	14	14	0.000061	0.000061
$K_{-1} \approx 4.0000058651 \approx 2^2$				
$K_1 \approx 0.5000096615 \approx 2^{-1}$				

In case $\sigma_i(n+i)$ is given for all i, the operation of the CORDIC is referred to as *rotation*, while in case $\sigma_i(n+i)$ is computed from the data (i.e., $[x_0(n),y_0(n)]^t$), the operation of the CORDIC is referred to as *vectoring*. In CORDIC terminology, the value of $m_i(n)$ specifies the *coordinate system* of the operations: the coordinate system is *circular* or *hyperbolic* if $m_i(n)=1$, or -1, respectively. A trivial case omitted here is $m_i(n)=0$, in which case, the coordinate system is called *linear*. Figure 8 shows the logical scheme of a micro-rotation (8.1). The cascade (8.2) is implemented in CMOS as a pipeline and is described in details in [9] (see Figure 9).

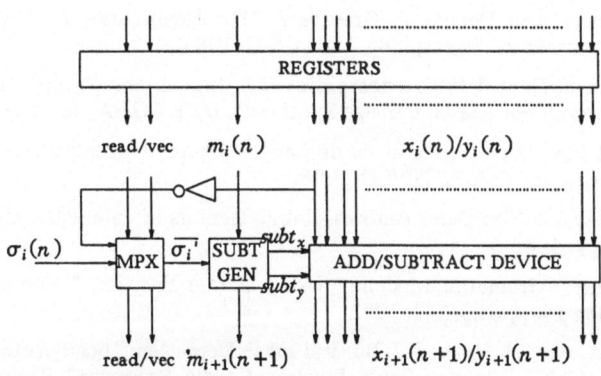

Figure 8. Logical Scheme of a Micro-Rotation.

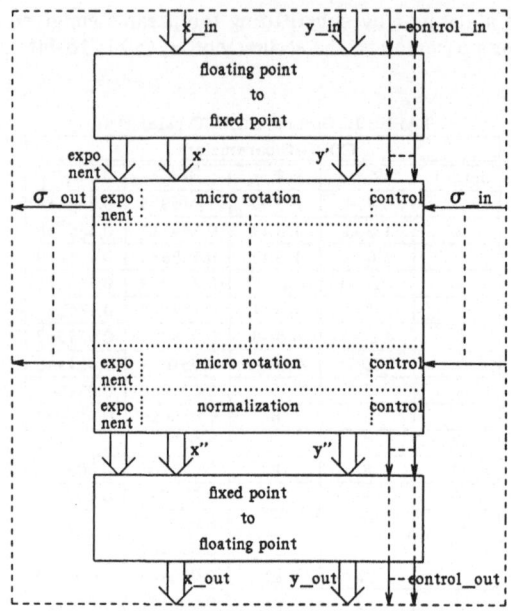

Figure 9. The CORDIC Processor Architecture.

9. REFERENCES

[1] Siegel, Robert and Howell, John R., "Thermal Radiation Heat Transfer," Hemisphere Publishing Corporation, Washington, 1978.

[2] Sparrow, E.M. and Cess R.D., "Radiation Heat Transfer," Hemisphere Publishing Corporation, Washington, 1978.

[3] Goral, Cindy M. Torrance, Kenneth E., Greenberg, Donald P., Battaile, Bennett, "Modeling the Interaction of Light Between Diffuse Surfaces," ACM Computer Graphics (proceedings 1984), pp.213-222.

[4] Michael F. Cohen and Donald P. Greenberg, "The Hemi-Cube, A Radiosity Solution for Complex Environments," Siggraph'85, Vol. 19(3), 1985.

[5] Michael F. Cohen, Donald P. Greenberg, David S. Immel, and Philip J. Brock, "An Efficient Radiosity Approach For Realistic Image Synthesis", IEEE CG&A, 26-35, march 1986.

[6] Jichun Bu, Ed F.A. Deprettere and A. de Lange, "On the Optimization of Pipelined Silicon CORDIC Algorithms," Proc. EUSIPCO-1986.

[7] Foley, James D., and Van Dam, Andries, "Fundamentals of Interactive Computer Graphics", Addison-Wesley, 1982.

[8] Donald Meagher, "Geometric Modeling Using Octree Encoding," Computer Graphics and Image Processing 19, pp.129-147, 1982.

[9] Lange, A. de, A. van der Hoeven, J. Bu, and Ed F. Deprettere, "Semi-Automatic Silicon Compilation of a CMOS Floating-Point Pipeline Cordic Processor," Technical Report Delft University of Technology, Delft, The Netherlands, Jan. 1987.

[10] Volder, J.E., "The Cordic Trigonometric Computing Technique," IRE Trans. Electronic Computers, Vol. EC-8(3), pp.330-340 (1959).

BIOGRAPHIES

Jichun Bu was born in ChangChun, China, on March 22, 1960 and is a student member of the IEEE. He graduated from the Delft University of Technology, Delft, The Netherlands, in 1985. Currently he is doing his Ph.D. at this university, in the department of Electrical Engineering, Network Theory Section. His interests are mainly in dedicated VLSI systems for computer algorithms, VLSI for computer graphics and systolic arrays.

Dr. Ed F.A. Deprettere (M'1980) was born in Roeselare, Belgium, on August 10, 1944. He received the MS degree from the Gent State University, Gent, Belgium, in 1968 and the Ph.D. degree from the Delft University of Technology, Delft, The Netherlands, in 1981.

In 1970 he became a research assistant and lecturer at the DUT and is now an associate professor at this university, department of electrical engineering, Network Theory Section, Signal Processing Group. His current research interests are in VLSI and Modern Signal Processing, computer graphics, VLSI systolic/wavefront array processing and mappings of signal processing algorithms and matrix equations on silicon.

Authors Address: Department of Electrical Engineering, Section Network Theory, Delft University of Technology, 2628 CD Delft, The Netherlands.

Chapter 5

Computational
Geometry

B2-Splines

A Local Representation for Cubic Spline Interpolation

Charles D. Woodward

ABSTRACT

The cubic B-spline representation provides the local interaction properties and the order of continuity that are sufficient for many free-form curve and surface modeling tasks in CAD. Basic problems are nevertheless met when applying the B-splines to interpolation, where they have global behavior. We present a new class of cubic splines, the $B2$-splines, providing increased locality to the curve and surface interpolation tasks. Applications are also given with the skinning method for interactive surface modeling.

Keywords: free-form modeling, interpolation, interaction, B-splines

1. INTRODUCTION

Ever since their advent into computer graphics in the early '70s, the *cubic B-splines* (Riesenfeld 1973) have been one of the most favored mathematical models for free-form curve and surface representation in CAD. Factors that have contributed to this are, most importantly, the C^2-continuity of the cubic B-splines that is not possessed by the cubic Bézier form or Coons patches, and local behavior, whereas e.g. the cardinal splines have global construction (Faux and Pratt 1979). Compared with the more recently introduced β-splines with the local *shape parameters* available (Barsky 1981), the B-splines on the other hand are computationally simpler, and they also support more flexible parametrization (only uniform β-splines are used in practice).

Nonetheless, the B-splines have their defects as well. In interactive design work, a disturbing fact the B-spline users must meet is that the B-spline control points are dislocated from the B-splines themselves. When a control point is moved, the B-spline curve or surface is changed in an intuitively natural manner, but adjusting the B-spline to smoothly match given exact locations is not so simple.

For *interpolating* a set of points, the B-spline curve is computed with the globally determined B-spline inversion procedure, where fluctuations and even loops are easily induced to the curve. If the interpolating B-spline curve is afterwards locally adjusted by moving the control points (or manipulating the knot vector), the interpolation property will be lost. On the other hand, relocating an interpolation point requires a recomputation of the interpolation curve, changing the curve shape globally, though only a local change near the interpolation point might rather be desired.

Equal considerations apply to interpolation with B-spline surfaces. And further, B-spline surface *modeling* and *interaction* techniques often involve interpolation as well, so the global properties of B-spline interpolation set up a general limit to the B-spline surface modeling range.

To gain locality for the B-spline interpolation, we abandon the convention of interpolating a given number of points with equally many spline segments. Instead, *two B-spline segments* are used for each interpolation point. The resulting class of splines, called as the *B2-splines*, are thus closely related to the double-quadratic (dq) representation of Varady (1985), correspondingly increasing the modeling power of the quadratic forms by compounding two quadratic segments into one dq-segment.

Besides interpolation, applications of the $B2$-spline formulation are discussed with the *skinning* (or *lofting*) method for surface modeling. Having every other control point located on the curves themselves, the $B2$-splines are also directly attractive for interactive design of curves. As a superset of the B-splines, the $B2$-splines are easily implemented to increase the modeling domain of already existing B-spline modeling systems.

2. B-SPLINES

For compactness, we will carry out our discussion with the *uniform cubic B-spline* representation. The straightforward, but somewhat laborous generalizations to the general non-uniform B-splines (deBoor 1978) are pointed out in section 7.

By definition, splines are parametric piecewise polynomial curves of order k, whose neighboring segments meet at the parameter *knots* with the parametric continuity of the $k-1$ first derivatives. Cubic splines have continuous first and second derivatives everywhere, which is referred to as C^2-continuity.

A uniform cubic B-spline curve $Q(\mathbf{u})$ is defined piecewise with the so-called *control points* V_i, $i = 0, \ldots, n+1$,

$$Q_i(u) = \sum_{r=-1}^{2} V_{i+r} b_r(u), \qquad u \in [0,1], \quad i = 1, \ldots, n-1,$$

where the B-spline *basis functions* $b_r(u)$ are

$$\begin{cases} b_{-1}(u) = (1 - 3u + 3u^2 - u^3)/6 \\ b_0(u) = (4 - 6u^2 + 3u^3)/6 \\ b_1(u) = (1 + 3u + 3u^2 - 3u^3)/6 \\ b_2(u) = u^3/6. \end{cases}$$

The B-spline curve does not pass through the control points, but imitates smoothly the path of the control points (control polygon). As each control point is involved in only four B-spline segments, moving a control point to a new location will change the B-spline curve shape locally near the modified control point. After some exercise, such local changes become easy to predict by the user, which makes the B-splines especially suitable for interactive design of free-form curves.

Bicubic uniform B-spline surfaces are defined analogously with a rectangular control mesh

$$\{\ V_{i,j}, \qquad i = 0, \ldots, m+1, \quad j = 0, \ldots, n+1\ \},$$

as the tensor product of B-spline curves

$$S_{i,j}(u,v) = \sum_{r=-1}^{2} \sum_{s=-1}^{2} V_{i+r,j+s} b_r(u) b_s(v), \qquad u,v \in [0,1], \quad i = 1, \ldots, m-1, \quad j = 1, \ldots, n-1.$$

Moving the control mesh points produce local surface changes, where sixteen (four times four) surface patches are affected by each control point $V_{i,j}$.

3. B-SPLINE INVERSION

In the B-spline inversion procedure, the B-spline curve is computed to interpolate a set of points P_i, $i = 1, \ldots, n$. This is accomplished by formally matching the B-spline knot points with the interpolation points,

$$\begin{cases} Q_i(0) = P_i, & i = 1, \ldots, n-1, \\ Q_{n-1}(1) = P_n, \end{cases}$$

yielding a set of linear equations for the B-spline control points:

$$V_{i-1} + 4V_i + V_{i+1} = 6P_i, \quad i = 1, \ldots, n. \tag{3.1}$$

To complete the set of equations, closed curves $(P_1 = P_n)$ require $V_0 = V_{n-1}$ and $V_{n+1} = V_2$ for the C^2-continuity at the boundary joint, For open curves, the two additional conditions can be determined arbitrarily, e.g. $V_0 = V_1$ and $V_{n+1} = V_n$. [1]

The resulting matrix equation is diagonally dominated, and it can be confidently solved with standard numerical methods. With Seidel iteration, the control points V_i are taken from (3.1) as

$$\begin{aligned} V_i^k &= (6P_i - V_{i-1}^k - V_{i+1}^{k-1})/4 \\ &= P_i + (P_i - (V_{i-1}^k + V_{i+1}^{k-1})/2)/2, \quad i = 1, \ldots, n, \end{aligned}$$

where k denotes iteration, and the V_i can be thereby computed in integer arithmetic with mere addition and logical shift operations (Yamaguchi 1978).

The B-spline surface inversion for a rectangular array of interpolation points

$$\{ \quad P_{i,j}, \quad i = 1, \ldots, m, \quad j = 1, \ldots, n \quad \},$$

can also be brought down to just curve interpolation computation. First, the points $P_{i,j}$ are interpolated in the cross-sectional direction, with m *section curves* for the data rows of constant i values. In the second phase, the control points of the section curves are interpolated in the longitudinal direction of constant j values, with $n + 2$ *control curves*. Connecting the control polygons of the control curves as a surface control mesh, the interpolation surface for $P_{i,j}$ becomes defined. As an additional result, the section curves will be also located on the interpolation surface. For a detailed description of the method, see e.g. (Woodward 1987).

4. B2-SPLINE CURVES

In the B-spline curve equation, each control point V_i is involved with three knot points $Q_j(0)$, $j = i-1, i, i+1$, which will all be altered when the curve shape is modified by moving V_i. Assigning a new value to one knot point $Q_i(0)$ at a time can only be accomplished through global modifications of the B-spline curve.

To achieve locality for interpolation curve interaction, we introduce an additional degree of freedom to the interpolation curves by joining every two B-spline segments $Q_{2i-1}(u)$ and $Q_{2i}(u)$ together, and assigning the interior knot points $Q_{2i}(0)$ only secondary meaning. The interpolation property will be required only of the impair knot points $Q_{2i-1}(0)$, which can then be independently controlled.

---

[1] We assume these conditions to keep the discussion similar for open and closed curves; in fact, *triple* boundary control points (Barsky 1982) are used in the figures.

Denoting the resulting representation as the *B2-splines*, the *B*-splines will serve as an underlying mathematical model for them, but filtered through a different modeling interface. Thus, in the composite *B2*-spline curve interface the *interior control points* V_{2i} are immediately displayed, but V_{2i-1} are updated only in the computer memory. Instead, the *B2-spline knot points*

$$P_i = Q_{2i-1}(0) = (V_{2i-2} + 4V_{2i-1} + V_{2i})/6. \tag{4.1}$$

are marked on the curve. A new value P_i can then be assigned to the *B2*-spline knot point $Q_{2i-1}(0)$ by adjusting the corresponding *B*-spline control point V_{2i-1} with

$$V_{2i-1} = (6P_i - V_{2i} - V_{2i-2})/4. \tag{4.2}$$

The control point V_{2i-1} influences only in the *open* interval $(Q_{2i-3}(0), (Q_{2i+1}(0))$, so no other *B2*-spline knot point than $Q_{2i-1}(0)$ will be affected in the procedure (fig. 1a).

On the other hand, if one of the interior control points V_{2i} is changed, then V_{2i-1} can be again adjusted by (4.2) to preserve $Q_{2i-1}(0) = P_i$. For maintaining also $Q_{2i+1}(0) = P_{i+1}$, the control point V_{2i+1} is similarly corrected (fig. 1b).

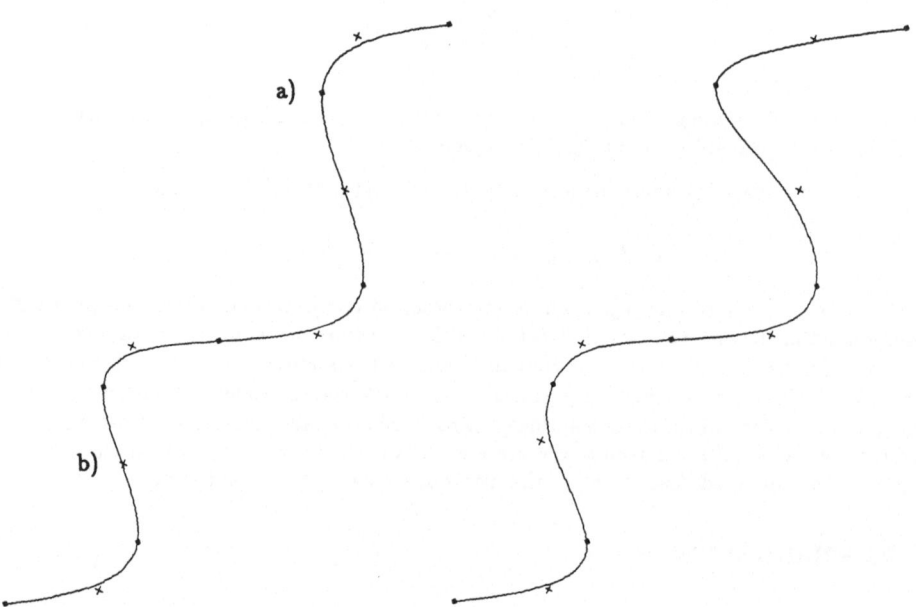

Fig. 1. *B2*-spline curve modifications

Any *B*-spline curve with impair number of control points can be interpreted as a *B2*-spline, but this does not yet solve the *B2*-spline inversion problem to match the *B2*-spline knot points with given interpolation points. To represent an interpolating *B*-spline curve as a *B2*-spline, it must first be *reparametrized* with $u \leftarrow 2u$. The subdivision method of Catmull and Clark (1978) gives the necessary formulas:

$$\begin{cases} V_{2i-1} \leftarrow (V_{i-1} + 6V_i + V_{i+1})/8, & i = 1, \ldots, n \\ V_{2i} \leftarrow (V_i + V_{i+1})/2, & i = 0, \ldots, n. \end{cases}$$

The corresponding $B2$-spline curve has then the V_{2i} acting as the interior control points, with the original interpolation points inherited as its knot points

$$\begin{cases} Q_{2i-1}(0) \leftarrow Q_i(0) = P_i, & i = 1, \ldots n-1, \\ Q_{2n-2}(1) \leftarrow Q_{n-1}(1) = P_n. \end{cases} \tag{4.3}$$

Figure 2 shows a B-spline curve first reparametrized, and then modified within the $B2$-spline representation by moving the interior control points V_{2i}. Both the curves interpolate the same data P_i, for which the interpolating B-spline curve becomes uniquely determined, whereas the $B2$-spline curve can be further adjusted to correspond with the shape of the underlying reality model.

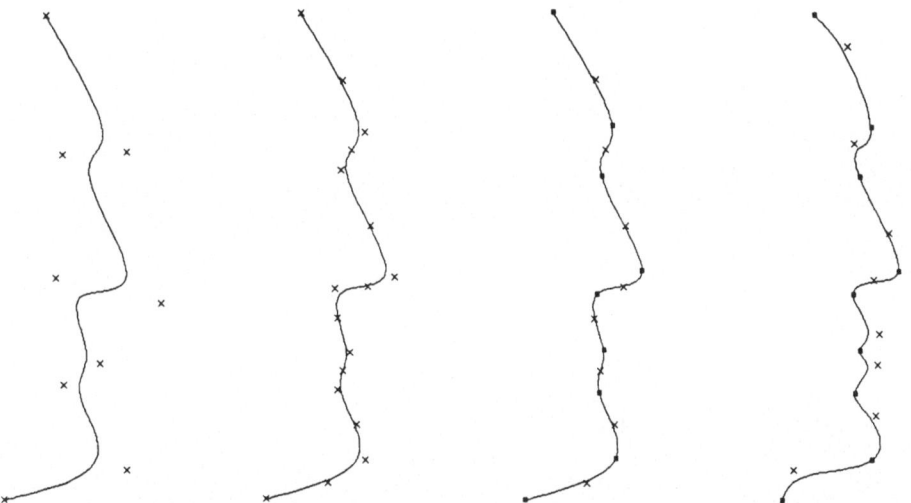

Fig. 2. B-spline curve reparametrized, and modified within the $B2$-spline representation

Although the reparametrization splits each of the original B-spline segments into two, $Q_{2i-1}(u)$ and $Q_{2i}(u)$, these will still represent just one parametric polynomial, and the segments meet at the interior knot $Q_{2i}(0)$ with third derivative continuity (with the value $8\,Q_i^{(3)}(1/2)$ of the original B-spline segment). This observation gives us a direct construction method for the $B2$-splines, where no B-spline interpolation or reparametrization is explicitly done. Demanding immediately for the C^3-continuity at the intermediate knots

$$Q_{2i-1}^{(3)}(1) = Q_{2i}^{(3)}(0), \quad i = 1, \ldots, n-1, \tag{4.4}$$

and interpolation of the P_i (equations (4.3)), leads to the set of equations

$$V_{2i-2} + 4V_{2i} + V_{2i+2} = 3(P_i + P_{i+1}), \quad i = 1, \ldots, n-1. \tag{4.5}$$

The unknowns V_{2i} can be thereby solved as discussed with the equations (3.1), and the control points V_{2i-1} are then available by the equation (4.2).

The C^3-continuity at the interior knots identifies the interpolating $B2$-spline geometrically with the B-splines. However, this is not necessary for the interpolation task as such, and some or all of the equations (4.4) can be replaced with other suitable restrictions, better matching the requirements of the specific application. This makes it possible to incorporate completely local interpolation criterion at some curve parts, while the B-spline behavior is maintained elsewhere.

As an important special case, when three interpolation points lie on a same line it is usually desirable to interpolate them with a straight line instead of a curved spline. With the $B2$-splines, this is accomplished by projecting the interior control points $V_{2(i+k)}$, $k = -2, -1, 0, 1$, onto the line connecting P_{i-1}, P_i and P_{i+1}. The actual positions of the control points on the line can be afterwards interactively adjusted, to determine how the $B2$-spline curve imparts from P_{i-1} and P_{i+1},

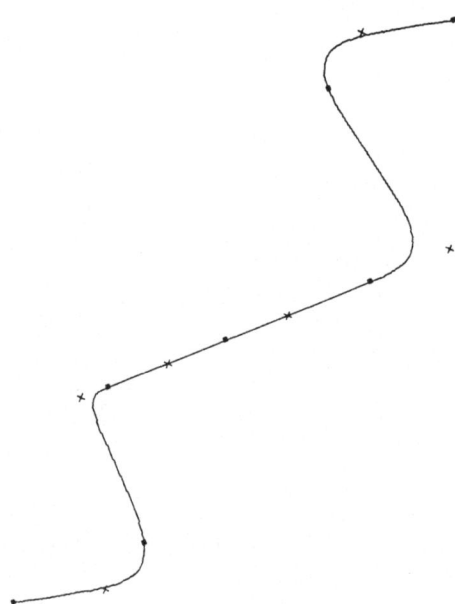

Fig. 3. $B2$-spline construction by the straight-line rule

5. B2-SPLINE SURFACES

Just as B-spline surface interpolation is based on curve interpolation, interpolating $B2$-spline surfaces can be constructed with $B2$-spline curve interpolation (4.5) in cross-sectional and longitudinal directions of the interpolation data. Alternatively, the B-spline surfaces can be explicitly converted into the $B2$-spline representation with the Catmull-Clark subdivision, replacing $u \leftarrow 2u$ and $v \leftarrow 2v$. Local $B2$-spline surface construction, for instance to create planar facets to the interpolation surfaces, can be similarly generalized from the theory.

Writing out the surface equation at the $B2$-spline knot

$$S_{2i-1,2j-1}(0,0) = \sum_{r=-1}^{2} \sum_{s=-1}^{2} V_{2i-1+r,2j-1+s} b_r(0) b_s(0) = P_{i,j},$$

and solving the $V_{2i-1,2j-1}$, the analog of the correction operation (4.2) for the $B2$-spline surfaces becomes

$$V_{2i-1,2j-1} = (36P_{i,j} - 4(V_{2i-2,2j-1} + V_{2i,2j-1} + V_{2i-1,2j-2} + V_{2i-1,2j})$$
$$- (V_{2i-2,2j-2} + V_{2i,2j-2} + V_{2i-2,2j-2} + V_{2i,2j}))/16. \tag{5.1}$$

There are four cases to be considered for local interaction with the $B2$-spline surfaces:

1) $P_{i,j}$ changed $\Rightarrow$ correct $V_{2i-1,2j-1}$
2) $V_{2i,2j-1}$ changed $\Rightarrow$ correct $V_{2i-1,2j-1}$ and $V_{2i+1,2j-1}$
3) $V_{2i-1,2j}$ changed $\Rightarrow$ correct $V_{2i-1,2j-1}$ and $V_{2i-1,2j+1}$
4) $V_{2i,2j}$ changed $\Rightarrow$ correct all four $V_{2i\pm1,2j\pm1}$.

The control points $V_{2i-1,2j-1}$ will thus hold the surface at the interpolation points $P_{i,j}$, meanwhile the surface shape can be adjusted with the remaining control points. How the control data are actually displayed for the $B2$-spline user are matters of application and taste. In fig. 4, only the stationary interpolation points $P_{i,j}$ are marked on the surfaces.

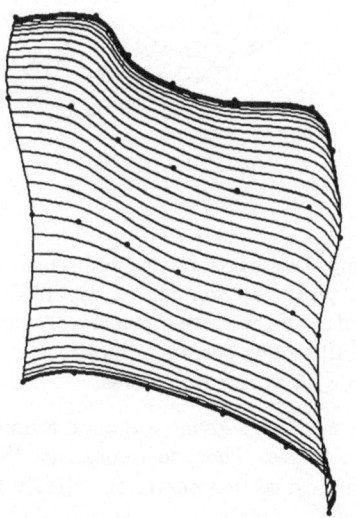

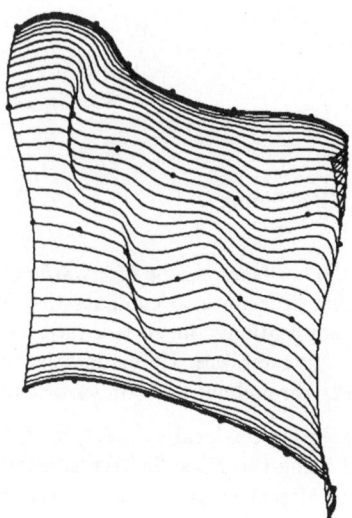

Fig. 4. $B2$-spline surface modifications

6. SKINNING INTERACTION

The $B2$-spline surface modification operations given in the previous section apply especially for surface interpolation interaction. Nonetheless, many surface construction methods in free-form *modeling* applications are likewise based on interpolation, and the $B2$-spline representation makes it again possible to increase the interaction locality there.

In B-spline *skinning* (Tiller 1983), the central task is to fit a surface through a set of section curves

$$Q^i(\mathbf{u}), \quad i = 1, \ldots, m,$$

with $n+2$ control points V_j^i, $j = 0, \ldots, n+1$, each. This is accomplished as the second phase of the surface inversion procedure, interpolating the control points of the section curves longitudinally with the control curves

$$C^j(\mathbf{v}), \quad j = 1, \ldots, n,$$

whose $(m + 2) \times (n + 2)$ control points define the skin surface control mesh $W_{i,j}$.

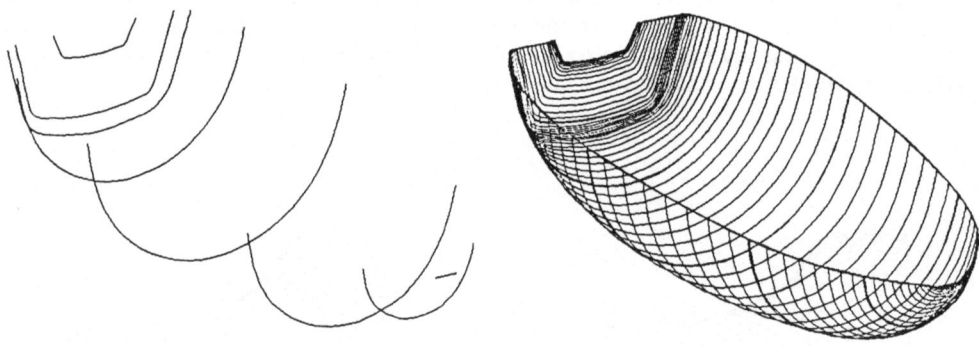

Fig. 5. Skinning

The skin surfaces can be afterwards modified by changing the section curves, and repeating the skinning procedure to compute the new surface. With planar section curves, as sufficient for most applications, the surface interaction is thus reduced from the three-dimensional space into plane curve analysis. Unfortunately, the influence of (local) section curve modifications is spread globally throughout the skin surface in the interpolation with the control curves.

The solution for local skinning modifications (fig. 6 on next page giving a drastic example) is found using the $B2$-spline representation for the control curves. Then, to reconstruct the skin surface after a control point V_j^i has been changed in the ith section curve, one simply has to adjust the jth control curve with (4.2) to match $C_{2i-1}^j(0) = V_j^i$. In terms of the skin surface control mesh, this is expressed as

$$W_{2i-1,j} = (6V_j^i - W_{2i,j} - W_{2i-2,j})/4.$$

Here the section curves may have either the B-spline or the $B2$-spline formulation. Note also, that the the skin surface modification is now carried out with a local procedure, instead of the global recomputation of the control curves as in B-spline skinning.

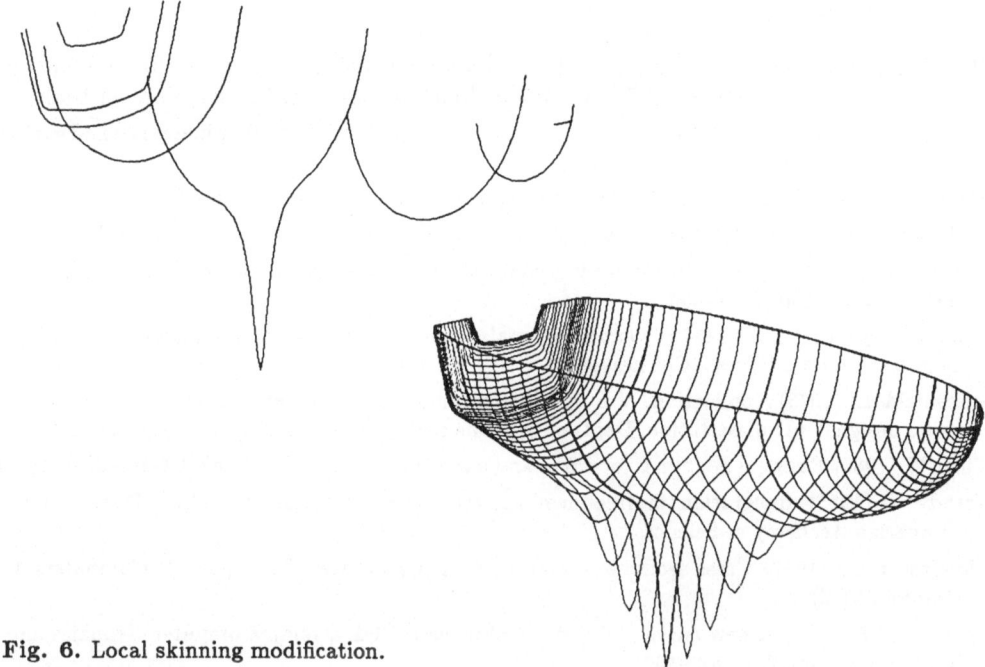

Fig. 6. Local skinning modification.

7. GENERALIZATIONS

The theory for the non-uniform B2-spline curves can be evaluated writing out the equations (4.1) and (4.3−4) in the general form instead of (4.2) and (4.5). Non-uniform $B2$-spline surfaces follow with analogous reasoning. The method of Boehm (1980) is available for explicitly converting non-uniform B-spline curves or surfaces into the $B2$-spline representation.

8. CONCLUSIONS AND FUTURE WORK

The $B2$-spline representation provides a local interface to B-spline interpolation, obtained with a simple reparametrization of the B-splines, or independently with local criterion. The B-spline modeling range is thus extended with local interaction operations for interpolation curves and surfaces, and local cross-sectional access to surfaces defined with skinning, as described in the paper. Applications to other modeling tasks where increased interpolation locality is required, e.g. offset surface construction and adjustment, can be evaluated accordingly.

Local construction of interpolation curves and surfaces has been discussed here with the special case of straight-line interpolation segments, or planar patches. Further development of $B2$-spline interpolation strategies, for instance to indicate tangent directions at the interpolation points, is another topic for future research.

ACKNOWLEDGEMENTS

This work has been supported by the Technology Development Center of Finland and Olaf Öflund Foundation. Mr. Panu Rekola gave me valuable help in the preparation of this paper.

REFERENCES

Barsky BA (1981) The beta-spline: a local representation based on shape parameters and fundamental geometric measures. PhD dissertation, Dept. of Computer Science, Univ. of Utah

Barsky BA (1982) End conditions and boundary conditions for uniform B-spline curve and surface representations. Computers in Industry 3(1/2): 17-29

Boehm W (1980) Inserting new knots into B-spline curves. CAD 12(4): 199-201

deBoor C (1978) A practical guide to splines. Springer, Berlin Heidelberg New York Tokyo

Catmull E, Clark J (1978) Recursively generated B-spline surfaces on arbitrary topological meshes. CAD 10(6): 350-355

Faux ID and Pratt MJ (1979) Computational geometry for design and manufacture. Ellis Horwood/Halstead Press, Chichester

Riesenfeld RF (1973) Applications of B-spline approximation to geometric problems of computer-aided design. PhD dissertation, Dept. of Systems and Information Science, Syracuse Univ.

Tiller W (1983) Rational B-splines for curve and surface representation. IEEE CG&A 3(6): 61-69

Varady T (1985) Integration of free-form surfaces into volumetric modeller. Dissertation, Hungarian Academy of Sciences

Woodward CD (1987) Cross-sectional design of B-spline surfaces. To appear in Computers & Graphics 11(2)

Yamaguchi F (1978) A new curve fitting method using a CRT display. Computer Graphics and Image Processing 7(3): 425-437

Charles D. Woodward received his MSc degree in mathematics from Helsinki University in 1984. Since then, he has worked as lecturer at the Helsinki University of Technology and research scientist with the CAD-project of the Technology Development Center.

Woodward is currently completing his PhD studies in computer science for the Helsinki University of Technology with his thesis on parametric curve and surface modeling methods. Besides free-form modeling, his interests in computer graphics include solid modeling, user interfaces, and visualization techniques in CAD.

Address: Helsinki University of Technology, Laboratory of Information Processing Science, Otakaari 1, SF-02150, Espoo 15, Finland.

Real Scan-Conversion of Shape Contours

Roger D. Hersch

ABSTRACT

Traditional scan-conversion involves rounding of segment departure and arrival points. Rounding of shape vertices introduces distorsions which may be harmful for shape segmentation, curve approximation and shape filling. Real scan-conversion is introduced as an extension of traditional integer based scan-conversion. It allows avoiding rounding operations. Real scan-conversion of circular arcs needs special care. Minimization of quadratic error coefficient $|C_k| = |x_k^2 + y_k^2 - r^2|$ for real scan-conversion may introduce an additional error of a few percent of one grid unit. To assure discrete continuity at the join between two segments and to allow scan-conversion of degenerated segments, conditions for the occurrence of continuity pixels are analysed. Real scan-conversion as well as the definition of starting, ending and continuity pixels allow scan-converting shapes scaled down by any factor. By keeping track of real shape coordinates and by eliminating rounding operations, subdivision and segmentation algorithms can be applied without modifying the original shape topology.

Keywords

raster graphics, real scan-conversion, discrete continuity, segment degeneration

1. INTRODUCTION

Scan-conversion of shape contours described by pieces of straight line segments, arc segments or spline segments allows drawing contours or filling complex shapes. Well known algorithms exist for scan-conversion of straight line and arc segments with integer departure and arrival points [BRESENHAM65], [BRESENHAM77]. Splines are often approximated by polylines connecting many real intermediate spline points.

Harmful side effects may appear if one generates a contour in raster memory by first rounding contour segments and then scan-converting them. Real scan-conversion is introduced for the scan-conversion of straight line and circular arc segments having real departure and arrival points, as well as real parameters like slope or radius. Real scan-conversion is needed for the solution of many problems like shape segmentation, curve approximation and shape filling.

Discrete continuity between adjacent segments and degeneration effects are analysed. An elegant solution based on intersections between grid lines and real segments is proposed. It assures discrete continuity between segments and allows scan-converting degenerated shapes.

2. HARMFUL ROUNDING BEFORE SCAN-CONVERSION

The traditional method of rounding the vertices of a shape for later scan-conversion is harmful.
When using subdivision algorithms, the discrete line is not the same before and after subdivision
(Figure 1)

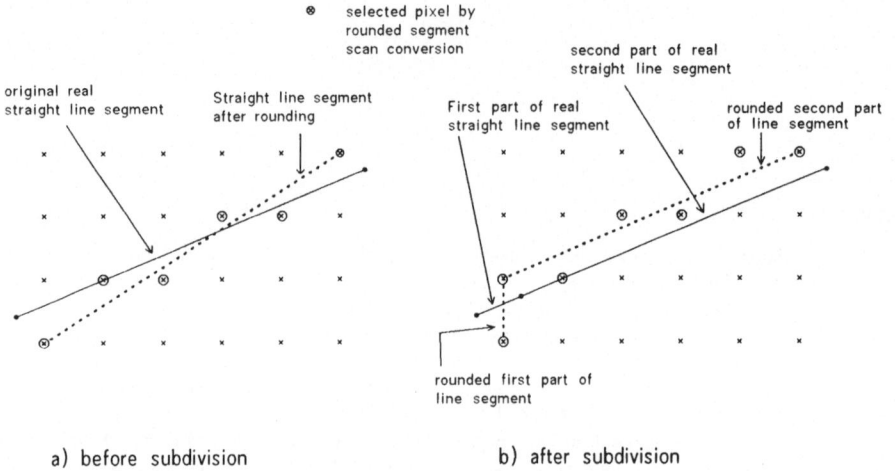

a) before subdivision   b) after subdivision

Fig. 1   Scan-conversion of a rounded straight line segment before and after
subdivision

Rounding of shape vertices may change the original shape topology (Figure 2). Such a change
cannot be accepted by some filling algorithms [HERSCH86].

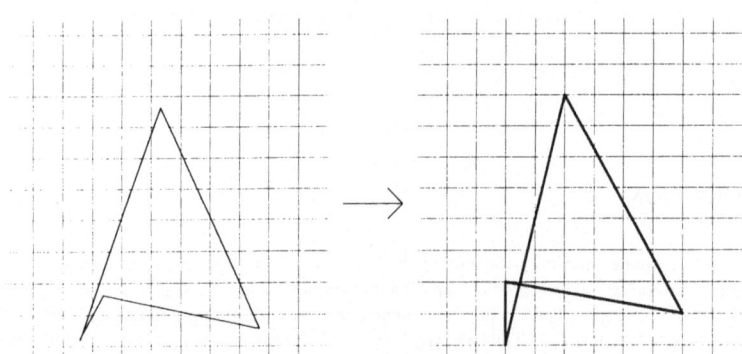

Fig. 2   Topology change produced by rounding of vertex coordinates

Subdivision techniques are used to generate simple trapezoidal shapes from complex shapes. In
image processing, shape contours are often approximated by many straight line and circle segments
[FAH82]. Splines may be recursively subdivided and approximated by polylines. In these
applications, it is essential that scan-conversion of a subdivided straight line or circular arc segment
generates the same pixels than those which would have been generated by scan-conversion of the
original straight line or circle segment. This leads to the conclusion that scan-conversion algorithms
should be applied directly on segments described by real parameters (departure and arrival points,
slope, radius, etc...).

The new category of real scan-conversion algorithms should exhibit the following properties :

1) Straight line and circular arc scan-conversion should generate exactly the same pixels, independently of how much the original straight line or circular arc has been subdivided.

2) There should be an 8-connected [PAVLIDIS82] continuity between the generated discrete pixels, especially on joins between adjacent segments.

3. REAL SCAN-CONVERSION OF STRAIGHT LINE SEGMENTS

The original algorithm [BRESENHAM65] for scan-conversion of straight line segments with integer departure and arrival points is easily extended for scan-conversion of segments having real departure and arrival points.

Let us consider a line segment with real extremities lying on its support line. Real scan-conversion applied to the considered segment should generate exactly the same discrete pixels as if they had been generated by scan-conversion of the support line (figure 3).

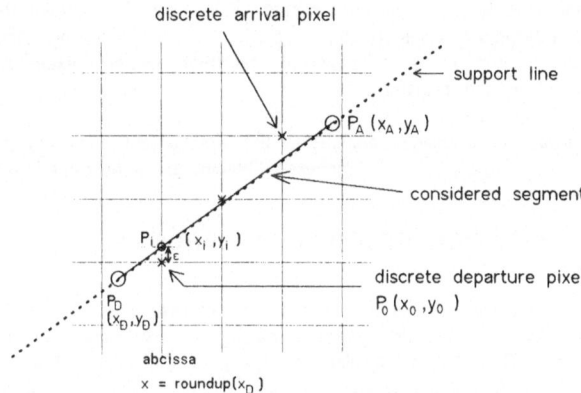

discrete arrival pixel

support line

$P_A (x_A, y_A)$

considered segment

$P_i (x_i, y_i)$

discrete departure pixel
$P_0 (x_0, y_0)$

$P_D (x_D, y_D)$

abcissa
$x = \text{roundup}(x_D)$

Fig. 3 Support line, real segment and associated pixels

A real straight line segment $\overline{P_D(x_D,y_D)P_A(x_A,y_A)}$ lying in the first octant will have after scan-conversion one pixel on each integer abcissa intersecting it. The discrete departure pixel $P_0(x_0,y_0)$ is the closest grid pixel to the intersection point $P_i(x_i,y_i)$ of the real segment with the integer abcissa on the right of departure point P_D.

Coordinates of intersection point $P_i(x_i, y_i)$:

x_D, y_D, x_A, y_A, y_i :
real numbers in fixed point representation
x_0, y_0, x_i : integer numbers

$$x_i = \text{roundup } (x_D) \qquad\qquad (1)$$

$$y_i = y_D + \frac{y_A - y_D}{x_A - x_D} (x_i - x_D) \qquad\qquad (2)$$

Discrete departure pixel $P_0(x_0,y_0)$:

$$x_0 = x_i \qquad\qquad (3)$$

$$y_0 = \text{round } (y_i) \qquad\qquad (4)$$

To run the extended Bresenham algorithm, the initial error $\varepsilon_0 = y_i - y_0$ is used for the computation of error e_1 which helps to select next grid pixel P_1. The following recurrence formula is used to get pixel P_{K+1} from pixel P_K and error coefficient ε_K.

$$e_{K+1} = \varepsilon_K + \frac{y_A - y_D}{x_A - x_D} \qquad\qquad (5)$$

$$x_{K+1} = x_K + 1 \qquad\qquad (6)$$

$$y_{K+1} = y_K + \text{round}(e_{K+1}) \qquad\qquad (7)$$

$$\varepsilon_{K+1} = e_{K+1} - (y_{K+1} - y_K) \qquad\qquad (8)$$

This recurrent formulation is equivalent to Bresenham´s algorithm but real error and slope coefficents are expressed in fixed point digital representation (for exemple 16 bit signed integer part and 16 bit fractional part). Applying program transformations [SPROULL82], this formulation can be made even more efficient. The last discrete pixel is the one lying on the integer abcissa on the left of real line arrival point P_A.

Thus, the number n of discrete pixels to be generated :

$$n = \text{trunc}(x_A) - \text{roundup}(x_D) + 1 \qquad\qquad (9)$$

For straight line segments not lying in the first octant, it is possible to build their image segments in the first octant by interoctant transformation (rotation and/or mirroring along x, y, and y=x axis). Then, the image segments are scan-converted and their discrete pixels in the original octant are obtained by reverse interoctant transformation.

A segment is *degenerated*, if its image segment in the first octant does not intersect any integer abcissa. The processing of contours having degenerated segments is described in section 7.

4. REAL SCAN-CONVERSION OF CIRCULAR ARCS

Except in a very small range, the original incremental scan-conversion algorithm [BRESENHAM77] can be extended for scan-conversion of circular arcs having a real center point, as well as real departure and arrival points. Consider a circular arc lying in the first octant (figure 4). Discrete departure pixel P_0 is one of the candidate pixels $T_0(x'_{T0}, y'_{T0})$, $T_1(x'_{T1}, y'_{T1})$ or $T_2(x'_{T2}, y'_{t2})$.
For the rest of this section, all coordinates are given in the coordinate system, whose origin passes through the center of the considered arc segment.
Compute, in coordinates relative to the center of the arc the error criterion

$$C_i = x_i^2 + y_i^2 - r^2 \qquad\qquad (10)$$

for each of the candidate pixels T_0, T_1, T_2. In the general case, select as the first discrete pixel P_0 the candidate pixel T_i for which $|C_i|$ is minimal.

In absolute coordinates:

$P_D : (x_D, y_D)$ real departure point

$P_A : (x_A, y_A)$ real arrival point

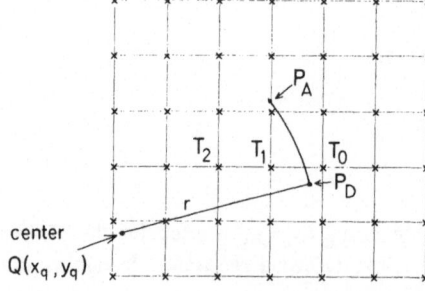

in absolute coordinates:

T_0 : $x'_{t0} = \text{roundup}(x_D)$
 $y'_{t0} = \text{roundup}(y_D)$

T_1 : $x'_{t1} = \text{trunc}(x_D)$
 $y'_{t1} = \text{roundup}(y_D)$

T_2 : $x'_{t2} = \text{trunc}(x_D)-1$
 $y'_{t2} = \text{roundup}(y_D)$

in coordinates relative to the center of the arc:

$x_{t0} = x'_{t0} - x_q$
$y_{t0} = y'_{t0} - y_q$

$x_{t1} = x'_{t1} - x_q$
$y_{t1} = y'_{t1} - y_q$

$x_{t2} = x'_{t2} - x_q$
$y_{t2} = y'_{t2} - y_q$

Fig. 4 Candidate pixels T_0, T_1, T_2 for discrete departure pixel P_0

From departure pixel P_0 the next pixels are selected using the following recurrent relations (figure 5):

$$\text{candidate pixels}: \begin{array}{l} P_{K+1L} \ (x_K-1, y_K+1) \\ P_{K+1R} \ (x_K, y_K+1) \end{array}$$

Computation of correspondent error coefficients:

$$C_{K+1L} = (x_K-1)^2 + (y_K+1)^2 - r^2 = C_K - 2x_K + 2y_K + 2 \qquad (11)$$

$$C_{K+1R} = (x_K)^2 + (y_K+1)^2 - r^2 = C_K + 2y_K + 1 \qquad (12)$$

In the general case select the candidate pixel P_{K+1} for which $|C_{K+1}|$ is minimal.

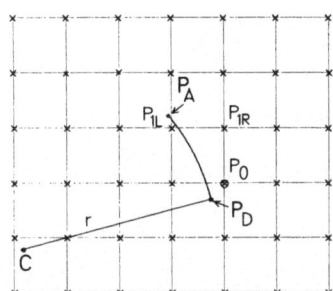

$P_0 : (x_0, y_0)$ departure pixel

$P_L : (x_{1L}, y_{1L})$ candidate for next pixel to the left of the arc

$P_{IR} : (x_{1R}, y_{1R})$ candidate for next pixel to the right of the arc

Fig. 5   Candidate pixels P_{K+1L} and P_{K+1R} for next pixel P_{K+1}

The above description of real scan-conversion is only true if the minimization of the real radial error criterion $D_K = \sqrt{x_K^2 + y_K^2} - r$ agrees with the minimization of the quadratic error criterion $C_K = x_K^2 + y_K^2 - r^2$. In fact, the real radial error D_K has to be minimized. Bresenham demonstrated that minimization of radial error criterion D_K and quadratic error criterion C_K agree for integer circle center and integer arc departure points.

As was demonstrated [MCILROY83], minimization of D_k and C_k may disagree within a certain range, for real center and departure points. This disagreement occurs under the following conditions (see Appendix, A.18):

$$x_K + \frac{1}{4} < |C_{KL}| < x_K + \frac{1}{2} \quad \text{(in coordinates relative to the center of the arc)} \qquad (13)$$

where C_{KL} is the quadratic error criterion for pixel P_{KL} lying on the left of the real arc segment (first octant).

Figure 6 shows the maximum domain of disagreement, in function of radius length r, expressed in % of one grid unit. It has been obtained by computing the range of radii, for which quadratic and radial error minimization disagree (see Appendix, A.11 to A.16). This range, at a particular ordinate connecting two discrete pixels is given by the set of circular arcs with radius r in the following range:

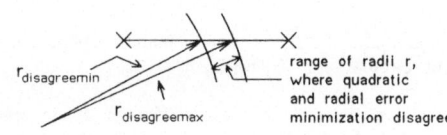

range of radii r, where quadratic and radial error minimization disagree

$$r_{disagreemin} < r < r_{disagreemax}$$

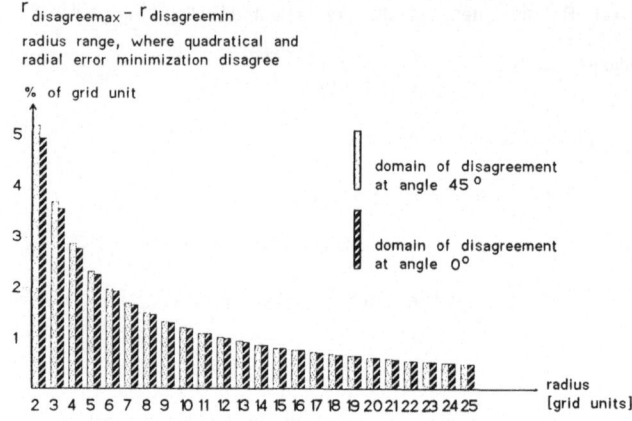

Fig. 6   Max. domain of disagreement in function of radius length

Upon disagreement, one can decide to minimize the absolute value of radial error criterion

$$D_{K+1L} = \sqrt{(x_K-1)^2 + (y_K+1)^2} - r$$

$$D_{K+1R} = \sqrt{x_K^2 + (y_K+1)^2} - r$$

to decide which will be the next pixel P_{K+1}. This operation should occur with a frequency of less than 2%. Square root extraction will thus not significantly reduce overall performance. If one is willing to admit a scan conversion error of a few percent of the grid unit in addition to the maximal error of Bresenham's scan-conversion algorithm, it is possible to rely entirely on the minimization of the quadratic error criterion

$$C_K = x_K^2 + y_K^2 - r^2$$

For arcs not lying in the first octant, scan-conversion is done on their image arc in the first octant and pixels in the original octant are obtained by reverse interoctant transformation. We define that a circular arc is *degenerated* if it's image arc in the first octant does not cross any integer ordinate.

5. REAL SCAN-CONVERSION OF SPLINE SEGMENTS

Several methods exist for the approximation of spline segments by straight line segments or by circle segments. Bézier spline segments can be recursively subdivided until the control polygons are sufficiently close to the original splines [DE BOOR74]. B-Splines can be subdivided in a similar way [RIESENFELD75], [KOHEN80].

Another method for spline generation consists of fast computation, by forward differentiation of closely spaced real points along the parametric curve segment [NEWMAN79]. For the purpose of scan-conversion, these real points can be considered as the vertices of a large polyline.

A further method allows approximating spline segments with known tangents at their vertices by pairs of circular arcs [HOURDEQUIN79].

The common ground of these different spline generation methods is that each spline segment is approximated by a large series of adjacent straight line or circular arc segments. Therefore, scan-conversion of connected adjacent real segments is of particular importance.

6. DISCRETE CONTINUITY BETWEEN SCAN-CONVERTED REAL SEGMENTS

The real scan-conversion algorithms presented in sections 4 assure 8 point-connectivity within the scan-converted segment. This connectivity however may be non-existent at the join between two adjacent segments (figure 7).

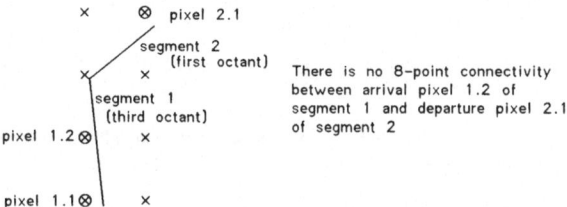

Fig. 7   Illustration of two unconnected adjacent discrete line segments

For segments with slope $\dfrac{\Delta y}{\Delta x}$, where $|\Delta y| \geqslant |\Delta x|$ (primary direction : vertical), real scan-conversion is the process of intersecting integer ordinates passing through pixel centers with the segment, and selecting those pixels which are the closest to the intersection points (figure 8a).

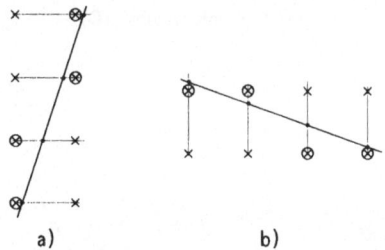

a)   b)

Fig. 8   Scan-conversion considered as selection of the closest pixels to intersection points between real segments and integer ordinates or abcissas

For segments with horizontal primary direction ($|\Delta x| > |\Delta y|$), real scan-conversion means the selection of pixels closest to intersection points between segment and integer abcissas (figure 8b)

Lack of discrete connectivity between adjacent line segments (figure 7) may occur on joins between segments having different primary directions. To assure discrete continuity, it may be necessary to look upon the intersection of the segment at its ends with its corresponding integer abcissa and ordinate (figure 9).

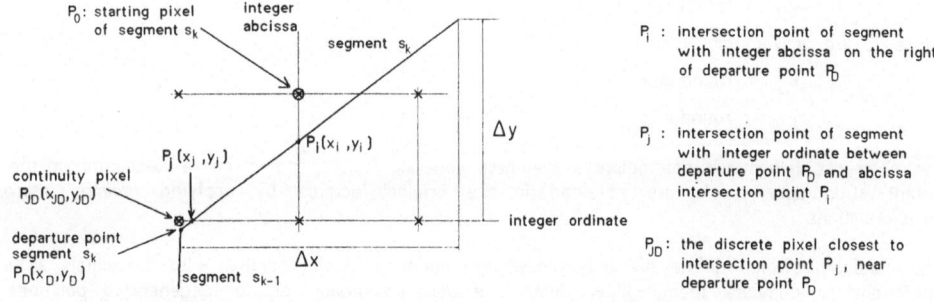

Fig. 9   Intersection points P_i and P_j between segment and integer grid lines (first octant)

Intersection point P_j is the first (last) intersection of a segment lying in primary direction with integer ordinates. For a segment lying in vertical primary direction, it is the first (last) intersection with an integer abcissa. We shall consider intersection point $P_j(x_j, y_j)$ and get *continuity pixel* $P_{JD}(x_{JD}, y_{JD})$, respectively $P_{JA}(x_{JA}, y_{JA})$ under the following conditions :

1) PrimaryDirection(S_K) ≠ PrimaryDirection (S_{K-1}) for two non-degenerated segments S_K, S_{K-1}

2) Departure point P_D (arrival point P_A) does not lie in the unit square, of which discrete starting pixel P_O (ending pixel P_{n-1}) is one corner.

These two conditions are very general and can be applied to straight line and circular arc segments in any octant.

For a straight line segment in the first octant, assuming that the above mentioned conditions are valid, coordinates of continuity pixel P_{JD} (P_{JA}) can be directly obtained.

At the departure point $P_D(x_{JD}, y_{JD})$ of a straight line segment :

$$x_{JD} = \text{trunc}(x_D)$$
$$y_{JD} = \text{roundup}(y_D)$$

At the arrival point $P_A(x_{JA}, y_{JA})$:

$$x_{JA} = \text{roundup}(x_A)$$
$$y_{JA} = \text{trunc}(y_A)$$

For a circular arc segment lying in the first octant (figure 10) :

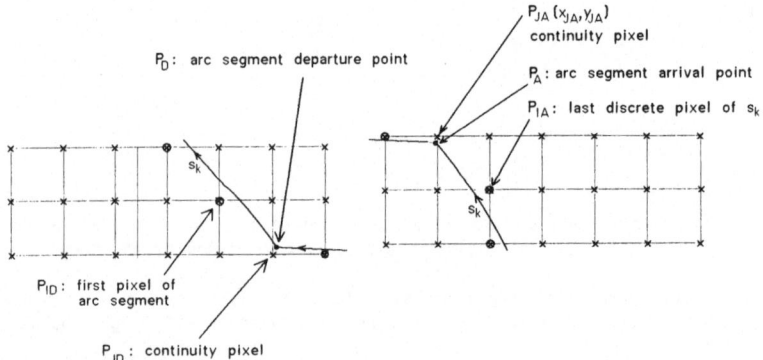

Fig. 10 *Continuity pixels P_{JD} and P_{JA} at arc departure and arrival points*

Close to arc departure point P_D :

$$x_{JD} = \text{trunc}(x_D)$$
$$y_{JD} = \text{trunc}(y_D)$$

Close to arc arrival point P_A :

$$x_{JA} = \text{roundup}(x_A)$$
$$y_{JA} = \text{roundup}(y_A)$$

For segments lying in other octants, we first generate corresponding image segments in the first octant. Continuity pixels are obtained in the original octants by applying reverse interoctant transformations.

The conditions which define the occurrences of continuity pixels together with the simple arithmetic operations to compute them, allow doing real scan-conversion of non-degenerated polylines and polyarcs while preserving discrete pixel continuity.

7. REAL SCAN-CONVERSION OF DEGENERATED SEGMENTS

Individual contour segments of a scaled shape are degenerated if they do not have discrete departure pixels. This section shows how to proceed with a contour having degenerated segments (figure 11).

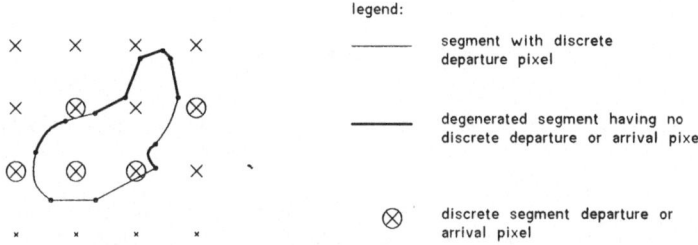

Fig. 11 Scaled shape with contour containing many degenerated segments

We want to select by scan-conversion those pixels which are the closest to the contour and to assure discrete pixel continuity. Many degenerated segments may form a fairly long contour part (figure 12).

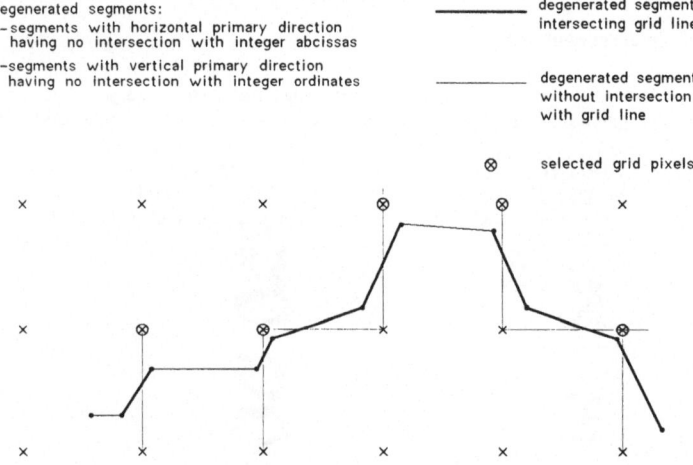

Fig. 12 Scan-conversion of contour part formed by degenerated segments

One possible way to process degenerated line segments is to concatenate and accumulate them in order to form valid segments [HERSCH86]. There is however an easier way to handle them by using the concept of continuity pixels introduced in section 7. We can assure discrete continuity if we consider only those segments which intersect integer grid lines (figure 12). If such an intersection point exists, it is computed and the pixel closest to it is chosen to be part of the discrete contour.

For a degenerated circular arc crossing a grid line, pixel P_K close to intersection point P_J is selected, for which the criterion for circular arc generation is minimal.

8. GENERAL REAL SCAN-CONVERSION ALGORITHM FOR SCALED CONTOUR PARTS

Let us assume that splines are approximated by real straight line and circle segments (section 6). The general real scan-conversion algorithm is the following :

Input: Contour given by a list of segments

Output: List of selected pixels representing the scan-converted contour

For all segments in the input list **do**

    If the current segment is *degenerated*, test if it intersects an integer grid line. If yes, put the corresponding *continuity pixel* on the output pixel list.
    Endif

    If the current segment is *valid*, test if the conditions for the occurence of a *continuity pixel* close to the departure point are satisfied. If yes, compute it and put it on the output pixel list.

    Execute *real scan-conversion* on the current segment. Put pixels P_0 to P_{n-1} on the output pixel list.

    Check if the conditions for the occurrence of a *continuity pixel* close to the segment arrival point are satisfied. If yes, compute and add the continuity pixel on the output pixel list.
    Endif
Endfor

Example of real scan-conversion:

The typographic characters used in figure 13 are described by straight line and circular arc segments. They are generated at the same size, with different horizontal and vertical subpixel displacements.

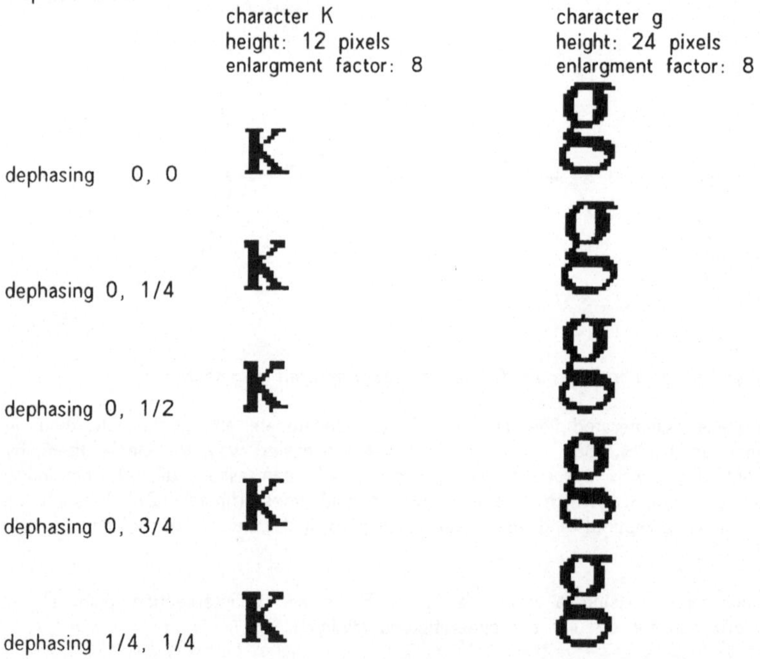

character K
height: 12 pixels
enlargment factor: 8

character g
height: 24 pixels
enlargment factor: 8

dephasing   0, 0

dephasing 0, 1/4

dephasing 0, 1/2

dephasing 0, 3/4

dephasing 1/4, 1/4

Fig. 13 Characters drawn with different horizontal and vertical subpixel dephasing factors

9. CONCLUSIONS

Scan-conversion is the basis of many drawing algorithms in computer graphics. The standard algorithms are extended for the scan-conversion of real contour segments on a discrete grid. Discrete continuity is assured and the elimination of contour rounding operations keeps the original contour topology unchanged. Processing is done in real numbers, using fixed point arithmetics. Contour parts can be broken into small or very small segments, without introducing changes in the discrete pixels selected by scan-conversion.

This significant extension of traditional scan-conversion algorithms opens new opportunities for shape filling, shape segmentation, shape scaling and character generation.

10. ACKNOWLEDGEMENTS

This work was partly accomplished during a four months leave at Vrije Universiteit Brussel. The discussions there with Prof. Theo d'Hondt were very stimulating. Many thanks to Prof. Nicoud and my colleagues at Laboratoire de Microinformatique for the hardware and software support they provided.

REFERENCES :

[BRESENHAM65] J.E. Bresenham, "Algorithm for computer control of a digital plotter," *IBM Systems Journal*, Vol 4, No 1, 1965, pp 25-30

[BRESENHAM77] J.E. Bresenham, "A Linear Algorithm for Incremental Digital Display of Circular Arcs," *Communications of the ACM*, Vol 20, No 2, Febrary 1977

[FAH82] P. Fäh, M. Kunt, "Efficient coding of high resolution typographic characters," *Proceedings ICASSP 82*

[HERSCH86] R.D. Hersch, "Descriptive Contour Fill of Partly Degenerated Shapes," *IEEE Computer Graphics and Applications*, Vol 6, No 7, pp. 61-71, July 1986.

[HOURDEQUIN79] M. Hourdequin, P. Coueignoux, "Specifying arbitrary planar smooth curves for fast drawing", Proceedings Eurographics Conference, Bologna 1979, pp 193-211

[KOHEN80] E. Cohen, T. Lyche, R. Riesenfeld, "Discrete B-Splines and Subdivision Techniques in Computer-Aided Geometric Design and Computer Graphics," *Computer Graphics and Image Processing*, Vol 14, pp. 87-111, 1980

[MCILROY83] M.D. McIlroy, "Best Approximate Circles on Integer Grids," *ACM Transactions on Graphics*, Vol. 2, No 4, pp 237-263, Oct 83.

[NEWMAN79] W.M. Newman, R.F. Sproull, *Principles of Interactive Computer Graphics*, McGraw-Hill, 1979

[PAVLIDIDIS82] T. Pavlidis, *Algorithms for Graphics and Image Processing*, Springer Verlag, Berlin, 1982, pp 167-193.

[RIESENFELD75] R.F. Riesenfeld, "On Chaikin's Algorithm," *Computer Graphics and Image Processing*, Vol 4, pp 304-310, 1975

[SPROULL82] R.F. Sproull, "Using program transformations to derive line-drawing algorithms," *ACM Transactions on Graphics*, Vol. 1, No 4, pp. 259-273, Oct. 1982

APPENDIX A

Derivation of conditions when pixel selection based on minimization of quadratic error coefficient $|C_K| = |x_K^2 + y_K^2 - r^2|$ and pixel selection based on minimization of radial error coefficient $|D_K| = |\sqrt{x_K^2 + y_K^2} - r|$ disagree.

P_{KL} is the pixel on the left of the arc (interior pixel) and P_{KR} is the pixel on the right of the arc (exterior pixel) in the first octant. The origin of the coordinate system is the center of the considered arc segment.

Therefore $C_{KL} < 0$ and $C_{KR} > 0$ (A.1)

Disagreement of minimal quadratic and minimal radial error coefficients :

Condition 1 : $|C_{KL}| < |C_{KR}|$ and $|D_{KL}| > |D_{KR}|$ (A.2)

Condition 2 : $|C_{KL}| > |C_{KR}|$ and $|D_{KL}| < |D_{KR}|$ (A.3)

The same conditions can be expressed in the following way :

Condition 1 : $r^2 - (x_K^2 + y_K^2) < ((x_K+1)^2 + y_K^2) - r^2$ (A.4)

$$r - \sqrt{x_K^2 + y_K^2} > \sqrt{(x_K+1)^2 + y_K^2} - r \quad\quad (A.5)$$

Condition 2 : $r^2 - (x_K^2 + y_K^2) > ((x_K+1)^2 + y_K^2) - r^2$ (A.6)

$$r - \sqrt{x_K^2 + y_K^2} < \sqrt{(x_K+1)^2 + y_K^2} - r \quad\quad (A.7)$$

Let us first look at condition 2. By dividing (A.6) by (A.7) we obtain

$$r + \sqrt{x_K^2 + y_K^2} > \sqrt{(x_K+1)^2 + y_K^2} + r \quad\quad (A.8)$$

The above inequality can never be true for $x_K > 0$. Therefore condition 2 is discarded.

Let us focus on condition 1: from (A.5) we obtain

$$2r > \sqrt{(x_K+1)^2 + y_K^2} + \sqrt{x_K^2 + y_K^2}$$

and squaring both sides

$$4r^2 > 2x_K^2 + 2y_K^2 + 2x_K + 1 + 2\sqrt{x_K^2 + y_K^2}\,\sqrt{(x_K+1)^2 + y_K^2} \quad (A.9)$$

Function $f(y_K) = \sqrt{x_K^2 + y_K^2}\,\sqrt{(x_K+1)^2 + y_K^2} - y_K^2$ takes the minimum value $x_K(x_K+1)$, when $y_K = 0$.

Therefore $\sqrt{x_K^2 + y_K^2}\,\sqrt{(x_K+1)^2 + y_K^2} \geq x_K(x_K+1) + y_K^2$

Together with (A.4) we obtain

$$x_K^2 + y_K^2 + x_K + \frac{1}{4} < r^2 < x_K^2 + y_K^2 + x_K + \frac{1}{2} \quad\quad (A.10)$$

This is the only condition, when minimum quadratic and minimum radial error may disagree. The previous development is taken from [MCILROY83].

Let us compute the range of radii, for which quadratic and radial error coefficient disagree. We introduce the new variables :

$$\rho = \sqrt{x_k^2 + y_k^2}$$

$$\varphi = \text{arctg } \frac{y_k}{x_k}$$

$$a = r - \rho$$

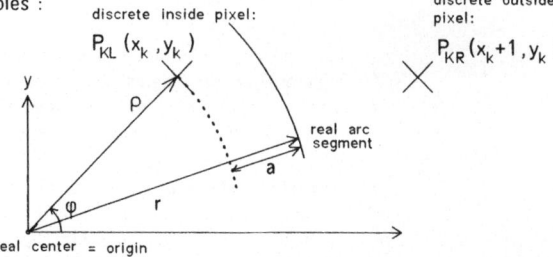

Condition (A.10) expressed with discrete radius ρ, angle φ and radial difference a :

$$\rho^2 + \rho\cos\varphi + \frac{1}{4} < (\rho + a)^2 \tag{A.11}$$

$$\rho^2 + \rho\cos\varphi + \frac{1}{2} > (\rho + a)^2 \tag{A.12}$$

From (A.11), let us express the condition for a :

$$a^2 + 2a\rho - (\rho\cos\varphi + \frac{1}{4}) > 0$$

$$a_{min} = -\rho + \sqrt{\rho(\rho + \cos\varphi) + \frac{1}{4}} \tag{A.13}$$

From (A.12)

$$-a^2 - 2\rho a + \rho\cos\varphi + \frac{1}{2} > 0$$

$$a_{max} = -\rho + \sqrt{\rho(\rho + \cos\varphi) + \frac{1}{2}} \tag{A.14}$$

For positive a, a_{min} gives the lowest bound and a_{max} the highest bound for possible disagreement between quadratic and radial error minimization.

The domain of radii where quadratic and radial error minimization disagree is given for arcs passing between pixel $P_{KL}(x_k, y_k)$ and pixel $P_{KR}(x_k+1, y_k)$ by a minimum radius $r_{disagreemin}$ and a maximum radius $r_{disagreemax}$.

$$r_{disagreemin} = \rho + a_{min} = \sqrt{\rho(\rho + \cos\varphi) + \frac{1}{4}} \tag{A.15}$$

$$r_{disagreemax} = \rho + a_{max} = \sqrt{\rho(\rho + \cos\varphi) + \frac{1}{2}} \tag{A.16}$$

Now that the lowest and highest bounds have been calculated, let us compute the range of the quadratic error coefficient C_{KL}, in which disagreement could occur :

From (A.10) :

$$x_k + \frac{1}{4} < r^2 - \rho^2 < x_k + \frac{1}{2} \tag{A.17}$$

$$|C_{KL}| = r^2 - \rho^2$$

Therefore disagreement between quadratic and radial error minimization can occur when

$$x_k + \frac{1}{4} < |C_{KL}| < x_k + \frac{1}{2} \tag{A.18}$$

Roger D. Hersch is a lecturer at the Swiss Federal Institute of Technology (EPFL) and at the University of Lausanne. During the last four years, he helped develop a printer server for the generation of high-quality documents and supervised the design of a special-purpose display controller for photogrammetric stereo image injection and superimposition. In summer 1986, Hersch was a visiting professor at Vrije Universiteit Brussel, where he worked on algorithms for analytical character generation. His current research interests are efficient graphic display algorithms, specialized display hardware and multiprocessor systems. Hersch received his Diploma in electrical engineering from ETH Zürich in 1975 and his PhD degree from EPFL in 1985.

Address: Laboratoire de Microinformatique, Ecole Polytechnique Fédérale de Lausanne, 37 Av. de Cour, 1007 Lausanne

Equations of Digital Straight Lines

Son Pham

ABSTRACT

Digitization of a real straight line is defined as the set of closest pixels to the line. These pixels form a digital straight line. This paper defines equation of a digital straight line as equation of the corresponding real straight line $y = a^*x + b$, where $a = p/q$ with $(p, q) = 1$ is the slope and b is the real-number offset. First, the paper provides an algorithm to digitize real straight lines, then discusses the relationships among slopes, offsets, permutations, and shifts of digital straight lines of different offsets. It will prove that digitization of $y = a^*x+b$ remains unchanged if b is in interval $[i/q, (i+1)/q)$, for integer i. From one interval of b to the next interval of b, the digitization is shifted or permuted. Number of shifts and position of permutations are calculated by explicit formulas. The concept of parallel digital straight lines is discussed as a consequence of these mentioned-above results.

Categories and Subject Descriptors: I.3.3 [Computer Graphics]: Picture/Image Generation; F.2.2 [Analysis of Algorithm and Problem Complexity]: Geometrics Problems and Computations.

General Terms: Digital straight lines, chain codes of directions, pixel, shift, equation, distance, digitization, closest pixels, algorithm, loop invariant, parallel and overlapped digital straight lines, intersection, permutation.

1. INTRODUCTION

A system of integer xy coordinates is called a *grid*, and a point of integer coordinates is called a *pixel* or *digital point*. Let (i, j) be a pixel. The eight pixels (i+1, j), (i+1, j+1), (i, j+1), (i-1, j+1), (i-1, j), (i-1, j-1), (i, j-1), and (i+1, j-1) are called eight neighbors of (i, j). They are labeled numerically, 0, 1, 2, 3, 4, 5, 6, and 7, respectively. These numbers are numbered counterclockwise with respect to the relative positions of neighbors of (i, j). (See Figure 1 for eight neighbors.)

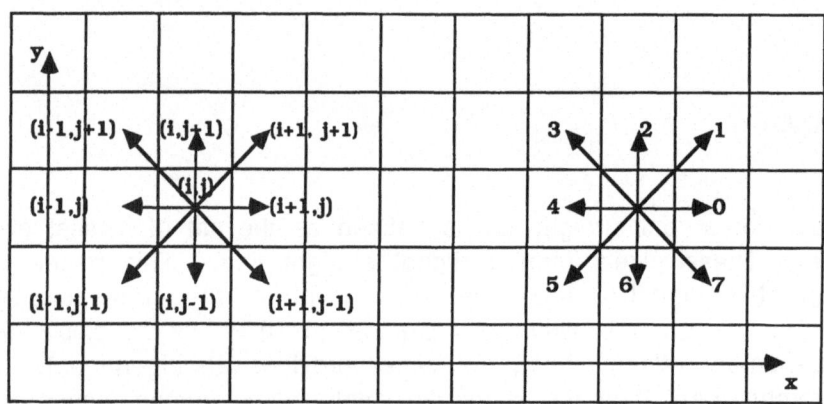

FIGURE 1: Eight Neighbors and Eight Corresponding Directions

A set of pixels is called a *chain code* or *digital arc* if every pixel except two (the first and last) in the set has exactly two neighbors, where the neighbors are elements of the set. The first and last pixels have only one neighbor. (See Figure 2 for an example of a digital arc.)

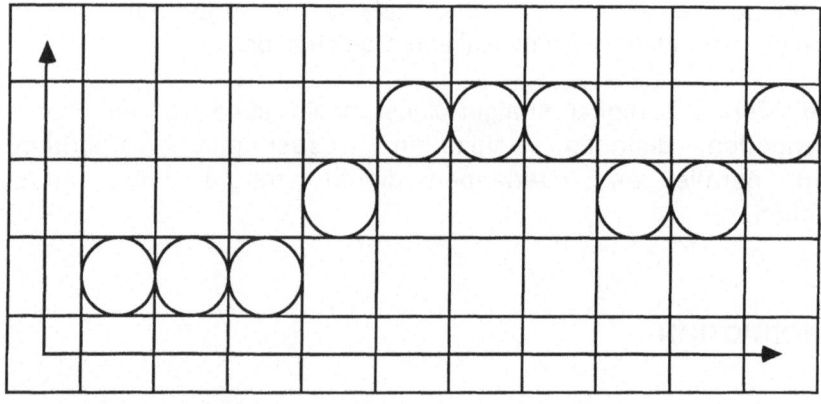

FIGURE 2: Digital Arc of Chain Code 0 0 1 1 0 0 7 0 1

Select the starting pixel which is one of the two pixels of having only one neighbor. Identify the neighbor of the starting pixel and record the relative positional number 0-7. From this neighboring pixel, identify its unselected neighbor and record the positional number. (We note that one of its two neighbors is the starting pixel.) From this new neighbor, identify its unselected neighbor and so on until the ending pixel is found. Hence, the process is similar to tracing the chain links until it reaches the last link. Therefore, the chain code can be reconstructed from a starting pixel and the sequence of neighboring numbers. This sequence is called chain code of *directions* .

Suppose a real straight line is drawn by pencil and ruler on a grid. Digitizing this real straight line is to find a set of closest pixels to the real straight line. The set will form a digital arc which is called a digital straight line. (See Figure 4 for a digitization of a real straight line.) We use the abreviations *rsl* and **dsl** for real straight line and digital straight line respectively. Here is a definition of dsl.

Definition 1.1. A given digital arc is a dsl if there is a rsl whose digitization is exactly the given digital arc.

Other definitions of dsl will be based on criteria or characteristics of a class of digital arcs.

Definition 1.2. A digital arc is called straight if it satisfies the Freeman's three criteria. Here are three criteria:
(1) At most two basic directions are present and these can differ by unity.
(2) One of these values always occurs singly.
(3) Succesive occurences of the principal direction occuring singly are as uniformly spaced as possible.

These three criteria are defined mathematically in Pham (1986).

Defintion 1.3. A digital arc is called straight if it satisfies the Rosenfeld's chord property. (Rosenfeld, 1982)

Definition 1.4. A digital arc is called straight if it has the absence of unevenness property. (Hung, 1986)

The importance of straightness has been studied extensively by Kim (1982) and Kim and Rosenfeld (1982), and numerous authors have studied the equivalent characterizations for the straightness and the related properties (Arcelli and Massaroti, 1975, Bresenham, 1965; Pfaltz and Rosenfeld, 1967; and Rosenfeld, 1974, 1969). Algorithms for these characterizations are also studied (Brons, 1974; Chang, 1971; Wu, 1982). In general, there are two main topics in raster graphics: one is to generate the digital objects and the other is to recognize or characterize them. For the objects as digital straight lines, the generation can be approached algebraically by the linear property of the lines (Pham, 1986), analytically (Dorst and Smeulders, 1984), or approximately by the method of rounding-off (Bresenham, 1965).

The recognition of lines to be straight is to verify their chain codes satisfy the criteria or the conditions of characterization. Hence, it leads to complex algorithms (Brons, 1974; Chang 1971, Wu, 1982). To reduce the complexity of the algorithm, a relaxation on the criteria of straightness is introduced (Pham, 1986). The idea is to determine the position of the chain code in the area bounded by two digital straight lines. Because generating digital straight lines is quite simple, the determination of the chain code becomes straightforward, but the chain code in the area does not guarantee its straightness.

Result of this Paper.

In this paper we will deal with the equation of digital straight lines. The equation is of the form $y = a*x + b$ such that its digitization is the given digital straight line. The case a is a rational number is studied rigorously. It is proven that the coefficient b will fall in some interval range to maintain the same digitization. Relationships among the dsl's with different ranges of b's are also investigated. It is proven that these dsl's of the same a and different b's have chain codes shifted from each others. In other words, all parallel real straight lines have digitization of the same chain code except for the numbers of shifts. Formulas to calculate the numbers of shifts are given explicitly. Conversely, the equation of dsl which is shifted from one dsl with given equation is also studied. More precisely, if a number of shifts is given, then the offset of real straight line can be calculated. Moreover two digital straight lines whose offsets are different by $1/q$ are permuted from each other. I.e., only two directions in a chain code are exchanged in order to get the other. The position of permutation is calculated explicitly by formulas.

As a consequence, a concept of parallel and overlapped digital straight lines is introduced. Two dsl's are parallel if their chain codes are the same except for a finite number of shifts, and they are overlapped if they are identical and start at the starting pixel. The number of shifts will determine the difference of their offsets. An equivalent definition of parallel dsl's with the concept of perputation can be given. Two dsl's are parallel if their chain codes are the same except for a finite number of permutations. Also this number of permutations can be used to calculate the difference of offsets.

2.   ALGORITHM TO FIND CLOSEST POINTS TO Y=A*X+B.

In this section an algorithm to find the closest pixels to the real straight line y = a*x+b is given. Let a = p/q, where $0 < p < q$ and (p, q) = 1. We assume without loss of genrality that b is in the interval [-0.5, 0.5). (**Note:** The notation [-0.5, 0.5) indicates the interval is closed at -0.5 and open at 0.5. It is defined mathematically to be {x : $-0.5 \leq x < 0.5$}). The b's outside can be reduced to the ones in this interval and they are discussed at the end of this section.

First, the evolution of this algorithm is presented (See Algorithms 1-3), then a loop invariant is discovered. The final algorithm, Algorithm 4 will contain only integer arithmetic operations of addition and subtraction. This algorithm for clarity also presented in flowchart form and a loop invariant is discovered which is used widely in the later sections.

We denote Plot(x, y) the subroutine to display the pixel of coordinates (x, y) on the screen and PlotDir(d) the subroutine to display the neighbor d of the most recent displayed pixel. The function Floor(x) and RoundOff(x) of any real number are defined as follows:

Floor(x) = the largest integer which is less than or equal x,

RoundOff(x) = Floor(x + 0.5).

Algorithm   1:

for i : =1 to q do Plot (i, RoundOff ((p/q) * i + b))

Algorithm   2:

```
Plot  (0,0)
LeftOver := b
for i := 1 to q do
     if LeftOver + p/q < 0.5
          then PlotDir(0); LeftOver := LeftOver;
          else PlotDir(1); LeftOver := LeftOver -1;
     LeftOver := LeftOver + p/q;
endfor
```

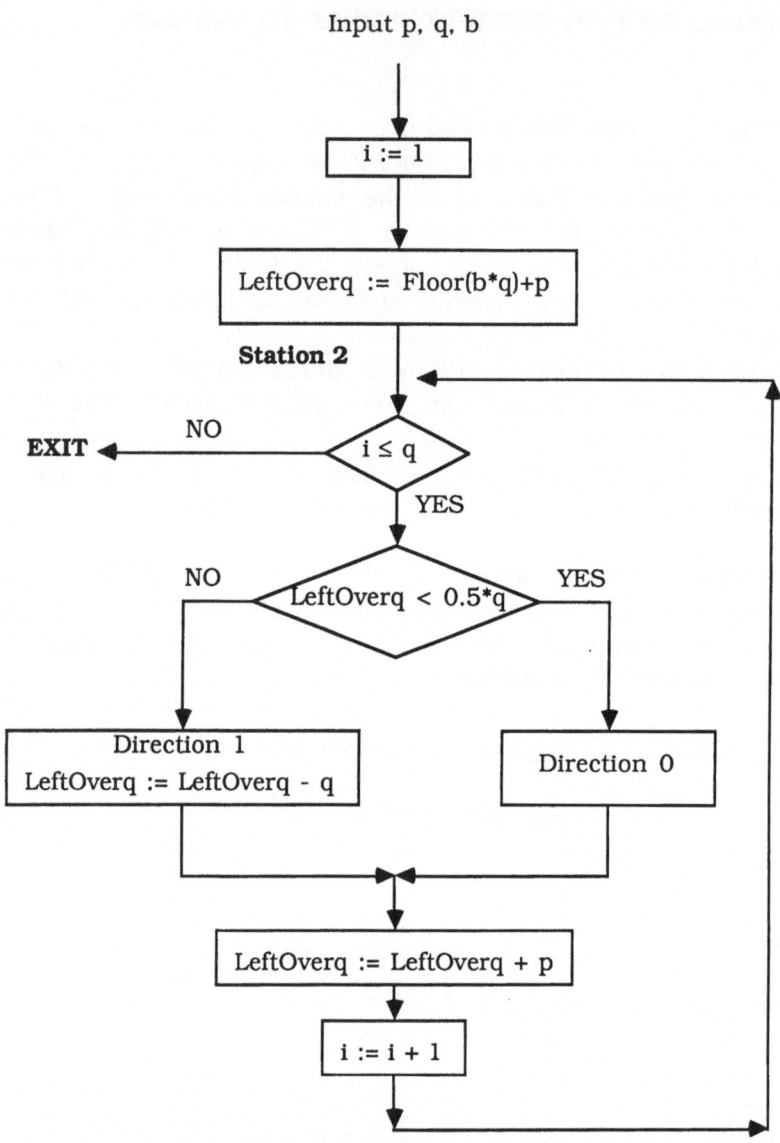

Input p, q, b

i := 1

LeftOverq := Floor(b*q)+p

Station 2

i ≤ q

NO → **EXIT**

YES

LeftOverq < 0.5*q

NO → Direction 1
LeftOverq := LeftOverq - q

YES → Direction 0

LeftOverq := LeftOverq + p

i := i + 1

**FIGURE 3: Standard Flowchart for Algorithm to Generate
Digital Straight Line of Equation y = a*x+b,
where a = p/q, 0<p<q, (p,q) = 1, and -0.5≤b<0.5**

**Loop Invariant at Station 2:
LeftOverq = p*i + Floor(b*q)   mod q**

Algorithm   3:

Let n = b * q. We transform in Algo. 2 the variable LeftOver by LeftOver * q
and denote LeftOver * q by LeftOverq in order to obtain Algorithm 3.

```
Plot(0,0)
LeftOverq := Floor(b*q)
for i := 1 to q do
     if LeftOverq + p < 0.5 * q
          then PlotDir(0); LeftOverq := LeftOverq +p;
          else PlotDir(1); LeftOverq := LeftOverq -q;
       LeftOverq := LeftOverq + p;
endfor
```

Algorithm 4:

(Remove p in the if-statement to the initial value of LeftOverq).

```
Plot(0,0)
LeftOverq := Floor(b*q) + p
for i := 1 to q do
     if LeftOverq < 0.5 * q
          then PlotDir(0); LeftOverq := LeftOverq;
          else PlotDir(1); LeftOverq := LeftOverq - q;
       LeftOverq := LeftOverq + p;
endfor
```

Algorithm 4 also is represented in an IBM standard flowchart. (see Flowchart). We denote station 2 before the for-do loop. The following result indicates a loop invariant at station 2.

Theorem 2.1: Loop invariant at Station 2 of Flowchart of Algorithm 4 is

$$LeftOverq = p*i + Floor (b*q) \qquad mod \ q.$$

Proof: Proof is skipped to avoid complexity of the paper.

The Interested Range of b's: [-0.5, 0.5)

The offset value b can be any real number. We are able to restrict the value of b in the interval [-0.5, 0.5) because of the following reason. For any offset b, it can be decomposed as a sum of the integer part and a fraction part:

$$b = I + b_{new}, \qquad where \ \ I = RoundOff(b), \ and$$
$$b_{new} = b - RoundOff(b).$$

Hence the fraction part b_{new} is in the interval [-0.5, 0.5).

We have in Algorithm 1,

$$\text{RoundOff}((p/q)*i + b) = I + \text{RoundOff}((p/q)*i + b_{new}).$$

Hence Algorithms 2-4 remained the same except for the first line which should be Plot(0, I) and b is substituted by b_{new}. In other words, they are:

Algorithm 2':

```
Plot (0, I)
LeftOver := bnew
for i := 1 to q do
    if LeftOver + p/q < 0.5
        then PlotDir(0); LeftOver := LeftOver;
        else PlotDir(1); LeftOver := LeftOver -1;
    LeftOver := LeftOver + p/q;
endfor
```

Algorithm   3':

Let $n = b_{new} * q$. In order to obtain Algorithm 3' we transform in Algorithm 2 the variable LeftOver by LeftOver * q and denote LeftOver * q by LeftOverq.

```
Plot(0, I)
LeftOverq := Floor(bnew*q)
for i := 1 to q do
    if LeftOver + p < 0.5 * q
        then PlotDir(0); LeftOverq := LeftOverq + p;
        else PlotDir(1); LeftOverq := LeftOverq - q;
    LeftOverq := LeftOverq + p;
endfor
```

Algorithm 4':

(Remove p in the if-statement to the intial value of LeftOverq).
```
Plot(0, I)
LeftOverq := Floor(bnew *q) +p
for i := 1 to q do
    if LeftOverq < 0.5 * q
        then PlotDir(0); LeftOverq := LeftOverq;
        else PlotDir(1); LeftOverq := LeftOverq -q;
    LeftOverq := LeftOverq + p;
endfor
```

As a consequence the directions which are produced by Algorithm 4 and Algorithm 4' are identical. We summarize the above results in the following theorem.

Theorem 2.2: The chain code of the equation $y = a^*x + b$ is identical to the chain code of the equation $y = a^*x + b_{new}$, where

$$b_{new} = b - RoundOff(b).$$

In the remaining of the paper we assume b is in the interval [0.5, 0.5).

The Interested Range of a's: the First Octant.

The slope in this paper is restricted in the first octant, Octant 0, i.e., the first 45 degrees. Table 2.1 will show the relationships of chain codes from other octants to Octant 0. (see Pham (1986) for more details). Table 2.1 is as a consequence of the following theorem.

Table 2.1: Eight different Cases of Slopes p/q

Geometric Region	Angle Range (in Degrees)	Slope p/q (p, q)=1	Periodic Sequence of Directions	Possible Directions	Formula and Relationships
	0 -45	$0<p<q$	$d_1 d_2 \ldots d_q$	0, 1	
	45 - 90	$0<q<p$	$(d_1 +1)(d_2 +2)\ldots(d_p +1)$	1, 2	$d_1 d_2 \ldots d_p$ is the chain code of the line with slope $(p-q)/p$
	90 -135	$0<|q|<|p|$	$(3-d_1)(3-d_2)\ldots(3-d_{|p|})$	2, 3	$d_1 d_2 \ldots d_p$ is the chain code of the line with slope $(|p|-|q|)/|p|$
	135 - 180	$0<|p|<|q|$	$(4-d_1)(4-d_2)\ldots(4-d_{|q|})$	3, 4	$d_1 d_2 \ldots d_q$ is the chain code of the line with slope $|p|/|q|$
	180 -225	$0<|p|<|q|$	$(d_1 +4)(d_2+4)\ldots(d_{|q|} +4)$	4, 5	$d_1 d_2 \ldots d_q$ is the chain code of the line with slope $|p|/|q|$
	225 - 270	$0<|q|<|p|$	$(d_1 +5)(d_2+5)\ldots(d_{|p|} +5)$	5, 6	$d_1 d_2 \ldots d_p$ is the chain code of the line with slope $(|p|-|q|)/|p|$
	270 - 315	$0<|q|<|p|$	$(7- d_1)(7- d_2)\ldots(7-d_{|p|})$	6, 7	$d_1 d_2 \ldots d_p$ is the chain code of the line with slope $(|p|-|q|)/|p|$
	315 - 360	$0<|p|<|q|$	$(8- d_1)(8- d_2)\ldots(8-d_{|q|})$	7, 0	$d_1 d_2 \ldots d_q$ is the chain code of the line with slope $|p|/|q|$

Theorem 2.3 (Pham, 1986): The dsl of $y = (p'/q') x$ with $p'>q'>0$ and $(p', q') = 1$ is the periodic sequence $(d_1+1)(d_2+1)...(d_q+1)$, where the periodic sequence $d_1 d_2...d_q$ is the chain code of the dsl of $y = (p/q) x$ with

$$p = p' - q'$$

and $$q = p'.$$

Therefore the properties on the chain codes in the first octant are also valid for the other octants. Hence, the assumption $0<p<q$ and $(p, q) = 1$ is used without loosing the generality.

3. DEMONSTRATION ON EQUATIONS OF DSL'S

In this section an example is given. The equation of the straight line is $y = 5/12^*x$, and the values of offset b are 0/12, 1/12,..., 5/12, -6/12, -5/12,..., -1/12. That means the values of b will range from -0.5 to 0.5. The relationships of $y = 5/12^*x + b$ with different b, the corresponding chain codes, and the numbers of shifts are displayed. The loop invariant for different equations is also included. These results will be proven rigourously in the next section.

equation : $y = a^*x + b$
slope : $a = 5/12; p = 5; q = 12$
y offset : $b =$ 0/12, 1/12, 2/12, 3/12, 4/12, 5/12,
-6/12, -5/12, -4/12, -3/12, -2/12, -1/12

Table 3.1 Chain Codes and Number of Shifts.

n=12*b	Loop invariant: $p*i+n \bmod 12, i = 1, 2,..., 12$	Chain codes of directions	# of shifts
0	5 10 3 8 1 6 11 4 9 2 7 0	0 1 0 1 0 1 0 0 1 0 1 0	0
1	6 11 4 9 2 7 0 5 10 3 8 1	1 0 0 1 0 1 0 0 1 0 1 0	5
2	7 0 5 10 3 8 1 6 11 4 9 2	1 0 0 1 0 1 0 1 0 0 1 0	10
3	8 1 6 11 4 9 2 7 0 5 10 3	1 0 1 0 0 1 0 1 0 0 1 0	3
4	9 2 7 0 5 10 3 8 1 6 11 4	1 0 1 0 0 1 0 1 0 1 0 0	8
5	10 3 8 1 6 11 4 9 2 7 0 5	1 0 1 0 1 0 0 1 0 1 0 0	1
6-12	11 4 9 2 7 0 5 10 3 8 1 6	0 0 1 0 1 0 0 1 0 1 0 1	6
7-12	0 5 10 3 8 1 6 11 4 9 2 7	0 0 1 0 1 0 1 0 0 1 0 1	11
8-12	1 6 11 4 9 2 7 0 5 10 3 8	0 1 0 0 1 0 1 0 0 1 0 1	4
9-12	2 7 0 5 10 3 8 1 6 11 4 9	0 1 0 0 1 0 1 0 1 0 0 1	9
10-12	3 8 1 6 11 4 9 2 7 0 5 10	0 1 0 1 0 0 1 0 1 0 0 1	2
11-12	4 9 2 7 0 5 10 3 8 1 6 11	0 1 0 1 0 0 1 0 1 0 1 0	7

In Table 3.1 the first column shows values of 12*b. For each value, there are a series of 12 residues of a*x mod 12 for x = 1, 2, ..., 12. These 12 residues are used to determine 12 directions. The last column will indicate the numbers of shifts to be applied to the chain code in the first line (case 12*b = 0) in order to get the one in the current line.

Note: The brackets in Table 3.1 show the permutations of two consecutive chain codes in the table. The last chain code in the table is wrapped to the first one and brackets show a permutation between these two. Permutations on chain codes are studied later.

Equations and Number of Shifts:

Consider the chain code 0 1 0 1 0 1 0 0 1 0 1 0 which is a digitization of the line y = 5/12 x. The chain code is provided by Algorithm 4 to select the closest pixels to the real line of the above equation. with the same algorithm, there are the chain codes for the equations y = a*x + b, where a = 5/12 and b = 1/2, 2/12, 3/12, 4/12, 5/12, - 1/12, -2/12, -3/12, -4/12, -5/12, and -6/12. Here is Table 3.2 to indicate the relationships among the equations and the number of shifts from the chain code of the case b = 0.

Table 3.2: Equations of Numbers of Shifts.

Equations	Number of Shifts	Equations	Number of Shifts
y = a*x	0	y = a*x - 6/12	6
y = a*x + 1/12	5	y = a*x - 5/12	11
y = a*x + 2/12	10	y = a*x - 4/12	4
y = a*x + 3/12	3	y = a*x - 3/12	9
y = a*x + 4/12	8	y = a*x - 2/12	2
y = a*x + 5/12	1	y = a*x - 1/12	7

Classes of b's Having the Same Chain Code

In the following table, Table 3.3 we will list the ranges of b's having the same chain code. Let's denote dsl_0 as the chain code 0 1 0 1 0 1 0 0 1 0 1 0; dsl_1 as a shift of dsl_0 to the right side; dsl_2 as a shift twice of dsl_0 to the right side; and so on. The value of b will range from -0.5 to 0.5. This interval is subdivided into 12 different subranges [i/12, (i+1)/12) for i = -6, -5, ..., 0, 1, ..., 5. The second column indicates figures which represent the digitizations.

Permutations of dsl's

We observe that the two chain codes in two consecutive figures (Figure 4.i, i=-6..5) are identical except for two consecutive directions. For examples, the two corresponding chain codes in Figures 4.0 and 4.1 are 010101001010 100101001010 and the first two directions are permuted to make one chain code to be the other.

Let denote p_i the permutation at the ith and (i+1)th directions. That means the directions at i and i+1 are exchanged. Mathematically speaking we have:

$$p_1(d_1, d_2, d_3, ...) = (d_2, d_1, d_3, ...),$$
$$p_2(d_1, d_2, d_3, ...) = (d_1, d_3, d_2, ...),$$
$$\text{..}$$
$$p_i(d_1, ..., d_i, d_{i+1}, ...) = (d_1, ..., d_{i+1}, d_i, ...),$$

where d's are directions of a chain code.
The last column of Table 3.3 shows a relationship between a dsl and its next one. The subscript of p_i will indicate the position of permutation. We observe that the subscript i can be calculated by the formula

$$i = 1 + 7*\ Floor(12*b)\ mod\ 12$$

(See Example at the end of Theorem 6.2 for an explanation.)

<u>**Table 3.3:**</u> **The classes of b's and dsl's of y = a*x + b**

Subintervals	Figure	Corresponding dsl	Permutation
$-0.5 \le -6/12 \le b < -5/12$	Fig.4.-6	dsl_6	$p_7(dsl_6) = dsl_{11}$
$-5/12 \le b < -4/12$	Fig.4.-5	dsl_{11}	$p_2(dsl_{11}) = dsl_4$
$-4/12 \le b < -3/12$	Fig.4.-4	dsl_4	$p_9(dsl_4) = dsl_9$
$-3/12 \le b < -2/12$	Fig.4.-3	dsl_9	$p_4(dsl_9) = dsl_2$
$-2/12 \le b < -1/12$	Fig.4.-2	dsl_2	$p_{11}(dsl_2) = dsl_7$
$-1/12 \le b < 0$	Fig.4.-1	dsl_7	$p_6(dsl_7) = dsl_0$
$0 \le b < 1/12$	Fig.4.0	dsl_0	$p_1(dsl_0) = dsl_5$
$1/12 \le b < 2/12$	Fig.4.1	dsl_5	$p_8(dsl_5) = dsl_{10}$
$2/12 \le b < 3/12$	Fig.4.2	dsl_{10}	$p_3(dsl_{10}) = dsl_3$
$3/12 \le b < 4/12$	Fig.4.3	dsl_3	$p_{10}(dsl_3) = dsl_8$
$4/12 \le b < 5/12$	Fig.4.4	dsl_8	$p_5(dsl_8) = dsl_1$
$5/12 \le b < 0.5$	Fig.4.5	dsl_1	$p_{12}(dsl_1) = dsl_6$

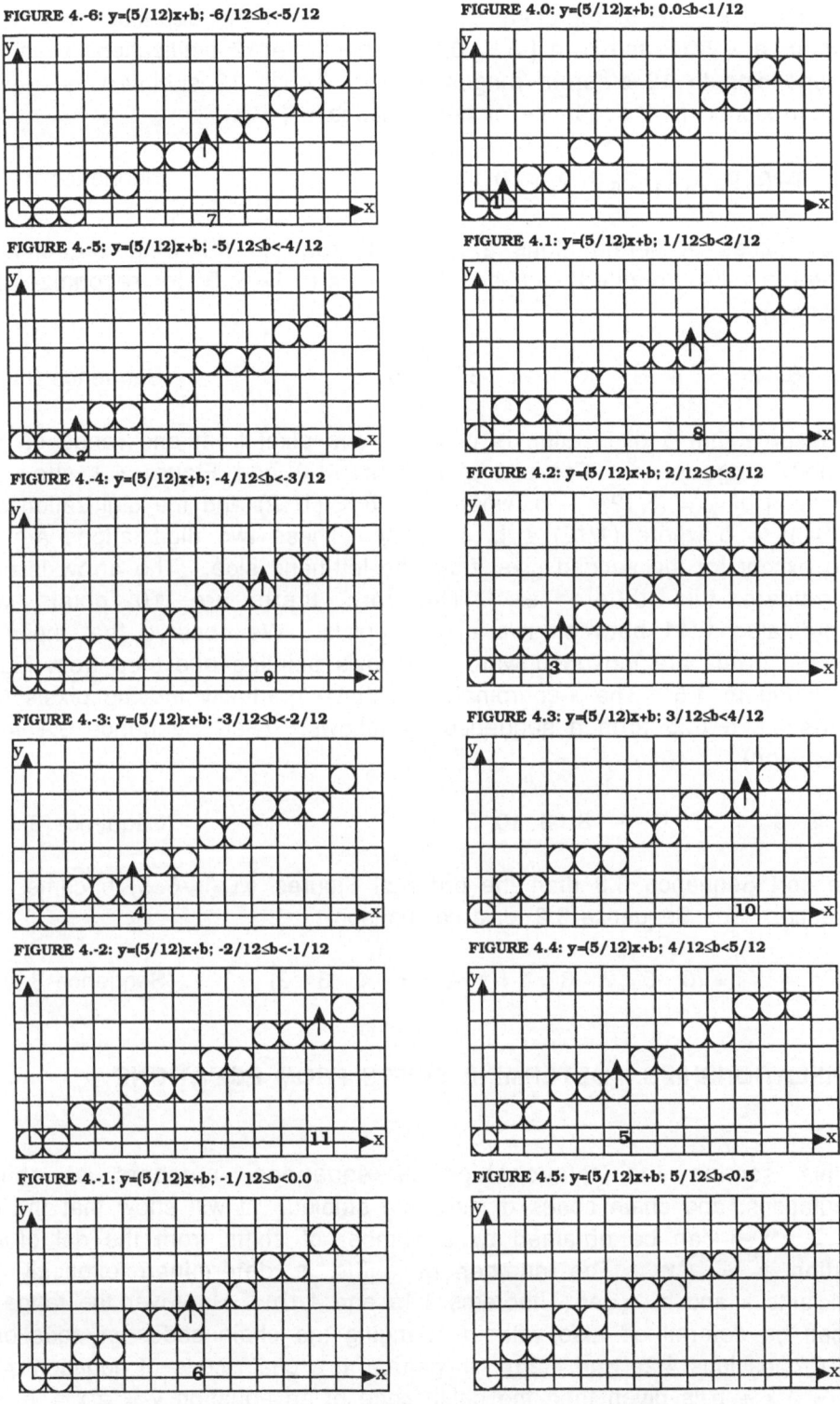

FIGURE 4.-6: y=(5/12)x+b; -6/12≤b<-5/12

FIGURE 4.0: y=(5/12)x+b; 0.0≤b<1/12

FIGURE 4.-5: y=(5/12)x+b; -5/12≤b<-4/12

FIGURE 4.1: y=(5/12)x+b; 1/12≤b<2/12

FIGURE 4.-4: y=(5/12)x+b; -4/12≤b<-3/12

FIGURE 4.2: y=(5/12)x+b; 2/12≤b<3/12

FIGURE 4.-3: y=(5/12)x+b; -3/12≤b<-2/12

FIGURE 4.3: y=(5/12)x+b; 3/12≤b<4/12

FIGURE 4.-2: y=(5/12)x+b; -2/12≤b<-1/12

FIGURE 4.4: y=(5/12)x+b; 4/12≤b<5/12

FIGURE 4.-1: y=(5/12)x+b; -1/12≤b<0.0

FIGURE 4.5: y=(5/12)x+b; 5/12≤b<0.5

FIGURES 4.i; i=-6..5. ↑ indicates the pixel will be moved for the next figure.

Figures 4.x (x = -6..5) represent the digitizations of the equations y = a*x + b, where a = 5/12 and b in [-0.5, 0.5). There are 12 digitizations which are corresponding to 12 different ranges of b's. These 12 subintervals (i=-6..5) of b correspond to a sequence of permutations

$$P_7\ P_2\ P_9\ P_4\ P_{11}\ P_6\ P_1\ P_8\ P_3\ P_{10}\ P_5\ P_{12} \qquad \text{(Sequence 3.1)}$$

If the indices of permutations are sorted then the following sequence of subintervals is obtained: (See Figures 4.i, i=-6..5 to recognize this sequence.)

$$0\ \text{-5}\ 2\ \text{-3}\ 4\ \text{-1}\ \text{-6}\ 1\ \text{-4}\ 3\ \text{-2}\ 5 \qquad \text{(Sequence 3.2)}$$

We observe that a digitization is changed one pixel from one range of b to the next range of b. For example Figure 4.0 and Figure 4.1 show the digitization of y = (5/12)x + b, where 0 ≤ b < (1/12) and the digitization of y = (5/12)x + b where (1/12) ≤ b < (2/12). These two digitizations are the same except for the second pixel from the left-hand side. The arrow is used to indicate this difference. Therefore there are 10 pixels with x-coordinates 1..11 between two ending pixels. We observe that these 10 -between pixels are moved upward by arrows pointing one step from Figure 4.-6 to Figure 4.5. The x-coordinates of these gradually moving pixels from Figures 4.i, i=-6..5 form a sequence as follows: (See Sequence 3.1 for a comparison)

$$7\ 2\ 9\ 4\ 11\ 6\ 1\ 8\ 3\ 10\ 5 \qquad \text{(Sequence 3.3)}$$

If we sort Sequence 3.3 then the order of Figures 4.i (i=-6..5) becomes the sequence: (See Sequence 3.2 for a comparison)

$$\text{Fig. 4.i;}\ i = (0\ \text{-5}\ 2\ \text{-3}\ 4\ \text{-1}\ \text{-6}\ 1\ \text{-4}\ 3\ 2) \qquad \text{(Sequence 3.4)}$$

4. RELATIONSHIPS: DETERMINE SHIFTS FROM EQUATIONS

In this section the relationships of equations, numbers of shifts, permutations, and chain codes of dsl's are studied. It will show that the dsl of y = a*x+b can be obtained by a number of shifts from the dsl of the equation y = a*x. The number of shifts is determined explicitly by coefficients a and b. (See Theorems 4.1a and 4.1b). Moreover the range of b's can be determined also without changing the chain codes of equations. (See Propositions 4.2a and 4.2b). In general if a chain code of equation such as y = a*x + b is given then the chain code of an equation y = a*x + b + e where e is an additional offset of b, can be determined by a number of shifts. (See Propositions 4.3a and 4.3b, 4.4a and 4.4b). The above mentioned results are similar for the cases b in the intervals [0, +0.5) and [0.5, 0). Therefore for a convenience we use the suffices a and b after propositions and theorem to indicate two cases respectively.

Lemma 4.1: If $x = k$ is a solution of $px = 1 \pmod{q}$, then $x = q-k$ is a solution of $px = -1 \pmod{q}$. In other words,

$$pk = 1 \pmod{q} \implies p(q-k) = -1 \pmod{q}.$$

We denote k the smallest value so that $pk = 1 \pmod{q}$ and hence q-k the smallest value so that $p(q-k) = -1 \pmod{q}$.

Proof: We have $p(q-k) = pq - pk$, but $pk = 1 \pmod{q}$; i.e., $pk = nq +1$ for some n, therefore,

$$p(q-k) = pq - nq - 1$$
$$= (p-n)q - 1.$$

Hence $p(q-k) = -1 \bmod q$.   Q.E.D.

Proposition 4.1a: If dsl_0 is dsl of equation $y = a*x$, where $a = p/q$, $0 \le p < q$, $(p, q) = 1$, then dsl_k is dsl of equation $y = a*x + (1/q)$, where k is the smallest solution of $pk = 1 \bmod q$.

Proof: Let $b = 1/q$, then $Floor(b*q) = 1$. The loop invariant in the algorithm becomes

$$LeftOverq1_i = p*i + Floor(b*q) \bmod q$$
$$= p*i + 1 \bmod q, \qquad \text{for all } i.$$

The subscript i is used to indicate the repetition in the for-loop. (See Algorithm 4 and Theorem 2.1.) The value 1 is appended to the variable LeftOverq to indicate the value $b = 1/q$ being used in the algorithm Similarly, the value 0 is used for $b = 0/q$ in the algorithm. We have

$$LeftOver0_i = p*i \bmod q.$$

To prove dsl of equation $y = a*x + 1/q$ is the shift k times of dsl_0, we prove that

$$LeftOver0_{i+k} = p*(i+k) \bmod q$$
$$= p*i + p*k \bmod q$$
$$= LeftOverq1_i \qquad \qquad \text{Q.E.D.}$$

We notice that Floor(b*q) = 1 for all b in the interval [1/q, 2/q). Therefore the proof of Prop. 4.1a remains unchanged for all b in the interval [1/q, 2/q). Hence, Prop. 4.1a is true for all b in [1/q, 2/a).

Proposition 4.2a: If dsl_0 is dsl of equation y = a*x, where a = p/q, 0 < p < q, (p, q) = 1, then dsl_k is dsl of equation y = a*x+b, where (1/q) ≤ b < (2/q) and k is the smallest solution of pk = 1 mod q.

Moreover, the proof of Prop. 1 can be reindexed to have the following results.

Proposition 4.3a: If dsl_n is dsl of the equation y = a*x +i/q, the dsl_{n+k} is dsl of equation y = a*x + (i+1)/q.

Proposition 4.4a: If dsl_n is dsl of the eqation y = a*x + b where i/q ≤ b < (i+1)/q for some positive integer (i-1) < 0.5*q, then dsl_{n+k} is dsl of equation y = a*x+b where

$$(i+1)/q \le b < (i+2)/q.$$

With the above propositions, we have the following theorem:

Theorem 4.1a: If dsl_0 is denoted as dsl of equation y = a*x, where a = p/q, 0<p<1, and (p,q) = 1, then dsl of equation y = a*x + b for 0 ≤ b < -0.5 is dsl_j, where j is calculated as follows:

$$j = ([Floor(q*b)] * k) \quad mod\ q.$$

Proof: For each b, an element in the interval [0, 0.5), there is a positive integer i such that

$$i/q \le b < (i+1)/q, \quad where\ i < 0.5 * q.$$
$$(or\ i \le q*b < i+1$$
$$or\ i = Floor(q*b).)$$

We can use recursive proof with Propositions 3 and 4 to have i*k mod q as the number of shifts to dsl_0 to get dsl of equation y = a*x +b.

Q.E.D.

Similarly, in this section we will discuss dsl's of equation y = a*x + b with negative offset b, i.e., b [-0.5, 0). Propositions and Theorems are appended letter b for easy comparison with the ones with suffix letter a.

Proposition 4.1b: If dsl_0 is dsl of equation $y = a^*x$, where $a = p/q$, $0 \leq p <$ q, $(p, q) = 1$, then dsl_k is dsl of equation $y = a^*x + (-1/q)$, where $u = q - k$ is the smallest solution of $p^*u = -1 \bmod q$.

Proof: Let $b = -1/q$, then $Floor(b^*q) = -1$. The loop invariant in the algorithm becomes

$$\begin{aligned} LeftOver1_i &= p^*i + Floor(b^*q) \bmod q \\ &= p^*i - 1 \bmod q, \qquad \text{for all i.} \end{aligned}$$

The value 1 is appended to the variable LeftOver to indicate the value $b = -1/q$ being used in the algorithm. Similarly, the value 0 is used for $b = 0/q$ in the algorithm. We have

$$LeftOver0_i = p^*i \qquad \bmod q.$$

To prove the dsl of equation $y = a^*x - 1/q$ is the shift $q-k$ times of dsl_0, we prove that

$$\begin{aligned} LeftOver0_{i + q-k} &= p^*(i+q-k) \bmod q \\ &= p^*i + p^*(q-k) \bmod q \\ &= LeftOver1_i \qquad \text{Q.E.D.} \end{aligned}$$

We notice that $Floor(b^*q) = -1$ for all b in the interval $[-1/q, 0/q)$. Therefore the proof of Prop. 1b remains unchanged for all b in the interval $[-1/q, 0/q)$. Hence, Prop. 4.1b is true for all b in $[-1/q, 0/q)$.

Proposition 4.2b: If dsl_0 is dsl of equation $y = a^*x$, where $a = p/q$, $0 < p <$ q, $(p, q) = 1$, then dsl_{q-k} is dsl of equation $y = a^*x + b$, where $(-1/q) \leq b <$ $(0/q)$ and $u = q-k$ is the smallest solution of $p^*u = -1 \bmod q$.

Moreover, the proof of Prop. 4.1b can be reindexed to have the following results.

Proposition 4.3b: If dsl_n is dsl of the equation $y = a^*x - i/q$, then dsl_{n+q-k} is dsl of equation $y = a^*x - (i+1)/q$.

Proposition 4.4b: If dsl_n is dsl of the equation $y = a^*x + b$ where $-i/q \leq b$ $< (-i+1)/q$ for some positive integer $(i+1) \geq 0.5^*q$, then $dsln+q-k$ is dsl of equation $y = a^*x+b$ where

$$(-i-1)/q \leq b < -i/q.$$

With the above propositions, we have the following theorem:

Theorem 4.1b: If dsl_o is denoted as dsl of equation $y = a*x$, where $a = p/q$, $0<p<q$, and $(p, q) = 1$, then dsl of equation $y = a*x + b$ for $-0.5 \leq b < 0$ is dsl_j, where j is calculated as follows:

$$j = (\ [\text{Floor}(q*b)]\ * (q-k)\ ), \qquad \text{mod } q.$$

Proof: For each b, an element in the interval $[-0.5, 0)$, there is a positive integer i such that

$$-i/q \leq b < (-i+1)/q, \qquad \text{where } i \leq 0.5 * q.$$

$$(\text{ or } -i \leq q*b < -i+1$$
$$\text{or } -i = \text{Floor}(q*b).\ )$$

We can use recursive proof with Propositions 3b and 4b to have $i*k(q-k)$ mod q as the number of shifts to dsl_o to get dsl of equation $y = a*x + b$.

Q.E.D.

5. RELATIONSHIPS: DETERMINE EQUATIONS FROM SHIFTS.

In this section we will find equations of dsl_s, where s is a given integer.

Theorem 5.1: Given an integer s, the equation of dsl_s is $y = (p/q)x + b$, where b is calculated as follows:
Case 1:   b is in the interval $[i_0/q, (i_0 + 1)/q]$,
$\qquad i_0 = (s * p) \text{ mod } q$ if $(s * p) \text{ mod } q < 0.5 * q$;
Case 2:   b is in the interval $[-io/q, (-io + 1)/q]$,
$\qquad i_0 = (s * (q - p)) \text{ mod } q$ if $(s * (q - p)) \text{ mod } q \geq 0/5 * q$.

Proof:
Case 1:   Assume $(s * p) \text{ mod } q < 0.5 * q$. Let $i = (s * p) \text{ mod } q$. Therefore, $i/q < 0.5$. By Theorem 1a, dsl of equation $y = (k/q) * x + (i/q)$ is dsl_{shift} where

$$
\begin{aligned}
\text{shift} \quad &= (i * k) \text{ mod } q \\
&= (((s * p) \text{ mod } q) * k) \text{ mod } q \\
&= (s * p * k) \text{ mod } q \\
&= s \text{ mod } q
\end{aligned}
$$

Hence dsl_s is dsl of the equation $y = (k/q) * x + (i/q)$. Similarly by Theorem 2a, dsls is also dsl of equation $y = (p/q) * x + b$, where $i/q \le b < (i+1)/q$.

Case 2: Assume $(s * p) \bmod q \ge 0.5 * q$. Let $i_0 = (s * (q - p)) \bmod q$. (Hence io $\le$ 0.5.) By Theorem 1b, the dsl of equation $y = a*x -(i_0)/q$ is dsl_{shift} where

$$\begin{aligned}
shift &= (i_0 * (q -k)) \bmod q \\
&= (((s * (q -p) \bmod q) * (q -k)) \bmod q \\
&= (s * (q -p) * (q -k)) \bmod q \\
&= s.
\end{aligned}$$

Hence dsl_s is dsl of the equation $y = a*x -(i_0)/q$. By Theorem 2b, dsl_s is also dsl of equation $y = a * x + b$, where $-i_0/q \le b < -(i_0 + 1)/q$.   Q.E.D.

Corollary 5.1: Given dsl_i which is i-shift dsl of dsl_0, and an integer s. The equation of dsl_{i+s} is evaluated by a similar method in the above theorem where i is substituted by (i+s).

6. RELATIONSHIPS: DETERMINE PERMUTATIONS FROM EQUATIONS.

Assume the slope a is fixed and the offset b varies. For each offset b, there corresponds a digitization which can be represented by chain code of directions. Consider chaiin code is a function of offset b. When the offset b increases, the chain code remains unchaged up to a value of b. At this value the chain code will permuted its two consecutive directions.   (**Note:** Definition of permutation is given in Section 3.) Then the chain code remains unchanged until the offset b reaches another set-point value.   These set-point values are multiple of 1/q, where q is the denominator of the slope $a = p/q$ with $(p, q) = 1$. In this section, the permutations of chain codes will be studied.   In other words, the positions of directions to be permuted in order to get the next chain code when b increases will be determined explicitly.

Lemma 6.1: The values $LeftOverq_i$, $i = 1,...,q$ are all different and form the set $\{0,1,...,q-1\}$.

Proof: This proof is omitted.

Corollary 6.1: For each n in the set $\{0,1,...,q-1\}$ there is one solution i such that
$$p*i + n = Floor(0.5*q) \quad \bmod q.$$

Theorem 6.1: For each n in $\{0,1,...,q-1\}$, let denote $\mathbf{d} = (d_1,d_2,...,d_q)$ the chain code of $y = (p/q)^*x + b$ with b in Interval$_n$, and $\mathbf{d'} = (d'_1,d'_2,...,d'_q)$ the chain code of $y = (p/q)^*x + b$ with b in Interval$_{n+1}$. There exists only one j such that

$$d_i = d'_i \quad \text{for all i such that } i \neq j \text{ and } j+1,$$
$$d_j = d'_{j+1},$$
$$d_{j+1} = d'_j.$$

The unique value j is denoted by s(n), and hence $\mathbf{p}_{s(n)}$ is the permutation on $\mathbf{d}$ to be $\mathbf{d'}$.

Proof: Denote LeftOverq$_i$ $i = 1,2,...,q$ be the values of variable LeftOverq in the loop of Algorithm 4 with b in Interval$_n$. Similarly denote LeftOverq'$_i$, $i=1,...,q$ be the values of LeftOverq in the loop of Algorithm 4 with b in Interval$_{n+1}$. By Theorem 4.1 (loop invariant), we have

$$\text{LeftOverq}_i = p^*i + n, i = 1,2,...,q,$$
$$\text{LeftOverq'}_i = p^*i + n+1, i = 1,2,...,q.$$

Therefore LeftOverq$_i$ + 1 = LeftOver'i for all $i = 1,2,..,q$. By Lemma 6.1, there is one j such that LeftOverq$_j$ < 0.5^*q ≤ LeftOverq$_j$ + 1. Hence LeftOverq$_j$ < 0.5^*q ≤ LeftOverq'$_j$, therefore $d_j = 0$ and $d'_j = 1$.

Moreover, by Algorithm 4

$$\text{LeftOverq}_{j+1} = \text{LeftOverq}_j + p$$
$$\text{LeftOverq'}_{j+1} = \text{LeftOverq'}_j + q\text{-}p.$$

Hence LeftOverq$_{j+1}$ ≥ 0.5^*q (because of 0<p) and

$$\text{LeftOverq'}_{j+1} < 0.5^*q \text{ (because of p<q)},$$

therefore $d_{j+1} = 1$ and $d'_{j+1} = 0$.

To prove the remaining results of Theorem 5.1 we need to show that $d_i = d'_i$, for all $i \neq j$ and $i \neq j+1$. Indeed for the other cases of i we have:

$$\text{not (LeftOverq}_i < 0.5^*q \le \text{LeftOverq}_i + 1).$$

Hence two possible cases can be
(1) both $LeftOverq_i$ and $LeftOverq'_i$ are less than 0.5^*q;
(2) both $LeftOverq_i$ and $LeftOver'q_i$ are greater or equal 0.5^*q.
For the former case $d_i = d'_i = 0$, and the later one $d_i = d'_i = 1$.   Q.E.D.

For each n, denote s(n) as the subscript of the permutation $\mathbf{P}_{s(n)}$ which transforms the chain code of $y = (p/q)^*x+b$, with b in Interval$_n$ to the chain code of $y = (p/q)^*x+b$, with b in Interval$_{n+1}$. In the following section, the subscript s(n) will be determined explicitly.

Theorem 6.2: The following results are true:
(1)   s(0) is the solution of $p^*s(0) = $ Floor (0.5^*q) mod q.
(2) $s(n+1) = s(n) + q-k$, where k is a solution of $p.k = 1$ mod q. Hence for all integer n

$$s(n) \quad = s(0) + (q-k)^*n \qquad mod\ q,$$
$$s(n+1) = s(1) + (q-k)^*n \qquad mod\ q,$$

(3) $s(-1) = k-s(0)$. Moreover s(-1) is also a solution of

$$(q-p)^*s(-1) = Floor(0.5^*q) \qquad mod\ q,$$

(4) $s(-n) = k^*n - s(0)$ mod q, for all strictly positive n.

Proof of (1): By the proof of Theorem 5.1, s(0) is the integer j such that

$$LeftOverq_j < 0.5^*q \le LeftOverq_j + 1.$$
Hence $LeftOver_j = $ Floor(0.5^*q) mod q, or $p^*j = $ Floor(0.5^*q) mod q.

Proof of (2): For each nonnegative n, we have :(See Proof of Theorem 5.1)

$$LeftOverq_i = p^*i + n\ mod\ q, \text{ for } i=1,2,...,q,$$
$$LeftOverq'_i = p^*i + n+1\ mod\ q, \text{ for } i=1,2,...,q,$$

where LeftOverq and LeftOverq' are notations for variable LeftOverq in Algorithm 4 with b in Interval$_n$ and Interval$_{n+1}$ respectively. To prove that $\mathbf{P}_{s(n)\ +\ q-k}$ is the permutation to transform the chain code of $y=(p/q)^*x + b$ with b in Interval$_n$ to the one with b in Interval$_{n+1}$, we need to show $s(n+1) - s(n) = q-k$ mod q. Therefore we need to solve the equation:

$$LeftOverq'_{i+x} = LeftOverq_i \qquad mod\ q, \text{ for all } i = 1,2,...,q.$$

Or $\qquad$ $p^*(i+x) + n +1 = p^*i + n,$ $\qquad$ mod q.

Hence we need to solve $p.x = -1$ mod q. Therefore $x = q-k$, where k is the solution of $p.k=1$ mod q. As a consequence of the recursion, we have

$$s(n) = s(0) + (q-k)^*n \text{ mod } q.$$

Proof of (3): With a similar argument in Proof of (2), we have

$$
\begin{aligned}
s(0) &= s(-1) + q-k \quad \text{mod q.} \\
\text{Therefore} \qquad s(-1) &= s(0)-q+k \qquad \text{mod q.} \\
\text{Or} \qquad s(-1) &= k - s(0) \qquad \text{mod q.}
\end{aligned}
$$

Proof of (4): Proof of (2) can be generalized for negative offset. We have

$$
\begin{aligned}
s(-n) &= s(-n-1) + q-k \text{ mod q.} \\
\text{Hence} \qquad s(-n-1) &= s(-n) + k \text{ mod q.} \\
\text{By induction we have} \qquad s(-n) &= s(-1) + k^*(n-1) \text{ mod q.}
\end{aligned}
$$

$$\text{Q.E.D.}$$

Example: Let p=5 and q=12. We have:

$$
\begin{aligned}
k &= 5, \qquad (\text{ it is the solution of } 5 * k = 1 \quad \text{mod 12}), \\
s(0) &= 6, \qquad (\text{ it is the solution of } 5 * k = 6 \quad \text{mod 12}), \\
s(1) &= 1, \qquad (\text{since } s(1) = s(0) + 12 - 5 \quad \text{mod 12}), \\
s(n+1) &= 1 + (12 - 5) * n \quad \text{mod 12}, \\
&\qquad (\text{since } s(n+1) = s(1) + (q-k) * n \text{ mod q}).
\end{aligned}
$$

Discussion

(1) Let denote $\text{Interval}_i = [i/q, (i+1/q)$, where i is an integer. The chain code of the digital straight line of $y = (p/q) x + b$ remains unchanged for all b in the interval $[i/q, (i+1)/q)$ for all integer i. This result is a consequence of Propositions 4.2a and 4.2b.

(2) Consider two consecutive intervals $\text{Interval}_i = [i/q, (i+1)/q)$ and $\text{Inteval}_{i+1} = [(i+1)/q, (i+2)/q)$. We assume that both intervals are included in $[-0.5, 0.5)$. That means $-0.5 \leq (i-1)/q$ and $(i+1)/q < 0.5$. These two inequalities are equivalent to $-0.5^*q + 1 \leq i < 0.5^*q - 1$. The differences between two chain codes whose offsets are in these two consecutive intervals are determined by permutations. More precisely, there are only two consecutive directions which are interchanged. The location of

interchanging is determined explicitly. Let s(n) is the index of the interchanging (i.e., directions at s(n) and s(n) + 1 are interchanged when b crosses from one subinterval to the next one.) The s(n+1) = s(n) + q-k mod q, where n can be negative number. We are able to compare this result with the result of shifting the chain codes. The chain codes are shifted k times when b crosses from one subinterval to the next interval.

(3) As a consequence of the previous results we are able to associate each $Interval_n$ of offset b with a fixed chain code of directions. Two chain codes of directions say, $d = (d_1, d_2, ..., d_q)$ and $d' = (d'_1, d'_2,..., d'_q)$ which are permuted from each other, can be used to calculate the different of corresponding offsets b by the formula

$$d_i \oplus d'_i = [Floor(b-b')]^*q/2, \tag{1}$$

where $\oplus$ is the exclusive-or operator. For an arbitrary pair of chain codes their difference of b's can be calculated by the number of permutations from one chain code to the other. It can not be used equation (1) without looking the positiveness of b's. In other words, if b and b' are both positive (or negative), equation (1) can be used to calculate the diffference between b and then equation (1) needs to be modified. We are not going to discuss in here the topic of evaluating b-b' from two chain codes by exclusive-or operator.

7. SUMMARY OF RESULTS

Propositions 4.4a,b indicate that $Interval_n$ to $Interval_{n+1}$ the $dsl_{s(n)}$ become $dsl_{s(n)+k}$ where k is the smallest solution of p.k=1 mod q. In reverse, if b decreases from $Interval_{n+1}$ to $Interval_n$, the $dsl_{s(n+1)}$ becomes $dsl_{s(n+1)+q-k}$ where q-k is the smallest solution of p.(q-k) =-1 mod q.

For permutation, if b increases from $Interval_n$ to $Interval_{(n+1)}$ the permutation will change from p_x to $p_{(x+q-k)}$. In reverse if b decreases from $Interval_{(n+1)}$ to Intervaln, the p_y become p_{y+k}.

Equation: $y = a^*x+b$;   slope a = p/q, where 0<p<q and (p,q) = 1
offset b is in the interval [-0.5, 0.5]

Interval$_n$: $[n/q, (n+1)/q)$;
        where $n =$ Floor($b*q$)

Loop invariant:
        LeftOverq$_i$ $= p*i + n$, $i = 1,2,...,q$ **Ref: Theo. 2.1**

Chain code: dsl$_j$, where j is number of shifts
        case $n \geq 0$: $j = n*k$ mod q,   **Ref: Theo. 4.1a**
        case $n < 0$: $j = n*(q-k)$ mod q,   **Ref: Theo. 4.1b**
        where k is the smallest solution
        of the equation p.k = 1 mod q. As a
        consequence p.(q-k) = -1 mod q.   **Ref: Lemma 4.1**

Offset b: $i_0/q \leq b < (i_0 +1)/q$, where
                $i_0 = j*p$ mod q, if $j*p$ mod q $\leq 0.5*q$
        $- i_0 /q \leq b < (- i_0 +1)/q$, where
                $i_0 = j*(q-p)$ mod q, if $j*(q-p)$ mod q $> 0.5*q$
                        Ref: Theo. 5.1

Permutation:
        s(n) : the position to permute dsl$_n$ to be dsl$_{n+1}$.
        s(0) : the solution of $p*s(0) =$ Floor($0.5*q$) mod q.
        s(n+1) = s(n) + q-k mod q, for all n   **Ref: Theo. 6.2**

Other Results:

        * offset b is not in [-j0.5, 0.5). It can be
          reduced to the case b is in [-0.5, -0.5)
                        Ref: Theo. 2.2
        * slope a is not in the first octant. It can be
          reduced to the case a is in the first octant.
                        Ref: Theo. 2.3

8. PARALLEL AND OVERLAPPED DIGITAL STRAIGHT LINES

Two dsl's can be parallel, overlapped, or intersected. The last case has been
discussed in Pham(1986). To detect the cases parallel or overlapped, we
will define the parallel and overlapped dsl's and overlapped dsl's and discuss
distances on the vertical line x=a (we call x-distance for short). Moreover,
we will discuss the case that two dsl's are not totally overlapped but they

are shifted from each other. (See Figure 5 for parallel and overlapped dsl's.) Hence, a rational distance on two parallel dsl's is introduced which is the difference between two corresponding offsets b's. similar results are obtained also for y-distances.

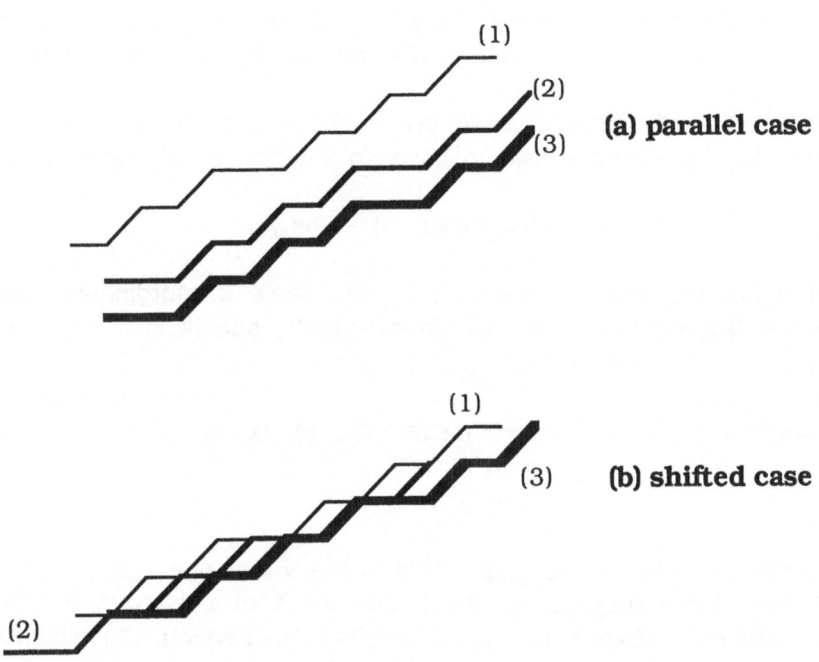

FIGURE 5: Parallel and Shifted dsl's

line (1): dsl 0 1 0 1 0 0 1 0 1 0 1 0
line (2): dsl 0 0 1 0 1 0 1 0 0 1 0 1
line (3): dsl 0 0 1 0 1 0 1 0 0 1 0 1

Notes: (2) is shifted 4 times from (1)
(2) and (3) are identical except for starting pixels
The dsl's in case (a) are the ones in case (b).

Definitions.

Definition of x-dsl: Vertical dsl is a dsl of one direction which can be 2 or 6.   It contains the pixels of the same x coordinate.   The equation for vertical dsl is x = c, where c is an integer constant, so it is called x-dsl for short.   Similarly, horizontal dsl is a dsl of one direction which can be 0 or 4. It contains the pixels of the same y coordinate.   The equation for horizontal dsl is y = d, where d is an integer constant, so it is called y-dsl for short. We have not defined the parallel dsl's yet, but we can say that x-dsl's are visually parallel to the y axis and y-dsl's are visually parallel to the x axis.

Definition of x-distance: Two pixels (x, y) and (u, v) of the same x coordinates (i.e., x = u) are said to have an x-distance calculated as follows:

$$\text{x-distance}[(x, y), (u, v)] = abs(y-v).$$

If A and B are two sets of pixels having the same x coordinates, then their x-distance is the x-distance of two closest pixels, one is in A and the other is in B, i.e.,

$$\text{x-distance}(A, B) = \text{minimum } (\text{x-distance}[(x, y), (x, v)])$$
$$(x, y) \text{ in A}$$
$$(x, v) \text{ in B}$$

The distance on x-dsl of two given dsl's is the x-distance between A and B, where A and B are respectively the intersections of x-dsl with one dsl and with the other dsl.   (See Figure 8 for details.)   In general, the distance may vary on different x-dsl's.

Suppose two dsl's are intersected at (x_l, y_l), then the distance on x_l-dsl is zero.

Definition of parallel and overlapped dsl's: Two dsl's are parallel if they have the same chain code of directions.   They overlap each other if they are identical, i.e., they generate the same set of pixels from their chain codes and their starting pixels.

With the above definition the x-distances are   a constant value for two parallel dsl's and zero for overlapped ones.

Discussion:
(1) In the case the chain codes are shifted from each other, do we consider them parallel or overlapped?   If so, what are their x-distances and are they constant?   The results of the previous sections will provide rigourous

answers for these questions. Indeed, two chain codes are shifted from each other and they start from the same pixel will not in general generate the same set of pixels. Their x-distances are 0 or 1.

On the other hand, they are not totally separated nor intersected at a few pixels. Their common pixels of both dsl's are distributed uniformly among the uncommon pixels. By the study of the previous sections, the two such dsl's having equations of the same slope but different offsets b's, and their offsets are differeng by a fraction. Therefore we provide in the following more rigourous definitions of parallel dsl's and their x-distances.

(2)More rigourous definitions of parallel dsl's and their distances.
Two dsl's are parallel if they have the same chain code of directions or their chain codes are different by a finite number of shifts. Their x-distance is a constant and is the difference between two corresponding b's of the two dsl's.

Acknowledgment: The author would like to express his gratitude to his wife KimThư for her assistant and encouragement.

REFERENCES

Arcelli C. and Massarotti A., "Regular Arcs in Digital Contours," *Comput. Graphics Images Process.*, Vol. **4**, 1975, pp 339-360; Erratum, *Comput. Graphics Images Process.*, Vol. **5**, 1976, p 280.

Bresenham J. E., "Algorithm for Computer Control of a Digital Plotter," *IBM Systems J.*, **4**, 1965, pp 25-30.

Brons R., "Linguistic Methods for the Description of a Straight Line on a Grid," *Comput. Graphics Image Process.*, Vol. **3**, 1974, pp. 48-62.

Chang S. K., "Picture Processing Grammar and its Applications," *Inform. Sci.* Vol. **3**, 1971, pp. 121-148.

Dorst L. and Duin R. P. W., "Spirograph Theory: a Framework for Calculations on Digitized Straight Lines," *IEEE Trans. Pattern Anal. Mach. Intell.* **PAMI 6**, No. 5, 1984, pp. 632-639.

Dorst L. and Smeulders A. W. M., "Discrete Representation of Straight Lines," *IEEE Trans. Pattern Anal. Mach. Intell.*, **PAMI 6**, No. 4, 1984, pp. 450-463.

Hung S. H. Y., "On the Straightness of Digital Arcs," *IEEE Trans. Pattern Anal. Mach. Intell.,* **PAMI-7**, No. 2, 1985, pp. 203-215.

Kim C. E. and Rosenfeld A., "Digital Straight Lines and Convexity of Digital Regions," *IEEE Trans. Pattern Anal. Mach. Intell.,* **PAMI-4** 1982, pp. 149-153.

Kim C. E., "On cellular Straight Line Segments," *Comput. Graphics Image Process.,* **18**, 1982, pp. 369-381.

Pfaltz J. L. and Rosenfeld A., "Computer Representation of Planar Regions by their Skeletons," *Comm. Asso. Comput. Mach.,* **10**, 1967, pp. 119-125.

Pham S. , "Digital Straight Segments," Comput. Vision, *Graphics and Image Processing,* **36**, 1986, pp. 10-30.

Pham S. , "On the Boundary of Digital Straight Line Segments," *International Computer Graphics Conference,* Tokyo, April 22-25, 1986, pp. 79-109.

Pham S. , "Parallel, Overlapped and Intersected Digital Straight Lines," *Second International Conference on Computers and Applications,* IEEE Computer Society, Beijing, China, June 23-27, 1987.

Rosenfeld A., "Digital Straight Line Segments," *IEEE Trans. Comput.,* **C-23**, 1974, pp. 1264-1269.

Rosenfeld A., *Picture Processing by Computer,* Academic Press, New York, 1969.

Wu L. D., "On the Chain Code of a Line," *IEEE Trans. Pattern Anal. Mach. Intell.* **PAMI-4**, No. 3, 1982, pp. 347-353.

An Extended Rounding Operation for Modeling Solids with Free-Form Surfaces

Hiroaki Chiyokura

ABSTRACT

The authors propose an extended rounding operation as a tool for modeling solids with free-form surfaces. Using the rounding operation, the edges and vertices of a solid can be locally rounded, and those parts of the solid are changed to free-form surfaces. The user inputs information about which edges should be rounded and about radii of curves generated by the operation. This facility has been implemented in our solid modeling system DESIGNBASE.

KEYWORDS: free-form surface, solid modeling, rounding operation

1. Introduction

The importance of a solid modeling system in CAD/CAM (Computer Aided Design and Manufacturing) has been widely recognized. At present, many solid model based CAD systems are used in the design of mechanical products. However, there are several problems in the practical usage of a solid modeling system. One of the most important problems is that the range of shapes generated in a solid modeling system is limited. Although it is easy to model a polyhedra in conventional solid modeling systems, it is not easy to model free-form and fillet surfaces. Therefore, we propose a **rounding operation,** a local operation for modeling a solid with free-form surfaces. Using the rounding operation, edges and vertices of a solid can be locally rounded, and those parts of a solid are changed to free-form surfaces.

Chiyokura and Kimura [1983] proposed a rounding operation, but there were several restrictions about the shapes that could be rounded. For example, it was difficult to specify the radii of curves generated in the rounding operation. The rounding of curved edges was also not considered. In our new method, these problems are solved. Further, the rounding operation is extended so that edges and vertices can be rounded by specifying different radii to the several edges which are connected to the same vertex. Our new extended rounding operation has been implemented in our solid modeling system, DESIGNBASE [Chiyokura 1987] whose internal model is a boundary representation.

2. Free-form surfaces in solid modeling

Recently, many research works have been reported in modeling free-form surfaces and fillet surfaces in a solid modeling system have been done. Broadly speaking, these methods form three groups. One uses Boolean operations of free-form surfaces [Riesenfeld 1983; Srraga and Waters 1984; Thomas 1985]. To implement the Boolean operation, the computation of intersecting curves between two different free-form surfaces is required. This computation takes a long computation time and the algorithm is unreliable for calculating intersecting curves. The second group is a method for constructing fillet and blend surfaces which smooth between two different surfaces [Hoffmann and Hopcroft 1985; Middleditch and Sears 1985]. These methods are not generally applied to modeling of free-form surfaces. The third group of methods is to generate free-form surfaces from a polyhedron. This method was first proposed by Doo, Sabin [1978], Catmall and Clark [1978]. Then Chiyokura an Kimura [1983] proposed rounding of a polyheron as a local operation for intergrating solid modeling and free-form surface modeling. The method of rounding a polyhedron has been recently expanded [Beeker 1986; Fjällström 1986; Séquin 1986; Tan and Chan 1986; Wijk 1986]. As the complex calculations are not usually needed, computation time and reliability are not a problem. However, there are several restrictions in the range of of shapes generated.

To extend the range of shapes that can be generated in a solid modeling system, it is necessary to solve the problems of the three facilities of methods. This paper deals with the third group of methods, rounding of a polyhedron. In conventional methods of rounding a polyhedron, the control of free-form surfaces generated were not adequate. To modify the free-form surfaces, a user usually changes the shape of the original polyhedron. In design of mechanical objects, radii of curves in the object are often important, and a designer is familiar with the shape definition using the radii. Therefore, we expanded the rounding operation so that a user can specify the radii of rounded edges. In addition, curved edges can be rounded. This paper describes the new version of the rounding operation.

3. Rounding specifications

For the rounding operation, the user specifies the **rounding values** of all the edges and the **rounding flags** of all the vertices. These are described below.

3.1 Rounding values of edges

There are five rounding values of edges (0, 1, 2, 3, and 4) as shown Figure 1. Figure 1(a) shows edge E_0, which is connected to vertices V_1 and V_2. The edge E_0 is attached to four edges E_1, E_2, E_3 and E_4. The edge E_0 is rounded according to five rounding values as follows:

0... The edge is rounded, as shown in Figure 1(b). First, edge E_0 is deleted. Then, curve C_1 replaces edges E_1 and E_2. Points P_1 is made in the center of edges E_1 and point P_2 in the center of E_2. Similarly, curve C_2 is made from E_3 and E_4. In this rounding, the user cannot specify the radii of the curves.

1... The edge is not rounded. If edge E_0 and all the edges connected to it have rounding value 1, edge E_0 is not changed. However, if edge E_0 has rounding value 1 but some of edges connected to it are rounded, edge E_0 is changed to a curved edge, as shown in Figure 1(c).

2... The edge is rounded. The user can specify a radius r_1 of a cross-section curve between a generated surface and a flat plane perpendicular to edge E_0, as shown in Figure 1(d).

3... The edge is rounded. The user specifies the distances D_1 and D_2 between the original vertex and the end point of the generated curve, as shown in Figure 1(e). The distances D_1 and D_2 are defined as follows:

$$D_1 = |V_1 - P_1| = |V_1 - P_2| \qquad D_2 = |V_2 - P_3| = |V_2 - P_4|$$

4... The edge is rounded. The user specifies radius r_1 of curve C_1 and r_2 of C_2. These radii may differ, as shown in Figure 1(f).

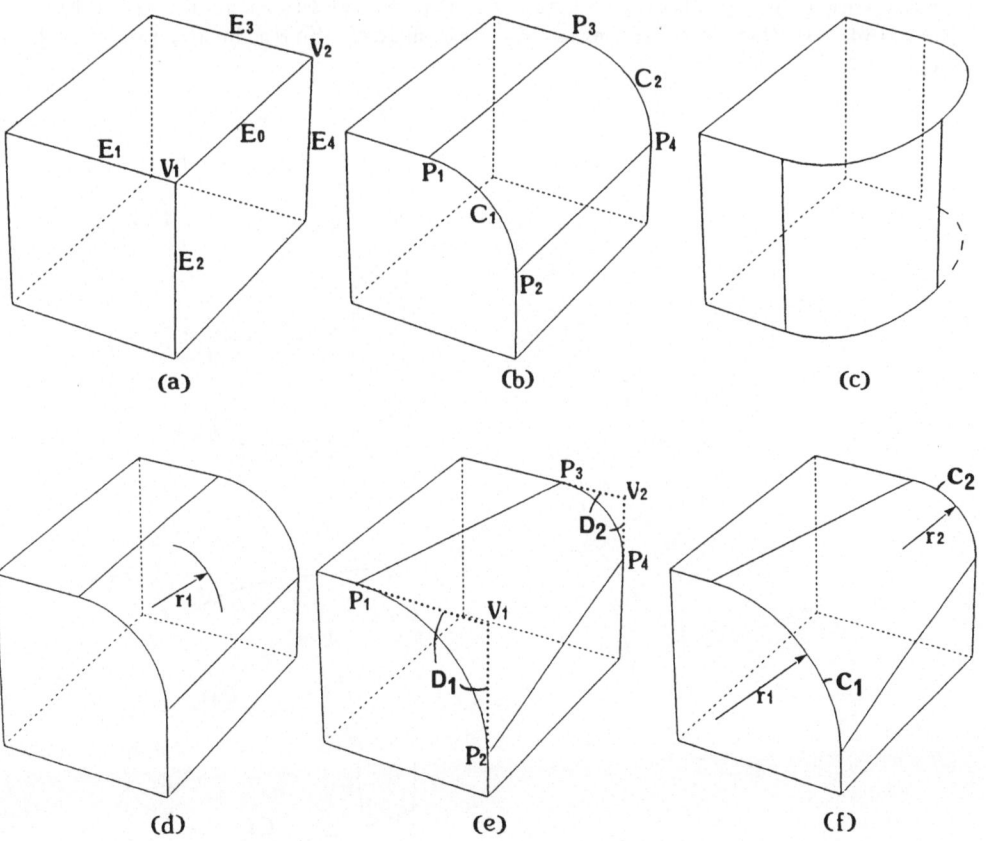

Figure 1. Rounding values for edges

3.2 Rounding flags of vertices

To round a vertex, the user assigns a rounding value other than 1 to edges attached to the vertex, and specifies a rounding flag (0 or 1) to the vertex. We describe the rounding flag, using Figure 2. Figure 2(a) shows vertex V_1 which is connected to three edges E_1, E_2 and E_3. These edges are given rounding value 2. Different radii r_1, r_2 and r_3 are specified for edges E_1, E_2 and E_3, respectively. If rounding flag 0 is given to the vertex V_1, edges E_1, E_2 and E_3 are replaced by curved edges, as shown in Figure 2(b). In this figure, curved edges $C_{1,1}$ and $C_{1,2}$ are generated to replace edge E_1. Similarly, curved edges $C_{2,1}$ and $C_{2,2}$ are generated to replace edge $E2$, and $C_{3,1}$ and $C_{3,2}$ are generated to replace edge $E3$. The radii of these curved edges have values specified by the user. However, the user occasionally wants the vertex rounded more smoothly. In such a case, he or she specifies rounding flag 1, which cause a rounding operation to generate the curve mesh model shown in Figure 2(c). In the curve mesh model, curves $C_{1,2}$, $C_{2,2}$ and $C_{3,2}$ have the specified radii, but curves $C_{1,1}$, $C_{2,1}$ and $C_{3,1}$ have different radii. Another example is shown in Figure 3. In this example, concave corner V_1 shown in Figure 3(a) is rounded. If rounding flag 0 is given to vertex V_1, the model shown in Figure 3(b) is created. If flag 1 is given to V_1, the model shown in Figure 3(c) is created.

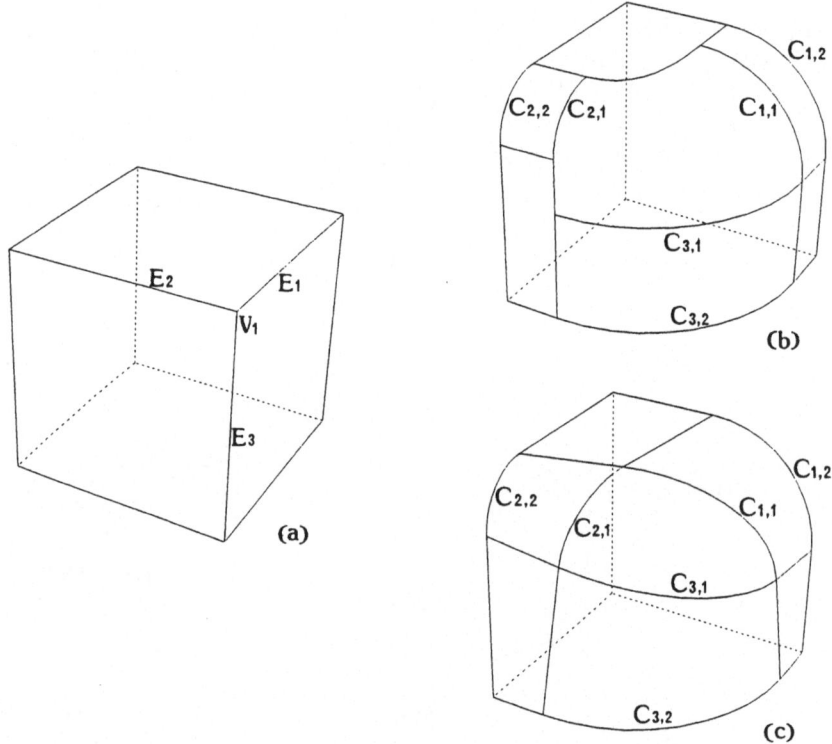

Figure 2. Rounding flags for vertices

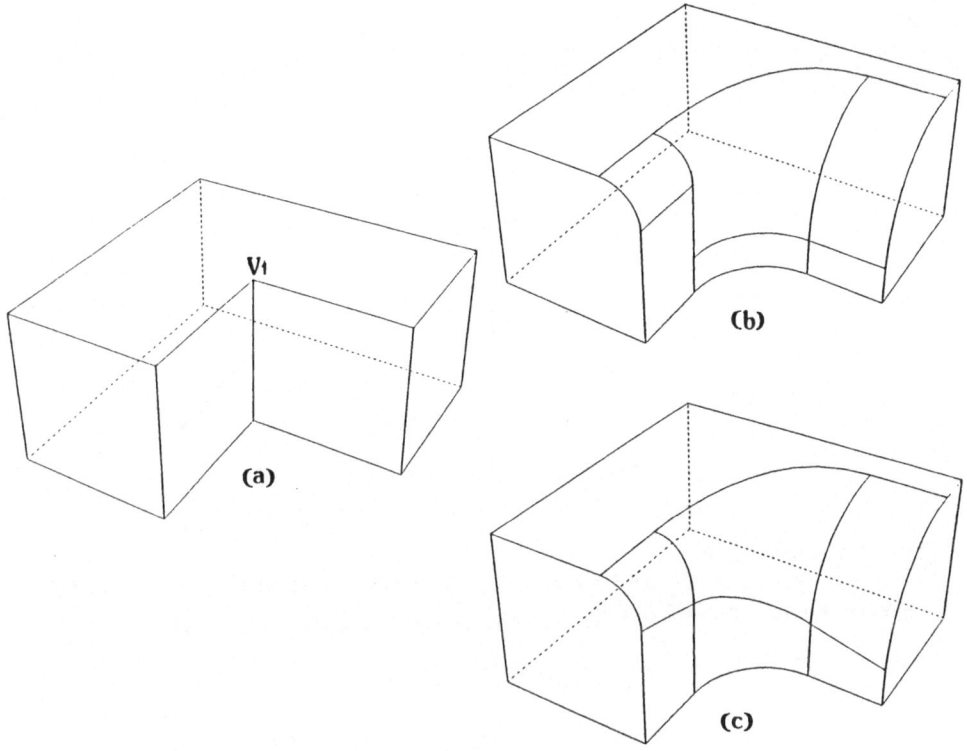

Figure 3. Rounding flags for vertices

4. Rounding operation

4.1 Primitive operations

In DESIGNBASE, all high-level operations such as Boolean operations and local operations create or modify a solid by using primitive operations [Chiyokura and Kimura 1985]. These primitive operations are stored in a tree-structure enabling undo and redo operations [Toriya, Satoh, Ueda and Chiyokura 1986]. This section explains the primitive operations used in the rounding operation.

(1) MVE and KVE

MVE makes vertex V_1 on edge E_1, as shown in Figure 4. KVE is the inverse operation of MVE.

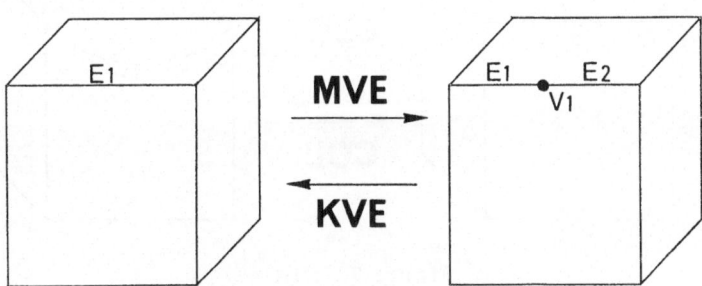

Figure 4. MVE and KVE

(2) MEL and KEL

MEL makes edge E_1 in loop L_1, as shown in Figure 5. KEL is the inverse of MEL.

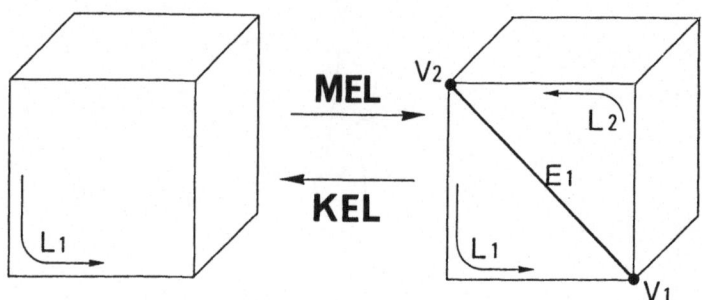

Figure 5. MEL and KEL

(3) MEV and KEV

MEV makes edge E_1 and vertex V_1 in loop L_1, as shown in Figure 6. KEV is the inverse of MEV.

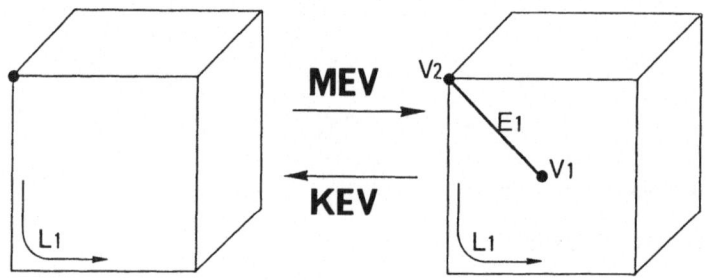

Figure 6. MEV and KEV

(4) CLC

CLC changes straight line edge E_1 to the curved edge E_1, as shown in Figure 7.

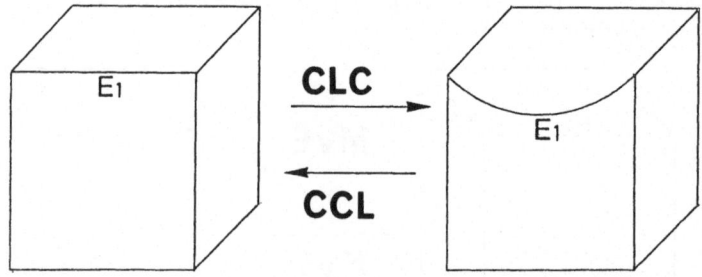

Figure 7. CLC

4.2 Overview of the rounding operation algorithm

The algorithm of the rounding operation consists of the following three phases.

(1) Vertex generation on edges

Figure 8(a) shows a solid to be rounded. V_1 is a **flat vertex,** a vertex between two edges that lie on the same straight line. The edges with mark 2 have rounding value 2. All the other edges have rounding values 1. Radii are specified for the edges with value 2. In phase 1, one or two vertices are generated on edges with value 2 by using a MVE primitive operation. One or two vertices are also generated, on edges connected to the edges with value 2. In Figure 8(b), new vertices are shown as markers. These vertices divide each original edge into two or three edges. Each new edge inherits the rounding value assigned to the original edge.

(2) Edge generation on faces

As shown in Figure 8(c), edges are generated between the vertices created in phase 1 by using MEV and MEL primitive operations. In this way the original faces are subdivided.

(3) Curved edge generation

Some of edges connected to the original vertices are deleted by using KEL and KEV operations. Also, edges connected to vertices made in phase 1 are deleted. Then curved edges are created from two straight edges. Figure 8(d) shows a curve mesh model created using the rounding operation.

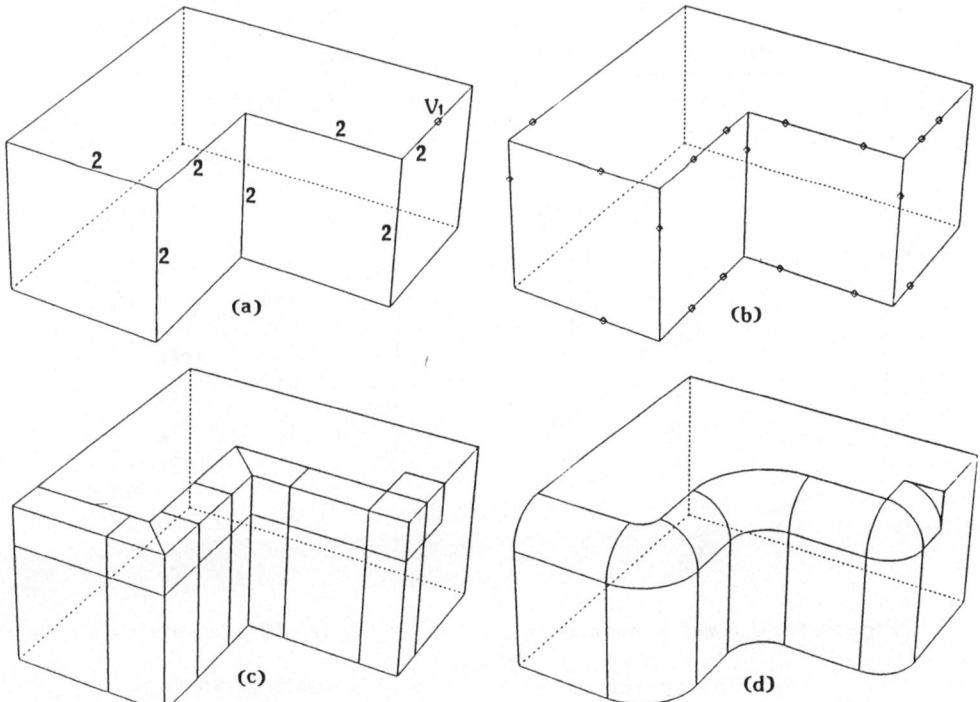

(a)

(b)

(c)

(d)

Figure 8. Overview of the rounding operation

The internal model in DESIGNBASE does not store surface equations interpolating faces. When surface equations are necessary, the Gregory patches interpolating the faces are locally generated from the boundary curves attached to the face [Chiyokura 1986].

5. Vertex generation on edges

This section describes phase 1 of the algorithm for the rounding operation. This phase consists of the following two steps:

5.1 Making the tables for edges

In the first step of phase 1, tables of subdivision points on edges are made. Figure 9 shows edge E_0, which runs between vertices V_5 and V_6. The rounding value of E_0 is either 2, 3, or 4. Edge E_0 is connected to edges E_1, E_2, E_3 and E_4, which is attached to vertices V_1, V_2, V_3 and V_4, respectively. Curves C_1 and C_2 drawn as dotted lines are to be made in phase 3 of the rounding operation. The radii r_1 and r_2 of curves C_1 and C_2 are assigned to edge E_0 by the user. Subdivision points P_1, P_2, P_3 and P_4 on edges E_1, E_2, E_3 and E_4 are computed so that the radii of curves C_1 and C_2 correspond to r_1 and r_2. The subdivision points P_1 and P_2 are the end points of curve C_1. P_3 and P_4 are the end points of curve C_2. The positions of subdivision points are represented as parameter value $t_i(i=1,2,3,4)$ $(0 \le t_i \le 1)$. The parameter values are

$$t_1 = \frac{(P_1 - V_5) \cdot (V_1 - V_5)}{(V_1 - V_5)^2} \qquad t_2 = \frac{(P_2 - V_5) \cdot (V_2 - V_5)}{(V_2 - V_5)^2}$$

$$t_3 = \frac{(P_3 - V_6) \cdot (V_3 - V_6)}{(V_3 - V_6)^2} \qquad t_4 = \frac{(P_4 - V_6) \cdot (V_4 - V_6)}{(V_4 - V_6)^2} .$$

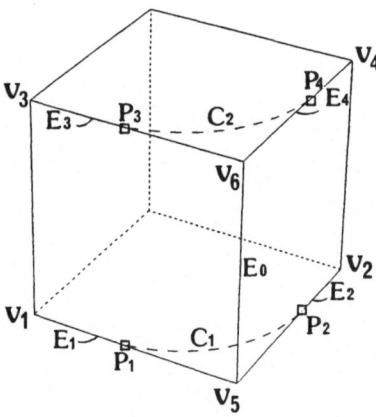

Figure 9. Curves generated

in the rounding operation

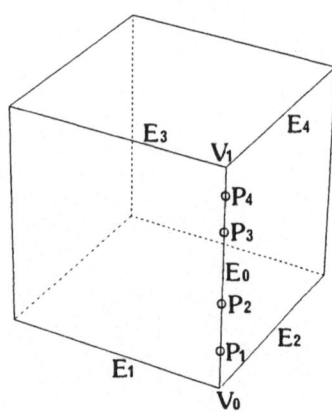

Figure 10. Subdivision

points on an edge

For each edge with a rounding value of either 2, 3 or 4, four subdivision points are computed. If the parameter value is larger than 1 or smaller than 0, it is difficult to generate a curve having the radius specified by the user, since the point is not on the edge. In such a case, the user must specify a different radius. If the parameter value is larger than 0 and smaller than 1, it is stored in the table of edges. The table of an edge to be subdivided is

```
struct EdgeTable {
        double StartLeft;
        double StartRight;
        double EndLeft;
        double EndRight;
}.
```

Four or fewer subdivision points are given   to each edge of a solid. In Figure 10, if the four winged-edges E_1, E_2, E_3 and E_4 of edge E_0 are rounded, subdivision points P_1, P_2, P_3 and P_4 on E_0 are computed. The parameter values of these points are stored in **StartLeft, StartRight, EndLeft** and **EndRight** of the table of edge E_0, respectively. If edge E_1 is not rounded, a number larger than 1 (e.g., 2) is stored in StartLeft of the table of the edge E_0. So the table represents the number and position of the subdivision points.

Figure 11 shows edge E_0 which runs between two vertices V_1 and V_2. E_0 is connected to face F_1 and three edges E_1, E_2 and E_3. The angle of corner V_1 of face F_1 is greater than 180 degrees and is called a   **concave corner.** The corner with an angle smaller than 180 degrees is also called **convex corner.** The corner at flat-vertex V_2 is called a **flat corner.** The rounding value of E_0 is either 2, 3 or 4. Curves C_1 and C_2 drawn as dotted lines are to be made in the third phase of the rounding operation. If a rounded edge is connected to a concave corner, no subdivision point is computed on the other edge connected to the corner. Thus, although subdivision point P_1 is computed on edge E_1, no point is computed on E_2. Also, if edge E_0 is connected to flat corner V_2, no subdivision point is computed.

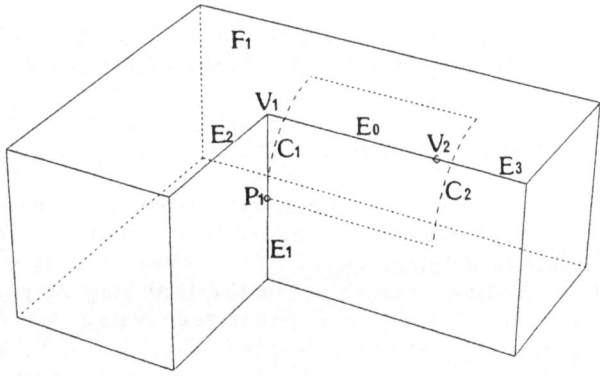

Figure 11. Curves generated in the rounding operation

5.2 Making vertices on edges

In the second step of phase 1, from the table of subdivision points, four or fewer subdivision points are given to an edge. On the subdivision points of the edge, vertices are made by using MVE primitive operations. In Figure 10, vertices V_0 and V_1 have rounding flag 0. Here, let the parameter value of the position at vertex V_0 be 0. The parameter value at vertex V_1 is 1. First, the system checks the parameter value of subdivision points to make curves with radii specified by the user. To make these curves, the parameter values t_1, t_2, t_3 and t_4 of the points P_1, P_2, P_3 and P_4 must satisfy the following condition:

$$t_1 < t_3, \quad t_1 < t_4, \quad t_2 < t_3 \quad \text{and} \quad t_2 < t_4$$

If the above condition is not satisfied, the system warns the users that the radii specified for curves are too large, and stops the rounding operation. If the condition is satisfied, the rounding operation continues.

After the check, vertices are created on two of four subdivision points. If the parameter value t_2 is larger than t_1, a vertex is made on P_2 by using a MVE primitive. If t_1 is larger than t_2, a vertex is produced on the position of P_1. If t_3 is smaller than t_4, a vertex is produces on P_3. If t_4 is smaller than t_3, a vertex is produced on P_4.

When the rounding flag of a vertex is 1, it is not necessary to make curves with specified radii to smooth the vertex. In figure 10, if the rounding flag of vertex V_0 is 1, a new vertex is made at the center point between P_1 and P_2. Similarly, if the flag of vertex V_1 is 1, a vertex is made at the center point between P_3 and P_4. When winged-edges E_1, E_2, E_3 and E_4 of E_0 all have rounding value 1, no vertex is made on E_0 since the winged-edges are not rounded. If some of the edges E_1, E_2, E_3 and E_4 have rounding value 0 and the other edges have 1, a new vertex on edge E_0 is made at the center point between V_0 and V_1.

6. Edge generation on faces

In phase 2, edges are generated on faces of a solid, and then the faces are subdivided. This phase consists of the two steps described below.

6.1 Generation of edges at corners

Figure 12(a) shows a solid after phase 1. The markers show flat-vertices. V_1 is a vertex made before the rounding operation. We call such a vertex an original vertex. The other vertices were made in phase 1 of the rounding operation. In the first step of phase 2, edges attached at corners of faces are generated, using MEV and MEL operations. Figure 12(b) shows new edges E_1, E_2, E_3, E_4 and E_5 made on face F_1. The way to make such edges varies according to whether the corner attached to the vertex is a convex corner, a flat corner or a concave corner.

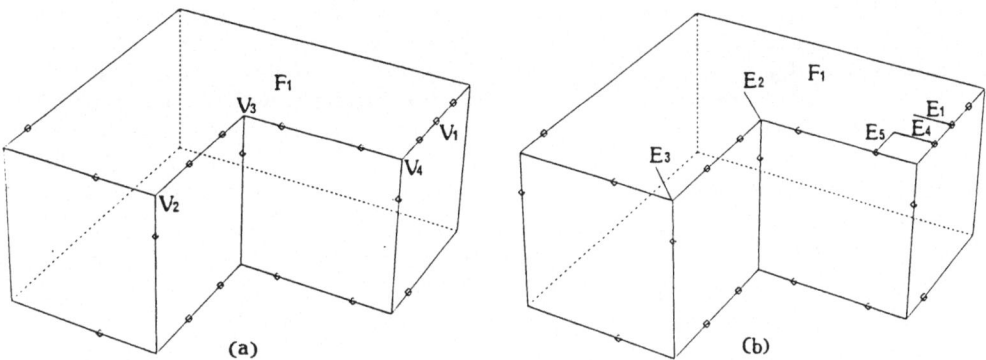

Figure 12. Generation of edges in a loop

6.2 Generation of edges between new vertices

Figure 13(a) shows a solid after the first step of phase 2. Vertices V_1, V_2, V_3 and V_4 were made in step 1. In step 2, MEL operations are used to make new edges between vertices made in step 1. Figure 13(b) shows new edges E_1, E_2 and E_3. If no edge is made at corner, an edge is made between a vertex made in phase 1 and a vertex made in step 1 of phase 2. Edge E_4 is an example of this case. Then edges are made between vertices on the original edges and points on new edges using MVE and MEL operations. These edges are perpendicular to the original edges. Figure 13(c) shows these edges E_5, E_6, E_7 and E_8. The procedure in phase 2 is applied to all faces of a solid.

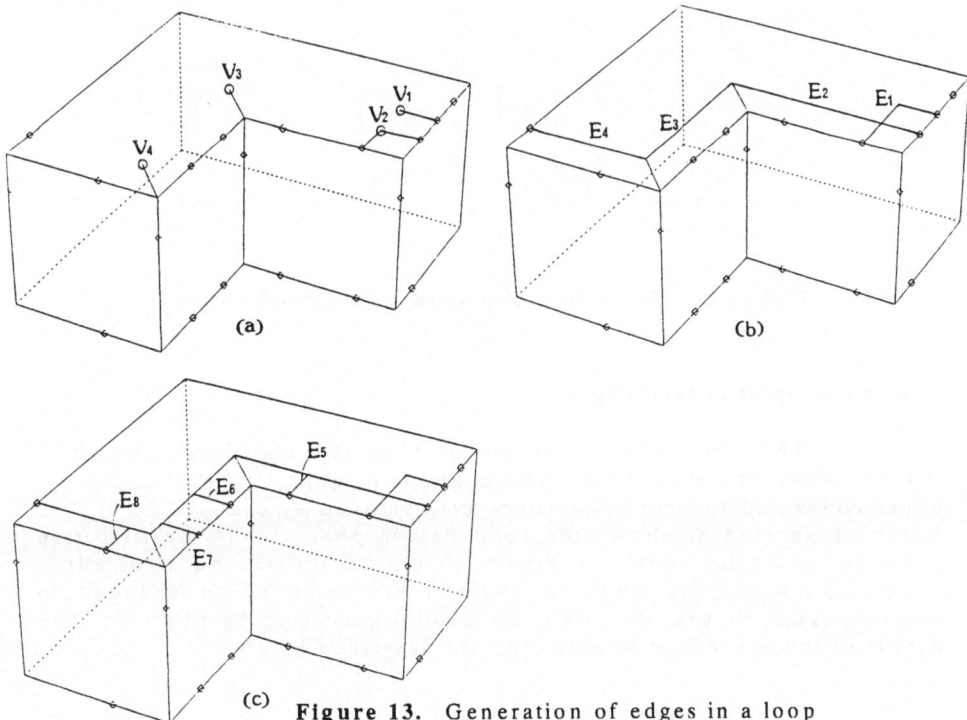

Figure 13. Generation of edges in a loop

Figure 14 shows the process of rounding a solid with curved edges. Figure 14(a) shows the original solid before the rounding. Edges E_1, E_2 and E_3 have rounding value 2. If the procedures of phases 1 and 2 are applied to the solid, the solid shown in Figure 14(b) is made. Here, the shapes of edges E_3 and E_4 are changed to offset curves of edge E_2, as shown in Figure 14(c). Furthermore, if the procedure of phase 3 is applied, the solid shown in Figure 14(d) is made.

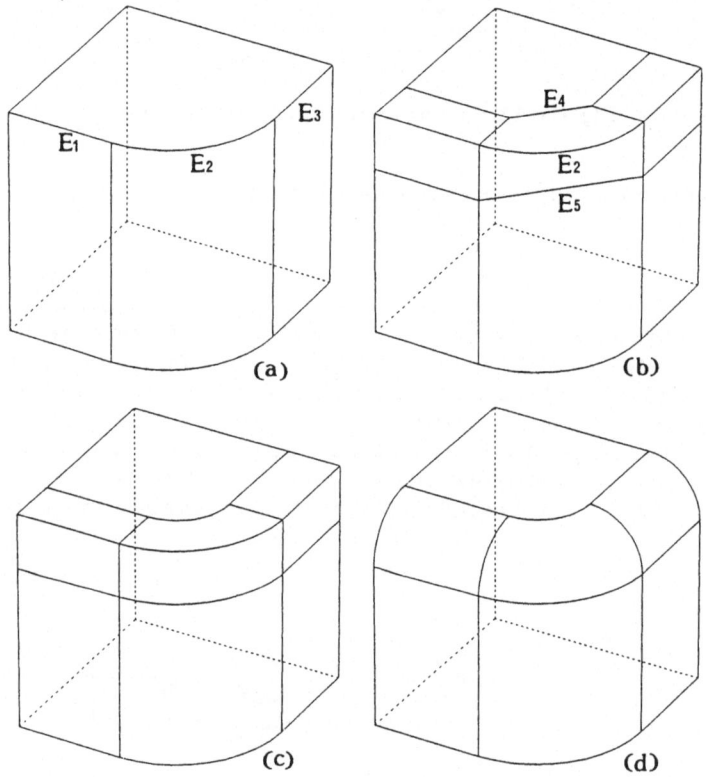

Figure 14. Rounding of a solid with curved edges

7. Generation of curved edges

This section explains phase 3 of the algorithm, in which curved edges are generated. These are two steps. In the first step, edges connected to original vertices are removed or changed to curved edges. Figure 15(a) shows the solid before phase 3. If the first step generates the solid shown in Figure 15(b). In the second step, edges connected to vertices made in phase 1 are removed or changed to curved edges. Figure 15(c) shows the solid generated by phase 3. The details of the procedure in each step are described below.

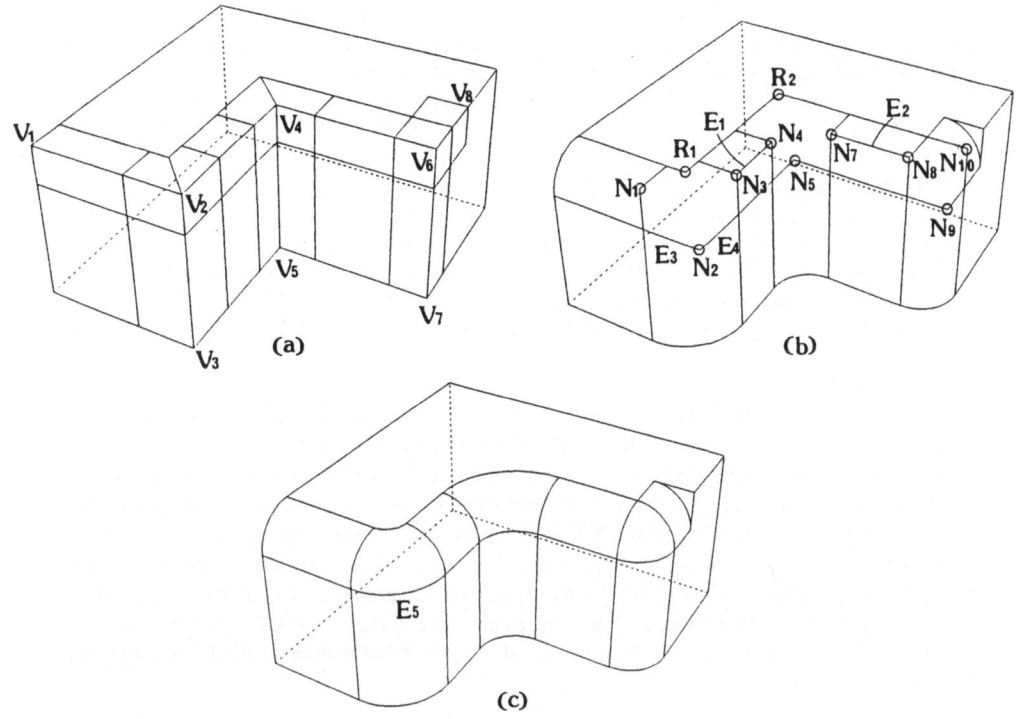

Figure 15. Generation of curved edges

7.1 Edges attached to the original vertex

Figure 16 shows vertex V_1 which is included in the original solid. Vertex V_1 is connected to edges E_1, E_2, E_3 and E_4. These edges are respectively attached to vertices N_1, N_2, N_3 and N_4 formed in phase 1 of the rounding operation. In the first step, some of edges attached to vertex V_1 are deleted, and curved edges are generated.

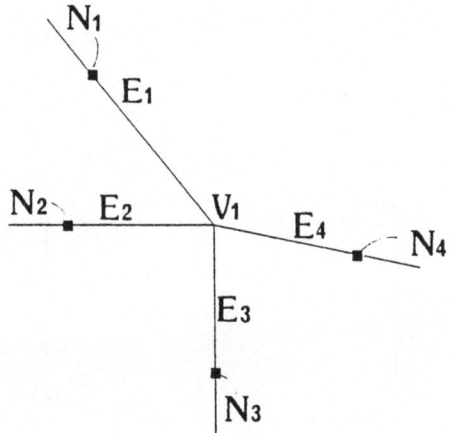

Figure 16. A vertex attached to several edges

First, all rounding values 2, 3 and 4 given to edges are replaced by value 0 so that all the edges have a rounding value of 0 or 1. The first step entails four procedures as follows:

Procedure 1

If the rounding values of all edges attached to vertex V_1 are 0, vertex V_1 and all the edges are deleted, as shown in Figure 17(a). Deleted edges are drawn as dotted lines. To delete four edges, a KEL operation is used three times, and then a KEV operation is used. If one of the edges has rounding value 1, and the other edges all have 0, all the edges and the vertex are deleted. In Figure 15(a), procedure 1 was applied to edges connected to vertices V_2, V_4 and V_6.

Procedure 2

If two of the edges attached to vertex V_1 have rounding value 1 (e.g., if E_1 and E_3 have 1), and the values of the other edges are 0, vertex V_1 and all the edges are deleted. A curved edge is then generated between vertices N_1 and N_3, as shown in Figure 17(b). The tangents of this curve at end points N_1 and N_3 are lines N_1V_1 and N_3V_1, respectively. For procedure 2, edges E_2 and E_4 are first deleted using KEL operations. Then vertex V_1 is deleted using a KVE operation. Lastly, the straight edge is changed to a curved one using a CLC operation. In Figure 15, the procedure 2 was applied to edges connected to vertices V_1, V_3, V_5 and V_7.

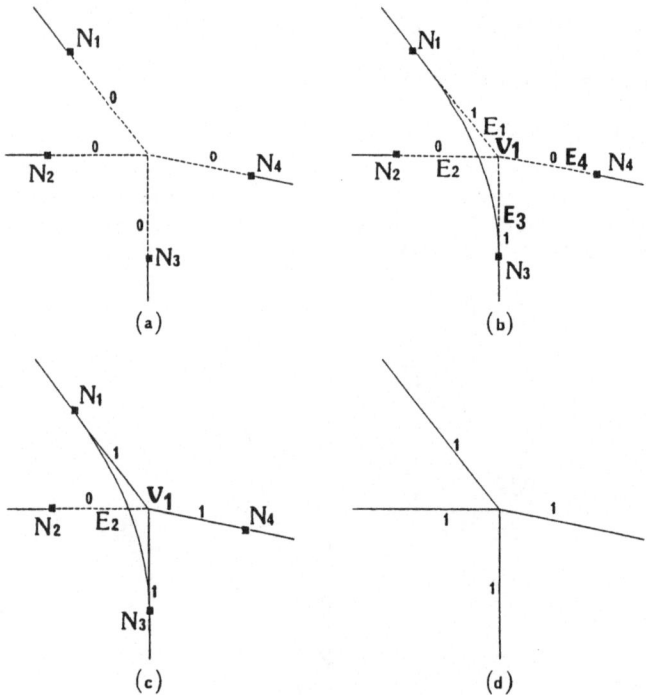

(a)

(b)

(c)

(d)

Figure 17. Procedure in Phase 3

Procedure 3

If one of the edges has rounding value 0 (e.g., if edge E_2 has 0), and the values of the other edges are 1, the edge with value 0 is deleted. A curved edge is then generated between vertices N_1 and N_3, as shown in Figure 17(c). The tangents of this curve at end points N_1 and N_3 are line N_1V_1 and N_3V_1, respectively. In procedure 3, edge E_2 is deleted using a KEL operation. A new edge is created between vertices N_1 and N_3 using a MEL operation. Then the edge is lastly changed to a curved one using a CLC operation. In Figure 15, procedure 3 was applied to edges connected to vertex V_8.

Procedure 4

If the rounding values of all the edges are 1, no action is taken, as shown in Figure 17(d).

7.2 Edges attached to vertex made in phase 1

In Figure 15(b), $N_i(i=1,...,10)$ are vertices made in phase 1. If these vertices are connected to the original edges or the edges made in phase 1, those edges are deleted. In Figure 15(b), edges E_1 and E_2 are deleted using KEL operations. Then a vertex made in phase 1 and two edges attached to the vertex are deleted, and a curved edge is generated. For example, vertex N_2 and edges E_3 and E_4 shown in Figure 15(b) are replaced by curved edge E_5 shown in Figure 15(c). In this procedure, KVE and CLC operations are used. Lastly, if any vertex remains that is connected to two edges, such as vertices R_1 and R_2 in Figure 15(b), they are replaced by curved edges. Figure 15(c) shows the solid that results after all the procedures in the rounding operations has been applied.

Figure 18, 19 and 20 show examples of solids which result from the rounding operations in DESIGNBASE. While Figure 18(a) shows a solid before the rounding operation, Figure 18(b) shows a solid after the operation. Figure 21 and 22 show color shaded images of the solid models generated by using ray tracing.

8. Conclusion

We proposed an extended rounding operation to create a solid with free-form surfaces. Using the extended rounding operation, the edges and vertices of a solid can be locally rounded, specifying the radii of rounded edges. Curved edges can be also rounded. This facility was implemented in our solid modeling system, DESIGNBASE.

Our future work is to extend the rounding of curved edges. In the present version, although a vertex attached to only one curved edge can be rounded, it is not possible to round a vertex attached to two or more curved edges. We will solve this problem in the near future.

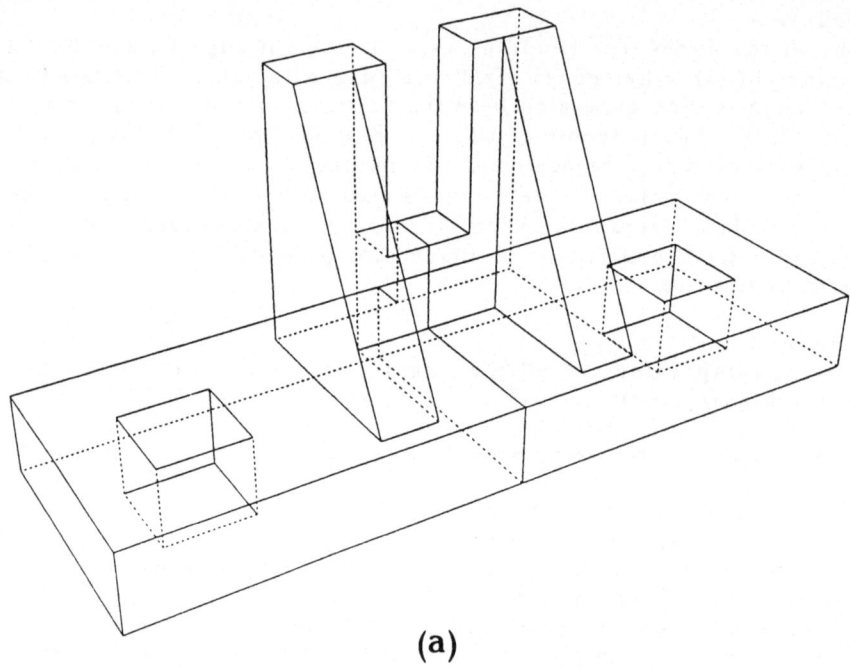

(a)

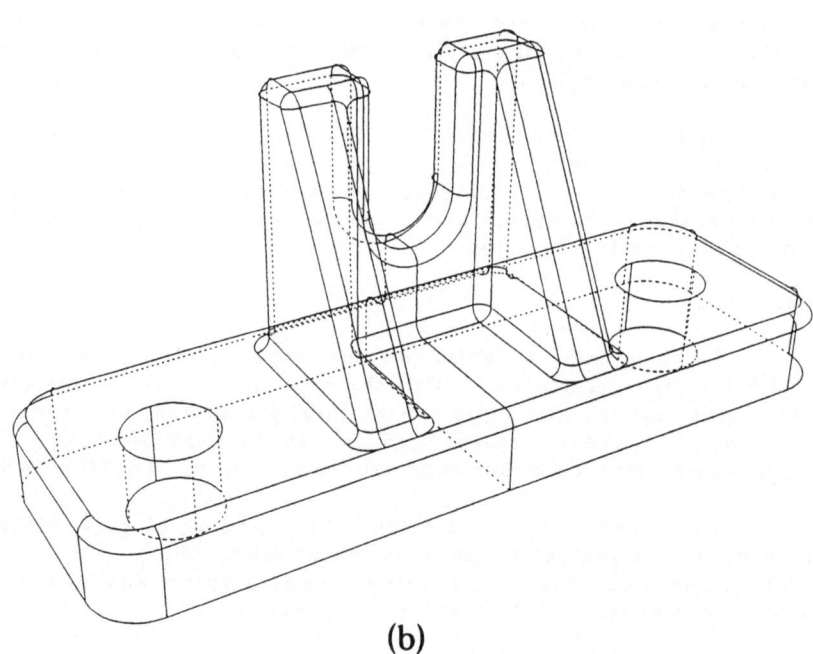

(b)

Figure 18. Mechanical part

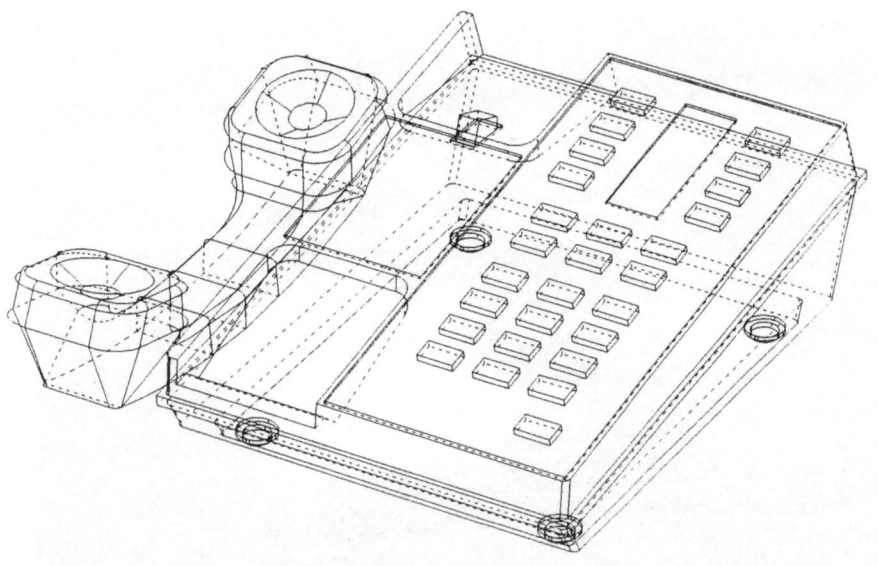

Figure 19. Telephone

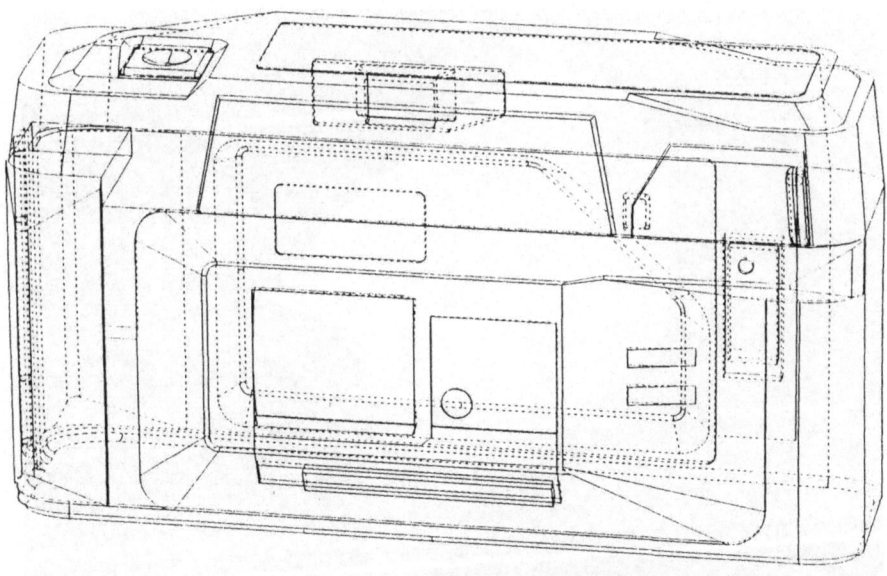

Figure 20. Camera

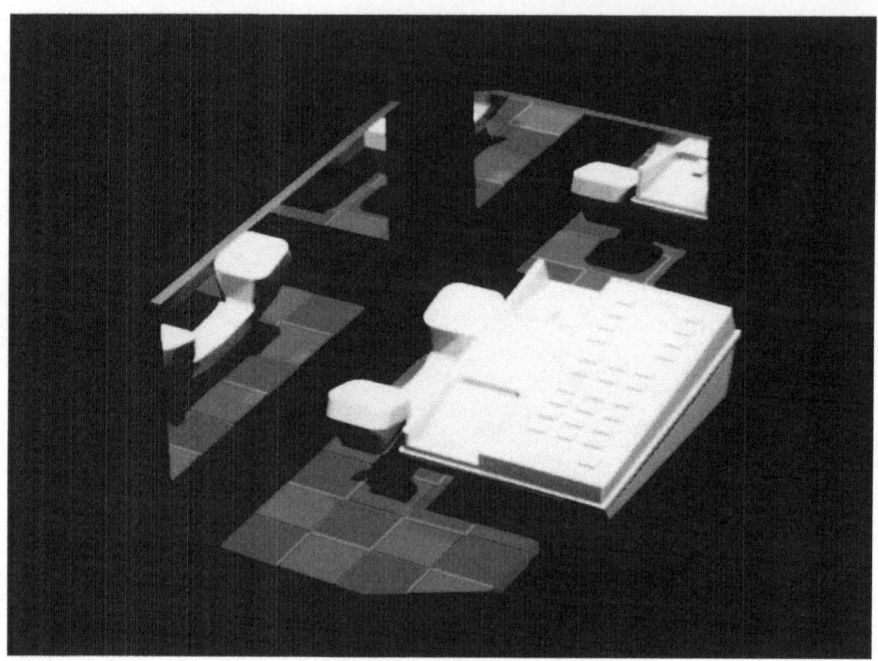

Figure 21. Telephone

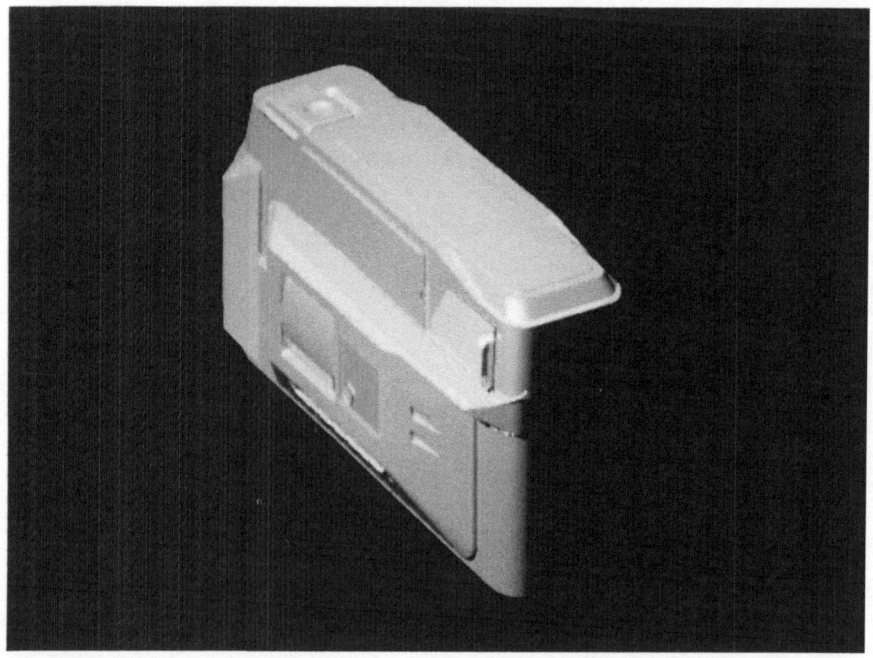

Figure 22. Camera

Acknowledgement

We would like to thank Professor Fumihiko Kimura in the University of Tokyo for his valuable suggestions; Teiji Takamura for the implementation of a ray tracing program.

REFERENCE

Beeker, E. [1986]. "Smoothing of Shapes Designed with Free-Form Surfaces," *Computer Aided Design,* Vol.18, No.4 May, pp.224-232.

Catmull, E. and Clark, J. [1978]. "Recursively Generated B-spline Surfaces on Arbitrary Topological Meshes," *Computer Aided Design,* Vol.10, No.6, November, pp.350-355.

Chiyokura, H. and Kimura, F. [1983]. "Design of Solids with Free-form Surfaces," *Computer Graphics (SIGGRAPH'83 Proc.),* Vol.17, No.3, July, pp.289-298.

Chiyokura, H. and Kimura, F. [1985]. "A Representation of Solid Design Process using Basic Operations," in *Frontiers in Computer Graphics - Proc. Computer Graphics Tokyo 84,* T. L. Kunii (ed.), Springer-Verlag, Tokyo, pp. 26-43.

Chiyokura, H. [1986]. "Localized Surface Interpolation for Irregular Meshes," *Advanced Computer Graphics - Proc. Computer Graphics Tokyo 86,* T. L. Kunii (ed.), Springer-Verlag, Tokyo, pp.3-19.

Chiyokura, H. [1987]. *Solid Modelling: Theory and Implementation,* Addison-Wesley, London, to appear.

Doo, D. [1978]. "A Subdivision Algorithm for Smoothing Down Irregular Shaped Polyhedrons," *Proc. Conf. Interactive Technique in CAD,* Bologna, Italy, pp.157-165.

Doo, D. and Sabin, M.A. [1978]. "Behaviour of Recursive Division near Extraordinary Points," *Computer Aided Design,* Vol.10, No.6, November, pp.356-360.

Fjällström, P. [1986]. "Smoothing of Polyhedra Models," *Proc. ACM Symposium on Computational Geometry,* Yorktown Heights, New York, pp.226-235.

Hoffmann, C. and Hopcroft, J. [1985]. "Automatic Surface Generation in Computer Aided Design," *Visual Computer,* Vol.1, No.2, pp.92-100.

Middleditch, A.E. and Sears, K.H. [1985]. "Blend Surfaces for Set Theoretic Volume Modelling," *Computer Graphics (SIGGRAPH'85 Proc.),* Vol.19, No.3, July, pp.161-170.

Riesenfeld, R.F. [1983]. "A View of Spline-Based Solid Modelling," *Proc. AUTOFACT 5,* SME.

Sarraga, R.F. and Waters, W.C. [1984]. "Free-Form Surfaces in GMSolid: Goals and Issues," in *Solid Modeling by Computers from Theory and Applications,* M.S. Pickett and J.W. Boyse (eds.), Plenum Press, New York, pp.237-253.

Séquin, C.H. [1986]. "Procedural Spline Interpolation in UNICUBIX," *USENIX Computer Graphics Workshop Proc.* December.

Tan, S.T. and Chan, K.C. [1986]. "Generation of High Order Surfaces over Arbitrary Polyhedral Meshes," *Computer Aided Design,* Vol.18, No.8, October, pp.441-423.

Thomas, S.W. [1985]. "The Alpha-1 Computer-Aided Geometric Design System in the UNIX Environment," *Login,* Vol.10, No.4, October, pp.54-64.

Toriya, H., Satoh, T., Ueda, K. and Chiyokura, H. [1986]. "UNDO and REDO Operations for Solids Modeling", *IEEE Computer Graphics and Applications,* Vol.6, No.4, April, pp.35-42.

Wijk, J.J. van [1986]. "Bicubic Patches for Approximating Non-Rectangular Control-Point Meshes," *Computer Aided Geometric Design,* Vol.3, No.1, May, pp.1-13.

Hiroaki Chiyokura directs the 3-D CAD project in the Software Research Center of Ricoh Co.,Ltd. His research interests are solid modeling, computer graphics and their applications to computer aided design and manufacturing. He received his BS. and MS. degree in mathematics from Keio University in 1979 and 1981. He earned his Dr.Eng. in precision machinery engineering from the University of Tokyo in 1984. He is a member of ACM Siggraph.

The auther's address is Software Research Center, Ricoh Co.,Ltd., 1-1-17, Koishikawa, Bunkyo-ku, Tokyo 112 JAPAN.

Optimal Sequential Disassembly in the Plane

Tony C. Woo

ABSTRACT

We map the boundary representation of an assembly to a tree structure
called Disassembly Tree (DT). An assembly is first classified by the
logical complexity of its DT and by the geometric complexity of the
nodes in a DT. Whether a component can be removed in one motion is
next described as a predicate. The predicate is then used in an
algorithm for constructing a DT in $O(N)$ time, where N is the total
number of edges in the plane.

Keywords: robotics, automatic assembly, automatic disassembly, data
structure, algorithm

1. INTRODUCTION

Motion planning in robotics can be described informally as navigating
an object in a room with obstacles. The "Sofa Moving Problem" (Reif
1979) is an instance in which a collision-free path from source to
destination is sought. If we associate a sofa in a warehouse to a
component in an assembly then motion planning is concerned with the
generation of a geometric solution that achieves some objective
function (shortest path from initial to final position, for example),
under certain constraints (without collision, using straight line
motions, for example). Assembly planning is concerned with the
generation of a logical sequence of steps each of which is a motion
plan. The "Warehouseman's Problem" is an apt characterization of the
assembly planning problem in which several sofas are to be unstacked
in order to reach a particular sofa, which is proven to be PSPACE-
complete (Hopcroft et al, 1984).

One of the difficulties of motion planning and assembly planning lies
in the degrees of freedom of the object under consideration. If we
restrict the motion to translation, significant improvement can be
made in the efficiency of the algorithm from doubly exponential
(Schwartz et al 1983) to polynomial time. For example, if N is the
number of walls, the motions for a circular disk can be planned in
$O(N\log N)$ time (O'Dunlaing et al 1985), and for two disks in $O(N^3)$
time (Schwartz et al 1985). We are motivated by the practicality of
restricting our assembly robot to translational motions (with two
degrees of freedom in the plane).

We study the problem of assembly from the point of view of disassembly.
If we visualize the process of assembly as having a finite number of
"states", each captured by a single frame on film, then rolling the
film backward corresponds to disassembly. The process of disassembly
is reversable, if the components are rigid and there is no internal

energy stored.   (Such would not be the case with components of variable
geometry such as a spring or a clip fastener, for example.)

To define the domain of this paper, we first characterize the inherent
difficulty of the problem by the logical complexity of the solution.
Let the solution to disassembly be represented by a tree, the nodes of
which represent the components.   In Fig. 1.1(a), the assembly A can be
disassembled not individually but only by removing a subassembly
$(a_1 a_2)$ first.

Definition 1.1:   An assembly is k-parallel if the disassembly of a
component requires an immediately prior clearing of k other components
in parallel.

The criterion for "clearing" a component from a subassembly may be one
of the following:

C1.   that the convex hull of the component in question does not inter-
        sect the convex hull of the subassembly; or

C2.   that the component can be translated to the perimeter of a circle
        of sufficiently large radius; or

C3.   that the component can be translated to infinity.

For simplicity, we adopt C3 as the criterion in this paper.

The tree in Fig. 1.1(b) shows that the disassembly of a component is
possible only after k of its neighbors have been removed.

Definition 1.2:   An assembly is k-sequential if the disassembly of a
component requires an immediately prior clearing of k other adjacent
components in sequence.

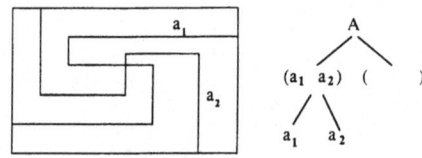

(a) Parallel Assembly

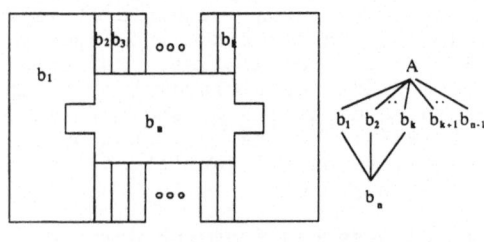

(b) Sequential Assembly

Fig. 1.1 Partially Ordered Assemblies

It may be noted that parallelism is a necessity while sequentialism is sufficiency. In other words, a k-sequential assembly can be disassembled by using k manipulators operating in parallel whereas the converse is not necessarily true.

Thus, observing the number of "parents" for a node in a disassembly tree, we have a characterization of assemblies by logical ordering.

Definition 1.3: An assembly is partially ordered if the disassembly of a component requires the prior disassembly of k other components. If k < 2, the assembly is totally ordered.

Now consider Fig. 1.2. The disassembly of component a_1 in Fig. 1.2(a) requires two translations. Recalling the "Sofa Moving Problem" versus the unstacking of sofas in the "Warehouseman's Problem", we see that the number of motions to clear a single component is a complexity measure independent of the number of parents for a node in a disassembly tree. Thus, we have a characterization of an assembly by the geometric complexity of each node in its corresponding DT.

Definition 1.4: A component is m-disassemblable if m motions are required to clear it.

Constructing a disassembly tree for totally-ordered, 1-disassemblable components is not entirely trivial. The difficulty comes from the observation that the ordering of the components affect the m-disassemblability of each component. Consider Fig. 1.2(b) in which there are L components on the left and R components on the right. If removed first, each of the L components are 2-disassemblable. However, after all R components are first removed, the L components become 1-disassemblable. To determine which one of the k = (L + R) components is 1-disassemblable suggest a decision procedure that could take k + (k-1) + (k-2) + ... steps leading to an $O(k^2)$ time algorithm. In this paper, we give a linear time algorithm for disassembling a totally ordered 1-disassemblable assembly.

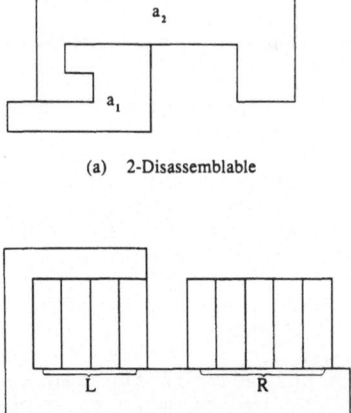

(a)   2-Disassemblable

(b) 1-Disassemblable

Fig. 1.2   Totally Ordered Assemblies

The paper is organized as follows. Section 2 discusses the determination of 1-disassemblability. Section 3 presents an algorithm for totally ordering the components in the form of a disassembly tree. Section 4 considers the application of removing more than one component from a given assembly.

2. DISASSEMBLABILITY

For simplicity, we shall first consider assemblies with only two components -- one being the component under consideration for removal and the other representing the subassembly (the rest of the assembly). Observe the two examples in Fig. 2.1. It is clear that the component c in Figure 2.1(a) is disassemblable while the one in Figure 2.1(b) is not. We distinguish these two cases by computing a range of directions along which a component can be translated such that it does not interfere with the subassembly S.

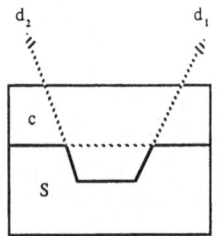

(a) Component c is disassemblable from subassembly S

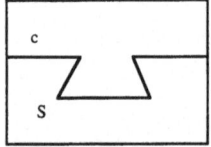

(b) Component c is not disassemblable

Fig. 2.1   Linear Disassemblability and Visible Region

Definition 2.1: A component c is said to be 1-disassemblable (or just disassemblable, for short) from a subassembly S in the direction d if, for all points p in c, a RAY (p,d), which is a semi-infinite line from p in the direction d, does not intersect S.

Definition 2.1 implies that component c, if disassemblable, can be gripped at any point p in c and pulled in the direction d without interference. If p is the center of mass for c then there is no angular moment when c is pulled. If the center of mass lies outside c (or lies in a hole of c), two or more grip points will ensure an interference-free removal (Wolter et al 1985). In Fig. 2.1(a), the direction d lies between d_1 and d_2.

The range of directions can be determined from the mating edges, the sequence of edges shared by c and S. If a viewer (the robot) can "see" (from infinity in the oposite direction of the ray) all points p on the mating edges without having to go through S then c is removable. We need the notion of a region in which the viewer should reside.

Definition 2.2: A visible region VR ({e_i}) for a sequence of edges {e_i} is the intersection of half space HS (e_i) induced by edge e_i.

We are ready to state the condition for disassembling c from S and the determination for the existence of such a condition.

Lemma 2.1: A component c is disassemblable from a subassembly S if the visible region VR ({e_i}) is unbounded.

[Proof]   If the visible region is bounded, by Definitions 2.1 and 2.2, there cannot be a point at infinity from which a ray reaches all points x on the edges {e_i}, and vice versa.

An edge e_i of a polygon naturally partitions a two-dimensional space into two half spaces -- the inside and the outside of a polygon. When the notion of a visible region is applied to the inside of a polygon and when the sequence of edges is the entire boundary of the polygon, we recall the definition of a kernel (Lee et al 1979).

Definition 2.3: A kernel with respect to a set of edges {e_i} is a region R such that, for any point p in R, and another point q on any edge e_i, the line segment pq lies entirely in R.

A kernel applies to "internal" visibility because it always lies inside a polygon. A visible region, by contrast, applies to external visibility as the viewer is assumed to be at infinity. Since a kernel can be constructed in time linear in the number of edges (Lee and Preparata 1979), we have a linear construction time for a visible region.

Lemma 2.2: A visible region VR ({e_i}) can be constructed in $O(n)$ time, where n is the number of mating edges in {e_i}.

Since an unbounded VR is necessarily convex, there must be two halflines or rays extending to infinity. As illustrated in Fig. 2.2(a), we denote these two rays by their polar angles in the counter-clockwise direction.

Definition 2.4: If c is disassemblable from S the visible region VR ({e_i}) is said to span a cone of visibility CV (d_1, d_2) with angle $d_2 - d_1$.

A special case for computing CV (d_1, d_2) arises when $d_1 = d_2$. This situation as illustrated in Figure 2.2(b) occurs when two halfplanes HS(e_i) and HS(e_j) are parallel (intersecting at infinity). As an alternative, we can decompose the mating edges {e_i} into subsequences, find their respective CVs, and compute the intersection of the CVs. This motivates the following lemma.

Lemma 2.3: A cone of visibility CV (d_1, d_2) can be computed from the intersection of CV_i (d_1, d_2), each corresponding to the cone of visibility of a subsequence in {e_i}, if they exist.

[Proof]   We are concerned with the efficiency of finding the maximum and the minimum of the spanning angles of the individual cones. Given a set of d_1s and d_2s, the maximum of the d_1s and the minimum of the d_2s can be found in $O(n)$ time. Hence, the method by Lemma 2.3 has the same time complexity as the one inferred by Lemma 2.2.

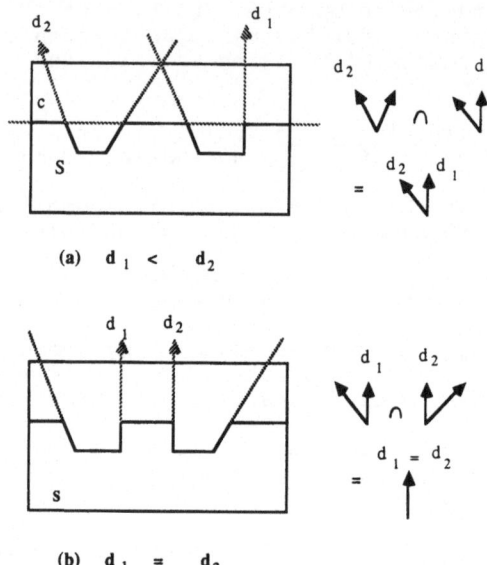

Fig. 2.2   Intersection of Cones of Visibility

Disassembly of a component c with respect to a subassembly S can now be expressed as a predicate.

<u>Function</u> Disassemblable (c,S)

1. From the mating edges of c and S, construct a visible region VR.

2. If the VR is bounded, return 'false'. Otherwise, return a cone of visibility $CV(d_1, d_2)$.

Step 1 of the function can be done in $O(n)$ time, where n is the number of mating edges for c with respect to S. Step 2 involves traversing the boundary of the VR to detect closure which is again $O(n)$ time. Thus, we have the following result:

<u>Lemma 2.4</u>: The disassemblability of a single component c can be determined in $O(n)$ time, where n is the number of mating edges between c and the subassembly S.

3. DISASSEMBLY TREE

We are ready to consider an assembly with more than two components. First, we describe the data structure to be used by the algorithm. The assembly is given as a <u>boundary graph</u> BG of vertices, edges and faces. Each vertex points to all of its incident edges. Each face points to all of its surrounding edges. Each edge points to its two end points that are vertices, its two faces that are mating components, and four edges with two at each end (Woo 1985). If one of the two faces of an edge is the background then it is a <u>boundary edge</u>. Otherwise, it is a <u>mating edge</u>. In Fig. 3.1(a), edge e_{14} is a boundary edge while edge e_{17} is the mating edge for components a and b. Note that an edge with more than one mate is split. Thus, every edge in the BG has exactly two mates. From the BG, we construct a dual <u>mating</u>

graph MG. The arcs in MG connect nodes that are mating components.
As illustrated in Fig. 3.1(b), component a mates with components b and
d as well as with the background B. As there are k components, and
each access in the boundary graph involves constant time (Woo 1985),
the planar graph MG can be constructed from BG in time linear in k.

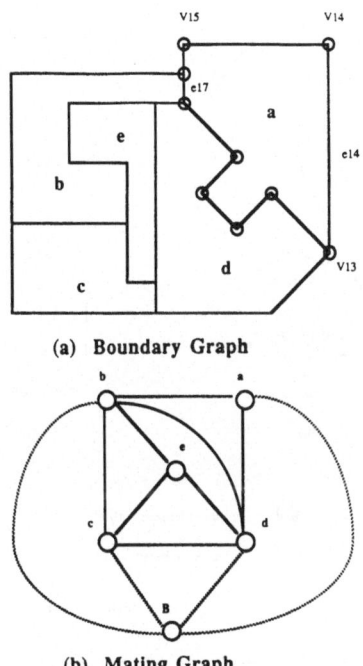

(a) Boundary Graph

(b) Mating Graph

Fig. 3.1 Data Structures

We begin the construction of disassembly tree DT by determining if
components with boundary edges can be disassembled first. Using the
example from Fig. 3.1, we find four candidates a, b, c and d. We next
determine if these candidates should be attached as nodes to the root
of the tree denoted by A, the assembly. In Fig. 3.2(a), each of the
candidates is tested for disassemblability with respect to a subassembly. For component d, the subassembly is S = A - d. If it is found
to be false after calling the function Disassemblable (d,S) then it
is not attached to the tree as illustrated by a shaded circle. The
total number of attached nodes, not counting the root node A, is
recorded in an integer variable NODES.

We next expand the tree by retrieving the mates of each of the leaf
nodes and by testing their disassemblability. From the mating graph,
the non-background mates are retrieved for each of the newly attached
leaves. If a retrieved mate occurs elsewhere in the tree, it is discarded from further consideration. In Fig. 3.2(b), the component a
has two mates b and d. Since b occurs previously, it is marked by a
circle and not considered for further testing. The mate d has not
occurred previously and is tested for disassemblability against subassembly S = A - a - d. (The new boundary for S is updated by replacing all occurrences of a and d by background B for all edges in
the boundary graph.) Following the example, it is found that d is
disassemblable, hence inserted in the tree and NODES is incremented by
1. Next, the mates for component b are retrieved. They are shown as
a, c, d, e in Fig. 3.2(c). Since a, c, d has occurred previously,

they are excluded from further consideration. The mate e is tested
and found to be disassemblable. At this point, the count for NODES
equals the total number of components in the assembly and the process
terminates. The resulting tree is shown in Figure 3.2(d).

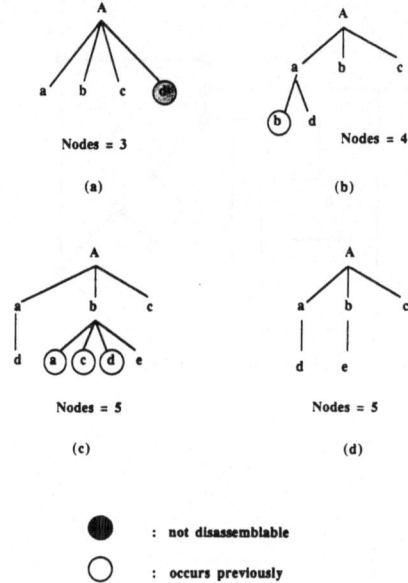

Fig. 3.2 Generation of the Disassembly Tree

The algorithm for generating such a disassembly tree can be described
as follows:

Algorithm Disassemble

input: boundary graph BG and mating graph MG
output: disassembly tree DT

[Initialization]

    1. NODES <-- 0

        TOTAL <-- total number of non-background nodes in MG.

    2. Make a root node A for the empty tree DT.

[First level]

    3. Identify all components in MG that are connected to the
        boundary B.

    4. For each component c

           If c is disassemblable

               then insert c as a leaf in DT

                    NODES <-- NODE + 1

               else return 'failure'.

[Subsequent levels]

    5.   While NODES < TOTAL do

        5a. For each leaf L in DT

            retrieve its mates from MG

        5b. For each mate M

            If M is not in DT and is disassemblable

              then insert M as a leaf node of L

                  NODES <-- NODES + 1

              else return 'failure'.

We show that the DT constructed by Algorithm Disassemble gives a minimal sequence. This is done by induction on the height of the tree. Steps 1 and 2 of the algorithm give level 0 of the tree. Steps 3 and 4 give level 1 of the tree. Components in level 1 cannot occur in level 0, by construction. Now, suppose there are (v-1) levels in the tree and we examine a leave node L at level v. There are three possibilities.

Case 1. [L occurs at level < v]

      By Step 5b, this is not possible. For a mate M to become a leaf L, it must not already be in DT.

Case 2. [L occurs at level = v]

      Again, by Step 5b, this is not possible, unless it is disassemblable. And, if so, there is only one occurrence of L anywhere in the tree, including level v.

Case 3. [L occurs at level > v]

      A leaf L that should occur later in the tree gets mistakenly placed at level v is not possible. By Step 5a, only mates that are leaf candidates at level v are retrieved.

This proves the minimality of the sequence obtained from traversing a DT, hence the following theorem.

Theorem 3.1: Algorithm Disassemble generates a DT the traversal of which yields a minimal number of removals for the disassembly of a single component.

4. ALL DISASSEMBLY SEQUENCES

The DT generated by Algorithm Disassemble gives a minimal sequence if a single component is to be removed. However, if multiple components are to be removed from the assembly, Algorithm Disassemble may not give the optimal solution. Consider the assembly in Figure 4.1(a) and suppose that two components c and d are to be removed from it. The Algorithm Disassemble could generate a tree with root A requiring the removal of three components a, d, and c. On the other hand, if the components to be removed (c and d) are in the same path in the tree with root B, as shown in Figure 4.1(b), only two removals are necessary.

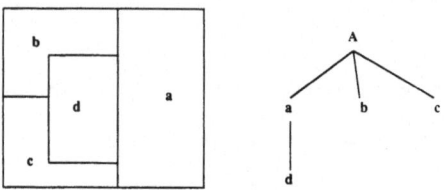

(a) One Disassembly Sequence

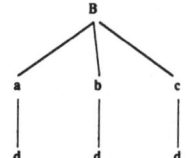

(b) All Disassembly Sequences

Fig. 4.1   Multiple Disassembly

To generate all optimal sequences for multiple component removal, two modifications to Algorithm Disassemble are necessary. First, disqualifying a retrieved mate M from disassemblability test should be postponed. Second, the termination condition for the algorithm should not be the total number of components. The first modification can be effected by changing, in step 5b of Algorithm Disassemble, "If M is not in DT and ..." to "If M is not at a higher level in DT and ...". the second change can be effected by noting the situation when the tree ceases to grow. In other words, if none of the retrieved mates M at that level are added to the tree then the algorithm should terminate.

We now present Algorithm Multiple_Disassemble reflecting two modifications. It is made compact by treating the first level of the tree as components that mate with the boundary. Thus, the root (the first new leaf of an empty tree) of the DT is the boundary B.

Algorithm Multiple_Disassemble

input: boundary graph BG and mating graph MG
output: disassembly tree DT with multiple occurrences of components

[Initialization]

    1.   Insert boundary B as NEW_LEAF in DT

    2.   LEVEL <-- 0

[Grow tree]

   3. While NEW_LEAF at LEVEL is not empty do

      For each NEW_LEAF at LEVEL

         retrieves its mates from MG

         LEVEL <-- LEVEL + 1

      For each mate M at LEVEL

         If M is not at level < LEVEL and M is disassemblable

            then insert M as NEW_LEAF in DT

            else return 'failure'.

As a component can now appear more than once at the same level in the tree, Algorithm Multiple-Disassemble performs more work. However, we shall show that its time complexity is still O(N), on the average.

Within the same level, a component can appear as many times in the tree as the number of mates it has in the mating graph MG. Given k components in an assembly, it is known that its MG is maximally connected if the k nodes form a triangulation graph. In other words, there can be a total of

$$m = 3k - 6$$

possible edges in MG. Averaging m over k components, we have

$$\frac{m}{k} = \frac{3k - 6}{k} = 3 - \frac{6}{k} .$$

Hence the average number of edges per node in MG is bounded by 3. Since each mating edge is tested at most twice (for its two mating components), the total work for Algorithm Multiple_Disassemble is at most 6N or O(N). This proves our next theorem.

Theorem 4.1: All minimal sequences for multiple disassembly can be constructed on the average in O(N) time, where N is the total number of mating edges in the assembly.

5. DISCUSSION

We have presented two algorithms for computing disassembly sequences by generating a disassembly tree DT. Traversing a DT in in-order yields a disassembly sequence. Traversing it in pre- or post-order yields an assembly sequence. We showed that any such sequence is the shortest possible, hence optimal. Algorithm Disassemble constructs a DT for the case in which one component is to be removed from the assembly. Algorithm Multiple_Disassemble constructs a DT for the case in which the removal of more than one component is desired. The latter is shown to run in time linear in the number of mating edges in the assembly, on the average. If there are k components with a total of N mating edges, it is possible that in the worst case it takes O(k) time to construct a DT. Since it handles multiple components O(k) time is the best case as well. Since multiple disassembly subsumes single disassembly, our algorithms are optimal.

The two algorithms extend naturally to three dimensions. A visible region for a set of n mating faces involves the intersection of n half-planes and a visible cone will be a solid angle bounded by at most n such half-planes. However, computing a disassembly sequence for a <u>parallel</u> assembly is expected to take more than linear time since the components must be grouped in combinations of two, three, ... up to (k-1), where k is the total number of components.

ACKNOWLEDGEMENT

The author wishes to thank J. D. Wolter of The University of Michigan for his keen insights. The author also acknowledges Professor T. L. Kunii of the University of Tokyo who initiated the author to the idea of disassembly during one of his visits to Ann Arbor. The meticulous preparation of this manuscript by P. Post is also gratefully acknowledged.

REFERENCES

Lee DT and Preparata FP (1979) An Optimal Algorithm for Finding the Kernel of a Polygon. Journal of the ΛCM, Vol 26, 415-421

Hopcroft JE, Schwartz JT and M Sharir (1984) On the Complexity of Motion Planning for Multiple Independent Objects: PSPACE Hardness of the Warehouseman's Problem. Int. J. of Robotics Research, Vol 3, No 4, 76-88

O'Dunlaing C and Yap C (1985) A Retraction Method for Planning the Motion of a Disc. J. of Algorithms, Vol 6, 104-111

Reif J (1979) Complexity of the Mover's Problems and Generalizations. Proc. 20th IEEE Symp. on Foundations of Computer Science, 421-427

Schwartz JT and Sharir M (1983) On the Piano Movers' Problem: II. General Techniques for Computing Topological Properties of Real Algebraic Manifolds. Advances in Appl. Math, Vol 4, 298-351

Schwartz JT and Sharir M (1983) On the Piano Movers' Problem: III. Coordinating the Motion of Several Independent Bodies: The Special Case of Circular Bodies Moving Amidst Polygonal Barriers. Int. J. of Robotics Research, Vol 2, No 3, 46-75

Wolter JD, Volz RA, and Woo TC (1985) Automatic Generation of Gripping Positions. IEEE Trans. on Systems, Man and Cybernetics, Vol SMC-15, No 2, 204-213

Woo TC (1985) A Combinatorial Analysis of Boundary Data Structure Schemata. IEEE Computer Graphics and Applications, Vol 5, No 3, 19-27

Tony C. Woo is Associate Professor in the Department of Industrial and Operations Engineering at The University of Michigan at Ann Arbor. He is on the Editorial Board for The Visual Computer: An International Journal on Computer Graphics. He is active in Computer Graphics Society, having served on Program Committee for CG Tokyo 1985, CG Tokyo 1986, and CG International 87. He is also active in Institute of Industrial Engineers. He serves as Department Editor (Manufacturing Engineering) for IIE Transactions and is Division Program Chair for IIE Fall Conference 1987. With D. Dornfeld (UC Berkeley), they are Co-Editors of a twenty-module series in CIM for Addison-Wesley, six of which will appear in Winter 1987.

Woo received his Ph.D. in Electrical Engineering from The University of Illinois in 1975. At Michigan, he teaches courses in computer graphics, geometric modeling and computational geometry. His research is in algorithm development for CAD, CAM and robotics.

Address: Department of Industrial and Operations Engineering, The University of Michigan, 1205 Beal Avenue, Ann Arbor, MI 48109-2117, U.S.A.

Chapter 6

Ray Tracing

A Simple, General Method for Ray Tracing Bicubic Surfaces

Geoff Levner, Paolo Tassinari, and Daniele Marini

ABSTRACT

A software package for creating and ray tracing bicubic surfaces is described. The software supports Beta-splines as well as Bezier and Hermite surfaces. We present a simple algorithm for calculating the intersection of a ray with a surface, and also an interactive modeler for creating bicubic surfaces.

Keywords: ray tracing, Beta-splines, ray surface intersection, surface modeling

1. INTRODUCTION

The ray tracing of parametric surfaces in general, and of bicubic surfaces in particular, is usually done in one of two ways. The simpler way is to generate a polygonal approximation of the surfaces to be rendered, and then perform the ray tracing on the resulting polygons. This is relatively easy because the calculation of the intersection of a ray with a polygon is easy. The second method, a variation of which is presented here, is to render the surfaces directly. The intersection of a ray with a parametric surface can be a hairy problem, however.

The direct intersection of a ray with a parametric surface has generally been done using either rather sophisticated numerical methods of multivariate Newton iteration (Faux and Pratt 1979) or simpler but inefficient subdivision algorithms (Catmull and Clark 1978; Whitted 1980). In 1982 Kajiya introduced an algorithm based on techniques from algebraic geometry for ray tracing rational bivariate polynomial surface patches. Sederberg (1984) also used algebraic geometry to solve the problem of ray tracing Steiner patches. Toth (1985) introduced the use of techniques from interval analysis to calculate a reliable initial guess for a Newton process, in an algorithm applicable to generalized parametric surfaces.

Recently Sweeney and Bartels (1986) proposed a method for ray tracing B-spline surfaces which simplifies the numerical analysis involved almost to the point where it is comprehensible to non-numerical analysts. They used Riesenfeld's (1980) Oslo algorithm to create a tree of tightly fitting, nested bounding boxes, which locate a point of intersection nearly enough that little time or care need be spent on the Newton process which determines the exact point of intersection.

The Oslo algorithm, given a set of control points defining a B-spline, calculates a larger, "refined" grid of control points which define the same surface. Neither the Oslo algorithm nor other subdivision algorithms seem to be readily applicable to Beta-splines, however.

Our own goal was to incorporate Beta-spline surfaces into an existing ray tracing package, without resorting to polygonal approximations. Beta-splines are particularly useful for modeling curved surfaces because they retain the local control and geometric continuity of B-splines, while providing the flexibility of global and local parameters of bias and tension (Barsky 1981; Bartels et al 1985). To our knowledge, however, the problem of ray tracing Beta-splines specifically has not been addressed in the literature.

The solution presented here is an extension of Sweeney and Bartel's algorithm. While the algorithm was developed with Beta-splines in mind, it has been applied successfully to bicubic surfaces in general, and should in fact be applicable to any parametric surface. Unlike many existing algorithms for intersecting a ray with a parametric surface, however, the algorithm presented here is relatively simple to understand and implement.

Our algorithm differs from that of Sweeney and Bartels in that it uses a grid of sample points on the surface itself to create the tree of bounding boxes. As a result, the bounding boxes fit the surface more tightly. And since only the evaluation of points on the surface is required, the technique is applicable to any parametric surface, although our implementation is limited to bicubic surfaces. Moreover, since the entire intersection algorithm requires only the evaluation of surface points and their derivatives, it is independent of the blending functions actually used (here Beta-spline, Bezier or Hermite). The same code is used for any kind of surface.

The remainder of this document is organized as follows. Section 2 presents some of the mathematics involved in dealing with bicubic surfaces. Section 3 is a brief introduction to Newton's method as used in the intersection calculation algorithm. Section 4 describes the algorithm in detail. Section 5 describes the user interface for creating and rendering surfaces, including an interactive surface modeler. And section 6 presents some images created with our software, our conclusions and some work in progress.

Some familiarity with spline surfaces and mathematics is assumed here, though not a lot, and no knowledge at all of numerical analysis should be required. For a basic introduction to spline curves and surfaces, see Foley and Van Dam (1982) or Newman and Sproull (1979). For a more in-depth treatment see Faux and Pratt (1979) or Bartels et al (1985).

2. SPLINE MATHEMATICS

What follows is not intended to be an exhaustive introduction to spline surfaces or the mathematics involved in dealing with them. For that, see any of the introductory references listed above.

For the purposes of this document, we will merely note that the evaluation of a point $P(u,v)$ on a bicubic surface patch may be expressed as a matrix multiplication of the form:

$$P_x(u,v) = UMG_x MTVT$$

$$P_y(u,v) = UMG_y M^T V^T$$

$$P_z(u,v) = UMG_z M^T V^T$$

where u and v are assumed to be between 0 and 1. A "T" superscript indicates the transpose of a matrix. Henceforth, only the equations for x will be stated explicitly; y and z are exactly analogous. When G or P is referred to without subscript, it is understood to stand for any of the components x, y or z.

In the equations above, then, U and V are the vectors:

$$U = [u^3 \; u^2 \; u \; 1]$$

$$V = [v^3 \; v^2 \; v \; 1]$$

M is a 4 x 4 matrix containing the coefficients of the blending functions used (Beta-spline, Bezier or Hermite), and G is a 4 x 4 geometry matrix defining the surface patch.

Note that this is just a reformulation of the equation:

$$P(u,v) = \sum_i \sum_j G_{ij} B_i(u) B_j(v)$$

where the functions B are cubic blending functions, which are non-zero only over four adjacent intervals.

If a patch is a Beta-spline or a Bezier spline, G contains the coordinates of the 16 control points defining the patch; if it is a Hermite spline, G_x takes the following form:

$$G_x = \begin{bmatrix} x_{00} & x_{01} & \dfrac{dx}{dv}_{00} & \dfrac{dx}{dv}_{01} \\[2ex] x_{10} & x_{11} & \dfrac{dx}{dv}_{10} & \dfrac{dx}{dv}_{11} \\[2ex] \dfrac{dx}{du}_{00} & \dfrac{dx}{du}_{01} & \dfrac{d^2x}{dudv}_{00} & \dfrac{d^2x}{dudv}_{01} \\[2ex] \dfrac{dx}{du}_{10} & \dfrac{dx}{du}_{11} & \dfrac{d^2x}{dudv}_{10} & \dfrac{d^2x}{dudv}_{11} \end{bmatrix}$$

Here x are the four corner points of the patch, dx/du and dx/dv are the derivatives at the corners with respect to u and v, and the four values in the lower right corner of the matrix are the partial derivatives at the corners with respect to both parameters, sometimes refered to as "twist vectors".

The calculation of the derivative with respect to u and v at any point on a surface patch also reduces to a similar equation:

$$\frac{dx}{du}(u,v) = UM'G_xM^TV^T$$

$$\frac{dx}{dv}(u,v) = UMG_xM'^TV^T$$

where M' contains the coefficients of the derivatives of the blending functions.

The surface normal at a point on a surface patch is simply the cross product of the derivatives with respect to u and v:

$$N_x(u,v) = \frac{dx}{du}(u,v) \times \frac{dx}{dv}(u,v)$$

Note that when the evaluation of a point on a surface patch and its derivatives is reduced to matrix expressions as above, the expressions are the same regardless of the type of patch used, once the blending function and geometry matrices have been determined. This permits the same code to be used for any bicubic surface.

3. NEWTON'S METHOD

Newton's method is a procedure for calculating the root of a polynomial equation or system of polynomial equations. It works by generating a sequence of successively closer approximations to the solution; a first approximation which is reasonably close to the actual solution is a prerequisite.

In the case of a polynomial equation in one variable, Newton's method has a simple geometric interpretation. If x_0 is our initial guess for the solution to the equation $f(x) = 0$, we calculate the tangent $f'(x_0)$. The next approximation, x_1, is given by the point where the tangent crosses the x axis.

For a more thorough explanation of Newton's method, see Appendix 4 of Faux and Pratt (1979). In this document we will limit ourselves to the practical application of Newton's method to the problem at hand, namely the intersection of a ray with a bicubic surface patch. As will become evident in the next section, this problem reduces to the solution of a system of two polynomial equations in u and v.

Suppose then that we want to determine the values of u and v where $f(u,v) = g(u,v) = 0$, and we have two initial guesses u_r and v_r. Our next, usually closer, approximations are given by $u_{r+1} = u_r + \Delta u$, and $v_{r+1} = v_r + \Delta v$, where Δu and Δv are the Newton steps:

$$\Delta u = \frac{g \frac{df}{dv} - f \frac{dg}{dv}}{\frac{df}{du}\frac{dg}{dv} - \frac{df}{dv}\frac{dg}{du}} \qquad\qquad \Delta v = \frac{g \frac{df}{du} - f \frac{dg}{du}}{\frac{df}{dv}\frac{dg}{du} - \frac{df}{du}\frac{dg}{dv}}$$

In the above equations, all the functions and derivatives are assumed to be calculated at (u_r, v_r).

Once the Newton steps have been calculated and u and v iterated, the new values of u and v can be plugged into the same equations to get successively closer approximations to the solution. This iteration continues until f(u,v) and g(u,v) are sufficiently close to zero. Typically the number of correct significant digits doubles with each iteration.

4. THE ALGORITHM

The algorithm for intersecting rays with a bicubic surface may be divided into three steps: the evaluation of sample points and the construction of the tree, which occur during preprocessing, and then the actual intersection calculation.

Sampling the surface

The first step in the preprocessing of a surface is the evaluation of a grid of sample points over the entire surface. Given an integer parameter divisions, the legal parameter range of each patch comprising the surface is divided into a grid of divisions x divisions squares. Then points on the surface are evaluated at the corners of each square.

For example, if divisions is 4, then surface points are evaluated on each patch for u and v equal to 0, .25, .5, .75 and 1. If the surface is comprised of M x N patches, then the number of sample points calculated is (M * divisions + 1) x (N * divisions + 1).

The divisions parameter is specified by the user based on the size and complexity of the surface. See the section below on selecting the divisions and overlap parameters.

Constructing the tree

The second step in the preprocessing of a surface is to use the grid of sample points evaluated above to create a tree of bounding boxes. The bounding box at the root node of the tree is big enough to contain the entire surface. Every internal node of the tree contains pointers to its children, and its bounding box is just big enough to contain all of its children's boxes. Each leaf node holds representative

values of u and v for the section of the surface it represents; these
values will be used later as an initial guess for a Newton process.

The tree is created by a process which recursively subdivides the
legal parameter range of the entire surface. At each level of
recursion a node is created for the tree. If the parameter range for
that node contains only one square of the grid of sample points
evaluated previously, then recursion stops, and a bounding box and
initial guess are calculated as described below; otherwise the
parameter range is subdivided recursively, the node created is made to
point to its children nodes, and a box bounding its children's boxes
is calculated.

To describe the process at a lower level: a recursive subdivision
routine is passed an array of u values at which sample points have
been calculated, and an array of v values. Initially these arrays
contain all the sample values of u and v except the last, each value
in the array representing the start of an interval. These arrays are
divided in half until only one value remains in each. At this point a
leaf node is created representing that interval of the sample grid.

If the sample values remaining are u_i and v_j then the leaf node
represents the interval (u_i, v_j) to (u_{i+1}, v_{j+1}), and a bounding
box and initial guess are calculated for that interval.

The values of u and v stored in a leaf node are just the mean values
of u and v for that section of the surface:

$$u = \frac{u_i + u_{i+1}}{2} \qquad\qquad v = \frac{v_j + v_{j+1}}{2}$$

The bounding box stored in a leaf node is a box big enough to contain
the four sample points at the corners of the surface interval.

In order for the intersection calculation algorithm to work, every
point on the surface must be contained in at least one leaf node's
bounding box. Note, however, that if the bounding boxes stored at the
leaf nodes are only just big enough to contain their four sample
points, then the surface is not guaranteed to stay inside the boxes.
If a peak or a valley on the surface falls between sample points, in
fact, the surface will wander outside the bounding box for that
interval.

One way to avoid this problem would be to position the sample points
more intelligently. If the sample points were evaluated so as to
coincide with any maxima and minima on the surface, then the surface
would be guaranteed to fall within boxes formed by adjacent sample
points. Unfortunately though, finding the exact locations of maxima
and minima on a surface is not trivial.

The solution adopted here is that when the bounding box for a leaf
node is calculated, it is enlarged according to an overlap parameter
specified by the user. Specifically, the length of each side of a
bounding box, as defined strictly by four sample points, is increased
by a factor of overlap while maintaining the same center point. For
instance, if a box just barely containing the four sample points is a

cube centered at the origin with sides of length 10, and overlap is
0.1, then the new box will be a cube with sides of length 11, still
centered at the origin.

The same value of overlap is used over the entire surface; see the
section below on selecting the divisions and overlap parameters.

Calculating points of intersection

Once a surface has been preprocessed and the tree created as above,
the algorithm for computing the intersection of a ray with the surface
is as follows.

We maintain a list of tree nodes to be tested for intersection with
the ray, sorted by the minimum distance from the origin of the ray to
the bounding box of the node. Thus the next node in the list is
always the closest to the origin of the ray. Initially the list
contains only the root node of the tree (assuming the ray intersects
the bounding box -- if not, an intersection can be trivially
rejected).

A loop removes, at each iteration, the next node from the list (that
is, the closest to the origin of the ray). If the node is an internal
node, each of its children is tested in turn for possible intersection
with the ray. Those whose bounding boxes are intersected by the ray
are put back into the list, others are thrown away. If the node is a
leaf node, then a Newton process determines the actual point of
intersection if there is one. The loop exits when either the list of
nodes to be tested is empty, or an intersection is found whose
distance from the origin of the ray is less than the minimum distance
from the origin to the next node in the list.

In high-level pseudocode, the intersection routine looks like this:

```
intersect_surface (surface, ray, intersection)
{
    initialize empty list
    add root node of surface's tree to list

    while list not empty
        remove next node from list
        if node is a leaf node
            call Newton process
            if intersection was found, and is closer than any
            previous intersections found, save it
        else for each child of node
            if ray intersects bounding box
                add child node to list
        if saved intersection is closer than minimum distance to
        next node in tree, exit loop

    free list
}
```

The pseudocode procedure above glosses over the Newton process which
finds the exact point of intersection. The Newton process works as
follows. Since we need to solve for two variables (u and v), we
formulate the problem in terms of two polynomials in u and v which go
to 0 when u and v correspond to a point where the ray intersects the

surface. We can then use Newton's method as described in Section 3 to solve these two polynomials.

We express the intersection as two polynomials by thinking of the ray as the intersection of two planes, and simultaneously solving for an intersection with each of the planes. This formulation is exactly as in Sweeney and Bartels.

We have two planes passing through a point (x,y,z) on the surface expressed as

$$(A_1,B_1,C_1) \cdot (x,y,z) = D_1$$

$$(A_2,B_2,C_2) \cdot (x,y,z) = D_2$$

If the ray is expressed parametrically in terms of its origin and its direction as

$$(x_a,y_a,z_a) + t(x_b,y_b,z_b)$$

then we can determine two perpendicular planes whose intersection contains the ray:

$$(A_1,B_1,C_1) = (x_a,y_a,z_a) \times (x_b,y_b,z_b)$$

$$(A_2,B_2,C_2) = (A_1,B_1,C_1) \times (x_b,y_b,z_b)$$

$$D_1 = (A_1,B_1,C_1) \cdot (x_a,y_a,z_a)$$

$$D_2 = (A_2,B_2,C_2) \cdot (x_a,y_a,z_a)$$

Using the equations for the evaluation of a point on a surface from Section 2, we can then formulate two polynomials representing the intersections of the surface with plane 1 and plane 2 respectively:

$$E_1(u,v) = \sum_i \sum_j [(A_1,B_1,C_1) \cdot G_{ij}] B_i(u) B_j(v) - D_1 = 0$$

$$E_2(u,v) = \sum_i \sum_j [(A_2,B_2,C_2) \cdot G_{ij}] B_i(u) B_j(v) - D_2 = 0$$

Rewriting these equations in matrix notation we get:

$$E_1(u,v) = UMH_1 M^T V^T - D_1 = 0$$

$$E_2(u,v) = UMH_2 M^T V^T - D_2 = 0$$

where

$$H_{ij} = (A,B,C) \cdot G_{ij} \quad \text{for } i,j = 1,2,3,4.$$

Although we have not been stating it explicitly, it should be understood that the functions E are vector functions, with x, y and z components. Similarly, the matrices H_1 and H_2 each have x, y and z components.

We now have two polynomial equations which we can solve by Newton's method, exactly as described in Section 3. The partial derivatives of these functions, necessary for calculating the Newton step, are given by:

$$\frac{dE}{du} = UM'HM^{T}V^{T} \qquad\qquad \frac{dE}{dv} = UMHM'^{T}V^{T}$$

The Newton process starts with the initial guesses for u and v provided by the leaf nodes of the tree. At each iteration, the two functions E are evaluated at the given values of u and v. If the functions are sufficiently close to zero (see below for a definition of "sufficiently close"), the process stops. Otherwise the partial derivatives of the two functions are evaluated and used to calculate two new values for u and v.

Two conditions cause the Newton process to exit. The first, indicating that an intersection has been found, is when the approximations of u and v are sufficiently close to the root of the functions. More precisely, when the sum of the absolute values of the two functions is less than tolerance, success is reported. In the current software implementation, tolerance is fixed at 0.01, although it should really vary with the dimensions of the object space.

The second stop condition indicates that the ray and the surface do not intersect, and occurs when, after more than a certain number of iterations, the approximations of u and v are no closer to the root of the functions than were the last guess. That certain number is a constant called allowance, and a reasonable value is 2. Sweeney and Bartels also register a failure when u or v wanders outside the legal parameter range; in our implementation, u and v are clamped within the legal parameter range, rather than registering failure immediately.

In pseudocode, the Newton process looks like this:

```
newton (surface, treenode, ray, intersection, t, u, v)
{
    calculate plane1, plane2
    get initial values for u and v from tree node
    success = failure = FALSE

    while not success and not failure
        calculate E1, E2
        error = |E1| + |E2|
        if error < tolerance
            success = TRUE
        else if iterations >= allowance and error >= last error
            failure = TRUE
        else
            calculate Newton steps
            add Newton steps to u and v
            increment iteration count

    if success
        intersection = point on surface at (u,v)
        t = distance from ray origin to intersection point

}
```

Once the values of u and v have been determined for the intersection of a ray with the surface, it is straightforward to calculate the actual coordinates of the intersection point and the surface normal at that point, using the equations from Section 2.

Choosing divisions and overlap

As is now evident, every spline surface defined has two extra parameters associated with it, divisions and overlap. Unfortunately the user must specify these parameters explicitly, and needs to have some understanding of the rendering algorithm in order to choose them intelligently.

When choosing the divisions parameter, the user has to take into account the complexity of the surface, and the screen area occupied by the surface. Divisions should be large enough (and the bounding boxes thus small enough) that each box contains a reasonable guess as to the point of intersection. There is a point of diminishing return in subdiving a surface, however. If divisions is too big, the rendering process actually slows down, overburdened by the time spent traversing a large tree. Also, in cases where a bounding box is extremely small, errors sometimes result from a loss of numeric precision. A typical value for divisions is somewhere between 4 and 16; we almost always use 4.

The overlap parameter should be chosen so that the tree of bounding boxes contains the entire surface, but fits it as tightly as possible. This again depends on the complexity of the surface, and also on where the boundaries between boxes fall. In ideal cases where any peaks and valleys on the surface fall exactly on box boundaries, overlap may be 0. More typically, a value of about 0.05 seems to work.

If overlap is too small, holes will appear in the surface at regular intervals, which is sometimes an interesting visual effect. Holes will also appear, in a less predictable manner, if a patch is not subdivided enough. This happens when the initial guess for the intersection point is so inaccurate that the Newton process fails to find the actual intersection.

5. THE USER INTERFACE

Spline surfaces to be rendered by the ray tracing software are defined by text files specifying, for each surface, the control points defining the surface, the blending functions to be used, and any other parameters required. These files may be created by hand, but usually they are generated by a menu-driven interactive surface modeler, SCULFACE. This section describes, very generally, how a user goes about creating and rendering spline surfaces.

Surface types supported

Currently four types of bicubic surfaces are supported: uniformly shaped Beta-splines; continuously shaped Beta-splines; Bezier surfaces; and Hermite surfaces whose derivatives are calculated automatically according to bias and tension parameters specified by the user.

a. Bias and tension parameters

Barsky (1981) introduced the use of shape parameters which he called bias and tension in his development of the Beta-spline. Visually, altering the bias parameter at one or more control points defining a Beta-spline surface tends to push the surface in one direction or the other with respect to the control points altered. Increasing the tension parameter makes the surface more jagged, causing the surface to converge to the grid of control points itself as tension goes to infinity. Note that a Beta-spline whose bias and tension parameters are left at their default values is just a B-spline.

Uniformly shaped Beta-splines have only one bias parameter and one tension parameter, which are constant over the entire surface; continuously shaped Beta-splines have different values of bias and tension associated with each control point. Continuously shaped Beta-splines are more expensive to calculate, since the bias and tension parameters are blended between adjacent control points, as are the blending functions themselves.

The use of bias and tension parameters with Hermite blending functions was introduced by Kochanek and Bartels (1984) in an article on interpolating curves. (Reviewers inform us that the surface form has since been developed by Du et al 1987.) Bias and tension parameters are associated with each control point, and visually have much the same effect they have on Beta-splines. In this case, however, the blending functions remain constant; the parameters are used only to calculate the slope of the surface at each control point.

b. Approximating vs. interpolating surfaces

Beta-splines are approximating surfaces, meaning they generally do not actually pass through the control points defining them; Bezier surfaces pass through the control points at the corner of each patch; Hermite surfaces are fully interpolating, passing through every control point. Beta-splines may also be used as interpolating surfaces, however: given a grid of points to be interpolated, a SCULFACE utility will calculate for the user a new grid of points which, when used as control points for a B-spline, define a surface which interpolates the original points (Barsky and Greenberg 1980).

c. Boundary conditions

When using Beta-splines, the user also has the freedom of specifying one of several possible boundary conditions. These are useful for extending the edges of a Beta-spline surface, since in general a Beta-spline surface patch is much smaller than the grid of control points defining it.

Specifically, four boundary conditions are available, denominated single, double, triple and phantom. If single is specified, the grid of control points is used exactly as is. If double is specified, each control point on the edge of the grid, or boundary vertex, is doubled, so that a grid of size M x N becomes a grid of size M+2 x N+2. (The vertices at the four corners are actually replicated three times: once horizontally, once vertically, and once diagonally to define a new corner vertex; all other boundary vertices are replicated just once.) Doubling the boundary vertices has the effect of adding a strip of new patches around the edges of the original surface, bringing the surface closer to the boundaries of the original grid of control points.

The boundary vertices of a Beta-spline may be tripled in an analogous manner. This adds yet another strip of patches to the edges of the surface. In fact, the surface is guaranteed to interpolate the four corner points of the original control grid when the triple boundary condition is specified.

Finally, the user may specify the phantom boundary condition. In this case two rows and two columns are added to the original control points, just as when the boundary vertices were doubled. Here however the boundary vertices are not merely replicated, but new "phantom" vertices are calculated which cause the surface to interpolate the four corner vertices.

For a more detailed discussion of boundary conditions for curves and surfaces, see (Barsky 1982).

SCULFACE

SCULFACE is a menu-driven, interactive modeler for creating bicubic surfaces. The modeler has been implemented on an Evans and Sutherland PS300, a graphics workstation with vector and raster monitors, dials, keyboard and tablet.

Creating a bicubic surface essentially involves the specification of a grid of control points to generate the desired surface. This consists of an array of points in 3-space. The user may start out with either a default, flat grid, or with a grid of points from an existing model. Points in the grid may be positioned in any of three editing modes -- free editing, section editing and copy editing -- which are described below.

At any point during the editing of the control grid the user may view the scene in any parallel or perspective viewing transformation. Dials allow the user to translate, rotate and scale the scene in real time, and to observe the scene from any point in space.

The default editing mode for positioning the control points is called free editing. In free editing, dials are used to translate the control points, one at a time, with respect to the x, y and z axes. A flashing cursor marks the point being edited. At any time the user may press a button to return a control point to its original location.

In the second editing mode, section editing, the user traces cross sections of the object being modelled with a tablet. Each row or column of the control graph follows one of the cross sections. By default cross sections are understood to be perpendicular to the z axis, but they may also be considered perpendicular to the x axis. In the first case, each row of the grid of control points corresponds to one of the cross sections; in the second, each column corresponds to a cross section. For each section the user may explicitly specify the depth in z or x, or may use the default value supplied by the modeler.

The third editing mode, copy editing, allows the user to pick vertices from an existing three dimensional boundary representation model. The existing model is loaded and a wireframe representation is displayed on the screen, whereby the user may use the tablet to pick vertices from the model to insert into the control graph. The resulting control points are thus a "rectangular" subset of the vertices of the model being copied.

All three editing modes may be used to manipulate any grid of control points. These points may then be used to generate any kind of spline surface -- Beta-spline (approximating or interpolating), Bezier or Hermite. This flexibility is very useful for comparing the different kinds of surfaces which may be generated starting with the same set of control points.

The SCULFACE menu also allows the user to specify various parameters for the surface being created. Global parameters include divisions and overlap, and, if the surface is a uniformly shaped Beta-spline, global parameters of bias and tension. If the surface is a continuously shaped Beta-spline or a Hermite surface, the user may also want to specify local bias and tension parameters. Each point in the control graph has associated with it a bias value and a tension value, which the user may specify explicitly or leave at their default values. In addition, the user may specify the boundary conditions to be imposed on a grid of Beta-spline control points.

Rendering surfaces

Once a bicubic surface has been created, it may be rendered directly by SCULFACE on the PS300 or saved in a format understandable to the ray tracing software.

SCULFACE itself can create and render a polygonal approximation of the surface. The rendering is done automatically by the PS300, and may be either wireframe or shaded. Flat, Gouraud and Phong shading are supported. The polygonal approximation of the surface may be saved to a file, or else the actual surface definition may be saved for rendering by the ray tracing software.

In addition to bicubic surfaces, the ray tracer can handle solids in constructive solid geometry (CSG) representation, generated by performing boolean operations (subtraction, intersection, union) on solid primitives such as spheres, parallelepipeds and cones. CSG solids and bicubic surfaces may be freely intermixed. For the purposes of boolean operations, surfaces are treated as infinitely thin solids; that is, any time a ray intersects a surface it is actually assumed to intersect it twice, entering and immediately exiting again. The intermixing of bicubic surfaces and CSG solids is useful for cutting surfaces by intersecting or subtracting solids. However the inverse operation, cutting a solid with a surface, and unions of solids and surfaces, have little meaning.

Treating surfaces as very thin solids to simulate boolean operations is obviously a hack. In fact, it will not work correctly if a surface is planar and the ray intersecting it lies in the same plane, although that is not a common situation. More importantly, it does not allow the user to define a solid object bounded by a surface. Miller (1986) reviews some of the issues involved in incorporating free-form surfaces into solid models, and provides references to several solid modeling systems with at least experimental free-form surface capability.

6. RESULTS AND WORK IN PROGRESS

The ray tracing software has been implemented in C on a Data General Eclipse MV/8000 mainframe, and on various Apollo workstations. The SCULFACE modeler has been implemented in both C and Pascal on an Apollo, which is connected to an Evans and Sutherland PS300.

The slides show some images created with our software. Figures 1 to 3 are examples of the different surface types supported. Figure 1 is a Beta-spline surface with the boundary vertices doubled, fig. 2 a Bezier surface, and fig. 3 a Hermite surface showing the effects of altering the bias and tension parameters. Red spheres indicate the control points defining the surfaces.

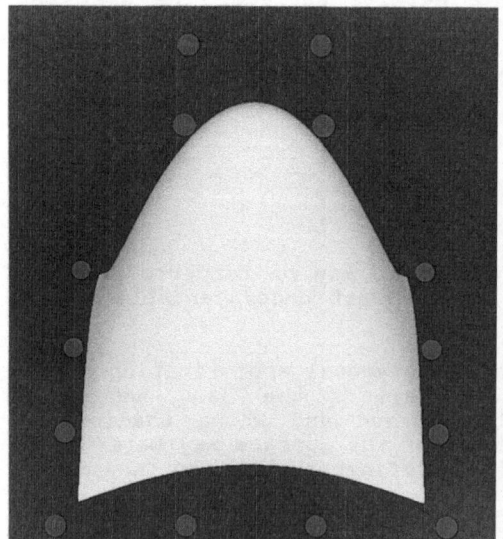 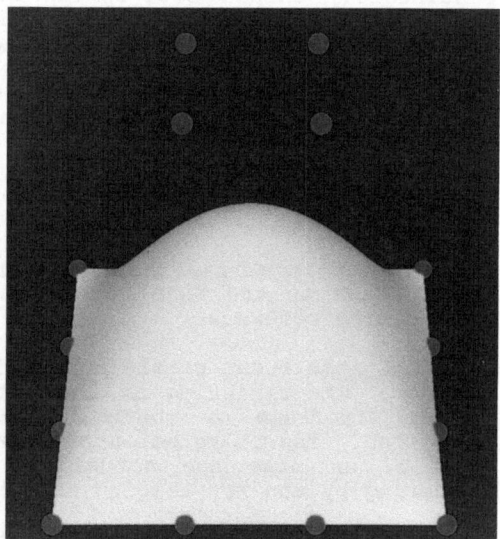

Fig. 1. Beta-spline surface.   Fig. 2.   Bezier surface.

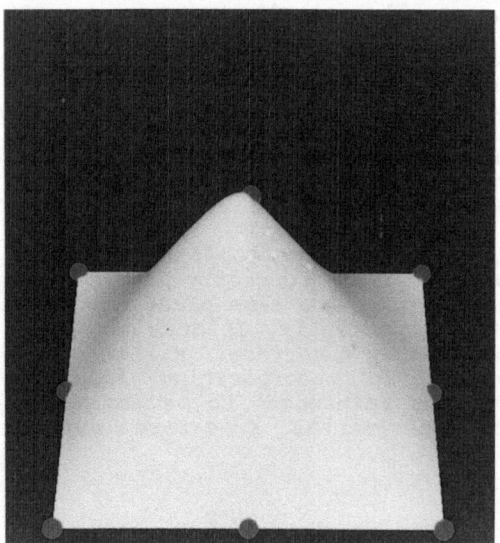

Fig. 3.
Hermite surface.

Figure 4 is an unfinished model of a Lancia Thema being created with a combination of Beta-spline surfaces and CSG solids. The car body and windows are constructed out of Beta-splines. So far the model contains 87 surfaces for a total of more than 1000 patches. The wheels, grill, mirror, steering wheel, etc., are CSG solids.

Fig. 4. Car created using Beta-spline surfaces and CSG solids.

The sample surfaces shown take between 20 and 40 minutes of CPU to generate, depending on the size of the surface, when calculated at a resolution of 512 x 512 on the Data General. The Data General is comparable to a VAX 11/780 speedwise. The car, calculated at the same resolution, without transparency, and with no antialiasing, takes about 2 hours. The image shown was calculated at a resolution of 2048 pixels, with transparent windows and 8 light sources, and took 62 hours to generate on an Apollo DN580 workstation. Preprocessing times range from less than a second for a simple surface to about a minute for the car.

The ray tracing software is not built for speed. In particular, it does not use any kind of space subdivision technique to reduce intersection calculations; every ray is tested for intersection with every surface in the scene. As for ray-surface intersections specifically, calculation time could be reduced, for instance, by varying the tolerance constant. We have been using a fixed value of 0.01, which for most surfaces is more demanding than necessary. Also, performing all calculations as matrix multiplications probably wastes a good deal of time on setting up the matrices and on redundant calculations, although it saved programming time and makes the code more readable.

We have found that the average number of Newton iterations per intersection test averages between 2 and 2.5. We are currently experimenting with reducing this number by taking advantage of image coherency. A ray-to-ray coherency scheme such as that proposed by Joy and Bhetanabhotla (1986) might be feasible.

There are some disadvantages to the approach we have taken for ray-surface intersection calculations. Most notably, it relies on two parameters, divisions and overlap, which must be explicitly specified by the user. Choosing the parameters can be tricky for a user who does not know much about spline surfaces. We have found, however, that we tend to choose the parameters from a very small, fixed set of values; specifically, 4 or 8 for divisions, and 0 or 0.05 for overlap. These values seem to do fine for all the images we have worked with. When in doubt, we choose the smaller values, then if calculation times or image quality are unacceptable we change them. A procedure for choosing these parameters automatically would obviously be very useful. More useful still would be an algorithm which subdivides a surface adaptively, stopping the subdivision process when the resulting surface fragment is sufficiently simple.

Another disadvantage is that Newton's method is by nature approximative, even though it can approximate a point of intersection to an arbitrary degree of accuracy. Imprecise intersection solutions can occasionally lead to problems with transparency and reflections, but precision can always be increased by modifying the tolerance constant.

Advantages of this method, on the other hand, are that it is conceptually relatively simple, and the code produced therefore is concise, easy to understand and easy to generalize. The resulting software package is flexible enough to handle surfaces using arbitrary blending functions, the quality of the images produced is good, and the calculation times are actually better than we had feared.

REFERENCES

Barsky Brian A, Donald P Greenberg (1980) Determining a Set of B-spline Control Vertices to Generate an Interpolating Surface. Computer Graphics and Image Processing 14:203-226

Barsky Brian A (1981) The Beta-spline: A Local Representation Based On Shape Parameters and Fundamental Geometric Measures. PhD dissertation, Department of Computer Science, University of Utah

Barsky Brian A (1982) End Conditions and Boundary Conditions for Uniform B-Spline Curve and Surface Representations. Computers in Industry 3(1/2):17-29

Bartels Richard H, John C Beatty, Brian A Barsky (1985) An Introduction to the Use of Splines in Computer Graphics. Notes for Siggraph 85 tutorial: The Use of B-Splines and Beta-Splines to Model Freeform Curves and Surfaces. University of Waterloo and University of California

Catmull E, J Clark (1978) Recursively Generated B-Spline Surfaces on Arbitrary Topological Meshes. Computer Aided Design 10(6):350-355

Du Wen-Hui, Francis JM Schmitt, Brian A Barsky (1987) Modeling Free-Form Surfaces Using Brown's Interpolant with Control Parameters. CADDM 87 conference proceedings

Faux ID, MJ Pratt (1979) Computational Geometry for Design and Manufacture. John Wiley, New York

Foley James D, Andries Van Dam (1982) Fundamentals of Interactive Computer Graphics. Addison-Wesley, Reading, MA

Joy Kenneth I, Murthy N Bhetanabhotla (1986) Ray Tracing Parametric Surface Patches Utilizing Numerical Techniques and Ray Coherence. Computer Graphics 20(4):279-285

Kajiya James T (1982) Ray Tracing Parametric Patches. Computer Graphics 16(3):245-254

Kajiya James T (1983) New Techniques for Ray Tracing Procedurally Defined Objects. Computer Graphics 17(3):91-102

Kochanek Doris HU, Richard H Bartels (1984) Interpolating Splines with Local Tension, Continuity, and Bias Control. Computer Graphics 18(3):33-41

Miller James R (1986) Sculptured Surfaces in Solid Models: Issues and Alternative Approaches. IEEE CG&A 6(12):37-48

Newman William M, Robert F Sproull (1979) Principles of Computer Graphics. McGraw-Hill, New York

Riesenfeld Richard, Elaine Cohen, Tom Lyche (1980) Discrete B-Splines and Subdivision Techniques in Computer-Aided Geometric Design and Computer Graphics. Computer Graphics and Image Processing 14(2):87-111

Sederberg Thomas W (1984) Ray Tracing of Steiner Patches. Computer Graphics 18(3):159-164

Sweeney Michael AJ, Richard Bartels (1986) Ray Tracing Free-Form B-Spline Surfaces. IEEE CG&A 6(2):41-49

Toth Daniel L (1985) On Ray Tracing Parametric Surfaces. Computer Graphics 19(3):171-179

Whitted Turner (1980) An Improved Illumination Model for Shaded Display. Communications ACM 23(6):343-349

Geoff Levner is a consultant for software development at Eidos in Milan. He received his BA in computer science from Brown University in 1985.

Paolo Tassinari is a student at the Universita' degli Studi di Milano, and is currently completing his thesis on the modeling of curved surfaces at Eidos. He is particularly interested in the use of curved surfaces for styling car bodies.

Daniele Marini is professor of computer science at the Istituto di Cibernetica of the Universita' degli Studi di Milano, vice president of Eidos, and vice president of the Associazione Italiana di Computer Graphics (Aicographics). He was co-founder in 1980 of Pixel, the first Italian scientific journal specializing in computer graphics and image synthesis. His research interests include software engineering, modeling of ecosystems and computer graphics.

All three authors may be reached at:

Eidos SpA
Via Fontana, 16
20122 Milano, Italy

Ray Coherence Theorem and Constant Time Ray Tracing Algorithm

Masataka Ohta and Mamoru Maekawa

ABSTRACT

The concept of ray coherence is formalized as a ray coherence theorem to decrease the amount of computation in a ray object intersection of the ray tracing algorithm. Using the theorem, the calculation time of ray object intersection in a ray tracing algorithm can be drastically decreased, by calculating a table which is used to limit the number of objects which may intersect with a given ray. The overhead of the algorithm is so small that it is effective even when there are only two objects. For more objects, the computation time of the ray object intersection remains almost constant.

Keywords: visible surface elimination, ray tracing, coherence, computational geometry, spherical geometry

1. INTRODUCTION

Ray tracing (Whitted 1980) is an algorithm which can produce the most realistic computer generated images. But, unfortunately, it is also the most time consuming algorithm. So the use of ray tracing has been applied only when great computational power is available or a very high quality image is required. Classical ray tracing is slow because it dose not use coherence to reduce the calculation of hidden surface elimination. So, nearly the same calculation must be done repeatedly for each ray in nearby pixels. The use of some sort of coherence has been a useful paradigm to shorten the computation time in computer graphics.

Recently, several improvements of the ray tracing algorithm have been proposed which use some sort of coherence. The coherence can be classified into three categories:

object-space coherence
> Object-space coherence means that an object tends to be continuous and different objects tend to be disjoint in three dimensional object-space, i.e if a point is occupied by some object, the neighborhood of the point is probably also be occupied by the same object.

image-space coherence
> Image-space coherence means that an object tends to be continuous and different objects tend to be disjoint in two dimensional screen after perspective transformation. Image-space coherence includes scanline coherence, which means consecutive scanlines are probably nearly the same, and pixel coherence, which means consecutive pixels probably have nearly the same color.

ray coherence
> Ray coherence means that rays which have nearly the same origin and nearly the same direction will probably intersect with nearly same object at nearly the same location.

All coherence can be used to accelerate ray tracing.

The object-space coherence is first used by Whitted (1980) as a bounding sphere technique which is used to reduce the calculation time of each ray-object intersection. But the improvement is only the order of a constant. Recent approaches (Fujimura 1983; Weghorst 1984; Matsumoto 1983; Glassner 1984; Fujimoto 1986; Satoh 1986) use the partitioning of the object-space into several sub-spaces. By object-space coherence, an object is expected to belong only to a number of sub-spaces. Thus actual ray-object intersection checks are needed only for the objects which are contained in sub-spaces which intersect with the ray. The efficiencies of the algorithms depend on how well the object-space is divided. Weghorst (1984) uses a hierarchy of bounding volumes for the partitioning. Others (Matsumoto 1983; Fujimure 1983; Glassner 1984) use an octree. In (Fujimoto 1986), the entire space is uniformly divided into congruent cubes, which results in better performance than the octree method.

The intersection between objects and sub-spaces are computed as pre-processing. The ray-object intersection problem is then solved in two steps, first all sub-spaces which intersect with the ray are listed, then in the second step, only the objects which are contained in these sub-spaces are actually checked for the intersection. With the increase of the number of sub-spaces, the number of the objects which need to be checked reduces. But at the same time, the number of the sub-spaces which intersect with the ray also increases. Thus the improvement is somewhat limited. By our analysis, Fujimoto's algorithm (1986) has time complexity of $O(N^{1/3})$ for N objects at its best.

Satoh (1986) use the same theorem as the ray coherence theorem 1 in section 2 of this paper. But, the theorem is used only to accelerate the computation on bounding spheres and to sort bounding spheres.

The image-space coherence is often used as a combination of the ray tracing and other hidden surface algorithm. Because the first generation rays directly cast from the eye have obvious coherence and regular structure, it is possible to replace tracing of the first generation ray by another hidden surface elimination algorithm. Weghorst (1984) uses a z-buffer algorithm to compute an image without reflection, refraction or shadows by z-buffering, then ray tracing is done in the direction of the reflection, refraction and light sources. Thus, the use of coherence is limited to the first generation rays. Speer (1985) tries to extract coherence by using the fact that rays from adjacent pixels pass nearly same space. A bounding cylinder around a ray is used to eliminate unnecessary computation of rays from adjacent pixels. But, by such weak coherence, no or only small amount of performance improvement is possible. Haines (1986) uses image coherence viewed from the light source to accelerate the calculation of shadow by computing a rough image from the point light source.

Ray coherence is used by Joy (1986), to efficiently compute the intersection between a ray and a parametric surface patch. For consecutive pixels in which the same patch is seen, solution of the previous pixel can be used as a initial value for the quasi-Newton iteration. Another interesting approach to use ray coherence is in (Heckbert 1984). By using only polygonal objects and by slightly changing the law of refraction, it is possible to maintain coherence and regular structure of first generation rays even after reflections and refractions. But the method can not handle curved surfaces.

Compared to object-space and image-space coherence, formal treatment of ray coherence is difficult because a ray has two components, origin and direction and ray coherence must treat both of them. But, it is expected that ray tracing can be most effectively accelerated by directly using ray coherence. In section 2, we give theorems which can be used to compute the coherence of the ray explicitly. Based on the theorem, in section 3, we give a ray tracing algorithm which uses ray coherence to accelerate the calculation of ray-object intersections. Section 4 gives a theoretical performance analysis of the algorithm. In section 5, actual performance data is presented, and section 6 concludes.

2. RAY COHERENCE THEOREM

In this section two theorems to treat ray coherence are given. They roughly mean that a object can be seen only in limited direction from the other objects. Following notations are used in the theorem.

$\vec{PQ}$
    is a vector from the point P to the point Q.
$dir(\vec{PQ})$
    is a function which maps non-zero vector $\vec{PQ}$, to its direction. $dir(\vec{PQ}) = \vec{PQ}/|\vec{PQ}|$.
$CH_3(\{P_0, \cdots, P_n\})$
    is a ordinary convex hull of points $P_0, \ldots, P_n$.
$CH_2(\{P_0, \cdots, P_n\})$
    is a convex hull of directions $P_0, \ldots, P_n$, represented by unit vectors and denoting
points on a unit sphere, based on spherical geometry of the unit sphere. The convex
hull on spherical geometry is defined as a minimum convex set which contains
$P_0, \cdots, P_n$, where the convex set C is a set which has the following property:

$$P,Q \in C \implies (\text{shortest path between } P \text{ and } Q) \sqsubseteq C.$$

Theorem 1: (ray coherence for spheres)

Let C_1 be a sphere with center o_1 and radius r_1 and C_2 be a sphere with center o_2 and radius
r_2 where $|o_1 o_2| > r_1 + r_2$. Then if point P is inside of C_1 and Q is inside of C_2, the following inequality holds:

$$(dir(\vec{PQ}), dir(o_1 o_2)) > \sqrt{1-((r_1+r_2)/|o_1 o_2|)^2}.$$

Proof:

Let the angle between $\vec{PQ}$ and $o_1 o_2$ be α ($0 \le \alpha < \pi/2$). Then, $\cos\alpha = (dir(\vec{PQ}), dir(o_1 o_2))$. From
Fig. 1, clearly, $\sin\alpha < (r_1+r_2)/|o_1 o_2|$. Moreover, $\cos\alpha, \sin\alpha \ge 0$. Thus, $(dir(\vec{PQ}), dir(o_1 o_2)) > \sqrt{1-((r_1+r_2)/|o_1 o_2|)^2}$.

Q.E.D.

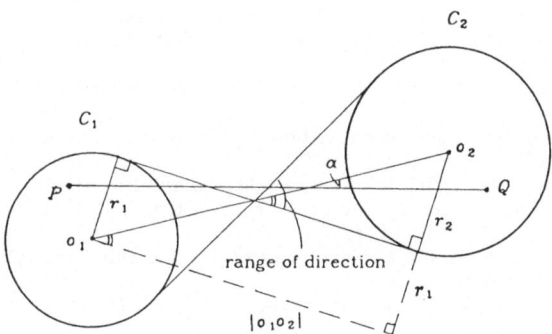

Fig. 1. Ray coherence theorem for spheres

Theorem 2: (ray coherence for convex hulls)
If point P is a member of $CH_3(\{p_1, \cdots, p_n\})$ and Q is a member of $CH_3(\{q_1, \cdots, q_m\})$, then
$dir(\vec{PQ})$ is a member of $CH_2(\{dir(p_1 q_1), \cdots, dir(p_1 q_m), \cdots, dir(p_n q_1), \cdots, dir(p_n q_m)\})$.

Proof:

It is enough to show that $\vec{PQ}$ is a non-negative linear combination of $p_1 q_1, \cdots, p_1 q_m, \cdots,$
$p_n q_1, \cdots, p_n q_m$ with at least one non-zero coefficients. Because $P \in CH_3(\{p_1, \cdots, p_n\})$
and $Q \in CH_3(\{q_1, \cdots, q_m\})$, $P = a_1 p_1 + \cdots + a_n p_n$ ($a_1, \cdots, a_n > 0$, $a_1 + \cdots + a_n = 1$) and
$Q = b_1 q_1 + \cdots + b_m q_m$ ($b_1, \cdots, b_m > 0$, $b_1 + \cdots + b_m = 1$). $\vec{PQ} = a_1 b_1 p_1 q_1 + \cdots +$
$a_1 b_m p_1 q_m + \cdots + a_n b_1 p_n q_1 + \cdots + a_n b_m p_n q_m$.

Q.E.D.

Figure 2 illustrates the theorem 2.

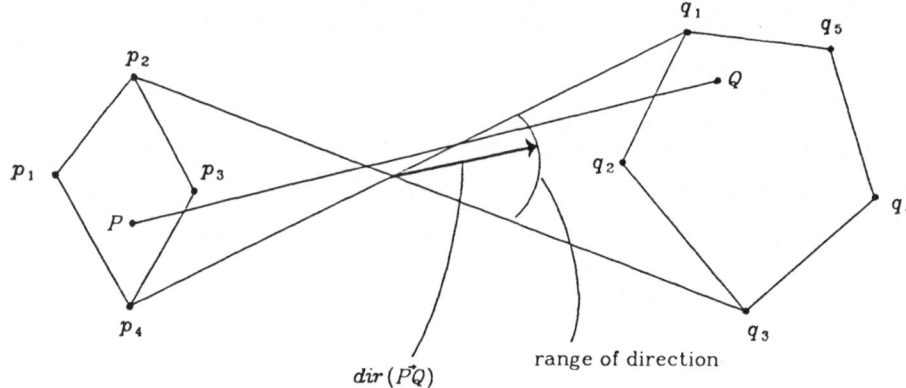

Fig. 2. Ray coherence theorem for convex hulls

3. THE ALGORITHM

Using the ray coherence theorem, we can construct a fast algorithm for ray tracing. The algorithm consists of two parts, which are combined using a two-dimensional array of the list of objects. The array contains information about what object can be seen from certain ray origins in certain directions. The former part is executed only once for an entire image as pre-processing to compute the table. The latter part is executed once for each ray, reducing the number of actual ray object intersection calculations by using the table.

To describe the algorithm, the following assumptions are used:

1) There are N objects. Each object is bounded by a sphere or a convex hull. Objects are numbered 1 to N.
2) There are M ray origins. Ray origins may be the eye, light source, or reflective/refractive objects. Each ray origin is bounded by a sphere or a convex hull. Ray origins are numbered 1 to M.
3) The direction space around the each ray origin is divided into D sub-directions. Sub-directions are numbered 1 to D.
4) There is a two dimensional array of lists of objects $O[1:M][1:D]$.

3.1. Pre-processing Algorithm

Using the ray coherence theorem, we can compute the array $O[j,d]$, where j is the index for the ray origin, d is the index of the sub-direction and $O[j,d]$ is a list of objects which can possibly be seen from the ray origin j in the sub-direction d.

Then the pre-processing algorithm is as follows:

Step 1.1)
    Initialize all elements of O to null.
Step 1.2)
    For each ray origin j, repeat the steps 1.3, 1.4 and 1.5.
Step 1.3)
    For each object i, repeat the steps 1.4 and 1.5.

Step 1.4)

Using ray coherence theorems, compute the subset $S_{i,j}$ of the direction from the point of the bounding volume of ray origin j to the point of the bounding volume of object i. If bounding volumes are spheres, $S_{i,j}$ is a circle, if bounding volumes are convex hulls, $S_{i,j}$ is a convex hull.

Step 1.5)

For each sub-direction d, which has non empty intersection with $S_{i,j}$, add object i to $O[j][d]$.

Step 1.6)

Compute the minimum distance $t_{i,j}$ between ray origin j and object i and sort the elements $O[j][d]$ by the increasing order of $t_{i,j}$.

After the completion of the algorithm, we have defined the array of lists of objects O. All objects which may be seen from the ray origin j in the sub-direction d are contained in $O[j,d]$.

3.2. Ray Object Intersection Algorithm

The ray object intersection algorithm is very simple. The following steps are repeated for each ray:

Step 2.1

Compute the index j of the ray origin and the index d of the sub-direction of the given ray.

Step 2.2

Perform the actual ray object intersection calculation for the objects in $O[j,d]$ from the top until:

a) there are no objects left.

b) the distance between the nearest intersection point and the ray origin is shorter than $t_{i,j}$ (i is the index of the currently tested object).

3.3. Implementation Details

To implement the algorithm, care must be taken in several places to obtain high performance. The most frequently executed part of the algorithm is steps 1.4, 1.5 and 2.1. For the efficient execution of these parts, partitioning of the direction space is the most important problem.

For large number of N, M and D, steps 1.4 and 1.5 of the algorithm are executed great number of times. So, its execution speed is also critical. In step 1.5, it is important to check only sub-directions near $S_{i,j}$. By careless implementation, step 1.5 has computational complexity of $O(N*M*D)$!

In step 2.1, the method to calculate the indices j and d is important. For the index of the ray origin, it will suffice to assign all objects indices, and use each as a ray origin index of a ray which originates from the object. But, the calculation of the index of the ray direction is more difficult. The direction space should be partitioned as evenly as possible to fully extract coherency. But, its shape should be simple because its computation speed is critical to the preformance of the algorithm. We use a partitioning method based on the cube. As in Fig. 3, the entire direction space is first divided into 6 sub-directions according to the 6 faces of a cube, and then, each face is divided into several rectangles. The method can be coded very efficiently using only a few floating point calculations as shown in Appendix A.

To use the ray coherence theorem with convex hulls, algorithms to treat convex hulls by spherical geometry are necessary. Such algorithms can be obtained by modifying similar algorithms for euclidean geometry. For example, it is possible to obtain an algorithm to compute a convex hull of a set of points by slightly modifying the termination condition of the usual convex hull algorithm by Graham (1972). But, in our implementation, at least, its speed and numerical stability are very poor. Though bounding by convex hulls is, in most cases, much tighter than by spheres, it is not practical to use it. It is better to use the union of several spheres as a bounding volume with strangely shaped objects.

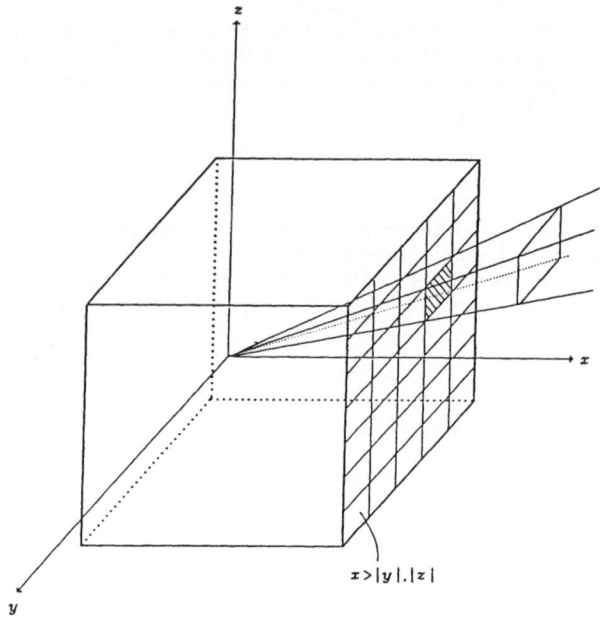

Fig. 3. Subdivision of the direction space

4. PERFORMANCE ANALYSIS

Because the algorithm utilize the coherence of the image, the efficiency of the algorithm heavily depends on the coherence of the image. If there is no coherence, no performance will be gained. And as it is difficult to define the coherence of an image numerically, detailed quantitative evaluation is impossible. In some sense, the performance of the algorithm itself can be a good measure of the coherence of the image.

Because most images have much coherence, the algorithm can compute them very fast. We show the analysis of two cases where ray can be traced in constant time regardless of the number of objects N. It is assumed that rays are randomly directed and have equal probability to have any directions.

The first case is when the sizes of the objects are very small relative to the distance between objects. In this case, even if N becomes large, the number of objects in $O[j,d]$ remain constant if D is increased proportional to N ($D=N\sim 3 \cdot N$ will be enough). Pre-processing takes $O(N \cdot M)$ time and $O(N \cdot M)$ space, and the expected number of ray object intersection calculation is approximately N/D and of course $O(1)$. It is worthwhile to note that nearly all images can be calculated in this very fast manner, if we can use unlimited pre-processing time and space. It is accomplished by dividing all large objects into many smaller ray origins.

The second case is when the sizes of objects are almost equal and are large relative to the distance between objects. The shapes of objects should also be well estimated by their bounding volumes. In such case, the number of objects in $O[j,d]$ is often very large. But the ordering of objects in step 1.6 and termination condition b) in step 2.2 become effective. Let α be the probability of actual ray object intersection when rays intersect with the bounding volume of the object. We assume D is set large enough. Roughly speaking (i.e. by neglecting the size of the ray origin and by assuming objects are disjoint each other), even if infinite objects are contained in $O[j,d]$, the possibility of testing second actual ray object intersection is only $1-\alpha$ and $(1-\alpha)^2$ for third $\cdots$. So, the expected number of objects to be tested remains constant $1+(1-\alpha)+ (1-\alpha)^2+ \cdots =1/\alpha$.

5. PERFORMANCE MEASUREMENT

Four types of measurements are performed to test the efficiency of the algorithm. Those are:

1) To compare the performance with the classical algorithm.
2) To check the former constant time property described in section 4.
3) To check the latter constant time property described in section 4.
4) To discover the efficiency of the algorithm in more general cases.

All measurements are done with randomly distributed spheres which themselves are used as bounding volumes. The resolution of the image is 512 by 512 without anti aliasing. Eye is located at (0,0,0) and directed to (0,0,1). Performance is measured by the time for pre-processing and for one ray object intersection calculation. The program is written in C and measured on SUN3/160 with floating point accelerator.

For case 1), several spheres are placed outside the view volume. Timing information for $N=1,2,3,...,20$, $D=1350$ and $M=N+1$ is illustrated in Fig. 4. The accelerated algorithm computes the image in very fast (as fast as the speed of the classical algorithm for one sphere) constant time.

For case 2), non-reflective/non-refractive diffuse spheres with radius 0.005 are randomly distributed in the unit sphere at (0,0,3) (Fig. 5a). Two light sources are located at (-4,0,-1) and (1,1,-3). Timing information for $N=100,200, \cdots ,1000$, $D=60000$ and $M=3$ (an eye point and two light sources) is illustrated in Fig. 6. Even for 1000 spheres, computation time is almost same as for 1 sphere as in case 1).

For case 3), non-reflective/non-refractive diffuse non-overlapping spheres with radius 0.06 are randomly distributed in the unit sphere at (0,0,3) (Fig. 5b). Two light sources are located at (-4,0,-1) and (1,1,-3). Timing information for $N=100,200, \cdots ,1000$, $D=60000$ and $M=3$ (an eye point and two light sources) is illustrated in Fig. 7. Timing information for sorting in step 1.6) and termination condition b) of step 2.2) is also shown. Without sorting, the computation time increases linearly with the increase of the number of spheres, but with sorting, the computation time is still very small and constant.

For case 4), reflective/non-refractive spheres with radius 0.05 are randomly distributed in the unit sphere at (0,0,0) with minimum distance between spheres of 0.05 (Fig. 5c). No light sources are provided. Timing information for $N=20,40,60,80,100,200,300,400,500$, $D=1350$ and $M=N+1$ is illustrated in Fig. 8. In this case, the computation time increases with the increase of the number of spheres, but the rate of the increase decreases.

6. CONCLUDING REMARKS

We have proved the effectiveness of the concept of ray coherence for the acceleration of the ray tracing. Though the idea is very simple, its effect is drastical. Because the algorithm use only fundamental properties of rays, it can be combined with several other techniques of ray tracing, for example, distributed ray tracing (Cook 1984), ray tracing with cones (Amanatides 1984) etc.

The performance can be estimated well from $O[j,d]$. So, automatic determination of D as a trade off between the memory requirement and the execution time may be an interesting problem. It is also useful to change the value of D according to the importance of ray origins. for example, directions around eye point and light sources should be divided finer than the directions around objects.

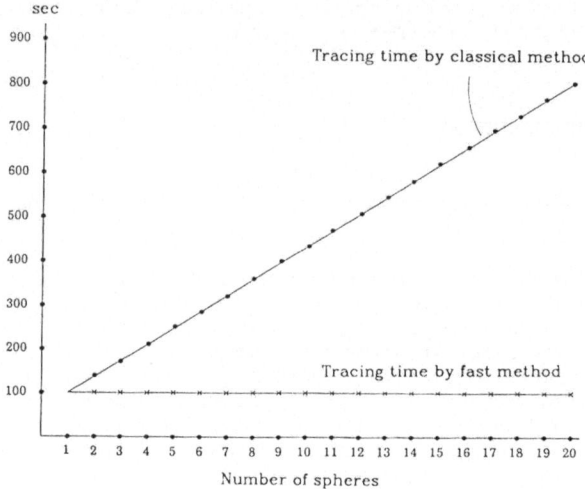

Fig. 4. Comparison of computation time for 1 ~ 20 spheres

a) 1,000 diffuse spheres (sparse)　　　b) 1,000 diffuse spheres (dense)

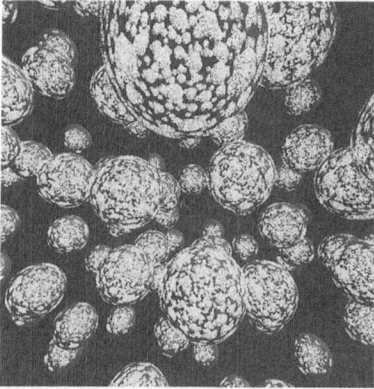

c) 500 reflective spheres　　　　　　Fig. 5. Pictures of spheres

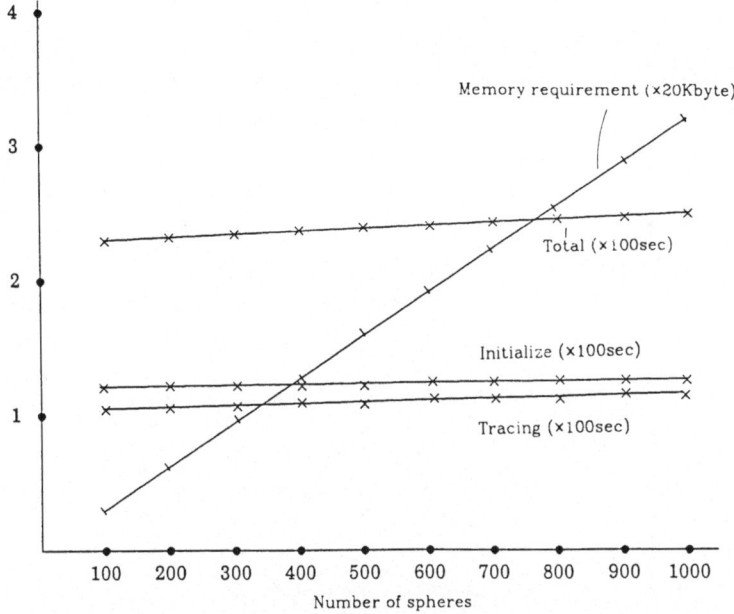

Fig. 6. Computation time and space for 100 ~ 1,000 sphere (sparse)

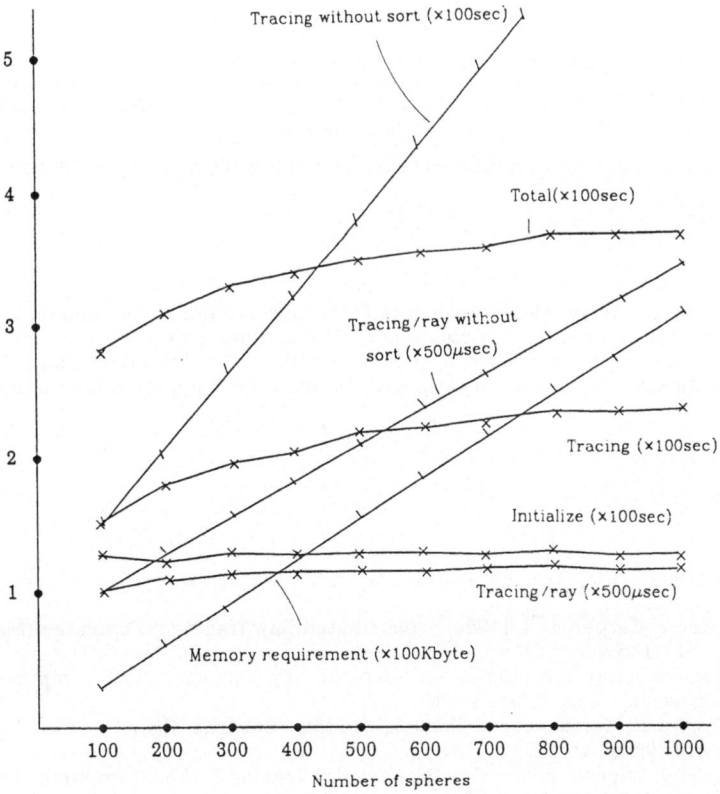

Fig. 7. Computation time and space for 100 ~ 1,000 spheres (dense)

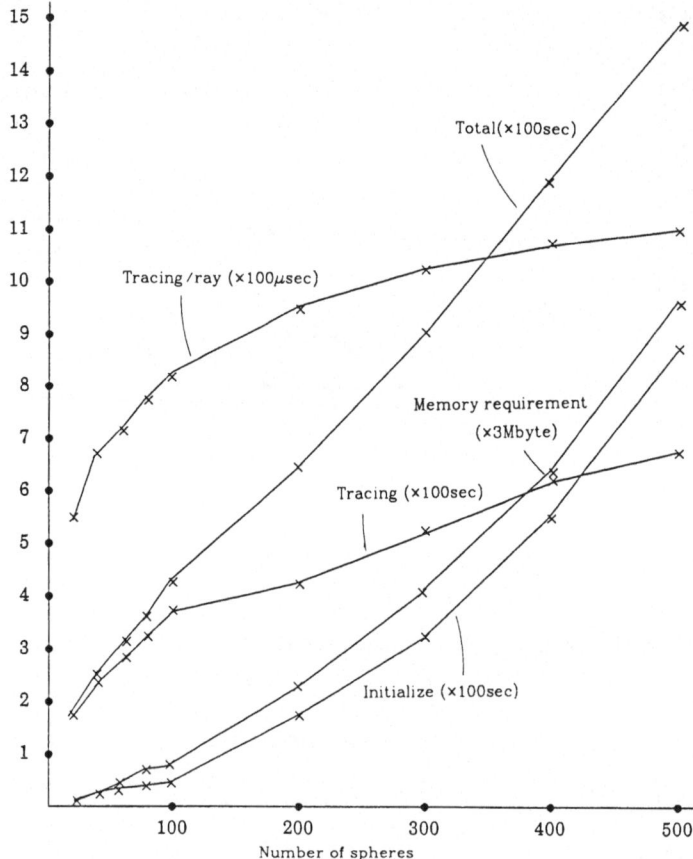

Fig. 8. Computation time and space for 100 ~ 500 spheres (reflective)

ACKNOWLEDGEMENTS

The authors appreciate precious comments from Dave Gordon. His comments were very helpful in clarifying the idea of ray coherence. The authors also thank for Tamiya Onodera for the proofreading of the manuscript and for pointing out several ambiguous descriptions and for Taiyo Kikaku corporation for willingly offering their equipment for the evaluation of the algorithm.

REFERENCES

Amanatides J (1984), "Ray Tracing with Cones," *Computer Graphics*, vol. 18, no. 3, pp. 129-135.

Cook RL , Porter T, Carpenter L (1984), "Distributed Ray Tracing," *Computer Graphics*, vol. 18, no. 3, pp. 137-145.

Fujimoto A, Tanaka T, Iwata K (1986), "Accelerated Ray Tracing," *IEEE Computer Graphics and Applications*, vol. 6, no. 4, pp. 16-26.

Fujimura K, Toriya H, Yamaguchi K, Kunii TL (1983), "Oct-tree Algorithms for Solid Modelling," *Proc. Intergraphics '83*.

Glassner AS (1984), "Space Subdivision for Fast Ray Tracing," *IEEE Computer Graphics and Applications*, vol. 4, no. 10, pp. 15-22.

Graham RL (1972), "An Efficient Algorithm for Determining the Convex Hull of a Finite Planar Set," *Information Processing Letters*, no. 1, pp. 132-133.

Haines EA, Greenberg DP (1986), "The Light Buffer: A Shadow-Testing Accelerator," *IEEE Computer Graphics and Applications*, vol. 6, no. 9, pp. 6-16.

Heckbert PS, Hanrahan P (1984), "Beam Tracing Polygonal Objects," *Computer Graphics*, vol. 18, no. 3, pp. 119-127.

Joy KI, Bhetanabhotla MN (1986), "Ray Tracing Parametric Surface Patches Utilizing Numerical Techniques and Ray Coherence," *Computer Graphics*, vol. 20, no. 8, pp. 279-285.

Matsumoto H, Murakami K (1983), "A Ray Tracing Technic Using Octree Data Structure," *Proceedings of the 27th Annual Convention IPS Japan (in Japanese)*, vol. 27, pp. 1535-1536.

Satoh A, Makino M, Oishi S, Horiuchi K (1986), "A High Speed Processing of Ray Tracing (in Japanese)," *Proc. of the Second Paper Context of NICOGRAPH*, pp. 39-47.

Speer LR, DeRose TD, Barsky BA (1985) "A Theoretical and Empirical Analysis of Coherent Ray-Tracing," in *Computer Generated Images - Proc. Graphics Interface '85*, ed. N. Magnenat-Thalmann and D. Thalmann, pp. 11-25.

Weghorst H, Hooper G, Greenberg DP (1984), "Improved Computational Methods for Ray Tracing," *ACM Transactions on Graphics*, vol. 3, no. 1, pp. 52-69.

Whitted T (1980), "An Improved Illumination Model for Shaded Display," *Communications of the ACM*, vol. 23, no. 6, pp. 343-349.

APPENDIX A. FUNCTIONS TO CALCULATE THE DIRECTION INDEX

The function *index*, written in C, computes the direction index of non-zero vector (x,y,z). The sphere is divided into $6 *N *N$ rectangles.

```
index(x,y,z)
register double x,y,z;
{       register double ax,ay,az;
        ax=(x>0)?x:-x;
        ay=(y>0)?y:-y;
        az=(z>0)?z:-z;
        if(ax>=ay&&ax>=az)
                if(x>0)
                        return index2(0,ay,az,ax);
                else
                        return index2(1,ay,az,ax);
        else if(ay>=ax&&ay>=az)
                if(y>0)
                        return index2(2,az,ax,ay);
                else
                        return index2(3,az,ax,ay);
        else
                if(z>0)
                        return index2(4,ax,ay,az);
                else
                        return index2(5,ax,ay,az);
}


index2(i,r,x,y)
register int i;
register double r,x,y;
{       register int m,n;
        m=(r+x)/(r*2)*N;
        if(m=N)
                m=N-1;
        n=(r+y)/(r*2)*N;
        if(n=N)
                n=N-1;
        return i*N*N+m*N+n;
}
```

Masataka Ohta received B. S. in computer science 1982 and then M. S. in 1984 from the University of Tokyo. At the same time, he engaged in creating computer graphics systems and computer generated images at Life Structure Institute, Seibu Digital Communications and FROGS. He is now studying on the multimedia communication as a graduate student of the University of the Tokyo.

Ohta is a member of ACM and the Information Processing Society of Japan.

Address: Department of Information Science, Faculty of Science, the University of Tokyo, 7-3-1, Hongo, Bunkyo-ku, Tokyo, 113 Japan.

Mamoru Maekawa received B. S. in applied mathematics and physics from Kyoto University in 1965. He then joined Toshiba Corporation to design operating systems. He spent 9 monthes to receive M. S. in computer science from the University of Minnesota in 1971, and then obtained Ph. D. in 1973 from the same institute. He taught at the University of Iowa, the University of Nebraska and the University of Texas. He also worked in system design for pattern information processing at Toshiba Central Research Laboratories. He is currently an associate professor in information science of the University of Tokyo. Dr. Maekawa is a member of the IEEE Computer Society, ACM and the Information Processing Society of Japan.

Address: Department of Information Science, Faculty of Science, the University of Tokyo, 7-3-1, Hongo, Bunkyo-ku, Tokyo, 113 Japan.

Sketches by Ray Tracing

Geoff Wyvill, Alistair Ward, and Tim Brown

Abstract

Ray tracing can show shadows and the effects of reflection and refraction. For this reason it is superior to other methods of rendering. It also enables us to make pictures directly from CSG models in a very general way which avoids the complication of finding intersections between primitive objects.

For many applications, we do not need the realism of the ray tracer, but we still value its generality. By using a sparse grid of rays and by following edges in the picture plane, we can extract most of the information from the model at greatly reduced cost.

Key words: CSG, Ray tracing, Geometric Modelling, Rendering

Introduction

Constructive solid geometry (CSG) is becoming increasingly popular as a technique in computer aided engineering design. In a CSG system, the designer works always in terms of solid objects and can remain unaware of their representation. Basic operations like welding and drilling are represented in a CSG system by adding or subtracting the volumes occupied by the objects. For example, the operation of drilling a hole is seen as the subtraction of a cylinder from the workpiece. For general information about CSG systems see Myers (1982) and Requicha and Voelker (1977, 1982). Recently, several systems have been described which represent the objects in a CSG system by means of a tree structure or an acyclic graph (Fujimoto 1986a, Wyvill 1986a, Woodwark 1986a). Pictures can be made from these structures directly, without converting them into a more conventional model.

Ray tracing has become the method of choice for rendering realistic synthetic images by computer. A ray tracer follows the paths of light rays backwards from the observer into the scene. Each time one of these rays intersects an object, operations are performed to determine the light observed from the intersection point. These operations can include generating secondary rays from the intersection to light sources. This is used to approximate diffuse illumination and find shadows. Other secondary rays can be used to show the effects of reflection or refraction.

Descriptions of ray tracing can be found in Whitted (1980), Weghorst (1984) and many other places. For the purpose of this paper it is sufficient to observe that:

1   Ray tracing can produce very high quality images,

2   The technique is expensive because of the very large number of rays required and

3   Ray tracers can operate directly on CSG models, avoiding, for example, the problems introduced when we represent curved surfaces by polygons or patches.

For many applications, a simple line sketch is as useful or even more useful than a photographic rendition of a design component. This paper describes how a ray tracer can be used to produce such a sketch. This, in itself, is not new. Scott Roth produced outline drawings in his now classic paper on solid modelling (Roth 1982). And, for line sketches alone, our method is the same as his. It turns out that line sketches can be made efficiently by this technique, and the designer can control closely the amount of detail revealed. We have also extended the method to make several other kinds of picture, useful in some applications.

Motivation

A capable human artist can represent a three dimensional object effectively with relatively few lines. More importantly, he can choose to emphasise certain features and leave out details which he does not want to show. Figures 1 to 4 are all representations of the same object: a crankshaft. Figure 1 is the most realistic, having been rendered with shadows and reflections. In Fig. 2, we have artificially coloured the curved and plane faces of the crankshaft to make it easier to identify each component. In Fig. 3, we have changed the lighting model so that the curved surfaces no longer show a variation of shading and Fig. 4 is a line sketch.

From the point of view of a design engineer, Fig. 1 is not the most useful. And the additional information provided by Fig. 2 or 3 may not justify the extra cost in producing them. Our main objective has been to find a cheap way to generate pictures like Fig. 4 from a CSG model.

Sometimes, we want to create a sketch which is deliberately unlike the photographic view. A good example is the cut-away sketch, Fig. 5. The effect of artificial colouring in Fig. 2 is to highlight the boundaries between different parts of one piece of metal. We may want to do the opposite and colour many components identically to draw attention to a particular detail. A secondary objective, therefore, is to be able to specify which features are important for our sketches.

It is an important feature of a line sketch that it is, in essence, artificial. Most of the lines we draw do not exist in the natural scene. What we are seeking to do, is to formalise the rules by which an artist chooses which lines to draw. Figure 6 shows two representations of a cylinder. In the first (a), there are no lines. In (b), there is no shading. The elliptical lines in (b) can be considered to be projections of the edges of the cylinder. But the vertical lines exist only by virtue of our viewpoint. When we observe this *profile* edge of a cylinder, we are really creating the edge. We choose to imagine a line lying between two areas of different colour or shade.

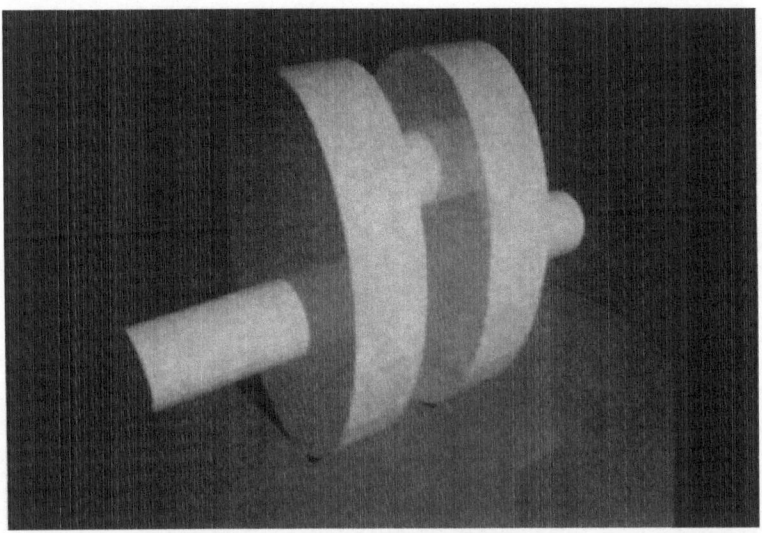

Fig.1: Ray tracing with shadows and reflections.

Fig. 2: Shading but no reflections

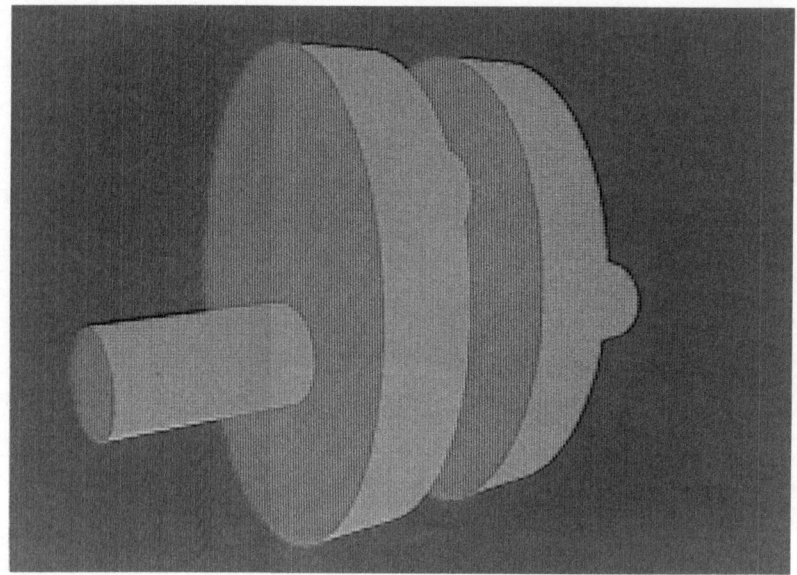

Fig. 3: Flatwash style.

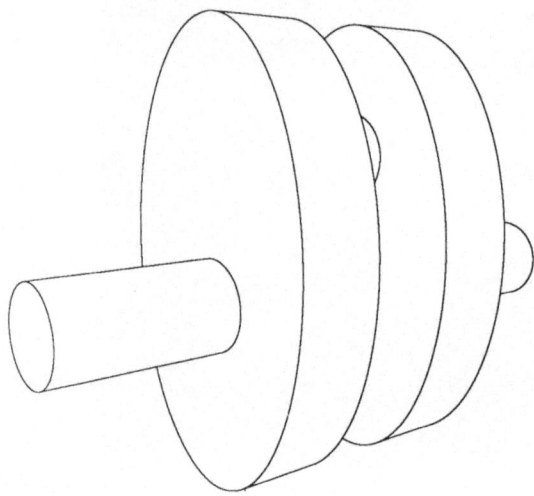

Fig. 4: Line sketch.

Our algorithm works by constructing lines along such edges. Which lines are drawn depends on where the differences of colour or shade occur. This can be specified in the CSG model.

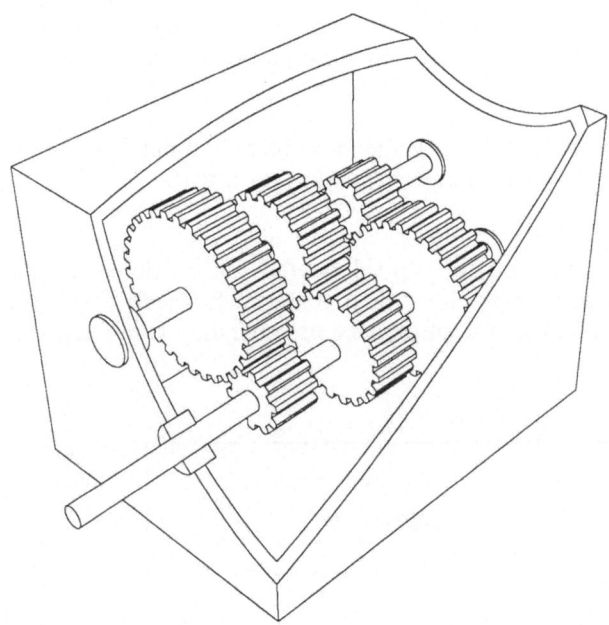

Fig. 5: Gearbox cut-away sketch.

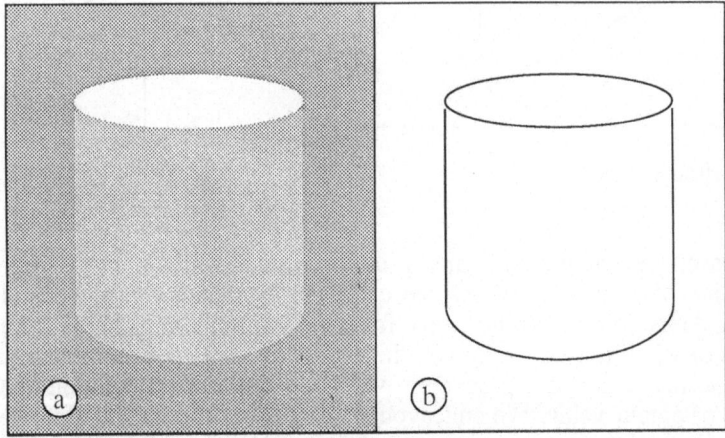

Fig. 6: Two representations of a cylinder.

Ray tracers

A ray tracer can be constructed as a procedure which finds the light level for a particular ray, projected into a scene. To create a picture, we have to decide which rays to trace. This is most simply done by defining an eyepoint and a picture frame in the three dimensional scene space. The picture frame corresponds to the display screen and for each pixel on the screen, there is a corresponding point in the frame. We trace a ray from the eyepoint in the direction of one of these corresponding points in order to find the intensity of a pixel. (See Fig. 7.)

Of course, this ray might produce other rays to gather information about lighting and reflections. The initial ray which we generate, corresponding to a particular pixel, we call the **primary** ray for that pixel.

Ordinarily, a primary ray is generated for every pixel on the screen. Some level of antialiasing can be achieved by generating more than one ray for each pixel. The algorithms described in this paper all make use of the idea of generating fewer rays than needed to cover the whole screen.

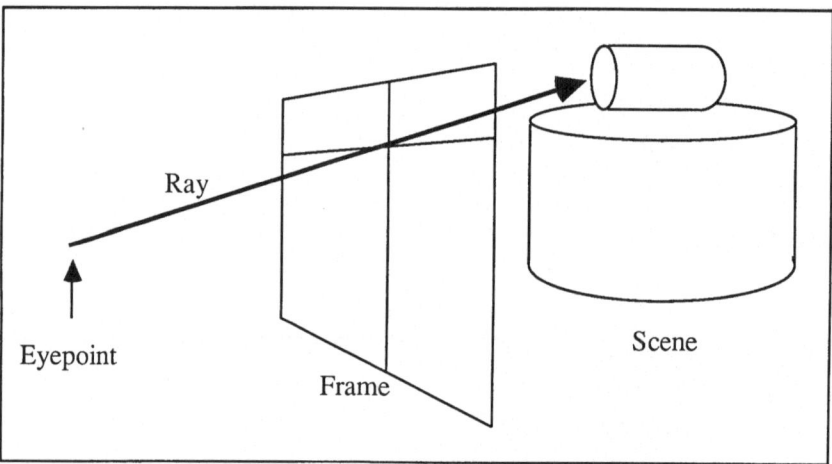

Fig. 7: Construction of primary rays.

In the most general case, we cannot omit any primary ray. But if we have some knowledge about the kind of picture to expect, we can usefully reduce the number of primary rays by making deductions about the image from the information gathered from rays cast so far. In most of what follows, we ignore the details of what goes on in the ray tracer itself. We treat the ray tracer as a procedure which accepts a pixel position and returns a light intensity or colour value. We endeavour to extract all the information we want about the pixels while calling this expensive procedure as little as possible. We have, in fact, already interfaced our algorithms to more than one ray tracing procedure.

A simple example of this strategy is the adaptive subdivision of pixels in regions of large changes in intensity or colour. This is used to get sub-pixel values for antialiasing. This technique, first described by Whitted (1980), is widely used and has set a standard for comparison with other approaches to antialiasing. Fujimoto (1986b) and Heckbert(1984), for example, both mention the method. Why can we not extend the idea to reduce the number of primary rays traced? It would be splendid, for example, to start with a very coarse grid (50 by 50 pixels) and, by recursive division, still obtain a high quality picture.

Figure 8 shows what can happen when we try to do this. The ellipse represents the object to be rendered. Suppose that all points inside the ellipse have one intensity value and points outside have a different value. Initial rays are cast at the intersections of the horizontal and vertical lines (a). Each group of four adjacent rays defines a square region. If the intensities at the four points are not equal the region is divided and more rays are cast. The shaded regions in a, b and c show which squares are divided. Figure 8d shows the result. Most of the edge of the ellipse has been rendered correctly, but because it overlapped one original square above itself without covering any corners of the square, the part of the ellipse falling in that square gets totally missed.

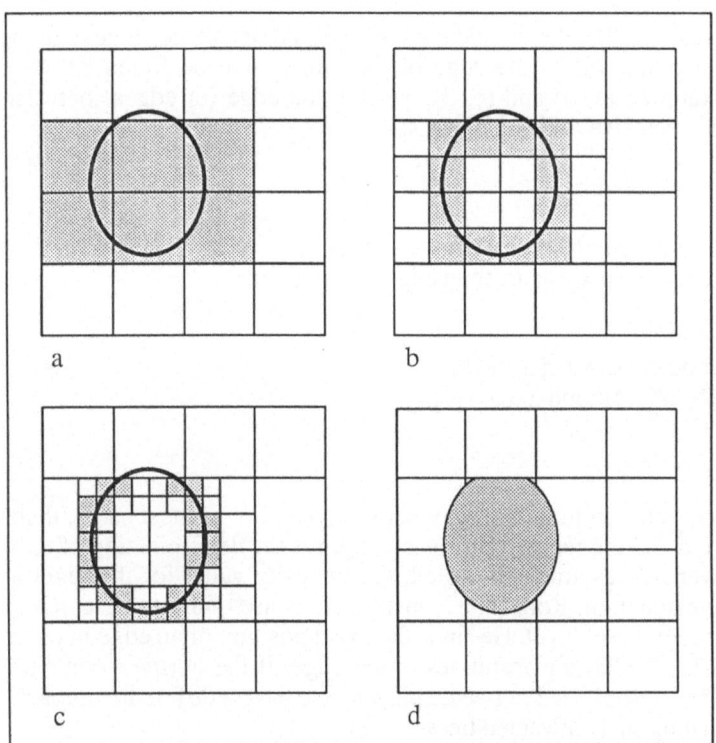

Fig. 8: Loss of detail through simple recursive division.

Heckbert and Hanrahan (1984) overcame this problem with their beam tracer for the special case of polygonal objects. Once a polygon has been found, its edges are generated by a scan line method. Our approach is different because we have no easy method of getting edges from our CSG model and, as mentioned, the profile edges exist only in the pixel buffer anyway.

The sketching algorithm

We can now describe the basic sketching algorithm. The line sketch is generated in three stages each of which calls the ray tracer as necessary.

In the first stage, rays are cast in a mesh of constant spacing across the field. This is the part where our knowledge of the scene is important. If we use too coarse a mesh, we may miss small objects. If the mesh is too fine, then the algorithm becomes slower. For views of common engineering objects, we can use a very coarse mesh, typically 20 to 50 points across a given scene.

In the second stage, we find edges. The exact criterion for recognising an edge depends on the way the ray tracer returns intensity values. For the moment, let us suppose that any two pixels with different intensities must be separated by at least one edge. In the original mesh, we examine every adjacent pair of sample points. If their intensities are different, we look for edges between them.

In Fig. 9, we see how this handles the problem of Fig. 8. Although no edge will be detected between adjacent points (a, b) the edge of the ellipse will be found between several other pairs, for example: (a, d) and (c, d). To find the edge (or edges) between two points, we use a simple, recursive division process:

```
procedure find_edges(a, b: point);
    begin
        if intensity(a) = intensity(b) then exit; {No edge}
        if a and b are only one pixel apart then edge_found(a, b);
        else
            begin
                find a point c between a and b;
                find_edges(a, c); find_edges(c, b)
            end
    end;
```

In practice, point c is always chosen to lie halfway between a and b. In most cases, there will be only one edge to find and the recursive division requires the determination of only a few intensities. Whenever the ray tracer is called, the intensity value for the pixel is retained to avoid a double evaluation. Roth (1982) mentions the use of a binary search to find edges, but this is at the sub-pixel level. He finds the exact position of an edge in order to compare surface normals of adjacent primitives at the edge. If the normals coincide, then the edge may be a false one and need not be displayed. We have a different approach, described below, for eliminating such unwanted lines.

In the third stage, we use an edge following algorithm to identify all the pixels adjacent to edges. This is illustrated in Fig. 10. The circles represent possible ray sampling points at the single pixel level. The shaded area indicates the presence of an edge in the scene. The letters are used to identify the squares formed by each four points. The algorithm proceeds by finding all the squares through which the edge passes. A record of which squares are to be processed is stored in a stack and a bit table is used to mark squares which have been put in the stack. In the example of the figure, an edge has been detected between points 10 and 11, and the square labelled e has been marked in the table and added to the stack. This is the function of the procedure *edge_found* in the algorithm above.

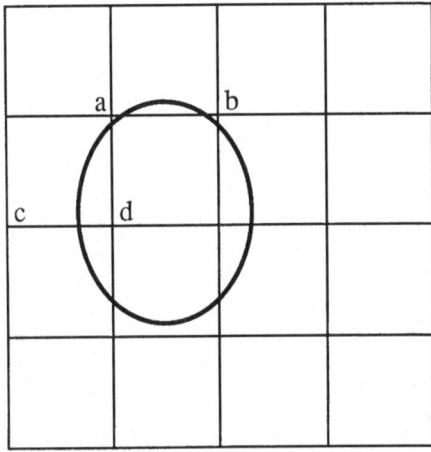

Figure 9: Edge finding.

To process square e, we start by finding the intensities of the points 6 and 7. Intensity at 10 and 11 has already been found, so this gives us values for the four vertices of square e. In this square, points 6 and 7 have different intensities indicating that an edge passes between them. Therefore, we must also examine square b, which is added to the stack. Similarly, points 10 and 11 have different intensities so we must process square h. We do not need to process square d, because the points 6 and 10 have the same intensity, and by examining 7 and 11 we see that we do not need to process square f. Squares b and h get processed in the same way and the squares b, c, e, h constitute the edge. Notice that we do not use the intensity values for points 1, 5, 9, 13, 12, 16, and these are never calculated.

We can express this algorithm for each square as follows:

```
while stack is not empty do
    begin
        get square from stack;
        for each side of square do
            if edge intersects side then
                begin
                    if neighbour is not marked then
                        begin
                            mark neighbour in the bit table;
                            add neighbour to stack
                        end
                end
    end;
```

A three dimensional version of this algorithm, for generating surfaces rather than edges, has been described (Wyvill 1986b) and a similar data structure is employed here.

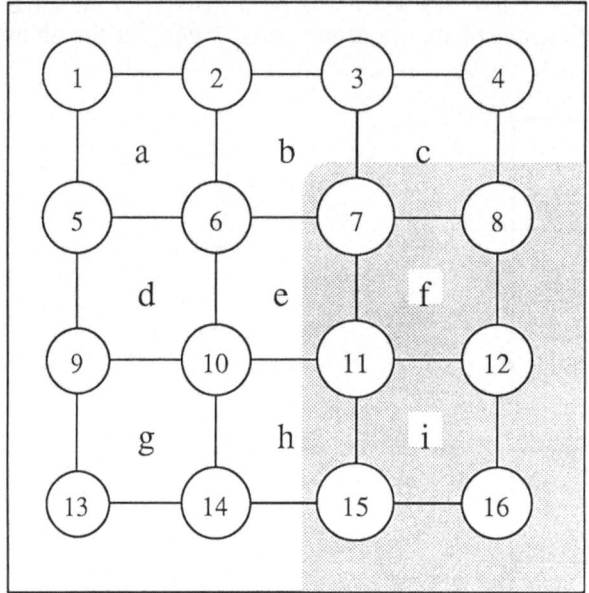

Fig. 10: Edge following.

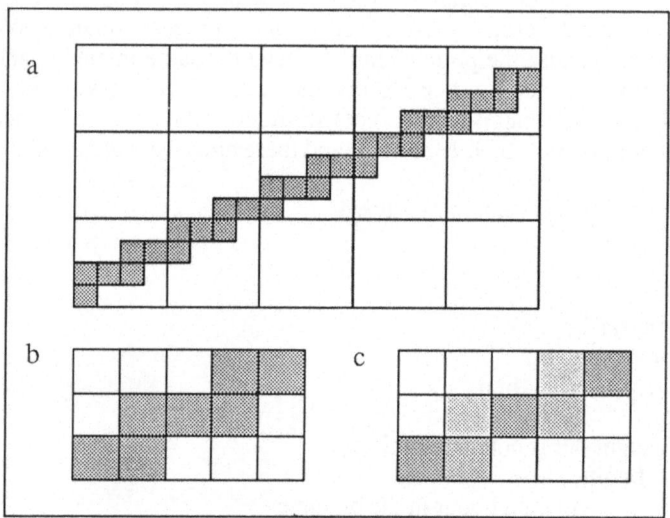

Fig. 11: Failure of antialiasing by supersampling.
  a) The sub-pixels
  b) The line at lower resolution
  c) The line antialiased

The edge following algorithm is suitable for a wide range of ordinary engineering scenes. It will fail if any object or feature is too small to be detected by the original coarse grid. For this reason, the method is probably not suitable for some scenes where texture mapping is employed. If there is a lot of detail, the initial grid can be made finer, but the time saving in this case is less.

Line sketches

Drawings like Fig. 4 are produced simply by plotting one dark pixel for every square considered to contain an edge. Figures 4 and 5 were produced on a laser printer and use a resolution of 1600 by 1600 pixels.

It is not reasonable to perform antialiasing on our line drawings because the pixels we have coloured represent the only definition we have of the lines. Even if we use supersampling as shown in Fig. 11, the result is mainly to reduce the intensity of the lines rather than to remove jagged edges. The reason for this is that the lines we have created, like the lines in nature, have no thickness. They have, therefore, no area to average.

Flatwash algorithm

Figure 3 shows a style of rendering which we call *flatwash*. It is reminiscent of the effect of colouring in a line sketch with just a few colours. The colours are useful for separating logically different parts of a scene, but the lack of shading makes this style less appealing than a shaded picture like Fig. 2.

We can make flatwash pictures from our line sketches very cheaply. After applying the edge follower algorithm, the pixel buffer contains cells which have been assigned colours (or shades) and a majority of cells which are unassigned. Every region of unassigned cells is surrounded by a border of cells, all the same colour. We can fill these regions with the following, very simple scanning algorithm:

```
for row := top to bottom do
    begin
        if pixel[row, left] = unassigned
        then pixel[row, left] := row_start
        else row_start := pixel[row, left];
        current := row_start;
        for column := left to right do
            if pixel[row, column] = unassigned
            then pixel[row, column] := current
            else current := pixel[row, column]
    end;
```

where top, bottom, right and left are the limits of the buffer. The algorithm works provided that the element pixel[top, left] is defined. But this one is always included in our original grid of sample points. Notice that this algorithm is faster than flood filling the regions. Only one comparison is made for each pixel plus one for each row.

Unlike the line sketches, flatwash pictures can be antialiased efficiently by supersampling. In this case, any one pixel is covered by some number of sub-pixels of different colours and a simple average is taken. Figures 12 and 13 show a pinwheel, coarsely rendered at a resolution of 250 by 250 pixels. Figure 13 is antialiased.

Lighting models

So far, we have referred to 'different intensities' or 'different colours' without defining these terms precisely. For the purpose of generating line sketches, the simplest choice is to regard each primitive object in the scene as having a different colour. That is, we use the identity of the primitive object instead of using a lighting model.

Alternatively, we can assign arbitrary numbers to represent the intensities of objects or collections of objects. If two surfaces have the same assigned colour, then no edge will appear between them. This is equivalent to using a lighting model with only ambient lighting and no reflections. Thus the observed colour of every surface depends only on its assigned colour. In this case, we create boundaries between components which have different colours, or we can suppress detail by a choice of colouring **within the solid model**.

Figure 14 provides an example of this. We have 'coloured' the teeth of the gearwheels of Fig. 5 so that they merge with the wheels. This is particularly useful in complicated scenes where unnecessary detail of an unimportant or small component can create a mass of lines which is at best expensive and at worst, actually confusing. The designer can choose the colouring of components comparatively easily and the suppression of detail happens automatically. It is not necessary for him to know which parts of a component will be visible in the final picture or even whether the component will be visible at all.

If we use a more conventional lighting model, the ray tracer will produce different intensities or colours according to the angles between surface normals and incident light. In this case the meaning of 'different colour', for the purpose of finding edges, must defined differently. We regard two pixels as different if their intensities differ by more than some threshold value. If the threshold is small enough, then our edge detector and line follower algorithms will produce a picture in which we have drawn all the boundaries of areas with detectably different colouring. If we apply the flatwash algorithm to such a picture, we obtain a shaded picture. Indeed, if our original grid is small enough that we have missed no details, the picture will be identical to that produced by 'full' ray tracing. Figure 15 shows the crankshaft portrayed by this method.

If we use a greater threshold value, we find edges only where there are sharp changes in intensity. The result of this is that we get a picture in which boundaries appear between areas of substantially different shade or colour. Within each area, we have also the colours of the original sampling points of our grid. Using all this information, we can use a simple interpolation algorithm to give us an approximation to the appearance of 'full' ray tracing, at little more than the cost of producing the line sketches. Such an interpolated picture is shown in Fig. 16. In Figs. 15 and 16, there are only sixteen levels of red, green and blue used, so the boundaries between areas whose colours differ by a minimum, are visible. Notice that these boundaries are not the same in the two figures. Figure 17 shows the edges detected in the production of Fig. 16. The other boundaries were generated by interpolation.

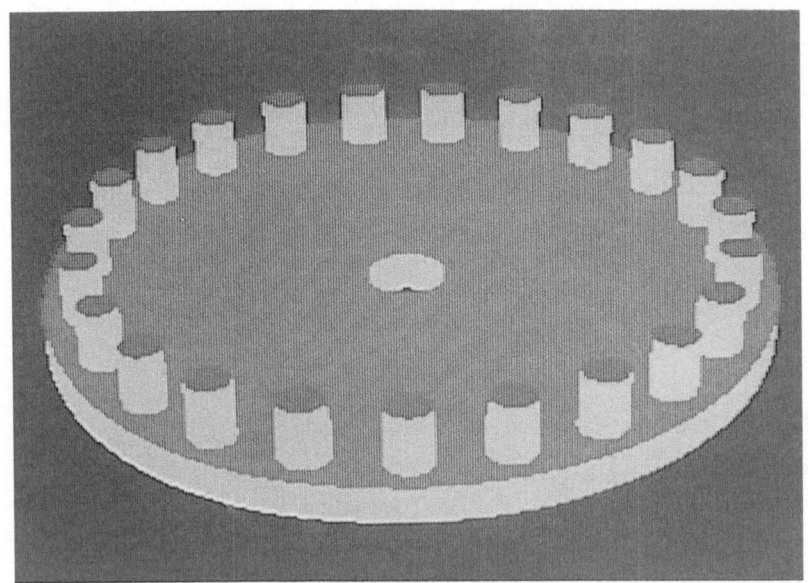

Fig. 12: Flatwash style, not antialiased.

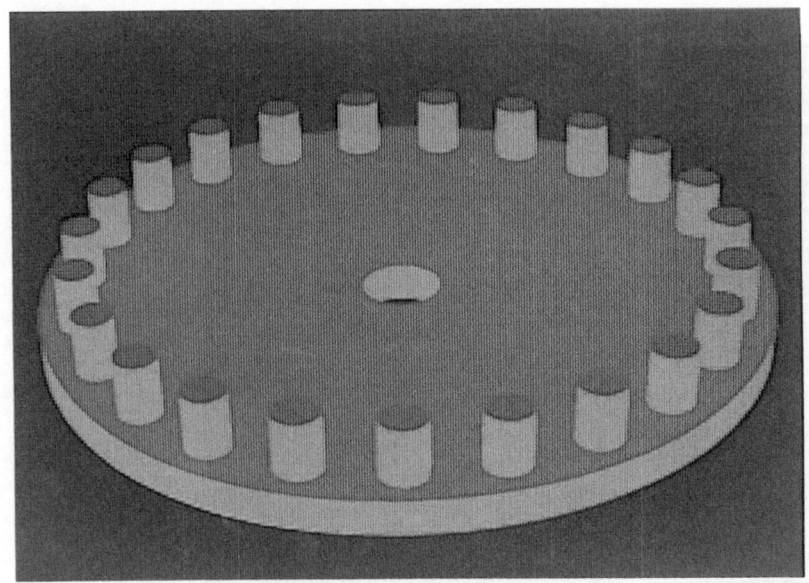

Fig. 13: Flatwash style, antialiased.

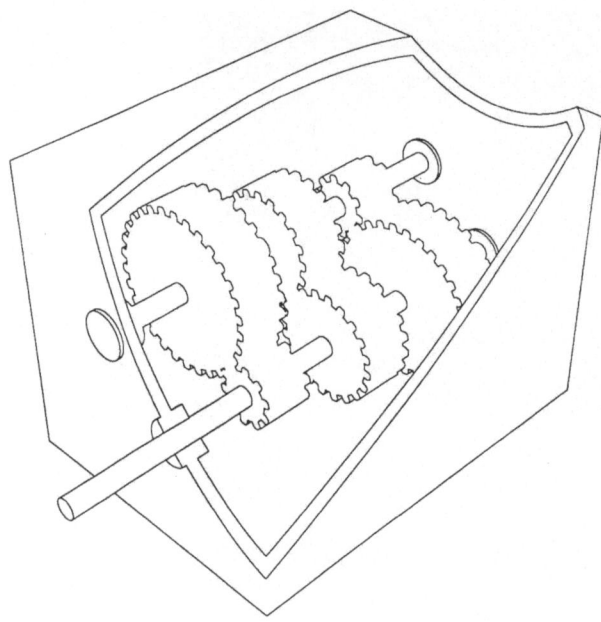

Fig. 14: Gearbox with detail suppressed.

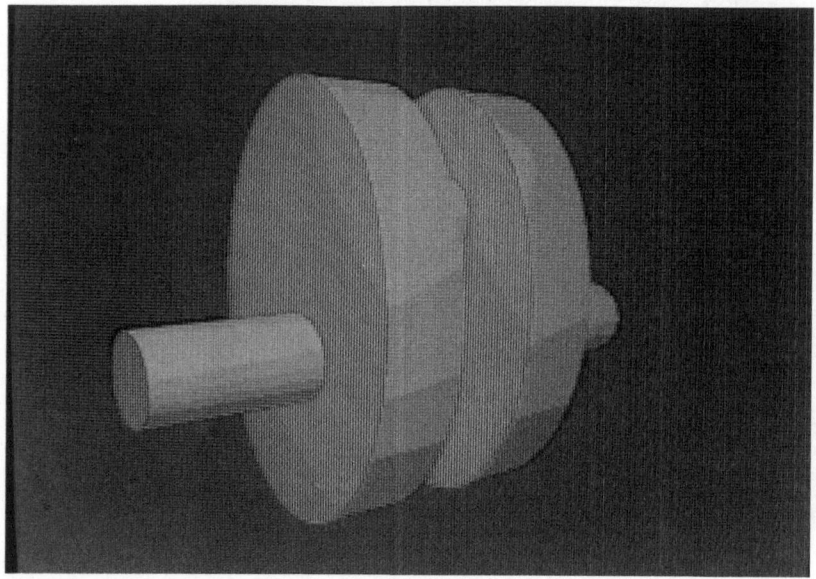

Fig. 15: Flatwash colouring, minimum threshold.

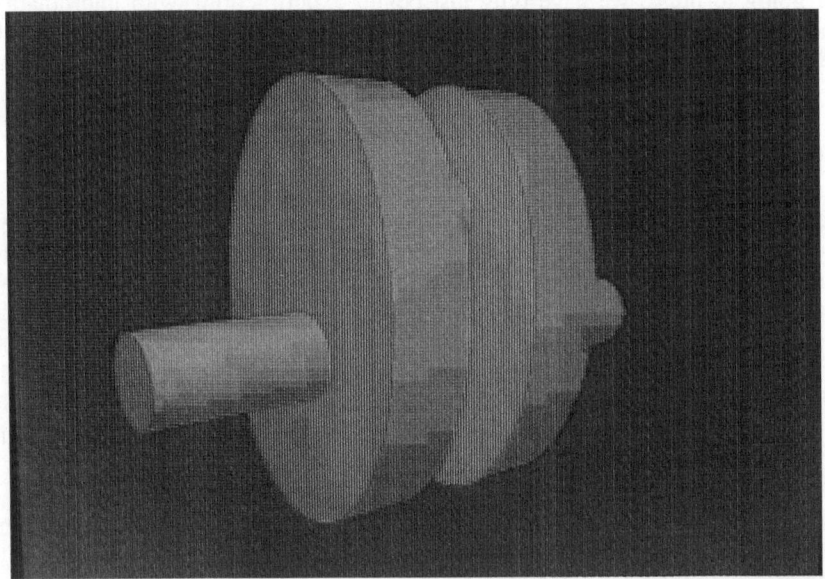

Fig. 16: Interpolated colours.

Fig. 17: Line sketch showing edges detected for Fig. 16.

At the time of going to press, we have only just begun experimenting with interpolation algorithms and we have no useful timing information yet. We hope to report on this aspect in a later article.

Efficiency of the algorithms

The current version of the ray tracer is not very fast. This is because it has been adapted from an experimental system (Wyvill 1986a) which was designed more with regard to generality than speed. Absolute timings are therefore less important than to observe the number of primary rays traced at each stage of the algorithm. In particular, Fig. 5, which was rendered at 1600 by 1600 pixels, needed only 93,717 rays compared with 2,560,000 for the whole grid. The time to render this in flatwash at 1600 x 1600, was 1390 seconds compared with 14,447 seconds to trace all the rays. Thus the ray tracer is performing 67 rays per second while sketching but 177 rays per second on average. Although our algorithms use fewer rays, these rays are the most expensive ones.

Table 1 shows execution times and number of rays traced at each stage of the algorithm. All of the software was written in C and the timings were measured on a Sun 3/50 workstation equipped with the 68881 floating point processor and running Unix BSD 4.2.

Table 1

Fig.	Resolution	Time secs	Stage 1	Stage 2	Stage 3	Total rays
3	250*	101	2601	1111	9459	13171
4	1600	164	2601	1312	16251	20164
5	1600	1357	2601	5681	85435	93717
12	250	97	2601	1267	4019	7887
13	250*	306	2601	2398	20745	25744
14	1600	976	2601	3435	48769	54805

*These are antialiased: equivalent to supersampling 4 x 4 in each pixel.

An interesting point to note about these timing results is that the saving achieved by using the line follower increases as the resolution increases. This is to be expected. If we improve the resolution by a factor, n, then we have n^2 times as many pixels. But the number of rays traced is roughly proportional to the total length of edges in the scene, so the ray-tracing time goes up roughly proportionally to n.

There are several ways in which we can speed up the ray tracer. We would like to be able to produce sketches directly from our CSG system, fast enough to allow interactive development of CSG models, without resorting to polygonal approximation. Our edge following algorithm is also suitable for adaptation to parallel processing. We believe that using these techniques, real-time animation of solid models is not far away.

Comparison with other work

Laidlaw (1986) has described a fast, robust method for rendering from a CSG model using a polygonal decomposition. The simple examples he shows are rendered much faster than ours. However, it is reasonable to expect that ray tracing may prove faster for scenes with a very large number of objects, especially if these objects are curved and would therefore require even larger numbers of polygons.

Woodwark (1986b) describes an elegant method of generating wireframe models from CSG trees. His trees, however, describe only faceted components whereas we are able to generate true profile edges for any curved surface for which we can write a ray intersection algorithm. Woodwark's wire frames are generated faster than our sketches, but our flatwash pictures appear to be faster than his shaded ones.

There have been several recent publications concerning the problem of finding curves of intersection of parametric surfaces. See Koparkar (1986) for example. It is worth noting that in a limited context, we have circumvented this problem. At present our CSG system has primitives for spheres, cylinders and planes only, although we can distort these in various ways. (Our gear teeth have elliptical profiles.) Our sketching algorithm will automatically generate visible edges of intersection for any pair of primitives for which ray intersection algorithms can be written.

Conclusion

We have produced a fast algorithm for producing line sketches directly from a ray tracer and tested it using a CSG modelling system. By choosing the colour of components we can reveal or conceal boundaries according to which features a particular sketch is intended to reveal. With a little extra post-processing, we can generate flatwash colour pictures and, in this case, we can include antialiasing of the edges. Because our method actually reduces the number of rays traced, the gains in speed are independent of the ray-tracing algorithm. Experiments show that the sketches require only a few thousand rays in cases where full ray tracing would need over a million to achieve similar resolution. However, precisely because the rays we select are the ones which yield the most information, they are also the most expensive rays. The gain in time is therefore less, typically a factor of ten to thirty.

If we apply our algorithm to a ray tracer which uses a more complete lighting algorithm, we obtain a picture in which the lines separate areas of different colour. That is, we generate contour lines across all surfaces where the perceived colour changes. Applying the flatwash algorithm to such a picture will produce a fully coloured, shaded picture as for normal ray tracing. We are currently investigating other ways to exploit the line following algorithm to produce high quality images at reduced cost.

Acknowledgments

This project was funded jointly by the University of Otago and the University Grants Committee of New Zealand. The CSG system and ray tracer were developed in Tokyo and this research was supported in part by RICOH Company Limited. Special thanks are due to the staff and students of the Kunii Laboratory of Computer Science for their help with the development of the CSG system, and to Mr Graham Furniss who helped to design some of the models for the figures.

References

Akira Fujimoto, Christopher G. Perrott and Kansei Iwata (1986a), "Environment for Fast Elaboration of Constructive Solid Geometry," *Advanced Computer Graphics,* (Proc. CG Tokyo '86), pp. 20-33

Akira Fujimoto, Takayuki Tanaka and Kansei Iwata (1986b), "ARTS: Accelerated Ray-Tracing System," *IEEE CG&A,* Vol. 6, No. 4, pp. 16-26

Paul S. Heckbert and Pat Hanrahan (1984), "Beam Tracing Polygonal Objects," *Computer Graphics,* (Proc. SIGGRAPH '84), Vol.18, No. 3, pp. 119-127

P.A. Koparkar and S.P. Mudur (1986), "Generation of continuous smooth curves resulting from operations on parametric surface patches," *Computer Aided Design,* Vol. 18, No. 4 pp 193-206

David H. Laidlaw, W. Benjamin Trumbore and John F. Hughes (1986), "Constructive Solid Geometry for Polyhedral Objects." *Computer Graphics,* (Proc. SIGGRAPH '86), Vol.20, No. 4, pp. 161-170

W. Myers (1982), "An industrial perspective on solid modeling," *IEEE CG&A,* Vol. 2, No. 2, pp. 86-97

A.A.G. Requicha and H.B. Voelker (1977), "Geometric Modelling of Mechanical Parts and Processes," *Computer,* Vol. 10, No. 12, pp. 48-57

A.A.G. Requicha and H.B. Voelker (1982), "Solid Modeling: A Historical Summary and Contemporary Assessment," *IEEE CG&A,* Vol. 2, No. 2, pp. 9-24

Scott D. Roth (1982) "Ray Casting for Modeling Solids," Computer Graphics and Image Processing, Vol. 18, pp 109-144

Hank Weghorst, Gary Hooper and Donald P. Greenberg, (1984) "Improved Computational Methods for Ray Tracing," *ACM Trans. Graphics,* Vol. 3, No. 1, pp. 51-69

Turner Whitted (1980), "An Improved Illumination Model for Shaded Display," *Comm. ACM,* Vol. 23 No. 6, pp. 343-349

John Woodwark and Adrian Bowyer (1986a), "Better and faster pictures from solid models," Computer-Aided Engineering Journal, February, pp 17-24

John Woodwark (1986b), "Generating wireframes from set-theoretic solid models by spatial division," *Computer Aided Design,* Vol. 18 No. 6, pp 307-315

Geoff Wyvill, Tosiyasu L. Kunii and Yasuto Shirai (1986a), "Space Division for Ray Tracing in CSG," *IEEE CG&A,* Vol. 6, No. 4, pp. 28-34

Geoff Wyvill, Craig McPheeters and Brian Wyvill (1986b), "Data structure for soft objects," *The Visual Computer,* Vol. 2, pp. 227-234

Geoff Wyvill graduated in physics from Jesus College, Oxford, and started working with computers as a research technologist with the British Petroleum Company. He gained MSc and PhD degrees in computer science from the University of Bradford where he lectured in computer science from 1969 until 1978. He is currently senior lecturer in computer science at the University of Otago. He is on the editorial board of The Visual Computer.

Tim Brown is a postgraduate student in computer science at the University of Otago where he completed a BSc in computer science in 1983. He worked for Textus NZ Limited from 1984 until 1986 designing automatic translation programs for European languages. He is currently working on the development of the Katachi solid modelling system.

Alistair Ward is a postgraduate student in computer science at the University of Otago where he completed a BCom in information systems in 1986. His research interests include computer graphics and its applications.

The authors can be contacted at: Department of Computer Science, University of Otago, Box 56, Dunedin, New Zealand

Bi-Directional Ray Tracing

Sudeb Chattopadhyay and Akira Fujimoto

ABSTRACT

Ray tracing is one of the most powerful techniques used in computer graphics. Although ray tracing techniques can take into account the effects of reflection from neighbouring surfaces, it has hitherto been impossible to completely account for the ambient or global illumination arising out of complex interreflections in an environment because of limitations of the number of rays that could be fired to render the scene in a span of time reasonable from the point of view of practical use. In this paper, a fast method based on positive and conventional (reverse) ray tracing techniques to take into account the complex interreflections in a scene is proposed. While the directionality of the illumination intensity from the secondary sources are not taken into account the description is viewer independent. Unlike the radiosity approach the present method can treat open systems since no limitations due to conservation of energy is imposed. The method is efficient and computationally inexpensive.

Keywords: Global illumination, Bi-directional ray tracing ,Conventional (Reverse) Ray Tracing, Positive Ray Tracing, Interreflection , Diffuse reflection

1. INTRODUCTION

With the recent developments of various accelerating techniques of ray tracing (Glassner 1984; Wyvill 1985; Fujimoto 1986; Joy 1986; Murakami 1986), attempts have been made to render hitherto difficult scenes even on personal computers. But it has been difficult to correctly simulate the global illumination effects in such a scene. Some aspects of the global illumination have been taken care of by considering the specular term (Whitted 1980). But this has been limited to only the mirror reflection or transmission direction at the point of intersection of the ray and the specific surface. Distributed ray tracing (Cook 1984) or ray tracing with cones (Amanatides 1984) are extensions to this approach and gather light from more than one point per ray, but still cannot model the real effects of global illumination properly. A radically new approach borrowed from thermal engineering called the "radiosity method" (Cohen 1985; Nishida 1985; Immel 1986) has been proposed to alleviate such problems. The results are promising but the model does not lend itself to commercial applications because of prohibitive computation time (of the order of weeks (Immel 1986)). Another new approach called the "integral equation technique" has been proposed (Kajiya 1986). While a significant improvement over conventional ray tracing rendering has been achieved, the computation time is still very long (of the order of days).

In view of the above, a fast and accurate method to simulate the effects of global illumination is proposed. The method named as bi-directional ray tracing combines two ray tracing techniques - the conventional (reverse) ray tracing and positive ray tracing. Positive ray tracing, unlike the conventional ray tracing, is employed in the preprocessing stage, where the rays are fired directly from the light sources to ascertain the prospective secondary light sources in a given scene. This makes the treatment of the secondary sources independent of the viewer. The conventional ray tracing is employed to render the scene once the position of the observer is known. We need only to repeat the rendering calculations if the position of the observer is changed. Thus to implement effects of global illumination in this method only some extra preprocessing time is required without changing the rendering time by any appreciable extent.

It is well known that in a ray tracing scheme the first generation rays along with the light source rays contribute maximum to the pixel intensity in terms of variance. In this context, it has been rightly pointed out (Kajiya 1986), that conventional ray tracing expends the vast bulk of the work on precisely those rays which contribute least to the variance of the image and in the process shoots too many rays of higher generations. In the positive ray tracing scheme a significant part of the light source rays is taken care of leaving only the first generation rays and a small portion of the light source rays to be taken into account in rendering by conventional (reverse) ray tracing. Thus our method of integrating conventional (reverse) ray tracing with positive ray tracing contributes essentially to efficiency and accuracy. Table 1 outlines the merits and demerits of the present method in comparison to radiosity (Immel 1986) and integral equation (Kajiya 1986) techniques.

To take into account the effects of global illumination we must treat all the surfaces that are illuminated by the primary light sources, as secondary light sources. This means, that first the surfaces receiving light from the primary sources must be identified. We must then specify an illumination model by which these surfaces can be treated as secondary light sources. The surfaces found to have an intensity level below a predetermined limit, are discarded. It remains then to ascertain the effect of these selected secondary surfaces on the others. Here also, the effects are ignored depending on the relative distance between two secondary sources even though they are in sight of each other. We can further save computation time at the expense of accuracy if we consider that the spectral intensity of the secondary sources are uniform in all directions. This means that for computing the intensity of the secondary sources in positive ray tracing, only the diffuse reflected intensity from the surfaces of the objects in the scene will have to be accounted for. We shall limit the discussions in this paper to this assumption. The treatment of directionality (surface lights, 3D lights or lights with specific intensity distribution) is a straightforward extension of the present method and will be the subject of a forthcoming paper. For the present study the specular reflected intensity will be taken care of only in the conventional (reverse) ray tracing where the level of reflections can be appropriately selected. The final intensity values of the secondary sources in such a scheme are obtained through iteration, starting with zero intensity for the secondary sources and gradually updating the intensity values till the difference between two successive steps falls within a tolerance limit. It is also assumed that the secondary sources do not alter the intensity of the primary sources but influence the intensity of other secondary sources only.

Table 1.   Comparison of Present Method with Radiosity and
           Integral Equation Methods

Present Method	Radiosity Method	Integral Equation Method
All surfaces with a diffuse reflection coefficient above a specified level and which are within an appropriate distance from the primary sources are treated as secondary sources	All surfaces are treated as secondary sources	Indirectly considered through path tracing (statistical)
Both open and closed systems can be treated	Only closed systems can be treated	Both open and closed systems can be treated
Directionality of secondary sources are not considered**	Directionality of the secondary sources are considered	Indirectly considered in path tracing
No special treatment for hidden surfaces are required	Needs the use of depth buffer for hidden surfaces	No special treatment for hidden surfaces are required
Treatment of secondary sources is viewer independent	Treatment of secondary sources is viewer independent	Treatment of secondary sources is not viewer independent
The method is not computation intensive (computation time of the order of minutes)	The method is very much computation intensive (computation time of the order of weeks)	The method is computation intensive (computation time of the order of days)

** this is under investigation

2.   THEORETICAL CONCEPTS

We start with the illumination model given by the following equation
after Hall (1983) without the wavelength dependent terms but with a
more general diffuse reflection term,

Intensity = Diffuse reflection term + Ambient term +
            Specular reflection term + Transmitted refraction term +
            Specular attenuation trem + Transmitted attenuation term

or, writing in mathematical notations,

$$I_m = k_d.I_{am} + k_a.I_a$$
$$+ k_s[\sum_j I_{lj} (\bar{n}.\bar{H})^n] + k_t[\sum_j I_{lj} (\bar{n}.\bar{H'})^{n'}]$$
$$+ k_s.I_s.F_e^{\Delta tr} + k_t.I_t.F_t^{\Delta tt} \qquad ----------- (1)$$

where,
        F_e - transmittance per unit length of environment
        F_t - transmittance per unit length of material
        $\bar{H}$ - unit bisector between $\bar{L}_j$ and $\bar{s}$

$\bar{H}'$ - unit normal vector for Torrance-Sparrow surface
        microfacet
$\bar{H}mp$ - unit bisector between $\bar{L}smp$ and $\bar{s}$
Im - illumination intensity
Ia - ambient intensity at the m-th secondary source
Iam - intensity (due to interreflection) of the m-th
        secondary light source
Ilj - intensity of the j-th primary light source
Is - intensity of reflected ray
It - intensity of transmitted ray
j - primary light source index
ka - material ambient reflection coefficient
kd - material diffuse reflection coefficient
ks - material specular reflection coefficient
kt - material transmission coefficient
$\bar{L}j$ - unit primary light source vector
$\bar{L}smp$ - unit secondary light source vector from p-th secondary
        source to the m-th secondary source
m - secondary light source index
$\bar{n}$ - unit normal vector at the point in question
n - exponent representing specular reflection scattering
n' - exponent representing specular transmission scattering
s - unit ray vector directed to the origin of the ray
 tr - distance travelled by the ray in the environment
 tt - distance travelled by the ray in the material

The first two terms are independent of the viewer and therefore can be
adequately treated in preprocessing. The rest of the terms are viewer
dependent. The first term in the above equation is the focal point of
this study. It must be noted that the intensity of a secondary light
source is the sum of the diffuse reflected intensity due to the
incident intensity from the primary sources as well as the rest of the
secondary sources. So, for the intensity of the m-th secondary light
source one can write,

$$Iam = \sum_{j} Ilj(\bar{n}.\bar{L}j) + \sum_{p \neq m} Iap\,(\bar{n}.\bar{H}mp) \qquad\qquad ----------(2)$$

p being the index of secondary sources . Here the first term denotes
the contribution from the primary sources and the second term denotes
the contribution from other secondary sources.

Treating interreflection in this manner means that a significant part
of the ambient reflection term (Ia) is taken into account in the
diffuse reflection term. Therefore, we can tune down the ambient
reflection term by an appropriate amount.

It must be noted here that the intensities of the seconadry sources
need to be determined in an iterative manner and hence we must
preprocess as much of information as possible regarding Iam in
equation (1) or (2).

3. PROCEDURE OF INTENSITY CALCULATION

First of all, the surfaces capable of significant diffuse reflection
are identified by checking the coefficient of diffuse reflection. The
surfaces possessing a diffuse reflection coefficient less than a
specified value are discarded.

The scene to be rendered is then divided into a number of cubical volumes or voxels. Next, rays are fired from the primary light source to the surfaces identified to be potential secondary sources beginning from the nearest one. A three dimensional line generator routine (Fujimoto 1986; Joy 1986; Murakami 1986) is used to check the prospective secondary light source surfaces that are hidden from the primary light source by an object in front of them. These hidden surfaces are deactivated to prevent any firing of rays to these surfaces. If there is only one light source these can be discarded outright. The reason they are only deactivated is that a second primary source may be capable of activating these surfaces hidden from the first primary source.

As soon as the intensity contribution to a certain surface from the primary light sources is established, this value is transferred to the vertices of the voxel which contains the surface by means of a weighting function. This means that the vertices of the voxel which contains an activated surface are automatically activated. In the next stage of calculation for mutual effects of the secondary sources, all these activated surfaces are therefore replaced by the activated vertices of the voxels. All references to secondary sources in the following stages would mean the activated vertices and not the surfaces. Two advantages are derived out of this. First, one can suitably reduce the number of secondary light sources in a case where there are more surfaces than the vertices. Secondly, one has the data at the voxel vertices and these can be directly used in rendering the scene without further manipulation.

After the effects of all the primary light sources are computed, the next stage is started in which the mutual effects of the secondary light sources are computed. An array SEE[N][N], each element of which occupies only one byte is constructed such that,

$$\text{SEE[i][j]} = \begin{cases} 1 & (\text{ point i sees point j }) \\ 0 & (\text{ otherwise }) \end{cases} \quad \text{------------ (3)}$$

where N denotes the total number of activated secondary sources (voxel vertices). The same three dimensional line generator routine is used to do this. A diagonally symmetric matrix with the diagonal elements zero is thus obtained. It must be mentioned here that the above matrix will be an enormous one requiring about 700 KB for a 32x32x32 voxel scheme. However, one can skip this step and generate the required information as and when required. This would mean that the same calculations have to be repeated for each iteration. Nevertheless, this will not seriously affect the computation time as one or two iterations may be sufficient for generating the desired effects.

The iterative calculations to determine the intensities of the secondary light sources are next started. The contribution from other sources to a particular source is first established. This is considered to be an increment of intensity over the contribution from the primary sources which are set to be constant for all iterations. After each iteration this increment is updated till the difference in increment from two successive iterations falls within a certain prescribed limit. As mentioned in the previous paragraph the iteration can be stopped before convergence has been achieved to cut back on computation time.

4. RESULTS

Figure 1 shows the effects of varying different parmeters in the
present method.   Frame 1 was obtained by conventional ray tracing.

Frame numbering

```
+---------------------------+
|  1 |  2 |  3 |  4 |
+---------------------------+
|  5 |  6 |  7 |  8 |
+---------------------------+
|  9 | 10 | 11 | 12 |
+---------------------------+
```

Symbol description

X (kd , ks , ka , I) , N
X - object name
kd - diffuse coefficient
ks - specular coefficient
ka - ambient coefficient
I - illumination model
[P - present model
  C - conventional model]
N - number of voxel in each
      direction (x,y,z)

Fig. 1   Effects of different parameters in the present method
[frame 1- (plane(0.5,0.5,0.0,C) , ball(0.6,0.9,0.0,C) , 9) ;
  frame 2- (plane(0.5,0.5,0.0,P) , ball(0.6,0.9,0.0,P) , 9) ;
  frame 3- (plane(0.2,0.5,0.0,P) , ball(0.6,0.9,0.0,P) , 9) ;
  frame 4- (plane(0.3,0.2,0.0,P) , ball(0.6,0.9,0.0,P) , 9) ;
  frame 5- (plane(0.5,0.5,0.3,P) , ball(0.9,0.6,0.3,C) , 9) ;
  frame 6- (plane(0.5,0.5,0.0,P) , ball(0.6,0.9,0.0,C) , 9) ;
  frame 7- (plane(0.5,0.5,0.0,P) , ball(0.6,0.9,0.0,C) , 12) ;
  frame 8- (plane(0.5,0.5,0.0,P) , ball(0.6,0.9,0.0,C) , 7) ;
  frame 9- (plane(0.5,0.5,0.0,P) , ball(0.6,0.9,0.0,C) , 5) ;
  frame 10- (plane(0.5,0.5,0.0,P) , ball(0.8,0.6,0.0,C) , 5) ;
  frame 11- (plane(0.5,0.5,0.0,P) , ball(1.0,0.6,0.0,C) , 5) ;
  frame 12- (plane(0.5,0.5,0.0,P) , ball(1.2,0.6,0.0,C) , 5) ;]

One can see that there is no color bleeding and the shadow cast is
sharp. In the present INTEGRA C-CUBE system different objects can be
treated with different illumination model. The other frames of figure
1 depict different combination of illumination models including
present model.   Frames 10, 11,   12 were obtained by gradually
increasing the diffuse reflection coefficient of the ball.   The ball
was rendered with conventional ray tracing and the flat surface was
rendered using the present model.   One can see that the color bleeding
increases with diffuse reflection coefficient.

Figure 2 shows a more complicated model. One can see the color
bleeding on the floor from the cubes nearest to the surface and also
from the red ball.   The shadow of the ball is clearly visible but that
formed by the cubes is not clear being illuminated by light bouncing
off the metallic yellow surfaces of the cubes.

Fig. 2 A scene exhibiting solid textures rendered with present model

(a) Conventional ray tracing

(b) Present model

Fig. 3 Comparison of rendering with present model and conventional ray tracing

Figure 3 shows another model with complex shadows rendered by the conventonal ray tracing and the present model. As can be seen, the complex interrefletions on the table surface is more realistically rendered by the present method. The computation time for the present model was about 20% less compared to conventional ray tracing.

5. CONCLUSION

A method in which preprocessing of shadows (viewer independent) and effects of interreflection can be taken into account by combining conventional (reverse) and positive ray tracing has been proposed. The preprocessing of shadows is very fast and the advantage of reduced computation time is more evident when the number of primary light sources in a particular scene is very large.

ACKNOWLEDGMENTS

The authors would like to thank all those who helped in software development and preparation of the article. Special thanks are extended to the reviewers for their helpful comments.

REFERENCES

Whitted, Turner (1980) An improved Illumination Model for shaded display. Communications of the ACM

Cook, Robert l., Porter, Thomas and Carpenter, Loren (1984) Distributed Ray Tracing. ACM Computer Graphics Proceedings , pp 137-145

Amanatides, John (1984) Ray Tracing With Cones. ACM Computer Graphics Proceedings, pp. 129-135

Cohen, Michael F., Donald P. Greenberg (1985) The Hemi-cube - A Radiosity Method for Complex Environment. ACM Computer Graphics Proceedings , pp. 31-40

Immel, David S., Michael F. Cohen, Donald P. Greenberg (1986) A Radiosity Method for Non-diffuse Environment. ACM SIGGRAPH Proceedings, pp. 133-142.

Nishita, Tomoyuki, and Eihachiro Nakamae (1985) Continuous Tone Representation of Three-Dimensional Objects Taking Account of Shadows and Interreflections. ACM Computer Graphics Proceedings, pp.22-30

Kajiya, James T (1986), The Rendering Equation. ACM SIGGRAPH Proceedings, pp. 143-150.

Hall, Roy A and Donald P. Greenberg (1983) A Testbed for Realistic Image Synthesis. IEEE CG&A, Vol. 3, No. 8, pp. 10-20

Glassner, A.S (1984) Space Subdivision for Fast Ray Tracing. IEEE Computer Graphics and Applications, Vol. 4, pp.15-22

Wyvill, G. and Kunii, T.L (1985) A Functional Model For Constructive Solid Geometry. The Visual Computer, Vol. 1, No. 1, pp.3-14

Fujimoto, Akira, Takayuki Tanaka and Kansei Iwata (1986) ARTS: Accelerated Ray Tracing System. IEEE Computer Graphics and Applications, Vol. 6, No. 4

Joy, Kenneth I (1986) A Dissection of Fujimoto's Algorithm. University of California, Davis, Division of Computer Science, Report CSE-86-6

Murakami, Koichi, Hirota Katsuhiko, Ota Masaaki, Kakimoto Tadanori, Sato Hiroyuki (1986) Modeling Language for Three Dimensional Animation (in Japanese). Nikkei Computer Graphics, 10(No. 1), pp.146-158.

Sudeb Chattopadhyay is an engineer with the Research and Development Division of Integra Incorporated, a company that produces intelligent image computing systems. His research interests include high level rendering, 3D solid modeling and application of artificial intelligence in computer graphics.

Chattopadhyay received his B.Tech. in Naval Architecture from Indian Institute of Technology,Kharagpur (India) and his ME from Yokohama National University and his Ph.D from the University of Tokyo. He is a member of the Society of Naval Architects of Japan.

Akira Fujimoto is President of Integra Incorporated which he founded in 1986. He was employed by Graphica Computer Corporation from 1981 to 1986 where he was a chief engineer and later Director with the Software Research Division. His research interests include computer graphics for raster-scan devices, application of computer graphics in scientific and engineering analysis and CAD.

Fujimoto received an ME in Mechanical Engineering from the Technical University Szczecin (Poland) and from the University of Tokyo, where he subsequently obtained his Ph.D. He is a member of the Society of Naval Architects of Japan, the Computer Graphics Society (CGS) and the GKS Japan committee of CGS.

The authors' address is Integra Incorporated, Hime Bldg. 2F, 2-7-11 Komagome, Toshima-ku, Tokyo 170, Japan. Tel. (3)949-6620, Fax. (3)949-6640.

Chapter 7

Image Generation Techniques

Lens Effect on Synthetic Image Generation Based on Light Particle Theory

Yong C. Chen

ABSTRACT

The synthetic image generation with the lens effect consists of two consecutive processors: the hidden-surface processor, and the focus processor. The normal ray-tracing algorithms are used in the first processor. The second processor involves the computing of Lommel's function, which is an infinite series of Bessel functions. In order to avoid the complicated calculation and the huge memory consumption, an approximation method based on the light particle theory is developed. No noticeable differences can be detected between the results from approximation method and those from the exact calculation.

Keywords: computer graphics, synthetic image generation, lens effect, blurry image, light particle theory, camera model

1. INTRODUCTION

In rendering realistic scenes on the raster display, several factors such as shading, color, texture, wrinkle, shadow and blurring, affect the realism of the visual system (Newman 1973; Foley 1982). Smooth shading presents the 3rd dimension of real objects by displaying surfaces as illuminated from both the ambient light and the direct light sources. Color greatly enchances the intelligibility and perceived quality of an image. Texture and wrinkles on objects provide additional cues for the relative size of objects and their relationships to one another. Shadows help distinguish directions toward light sources. Blur on objects provides the viewers with the feeling of the distances to objects. Any realistic scence captured by either camera or humman perception system is through a lens and an aperture. The lens and the aperture can blur the image of the objects in the screen, if the objects is out of focus. This paper addresses the effect of one of thefactors, the blurring, on the synthetic image.

The usefulness of lens effect on the synthetic image generation is several folds. Through the lens effect one can select highlighting and direct the viewers' attention to a particular portion of the image. It is also useful for many commonly used cinematographic techniques for animated sequences, such as fade-in and fade-out. In addition, this effect provides the viewers with three dimensional feeling by the effect of the depth of field.

The processor of generating the synthetic image under the lens and the aperture effects can be decomposed into two independent sub-processors: the hidden-surface processor and the focus-processor

(Potmesil 1981, 1982). The hidden-surface processor calculates the information of each sample point on the intermediate image plane by using a geometric pin-hole camera model (a reduced camera in which the aperture size is zero and it contains no lens). The data stored in each sample point on the intermediate image plane contains RGB (red, green and blue) intensities, z depth distance and identification of the visible surface. The hidden-surface processor is equivalent to any ray-tracing algorithm (Whitted 1980; Kay 1979), which renders three dimensional scenes on the two dimensional raster display.

The focus-processor, which combines the data created by the hidden-surface processor and the characteristics of the lens and the aperture, generates the synthetic image. Because the characteristics are based on the complicated diffraction effect of the light, the focus-processor involves numerous calculations which typically consume much CPU time (Potmesil 1982; Cook 1984). For this reason the development of a simplified method is proposed.

The improved algorithm proposed here reduces the computational time,while it does not sacrifice accuracy to any noticeable degree. This is accomplished by using the particle theory of light instead of the electromagnetic wave pheonomenon. The core problem, the diffraction of light, is avoided, resulting in the reduction of CPU computational time. The accuracy of the results will then be demonstrated. The basic motivation to derive approximation formulas is based on the fact that the very fine structure of the diffraction pattern is covered by the finite size pixels, and thus cannot contribute to a displayed pixel intensity to any noticeable degree.

2. THE HIDDEN-SURFACE PROCESSOR

The hidden-surface processor provides a projection of a point in the three dimensional scene to a two-dimensional intermediate image plane. A pin-hole camera is shown in Figure 1, which contains an obstacle plane O with an infinitesimal hole H in the center and an image plane P. A plane with such infintesimal hole does not exist in the real physical world. However, it is used as a mathematical model to simplify the calculations.

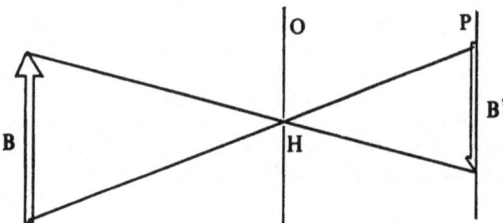

Fig.1. The principle of pin-hole camera

The image plane P is equivalent to the raster display on which the synthetic image is generated. Thus, one can assume that the image plane P consists of an array of pixels, and each pixel is a sample point of the hidden-surface processor. The processor calculates RGB intensities and the corresponding depth z of each sample point, then these data are passed to the next processor, the focus-processor.

The principle of forming an image by the pin-hole camera can be seen from Figure 1. When the arrow-shaped object B is illuminated, the light is reflected from all points on the object B. The reflected light is in all directions but only one ray from each point can pass through the infinitesimal pin-hole and reach the image plane P. The intersection of each ray and the plane P is a sharp point instead of a small light spot; therefore, the image of the object B is a well-defined image B'.

The hidden-surface processor traces the ray from each sample point through the pin-hole to the object and then to the background. Many ray-tracing and hidden-surface algorithms (Whitted 1980; Kay 1979) can be used in this processor and they will not be discussed in any detail in this paper.

3. THE FOCUS-PROCESSOR

The focus processor generates the synthesized image on the graphic raster display by using the information of each pixel on the intermediate image plane. The information contains RGB intensities and the depth z of the sample point on the object. Each pixel on the intermediate image plane can be considered an imaginary point light source q_j located at distance z from the lens with three intensities for the three primary colors (RGB). Q_{ij}, the intensity of the ith pixel on the raster display contributed by the imaginary light source q_j, can be expressed as

$$Q_{ij} = f_{ij} \cdot q_j ,$$

where the coefficient f_{ij} is the percentage of light intensity of the pixel j contributed to the pixel i. The value of the coefficient f_{ij} will be discussed later in the section. The final intensity Q_i of pixel i is computed as the weighted average of all the input sample points (Potmesil 1982). Thus,

$$Q_i = \sum_j f_{ij} \cdot q_j / \sum_j f_{ij} , \tag{1}$$

where the index j sums over all pixels on the intermediate image plane.

The coefficient f_{ij} represents the percentage contribution of light energy from pixel j to pixel i. In order to calculate f_{ij}, one must study the light energy distribution of a point light source behind a lens and an aperture.

Due to the effects of light diffraction, the image of a point light source through a finite size aperture spreads over a large area on the image plane. The diffraction phenomenon can be described by the Huygens-Fresnel principle (Beiser 1964) which states that, when a light wave passes through an aperture, every point in the wave front of the light can be considered as a new lights source. The total intensity of a point on the image plane is the superimposition of the intensities from these new light sources. Because of the constructive and the destructive interferences of these new light sources, the diffraction pattern contains a number of light and dark fringes.

If there is a point light source located at the origin of the coordinate system, then the wave field at the point P can be written as a complex function,

$$U(\vec{P}) = A_o \frac{1}{|\vec{P}|} e^{-i\phi(\vec{P})},$$

where A_o is the strength of the light source, $\phi(\vec{P})$ is the phase of the wave at the point P, and $\vec{P}$ is the position vector of P. The relation between the intensity energy of the light and the wave field at the point P is defined as $I(\vec{P}) = |U(\vec{P})|^2$. The wave field of a point P' on the aperture is $A_o \frac{1}{|\vec{P'}|} e^{-i\phi(\vec{P'})}$. From the Huygens-Fresnel principle, one can consider P' a new point light source with the strength $A_o \frac{1}{|\vec{P'}|} e^{-i\phi(\vec{P'})}$. Finally the wave field at a point P" on the image plane can be carried out by the integral over the entire aperture. Thus,

$$U(P'') = \int\limits_{\text{aperture}} A_o \frac{1}{|\vec{P'}|} e^{-i\phi(\vec{P'})} \cdot \frac{1}{|\vec{P''}-\vec{P'}|} e^{-i\phi(\vec{P''}-\vec{P'})} d\vec{P'},$$

where $\vec{P''}-\vec{P'}$ is the relative position vector from the point P" to the point P'. If a circular aperature is used (Figure 2), then the wave field of a point (x_o, y_o) on the image plane can be obtained by integrating over the aperture coordinate system (X_1, Y_1) according to

$$U(x_o, y_o) = \int h_o(x_o, y_o, x_1, y_1) U(x_1, y_1) dx_1 \, dy_1,$$

$$d/2 > r_1$$

$$\tag{2}$$

where $\quad h_o(x_o, y_o, x_1, y_1) = (1/j\lambda)(e^{kr_{01}}/r_{01})\cos(\vec{n} \cdot \vec{r}_{01}),$

$\vec{n}$ is the normal direction of the aperture,
d is the diameter of the aperture,
λ is the wave length of the light,
k is the wave vector of which the value equals $2\pi/\lambda$,
$r_{01} = [z^2 + (x_o - x_1)^2 + (y_o - y_1)^2]^{1/2}$,
and $r_1 = (x_1^2 + y_1^2)^{1/2}$.

Since, the wave field $U(x_o, y_o)$ is symmetric about the origin $(0,0)$ in $(X_o Y_o)$ system, the Equation (2) can be simplified using the radius coordinates $r_o = (x_o + y_o)^{1/2}$ and the distance between the image plane and the aperture z. The distribution of the intensity is then given by the equation,

$$I(r_o) = \left(\frac{kd^2}{8z}\right)^2 2\left(\frac{J_1(kdr_o/2z)}{kdr_o/2z}\right)^2 A_o^2,$$

$$\tag{3}$$

which is the well-known Airy pattern (Born 1970). In Equation (3), J_1 is Bessel function of the first order. This function is shown in Figure 3 where the Y-axis represents the intensity I in the unit of A_o^2 and the X-axis represents the coordinate r_o in the unit of $(kd/2z)$. From the law of the conservation of energy, the area under the curve in Figure 3 must equal A_o^2. The major peak in the center of the curve indicates that over 84% of the intensity is distributed in the forward direction, but there is still a small amount of the energy spreading over the image plane. This is due to the effect of the diffraction, which contradicts our intuition that the light follows a straight line path.

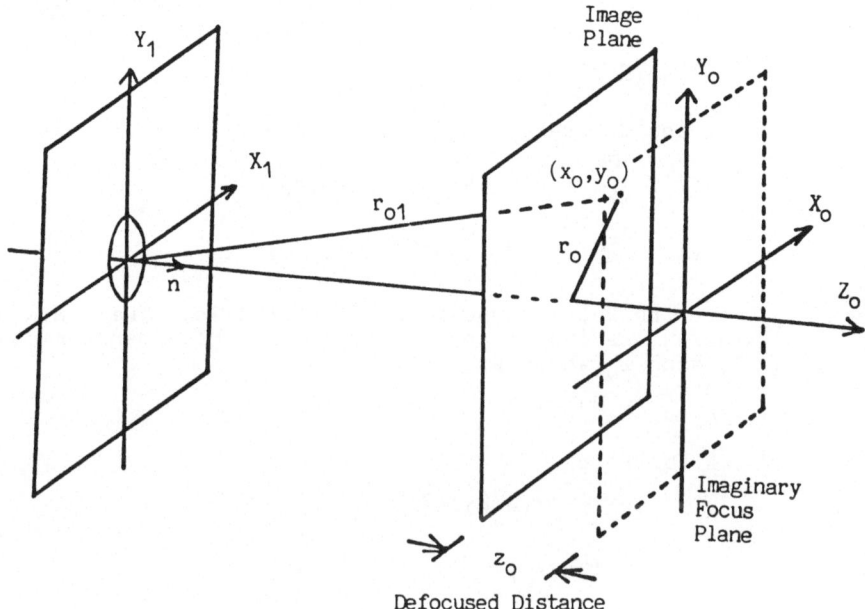

Fig.2. The coordinates system of the circular aperture diffraction

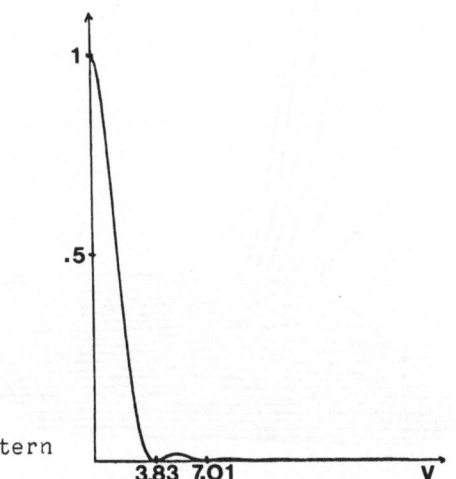

Fig.3. The Airy pattern

When a lens is added to the aperture, the distribution of the light not only depends on r_o but also on z_o, the defocused distance which is defined as the distance between the image plane and the focal point (Figure 2). The distribution of intensity in this case was first given by E. Lommel (Born 1970), which has two equivalent expressions:

$$I(u,v) = (2/u)^2 \ [U_1^2(u,v) + U_2^2(u,v)] \ I_o \quad (4)$$

and

$$I(u,v) = (2/u)^2 \ [1 + V_0^2(u,v) + V_1^2(u,v)$$
$$- 2V_0(u,v)\cos(0.5(u + v^2/u))$$
$$- 2V_1(u,v)\sin(0.5(u + v^2/u)) \ ] \ I_0,$$

(5)

where $I_0 = (kd^2/8F)^2 A_0^2$,

and V_0, V_1, U_0 and U_1 are Lommel functions defined as follows:

$$U_n(u,v) = \sum_{s=0}^{\infty} (-1)^s \ (u/v)^{n+2s} \ J_{n+2s}(v)$$

and

$$V_n(u,v) = \sum_{s=0}^{\infty} (-1)^s \ (v/u)^{n+2s} \ J_{n+2s}(v),$$

where J_{n+2s} are the Bessel functions of order n+2s. The v and u are the dimensionless radius coordinate r_0 and the dimensionless defocused distance z_0 which are defined as

$$u = k \ (d/2F)^2 \ z_0,$$

and

$$v = k \ (d/2F) \ r_0$$
$$= k \ (d/2F) \ (x_0^2 + y_0^2)^{1/2}.$$

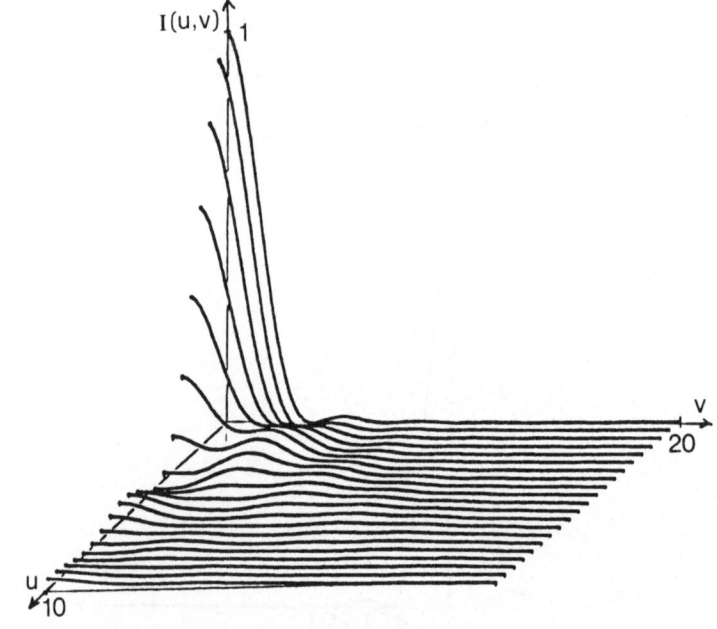

Fig.4. A 3-D drawing of the intensity distribution function I(u,v)

Because of the requirement of convegence of the infinite series, Equation (4) is for the range v≥u and Equation (5) is for the range u≥v. For the sake of conveniency, we shall assume $A_0^2 = 1$. Then the intensity distribution function can be considered the percentage of the intensity being distributed to the position (u,v).

The distribution function is shown as the three dimensional drawing in Figure 4. The Z axis represents the intensity I. The X axis represents the variable u which is proportional to z_0 and the Y axis represents the variable v which is proportional to r_0.

The quantity $I(z_j, [(x-x_j)^2 + (y-y_j)^2]^{0.5}) dx.dy$ represents the percentage of the contribution of the source q_j to the point (x,y). The coefficient f_{ij} is defined as the percentage of the contribution of the source q_j to the pixel i on the raster display. Therefore, f_{ij} can be expressed in terms of the integration of $I(x,y)$ over the pixel area i.

$$f_{ij} = \int_{x_i-\Delta x}^{x_i} \int_{y_i-\Delta y}^{y_i} I(z_j, x, x_j, y, y_j) dx.dy, \tag{6}$$

where (x_i, y_i) is the coordinate of a corner of the pixel i, and x and y are the length measurements of the pixel i in the x and the y direction (Figure 5). The straightest way to compute the f_{ij} is to subdivide the pixel i into smaller regions where the intensity function I has approximately a constant value. f_{ij} can be expressed as,

$$f_{ij} = \sum_{\text{all } n} I_n A_n,$$

where A_n is the area of the nth subdivision in the pixel i, and I_n is the approximated value of the intensity function I in the nth subdivision. Because the intensity function I depends on the radius coordinate r, the best way to subdivide the pixel is to dissect it into small arcs (Figure 5). In pixels adjacent to the origin, a large number of subdivisions (in the order of 100 subdivisions) are required to obtain the reasonable approximation, consuming excessive CPU time. In order to save computing time in these pixels, the integral from $L(u,v)$ of the Lommel's formula must be used.

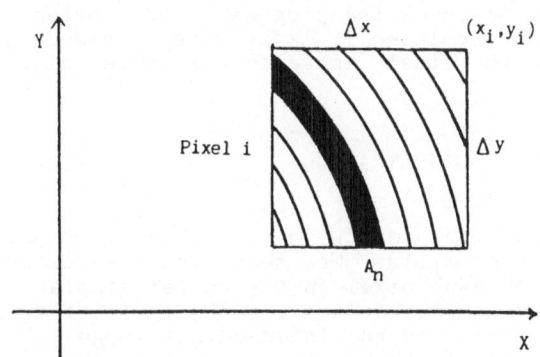

Fig.5. Subdivisions of pixel

The Lommel's formula $L(u,v)$ with respect to the radius coordinate r can be found as follows (Wolf 1951). In the case $v/u \geq 1$,

$$L(u,v) = 1 - \sum_{s=0}^{\infty} (-1)^s/(2s+1).(u/v)^{2s} Q_{2s}(v), \tag{7}$$

where

$$Q_{2s}(v)=\sum_{p=0}^{2s}(-1)^2[J_p(v)J_{2s-p}+J_{p+1}(v)J_{2s+1-p}(v)].$$

In the case $1 \geq v/u$,

$$L(u,v)=(v/u)^2[1+\sum_{s=0}^{\infty}(-1)^s/(2s+1).(v/u)^{2s}Q_{2s}(v)]$$

$$-(4/u)[Y_1(u,v)\cos(uu)+Y_2(u,v)\sin(uu)],$$

(8)

where $uu=(u+v^2/u)/2$, $\quad$ Y_1 and Y_2 are the two functions

$$Y_n(u,v) = \sum_{s=0}^{\infty}(-1)^s(n+2s)(v/u)^{n+2s}J_{n+2s}(v)$$

$$=0.5[(v^2/u)V_{n-1}(u,v) + uV_{n+1}(u,v)].$$

Because of the difficulties of computing the coefficient f_{ij}'s by
the exact formula, the conventional wisdom is to avoid repeating
calculation of f_{ij}. All f_{ij}'s are calculated once and stored for
future use. The focus-processor proceeds in two steps (Potmesil
1982) First, the program computes tables of the coefficient f_{ij}'s
at equally spaced intervals along z' (the defocused distance between
the nearest and the farthest points in the image for the given lens
and aperture parameters). Theoretically, the intensity function
extends to infinity, i.e., all f_{ij}'s are non-zero. Thus, there can
be no way to store all f_{ij}'s in the memory. The necessary
truncations are made at the boundary of circle of the confusion
(Potmesi 1982) (similar to the geometry shadow defined in section
V). Since f_{ij} is radially symmetric, values in only one quadrant
are actually computed and stored. For any value of z' whose f_{ij}
values are not listed, the corresponding values can be obtained from
two nearest tables by linear interpolation. In order to achieve more
accuracy, the spacing of the z' at which the tables are pre-
calculated are sufficiently small, affecting the menory requirements
and the execution speed of the program. The program of the second
step uses the pre-calculated f_{ij}'s and the stored data of each
pixel to generate the final image on the raster display.

4. THE MOTIVATION OF SIMPLICATION

The focus-processor includes two parts. The first part is to
calculate coefficient f_{ij}'s. The second part is to computer the
final intensity for each pixel on the raster display, using the
information stored for each pixel and the tables of f_{ij}. Because
imaginary light sources on the intermediate image plane only
contribute to the pixels around their forward directions, most
f_{ij}'s are close to zero. Thus the operation of the second part
is relatively simple, whereas the first part, calculating the
coefficient f_{ij}, is the major operation in the focus-processor.

The integral intensity function L(u,v) in Equation (7) and Equation
(8) contains an infinite series. Each term of the series contains
Bessel functions, which is an infinite series itself. Therefore, in
computing the function L(u,v), the convergence of the infinite series
is the most critical problem.

Even some software packages are capable of accurately computing the Bessel function, the logical complexity and the problem of excessive CPU time in the focus processor remains. A simpler algorithm is therefore desirable.

The fade-in and the fade-out animated sequences in cinematographic applications move objects back and forth; this changes the range of the defocused distance z'. When objects move, more tables should be added to the program; this decreases the speed of the calculation and requires more memory. Furthermore, in a system containing a very large number of small objects, the tables for the gaps between two objects become superfluous.

The truncation of the intensity function and the linear interpolation between two tables increase the computational error. Therefore, the precisely pre-calculated f_{ij}'s, which requires a great deal of memory space and tremendous computing effort, may turn out to be wasteful. This constitutes another reason for searching a simpler method of computing f_{ij}'s.

In order to determine the possibility of simplification, one should analyze the behavior of Lommel's formula. The major behavior of a function is controlled by the local minima and the local maxima. The following theorem gives a complete description of these critical points of the intensity distribution function $I(u,v)$.

THEOREM: For any fixed u, the distance between two adjacent critical points of the intensity function $I(u,v)$ is smaller than the first root of the equation $J_1(v)/v = 0$, which approximately equals 3.8.

PROOF: At a fixed u, the locations of the critical points of intensity function $I(u,v)$ are roots of the first derivative of $I(u,v)$ with respect to v. That is

$$dI(u,v)/dv = (2/u)^2 (2U_1(u,v)U_1'(u,v) + 2U_2(u,v)U_2'(u,v))$$

$$= 0,$$

(9)

where the prime represents the first derivative of the function with respect to v. Equation (9) implies that

$$U_1(u,v) \cdot U_1'(u,v) + U_2(u,v) \cdot U_2'(u,v) = 0$$

(10)

The derivative of Lommel's function U_m with respect to v is

$$U_m'(u,v) = \sum_{s=0}^{\infty} (-1)^s u^{(m+2s)} (v^{-(m+2s)} J_{m+2s}(v))'.$$

From an identity of Bessel functions (Arfken 1973),

$$\frac{d}{dx}(x^{-n} \cdot J_n(x)) = -x^{-n} \cdot J_{n+1}(x),$$

$U_m'(u,v)$ can be simplified as

$$U_m'(u,v) = \sum_{s=0}^{\infty} (-1)^s u^{m+2s} (-1) v^{-(m+2s)} J_{m+2s+1}(v)$$

$$= -(v/u) \sum_{s=0}^{\infty} (-1)^s u^{m+2s+1} v^{-(m+2s+1)} J_{m+2s+1}(v)$$

$$= -(v/u) U_{m+1}.$$

(11)

From the result of Equation (11), the left hand side of the Equation (10) can be separated into two factors,

$$U_1 U_1' + U_2 U_2' = U_1(-v/u)U_2 + U_2(-v/u)U_3$$

$$= (-v/u) \cdot U_2 \cdot (U_1 + U_3)$$

Therefore, the roots of Equation (10) can be obtained from

$$U_2(u,v) = 0$$

or

$$U_1(u,v) + U_3(u,v) = 0.$$

The expression $U_1 + U_3$ can be simplified by the definition of Lommel's function,

$$U_1 + U_3 = \sum_{s=0}^{\infty} (-1)^s (u/v)^{1+2s} J_{1+2s}(v) +$$

$$\sum_{s=0}^{\infty} (-1)^s (u/v)^{3+2s} J_{3+2s}(v)$$

$$= J_1(v)/v - \sum_{s=2}^{\infty} (-1)^s (u/v)^{1+2s} J_{1+2s}(v)$$

$$+ \sum_{s=0}^{\infty} (-1)^s (u/v)^{3+2s} J_{3+2s}(v)$$

$$= J_1(v)/v - \sum_{t=0}^{\infty} (-1)^t (u/v)^{3+2t} J_{3+2t}(v)$$

$$+ \sum_{s=0}^{\infty} (-1)^s (u/v)^{3+2s} J_{3+2s}(v)$$

$$= \frac{J_1(v)}{v} \quad ,$$

which is independent of u. The plots of $U_2 = 0$ or $J_1(v)/v = 0$ are shown in Figure 6. The vertical lines are roots of $J_1(v)/v = 0$ (Beattie 1958) and the curves are the roots of $U_2 = 0$. As v increases, two adjacent vertical lines become closer. Thus the distance between any adjacent critical points is smaller than 3.8, i.e., the first root of $J_1(v) = 0$.
Q. E. D.

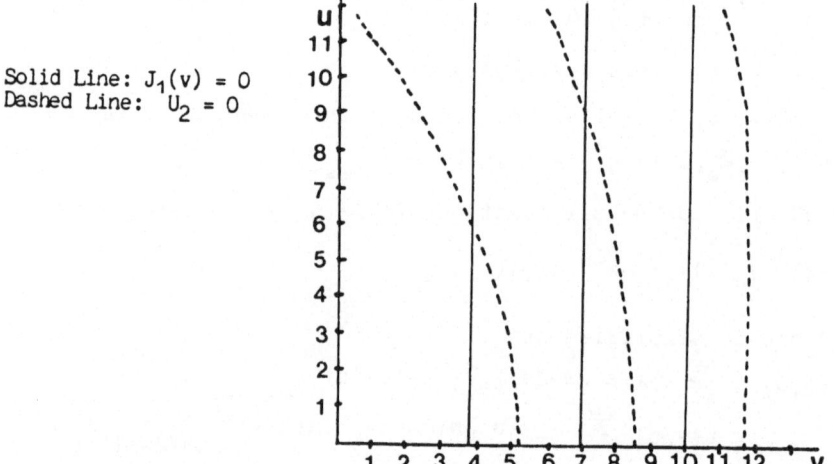

Solid Line: $J_1(v) = 0$
Dashed Line: $U_2 = 0$

Fig.6. Critical points of the intensity distribution function I(u,v)

The theorem predicts that the distance between any two adjacent peaks of the intensity function I(u,v) is less than v = 7.6. In order to compare v = 7.6 with the pixel size, we assume that the lens and the raster display used here have the following parameters: pixel size Δr^2 = 0.11 mm x 0.11 mm, the focal length of the lens F = 55 mm, the aperture diameter d= 5.0mm, and the wave length of visible light λ = 5×10^{-4}mm. The dimensionless pixel size can be computed by

$$v = (2\pi/\lambda).(d/2F).\Delta r$$
$$= 63.$$

Thus, under these parameters, more than 8 peaks are inside a single pixel. In other words, the resolution of the raster display is insufficient to display the details of the function. Consequently, the detailed descriptions of the functions I(u,v) or L(u,v) are not necessary, and approximation methods can be used to obtain a realistic description of the situation.

The final intensity of each pixel on the raster is the summation of contributions from different imaginary light sources on the intermediate image plane. The summation may also smear out the fine structure of the intensity distribution function. This is still another reason why certain approximation methods are adequate.

5. PARTICLE THEORY OF LIGHT

The conventional treatment of lens effect is based on the wave theory of light. The calculations involved are tedious and time consuming. In this work, an attempt is made to simulate the lens process using the particle theory because of the anticipated simplification of computational efforts and the fact that this theory can account for the law of refraction. If the intensity distribution function derived from the particle theory can give an adequate represention of the exact formula, then this approximation has two important implications: the simplification of computation and better understanding of the relationship between the raster display and the lens effect.

An illustration of how the light particles are focused on the image plane is shown in Figure 7. The light source emits light particles in all directions. Some light particles hitting the object are reflected back; other light particles which pass through the lens will be bent towards the image point A on the image plane. The image plane is located at a distance p away from the lens satisfying the relationship,

$$\frac{1}{q} + \frac{1}{p} = \frac{1}{F},$$

where q is the object distance and F is the focal length.

If one moves the image plane backward to a distance z' from the position p (Figure 7), all light particles through the lens still focus at the point A. Since the image plane has been moved, particles traveling farther along their individual directions reach the image plane in a new position. The image is formed by the spread of the light particles resulting in a relatively large light spot rather than a sharp point.

The light intensity of a point in the light spot can be obtained by the inverse-square rules of light (Figure 7),

$$I(r) = \frac{(p+q+z')^2}{(\sqrt{p^2+b^2} + \sqrt{q^2+b^2} + \sqrt{z'^2+r^2})^2} I_{oo}$$

where I_{oo} is the light intensity on the image plane in the forward direction, r is the radius coordinate of the point of interest, and b is the radius coordinate of the point at which the particle passes through the lens.

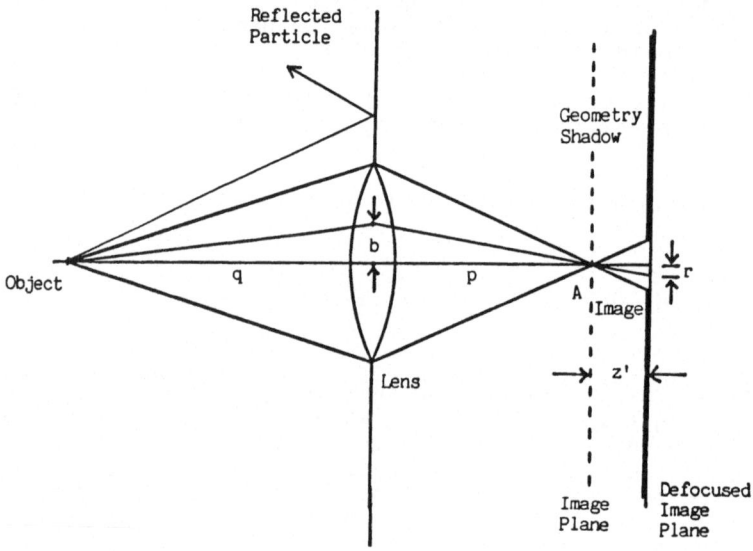

Fig.7. Light particles distribution on the defocused image

For a camera, the image distance q is large compared to the other quanities, p, r, b, and z'. The intensity function I can be reduced to a constant since

$$I(r) \approx \frac{q^2}{(\sqrt{p^2+b^2} + q + \sqrt{z'^2+r^2})^2} I_{oo}$$

$$\approx (q^2/q^2) I_{oo}$$

$$= I_{oo}$$

The only region on the image plane where light particles can land is a circular area centered at the forward direction of the light source. The whole image plane outside the circular area is the shadow, referred to as the geometry shadow. Thus,

$$I(r) = \begin{cases} I_{oo} & \text{..... inside the boundary of the geometry shadow,} \\ 0 & \text{........ outside the boundary of the geometry shadow.} \end{cases}$$

The integral intensity function then becomes

$$L(u,v) = 2\pi . \int_o^v I(u,x).x \, dx$$

$$= \begin{cases} \pi v^2.I_{oo} & \text{inside the boundary of the geometry shadow,} \\ 1 & \text{..... outside the boundary of the geometry shadow.} \end{cases}$$

If the total intensity within the boundary of the geometry shadow is 1; the intensity in the forward direction is $(\pi u^2)^{-1}$. The function $L(u,v)$ can then be simplified as

$$L(u,v) = \begin{cases} (v/u)^2 & \text{.....inside the boundary of the geometry shadow,} \\ 1 & \text{.. outside the boundary of the geometry shadow.} \end{cases}$$

Since the intensity function $I(u,v)$ is constant inside the geometry shadow, $L(u,v_o)$ is proportional to the area of the circle $v = v_o$. Therefore, every pixel inside the geometry shadow receives the same intensity, $f_{ij} = A/\pi v_o^2$, where A is the area of the pixel. The pixels outside the boundary receive nothing. A pixel i on the border only receives an intensity of $A_i'/\pi v_o^2$, where A_i' is the area of the portion inside the boundary.

The matrix element f_{ij} can now be calculated as

$$f_{ij}= \begin{cases} A/\pi v_o^2 & \text{..... for pixel i inside the boundary,} \\ A_i'/\pi v_o^2 & \text{..... for pixel i on the boundary,} \\ 0 & \text{............. for pixel i outside the boundary,} \\ 1 & \text{............. in the case } A > v_o^2. \qquad (12) \end{cases}$$

The coefficient f_{ij}'s in Equation (6) involve infinitive series of another infinitive series, but those in Equation (12) only include simple algebraic and trigonometric functions.

The value of A' does not affect f_{ij} inside or outside the boundary; it only give rise to errors for the pixels on the boundary. The number of pixels inside the boundary is proportional to the square of the radius of the boundary, but the number of the pixels on the border is only proportional to the radius. In order to save computational time for the case with large defocused distance (large u), the values of all A_i''s can be estimated as 1/2 of the pixel area, or one may even assume $A_i' = 0$ or $A_i' = $ the pixel area.

6. RESULTS

An scene (Figure 8) consisting of a wall (wooden table top), a rectangular box with two vese pictures and an ellipsoid with alphabets, was used to test the validity of the formulas derived in the previous sections. For anti-aliasing in this picture, the light intensities were resampled at the cornner of the subdivisions of pixels on the silhouettes or edges. For simplicity, black and white pictures were used. The distances of the wall, the rectangular box, and the ellipsoid to the lens were 1000mm, 550mm and 300mm, respectively. A point light source, 3500mm from the wall, 70 mm above and 400 mm right to the center of the box, was used to create shadows of the rectangular box and the ellipsoid on the wall. A 512x480 pixel raster display were used to display this 275x200 mm scene in all pictures. Figures 9-11 are the images generated by the focus-processor with the aperture diameters of 5mm and the lens focal length of 55 mm, focused at 300mm, 550mm and 1000mm, respectivly. The sharpest images were, therefore, formed for the ellipsoid (Figure 9), the rectangular box (Figure 10), and the shadow (Figure 11). The same process was used to produce images shown in Figures 12-14 with the exception that the aperture diameter was 9.8mm. Comparison of Figures 9-11 with 12-14 clearly indicates that with a larger aperture the images of the defocused objects appeare much more blurry as can be seen from the rectangular box and shadow of Figure 12, the ellipsoid and shadow of Figure 13, and the rectangular box and ellipsoid of Figure 14.

Fig.8. 3D Scene consists of a wall, a rectangular box, and a ellipsoid

It is important to compare the coefficient f_{ij}'s calculated by the approximation methods with those from the exact intensity distribution function. Tables 1 and 2 show the comparisions of f_{ij}'s between the approximation method and the exact formula in the display resolutions of 512 x 512 pixels and 1024 x 1024 pixels in a 9" x 9" display, respectively. In both tables, f_{ij}'s were calculated on the basis of the following parameters: aperture diameter of 9.8 mm, object in 2000 mm and focusing at 290 mm from the lens. The pairs of integers (i_x, i_y) in the first column of both tables represent the coordinates at the right upper corner of pixel i (Figure 15), provided that the origin lies on the forward direction of the pixel j on the intermediate image plane. Because the coefficient f_{ij}'s were radially symmetric, only half of the first quadrant was computed, i.e., f_{ij}'s with $i_x \geq i_y \geq 1$. The data in the second column are the coefficient f_{ij}'s from the exact formula, and the last column are that from the approximation. The percentage differences (PD) between f_{ij}'s from the approximated method and that from the exact formula are 1.2% in Table 1 and 1.4% in Table 2. PD is defined as

$$PD = \sum_i |f^a_{ij} - f^e_{ij}| / \sum_i f^e_{ij},$$

where the superscript 'a' indicating the f_{ij}'s is from approximation method and 'e' is from exact formula, and index i's denoting the summations are over all pixels in the first quadrant.

Fig.9. Image formed by focusing at ellipsoid with 5mm aperture diameter

Fig.10. Image formed by focusing at rectangular box with 5mm aperture diameter

Fig.11. Image formed by focusing at wall with 5mm aperture diameter

Fig.12. Image formed by focusing at ellipsoid with 9.8mm aperture diameter

Fig.13. Image formed by focusing at rectangular box with 9.8mm aperture diameter

Fig.14. Image formed by focusing at wall with 9.8mm aperture diameter

The values of f_{ij}'s depend on the size of the lens, the defocused distance z' and the resolution of displays. Further comparisons based on four resolutions: low resolution (512 x512 pixels in a 9" x 9" display), normal resolution (1024 x1024 pixels in a 9" x 9" display), high resolution (2048 x 2048 pixels in a 9" x 9" display), and super high resolution (4096 x4096 pixels in a 9" x 9" display); three focus distances: 290mm, 550mm, and 980 mm; and three sizes of lens: 9.8 mm, 5.00 mm, and 2.5 mm; in a total of 36 cases, were made. Only the average PD in each display resolution is listed as follows: 1.2% for low resolution, 1.25 % for normal resolutin, 4.87% for high resolution and 11.4 % for super high resolution.

In order to investigate the effect of the f_{ij} difference on the perception system, 10 images with the same lens characteristics and the focus distance as Figure 9 were generated. The f_{ij}'s used in these 10 images have the same average difference (PD=10%) from that of Figure 9. However, the individual f_{ij}'s vary from one image to another. For the naked eye, no noticeable difference can be found in the images. Figure 16 shows one of the 10 images. In this figure, the f_{ij}'s are 10% higher than that in Figure 9 if the sum of coordinates i_x and i_y is a even number and 10% lower if the sum of the coordinates is odd. The only difference one can detect in Figure 16 is that the highlight on the ellipsoid was slightly brighter than that in Figure 9. From the above experiments, even the super high resolution (PD=11.4%) display isused, the approximation formula from the light particle theory still can predict reliable results.

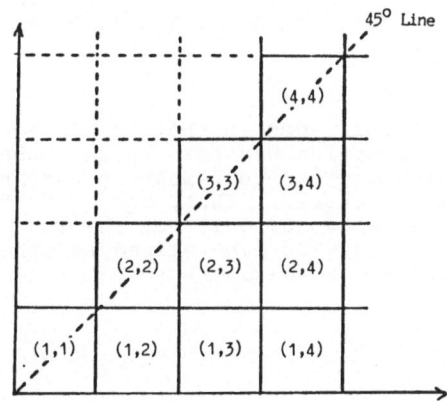

Fig.15. The pixel coordinate system

7. CONCLUSION

The core problem of the lens effect on synthetic image generation is the computation of the coefficient f_{ij}'s from the intensity distribution function I(u,v). An approximation method was developed for this purpose. The values of the coefficient f_{ij}'s from the approximation formulas were compared to that from the exact formula. The approximation can predict almost identical values of f_{ij}'s as those from the exact formula on the normal resolution displays. Even in the super high resolution display, the difference is around 11%, which is proved experimently that the amount of difference does not contribute detectable significance to our perception system.

Theoretically, all the coefficient f_{ij}'s computed from the exact
formula are non-zero. In order to be performed in a computer,
truncations at the circle of confusion must be made. Thus, the
values of f_{ij}'s from the exact formula are still only
approximations. It is difficult to judge which algorithms, the
direct calculation and the aaproximation, are closer to the real
values. Therefore, the term 11% difference (instead of 11% error) is
used.

Fig.16. Image formed by focusing at ellipsoid with 5mm aperture
diameter using PD = 10%

An interesting point of this work is that the fine structure of the
intensity distribution function has been shown to be within the order
of v = 3.8, which indicates that contemporary raster displays are not
adequate for the true structures. Thus, the validity of
the approximation may be good not only for the lens effect. It is my
belief that this approach may be generalized to other types of
modeling on raster display devices.

8. BIBLIOGRAPHY

Arfken G (1973) Mathematical Method for Physics. Academic Press, New
   York, NY
Beattie C (1958) Table of First 700 Zeros of Bessel Function. Bell
   Tech. J. (37):689
Beiser A (1964) The Science of Physics. Addison-Wesley, Reading, MA
Born M, Wolf E (1970) Principles of Optics, 4th ed. Pergamon,
   London
Cook L, Porter T, Carpenter L (1984) Distributed Ray-Tracing.
   Computer Graphics 18(3):137-145
Foley J, Van Dan A (1982) Fundamentals of Interactive Computer
   Graphics. Addison-Wesley, Menlo Park, CA
Kay D, Greenberg D (1979) Transparency for Computer Synthesied
   Images. Computer Graphics 13(2):158-164
Newman W, Sproull R (1973) Principles of Interactive Computer
   Graphics. McGraw-Hill, New York, NY
Potmesil M, Chakravarty I (1981) A Lens and Camera Model for
   Synthetic Image Generation. Computer Graphics 15(3):297-305

Potmesil M, Chakravarty I (1982) Synthetic Image Generation with a
  lens and Aperture Camera Model. ACM Transaction on Graphics 1(2):
  85-108
Whitted T (1980) An Improved Illumination Model for Shaded Display.
  CACM 23(6):343-349
Wolf E (1951) Light Distribution near Focus in an Error Free
  Diffraction Image. Proc. Roy. Soc. A(204):533-548

Table 1. Comparison of coefficient f_{ij} for a low resolution display

Pixel Coordinates		Exact * Calculation	** Approximation
1	1	0.060179	0.060378
2	1	0.060669	0.060362
2	2	0.041516	0.042281
3	1	0.013223	0.013746
3	2	0.000481	0.000343
3	3	0.000020	0.000000
4	1	0.000019	0.000000
4	2	0.000012	0.000000
4	3	0.000006	0.000000
4	4	0.000003	0.000000
5	1	0.000004	0.000000
5	2	0.000004	0.000000

Table 2. Comparison of coefficient f_{ij} for a normal resolution display

Pixel Coordinates		Exact * Calculation	** Approximation
1	1	0.015133	0.015095
2	1	0.015107	0.015090
2	2	0.015107	0.015089
3	1	0.015113	0.015088
3	2	0.015120	0.015090
3	3	0.015016	0.015089
4	1	0.015198	0.015089
4	2	0.015336	0.015090
4	3	0.012243	0.012405
4	4	0.001736	0.001840
5	1	0.008356	0.008406
5	2	0.004457	0.005141
5	3	0.000403	0.000275
5	4	0.000031	0.000000
5	5	0.000009	0.000000
6	1	0.000049	0.000000
6	2	0.000031	0.000000
6	3	0.000015	0.000000
6	4	0.000008	0.000000
6	5	0.000004	0.000000
6	6	0.000002	0.000000

* Average calculation time per pixel: 200 sec by IBM AT.
** Average calculation time per pixel: 0.2 sec by IBM AT.

Yong C. Chen is currently an assistant professor at the Department of Mathematical Sciences, Purdue University Calumet. His research interests include Computer Graphics, Geometric Modeling, Computer Vision, and Biomedical Image Processing. He is also a visiting scholar at the Urology Department, Northwestern University School of Medicine in charge of computer analysis of proteins separated by 2-dimensional gel electrophoresis.

Chen received the PhD degree in physics from University of Louisville, 1979 and the master degree in computer science from Illinois Institute of Technology, 1984.

Address:Dept. of Mathematical Sciences, Purdue University Calumet, Hammond, IN. 46323 U.S.A.

Reconstruction and Semi-Transparent Display Method for Observing Inner Structure of an Object Consisting of Multiple Surfaces

Kazufumi Kaneda, Koichi Harada, Eihachiro Nakamae, Mineo Yasuda, and Akinao G. Sato

ABSTRACT

A system of techniques is proposed for reconstructing the original object from multi-layered cross-section data including open contour lines and for displaying the inner structure as well as the outside using a stereoscopic semi-transparent image and cut-away views. The procedure is divided into three steps: 1) selection/construction of contour lines for each cross-section, 2) reconstruction of the object based on the contour line information including cutting away part of the reconstructed object with a convex polyhedron, and 3) display of the reconstructed image. Control parameters are provided to allow easy and reliable observation of multi-layered structures.

Keywords: Semi-transparent display, Triangle method, Contour lines, Multi-layered cross-section, Cut view, Stereoscopic display

1. INTRODUCTION

A widely used method for describing complicated three-dimensional objects composed of various elements (characteristics of each element are not the same in general) displays sets of two-dimensional cross-sections. Usually, each cross-section is perpendicular to the center line of the object, and is composed of a number of contour lines. Direct comprehension of the original geometry based on this form of data is almost impossible. Therefore, the following two technologies are very important for understanding the complicated three-dimensional object in detail: i) reconstruction of the original object based on sets of two-dimensional cross-sections, and ii) display of the inner along with the outer appearance of the object in a form that may be easily understood. These technologies are desired especially in the study of development in the field of anatomy.

Traditionally, in the field of anatomy, a number of cross-section images was prepared, each section being a thin slice of an organism. The observer had to create the entire geometry in his/her mind based on the set of sections. A simple and only solution to this situation was to obtain perspective drawings or 3-D models of the original object supplied by some researcher. This does not provide sufficient understanding if the interior geometry of the object is not simple.

This paper proposes a system of methods using computer graphics to solve this problem. The whole procedure is divided into three steps: 1) generation of contour lines based on each cross-section, 2) reconstruction of the object based on the contour line information, possibly cutting away a portion with a convex polyhedron, and 3) display of the reconstructed image.

In general, contour lines have been automatically generated by using a threshold value (Sumi, 1981). The elements of the two-dimensional data that exceed the value are selected, and then contour lines are generated using these elements.

Several modeling methods are available for reconstructing the original object from cross-sectional data. A surface model in which the objects represented as a set of surfaces is more appropriate than voxel modeling (Herman, 1979), because the interior geometry of the object is easily understood when each surface is displayed as a semi-transparent membrane.

A widely used method for object reconstruction is to fill the area between two consecutive contour lines with a triangular mesh. A typical triangular mesh technique using graph theory was reported by Fuchs et al (1977). However, this technique is not valid if elements branch off or join together between cross-sections.

Christiansen et al (1978) proposed a modified triangle method to handle this case. The algorithm is simple, and generates a good triangular mesh if there is no drastic change between two consecutive sections. However, they did not consider handling multi-surface cross-section data nor data in which open contour lines (such as a mouth) are allowed.

The reconstructed image could be displayed using a three-dimensional shading technique. However, to visualize the interior aspect more clearly, the surface of each element should be displayed as a semi-transparent membrane (Sungunoff, 1978), (Sumi, 1982). The semi-transparent image is obtained by mixing the color of the background picture calculated by conventional methods and the color of the object to be displayed as semi-transparent membrane (Newell, 1972). However, direct application of the method is known to produce low apparent transparency. A remedy for this problem is to introduce a transparency parameter (Kay, 1979). The transparency is high where the surface is perpendicular to the viewing direction, and it is low where the surface is parallel.

We have previously proposed a semi-transparent stereoscopic method (Nakamae, 1985). In our new system, generation of contour lines is carried out by manual input of the contour lines using a digitizing tablet. This is because there exist features in cross-section data in our application where automatic contour line detection using image processing technique is almost impossible.

For 3-D object reconstruction, two modifications have been made to Christiansen's method:

> (i) Any number of contour lines may be included
> in each cross-section.
> (ii) An appropriate triangular mesh is obtained
> even if drastic geometry change occurs between
> consecutive sections.

Display of the reconstructed object is specially designed to allow easy observation of the inner structure. This is because the most realistic semi-transparent representation of an object does not always offer the best information for observation. In our system, the displayed color of each point is related to the inverse of the cosine of the angle formed by the surface normal and the view direction. Thus, the area near the edge of each object seems less transparent, and is viewed more clearly, than the center region.

In this way, the semi-transparency effect is increased, and the shape of internal objects becomes clear. The transparency coefficient of each object may be adjusted, and any element of the entire object may be deleted or separately displayed to make observation easier. Two projected views are created, corresponding to left and right eye positions. The obtained stereoscopic effect enables three-dimensional observation of the object.

In our previous work, open contour lines were not allowed in a cross-section. However, open regions in the object, such as a mouth, are often important elements of the entire body. Thus, we have improved our previous reconstruction method to incorporate open regions in objects.

We also have modified our system to allow cut-away views to be generated by cutting with a convex polyhedron. In many cases it is desirable to display the inner structure of the reconstructed object. The intersection of the original object and a convex polyhedron is removed and the cut surfaces are therefore polygonal. Using cut-away views, one can easily observe the inner structure and the shape of elements on arbitrary sections.

An example of application of the new proposal follows the detailed description. It demonstrates the usefulness of our techniques.

2. RECONSTRUCTION OF THE OBJECT FROM CONTOUR LINE DATA

2.1 Data Structure

To improve Christiansen's method, we must first understand its limits of application. The method is designed for contour line data that changes gradually from one cross-section to another. Additionally, although multiple contours can exist on each cross-section, contours must not be contained within other contours. In order to determine which pairs of contours on consecutive cross-sections to connect, it considers the minimum bounding rectangle surrounding each contour. The pairs of rectangles that exhibit the maximum area of intersection when projected onto a plane parallel to the object's center line are considered to contain contour lines which should be connected. If cross-sections include multiple contour lines as in Fig. 1, this technique produces erroneous results.

A hierarchical data structure is introduced in the new proposal that consists of object elements, sub-objects, contour lines and contour points. Regions of different characteristics are assigned to different object elements. Therefore, each object element is a region sharing the same characteristics. An object element is divided into several sub-objects in general if it branches

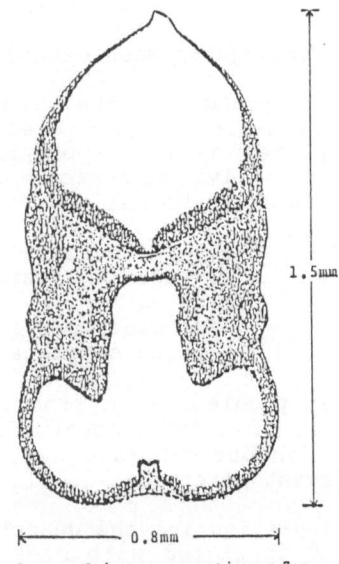

1.5mm

0.8mm

interval between sections : 7μm

Fig.1 Sectional photograph of mouse embryo.

out or comes together between cross-sections. Each contour line defined on a cross-section corresponds to one object element. Furthermore, a contour line is defined by a set of contour points. Fig. 2 illustrates an example of the hierarchy.

The sub-object information in our data structure eliminates the need for special processing to determine which pairs of contour lines on consecutive cross-sections should be connected. The user simply associates the name of the sub-object with its contour line on each cross section when digitizing the data. Thus, contour lines may contain other contour lines, and objects may exhibit branching structures like Fig 2.

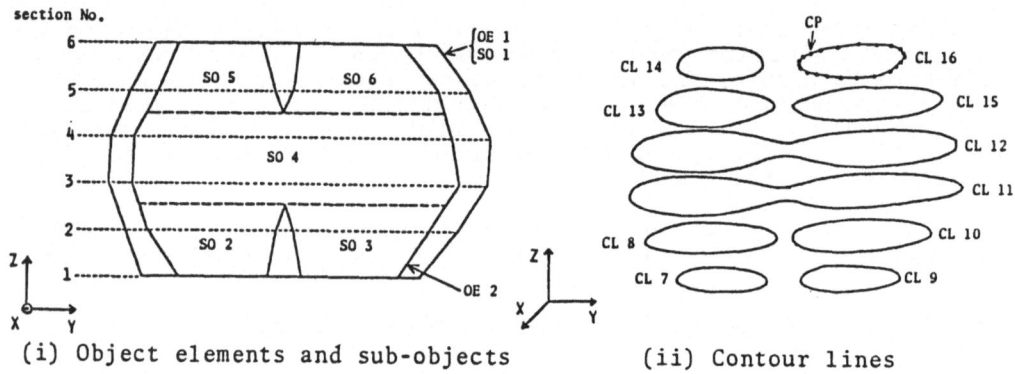

(i) Object elements and sub-objects   (ii) Contour lines

OE : object element
SO : sub-object
CL : contour line
CP : contour point

Fig.2 . Hierachical data structure.

2.2 Triangular Mesh Generation

In the proposed system, the triangular mesh generation is continued by checking if the generated mesh is appropriate or not. Therefore, the completed mesh is appropriate even if consecutive contour lines vary drastically. Cristiansen's algorithm on the contrary exhibits the following problems:

    (i) There exist defective triangles if two
    consecutive contour lines differ in the manner of
    Fig. 3.
    (ii) Clockwise and counterclockwise methods
    produce completely different reconstructions.

These problems stem from the fact that the triangular mesh generation begins from the closest pair of contour points (initial points) in the two contour lines. Then, a triangle is generated by connecting the adjacent point that is closest to one of the two initial points.

By investigating the defective triangles, it is found that one contour point is shared with many triangular elements. Moreover, the length of edges is much larger than the distance between the contour lines. This problem above may be avoided by introducing the following criterion :

    [Triangle Criterion]

For each triangle edge (shared by two triangles)
the shortest of the possible candidates is selected.

The criterion discards the segment $b_4 t_3$ in Fig.3, because it is longer
than the segment $b_4 t_6$. Instead, b_3 and t_4 are connected. Fig.4
illustrates the improved result over Fig. 3, showing the merit of the
criterion.

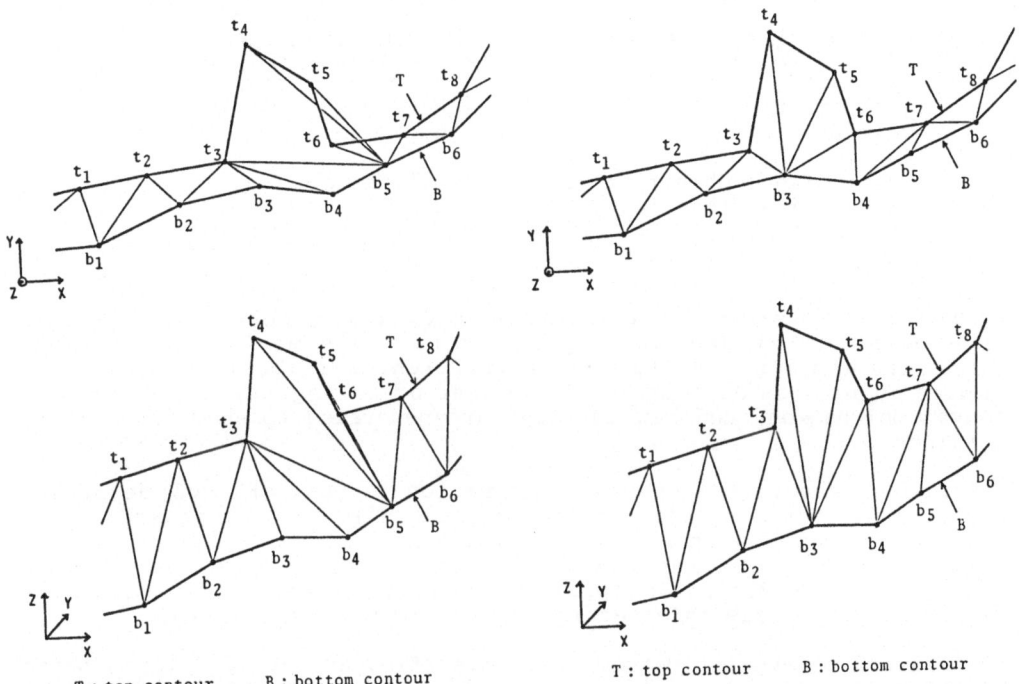

T : top contour   B : bottom contour

Fig.3 Application of
Christiansen's method to
contours of drastic shape
change。

Fig.4 Application of proposed
method to contours of drastic
shape change。

2.3 Open Contour Lines

If cross-sections include open regions such as a mouth there exist
open contour lines. Two combinations of consecutive cross-sections
are possible as shown in Fig. 5. For (a), both cross-sections are
open, and the triangular mesh generation is initiated with one terminal point from each section (P_1 and Q_1). For (b), one cross-section
is open, and one closed. This case is treated by first locating the
point P_i where the bifurcation occurs. Then the pair P_i and Q_1 are
used as the initial point for triangular mesh generation, and the
process ends at the pair P_i and Q_m.

Bifurcation points are located as follows (see Fig. 5):
   (1) The cross-sections are translated so that their centers
   line up.
   (2) P_j, the contour point nearest to Q_1, and P_k, the contour
   point nearest to Q_m, are located.
   (3) The point P_i ($k \le i \le j$), which satisfies $\overline{P_{i-1} Q_m} < \overline{P_{i-1} Q_1}$ and
$\overline{P_i Q_m} > \overline{P_i Q_1}$, is taken to be the bifurcation point.

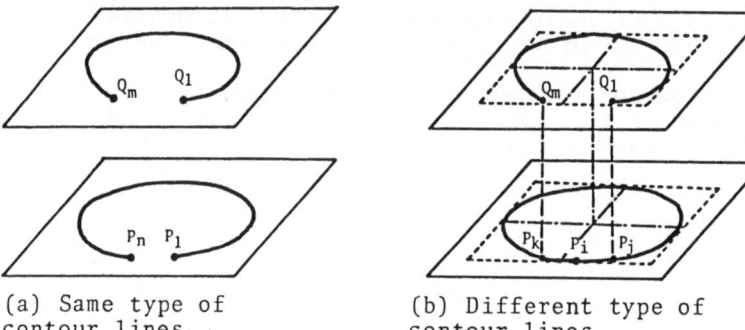

(a) Same type of
contour lines.

(b) Different type of
contour lines.

Fig.5 Two combinations of contour lines on
consecutive cross-sections.

2.4 Cut View

Appropriate cut-away views often facilitate better and easier
observation. This operation provides new information on the inner
structure and inter-relations of different surfaces. We allow the
entire object, as described by a number of triangles, to be cut by a
convex polyhedron, and new surfaces are generated to show the cutting
surfaces.

The basic idea of the cut-away operation is that the volume of the
object intersected by the cutting polyhedron is to be removed. Each
triangular patch of the object can be classified as lying totally
inside, totally outside, or intersecting the cutting polyhedron.
Those lying outside are displayed unchanged, those lying inside are
discarded, and those intersecting must be further processed.

Intersected triangular patches are classified as one of 7 types based
on the number of intersections with the polyhedron and the number of
vertices of the triangle contained within the polyhedron (See Fig.6).
Classifications 2' and 3' are also used for triangles which intersect
two edges of the polyhedron.

As shown in Fig 6, for each class of triangle, the shaded area is
removed (except for Type 7, where the area is considered neglectably
small), and the remaining area of the triangle is divided into new
triangles, as shown by the dotted lines. This helps simplify further
processing.

An efficient priority table technique, explained in Section 3, is used
for display. The efficiency of this application of the priority
table derives from the fact that the data is already partitioned
(because of the cross-sections) into parallel layers. We must be
careful to generate the new cut surfaces in the same way. Fig. 7
illustrates the generation of new surface elements for a pair of
concentric cylinders with an angular wedge cut away.

3. DISPLAY METHOD

3.1 Priority Table for Display

A test of depth from the view point is required for semi-transparent

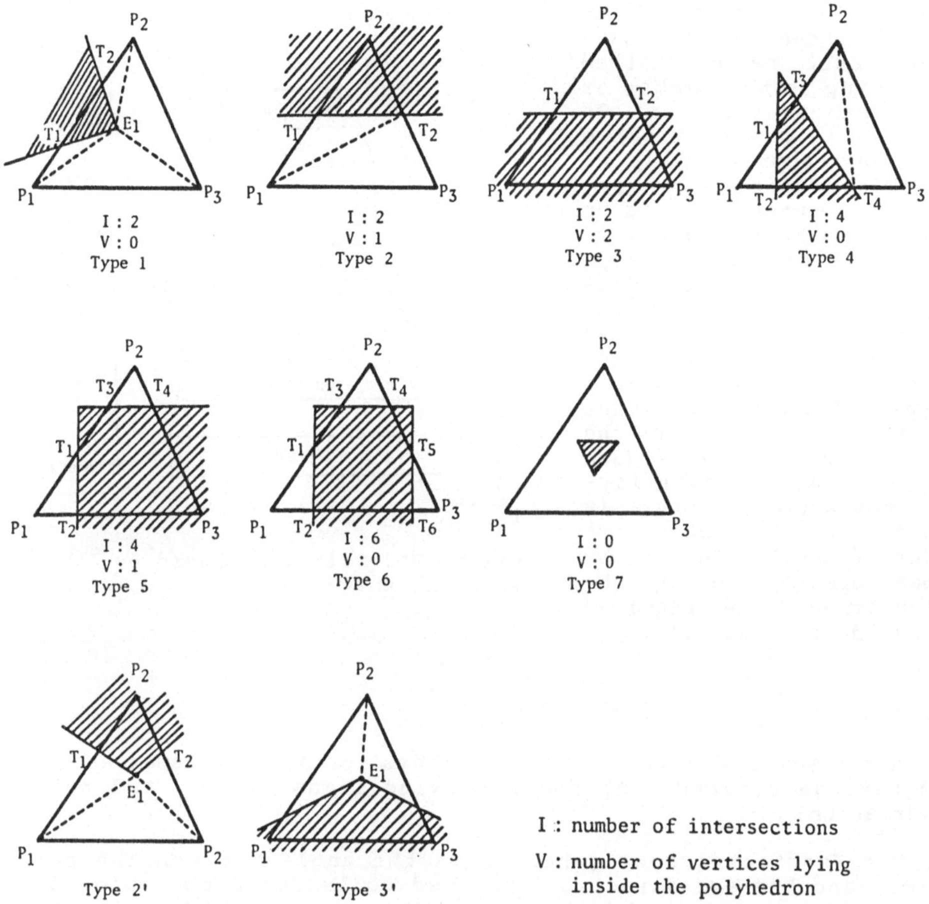

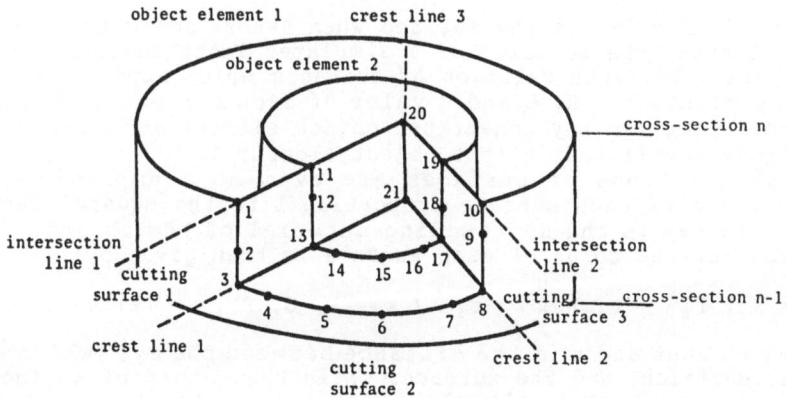

P₂ T₂ T₁ E1 P₁ P₃
I : 2
V : 0
Type 1

P₂ T₁ T₂ P₁ P₃
I : 2
V : 1
Type 2

P₂ T₁ T₂ P₁ P₃
I : 2
V : 2
Type 3

P₂ T₃ T₁ P₁ T₂ T₄ P₃
I : 4
V : 0
Type 4

P₂ T₃ T₄ T₁ P₁ T₂ P₃
I : 4
V : 1
Type 5

P₂ T₃ T₄ T₁ T₅ P₁ T₂ T₆ P₃
I : 6
V : 0
Type 6

P₂ P₁ P₃
I : 0
V : 0
Type 7

P₂ T₁ T₂ E₁ P₁ P₂
Type 2'

P₂ E₁ P₁ P₃
Type 3'

I : number of intersections

V : number of vertices lying
inside the polyhedron

Fig.6 Classification of triangular elements divided by
a polyhedron.

object element 1   crest line 3

object element 2

20
cross-section n

11
12 21 19 18
1   10
intersection   9   intersection
line 1   line 2
cutting   2 13
surface 1 3 14 15 16 17
4   5   6   7   8   cutting ___ cross-section n-1
surface 3
crest line 1   crest line 2

cutting
surface 2

Fig.7 Generation of new surfaces in cutting operation.

display because the displayed intensity of surfaces must be diminished according to the number of intervening surfaces. In the usual priority table technique, approximately n^2 depth comparisons are required to enter n surfaces into the table. Here, we take advantage of the layered nature of our data (imposed by the original cross sections) to improve the efficiency. We enter surfaces into the table a layer at a time, in order of the distance of the layer from the eye (see Fig. 8). Within each layer, the surface number is stored in the table in order of depth. This technique greatly reduces the calculation time required to build the priority table.

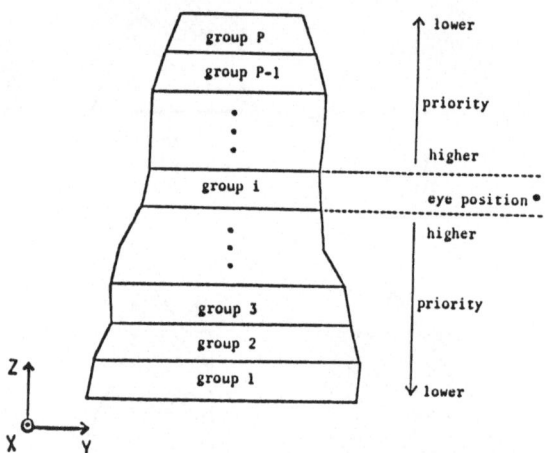

Fig.8 Priority test based on sectinal partition.

3.2 Semi-Transparent Display Method

We have researched a number of algorithms for semi-transparent display and have determined that the following leads to easy and reliable observation:

(1) The function $1/\cos\theta$ (where θ is the angle between the surface normal and the eye direction) is used to increase the color of the surface near edges and to decrease it near the eye position. The semi-transparent effect is emphasized by this method, and the shape of each object is easily understood. The color (R, G and B components) is calculated by the equation:

$$I_{k\theta} = I_{k0} / \cos(\theta-\alpha); \quad k=R, G, B. \quad (1)$$

I_{k0} is the original color of the surface when $\theta=\alpha=0$, and α is an angle parameter to control the position of a simulated light source.
(2) To make clear the depth relation of surfaces which appear overlaid from the view point, the R, G and B value of each surface is multiplied by t_i each time the ray penetrates object element i, where t_i is the transparency coefficient of the object element i.
(3) The depth relations of surfaces are even more emphasized by reducing the color of each surface proportional to the squared length of travel of the ray in the surrounding material of the object. The final equation for the color of each surface is then given by:

$$I_k = K (I_{k\theta} / r^2) \prod_{i=1}^{N}{}^{*} t_i \quad (k = R, G, B). \quad (2)$$

Where K is a constant and r is the distance between the eye (which may be set at any position) and the surface. N is the number of surfaces, and $\prod^{*}$ indicates that the multiplication takes place only if the surface is penetrated by the ray.
(4) Gouraud's smooth shading technique (1971) is applied in displaying the image. It smoothes over edges caused by the triangular mesh.

Thus, the observation becomes easier.

The proposed equations are evaluated by application to a simple set of objects, namely, a set of concentric cylinders. A pair of views has been produced to allow stereoscopic observation. The result demonstrates the semi-transparent effect, and the three-dimensional geometry is easily perceived (see Fig.9).

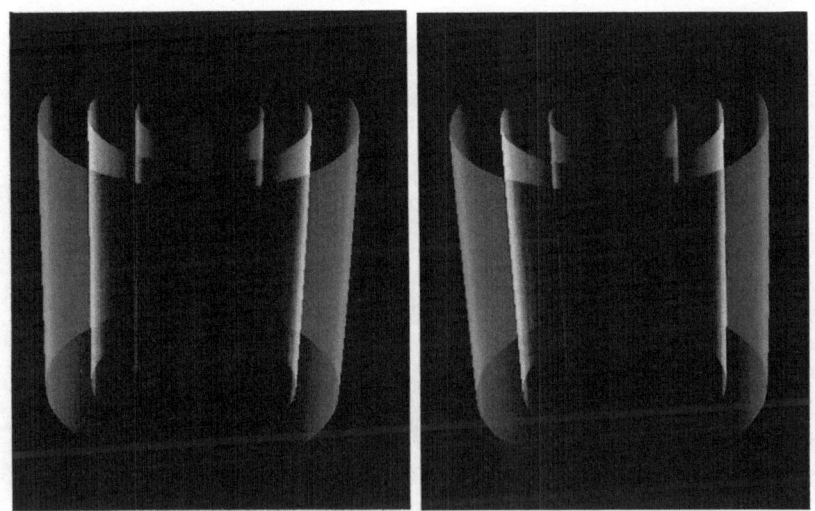

Fig.9   Semi-transparent stereographic display of concentric cylinders

3.3 Examples

The proposed system is applied to data from a mouse embryo. The data are composed of 69 cross-sections, and there are 8 object elements.

Fig.10 shows a stereoscopic representation of the entire object. $\alpha=0$, and each transparency coefficient t_i is set to 0.6. Detail near the center of the object is not easily observed in this representation. In Fig. 11, the angle parameter α is set to 90 degrees, and the surface of the object is more clearly observed. These examples demonstrate the effect of the angle parameter α.

Transparency coefficients may be used to emphasize some particular object elements among others. Fig.12 shows the result when the transparency coefficient of an object element is set to zero and the angle parameter is 90 degrees. With this parameter choice, the representation of the specified object element is the same as that of conventional (non-semi-transparent) methods.

Treatment of open contour lines is shown in Fig.13. The mouth object element is emphasized in this example by lowering its transparency coefficient and altering the view angle, as discussed above.

The cutting operation was used to obtain the image in Fig.14. The data is of the head of a mouse embryo with a portion cut-away by a rectangular solid. If it is desired to view the cutting surfaces, cut-away view with semi-transparent cut surfaces is displayed. Fig.15 demonstrates this application.

Appreciation of the size of each object element is made possible by
displaying scales along with the object image itself in stereoscopic
manner as shown in Fig. 16.   Various display options in our methods
have been illustrated separately in the current examples to demonstrate clearly each parameter's effect on the total image.   They may
be combined to produce the easiest and most reliable observation of
multi-layered structures.

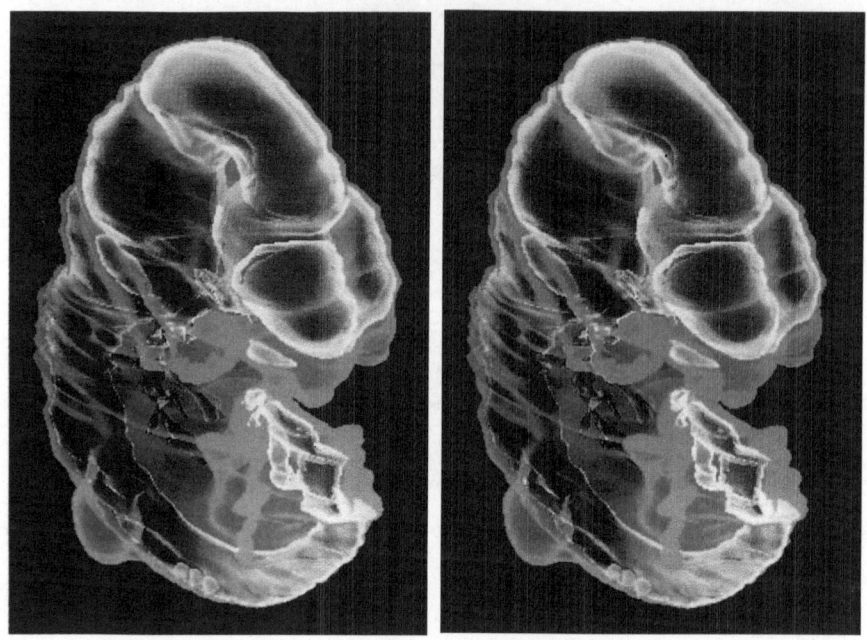

Fig.10   Semi-transparent stereographic display of mouse embryo

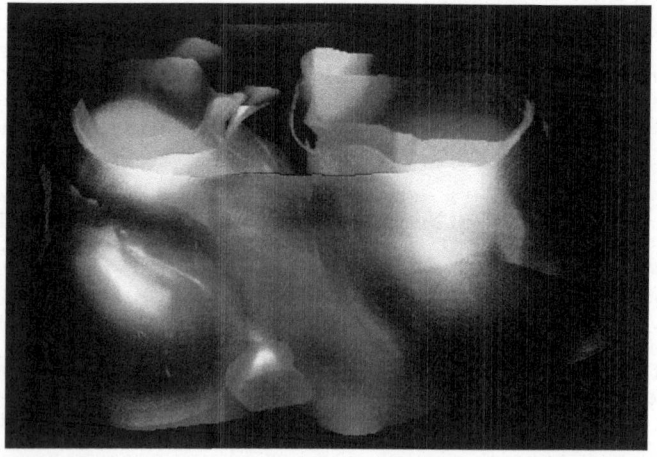

Fig.11   Effect of brightness phase

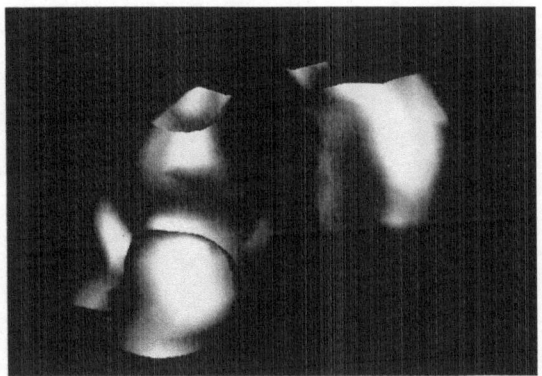

Fig.12 Selection of an object-element

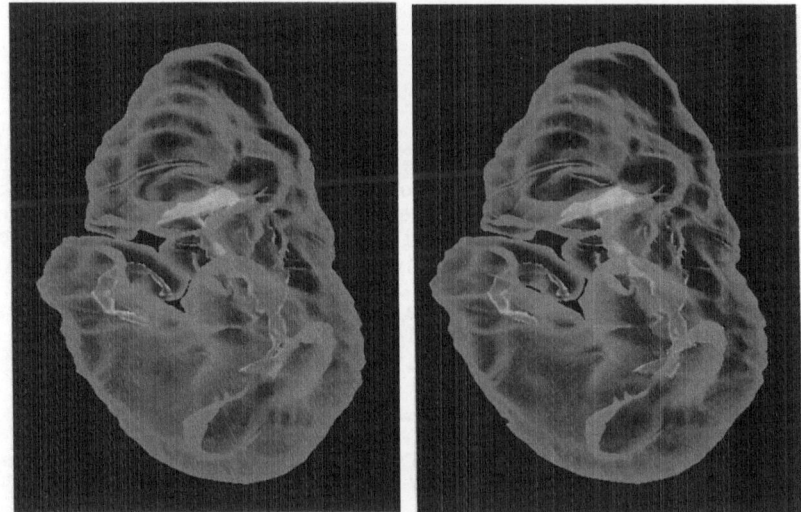

Fig.13 Semi-transparent stereographic display of mouth, which
includes open contours

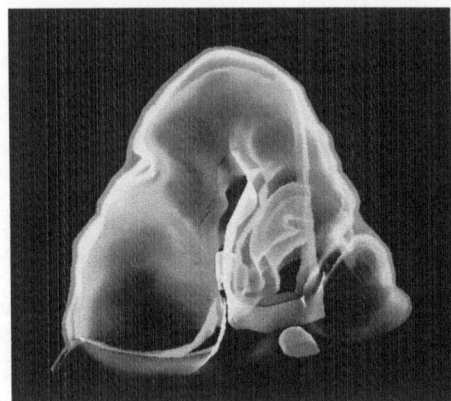

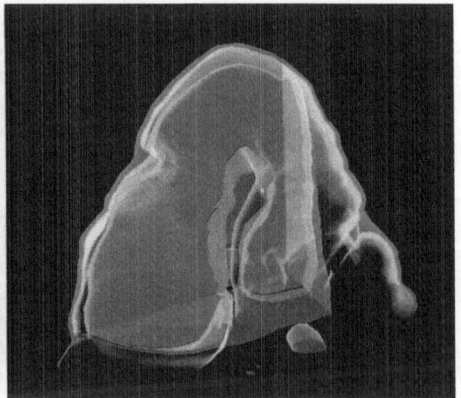

Fig.14 Cut-away view

Fig.15 Cut-away view with semi-
transparent cut surfaces

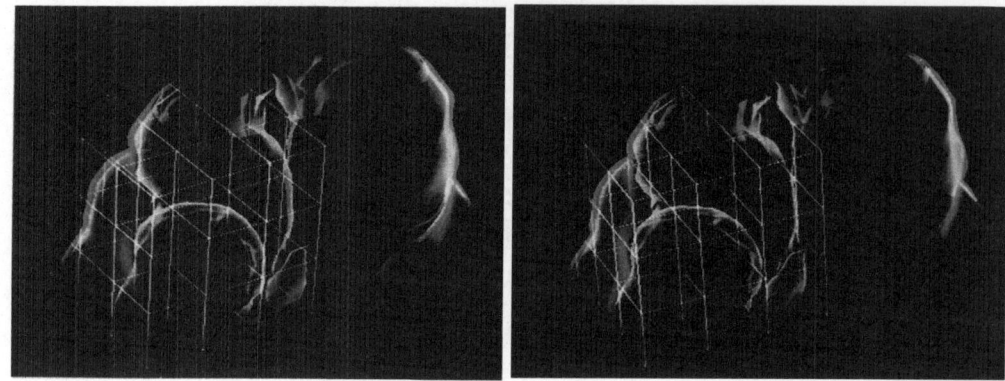

Fig.16   Display of an object along with three dimensional scales

4. CONCLUSIONS

A system of techniques has been proposed for reconstructing the
original object from multi-layered cross-section data and for
displaying it as a stereoscopic semi-transparent image. At the reconstruction step, the new sub-object oriented data structure enables
the handling of objects with multiple surfaces.   Even if sub-objects
exhibit branching, the original object is easily reconstructed.

The new triangular mesh generation technique guarantees good
triangular meshes even if consecutive cross-sections vary drastically.
Moreover, open contour lines may be processed, and the cutting
operation using a convex polyhedron allows better understanding of the
entire object.

Two control parameters, the transparency coefficients, and the light
source angle (Eqs. (1) and (2)) may be adjusted for ad hoc control of
the image to obtain the best image for specific observations.

ACKNOWLEDGMENTS

The authors wish to thank Bonnie G. Sullivan for going through and
commenting this manuscript.

REFERENCES

Christiansen H N and Sederberg T W (1978) Conversion of Complex
    Contour Line Definitions into Polygonal Element Mosaics, Proc. ACM
    SIGGRAPH'78, pp.187-192
Fuchs H, Kedem Z M and Uselton S P (1977) Optimal Surface Reconstruc-
    tion from Planar Contours, Comm. ACM 20(10), pp.693-702
Gouraud H (1971) Continuous Shading of Curved Surfaces, IEEE
    Transactions on Computers C-20(6), pp.623-628
Herman G T and Liu H K (1979) Three-Dimensional Display of Human
    Organs from Computed Tomograms, Computer Graphics and Image
    Processing 9, pp.1-21

379

Kay D S and Greenberg D (1979) Transparency for Computer Synthesized
   Images, Proc. ACM SIGGRAPH'79, pp.148-164
Nakamae E, Harada K, Kaneda K, Yasuda M and Sato A G (1985)
   Reconstruction and Semi-Transparent Stereographic Display of an
   Object consisting of Multi-Surfaces, Trans. IPSJ 26(1), pp.181-188
Newell M E, Newell R G and Sancha T L (1972) A New Approach to the
   Shaded Picture Problem, Proc. ACM Nat'l Conf.'72, pp.443-450
Sumi J, Yokoi S, Tsuruoka S and Miyake K (1981) A Three-Dimensional
   Display Method of a Human Head from Its CT Image Using Raster
   Graphic Display, IPSJ Workshop on Computer Vision 14-1
Sumi J, Yokoi S, Tsuruoka S and Miyake K (1982) A Three-Dimensional
   Display Method of a Human Head from Its CT Image Using Raster
   Graphic Display Part II, IPSJ Workshop on Computer Vision 19-7
Sungunoff A and Greenberg D (1978) Computer Generated Image for
   Medical Application, Proc. ACM SIGGRAPH'78, pp.196-202

Kazufumi Kaneda was born in Tottori Prefecture, Japan,
on October 1, 1959. He received the B.E. and M.E.
degrees in system engineering from Hiroshima University
in 1982 and 1984, respectively. After he graduated, he
worked at The Chugoku Electric Power Company Co.
Ltd., Japan, in 1984. From 1986 he is with the Faculty
of Engineering, Hiroshima University. At present, he
is a research associate. His current research
interests are in computer graphics and image
processing. He is a member of IEE of Japan, IPS of
Japan and IECE of Japan.
Address: Faculty of Engineering, Hiroshima University,
Saijo-cho, Higashi-hiroshima, 724 Japan.

Koichi Harada was born in Hiroshima, Japan, in June
1950. He received the B.E. in electrical engineering
from Hiroshima University, Hiroshima, Japan, in 1973,
and M.S. degree in electrical engineering and the Ph.
D. degree in 1975 and 1978, respectively, from Tokyo
Institute of Technology, Tokyo, Japan. He studied the
stability of ecological systems in TIT. After he
graduated, he worked at Takamatsu Technical College,
Kagawa, Japan, in 1978 and studied neural networks.
From 1979 he is with the Faculty of Engineering,
Hiroshima University. Now he is an assistant
professor. His research interests now are on data
interpolation and computer graphics. He is a member of ACM, IPS of
Japan, IEE of Japan and IECE of Japan.
Address: Faculty of Engineering, Hiroshima University, Saijo-cho,
Higashi-hiroshima, 724 Japan.

Eihachiro Nakamae was born in Hiroshima Prefecture, Japan, on April 11, 1929. He received the B.E., M.E. and D.E. degrees in 1954, 1956 and 1967, respectively, all from Waseda Universirty. He was appointed as Research Associate in 1956 and Professor in 1968 of the Fuculty of Engineering, Hiroshima University. He was Associate Researcher at Clarkson College of Technology, Potsdam, N.Y. in 1973-1974. His research interests include computer graphics and electric machinery. Dr. Nakamae is a member of IEEE, IEE of Japan, IPS of Japan and IECE of Japan.
Address: Faculty of Engineering, Hiroshima University, Saijo-cho, Hogashi-hiroshima, 724 Japan.

Mineo Yasuda is a professor of anatomy at Hiroshima University School of Medicine. His main interest area is teratology, the science of abnormal development of the individual. He intended to utilize computer graphics in his research and teaching, and began a collaborative study with Professor Nakamae in 1982. He served as president of the Japanese Teratology Society (JTS) in 1982-83, and is a director and a councillor of the JTS. He also serves as the associate editor of CONGENITAL ANOMALIES, the official journal of the JTS, and as the liaison editor of TERATOLOGY, an international journal published in the U.S. Yasuda received his M.D. in 1962, and Dr.Med.Sci. in 1975 from Kyoto University.
Address: Department of Anatomy, Hiroshima University School of Medicine, Kasumi 1-2-3, Minami-ku, Hiroshima, 734 Japan.

Akinao G. Sato is currently one of the teaching staffs in the Department of Anatomy, Hiroshima University School of Medicine. Since 1981, he has been working to establish a new system for teaching anatomy in which various kinds of stereoscopic photos, including X-ray photos as well as scanning electron microphotos, are fully utilized. His recent work is to provide some useful stereoscopic photos of the computer-reconstructed three-dimensional images from the microscopic serial sections of mammalian embryos under the collaboration with the Electric Machinery Laboratory, Hiroshima University. He received his BSc, MSc and DPh in zoology from Kyoto University in 1961, 1963, and 1968.
Address: Department of Anatomy, Hiroshima University School of Medicine, Kasumi 1-2-3, Minamiku, Hiroshima, 734 Japan.

Frequency Modulation Synthesis

Masa Inakage

ABSTRACT
The presence of texture substantially increases the reality in the synthesized image. However, the synthesis of texture has been computationally expensive. This paper describes a method for texture synthesis by means of frequency modulation. Frequency modulation synthesis technique is an inexpensive approach to approximate complex waveforms. A waveform is frequency-modulated by another waveform. This modulation process produces sideband frequncies which occur at multiples of the modulation frequency. The sidebands add complexity to the initial waveform. Only a few control parameters are required to control the frequency modulation. Natural phenomena such as clouds, terrain, and aurora borealis can also be synthesized.

keywords: texture, image synthesis, waveform, natural phenomena

1. INTRODUCTION
The addition of texture to a smoothly rendered surface produces highly realistic images. The texture can be functionally defined or scanned from the actual data. Mapping techniques are used for surface texturing of smooth surfaces in the image rendering. 2D texture mapping maps certain informations of the texture onto 3D rendered surfaces [4,10], while solid mapping uses 3D texture information to map onto 3D surfaces [14]. The texture can contain a number of surface attributes such as surface color [4], surface normal (known as "bump mapping") [3], specularity (known as "reflection mapping") [2], transparency [8], and surface displacement [5].

A number of techniques have been developed for texture generation. Stochastic techniques are employed in several texture synthesis techniques [7,9,11,12,17,18]. These techniques are suited for texture synthesis of spectrally irregular textures. Functional techniques have also received attention for texture synthesis. Schachter [16] used sums of a few long-crested, narrow-band waveforms. To avoid the regularities of the synthesized texture, stochastic parameters were added to the synthesis. Max [13] used the additive synthesis of linear wave fronts. These methods are either computationally expensive or memory intensive. Perlin [15] combined functions to achieve realistic textures. This approach provided an interactive image and texture generation environment, but different functions were required for different texture generations.

Intricate textures contain complex waveforms. The goal of this paper is the synthesis of complex waveforms. By Fourier analysis, complex waveforms can be separated into sums of sinusoids. Hence, sums of multiple sinusoids can effectively generate complex waveforms. This method is called the additive synthesis. The additive synthesis is computationally expensive [1].

This paper presents a texture synthesis algorithm called the frequency modulation synthesis. The frequency modulation synthesis is widely used in the digital sound synthesis domain [1,6]. The advantage of the frequency modulation synthesis is its simplicity for control and the inexpensive computation. The basic model of this algorithm requires only 2 simple sinusoids with a few control parameters for generating complex waveforms. A sinusoid frequency-modulates another sinusoid, which effectively produces sideband frequencies. These sidebands create complex waveforms from a simple sinusoid.

2. ALGORITHM
2.1 The Basic Model
The basic model assumes that a texture is one dimensional and composed of complex waveforms which are sums of sinusoids. Instead of summing large number of sinusoids to achieve complex waveforms, the frequency modulation technique is introduced.

A simple sinusoid is denoted by

$$y = a \sin(\theta) \ (0 \le \theta \le 2\pi)$$

By substituting $\theta = \omega t$, the equation is expressed as

$$y = a \sin(\omega t)$$

where a is the amplitude, and ω is the angular frequency in radian per second. The frequency modulation technique modulates a sinusoid by another sinusoid. $\theta = \omega_1 t + a_2 \sin(\omega_2 t)$ is substituted into the equation, the equation then becomes

$$y = a_1 \sin(\omega_1 t + a_2 \sin(\omega_2 t))$$

where a_1 is the amplitude of the carrier waveform, a_2 is the amplitude of the modulation waveform, ω_1 is the angular frequency of the carrier waveform, and ω_2 is the angular frequency of the modulation waveform.

The angular frequencies ω_1 and ω_2 can be rewritten in terms of frequencies

$$\omega_1 = 2\pi f_c \text{ and } \omega_2 = 2\pi f_m$$

where f_c is the carrier frequency, and f_m is the modulation frequency. The basic model of the frequency modulation synthesis is defined by

$$f(x) = a(x) \sin(2\pi f_c x + I(x) \sin(2\pi f_m x))$$

where a(x) is the amplitude of the waveform and I(x) is called the modulation index. Here, a(x) controls the overall amplitude in x-axis which acts as an envelope of the waveform.

The modulation index I(x), or the amplitude of the modulating waveform, determines the amount of modulation applied to the carrier waveform. The peak deviation of the carrier waveform due to the frequency modulation synthesis is the multiplication of the modulation index and the modulating waveform frequency. For example, when the carrier frequency at 10,000 Hz is modulated by the modulation frequency at 1,000 Hz with the modulation index 4, the output frequency deviates between 10,000 Hz ± 4,000 Hz. As the modulation index increases, the deviation of the output frequency deviates bewteen a wider range. The modulation creates multitples of sideband frequencies which add complexity to the initial waveform. Figure 1 is an example of the frequency modulation synthesis which is used for calculating the intensity of the pixel for a given x-axis location.

Fig. 1 Frequency-modulated sinusoid

383

2.2 Sequence

The basic model of the frequency modulation synthesis provides complex waveforms, but the level of complexity may not be sufficient for purposes such as texture synthesis. To accomplish further complexity to the waveform provided by the basic model, the concept of "sequence" is introduced. Here, the "sequence" is defined as a method of connecting multiples of the basic model. By sequencing the basic model, infinite variations of connection become available.

The basic model can be denoted as figure 2. Each block is called a "module" which has an input and an output. A module is a function of sinusoid at a certain frequency. The input waveform frequency-modulates the sinusoid of the module. If there is no input waveform coming in to the module, the output waveform of the module is a non-modulated waveform. Modules may be connected in series and in parallel.

Two typical examples of serial sequences are explained. Figure 3a shows the sequence of the modulation frequency f_{m1} being modulated by another modulation frequency f_{m2}. Since the modulation waveform adds the complexity to the carrier waveform, a complex modulation waveform is generated by this double frequency modulation technique. The carrier waveform is now frequency-modulated by a complex waveform instead of a simple sinusoid. An output example is shown in figure 4. Notice the difference between figure 1 and figure 4. The pattern of figure 4 is more complex than the pattern attained in figure 1. Figure 3b is another example of serial sequence. This technique provides similar effect that is generated by figure 3a. The modulation frequency is modulated in order to create complex waveform which is then used to frequency-modulate the carrier waveform. In this case, the modulation frequency is looped so that it is frequency-modulated by itself. This feedback process generates complex patterns.

Fig. 2 Sequence flow chart of the basic model

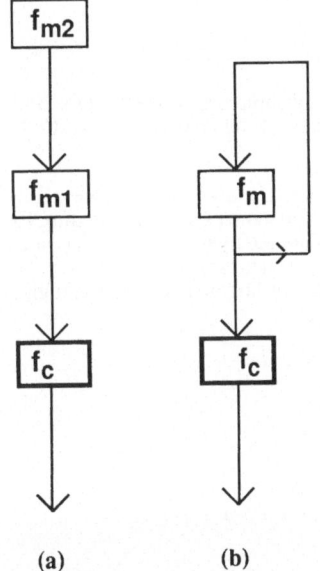

(a) (b)

Fig. 3(a) Frequency modulation of modulation frequency,(b) recursive frequency modulation of modulation frequency.

Fig. 4 Serially sequenced frequency modulation

The modules can be also connected in parallel. Figure 5a shows a parallel connection scheme where a non-modulated waveform is added with a frequency-modulated waveform. This technique is an additive synthesis with a simple sinusoid and a complex waveform. Depending on the ratio in the additive process, the non-modulated simple sinusoid dominates the waveform. From a texture point of view, the pattern will possess strong sinusoidal wave. However, if two frequency-modulated waveforms are sequenced in parallel as shown in figure 5b, the output becomes complex. As the sequence combinations increase, the output texture becomes more complex, and it will approach a noise.

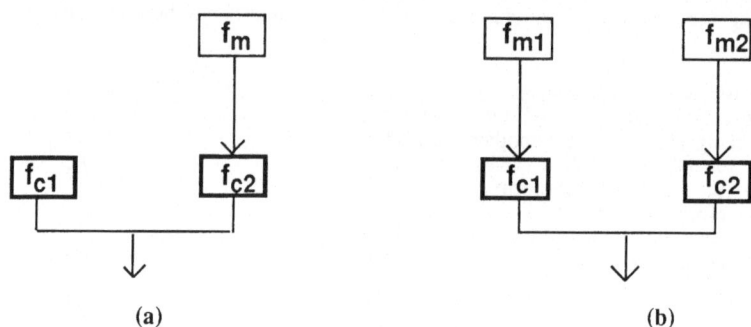

(a)   (b)

Fig. 5 (a) Summation of a frequency modulation and a sinusoid, (b) summation of 2 frequency modulated basic models.

3. 2D TEXTURE SYNTHESIS

The frequency modulation synthesis is extended to the two dimensional model for the texture generation. The formula can be expressed as

$$f(x,y) = a(x,y) \sin(2\pi f_c p(x,y) + I(x,y) \sin(2\pi f_m p(x,y)))$$

where $p(x,y)$ is a point on the plane.

If the frequency modulation synthesis outputs a texture with high frequency components, the Nyquist limit may be exceeded depending on the sampling resolution. Generally, the sampling resolution is set to the screen resolution. For such cases, filtering process is applied [10].

Since the function is sampled to the display resolution, the levels of detail can be easily achieved by controlling the sampling frequency. The frequency modulation synthesis guarantees a smooth texture for zooming in to the detailed area. The output $f(x,y)$ can be used to modulate parameters such as the pixel intensity, transparency, specularity, and color. This paper will describe a method for two dimensional tetxure synthesis of the pixel intensity. The explanation is focussed on the orthogonal model, although it can be easily adopted to the radial model for applications such as wave textures.
The intensity H for a given pixel $p(x,y)$ may be obtained from

$$H = H_x + H_y \qquad (-1.0 \le H \le 1.0)$$

where

$$H_x = a(x) \sin(2\pi f_c x + I(x) \sin(2\pi f_m x))$$
$$H_y = a(y) \sin(2\pi f_c y + I(y) \sin(2\pi f_m y)) \qquad (-1.0 \le H_x, H_y \le 1.0)$$

To obtain the pixel intensity value, NEWH = H*level*. For 8-bit intensity resolution, *level* is 255. An alternative for NEWH is: NEWH = H(*level* / 2) + (*level* / 2). The latter equation sets the lowest value of NEWH to zero. An output is shown in figure 6. If the modulation index is increased, the pattern becomes irregular. However, the grid structure still dominates the texture due to its orthogonality. In order to avoid the grid pattern, the frequency modulation synthesis is used to control the phase of other frequency modulation modules. The sequence module structure do not limit itself to the frequency modulation. Parameters such as phase and amplitude of the waveform can be also modulated (figure 7).

Figure 8 is another example of sequenced frequency modulation synthesis with the phase modulation. Figure 9 is an example which the frequencies used in figure 8 is shifted to lower frequencies. Notice that both images have similar texture quality, but figure 9 is not a simple magnification of figure 8.

4. APPLICATIONS: Clouds and Aurora Borealis

Gardner has produced clouds with varying transparency to the texture-mapped ellipsoids [8]. His texture synthesis function is based on the additive synthesis of sinusoids. The additive synthesis technique is expensive because many trigonometric calculations are demanded. To achieve the texture pattern for clouds, the frequency modulation synthesis may be used. The two dimensional texture is mapped on to the sphere or ellipsoid, and then the ellipsoid is digitally composited with transparency function of the texture. Figure 10 shows a cloud texture mapped onto the sphere. Minimal specularity and maximum diffused and ambient light functions are used for the shading parameters. Figure 11 is an example of clouds that is generated by digitally compositing the background sky and the textured sphere.

Aurora borealis can be characterized by its veil-like shape and transparency. To obtain the veil-like appearance, a low frequency carrier wave is set to dominate the output waveform. In order to vary the veil, a frequency-modulated waveform is used to control the phase of the modulation frequency in the basic model. The pixel intensity of the output texture determines the transparency value for the image compositing process. Figure 12 is an example of the synthesized aurora borealis.

Figure 13, "Beyond", is an art work where the frequency modulation synthesis is used to generate the aurora borealis, terrain map of the planet, clouds surrounding the planet, flame-like texture, and the artificial texture of the floor and the wall. The specularity and illumination maps are also synthesized by the frequency modulation synthesis.

Fig. 6 2 Dimensional texture by orthogonal approach

Fig. 7 Frequency modulation with phase modulation

Fig. 8 Serially connected frequency modulation with phase modulation

Fig. 9 Serially connected frequency modulation with phase modulation
using low frequency waveforms

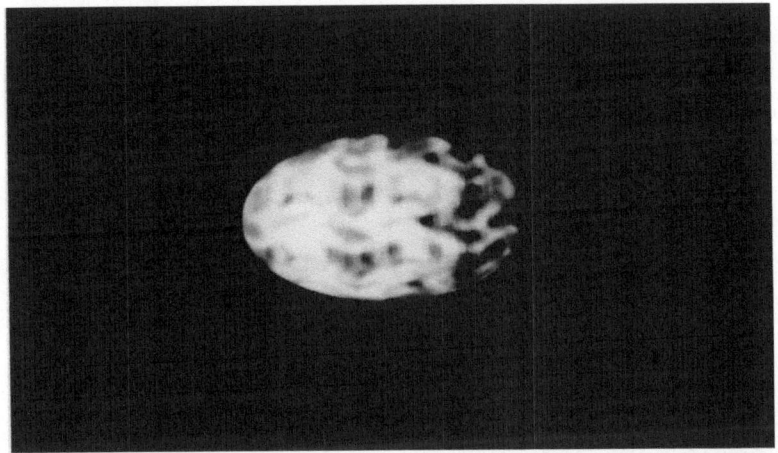

Fig. 10 Texture mapped sphere

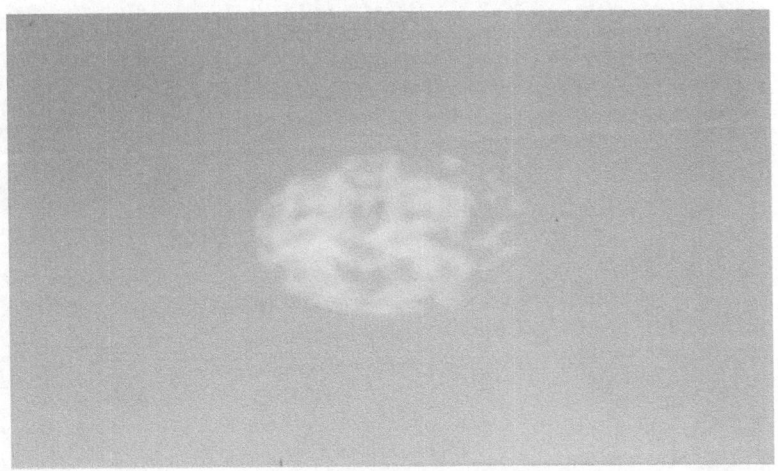

Fig. 11 Synthesized clouds

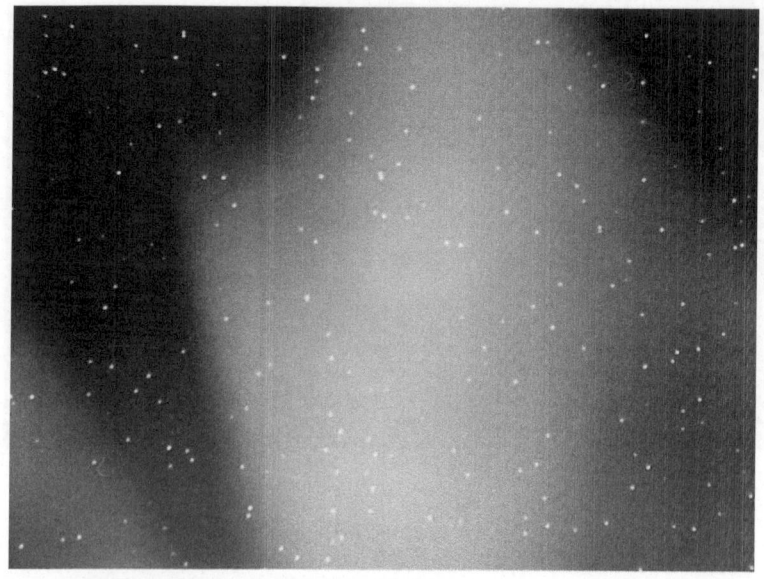

Fig.12 Synthesized aurora borealis

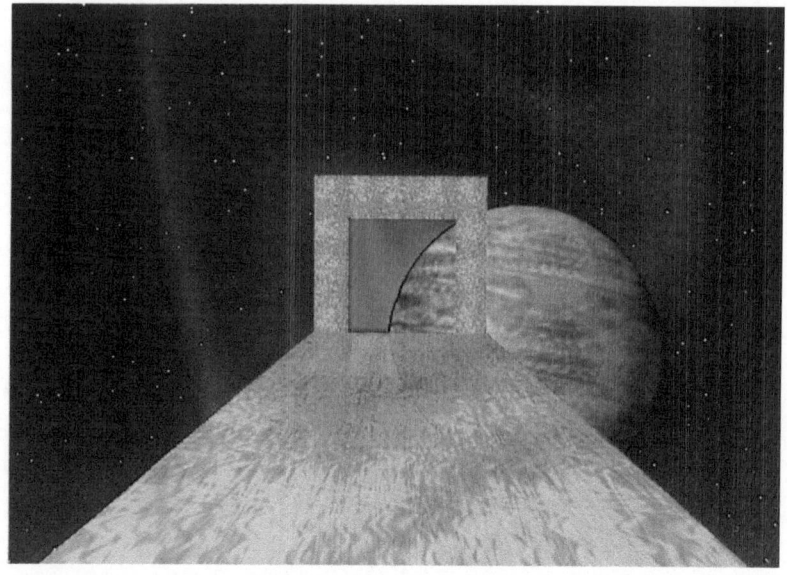

Fig. 13 Art work: "Beyond"

5. DISCUSSIONS

The frequency modulation synthesis can generate various patterns of complex waveforms. A "square" wave can be generated using the basic model by setting the modulation frequency f_m and the carrier frequency f_c to be $f_m = 2f_c$. A similar waveform can be achieved with the additive synthesis by summing

$$f(x) = \sum_{n=1}^{\infty} \sin(2\pi f_c(2n - 1)x)$$

This comparison of the additive synthesis and the frequency modulation synthesis shows that the frequency modulation synthesis can attain similar waveform with much less calculations.

The disadvantage of the frequency modulation synthesis is the difficulty of refining the waveform. Precise patterns are difficult to achieve with the frequency modulation synthesis while an approximated pattern can be easily achieved. This problem may be disregarded for texture synthesis of clouds, aurora borealis and waves because such textures require only the overall 'look' of the pattern.

For further research of this algorithm, the frequency modulation synthesis can be extended to the three dimensional model for applications such as height fields of ocean waves, landscapes, and solid texture generations.

6. CONCLUSIONS

The frequency modulation synthesis is applied to the texture synthesis. The frequency modulation synthesis requires very few parameters to define complex waveforms. This technique yields complex waveforms at relatively low cost compared to the existing algorithms such as the additive synthesis. Infinite variations can be made to the frequency modulation synthesis technique to achieve various effects. In this paper, the notion of 'sequence' is introduced to attain the variations.

One of the disadvantages with the use of frequency modulation synthesis is the difficulty of refining the waveform. Complex waveforms can be synthesized easily, but it is difficult to modify the waveform to match the precisely defined pattern. The algorithm is suited for non-precise textures. Another problem with this algorithm is the regularity in the pattern. The problem of regularity is the problem of non-stochastic synthesis algorithms. In this paper, the regularity is avoided by sequencing multiples of modules and by incorporating phase and amplitude modulation techniques into the frequency modulation synthesis. Nevertheless, the frequency modulation synthesis can produce interesting textures and phenomena such as clouds, terrain landscape, and aurora borealis.

Acknowledgements

The author would like to thank Noriyoshi Tezuka of IMÆDIA Corporation for photographic support. The images were rendered with YDK IM-9800 frame buffer.

References

[1] Batesman, W.A., *Introduction to Computer Music*, John Wiley & Sons Inc., New York, 1980.

[2] Blinn, J.F. and Newell, M.E., "Texture and Reflection in Computer Generated Images," *Comm. ACM 19*, 10, 1976, pp.542-547.

[3] Blinn, J.F., "Simulation of Wrinkled Surfaces," *Computer Graphics 12*, 3, 1978, pp.286-292.

[4] Catmull, E., "A Subdivision Algorithm for Computer Display of Curved Surfaces," Ph.D Dissertation, University of Utah, 1974.

[5] Cook, R.L., "Shade Trees," *Computer Graphics 18*, 3, 1984, pp.223-231.

[6] Chowning, J., "The Synthesis of Complex Audio Spectra by Means of Frequency Modulation," *Journ. of the AES 21*, 7, 1973, pp.526-534.

[7] Fournier A., Fussell, D., and Carpenter, L., "Computer Rendering of Stochastic Models," *Comm. ACM 25*, 6, 1982, pp.371-384.

[8] Gardner, G.Y., "Visual Simulation of Clouds," *Computer Graphics 19*, 3, 1985, pp.297-303.

[9] Haruyama, S. and Barsky, B.A., "Using Stochastic Modeling for Texture Generation," *IEEE Computer Graphics and Appl.*, March 1984, pp.7-19.

[10] Heckbert, P., "Survey of Texture Mapping," *IEEE Computer Graphics and Appl.*, Nov. 1986, pp.56-67.

[11] Lewis, J.P., "Texture Synthesis for Digital Painting," *Computer Graphics 18*, 3, 1984, pp.245-252.

[12] Lewis, J.P., "Methods for Stochastic Spectral Synthesis," *Graphics Interface 86 Proceedings*, pp.173-179.

[13] Max, N.L., "Vectorized Procedural Models for Natural Terrain: Waves and Islands in the Sunset," *Computer Graphics 15*, 3, 1981, pp.371-324.

[14] Peachey, D.R., "Solid Texturing of Complex Surfaces," *Computer Graphics 19*, 3, 1985, pp.279-286.

[15] Perlin, K., "An Image Synthesizer," *Computer Graphics 19*, 3, 1985, pp.287-296.

[16] Schachter, B., "Long Crested Wave Models," *Computer Graphics and Image Proc.*, 12, 1980, pp.187-201.

[17] Schachter, B. and Ahuja, N., "Random Pattern Generation Processes," *Computer Graphics and Image Proc.*, 10, 1979, pp.95-114.

[18] Voss, R., "Random Fractal Forgeries," SIGGRAPH 85 tutorial notes.

Masa Inakage is currently a freelance media artist and researcher. From 1985-1986, he was an executive producer at Japan Computer Graphics Lab., Inc., Tokyo. His research interests include graphics software for animation and various image synthesis tools for computer graphics art. He received his B.A. from Oberlin College, Ohio and M.F.A. in Video Art from California College of Arts and Crafts. He has been developing ray tracing algorithms, animation system, and image synthesis algorithms at the Media Lab., MIT. His art works and papers have been published internationally.

Adress: Masa Inakage, 23-12, Nakane 1-chome, Apt. 20-D, Meguro-ku, Tokyo, 152 Japan

Chapter 8

Graphics Interfaces, Languages and Databases

HutWindows

An Improved Architecture for a User Interface Management System

Marja-Riitta Koivunen and Martti Mäntylä

ABSTRACT

The design of HutWindows, a user interface management system intended for applications in mechanical computer-aided design is described. HutWindows features a three-layered internal architecture, where the presentation, dialogue control, and application processing layers are clearly separated from each other. This leads to increased simplicity and flexibility in user interface design over the more traditional situation where all of these layers are closely coupled.

Keywords and phrases: User Interface Management System, Logical Input Devices, Dialogue Control, Finite State Machines, Distributed Processing

1. INTRODUCTION

Everyone using computers has surely sometimes wished that the computer could understand our intentions without clumsy input devices and irritating dialogues which make us hope we could go back to the time of pencil and paper. To make this possible we would need communication means resembling telepathy. Unfortunately, these are not yet available in the stores, and we have to submit to more conventional techniques for the user interfaces and put our effort to improving human-machine interaction.

One area that has a lot of significance in making user-friendly techniques available to end-users is the development of tools for user interface design and implementation. Good tools will help the designers to be effective enough so that characteristics of different applications and users can be taken into account. They also encourage prototyping of user interfaces, and make the cost of improving an existing interface smaller.

So-called User Interface Management Systems (UIMS) [18, 21] are intended to offer a collection of user interface development tools to a designer, and to take responsibility for the operation of the user interface. Unfortunately the concept of the UIMS is still a vague one, and many mutually inconsistent approaches exist [2, 3, 8, 16, 17, 19].

Existing approaches to UIMS can be broadly classified in two families [21]. So-called internal control UIMS takes the form of a procedure library including user interface tools. These are activated under the control of the application program. In contrast, external control UIMS assumes a total responsibility of the operation of the interface, and calls the application procedures to perform application-oriented tasks. Hence the control resides in the user interface, not in the application.

Since 1984, our group has been involved in a research program for distributed CAD systems for mechanical applications. The importance of user interface tools was soon realized in the group. This paper describes the overall architecture of HutWindows, an external control type of a UIMS that resulted from this activity.

Our aim while developing HutWindows was to give the user the opportunity to influence her/his working environment not just in theory but also in practice. To ensure this, we wanted to give the user interface designer more powerful concepts for designing logical input operations and specifying dialogues than for instance those of GKS [7]. We also wanted the applications and user interfaces to be machine-independent. To encourage this, HutWindows includes a high level language HDL (HutWindows Definition Language) for defining the user interfaces.

In the architecture of HutWindows the user interface and the application are strictly separated from each other. In fact, they are implemented as two concurrent processes running in parallel. This makes the user interface independent of the application so that it can be modified without touching the application. This is unlike for example in [8], where some of the application data structures are visible to the user interface. In HutWindows the role of the application is to be a modeless program that executes the algorithms requested by the user through the user interface. Modelessness in an application is an equally desirable aim as in a user interface [9, 20]; too many modes in the application confuse the application programmer, particularly when some time has passed since she/he looked at the code.

The outline of the paper is as follows: First, the ordinary use of FSM's is introduced in Section 2. Section 3 describes the architecture of HutWindows in more detail. Section 4 gives additional information on the implementation of HutWindows. Section 5 describes some of the extensions currently contemplated. Finally, Section 6 summarizes the results of our work so far.

2. FINITE STATE MACHINES FOR DIALOGUE CONTROL

The use of finite state machines for dialogue control in interactive systems has its roots deep in the history of interactive graphics; see e.g. [5, 15]. In ordinary implementations, the FSM is a directed graph where the states correspond to states or modes of the interactive system. The arcs in the graph are labeled with physical input events caused by the user. A transition from one state to another causes some predefined operations to be invoked.

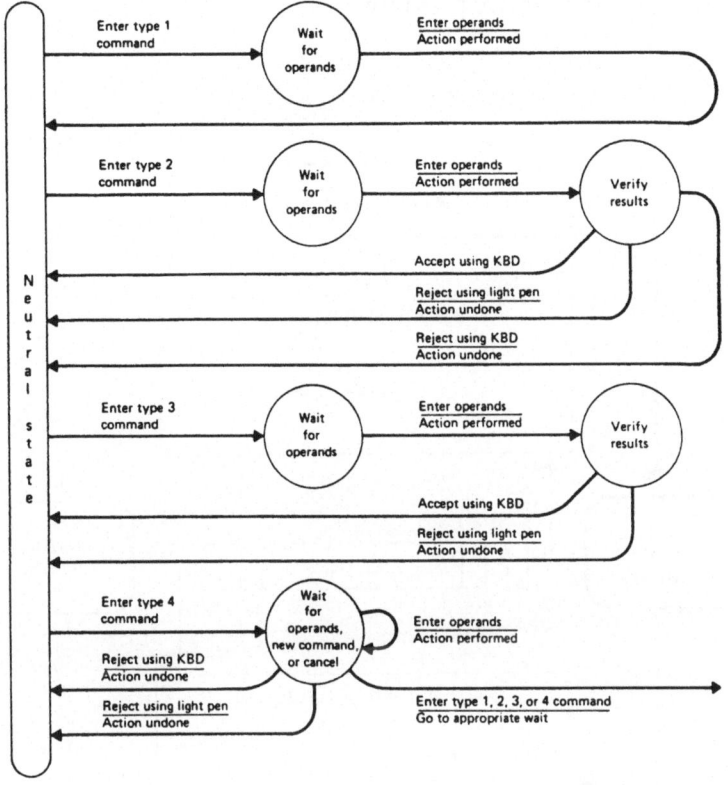

Fig. 1. A transition network [4]

In straightforward implementations the graph may easily become very cumbersome and difficult to define or modify. Because every possible action of the user must be described explicitly in the FSM, the number of states can become quite large even in relatively simple user interfaces. In particular, if the user has several possibilities in expressing a command, it must be handled in many locations of the FSM. So this desirable parallelism makes the size of the FSM even worse.

Another problem with straightforward uses of a FSM is that the kinds of possible dialogues is restricted. For example, a hierarchical structure of a system cannot be naturally expressed. Some improvements have been suggested to broaden the expressiveness of the FSM. For example, in [22] and [12] augmented transition networks have been used. However the problem of too low level input events still persists.

3. THE ARCHITECTURE OF HUTWINDOWS

3.1. Basics

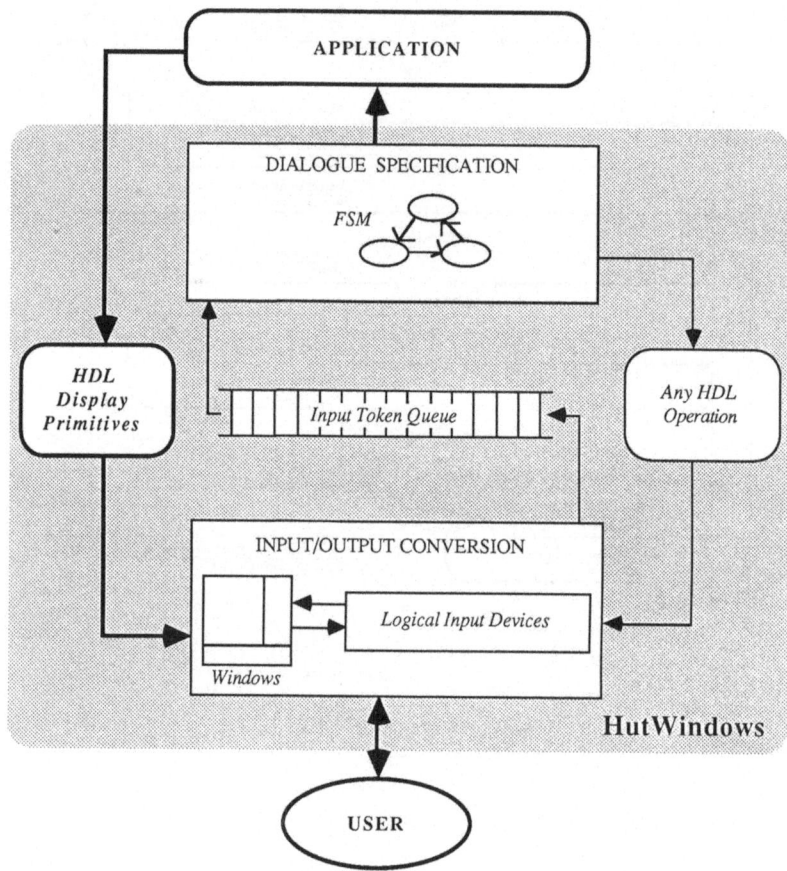

Fig. 2. Basic structure of HutWindows

HutWindows architecture consists of three layers, two layers in the user interface and one layer which is the HutWindows interface to the application. The user interface and the application are separate processes. The user interface is divided into a presentation part and a dialogue specification part to overcome the problems outlined in the above. The input conversion in the presentation part consists of high level logical input devices whose inputs are mapped to sequences of device independent input tokens buffered in an input token queue. The tokens are used to control the traversing of a FSM in the dialogue specification part.

By means of this additional layer of processing before the dialogue part, the dialogue specification of a user interface becomes independent not only from the application, but also from the logical input and output devices. This approach is similar to the division of labor in compilers [1], where the lexical and the syntactic processing are separated from the semantic processing.

To the arcs of the FSM, a sequence of HDL commands can be associated. These commands can modify the interpretation of user events in the presentation layer for instance by changing the layout or the means of interaction. Communication with the application process is achieved by sending character strings to the application by means of an explicit message operation and executing the primitives that are sent back. In this case the application process has control temporarily, but as soon as it sends acknowledgement or notifies an error to the user interface process, control goes back to the FSM. Further details are described in the following sections.

3.2. Window Layout

A HutWindows user interface takes the form of a rectangular area on the screen which is divided into windows with horizontal or vertical lines (Fig. 3). Each window is of a certain type, i.e. either a text, a graphics or an icon window. Empty windows can be used as placeholders for additional windows or just for esthetic reasons.

3.3. Input Operations

Communication with a window is achieved by associating some input operations with the window. The available input tools are predefined parameterized operations with which it is possible to generate input tokens. At the moment possible input operations are text, text key, icon key, menu key and function key input.

Text input can always be typed from a keyboard by defining the interpretation of text strings as tokens and associating the definition with a text window. Then tokens can be directly typed after moving the cursor inside the text window.

All other input types preserve the current position of the cursor, and cause another cursor symbol to be displayed during the operation. This ensures that the point of interest is not lost and users are able to use muscle memory for the operation. Icon key and menu key are used for selection, the former from a continuously available list and the latter from a pop-up list. Function keys are used for abbreviations of commands.

The logical input devices in HutWindows can use all the possibilities available in the actual physical input devices without having to worry about compatibility like for instance in GKS. The tokens created do not make any difference whether they come from an icon selected with a mouse key or from a keyboard. To cover the basic input operations that were presented by [6] a richer set of input operations have been planned. However we rather have a few operations easy to understand and use than all the possible alternatives.

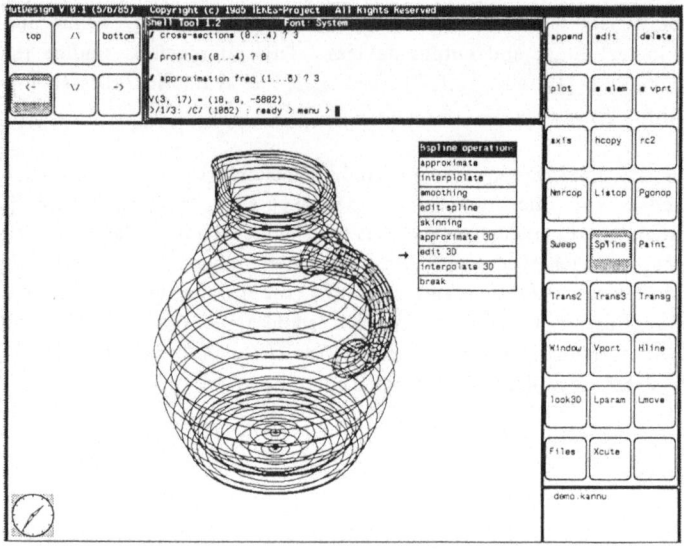

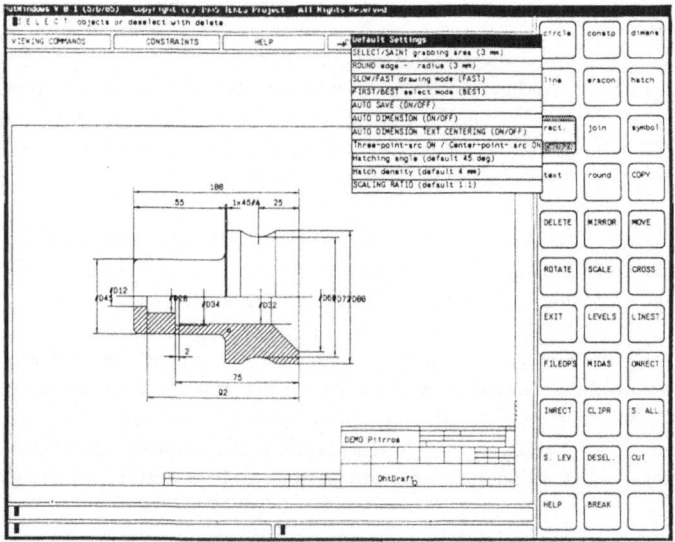

Fig. 3. Examples of HutWindows user interfaces

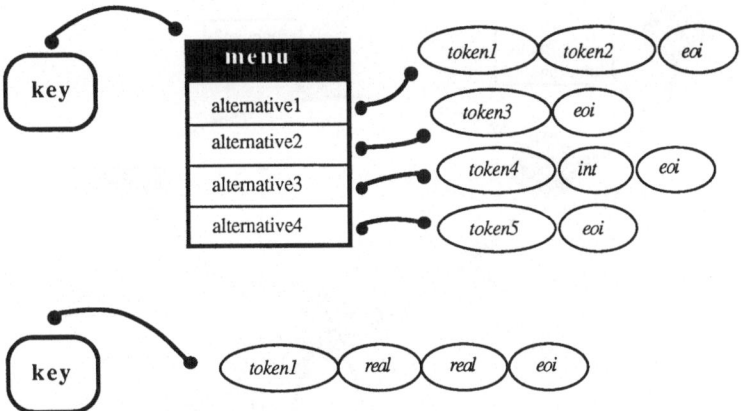

Fig. 4. Example of input conversion

Input conversion in presentation layer is implemented by associating objects that are used to cause input operations with a list of tokens. Token lists are either connected directly to keys to form function keys or to user interface objects which are then connected to keys (Fig. 4.). For example every icon in an icon block object is associated with a list of tokens, then the icon block is associated with an icon window and an icon key. When this key is hit, an icon from the icon window can be selected.

3.4. Output Operations

Output operations are primitives which can be used for displaying graphical or textual information in a window. These primitives can be used either from a FSM or from an application. An application can output only to those graphics or text windows which have been explicitly made visible to it. Each of those windows appears to the application as a graphics display or as an ordinary VDU terminal. All the primitives that are sent to a window are stored in the display list of that window.

3.5. Finite State Machine (FSM)

The dynamic operation of the user interface is described in HutWindows by means of a finite state machine. Every arc in the FSM is labeled with an input token and associated with a HDL function to be executed when the arc is traversed from one state to another. Functions consist of a list of HDL operations, optionally followed by a command to send a message to the application. HDL includes special operations for formatting the message.

Operation of a FSM starts from a designated initial state. Before starting the actual operation a special initialization function is executed. This function is intended to be used for object definitions, for giving initial values to objects and for starting applications. However, all these operations can also be done by means of the ordinary HDL functions.

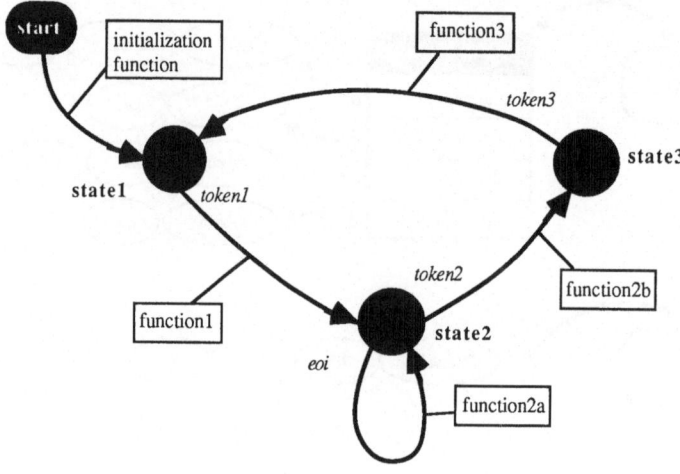

Fig. 5. A Simple FSM

3.6. Application Interface

The application communicates with the user interface process through the application interface. When an application is started it can first execute some initialization code. After this, the application gives the control back to the interface process, and makes handles to three procedures to be called by HutWindows available to the interface process. One of the procedures is used to announce a new window to the application, and another when a window is closed. The third routine makes the messages sent by HutWindows available to the application.

Output can be sent to HutWindows from the message handling procedure by calling interface procedures that generate output primitives or perform viewing operations. Besides these, no other HutWindows operations are permitted to be used by the application. After the primitives have been sent the application must return the control back to the user interface process.

4. IMPLEMENTATION NOTES

HutWindows is written in the C programming language [11]. Currently it runs on SUN workstations and VAXes under UNIX 4.2 bsd. It is also being ported to IBM PC under MSDOS.

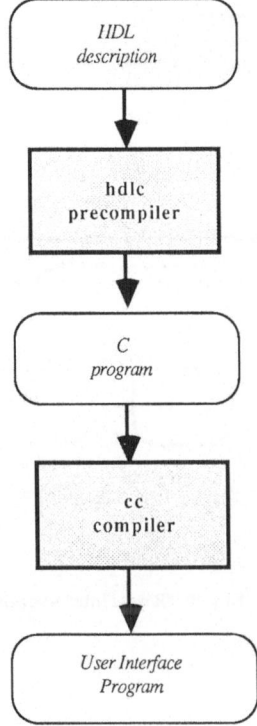

Fig. 6. Compile-time system

Creating a program with HutWindows consists of two stages. First, a compile-time system for the preparation of the user interface is used. The resulting run-time system is for the actual interactive operation.

A HutWindows user interface is defined with a high level language HDL specially designed for this purpose. The definition is compiled to a C program with the precompiler **hdlc**. Applications are compiled separately, and if the messages from the user interface process remain unchanged, the applications need not be touched even if the user interface is modified in other respects.

At run time, the user interface process is first started by the user. When a HDL function desires to start an application program, a special HutWindows server is first contacted to arrange the rendez-vous with the user interface and the application. Thereafter, the two processes will communicate directly with each other by means of interprocess communication primitives. As depicted in Figure 4.2, the two processes may well reside in two distinct nodes of a network. It is also possible to run several applications in different nodes at the same time or one after another.

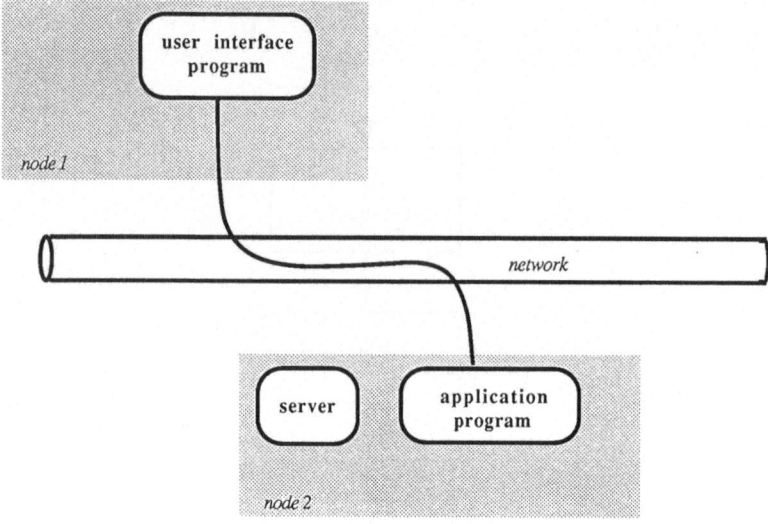

Fig. 7. Run-time System

5. EXTENSIONS

To great surprise of its authors, HutWindows has been successfully used to implement user interfaces for applications quite far from the originally targeted CAD realm. While this seems to suggest that something must be right in HutWindows as it is, there are extensions contemplated by us or requested by the users.

While the logical input devices currently available have been sufficient for the interfaces developed so far, there is a need for quantification and path type input devices. These would help the user to operate in a more visual level while giving commands and there is no reason not to allow this.

To be able to use HutWindows for example with applications performing simulation a special logical device, clock is needed. This device can be set to send input tokens to the FSM token queue at every alarm point. The user should naturally be able to adjust the time between alarms.

At the moment we have successfully used just a simple FSM for describing the interaction dialogues. The extension of using for instance a recursive transition network scheme, would certainly increase the descriptive power of the HDL language. However, the future inclusion of additional high level logical input devices may reduce the need for more powerful dialogue description facilities.

Instead there is growing need for a good interactive graphical user interface for developing graphical user interfaces. It should include tools like icon editors, layout editors, dialogue editor and user interface simulator. To implement the simulator, HDL would have to be interpreted instead of compiled.

To make the user interfaces to look more uniform and hence facilitate the learning process of users, we have planned to write a guide on the recommended style of using HutWindows. The guide would be aimed at the user interface designers. In different user communities and application areas the style recommendations can of course be different.

6. CONCLUSIONS

The division of an interactive system in three layers is very natural. It increases the independency of functional parts of the system and makes it easier to write and understand. However too much responsibility is usually given to the dialogue part; e.g. in [8] it sees parts of the application data structures. If the role of the layers is changed to make them more independent, then every layer can be modified without changing the others.

Applications become simpler because no interaction modes or states are needed. Hence, application programmers can concentrate on the essential algorithms of the system, in accordance with the modeless programming style. If necessary, the application can use tools such as LEX [14] or YACC [10] to parse the messages, because they take the form of character strings. However, the messages are unlikely to be very complicated. The independence of an application also makes it possible to use it over the network. This means that the user interface can be running e.g. in a PC and the application in a more powerful machine.

The goal of giving the user the opportunity to rule the system is accomplished in several ways. First, the user can have more influence on her/his working environment because the user interface can be changed separately from the application. A user interface designer can also embed into the interface possibilities for direct tailoring, even after the application has been frozen.

Second, by the design of HutWindows, it is the user that starts all the events and gives orders to the application through the interface, not vice versa. The selection of input devices available in HutWindows suggests the modeless operation paradigm, where the user can freely invoke operations without having to follow strict paths. Moreover, HutWindows encourages the use of standard methods of communication in all applications. This facilitates the learning of a new application.

The design of HutWindows certainly has drawbacks. Cursor tracking by the application has not been included, because its efficiency would be very sensitive to the network load. Applications that require direct manipulation of a raster display (e.g. by painting) cannot be supported. As a more subtle restriction, dynamically calculated pop-up menus are not possible in the current design, although HDL could be modified to accommodate them.

Nevertheless, for our applications the advantages brought about by HutWindows outweigh the problems. HutWindows has turned out to fulfill our needs and we have reached our aims to a reasonable degree. The designers find HutWindows useful both for prototyping and implementing a user interface. It also seems to support the development of user interfaces that are easy to use for the end-users.

ACKNOWLEDGEMENT

This work was performed as a part of the project "Distributed CAD Systems" funded by the State Technical Development Centre of Finland.

REFERENCES

1. Aho, A.V. and Ullman, J.D. (1974) Principles of Compiler Design. Addison-Wesley.

2. Buxton, W. and Lamb, M.R. (1983) Towards a Comprehensive User Interface Management System. Computer Graphics, Vol. 17, No. 3, p. 35-42.

3. Coutaz, J. (1985) Abstractions for User Interface Design. Computer, Vol. 18, No. 9, p. 21-34.

4. Foley, J.D. and van Dam, A. (1983) Fundamentals of Interactive Computer Graphics. Addison-Wesley.

5. Foley, J.D. and Wallace, L.V. (1974) The Art of Natural Graphic Man-Machine Conversation. Proceedings of the IEEE, Vol. 62, No. 4, p. 462-471.

6. Foley, J.D., Wallace, L.V. and Chan, P. (1984) The Human Factors of Computer Graphics Interaction Techniques. IEEE Computer Graphics and Applications, Vol. 4, No. 11, p. 13-48.

7. Graphical Kernel System (GKS) - Functional Description. ISO DP 7942, 1982.

8. Green, M. (1985) The University of Alberta User Interface Management system. SIGGRAPH'85 Proceedings, ACM, p. 205-213.

9. Inside Macintosh. Apple Computer Inc., 20525 Mariani Avenue, Cupertino, CA 95014, 1985.

10. Johnson, S.C. (1979) YACC - Yet Another Compiler-Compiler. Bell Laboratories, Murray Hill, N.J.

11. Kernighan, B. and Ritchie, D. (1978) The C Programming Language. Addison-Wesley.

12. Kieras, D. and Polson, P. G. (1983) A Generalized Network Representation for Interactive Systems. Proc. CHI'83 Human Factors in Computing Systems, p. 103-106.

13. Koivunen, M. and Mantyla, M. and Peltonen, H. (1986) HutWindows Version 0.3 User's Manual. Technical Report HTKK-TKO-C16, Helsinki University of Technology, Laboratory of Information Processing Science, Otakaari 1 SF-02150 Espoo, Finland.

14. Lesk, M.E. and Schmidt, E. (1979) Lex - A Lexical Analyzer Generator. Bell Laboratories, Murray Hill, N. J.

15. Newman, W.M. (1968) A System for Interactive Graphical Programming. SJCC, Thompson Books, Washington D.C., p. 47.

16. Newell, M. (1983) Perseus - A Programmable Interactive User Interface in a Multi-Window Environment. Proc. National Computer Graphics Conference, p. 451-458.

17. Schulert, A.J., Rogers, G.T. and Hamilton, J.A. (1985) ADM - A Dialog Manager. CHI'85 Proceedings, ACM, p. 177-183.

18. Pfaff, G.E. (ed.) (1985) User Interface Management Systems. Proceedings of the Workshop on User Interface Management Systems held in Seeheim, FRG, November 1-3, 1983. Springer-Verlag, 1985.

19. ten Hagen, P.J.W. (1983) Interactive Techniques. Eurographics Tutorials' 83. Springer-Verlag.

20. Tesler, L. (1981) The Smalltalk Environment. BYTE, Vol. 6, No. 8, p. 90-147.

21. Thomas, J.J. and Hamlin, G. (ed.) (1983) Graphical Input Interaction Techniques. Report on a workshop held at Battelle Seattle Conference Center, June 2-4, 1982. Computer Graphics, Vol. 17, No. 1, p. 5-30.

22. Woods, W.A. (1970) Transition Network Grammars for Natural Language Analysis. CACM, Vol. 13, No. 10, p. 591-606.

Marja-Riitta Koivunen is a research scientist with the Laboratory of Information Processing Science at the Helsinki University of Technology. She received her M.Sc. degree in Computer Science and Biophysics from the Helsinki University of Technology in 1986. Koivunen's research interests include user interface management, systems programming, and computer graphics. She is a member of the IEEE.

Address: Helsinki University of Technology, Laboratory of Information Processing Science, Otakaari 1, SF-02150 Espoo, Finland.

Martti Mäntylä is a senior research associate with the Laboratory of Information Processing Science at the Helsinki University of Technology, Finland; currently he also is an acting professor of Computing Technology. Mäntylä received his Ph.D. in 1983 in Helsinki University of Technology. In 1983-1984 he was a visiting scholar with the Computer Systems Laboratory at the Stanford University.

Mäntylä's research interests include computer applications in engineering, CAD, computer graphics, user interfaces, and data base management. He is an associate editor of the ACM Transactions on Graphics and a member of the ACM, the IEEE Computer Society, and the Eurographics Association.

A Gestural Representation of the Process of Composing Chinese Temples

Ranjit Makkuni

ABSTRACT.   This paper illustrates the design of a computing based design environment that can represent the process of composing facades of Chinese temples.

Temple compositions are constructed by generating tesselated vocabulary elements, relating vocabulary elements in a topological mosaic and integrating the mosaic into temple facades. Assuming this compositional machinery, the paper examines the design environment: presentation of the machinery, techniques by which a designer interacts with the machinery, methods to depict process and render process as an aesthetic experience.

In this environment, a gestural language provides the means to interact with the machinery as well as create the marks that record process. The gestural language furnishes the designer with mechanisms to experience process, realise and reflect upon process, and share and present process with members of a design studio. It enables compositional process to be represented in a temporal framework that reflects the designer's sense of presence: invoking gestures, engaging in gestural conversations, representing design scenes, and eventually, forming a design craft.

Keywords: design environment, representation of process, gestural interface, gestural conversation, scenes of process, design craft, machine mediated communication.

INTRODUCTION

Walking into a design studio of an architectural school or office, one witnesses a familiar scene: a group of designers huddled over a drawing board *(Fig. 1)*. Pinned upon their workspace and on the walls around them, are stacks of thin and transparent yellow tracing paper that bears the markings of a designer's project. Typically, one designer is explaining the markings on the board to the others who will in turn criticise them . . . the critics ponder the designer's remarks, browse the markings on the yellow paper and, eventually, one of them snatches a pencil and begins sketching, or tears another yellow sheet, places it over the original drawing and modifies the original. More often than not, crumpled wads of these sheets of yellow paper litter the floor after the critique.

Contained in the scene in the design studio are ideas about **representation, presentation, sharing, interpretation, evaluation, negotiation**, or in general, the **design environment**. Within the design environment, the designers' marks on the yellow paper, whether crumpled or on the drawing board and walls, are all shadows of the process of design. This research attempts to understand and capture, in computational form, some of the qualities of the design environment. In particular, it is an attempt to emulate and extend some of the properties of the thin yellow paper. This research is about using computers to make better shadows.

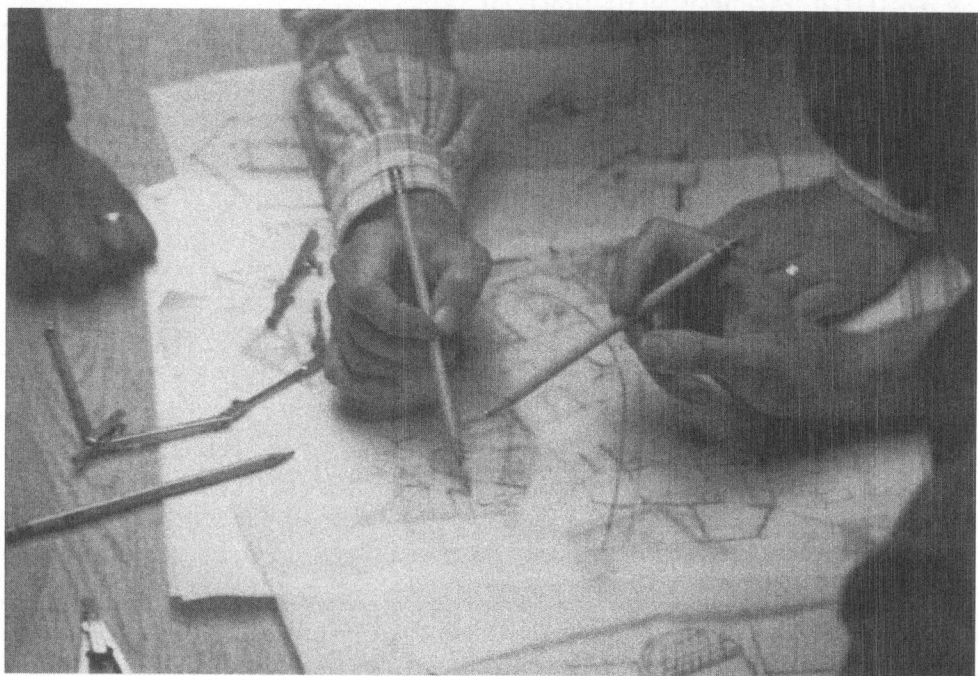

Figure 1. Scene in a design studio.

Today, Computer Aided Design, in a broad sense of the term, uses structured computing machinery to represent the products of a design process, the design artifacts. These vary from the invention of data structures that represent artifacts (Baer et al. 1977; Greenberg and Marcus, 1982), to techniques that manipulate these structures in order to synthesise a variety of design options (Stiny and Gips, 1972; Mitchell 1977; March 1976; Steadman 1973; Makkuni 1985).

Structured machinery amplifies a designer's actions, allowing a small input to cause greater effect, and therefore allows a designer to explore an open-ended range of design possibilities. The representations used by the machinery will differ in the properties of the artifacts that they represent. While the differences are important in terms of selecting representations for artifacts, the purpose of this paper is not to argue the merits of one representation over another, nor to state that the invention of novel representations can produce novel designs. The purpose is to look more at the process of marking than at the marks, to look more at the shadows of process made visible by the wads of yellow paper. Thus we are led to ask: **Assuming the use of structured machinery how does a designer interact with it? How is the machinery presented to the designer? How can we give computer-aided systems, whatever their particular capabilities, the quality of yellow tracing paper as a design medium? In general, what is the nature of a designer's experience while interacting with the machinery? Is the experience an aesthetic and joyous one, and one that is comparable to the experience with traditional media? Does the experience contribute to the social process of the studio?**

This paper casts these questions through an example of composing facades of Chinese temples, and in doing so looks toward the representation and experience of the compositional process. Chinese temples are illustrative of artifacts in a design environment in order to demonstrate that a "representation of process" (Lambert 1984; Stults1985; Stults 1986; Harrison 1986)is possible in a computational environment. The research does not address novel methods to design Chinese temples.

Inspired by Chinese calligraphy (Sullivan 1980; Whitfield 1980; Loehr 1980), this paper depicts the designer as a calligrapher, who expressively exercises a gestural language. The gestural language provides the means to interact with the machinery as well as create the marks that make process visible. It will furnish the designer with mechanisms to experience process, realise and reflect upon process, and share and present process with members in a design studio.

We will discover that the gestural language is an integral part of the design experience, the representation of process, and the eventual formation and preservation of a design craft -- for "Does the calligrapher write artistically for the sake of writing and not for the sake of reading?" (Coomaraswamy 1964) and "Does the designer gesture expressively for the sake of interacting with the machinery and not for the sake of sharing experience with members in a studio?"

CONSTRUCTING THE COMPOSITIONAL MACHINERY

Chinese Temples

Spanning over four thousand years, the architecture of China was an important factor contributing to the continuity of the Chinese civilisation (Ssu-ch'eng 1984). The architectural language employed by the Chinese remained homogeneous across time, over a vast distance, and despite repeated foreign invasions. The homogeneity across time and space in the indigenous system of construction that the Chinese use renders this an ideal domain to represent using structured machinery.

The basic characteristics of a Chinese temple consist of a raised platform forming the base of the structure with a timber post and lintel skeleton; this in turn supports a pitched roof with overhanging eaves *(Fig. 2)*. This construction allows freedom in wall placement and fenestration and, by the simple adjustment of the proportion between walls and openings, adaptation to a variety of climates and uses (Ssu-ch'eng 1984; Ch'en 1981).

Compositional Machinery

A Chinese temple facade may be tesselated or decomposed into an assemblage of cells by superimposing a two-dimensional lattice upon it. Each unit of decomposition, a rectangular cell, will be referred to as a **temple element**. Associated with each temple element are a set of parameters that denote the dimensioning and proportioning properties. When these properties are assigned, a particular instance of a temple element is constructed. The careful generation and the subsequent selection of instances of temple elements form a collection referred to as a **designer's vocabulary**; a member in this collection is referred to as a **vocabulary element**. Vocabulary elements need not be encapsulated in a cell. They can also be created from aggregations of clusters of cells. However, in this research, the latter is not considered.

Once a designer's vocabulary is established, vocabulary elements are positioned and related to each other in a cellular mosaic, and a temple composition is considered an assemblage of all the

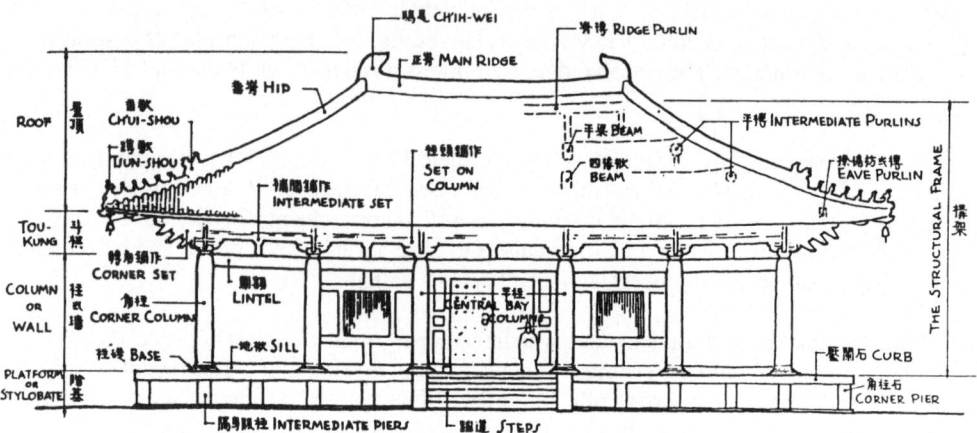

NAME/ OF PRINCIPAL PART/ OF A CHINE/E BUILDING
中國建築主要部份名稱圖

Figure 2. Basic characteristics of a Chinese temple. Copyright 1984 by the Massachusetts Institute of Technology. Reproduced with permission from: Ssu-ch'eng, Liang, A Pictorial History of Chinese Architecture, edited by Wilma Fairbank, MIT Press, Cambridge, 1984.

cells. However, when vocabulary elements are re-arranged and assembled, a communication network is used to transmit dependencies between vocabulary elements. These relationships may be derived from Chinese literature and encoded as dimensioning and proportioning dependencies between vocabulary elements, such as the expressions,

"the width of a roof element will be equal to eleven times the diameter of the column of the bay below a roof,"

"the width of a window bay is fixed by the number of tiles in a roof,"

or explicitly enforced by a Chinese temple designer.

Specifying relationships between vocabulary elements enables the designer to separate the essence of the compositional structure from a dimensioned and proportioned temple facade. Hence, in the presentation of a composition as an assemblage, an intermediate step is introduced to enable the quick and easy viewing of the compositional structure of a temple facade. This step defocusses an assemblage into its unconnected state -- a dimensionless and proportionless state -- called a **compositional topology map**.

Manipulating a compositional topology map allows the designer to quickly edit a temple structure, explore symmetries inherent in temple compositions by mirroring transformations, repeat clusters of cells, and substitute vocabulary elements for others in a composition. Later, the compositional topology map is integrated into a temple facade by enforcing the knowledge of dependencies.

In essence, the compositional machinery requires the designer to engage in three kinds of activities: 1) generating a vocabulary, 2) relating vocabulary elements in a topology map, and 3) integrating the map into a temple facade with the knowledge of dependencies *(Fig. 3)*.

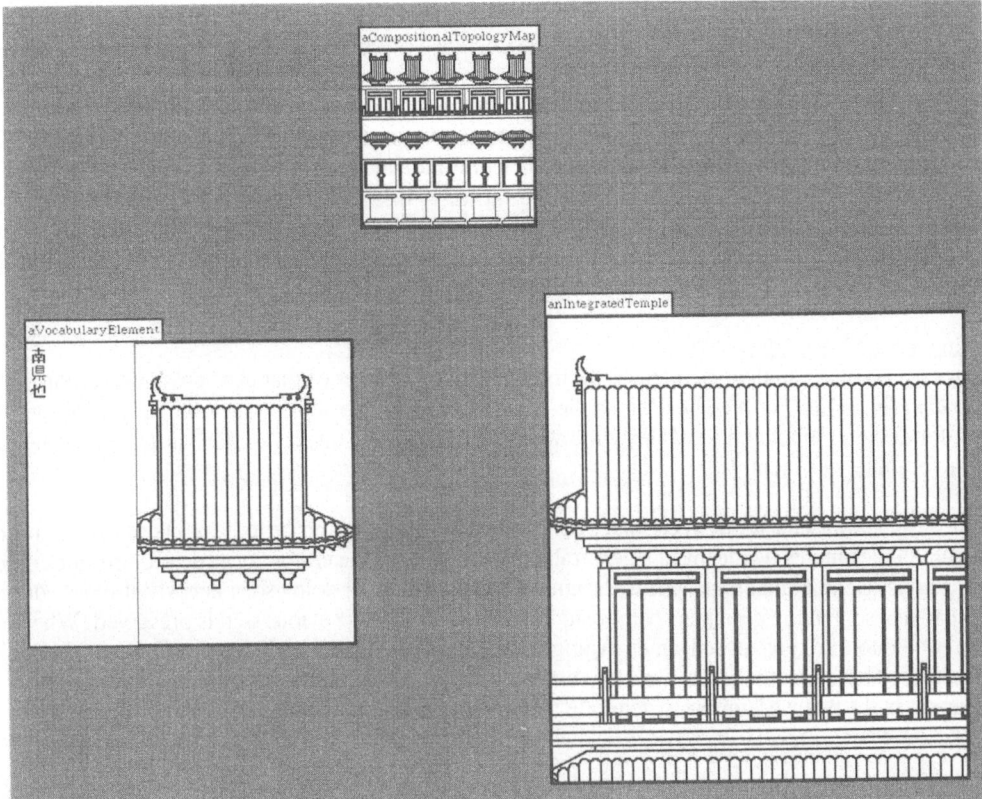

Figure 3. Representational schema for design activities. At the left) generating a vocabulary, top) relating vocabulary elements in a topology map, and right) integrating the map into a temple facade with the knowledge of dependencies.

Interaction & the Representation of Process

For purposes of clarity, this section will present compositional activities in discrete steps or stages. However, any particular notion of sequentiality is not intended. The interaction of a designer with the machinery was designed to respect **non-sequentiality** and, in the generation of temple facades, allows a designer fluidly to: 1) move between the different activities, i.e., generating vocabularies, exploring topologies and integrating temples; and 2) represent overlapping, partial and parallel temple compositions.

Defining Vocabulary Elements

Vocabulary elements as well as the compositional machinery are expressed in Smalltalk code (Goldberg 1983). In the Smalltalk-80 object-oriented programming environment, an object is a package of information and descriptions of its manipulation, a class is a description of one or more similar objects, and an instance is an object described by a particular class.

Every object is an instance of a class. A class may be modified to create another class: the first class is called the super-class and the second is called the sub-class. Hence, a sub-class is a class that is created by sharing the description of its super-class and modifying some aspects of that description (Robson 1981). This enables easy definition of classified objects according to shared and differing properties.

Paralleling the anatomy of a Chinese temple facade, roofs, windows and bases comprise the super-classes of vocabulary elements. For example, sub-classed under the class *Roof* are the different types of roofs, such as a pavilion roof, a mid-mezzanine roof. Sub-classed under *Window* are various windows. These do not exhaust the various windows or roofs that are used in Chinese facade compositions and are only a handful out of a host of actual possibilities. The intention below is to portray methods of easily defining a new class of windows or roofs by sub-classing the existing classes of roofs and windows and changing their properties.

Generating a Vocabulary
Once a class of vocabulary elements is defined, specific instances of that class are generated in a *Vocabulary Editor (Fig. 4)*. The form of the editor consists of two windows, an active window on the left for designer input and a passive window on the right for the display of the constructed instance of a vocabulary element.

The designer presents to the vocabulary editor the dimensioning and proportioning requirements of vocabulary elements by means of a gestural language. In turn the editor constructs an instance of a vocabulary element that matches the designer's requirements. In doing so, a new vocabulary editor is spawned so that the designer's compositional intention at the previous step is preserved. When the two editors are juxtaposed, an emerging temple facade's "process of becoming" (Klee 1961) is observed. Therefore, the active window shows the actions taken on the instance of a vocabulary element in the passive window to generate a new instance.

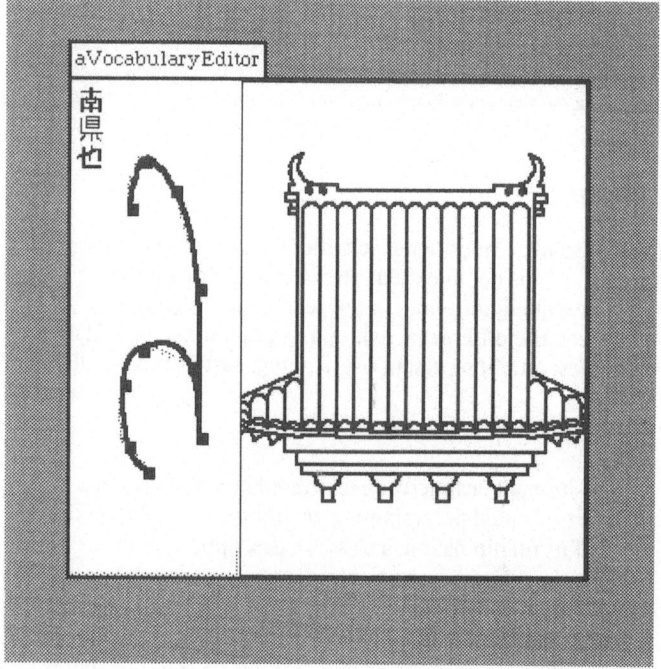

Figure 4. Vocabulary Editor showing an active window on the left for designer input and a passive window on the right for the display of the constructed instance of a vocabulary element.

*Figure 5a. A Gesture --
strokes taken from a
mouse.*

*Figure 5b. Gesturally
generating and exploring
a Pavilion Roof.*

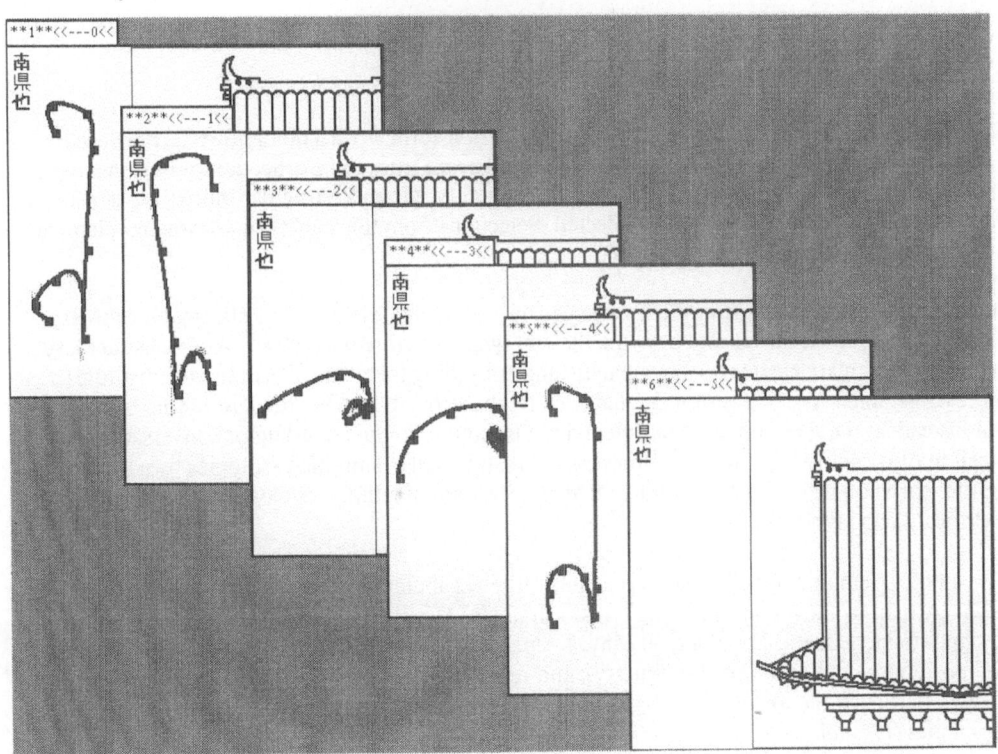

The Gestural Language: A gestural language is a collection of **gestures** -- strokes taken from an input device that the vocabulary editor recognises as a designer's intentions for creating and manipulating vocabulary elements *(Fig. 5a)*. The form of the machinery that constructs an instance of a vocabulary element is a parametric procedure, one whose arguments represent the design properties, that is, dimensioning and proportioning properties of a vocabulary element that a designer wishes to manipulate. The gestural language mediates between the designer's assignment of these arguments and the construction of an instance. *Figure 5b* illustrates a designer gesturally exploring possibilities for a Pavilion Roof.

A gesture is a stroke that denotes a designer's intention. Pictorially it may be viewed as a calligraphic stroke: part picture and part writing (Sullivan 1980; Whitfield 1980; Loehr 1980). The picture part is a path of points that contributes useful information, such as the height of a tile, the width of a tile, or increase or decrease in the number of tiles in a roof. The writing part is a notational transcript that records computationally the state of a designer interacting with the machinery.

The cycle of interacting by gestures, constructing instances of vocabulary elements, assaying instances and gesturing once again, is a design activity at the lowest grain. A history of these activities is called a **gestural conversation** *(Fig. 5c)* and is available as a historical sketch that illustrates computational changes in the state of the vocabulary elements over time and process. Designers will converse differently with the different sequences of gestures (different methods to manipulate the machinery); hence the gestural conversation, in the context of structured compositional machinery, can be viewed as a designer's signature portraying a designer's particular handling of the machinery towards a vocabulary element.

Exploring Topologies

Vocabulary elements generated in the vocabulary editor form a collection known as the design vocabulary. The interface to the vocabulary looks like a palette, i.e., a collection of buttons that represent the various elements of a designer's vocabulary. When a particular button is pressed, a corresponding vocabulary element is selected. Selections from this palette of vocabulary elements are used in the *Topology Editor (Fig. 6a)*.

A designer constructs and examines topologies by sprinkling (selecting and placing) vocabulary elements over a tiled canvas and assaying the emergent structure of a temple. At an abstract level, selecting vocabulary elements from a palette and sprinkling them on a tiled canvas constitutes a more constrained type of gestural language. Here, the stroke is not recorded as a series of points, but instead, as the selection and placement actions. Similar to the recording of conversation in the creation of vocabulary elements, the process of creating and examining topologies by a topological gesture spawns a new topology editor so that an evolution of temple topologies is observed and a historical sketch is maintained.

The topology editor provides functions to substitute vocabulary elements for others and to enlarge a topology map by the use of mirroring transformations. A mirroring transformation allows the designer to increase the size of a tiled canvas, repeat particular clusters of tiles (to produce temple compositions with translational symmetry), and reflect the topology map (bi-lateral symmetry) about a particular tile. By doing so, a designer is able to quickly explore symmetries in temple topologies *(Fig. 6b)*.

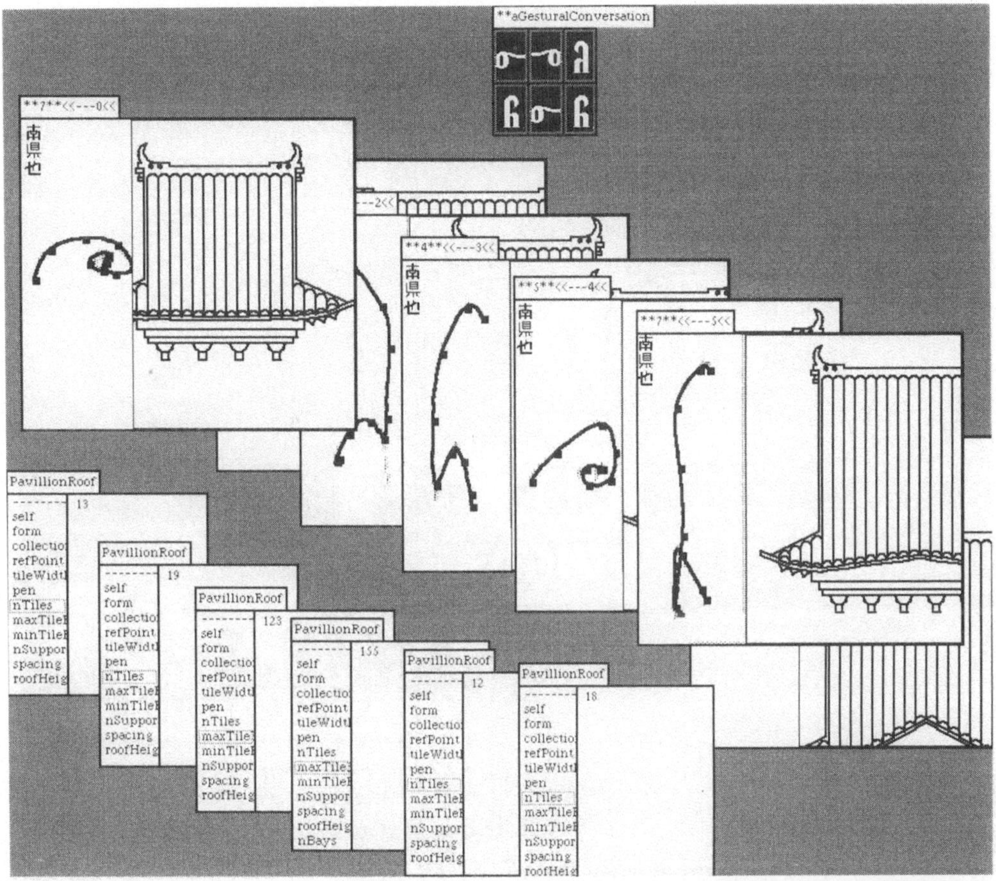

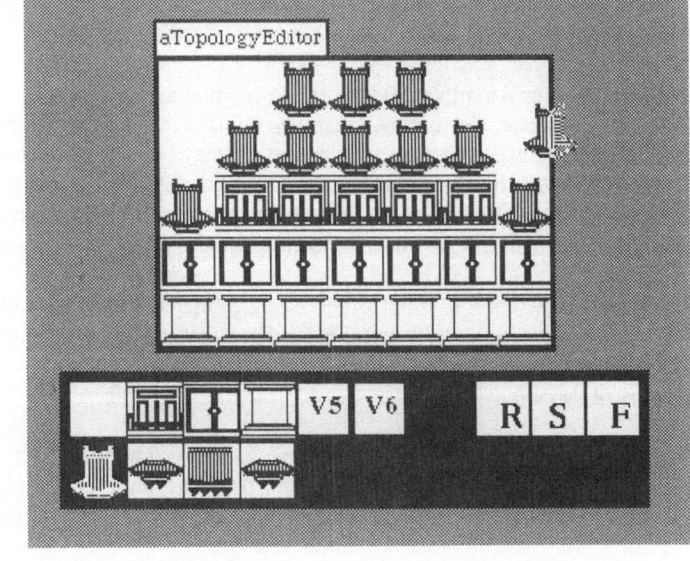

Figure 5c. Gestural conversation illustrating computational changes in the state of a Pavilion Roof element over process. At the top) notational representation of a conversation as a sequence of gestural icons, middle) gestural exploration of a Pavilion Roof, bottom) changes in state of the Pavilion Roof.

Figure 6a. Topology Editor showing a tiled canvas at the top and a palette of vocabulary elements at the bottom.

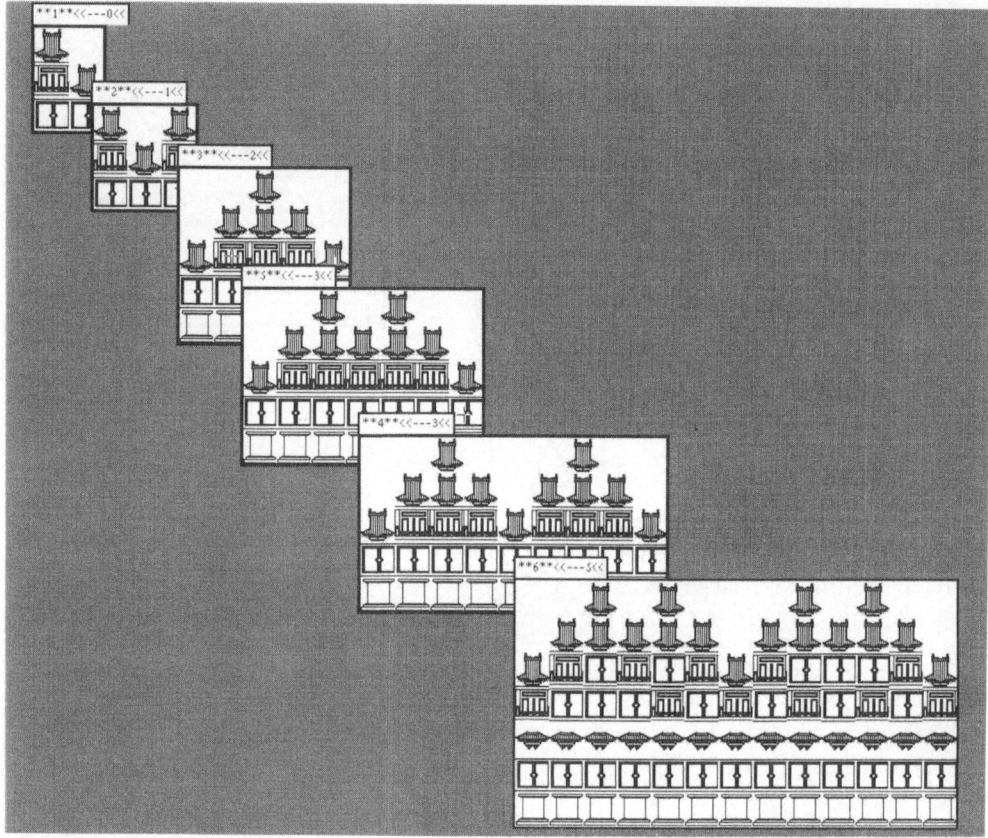

Figure 6b. Exploring symmetries in temple topologies by mirroring transformations.

Integrating Temple Facades

The journey from a compositional topology map to a description of a temple facade passes through a *Temple Integrator*. The temple integrator manages the transmission of the knowledge of dependencies between vocabulary elements. It may be viewed as a **book of rules** that enables the weaving of the various vocabulary elements in a topology map into a picture of a temple facade. It does this by aggregating like vocabulary elements into sub-assemblies and sizing details of each aggregated element to make the connecting elements flow into a seamless whole.

The integrator receives as input a tiled topology map of vocabulary elements, integrates this map into a single description of the temple, and presents it in a viewing window *(Fig. 7)*.

History of Process

In the process of composing temple facades, the three kind of activities that a designer engages in are: generating a vocabulary, constructing a topology, and integrating a temple. Given the nonsequentiality and fluidity that enable the designer to represent parallel, partial compositions,

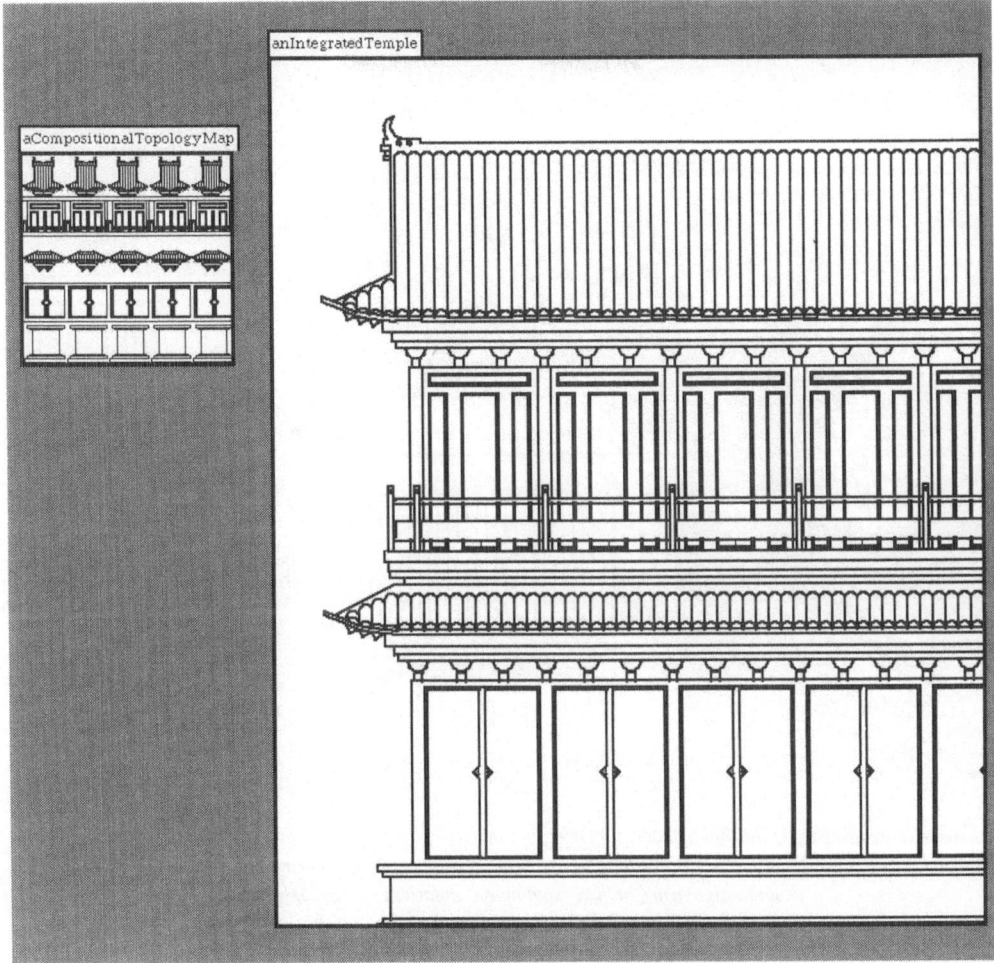

Figure 7. A temple topology and an integrated temple.

how is the history of process maintained? What mechanisms communicate and visually present a designer's flow of thought? In general, how is process sensuously depicted? This section will describe the attempt to capture and record in computational form "process", and through the act of recording provide a sensation of history (time) to the designer.

The perception of process and its depiction differs from traditional form (artifact) depiction. The notion of form depiction is subsumed in process depiction, i.e., through the evocative qualities of form. A **process depiction** illustrates not only form derivation and evocations, but presents phantoms of possibilities that lie in the future. Hence, process is "formation" depiction (Klee 1961). It is transitory in nature and its perception alludes to and invests in the importance of a designer's suggestiveness and intentionalities, rather than in view a particular frozen "compositional state" in a process as an end in itself or complete.

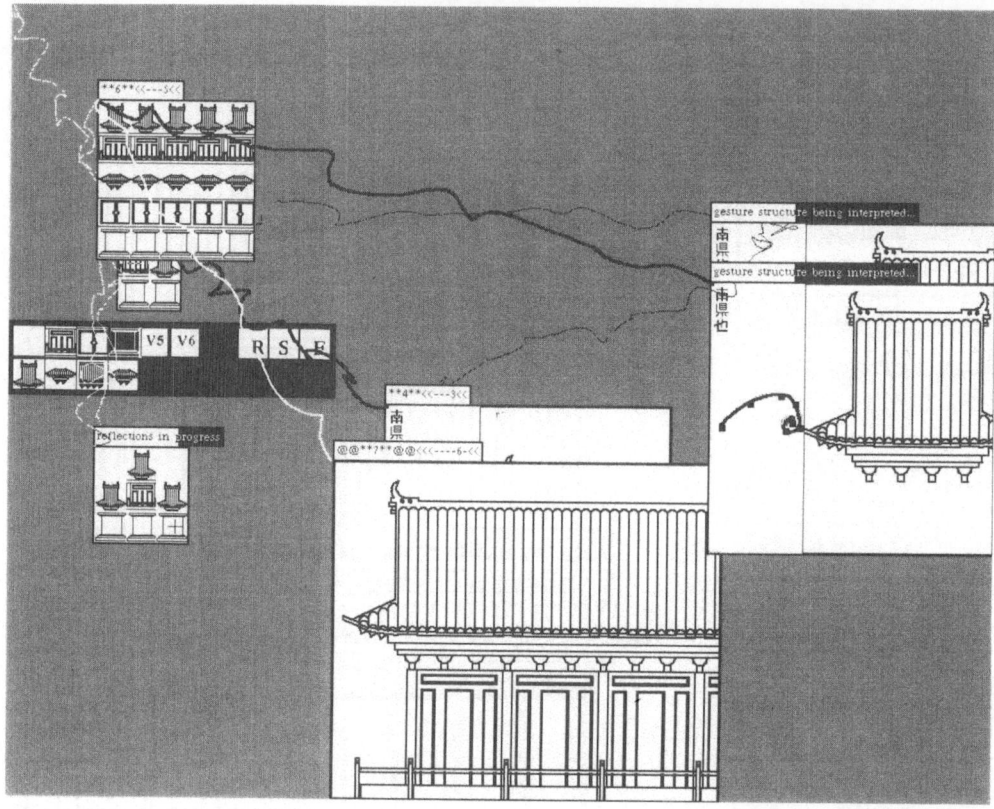

Figure 8a. Threads tying up the different activities over time in a designer's derivative process. Thin, fragile and slender threads denote weak transitions between activities (for eg., casually exploring vocabularies) and bold and confident threads denote assignment (for eg., assigning vocabularies to a topology map).

Compositional state, thus, is related to time. Its perception reflects the designer's sense of presence. A designer's **sense of presence** ranges from invoking a gesture (a second), engaging in a conversation (minutes), the context of composing a facade (an hour), to preserving design sessions (the length of a project), and eventually forming a design craft (many years). The form of the recording of "presence" ranges from a notational transcript of a gesture, a gestural conversation, the recording of a compositional scene, and the dissemination of craft in to public media such as video, books, or ballads.

Threads and Lineages
Each activity is connected to its history, the previous activities that spawned it. This connection elucidates the direction in the flow of a designer's thought. Visually, this connection is made by "threading" activities that are reproductive (give birth). The threads tie up the different activities over time in a designer's derivative process and, by its appearance, denote a designer's journey towards temple facades *(Fig. 8a).*

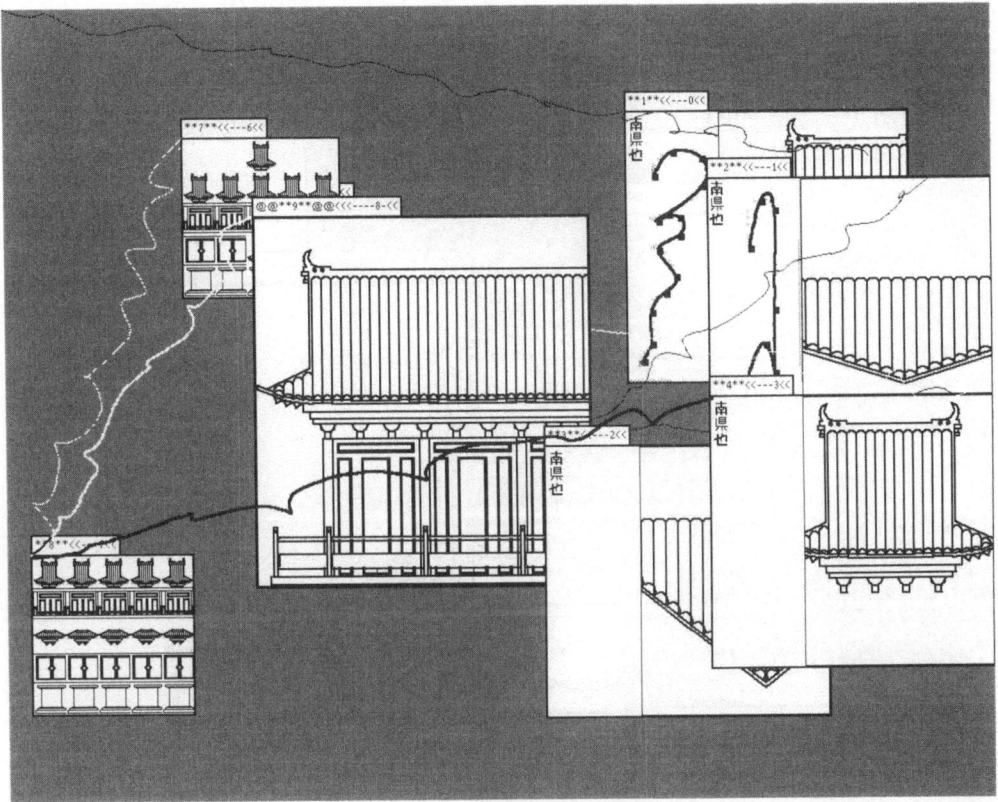

Figure 8b. Divergent exploration: many threaded editors bursting out from a topology editor.

A **thread** visually links two activities on the display screen, accentuating a direction in thought flow. Threads may be thin, fragile and slender like silk to denote weak transitions; or they may be bold and confident like iron wire or lightning to denote assignment, such as the assignment of vocabularies in the topology map. Visual appearance apart, threads allow the designer to attain a tactile sensation. Threads mediate between actions taken and the spawning of a new activity. The visual experience of a thread can be likened to the magic smoke from the genii's pot in Alladin's lamp. Beginning with a gesture and followed by a thread, a designer can feel the sensation of the act of creation, and witness birth.

When viewed in the whole, threads, along with the various editors they link constitute a roadmap of "process." A point in this roadmap may be the progenitor of much divergent exploration, made visible as many threaded editors bursting out from a particular editor -- like the roads in the center of a medieval city *(Fig. 8b)*. Or a point may terminate a thread showing an abandoned flow of thought, or an idea un-explored.

The Scene Editor
As the number of editors in a process begins to increase, threads outlive their utility, and we must look towards other mechanisms to present a designer's roadmap or the ranges of a designer's sense of presence. While threads preserve the immediate context of the designer's interactions with the

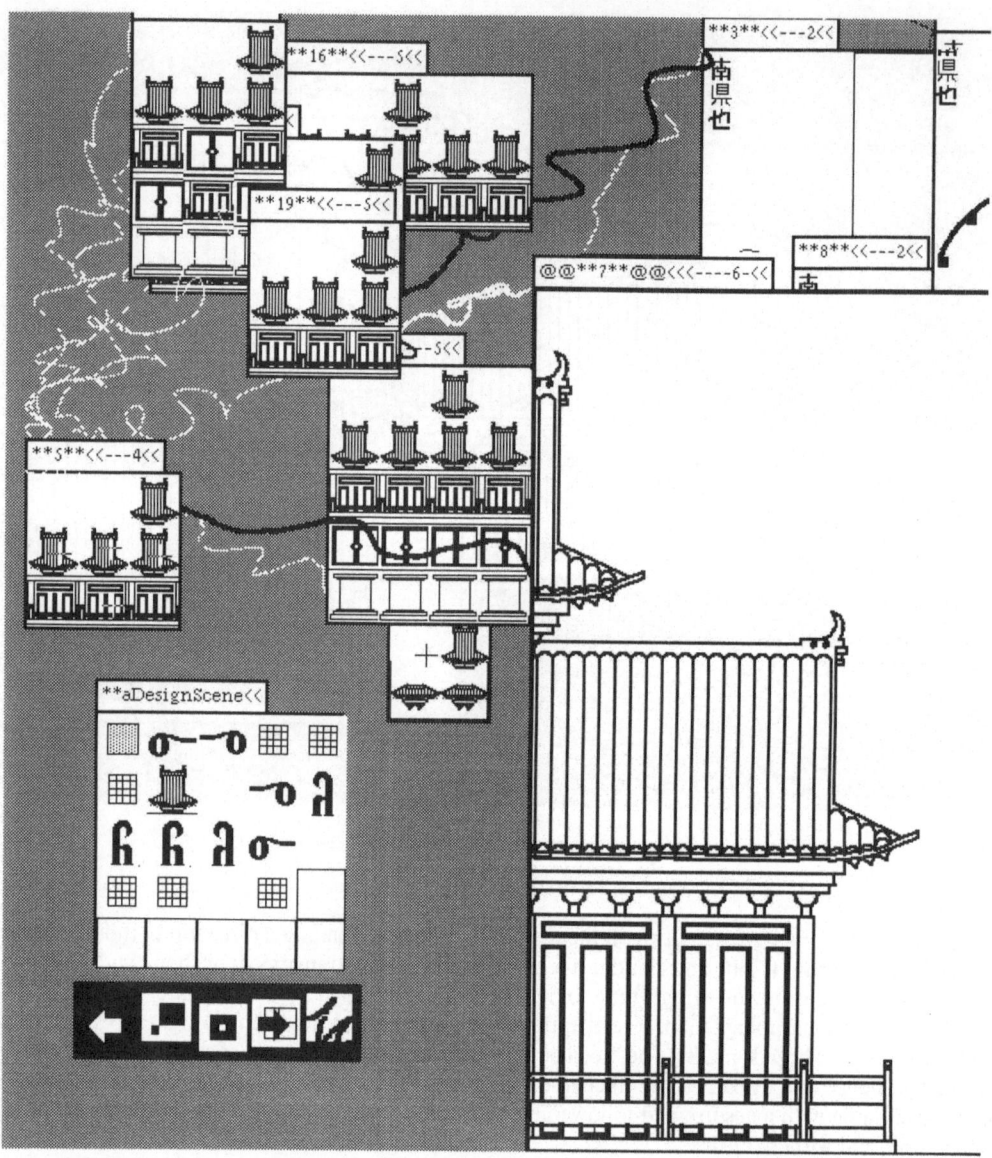

Figure 9. Scene Editor concisely representing the overall process. Each activity is represented as an icon on a tiled canvas. Activities or scenes may be browsed, inspected, scripted and re-enacted.

machinery, we need another mechanism to concisely represent the overall process. The overall process is referred to as a compositional **scene**. The *Scene Editor* allows a **backward glance at process** so that a designer can trace the course of a temple facade development, and examine all or part of the history to see how far one has come.

At this stage, it is important to make a distinction between interacting with the scene editor and the other history mechanisms the designer experiences during a process. The spawning of new editors, threading compositional activities, and inspecting a conversation may be considered as an **immediate glimpse of process** in comparison to a backward glance. A glimpse enables the designer to understand the genesis of ideas in one's immediate attention span, while editing in the scene editor is considerably different. The scene editor allows a designer to retrace all or parts of the process, and move freely between steps in process, and in doing so, **realise process**. However, there is fluidity in the course of the realisation -- a designer need not be strapped into realisation; in the course of realisation, the designer feels free to start a new process or change the steps in a process by editing the scene.

A designer can convert a backward glance at process into an **impression**, and share the impression with other members in a design studio. Latent in the term "impression" is the idea of the individualisation of a designer's process. A designer might wish to control the recording of process, and in doing so personalises process by placing preferences on particular situations over others in the recording of process, thereby presenting to the world one's "overall impression."

The presentation of an impression is accomplished by scripting activities important to a designer and re-enacting process to members in the studio. Scripting a scene allows a designer to re-arrange and regroup activities. Scripting a scene, similar in relationship to unifying a temple from its topological structure, affords the designer with diagramming the essence of a scene.

Visually, each activity in a scene is depicted by an icon. Similar to the realisation of topologies, a designer quickly explores alternative possibilities of scenes by shuffling icons of activities before they are re-enacted to the members of the studio *(Fig. 9)*. Re-enactment can aid designers temporally separated in a project to share process. Also, designers can reminisce and evaluate the development of process across projects.

Library and Craft
Now that process has a concise transcript, (i.e., a design scene capable of re-enactment), it can be preserved in a library. Notice that there is a fundamental shift in the term "process," for by concisely representing it, the process itself has become an artifact.

However, this artifact is special. Re-enactment of design scenes transcribed in the library is like the ritual dancing in praise of the greatness of the mythical figures that protect and provide prosperity to the farmers in Asia. Repeated re-enactments across projects preserve the knowledge of the techniques of a design culture, the **design craft**. The artifact of process is deceptively simple and, although denoted by a simple icon residing in a library *(Fig. 10)*, consists of memories and reflections of a designers' experiences.

The idea of preserving process in a library of craft and disseminating craft is in its infancy. For the purposes of this paper, the library is visually presented in a manner similar to the topology editor, i.e., a mosaic of tiled-icons. Each icon in the mosaic represents a scene (or an impression of process), and the mosaic in total, a collection of scenes of a "project-experience." When a particular icon is pressed, a corresponding scene is constructed for re-enactment. Scenes of process in a library can be categorised and summoned by descriptive conventions that a designer assigns.

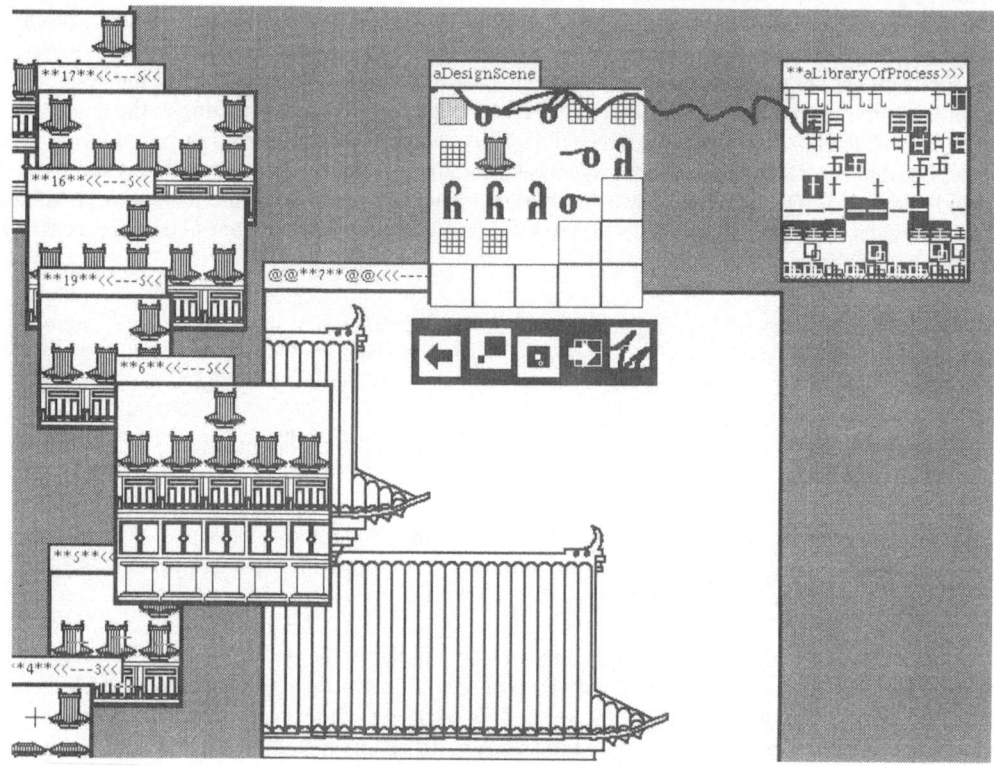

Figure 10. Each tile in the library represents a previously preserved scene capable of re-enactment.

Implementation

Figure 11a illustrates the major components of the compositional machinery and their connections. Except for the authoring of code to construct the compositional machinery, the interaction of a designer is gestural, i.e., generating and manipulating vocabulary elements by gestural strokes, generating topologies and scripting scenes by sprinkling gestures, integrating temples and summoning scenes and coversations by button pushes.

Figure 11b diagrammatically illustrates the implementation-framework in which the compositional process is represented. A *historian* mediates between *user input* and the *assignment of the machinery*. Like calligraphy, the input as gestural strokes, sprinkling gestures and button pushes, is separated into a *writing part* and a *picture part*. The writing part provides a notational mark, i.e., icons of gestures used in the presentation of history to the designer, and the picture part provides a transcript of the state of the key variables of the machinery such as dimensioning and proportioning properties. Together, the icon that lets a designer refer to a particular compositional activity in the process, and the transcript of the key variables, can subsequently reconstruct the activity. Similarly the output is separated into two parts: the *form-depiction part* and the *process-depiction part*. Associated with form depiction are the construction and display of vocabularies, topologies and descriptions of temples; and with process depiction are the threaded spawning of editors, gestural conversations, scenes of process and the preservation of scenes.

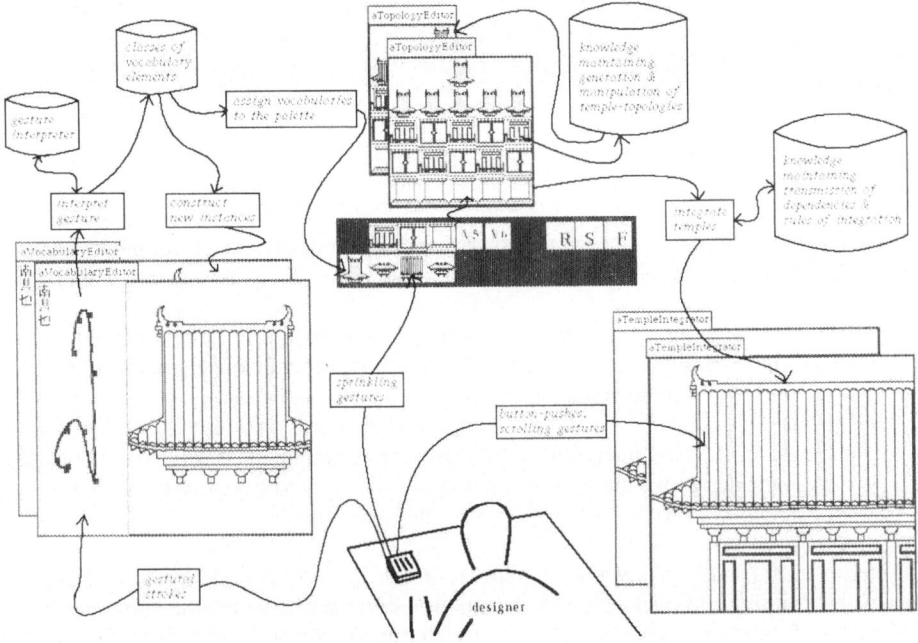

Figure 11a. Components of the compositional machinery and their connections.

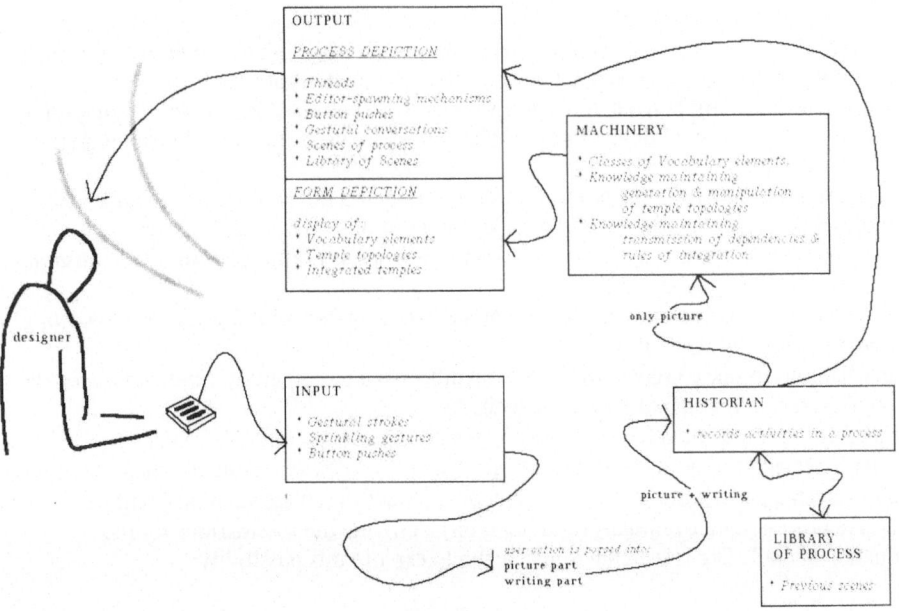

Figure 11 b. Implementation-framework in which the compositional process is represented.

The historian is constantly active through the life of a project and independantly accessed by temporally -- as well as spatially -- separated temple designers, and scenes of process re-enacted, transformed, and preserved.

CONCLUSION

In the beginning of this paper, an example consisting of the designer, the critic, and the thin transparent yellow tracing paper was presented. In this example, the yellow tracing paper mediated between:

1) *intentions* in the designer's mind and the ability of a designer to fluidly represent intentions by *marking*, or allowing a designer to trace over previous marks, modify, compare and realise these marks; and

2) *designer* and the *critic*, by affording them a common canvas on which the designer could trace the development of ideas, evaluate and negotiate ideas, while the critic tries to discern the designer's intentions, explores, transforms and develops them -- the canvas enables craft to be imparted, transformed and innovated.

In the studio, marks on the yellow tracing paper reflect the process of designers graphically experiencing, realising and developing ideas, and provide means by which the marks can be critiqued, transformed and explored. After repeated critiques, the crumpled wads of marked yellow paper, the shadows of a design process, lies abandoned on the floor as the designer drafts a polished presentation drawing. Representation of process is not merely an aid to a presentation drawing, but is valuable to the designer as a sketchpad illustrating the development of a project, designers' personal growth across projects, growth of a design craft, and most memorable of all, the diary of design experiences.

This paper illustrates the sensibilities of a computing-based design environment that can enable the representation of process, and points to the eventual dissemination of craft:

1) a **consistent gestural language** (*strokes, sprinkling gestures and button pushes*) providing the **means to interact** with the machinery as well as create marks that contribute to the **recording of process**;

2) **non-sequentiality within the process** of composition and the ability of a designer to **fluidly** represent overlapping, partial and parallel compositions;

3) mechanisms that enable a designer to **experience process** (*gestures, gestural conversations, threaded spawning of editors*);

4) mechanisms to **realise** and **reflect upon process** (*editing and scripting scenes, re-enacting scenes, preserving scenes*);

5) mechanisms to **share process** with other members in a design group (*presentation by the re-enactment of edited and scripted scenes*).

Although, some of these emulate yellow tracing paper, representation of process in a computing-based environment allows the designer not only to make visible the shadows of process (like yellow tracing paper), but to enact the shadows, render the shadows in different ways, re-enact and preserve process, and, eventually (and hopefully), provide the foundations for the dissemination of craft. The research has just begun to explore this possibility.

Can we walk into a design studio and witness this familiar scene: a group of designers huddled around a display screen? The display screen bears the representation of a designer's process, and in their hands are input devices, one in the hand of the critic, and one in the hand of the designer. The designer enacts process, describes experiences during the process . . . . The critic witnesses the enactment, forms an impression, and gestures with the input device. . . . Together, the designer, the critic and the design environment witness the birth of a new possibility . . . .

REFERENCES

Baer A, Eastman C, Henrion M (1977) A Survey of Geometric Modeling. Institute of Physical Planning Rep. 60, Pittsburgh

Ch'en Ming-ta (1981) Ying-tsao fa-shih ta-mu-tso yen-chiu (Research on timber construction in the Sung manual Building Standards). Wen-wu, Peking

Coomaraswamy DL, introduction in Coomaraswamy, AK (1984) The Arts and Crafts of India & Ceylon. Farrar, Straus and Company, New York

Goldberg A, Robson D (1981) Smalltalk-80: The Language and its Implementation. Addison-Wesley Publishing Company, Reading

Greenberg D, Marcus A (1982) The Computer Image: Applications of Computer Graphics. Addison-Wesley Publishing Company, Reading

Harrison S (1986) Shoptalk 2b: Steve's View of a Conversation, Video. Xerox PARC, Palo Alto

Klee P, edited by Spiller J (1961) Paul Klee: The Thinking Eye. George Witternhorn, New York & Lund Humphries, London

Lambert S (1984) Reading Drawings. Pantheon Books, New York

Loehr M (1980) The Great Painters of China. Harper and Row Publishers, New York

Makkuni R (1985) Experiments on a Grid, M.Arch thesis. University of California, Los Angeles

March L (1976) The Architecture of Form. Cambridge University Press, Cambridge

Mitchell WJ (1977) Computer Aided Architectural Design. Petrocelli Charter, New York

Robson D (1981) Object-Oriented Software Systems. Byte magazine, 6 (8): 74-86

Ssu-ch'eng L, edited by Wilma Fairbank, (1984) A Pictorial History of Chinese Architecture. MIT Press, Cambridge

Steadman P (1973) Graph-Theoretic Representation of Architectural Arrangement. Architectural Research and Teaching, 2 (3)

Stiny G, Gips J (1972) Shape Grammars and the Generative Specification of Paintings and Sculpture. Information Processing 71: 1460-1465

Stults R (1985) Shoptalk 1: Representing the Process of Design, Video. Xerox PARC, Palo Alto

Stults R (1986) Shoptalk 2a: Design Activities Using Computing and Video, Video. Xerox PARC, Palo Alto

Sullivan M (1980) The Three Perfections: Chinese Painting, Poetry and Calligraphy. George Braziller, New York

Whitfield R (1980) In Pursuit of Antiquity. The Art Museum, Princeton University and Charles E. Tuttle Company, Rutland

Ranjit Makkuni is a member of the research staff at the System Concepts Laboratory, Xerox Palo Alto Research Center. He is interested in the use of electronic technologies towards preserving and disseminating design craft.

Ranjit is a member of the American Committee for South Asian Art, American Craft Council, Japan Society of Northern California, and the Tibet Society. He is presently serving on the art advisory board of the Visual Computer.

Ranjit received a B.Arch from the Indian Institute of Technology, Kharagpur, and an M.Arch in design theory and methods from the University of California, Los Angeles.

Address: System Concepts Laboratory, Xerox Palo Alto Research Center, 3333 Coyote Hill Road, Palo Alto, CA 94304, USA.

Information Retrieval System for Optical-Disk-Filed Machine Drawings Based on Feature Description

Syunsuke Minami, Hitoshi Saji, Hideko S. Kunii, and Naomasa Nakajima

ABSTRACT

We propose a method to retrieve the contents of drawings, which employs descriptions of features of machine structures as retrieval keywords. A prototype retrieval system was developed that utilizes optical disks and an image scanner together with a DBMS. Feature Description (FD), on which studies have been promoted by Nakajima et al. at the University of Tokyo and Gossard et al. at MIT, was used as an expression method of machine structures. Feature Description Language (FD language), a language for designers based upon the FD, was employed as an aid for query formation of drawings. Machine structures expressed by the FD were managed by the DBMS based upon a graph data model. As an example, drawings of rolling bearings were stored in the system, and retrieval of combinations of shafts and bearings including fixtures and seals was conducted, which proved that retrieval by contents was effective.

KEYWORDS
information retrieval, feature description, machine drawing, optical disk, graph data model

1. INTRODUCTION

Design activities require various kinds of information. Especially today, high reliability is required for every product and standardization of design is strictly sought in order to attain cost reduction. Thus, it is very important to gather a large volume of relevant information and to refer to it during design processes. Also, the development of network technology has led us to share information which has been individually managed in each department.

For retrieval of documents, efficient systems have been developed with the progress of information processing technology. However, the retrieval of image and picture information such as drawings is prominently behind. Therefore, most of design drawings, the number of which is increasing year by year, are still kept useless.

An obstacle to the progress of retrieval systems of drawings is that a method of retrieval of drawings by the semantics is not yet established. In a management system of drawings, presently in the practical use, only annotational information such as titles, serial numbers, and dates of drawings is available for retrieval. Therefore, retrieval cannot be done against essential information on drawings such as machine structures.

This research aims at realization of an effective retrieval system for machine design drawings. For this purpose, a method to retrieve the contents of drawings is contrived with the use of features of machine structures as keys. Also, a prototype system for design drawing retrieval has been developed to investigate the validity of this method that utilizes a DBMS together with an optical disk driver and an image scanner.

2. RELATED WORK

Studies on image databases including drawings have vigorously been carried out. Above all, databases having keys to image contents, MIDAS [1] by Makeown et al. of Carnegie Mellon University and GRAIN [2] by Chang et al. of Illinois University are distinguished. A study on retrieval of the weather map image database in terms of the characteristics of the figure patterns was tried by Yamamori et al. [3]. However, there is no work on image databases of machine design drawings.

As an example of management of drawings using optical disks, there is YANMAR Specification Management System-Drawing Retrieval System (YMS-DRS System)[4] developed by Yanmer Group. In this system, retrieval can be done against the keys of drawing number, item name, GT code, size, material, and category. However, retrieval is restricted to components and cannot be done against assemblies. Since the key regarding the shape of a component is based upon the GT code for a machining process, the retrieval capability is limited when the system is used for information retrieval of the machine structure required for design.

Nakajima and Gossard [5] proposed a method of Feature Description (FD) to express assembled machines. Based on this, Ishida et al. proposed Feature Description Language (FD language), where its major objective is to detect of unanticipated functions of machines [6]. We express machine structures in terms of the FD. Also we avail ourselves of a subset of the FD language for storing and retrieving drawings.
In addition, a method to express machine components and other such relevant pieces based upon their features is recently reported in the study of Luby et al. [7].

3. EXPRESSIONS OF MACHINE STRUCTURES AND REALIZATION OF CONTENT RETRIEVAL OF DESIGN DRAWINGS

In referring to design drawings, the information on detailed structures of the machines related to a given design object is usually most important. A content retrieval of design drawings in this paper means the retrieval of the information related to machine structures. Adequate keys, or indexes must be provided for each machine structure in order to realize such content retrieval.
The aforementioned Feature Description (FD) is used to determine indexes to retrieve drawings. The FD is a method to express machine structures in terms of functional primitives (feature description elements, FD elements) such as a boss and a shaft, and relationships between elements such as contacts between faces, coincidences of center axes, and dimensional constraints between faces and center axes. The retrieval of drawings in terms of the FD is much effective than the one that only uses geometric information by the following reasons[8]:

- The FD elements include not only geometrical volumes such as a cylinder and a cube but also machine elements such as a shaft, a bearing, a chamfer, a key and a keyway which designers usually use.

- Assembled machines can be expressed.
- A function to define new FD elements of higher level is provided by using registered FD elements and the relationships among them. Thus, the machine can be expressed hierarchically in the way designers usually do.

The Appendix shows the grammar of the FD language with extension for registration and retrieval of drawings which will be described in the next section.

Fig. 1 illustrates a "cylinder" as an example of the FD element, which has "top", "bottom", and "side" as face and "center" as axis. These faces and axis are used to express relationships among elements.
In the retrieval of machine structures expressed by the FD, the FD elements play the role of keywords for retrieval. Fig. 2 shows the list of FD elements used to express rotational units using rolling bearings.

In describing relationships between contact faces and those between coincident axes, the following three terms are used.
- Join   A Contact between fixed faces or a coincidence of axes in the same components.
- Mate   A contact between movable faces or a coincidence of axes among different components.
- Seal   Seal status of lubrication oil on sealed contacting faces.

By using the FD, machine structures can be displayed by a graph in which an FD element is represented by a node and a contact between faces or a coincidence of axes is represented by an arc.   Fig. 3 illustrates a simple machine structure consisting of a stepped shaft and a ring. "Stepped Shaft & Ring" is the name of the assembly, and "Stepped Shaft" and "Ring" are the names of the components. "cyl1", "cyl2", and "cyl" are FD elements of the cylinder type, and "hole" is that of the hole type. "top", "bottom" and "side" are the names of a face, and "center" is the name of an axis.
Using the FD description of machine structures as indexes of the drawings makes it possible to retrieve drawings based on the relationships of features.
Retrieval is performed by structural matching to detect the types of elements, the hierarchical relationships among the elements, the kinds of axes or faces, the contacts between the faces, and the coincidences of the axes.

4. MACHINE DRAWINGS DATABASE

In constructing a database to store structure information, it is necessary to choose a data model adequate to explicitly express relationships between objects. In this study, Graph Data Model (GDM) [9], is adopted as a data model and a drawing database is constructed using G-BASE, DBMS based upon the GDM which is developed by Software Research Center of Ricoh Co., Ltd.
The schema of GDM consists of a set of record types and a set of link types. A record type is equivalent to a relation in a relational model. A link type represents a binary relationship between two record types that can be of an identical type. Link types are classified into two kinds: a real link type and a virtual link type. A real link type connects the occurrences of two record types via pointers. A virtual link type connects those occurrences by the values of compatible attributes of two record types. While the link occurrences of a real link type always physically exist, a virtual link type has physically no link occurrences.

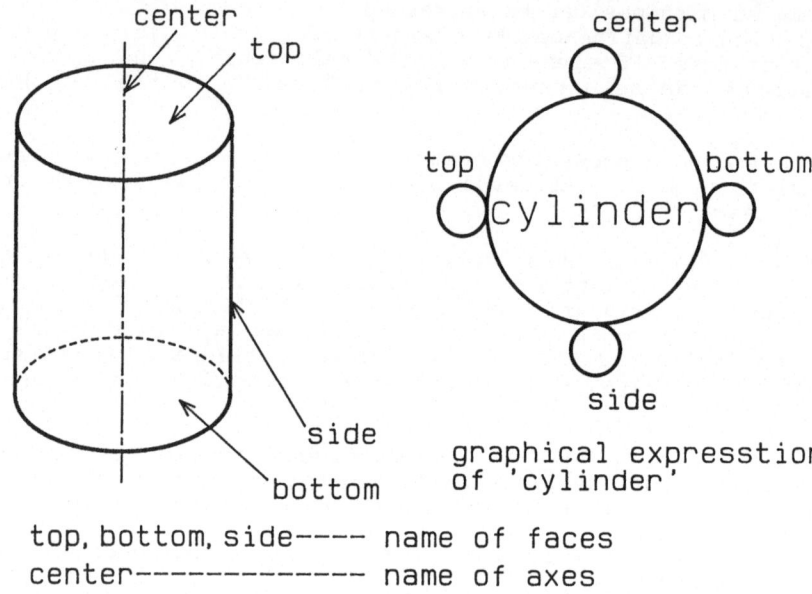

center
top

center

top   bottom

cylinder

side

side

graphical expresstion
of 'cylinder'

bottom

top, bottom, side---- name of faces
center------------- name of axes

Fig. 1 An example of a FD element, "cylinder"

〈geometric primitives〉

    cylinder
    hole
    cube
    prism
    cone
    ring

〈features〉

    boss
    spacer_ring
    flange
    inner_groove
    outer_groove
    inner_thread
    outer_thread
    bevel_gear
    spur_gear
    oil_groove

〈standard parts〉

    bolt
    nut
    washer
    oil_seal
    felt_ring
    retaining_ring

〈bearings〉

    deep_groove_ballbearing
    parallel_rollerbearing
    angular_ballbearing
    conical_rollerbearing
    needle_rollerbearing
    self_aligning_ballbearing
    thrust_ballbearing

Fig. 2 List of FD elements to express rotational units using
rolling bearings

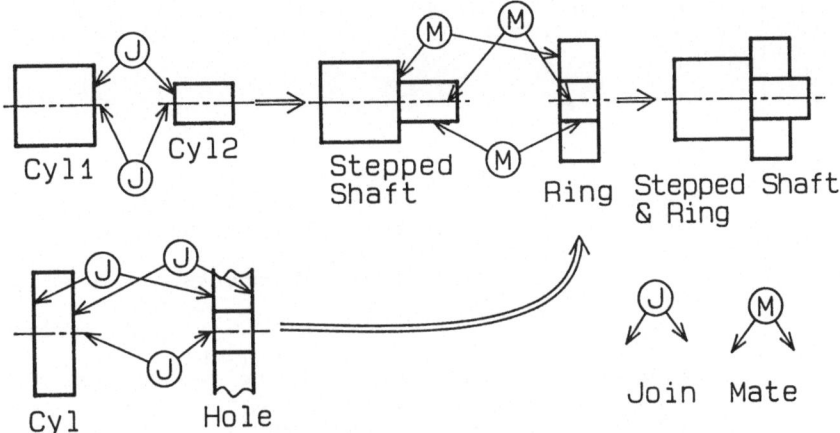

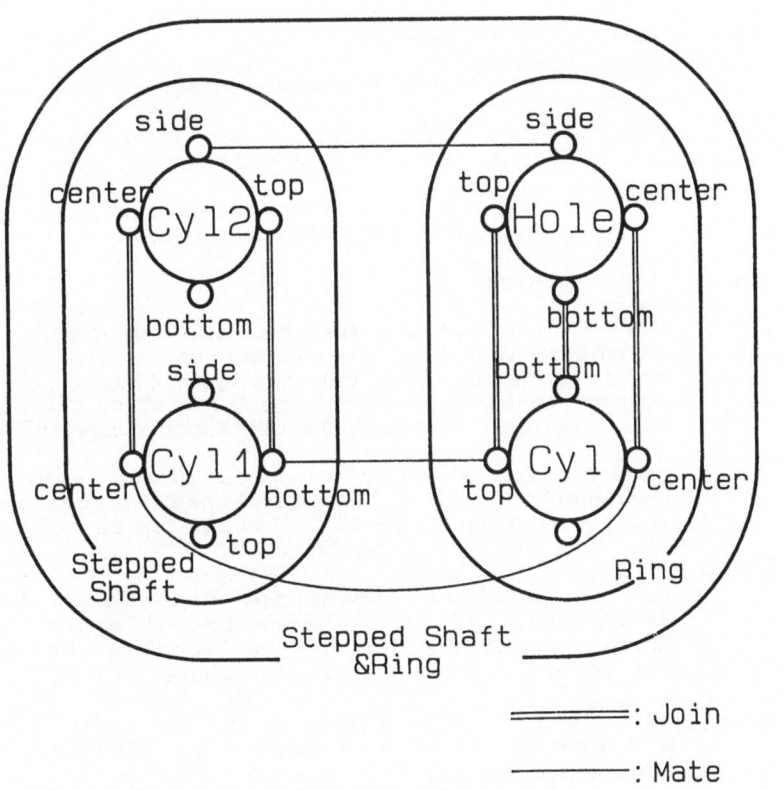

Fig. 3 A simple machine structure represented by the FD
      (Stepped Shaft & Ring)

Fig. 4 illustrates the schema of mechanical drawings database represented by GDM. The interpretation of record types and link types are as follows:

<Record type>	<Attribute>	<Meaning>
Drawing		drawings
	ID	identifier
	Name	name of the image file of a drawing
	Note	annotation of a drawing
Object		assemblies, components, or FD elements
	ID	identifier
	Parent	identifier of the parent record type "Object" of an object
	Drawing	identifier of the record type "Drawing" depicting an object
	Name	name of an object
Face		faces in FD elements
	ID	identifier
	Object	identifier of the record type "Object" that a face belongs to
	Name	name of a face
Axis		axes in FD elements
	ID	identifier
	Object	identifier of the record type "Object" that an axis belongs to
	Name	name of an axis
	No	axis numbers that of coincident axes are assigned the same value

<Link type>   <Meaning>
(virtual link types)

Drawing	association between assemblies, components, or FD elements, and the drawing depicting them: links an occurrence of the record type "Drawing" and an occurrence of the record type "Object" by the values of the attribute "ID" and the attribute "Drawing"
Parent	hierarchical relationships among assemblies, components, and FD elements: links two occurrences of the record type "Object" by the values of the attribute "ID" and the attribute "Parent"
OwnFace	possessional relationships of a face: links an occurrence of the record type "Object" and an occurrence of the record type "Face" by the values of the attribute "ID" and the attribute "Object"
OwnAxis	possessional relationships of an axis: links an occurrence of the record type "Object" and an occurrence of the record type "Axis" by the values of the attribute "ID" and the attribute "Object"
Meet	coincidences of axes: links two occurrences of the record type "Axis" by the values of the attribute "No"

(real link types)

Join,Mate,Seal	relationships of join, mate, seal among faces, respectively: links two occurrences of the record type "Face"

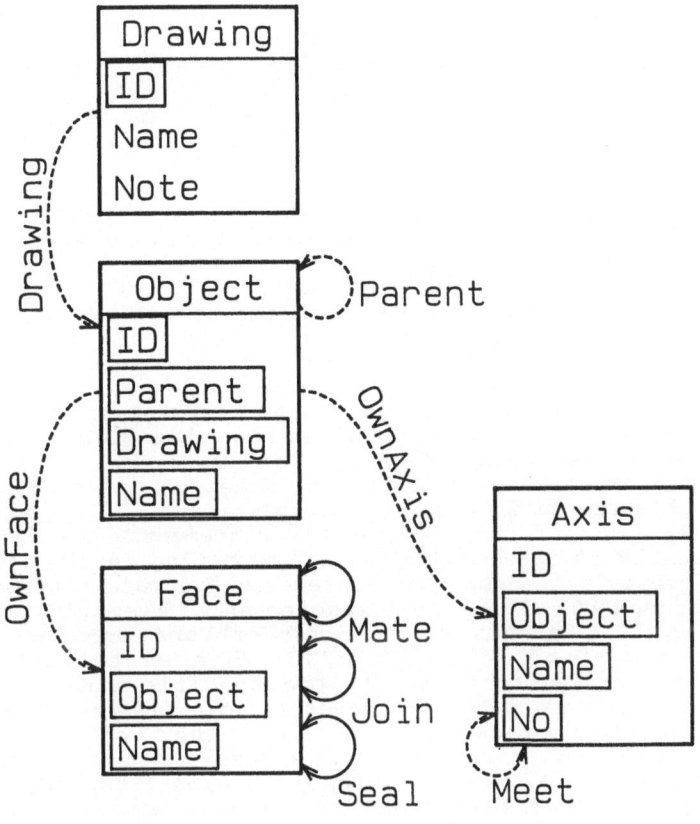

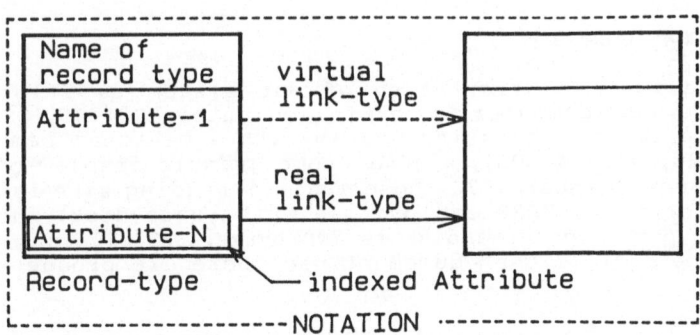

Fig. 4 The schema of machine drawings database represented by GDM

In the database, a coincidence of axes is represented by the virtual link type "Meet" while a contact between faces is represented by the real link type "Join", "Mate", or "Seal". The reasons are as follows:
- In the case of coincidence of axes, it is not necessary to distinguish a coincidence within a component from that among components.
- Where an axis "A" is coincident with an axis "B" and "B" is coincident with an axis "C", the coincident relationship between "A" and "C" holds true. In the case of contacts between faces, this predicate does not hold true.
- In the previous implementation of the FD, the retrieval of a coincidence of axes was realized by traversing links of coincidences [6]. In this study, a coincidence of axes can be retrieved by searching the virtual link type "Meet" without traverse.

Graph Data Language (GDL) is a data language based upon the GDM. The FD language is implemented using this GDL to facilitate registration and retrieval of drawings.

Fig. 5 shows a description of the index of the stepped shaft and the ring (illustrated in Fig. 3) in terms of the FD language. All the lines in the figure denote an assembly statement. The "generic name" of the assembly is "SteppedShaft&Ring" appearing in the line 1, whose structure consists of component statements and mate statements in the lines 2 through 16. The line 3 denotes an FD element statement. It defines two FD elements of a "cylinder" and provides them with "specific names" of "c1" and "c2". When we refer to these FD elements, we designate them with the specific names. The line 4 denotes a coincidence within components (join statement), which makes the faces of the "bottom" of "c1" and of the "top" of "c2" contact within the component. In the line 6 a specific name "shaft" is given to the "SteppedShaft", and parenthesized name "SteppedShaft" is the name of the drawing of this component. In the same way, the structure of "Ring" and the name of the drawing of the component are described in the lines 8 through 13. The line 14 is an example of a coincidence among components (mate statement), which indicates that the "bottom" (the face of the element "c1" in "shaft") and the "top" (the face of the element "c" in "ring") are contacted.

5. SYSTEM CONFIGURATION

The hardware configuration of our system is illustrated in Fig. 6. The host computer is a mini-computer 3B2/310 (OS: UNIX^{TM}). ID100 is an image processing system with a personal computer TS-5 (CPU: i80186, OS: MS-DOS), a monochrome graphic display of 1024x768 dots, an image scanner IS30 whose maximum reading size is A4, and an optical disk drive OD20 employing a write-once disk, whose memory capacity of each side of a disk is 700Mbytes. 3B2/310 is a product of AT&T and the rest of the equipment used here are products of Ricoh Co., Ltd.

The software is developed using a C programming language and an assembly language. G-BASE (3B2 version) developed by Ricoh Co., Ltd. is used as the DBMS.

The registration of drawings follows the next procedure. The image data of a given drawing is read by the image scanner, and filed in the optical disk. The index of the drawing described in the FD language is entered from the keyboard and stored in the database on

---

UNIX^{TM} is a trademark of AT&T

```
1          assembly SteppedShaft&Ring {
2              component SteppedShaft {
3                  feature cylinder c1,c2;
4                      c1->bottom /J/ c2->top;
5                      c1->center /J/ c2->center;
6                  } shaft ( SteppedShaft );
7              component Ring {
8                  feature cylinder c;
9                  feature hole h;
10                     c->top /J/ h->top;
11                     c->bottom /J/ h->bottom;
12                     c->center /J/ h->center;
13                 } ring ( Ring );
14                 shaft.c1->bottom /M/ ring.c->top;
15                 shaft.c2->side /M/ ring.h->side;
16                 shaft.c2->center /M/ ring.c->center;
17         } shaft&ring ( SteppedShaft&Ring );
```

Fig. 5 An example of an index of a drawing described in the FD
language (Stepped Shaft & Ring)

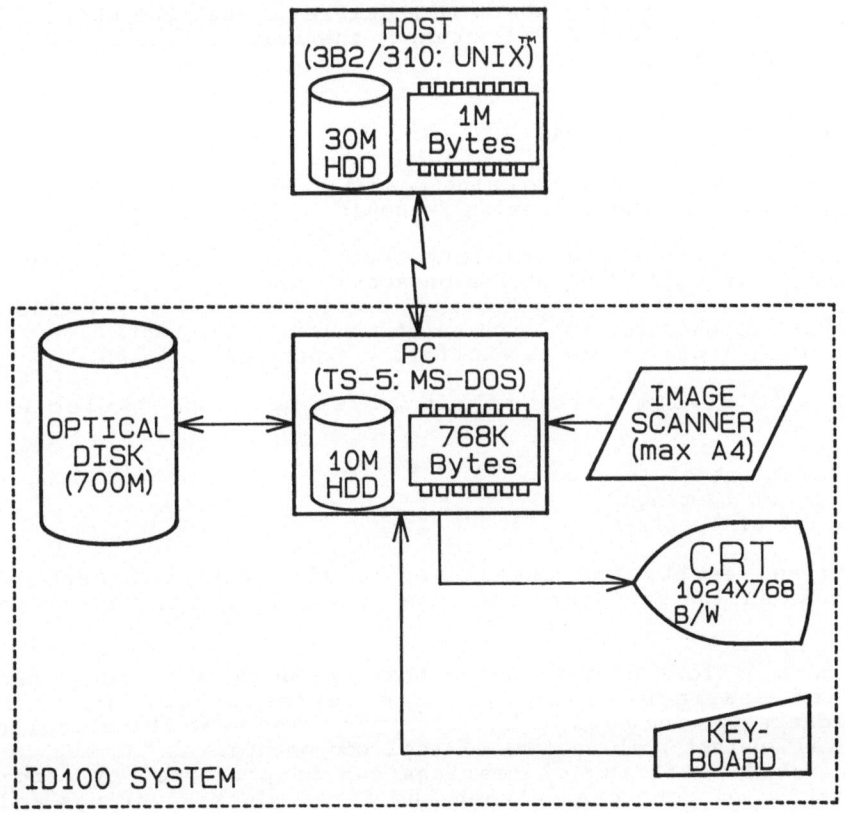

Fig. 6 System configuration

the host computer. The index information and the image data are linked with the name of the image data file.

A query to the database is performed as follows. A user describes a machine structure in the FD language and inputs it from the keyboard. The system retrieves indexes of drawings in the database and displays the list of the drawings which have the desired structure. The list consists of a title of the drawings and the annotational information. When more than one drawing are obtained, the user can either search them by looking at their annotations or browse them one by one. Then, the image data of the drawing is read from the optical disk and displayed on the CRT.

Fig. 7 illustrates an example of query. The query statements to retrieve the machine structure that a bearing is constrained by a shoulder of a stepped shaft in the axial direction is shown in (1). The statements in the lines 1 and 2 mean that one bearing (named "b") and two cylinders (named "c1" and "c2") exist in the structure. The line 3 means that the "bottom" face of "c1" and the "top" face of "c2" are joined. The line 4 represents a coincidence of the "center" axes of "c1" and "c2". The line 5 means that the "inside" face of "b" and the "side" face of "c1" are mated. The line 6 describes that the end face of the inner wheel of "b" (named "inside_bottom") and the "top" face of "c2" are mated. The line 7 means the coincidence of the "center" axes of "b" and "c1". When these statements are entered into the system, the list of the drawings is displayed with titles and annotations shown in (2). The "cnt" is the number of the structures which satisfy query statements in a drawing. When the number in the column "dno" is selected and entered, the image of the drawing shown in (3) is displayed.

6. EXPERIMENTS OF RETRIEVAL

A set of samples of rolling bearings is chosen as the data for our experiments by the following reasons:

- Rolling bearings are primitive machine elements and are often referred in various kinds of design activities.
- Various kinds of rolling bearings are available for selection, and retrieval requests for the machine structure is frequent.
- Retrieval requests can be explicitly expressed.

The following three retrieval examples are selected for experiments.

- Combinations of bearings.
- Fixing of bearings.
- Sealing of lubricating oil.

As a result, the usefulness of the retrieval method that utilizes machine structures as indexes was proved in the following cases.

- In combinations of the shafts that are held by no less than two types of bearings, retrieval was correctly performed using coincidences of the axes of the bearings. The same thing applies to retrieval against combinations of seal components.
- Retrieval of fixing of bearings can be performed by using the information on contacts between the faces of the bearings and the peripheral components. The same thing can be said for the retrieval of sealing lubrication oil by making a portion of a component into a peculiar shape and combining it.

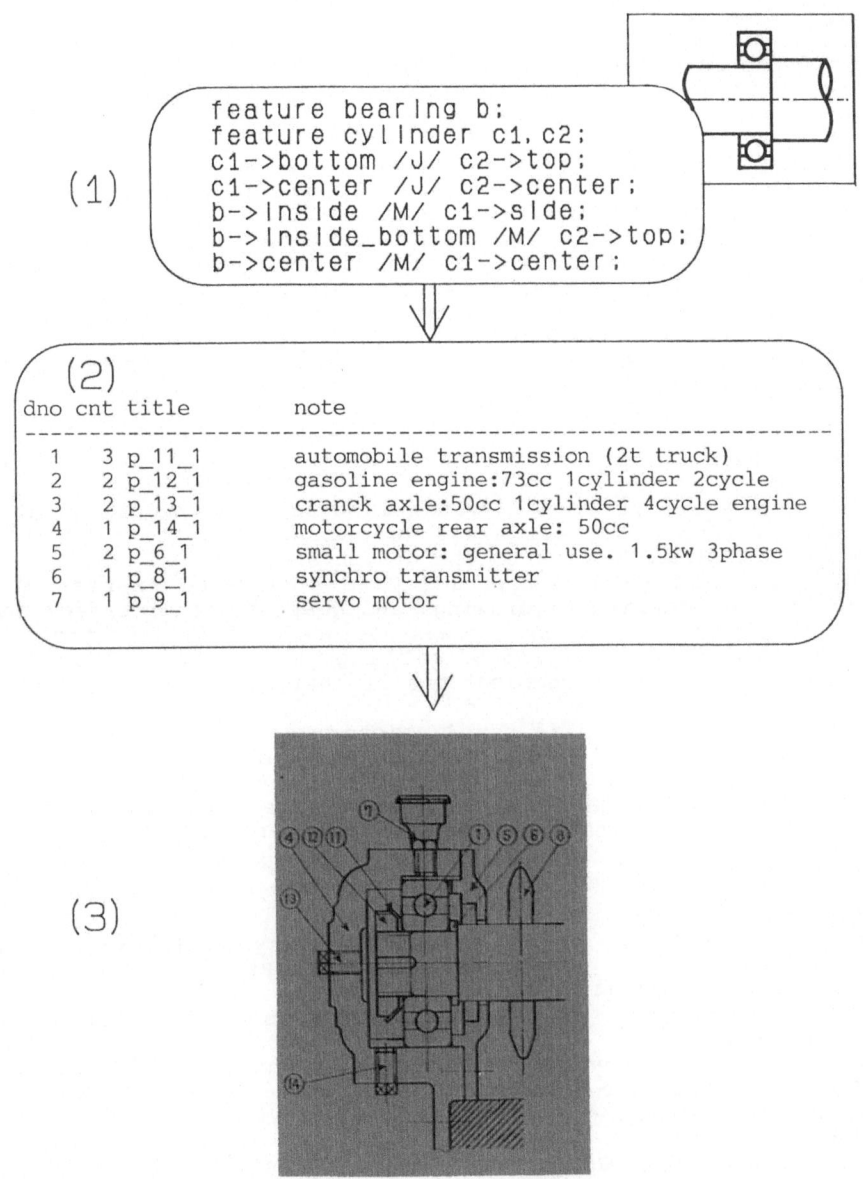

Fig. 7 An example query to the database

- Since most of peripheral components of the bearings are, in general, similar in geometrical configuration, retrieval can be performed by just referring to the names of the elements when the machine structures are expressed in terms of the elements which very clearly identify the functions such as FD elements.

However, there are a few problems in this method as shown below and they are left for the future work.

- Since the information on machine structures is used as indexes of drawings, detailed information such as contacts between faces and coincidences of axes must be available. Our efforts to reduce the work required for registration of drawings are made by adopting index registration based upon the FD language that is easy for designers to understand. One approach to reduce the input work is automatic indexing of design drawings by mechanical recognition.
- The same thing applies to queries. Since a query is realized by describing machine structures in the FD language, knowledge on the grammar of the FD language, the definitions of the FD elements, etc. is required. Also the machine structure should be described without any contradiction. Realizing a thesaurus as in a document retrieval system and also abstracting the FD elements from shape elements to functional elements are desirable.

7. CONCLUSION

(1) An information retrieval system in which machine design drawings were stored in optical disks was developed, adopting the feature description (FD) as indexes to the drawings.
(2) By using the FD language adequate enough to express machine structures for indexing of drawings and queries, an interface that is easy for designers to understand was designed and implemented.
(3) As a case study, drawings of rolling bearings were stored in the system and retrieval of combinations of shafts and bearings including fixtures and seals was conducted.
(4) By using GDM as a data model, machine structures based upon the FD was easily expressed in the database schema.

We acknowledge the financial aid by the Ministry of Education (trial study, representative, Nakajima) on this research.

REFERENCES
[1] P.M. Mckeown Jr. et al., "A hierarchical symbolic representation for an image database", Proc. of Workshop on Picture Data Description and Management, pp40-44. 1977.
[2] S.K. Chang et al., "A relational database system for picture", ibid., pp142-149.
[3] K. Yamamori, Y. Yoshida, T. Fukumura, "Encoding of Weather Maps and Its Application to Weather Map Database System", Transitions of Information Processing Society of Japan, Vol.26, No.6, 1985. (In Japanese)
[4] H. Kameoka, "YMS-DRS System in Yanmar Diesel", Office Management, Vol.25, No.3, 1986. (In Japanese)
[5] N. Nakajima, D.C. Gossard, "Basic Study on Feature Descriptor", MIT CAD Lab. Technical Report, 1982.
[6] T. Ishida, H. Minowa, N. Nakajima, "Detection of Unanticipated Functions of Machines" ISDS, July 1984.
[7] S.C. Luby, J.R. Dixon, M.K. Simmons, "Creating and Using A Feature Data Base", Computers in Mechanical Engineering, Nov. 1986.
[8] H. Takase, N. Nakajima, "A Language For Describing Assembled Machines", ISDS, July 1984.
[9] H.S. Kunii, "Graph Data Language: A High Level Access-Path Oriented Language", Ph. D. Dissertation of The University of Texas at Austin, May 1983.

Appendix

The Grammar of the FD Language in Backus-Naur form

```
        <index of drawing> ::= <assembly statment>

        <query> ::= <assembly structure>
                  | <component structure>
                  | <FD element structure>

        <assembly statement>
             ::= assembly <generic name> { <assembly structure> }
                   <list of specific names>
                   ( <name of drawing> ) ;
                 | assembly <generic name> { <assembly structure> }
                   <list of specific names>
                   ( <name of drawing> "<comment>" ) ;

        <assembly structure>
             ::= <assembly statement>
               | <component statement>
               | <assembly structure> <assembly statement>
               | <assembly structure> <component statement>
               | <assembly structure> <mate statement>
               | <assembly structure> <seal statement>

        <component statement>
             ::= compoent <generic name> { <component structure> }
                   <list of specific name>
                   ( <name of drawing> );
                 | component <generic name> { <component structure> }
                   <list of specific name>
                   ( <name of drawing> "<comment>" );

        <component structure>
             ::= <FD element statement>
               | <component structure> <FD element statement>
               | <component structure> <join statement>

        <FD element statement>
             ::= feature <generic name> { <FD element structure> }
                   <list of sepcific names> ;
                 | feature <name of defined FD element>
                   <list of specific names>;

        <FD element sturcture>
             ::= <FD element statement>
               | <FD element structure> <FD element statement>
               | <FD element structure> <join statement>

        <mate statement>
             ::= <path> -> <name of face> /M/ <path> -> <name of face> ;
               | <path> -> <name of axis> /M/ <path> -> <name of axis> ;

        <join statement>
             ::= <path> -> <name of face> /J/ <path> -> <name of face> ;
               | <path> -> <name of axis> /J/ <path> -> <name of axis> ;

        <seal statement>
             ::= <path> -> <name of face> /S/ <path> -> <name of face> ;

        <path> ::= <specific name> | <path> . <specific name>

        <list of specific names>
             ::= <specific name>
               | <list of specific names> , <specific name>
```

Syunsuke Minami* is a member of Hitachi, Ltd. His research interests include Computer Aided Design for machine.

He received B.E. and M.S. in mechanical engineering at the University of Tokyo in 1985 and in 1987, respectively.

Hitoshi Saji** is currently a research student of information science at the University of Tokyo. His research interests include database and its application to machine design.

He received B.E. in mechanical engineering at the University of Tokyo in 1987.

Hideko S. Kunii*** is currently the director of Software Research Center of Ricoh Co., Ltd., managing R&D projects in the areas of OS, DBMS, CAD/CAM, Document Processing, and AI. Her principal research interest is DBMS for engineering applications, multi-media DBMS, and distributed systems.

She received Ph. D. in computer sciences at The University of Texas at Austin in 1983, M.S. in electric engineering at The California State University at San Jose in 1976, M.S. in physics at Ochanomizu University in 1973, and B.S. in physics at Ochanomizu University in 1970.

Naomasa Nakajima**** is a professor of mechanical engineering at the University of Tokyo, where he has been teaching CAD/CAM and engineering design, and directs the research of graduate students and research associates in knowledge base CAD/CAM system and CAD/CAM education system. His research interests include not only CAD/CAM and computer graphics but also system design for autonomous energy system, autonomous building and welfare apparatus.

He received B.E., M.S. and Ph. D. in mechanical engineering at the University of Tokyo in 1964, 1966, and in 1969, respectively. He is a member of JSME and Computer Graphics Society.

Address:
* Hitachi, Ltd., 6, Kanda-Surugadai 4 chome, Chiyoda-ku, Tokyo 101, Japan
** Faculty of Science, The University of Tokyo, 7-3-1 Hongo, Bunkyo-ku, Tokyo 113, Japan
*** Software Research Center, Ricoh Co., Ltd., Tomin-Nissei-Kasugacho Bldg., 1-1-17 Koishikawa, Bunkyo-ku, Tokyo 112, Japan
**** Faculty of Engineering, The University of Tokyo, 7-3-1 Hongo, Bunkyo-ku, Tokyo 113, Japan

Chapter 9

Hierarchical Modeling

H-P Model

A Hierarchical Space Decomposition in a Polar Coordinate System

Yong C. Chen and Catherine M. Murphy

ABSTRACT

The hierarchical probe model, a geometric model, using hierarchical data structures to represent 2-D and 3-D objects, is developed. Many radial lines, called probes, are drawn from the origin. The intersection points of probes and the boundary of the object are stored in a tree and a number of lists. The piecewise boundaries of the object between adjacent probes are represented by the patches which are the interpolations of intersection points, also called control points, on the probes. The error of representation is defined to describe the details of the model representing an object. In the appendix, we prove that the basic theory which insures the model can represent any physical object with an error less than a given tolerance. The new model is evaluated and compared with the octree/quadtree model. Several advantages of the model are also discussed.

Keywords: geometric modeling, octree/quadtree model, cellular decomposition, hierarchical probe model

1. INTRODUCTION

The development of geometric models have led to important applications in CAD/CAM (Woo 1984), computer graphics, artificial intelligence, computer vision, simulation, and robotics. Some of the familiar methods for representation and organization of geometric information include wireframe, generalized cylinder (Lee 1982), graph based representation, transformational sweeping (Mortenson 1985), constructive solid geometry (Boyse 1982), analytic solid modeling (Casale 1985) and octree/quadtree representation (Jackins 1980; Samet 1984). Reviews of geometric models are described by Requicha (1983) and Mortenson (1985).

Among geometric models the octree/quadtree representation has received considerable attention recently. One reason is the use of the hierarchical data structures with the cellular decomposition scheme, which can reduce the computational complexity of data retrievals. For example, the computational complexities of the set operations, i.e. union, intersection, and difference, in the octree/quadtree representation are linear to the given trees. In addition to the above advantage, this scheme stores geometric and topological properties in the same data structure, which eliminates redundancy and is useful for analysis. However, some defects remain, including discontinuities of surface normals, measurement discrepancies of boundaries between objects and their representations (Chen 1987), and difficulties in scaling operations (Samet 1984). Several improvements and modifications to the octree/quadtree model have been reported (Samet 1984; Carlbom 1985). The connections to other models and the higher dimensional tree models are also investigated (Tamminen 1984; Yau 1983). In this paper an alternative version of the geometric model (Chen 1985), named the hierarchical probe (HP) model, is discussed and evaluated. This new model eliminates some limitations and yet retains the power of the tree structure. Especially, it provides a data structure to support real-time rotation of models of internal organs, for examples heart, brain and kidney, and provides surface normal data for shading.

2. 2-D HP MODEL

To simplify the analysis, the HP model for 2-D objects is presented prior to the introduction of the model for 3-D objects. Several terms are defined before the representation scheme and the associated data structure are introduced.

2.1 Terminology

The HP model is a cellular decomposition of the 2-D polar plane into wedges. A wedge $W(\theta_0, \theta_1)$, determined by $\theta = \theta_0$ and $\theta = \theta_1$, is the set of points (r, θ) with $\theta_0 <= \theta <= \theta_1$, and $r >= \emptyset$. $\theta = \theta_0$ is the right probe of the wedge and $\theta = \theta_1$ is the left probe of the wedge (Figure 1). $\alpha = \theta_1 - \theta_0$ is the angle of the wedge. If $W(\theta_0, \theta_1)$ and $W(\theta_1, \theta_2)$ are adjacent wedges, the ridge between them is the ordered pair (θ_1, θ_1). The first coordinate is for the wedge of $W(\theta_0, \theta_1)$ and is called the clockwise thread of the probe; the second coordinate is for the wedge of $W(\theta_1, \theta_2)$ and is called the counterclockwise thread of the probe (Figure 2). In other words, a probe contains two conceptual threads, one for each wedge adjacent to the probe. For our purposes, the probes are along lines of the form $\theta = 2k \pi/2^n$, where k and n are non-nagative integers. The angles of the wedges are $2\pi/2^m$, where k and m are non-negative integers with $k < 2^n$ (Figure 3). We define the integer m as the order of the wedge. Due to the decomposition of the 2-D space, the boundary of the object is also decomposed into small pieces (Figure 3). The piecewise boundaries in each wedge can be classified into three categories as follows:

Category I: In most cases, the boundary intersects with each edge probe of the wedge at the same number of points. The intersection points are called control points. It is assumed that each control point belongs to both threads of a probe. The boundaries within this wedge are approximated by the linear parametric equations,

$$r(t) = r_1 + (r_2 - r_1)t$$

$$\theta(t) = \theta_1 + (\theta_2 - \theta_1)t, \quad 0 <= t <= 1 \quad \text{(Figure 4)},$$

where (r_1, θ_1) and (r_2, θ_2) are the polar coordinates of the corresponding control points. Because of the linear relation between r and θ, the interpolation curves are spirals.

To measure the possible error created by the approximating procedure, one may define the error in one wedge as

$$error = \max \{ |(r_a, \theta(t)) - (r_b, \theta(t))|, \text{ for } 0 <= t <= 1 \},$$

where $(r_b, \theta(t))$ is a point on the real boundary and $(r_a, \theta(t))$ is the corresponding point on the approximating curve. This measurement can also be applied to the other two categories.

It can be proved that for a given object and a given $\varepsilon > 0$, one can find a $\Delta\theta$ so that the error in the wedges with $\alpha < \Delta\theta$ will be less than (Chen 1987) ε. The above statement insures that the approximate error of the HP model for any object can be smaller than the given tolerance.

Category II: In another case (Figure 5), part of the boundary coincides with the probe A between control points P_1 and P_2. Since P_2 is connected to P_3 along a path in the wedge X, P_2 is assumed to be on the clockwise thread of the probe A. By the same token, P_1 is on the counterclockwise thread. The boundary of the object in the wedges X and Y are represented by the spirals S_1 and S_2 as well as the line segment $\overline{P_1P_2}$.

Category III: In the last case (Figure 6), the wedge has a different number of control points on its edge probes A and B. To represent this situation, two different methods, the inner and the outer approximations, can be used. The inner approximation places both control points, P_1 and P_2, on the counter-clockwise thread of the probe A (Figure 7a). The shaded portion of object in the wedge X is truncated. The approximate boundary includes the line segment $\overline{P_1P_2}$. The outer approximation inserts two identical control points P_1' and P_2' ($P_1' = P_2'$), to the counterclockwise thread of the probe B (Figure 7b). The radial components of P_1' and P_2' equal the average of the radial components of P_1 and P_2. The approximate boundary contains spirals S_1' and S_2'. Apparently, the round-off procedure creates approximate errors, but the errors can be reduced to any small value by increasing the number of wedges (Chen 1987).

Now, in all cases, any wedge has the same number of control points on its edge threads. The spiral arcs can be constructed from the pairs of the corresponding control points. From another point of view, the HP model presents objects by a collection of primitives. Each primitive is a portion of a wedge bounded by the two edge threads and spirals (or one spiral). The control points are on the corners of the primitives (Figure 8).

The error of the HP model (representation) is defined as the maximum error of all the wedges and the order of the model is defined as the maximum order of all the wedges in 2-D space.

2.2 Data structure

The data structure of the HP model contains a binary tree and linked lists. The angles of wedges are stored in the tree, which represents the topological properties of the object. The linked lists, which are pointed to by the leaves of the tree, store the radial components of control points.

Each node of the tree, representing a wedge, contains two pointers, since each wedge is decomposed, if required, into two wedges. For an interior node, the left pointer points to the node of the counter-clockwise subwedge while the right pointer points to the clockwise one. For a leaf node, the left pointer points to the list of the radial components of the control points on the clockwise thread of the left edge probe of the wedge. The right pointer points to that of the counter-clockwise thread of the right edge probe. Since there may be more than one control point on a thread, each node in the lists contains a pointer which points to the radial components of the next control points. The lists of the radial components are simply called radial lists.

Figure 9 shows the space decomposition and the data structure of modeling a given object. At the beginning a probe is drawn in the $\theta = 0$ direction and the control point p_0 is sampled (Figure 9a). Node N (Figure 9b) representing the universal wedge W, the entire 2-D polar space, is created in the tree. Since the interpolated arc cannot represent the real boundary of the object within the given tolerance, more probes must be added to the space. P_4, at $\theta = \pi$, divides the universal wedge W into two wedges, W_0 and W_1. The corresponding nodes are N_0 and N_1, respectively. Suppose the approximate error in W_1 is within the given tolerance, then the decomposition in wedge W_1 is terminated, and N_1 becomes a leaf node. Its pointers point to the radial lists r_4 and r_0. W_0 is decomposed into W_{00} and W_{01}. W_{01} is decomposed into W_{010} and W_{011}, but no division is made in W_{00}. The decompositions are repeated until the approximate error in each wedge is smaller than the given tolerance. The inner and the outer approximations are made in the wedges W_{0101} and W_{0100}. Multiple control points are obtained on the edge probes of the wedge W_{0100}. The radial components of control points are linked one by one in the list (Figure 9b). Since most control points are duplicated, part of the data in the radial lists is redundant. In the case where the storage space is limited, one may combine identical radial lists into one list. Each node also includes another pointer pointing to its parent node or preceding node.

2.3 Examples

In the HP model, a circle with its center at the origin can be modeled by only one probe without error. Furthermore, the hierarchical probe representation of an object with a curved boundary tends to cause less error than that of one with a straight boundary. In a worst case, the modeling of a triangle with the mass center at the origin and the base in the $\theta = 0$ direction is shown in Figure 10. As the number of the probes increases, the approximation is improved. The shape of the object (triangle) looks like a leaf with 8 probes. For 32 probes, the sides of the approximated triangle are approaching straight lines. The top vertex of the triangle is found to be sharp, as one of the probes passes through it. The two base angles are inaccurate, for they are rounded off through the interpolation of a continuous curve. As the number of probes increases, eventually, distances from some probes to each vertex will be smaller than required. Figure 11 illustrates a circular object that does not include the origin. Again, the approximation is improved as the number of probes increases.

3. 3-D HP MODEL

The analysis of 2-D modeling can be generalized using a 3-D spherical coordinate system (r, θ, ϕ). The 3-D space is decomposed into a number of cones that are in the form of { $(r, \theta, \phi) \mid \theta \in [\theta_0, \theta_1]$ and $\phi \in [\phi_0, \phi_1]$, where $\theta_0 = k\pi/2^n$, $\phi_0 = 2m\pi/2^n$, $\theta_1 = \theta_0 + \pi/2^n$, $\phi_1 = \phi_0 + \pi/2^n$, and k, m, and n are non-negative integers with k and m $< 2^n$ }. The integer n is defined as the order of the cone. The diagram showing the spatial dependence of θ and ϕ is illustrated in Figure 12. Each divided area represents a cone in the 3-D space. The intersections of the vertical lines and horizontal lines are the locations of probes. The ranges of the polar and the azimuth angles are $0 <= \theta <= \pi$ and $0 <= \phi <= 2\pi$, respectively. In order to obtain the same measurement in the θ and the ϕ directions, the entire space is initially divided into two cones at $\phi = \pi$. After that, each cone is

decomposed into 4 smaller ones if desired. The approximated surface
of each cone can be interpolated from the control points on the probes
residing at the 4 corners (usually distinct except at $\theta = 0$ and $\theta = \pi$)
of the cone (Figure 13). The 3-D polar parametric equations of the
simplest form for the surface are found to be

$$r(s, t) = r_0 + (r_1 - r_0)s + (r_2 - r_0)t + (r_3 - r_2 - r_1 + r_0)st$$

$$\theta(s, t) = \theta_0 + (\theta_1 - \theta_0)s$$

$$\phi(s, t) = \phi_0 + (\phi_1 - \phi_0)t, \qquad 0 <= s <= 1 \text{ and } 0 <= t <= 1,$$

where r's, θ's and ϕ's are the spherical coordinate components of
the control points. $r(s, t)$ is a non-linear function of the parameters
s and t. However, in the edges of the piecewise approximate surface,
i.e., $s = 0$, $s = 1$, $t = 0$, and $t = 1$, $r(s, t)$ reduces to a linear
function. Being analogous to those of the 2-D case, the definitions
of the errors and the orders of the 3-D modeling are omitted.

Like the 2-D HP model, the data structure of the 3-D case also
contains a hierarchy tree and radial lists of control points.
Unlike the 2-D model, however, a quadtree is used instead of the
binary tree. For each interior node, there are four pointers pointing
to the children nodes. For each leaf node, they point to the radial
lists of control points. Several threads of each probe are required,
because each probe is located at the corners of more than one cone.
The number of threads varies in three different cases. In Figure 14,
four cones are attached to probe A. Therefore, 4 threads are required
for probe A. Three cones X, Y and Z are adjacent to probe B, but no
corners of X are located at probe B. Therefore, probe B only requires
two threads. One is for the cone Y and the other is for Z. All
probes have 2 or 4 threads, except the probes at $\theta = 0$ and $\theta = \pi$.
Since they are the degeneracy directions of the spherical coordinate
system, more than 4 threads are required here.

It is important to notice that there are discontinuities on the 3-D
approximate surfaces (Figure 15). Control point P_0 at probe A is
sampled from the surface of the object. P_1 is the intersection of the
edge of the approximate surface of cone X and probe A. Hence, the
approximate surface of cone X does not match the approximate surfaces
of cone Y_0 and cone Y_1. The problem only exists for the probes with
two threads. It may be solved by using the cones with the same order
through the whole model, but is will increase the size of the tree,
consuming tremendous amount of memory space. The best solution is
sampling the control points from the approximate surface of the
adjacent cone with lower order instead of the surface of the object.
After the entire space is decomposed into the desired cones, the
control points on the probes with two threads are resampled from
the approximate surfaces. The replacement will increase the approximate error, but the increments can be balanced by reducing the given
tolerance to a fractional factor. The existence of the factor has
been proven (Chen 1987) (see Appendix for the details).

Approximations of a cube are shown in Figure 16. The pattern fidelity
is improved as the number of probes increases. For the part of a unit
cube in the first octant shown in Figures 17a, 17b and 17c, the
tolerances are 0.05, 0.01 and 0.005, respectively. Unlike Figure
16, the cones in Figure 17 are unequally decomposed, since further
decomposition is not required when the approximate error of a cone is
smaller than the given tolerance. One can see three edges of the cube
clearly shown in Figure 17c. Again, the approximation is improved as
the number of probes increases or, in other words, the tolerance
decreases.

4. DISCUSSION

Both the HP and the octree/quadtree models store the geometric and the topological properties in the same data structure. It is a very important feature for geometric models, since the separated data sets may cause data redundancy and difficulties of analysis.

Another advantage of the octree/quadtree model is its simplicity for performing set operations, i.e., union, intersection, and difference (Samet 1984). The resulting tree can be obtained merely by traversing the given trees in parallel while the resulting tree is being constructed. The set operations are performed on each corresponding node. The algorithm of the set operations for the HP model is quite similar to that of the octree/quadtree, except for the numerical calculations on the radial lists.

It is trivial that an octree/quadtree can be enlarged or reduced by a power of 2 merely by rearranging some pointers of the tree. Rotations in multiples of 90 degrees can be easily performed by a similar method. However there is no simple algorithm for general transformations, rotations or scaling operations. Scaling an object in the HP model up or down becomes easier since the parameters that determine the physical size are listed separately. By rearranging some pointers of the HP tree, the object can be rotated in multiples of $2\pi/2^n$ along the ϕ direction (Chen 1987).

There is a major defect in the octree/quadtree model. The normal directions of the approximate surface are always along several fixed directions (Figure 18). There is a 90 degree discontinuity between two consecutive patches. It is extremely harmful to some important applications (e.g., the shading of the computer graphics which rely on the directions of the surface). Although the problem can be solved by adding the value of the surface normal to each leaf node of the tree, the enlarged tree will cause difficulties for storage and analysis. Another problem related to that of the surface normal is that the measurement of the approximate boundary does not converge to the boundary of the real object. In Figure 19, one can find that no matter how close the area of the approximation approaches the object, the perimeter of it always equals $4/(2+\sqrt{2})$ of the real boundary. The above difficulties do not exist in the HP model (Chen 1987).

The octree/quadtree provides better representation and less data storage for objects with boundaries parallel to X and Y (or X, Y and Z) axes, whereas the HP model shows its superiority for objects with a curved boundary. Any formal comparisons of both models based on particular objects may be unfair to either model. Therefore, an ad hoc comparison based on the worst cases is made. A square in the first quadrant is used as the worst case of the HP model (Figure 20). The quadrant is decomposed into 4 wedges. Eleven tree nodes and 4 list nodes are used. Suppose each pointer is an integer which takes 4 bytes and each radial component in the lists is a real number which also takes 4 bytes. Overall, 148 bytes are required. This figure is calculated on the basis of three pointers in each tree node and one radial component in each list node. The approximation error of this model is 0.021. On the other hand, a quarter of the circle residing in the first quadrant is chosen as the worst case for the quadtree model. The decomposition of the space is shown in Figure 21. Nine nodes are used, each node requiring 5 pointers. The total storage space for the tree is 180 bytes, more storage space than the HP model. Furthermore, the approximation error, 0.075, is larger than that of the HP model.

Like the other models, the HP model has some weaknesses: it does not easily handle non-convex objects and is sensitive to orientation. In addition its data structure contains real numbers. However, in many cases, it can be simplified by using fixed point arithmetic calculation, which is equivalent to integer calculation.

5. CONCLUSION

The hierarchical probe model for representing 2-D and 3-D objects has been developed. Pattern fidelity and approximate error can be determined by the number of probes being used. Several mathematical statements supporting the model are stated without detailed proof. The formal proofs will be shown in later articles (Chen 1987). From the comparison with the octree/quadtree model, the development of the HP model has been shown to be very encouraging.

6. REFERENCES

Woo T (1984) Interface Solid Modeling to CAD and CAM: Data Structures and Algorithms for Decomposing a Solid. IEEE Computer 12: 44-49

Lee Y, Requicha A (1982) Algorithms for Computing the Volume and Other Integral Properties of Solids. CACM 25(9): 635-641

Mortenson M (1985) Geometric Modeling. John Wiley & Son

Boyse J, Gilchrist J (1982) GM Solid: Interactive Modeling for Design and Analysis of Solids. IEEE CG&A 2(2): 27-40

Casale M, Stanton E (1985) An Overview of Analytic Solid Modeling. IEEE CG&A 5(2): 45-56

Jackins C, Tanimoto S (1980) Octrees and Their Use in Representing Three-Dimensional Objects. Computer Graphics and Image Processing 14: 249-270

Samet H (1984) Quadtree and Related Hierarchical Data Structure. Computing Surveys 16(2): 188-253

Requicha A, Voelcker H (1983) Solid Modeling: Current Status and Research Directions. IEEE CG&A 10: 25-37

Chen Y, Murphy C, Chen A (1987) Mathematical Aspects of the Hierarchical Probe Model. in preparation

Carlbom I, Chakravarty I, Vanderschel D (1985) A Hierarchical Data Structure for Representing the Spatial Decomposition of 3-D objects. IEEE CG&A 5(4): 24-31

Tamminen M, Samet H (1984) Efficient Octree Conversion by Connectivity Labeling. Computer Graphics 18(3): 43-51

Yau M, Srihari S (1983) A Hierarchical Data Structure for Multidimensional Digital Images. CACM 26(7): 504-515

Chen Y, Grace T (1985) Boundary Codes Consisting of Spiral Surfaces between Radial Probes. SIAM Conference on Geometric Modeling and Robotics: A16-17.

APPENDIX

Two results from (Chen 1987) are included here since overcoming the problem that adjacent approximating surfaces may not match up at their edges was crucial in developing the 3-D HP model.

Let $P_i(r_i, \theta_i, \phi_i)$, $0 <= i <= 3$, be control points on the real surface R, used to determine a cone and approximating surface (r, θ, ϕ) with error $\varepsilon > 0$. Let $P'(r'_i, \theta_i, \phi_i)$, $0 <= i <= 3$, be points along the four probes of this cone with $r'_i - r_i = \mathcal{E}_i$, $0 <= i <= 3$. Then error between the real surface R and the new approximating surface (r', θ, ϕ) is

bounded by $\max\{ |\mathcal{E}_0|, |\mathcal{E}_1|, |\mathcal{E}_2|, |\mathcal{E}_3| \} + \varepsilon.$

Proof:

$$r = r_0 + (r_1 - r_0)s + (r_2 - r_0)t + (r_3 - r_2 - r_1 + r_0)st.$$

$$r' = r'_0 + (r'_1 - r'_0)s + (r'_2 - r'_0)t + (r'_3 - r'_2 - r'_1 + r'_0)st.$$

Then $\Delta r = r' - r = \mathcal{E}_0 + (\mathcal{E}_1 - \mathcal{E}_0)s + (\mathcal{E}_2 - \mathcal{E}_0)t + (\mathcal{E}_3 - \mathcal{E}_2 - \mathcal{E}_1 + \mathcal{E}_0)st.$

Since

$$\left(\frac{\partial^2 \Delta r}{\partial s \, \partial t}\right)^2 - \left(\frac{\partial^2 \Delta r}{\partial s^2}\right) \cdot \left(\frac{\partial^2 \Delta r}{\partial t^2}\right) = \left(\frac{\partial^2 \Delta r}{\partial s \, \partial t}\right)^2 \geq 0,$$

then Δr has no relative maximum or minimum. Its extreme value must occur at a vertex of its domain, that is, when $s=0, t=0$; $s=1, t=0$; $s=0, t=1$; or $s=1, t=1$. At these points, Δr has values $\mathcal{E}_0, \mathcal{E}_1, \mathcal{E}_2, \mathcal{E}_3$, respectively. Therefore, the maximum of the function

$$\Delta r = \max \{ |\mathcal{E}_0|, |\mathcal{E}_1|, |\mathcal{E}_2|, |\mathcal{E}_3| \}.$$

The new error of the cone is

$$\max |r' - R| = \max |r' - r + r - R| \leq \max |r' - r| + \max |r' - R|$$

$$\leq \max \{ |\mathcal{E}_0|, |\mathcal{E}_1|, |\mathcal{E}_2|, |\mathcal{E}_3| \} + \varepsilon. \qquad \text{Q.E.D.}$$

We shall use this information to show that discontinuities between 3-D approximate surfaces caused by adjacent cones being of different orders can be smoothed out through resampling without exceeding the prescribed tolerance for the error.

Proof:

Probes of order 0 cones are never resampled. We need only be concerned with orders greater than or equal to 1. Let $\varepsilon > 0$ be given. We can find a 3-D HP representation of order n such that the error of representation is less than ε (Chen 1987). From above, if a cone of order 1 must be resampled, the error may increase to at most $\varepsilon + \varepsilon$. Similarly, the error of an order k cone may increase to $\varepsilon + k\varepsilon$.

To keep our error of representation less than ε, we must increase the order of representation to n+m, where m is an integer solution of $n+1 < 2^m - m$. In this higher-ordered representation, the error of representation is $\varepsilon' = \varepsilon / 2^m$ (Chen 1987). After resampling the maximum error is

$$\varepsilon' + (n+m) \varepsilon' = (n+m+1) \varepsilon' < 2^m \cdot \varepsilon' \leq \varepsilon. \qquad \text{Q.E.D.}$$

451

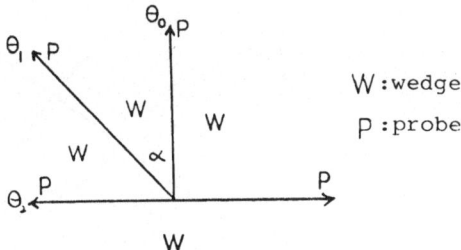

W:wedge

P:probe

Fig.1. Wedges and probes in 2-D space

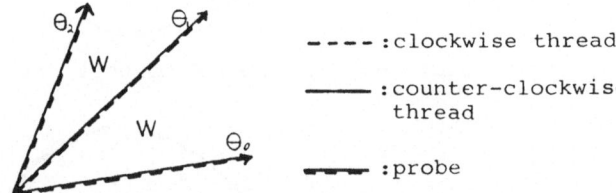

- - - - :clockwise thread

——— :counter-clockwise thread

—— :probe

Fig.2. Threads

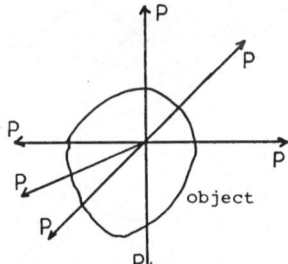

Fig.3. Decomposition of object in 2-D space

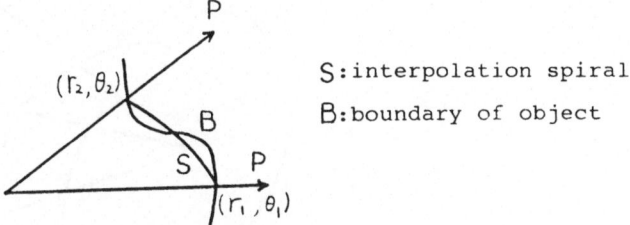

S:interpolation spiral

B:boundary of object

Fig.4. Real boundary and interpolation spiral

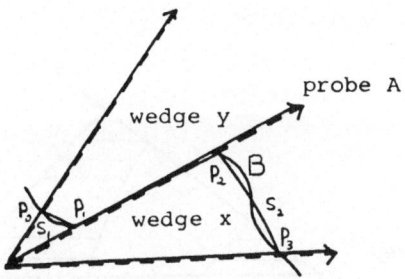

Fig.5. Boundary of object coincides with probe

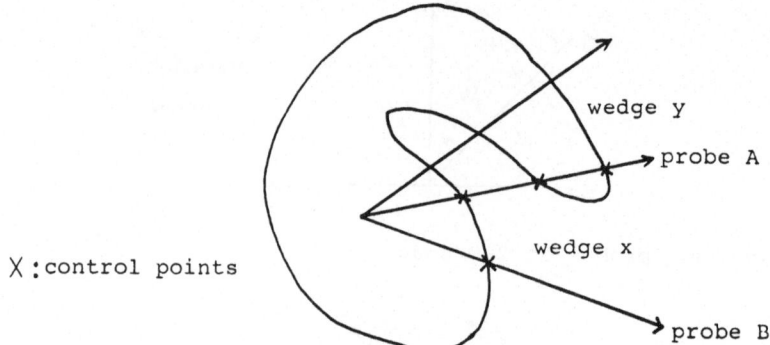

X:control points

Fig.6. Different numbers of control points on adjacent probes

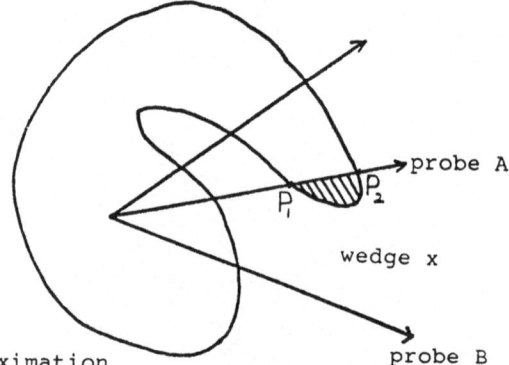

Fig.7a. Inner approximation

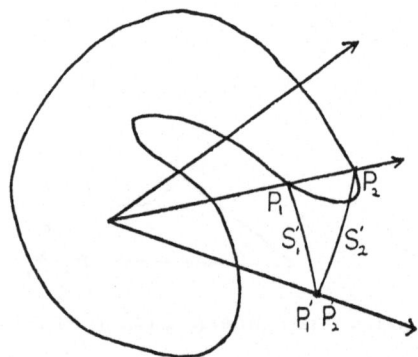

Fig.7b. Outer approximation

≡: Primitives

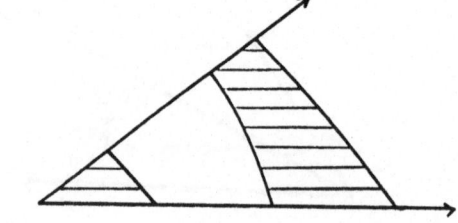

Fig.8. HP primitives

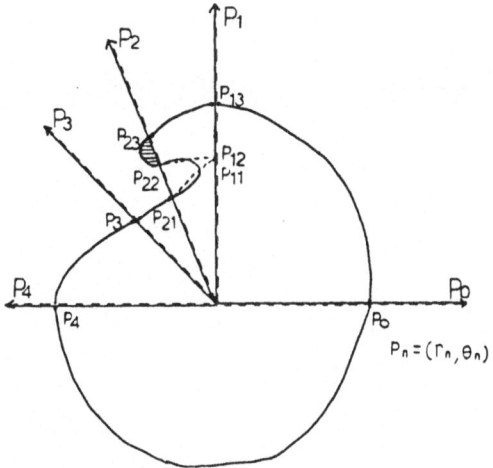

Fig.9a. Decomposition of object

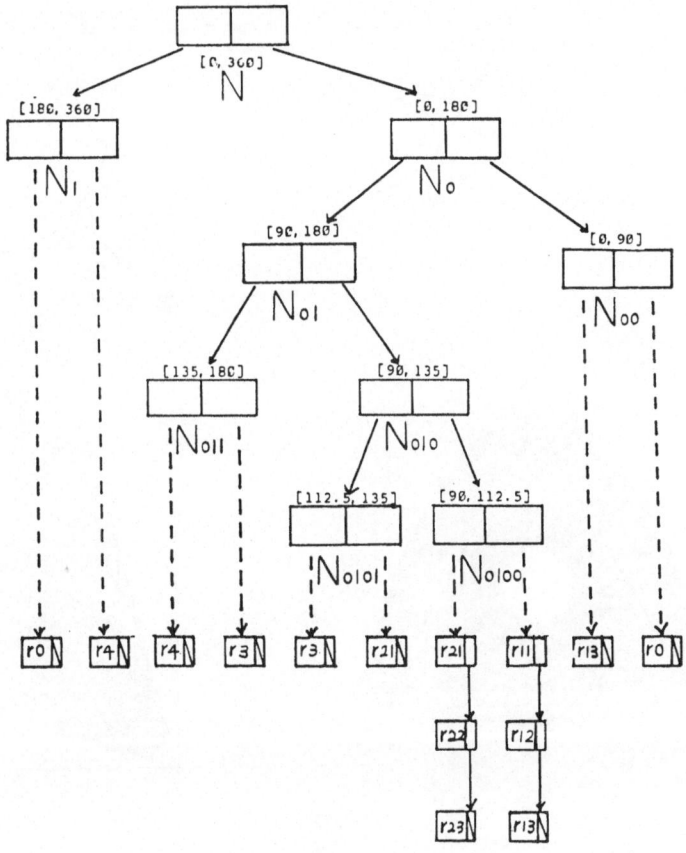

Fig.9b. HP data structure of object in Fig. 9a

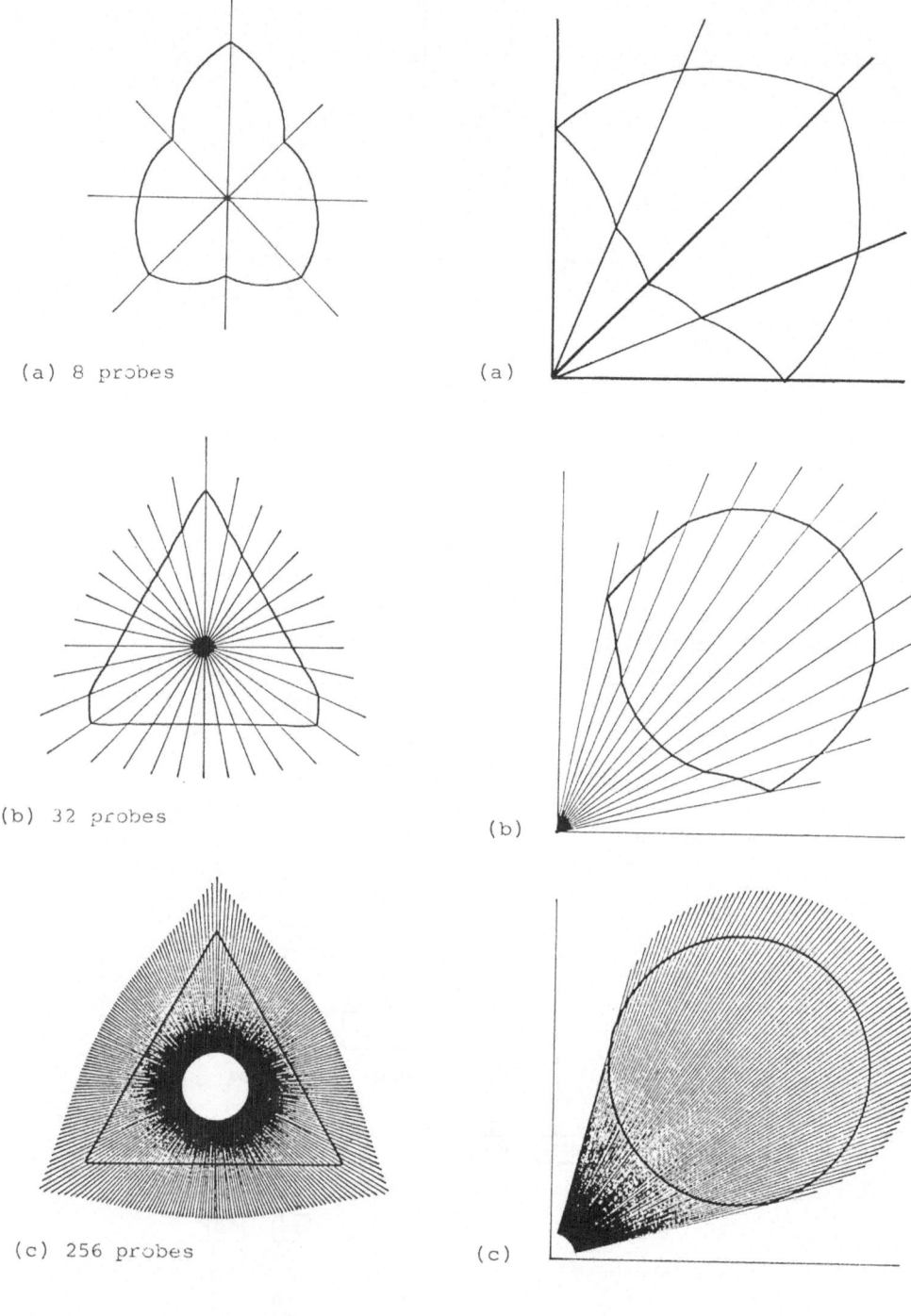

(a) 8 probes

(b) 32 probes

(c) 256 probes

Fig.10. HP representations
of triangle

(a)

(b)

(c)

Fig.11. HP representations
of circular object

455

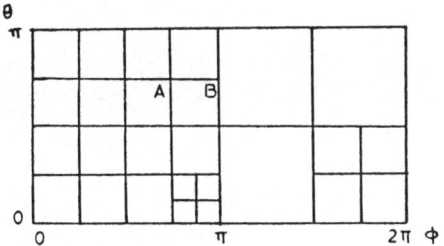

Fig.12. Θ-Φ Diagram

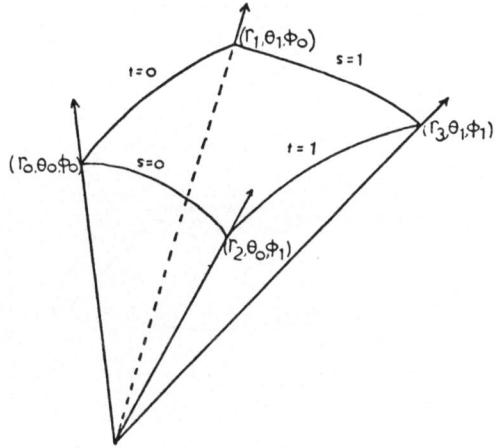

Fig.13. Cone in 3-D space

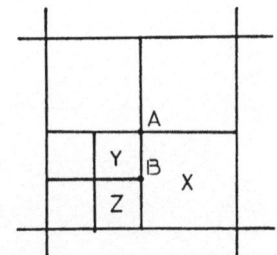

Fig.14. Locations of probes with 2 and 4 threads

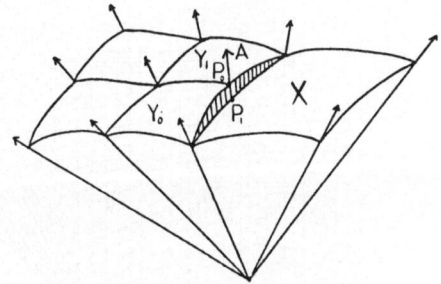

Fig.15. Surface discontinuity in 3-D HP model

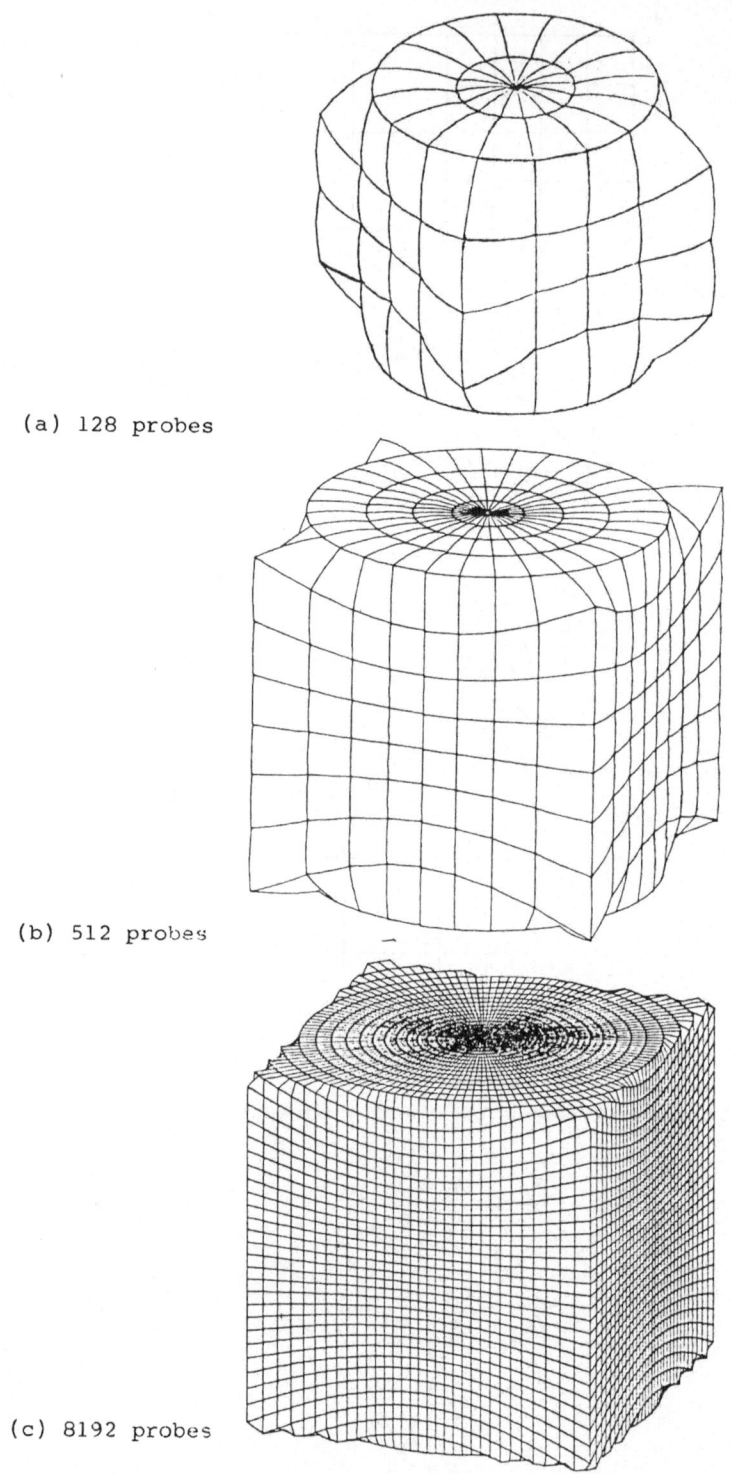

(a) 128 probes

(b) 512 probes

(c) 8192 probes

Fig.16. HP representations of cube

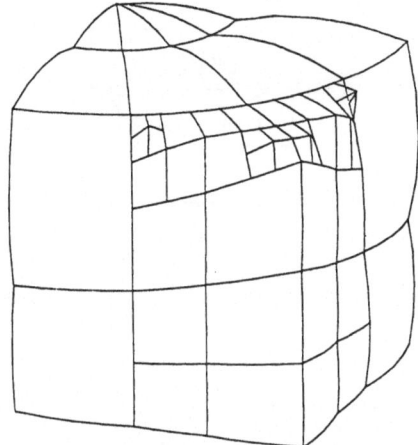

(a) tolerance = 0.05

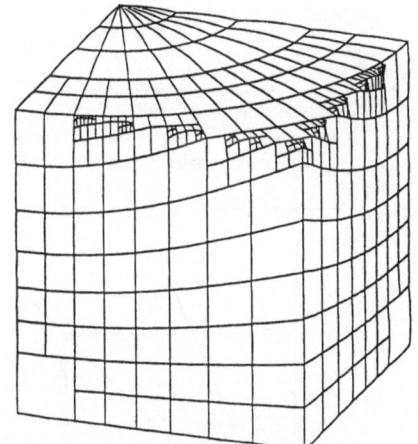

(b) tolerance = 0.01

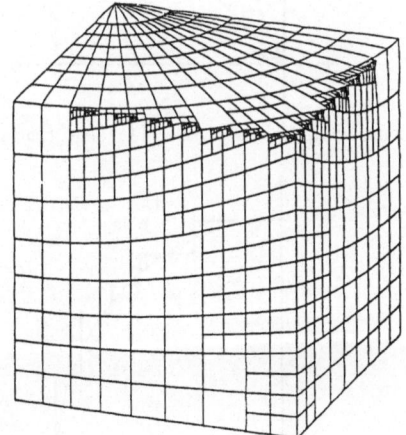

(c), tolerance = 0.005

Fig.17. HP representations of cube in first octant

458

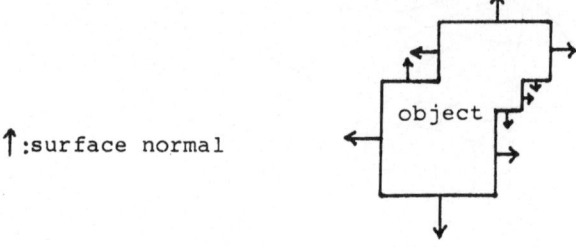

↑:surface normal

Fig. 18. Surface normals in quadtree representation

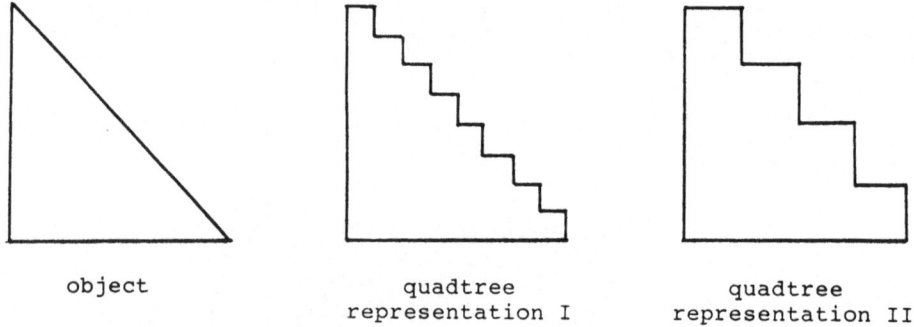

object   quadtree representation I   quadtree representation II

Fig. 19. Measurement discrepancies of boundaries in quadtree representation

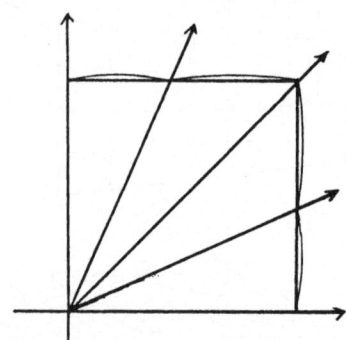

Fig. 20. One of worst cases (square) in HP model

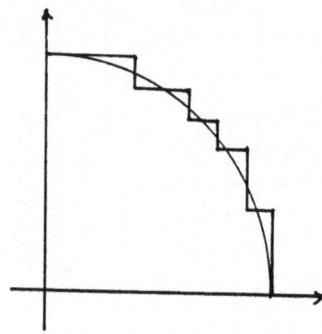

Fig. 21. One of worst cases (quarter of circle) in quadtree representation

Yong C. Chen is currently an assistant professor at the Department of Mathematical Sciences, Purdue University Calumet. His research interests include Computer Graphics, Geometric Modeling, Computer Vision, and Biomedical Image Processing. He is also a visiting scholar at the Urology Department, Northwestern University School of Medicine in charge of computer analysis of proteins separated by 2-dimensional gel electrophoresis.
Chen received the PhD degree in physics from University of Louisville, 1979 and the master degree in computer science from Illinois Institute of Technology, 1984.
Address:Dept. of Mathematical Sciences, Purdue University Calumet, Hammond, IN. 46323 U.S.A.

Catherine M. Murphy is currently an associate professor of Mathematics, and the head of the Department of Mathematical Sciences, Purdue University Calumet.
Address:Dept. of Mathematical Sciences, Purdue University Calumet, Hammond, IN. 46323 U.S.A.

Reconstruction and Cross-Section Generation of Hierarchically Represented 3D Gray-Scale Digital Images

Xiaoyang Mao, Tosiyasu L. Kunii, Issei Fujishiro, and Tsukasa Noma

ABSTRACT

This paper proposes G-octree as an extension of G-quadtree to 3dimensions. A G-octree reflects in its construction a hierarchy of gray-scale level value homogeneity, as well as that of spatial resolution. The paper also develops two-way G-quadtree/G-octree conversion procedures based on the algorithms for the binary case. These procedures provide an integrated processing environment for hierarchically represented 2D/3D images. Our approach is demonstrated with an application to the color-coding of macroautoradiography images taken from rat brains.

Keywords: gray-scale level value homogeneity, quadtree/octree, 3D image reconstruction, cross-section generation, macroautoradiography

1. INTRODUCTION

In the previous paper (Kunii 1986), we proposed G-quadtree (Gray-scale quadtree) as a new hierarchical representation scheme for 2D gray-scale digital images. A G-quadtree is an extended quadtree which reflects hierarchies both of spatial resolution and of gray-scale level value homogeneity. On G-quadtree images, we defined several effective graphics operations including: search for regions of particular levels, adaptive level interval division, and spatially-local subdivision of level intervals (Mao 1987).

G-quadtree has been implemented and tested in a color-coding system for macroautoradiography images of rat brains (Kunii 1986; Mao 1987). A linearly coded form of G-quadtrees called SKF (Simplified K-Formula) has been used for the purpose of space compression, and it has been proved that G-quadtrees with the aid of this form would play the role of a master representation of gray-scale images.

Our original color-coding system was designed to process 2D cross-section images representing local cerebral glucose concentration. But, since the region of interest to neurosurgeons is essentially in 3D, it is required to pile these 2D images up efficiently to reconstruct a whole 3D rat brain by computer graphics. The set of 2D graphics operations needs to be extended for the reconstructed 3D image. Furthermore, it is meaningful to cut the reconstructed image by an arbitrary plane to get a new cross-section image, which in reality cannot be obtained, because the generation process of the original cross-sections involves the cutting of the sample rat brain in a certain direction (Goochee 1980).

In order to fulfill these requirements in an extended system for color-coding of hierarchically represented images, this paper introduces Gray-scale octree (G-octree for short) as the 3D version of G-quadtree, and describes efficient two-way conversion procedures between a series of G-quadtrees and a G-octree based on the existing algorithms developed by Yau and Srihari (1983, 1984) for the binary case.

In the next section, we give an overview of G-quadtree. Section 3 presents a modified procedure for constructing a G-quadtree from an image array. This procedure constructs G-quadtrees of arbitrary precision efficiently, and its essential idea serves as a basis for the two-way G-quadtree/G-octree conversion procedures. After giving the formal definition of G-octree in Section 4, the conversion procedures are described in Section 5 and Section 6 with examples in macroautoradiography color-coding. Section 7 concludes the paper with the plans for some future researches.

2. OVERVIEW OF G-QUADTREE

2.1 Quadtree Approach to Gray-Scale Images

According to Samet's classification (Samet 1984), G-quadtrees are categorized as region quadtrees. But the type of data is not limited to "binary"; G-quadtrees are capable of dealing with "gray-scale" data in general.

So far, there has been research on hierarchical representation of gray-scale images in two directions. One is the exploration of the technique's effectiveness as a tool for image processing, and the other is the data compaction.

Among early works, Klinger and Dyer (1976) proposed, from the viewpoint of pattern recognition, the quadtree method for partitioning digital pictures into homogeneous blocks. The split-merge algorithm presented by Horowitz and Pavlidis (1976) performs picture segmentation by traversing a quadtree.

More recently, the groups at University of Maryland considered the deteriorated condition of space coherence of gray-scale images represented by quadtree (referred to as Q-images), and forced the quadtree approach to be dedicated to special image processing techniques; for example, edge enhancement (Ranade 1981a); image smoothing (Ranade 1981b); threshold selection (Wu 1982) and so on.

On the other hand, Oliver and Wiseman (1983) presented leaf codes as a pointer-less traversal form for large-sized four bit colored quadtrees with a set of efficient operations on it. Woodwark (1984) succeeded the similar approach to obtain his traversal codes. These data structures are thought of as a variant of linear quadtrees devised by Gargantini (1982) for binary images.

The aspect of compressed hierarchical forms for digital images is advanced independently by Kawaguchi et al (1983) as their Depth First (DF) expressions. We developed Simplified Krider Formula (SKF) as a compact gray-scale linear code for our G-quadtrees (Kunii 1986), which is a tree-constrained version of graph forms for image segmentation. In the binary case, SKF is equivalent to DF-expression.

2.2 G-Quadtree

Our G-quadtree, however, can be differentiated from these multi-valued quadtrees listed above in that it incorporates the hierarchy of gray-scale level value homogeneity, that is, level interval subdivision, into its data structure.

An original 2D image corresponding to a cross-section is given by a gray-scale square pixel array $A^{(t)}$ of size $2^n \times 2^n$. Each element of $A^{(t)}$ is a non-negative integer represented with t bits, that is,

$$a_{ij} = d_{t-1}d_{t-2} \cdots d_0,$$
$$a_{ij} \in [0,2^t), \quad 0 \le i,j < 2^n,$$

In a G-quadtree, the gray-level interval of $A^{(t)}$ is divided into 2^i ($0 < i < t$) grades in the following way: at first we bisect the entire data interval $[0,2^t)$, with 2^{t-1} as the threshold value, into the two grades "0" and "1". At this point, the grade value of every element of $A^{(t)}$ corresponds to the value of MSB (Most Significant Bit) d_{t-1}.

If further level interval subdivision is needed, then we again bisect the two subintervals to get four grades "0", "1", "2", and "3", which can be represented with $d_{t-1}d_{t-2}$. In the same way, we can divide the gray-level interval into at most 2^t grades. In this case the grade value becomes the level value $d_{t-1}d_{t-2}\cdots d_0$ itself.

The construction process of a G-quadtree of 2^i grades ($1 \le i \le t$) is summarized as follows: assume Binary Array-to-Quadtree Conversion (BAQC) algorithm (Samet 1980) is given. If $i = 1$ then we apply the BAQC algorithm to the MSB plane. The resulting binary-valued quadtree is the G-quadtree to be constructed. Otherwise, the BAQC algorithm is applied to each bit-plane of $A^{(t)}$ successively in the order of descending significance. And at each time, the binary-valued quadtree is merged one after another into the current G-quadtree by the modified pairwise superposition algorithm (Kunii 1986) to obtain a G-quadtree of more grades.

The above construction procedure naturally leads to a two-layered representation scheme for gray-scale images. Every time a G-quadtree of 2^k grades ($1 \le k \le t$) is obtained, the whole information of the image is divided into two and stored separately in the G-quadtree of 2^k grades and in the current image array $A^{(t-k)}$. Every element of $A^{(t-k)}$ is the lower (t-k) bits of $A^{(t)}$. Note that any two stages associated with two different k's are mutually reachable. This characteristic offers a more suitable environment for interactive image processing than any other quadtree approaches.

Figure 1 shows an example of G-quadtree images of 16 $(= 2^4)$ grades, which is constructed from $A^{(8)}$, where n = 7 (2^n = 128).

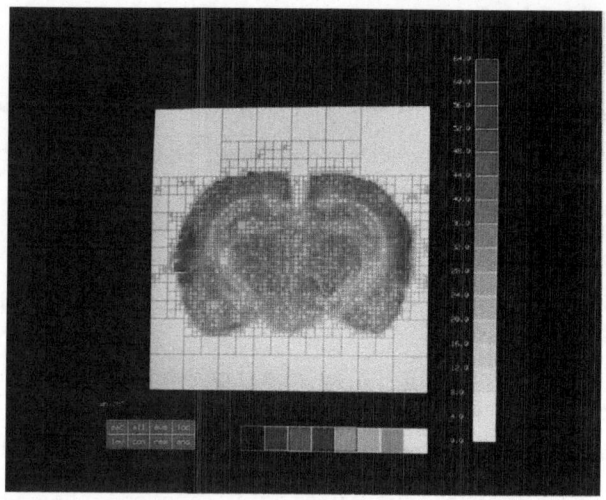

Fig. 1. A G-quadtree image (resolution 128x128; 2^4 grades).
Note that quadrant boundaries are shown as blue lines.

Furthermore, taking advantage of the hierarchy of both spatial resolution and gray-scale level value homogeneity, we can define several graphics operations on G-quadtree images which were not available previously. Among these operations, most important are the adaptive level interval division and the spatially-local subdivision of level intervals.

In Fig. 2(a), the grade "2" representing the level interval [32, 48) is further divided into four subgrades. This situation is illustrated using the grade-division tree (see Fig. 2(b)). In a grade-division tree, every node corresponds to a grade, and every non-leaf node stores a threshold value equal to the mean value of the level interval it is associated with. The grade of each node below the left edge of a non-leaf node falls below the threshold value of the non-leaf node, and the grade of each node below the right edge falls on or above the value. The level interval subdivision/concatenation operations change this grade-division tree to obtain more appropriate images. The operations can be easily implemented by paying attention to particular grade values while traversing the current G-quadtree.

The image shown in Fig. 3 is an example of spatially-local subdivision of level intervals. Within the polygon which is specified interactively, the image is represented with 8 grades; while the remainder of the image is represented with 2 grades. Note that, even after such an operation, a single G-quadtree is sufficient to hold the displayed image in its entirety. This operation is realized by a further application of the G-quadtree construction procedure to the set of quadrants corresponding to the specified region.

Two types of "<u>adaptive</u>" G-quadtrees, as delineated above in Figs. 2 and 3, play an important role in representing the necessary and sufficient information concerning gray-scale images with sparsity distribution in terms of level and space.

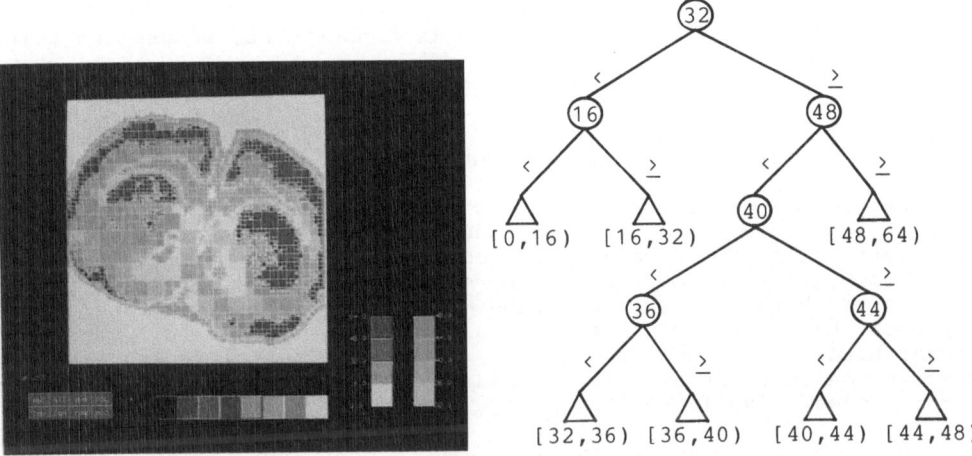

(a) G-quadtree image   (b) Grade division tree
(resolution 128x128)

Fig. 2. An example of adaptive level interval subdivision.

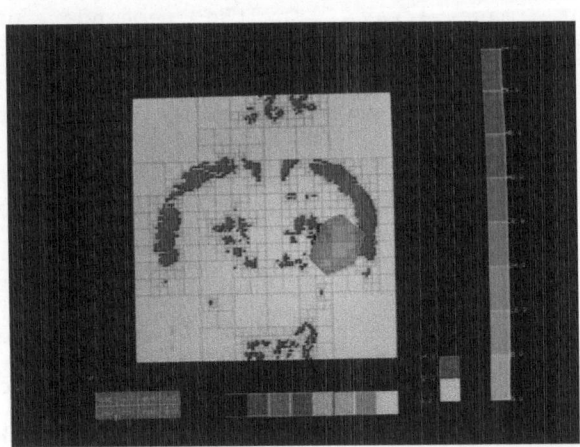

Fig. 3. An example of spatially-local subdivision of level intervals (resolution 128x128; 2^3 grades within the specified polygon, 2^1 grades outside).

3. AN IMPROVED G-QUADTREE CONSTRUCTION

The G-quadtree construction procedure described in the previous section may be considered inefficient when the desired precision of images is given from the beginning. In this section, we improve the G-quadtree construction procedure from the viewpoint of efficiency.

Let us examine the direct application of BAQC to gray-scale images. Whenever a G-quadtree of 2^k grades is constructed, we use the value represented with $d_{t-1}d_{t-2}\cdots d_{t-k}$ (higher k bits of $A^{(t)}$) as the grade value, and recursively subdivide $A^{(t)}$ into quadrants until every quadrant consists only of the elements with the same grade value.

Obviously, the time required to construct a G-quadtree of 2^k grades with an arbitrary k with this procedure equals that of BAQC, more efficient than our previous method. We call this method Gray-scale Array to G-Quadtree Conversion (abbreviated to GAGQC) in this paper. To the authors' knowledge, some researchers on the quadtree/octree approach have probably used a similar algorithm to construct hierarchical multi-colored images, but have not given any explicit description in their articles (Ranade 1981a, 1981b; Wu 1982; Oliver 1983; Woodwark 1984).

As for space efficiency, however, GAGQC does not allow users to construct G-quadtrees with different k's interactively in spite of keeping the whole image array resident in memory all the time.

Incorporating the merits of our two approaches, we propose here a new procedure which constructs G-quadtrees with any k in at most the same time as BAQC. Instead of repeatedly building a binary-valued quadtree and merging it to the current G-quadtree to get a G-quadtree of more grades, we just modify the existing G-quadtree with the superior bits of the current image array. In the remainder of the paper, a pointer-oriented data structure is assumed for G-quadtree/G-octree. Needless to say, the essentials of the procedures are invariant even if other data structures including SKF are used. An informal description of the procedure is as follows:

PROCEDURE A (G-QUADTREE CONSTRUCTION)

Input: (I) The original image array $A^{(t)}$ of size $2^n \times 2^n$, (Note that no G-quadtree has yet been created.)

or

(II) A G-quadtree of 2^1 grades (hereafter referred to as $Gq^{(1)}$) ($1 \leq 1 \leq t$) together with the current image array $A^{(t-1)}$;

Output: A G-quadtree of 2^k grades ($Gq^{(k)}$) ($1 \leq k \leq t$, $k \neq 1$);

There are two different treatments depending on the type of input:

I. In this case, we take the higher k bits $d_{t-1}d_{t-2}\cdots d_{t-k}$ as the grade value, and directly apply GAGQC to $A^{(t)}$ to construct the $Gq^{(k)}$.

II. Let d = k-1;
  There are two cases to be considered:
  a) d < 0;
   We are to construct a G-quadtree of fewer grades than the given G-quadtree. $Gq^{(k)}$ can be constructed by right-shifting the value of each node of $Gq^{(l)}$ by d bits and compressing the resulting tree.
  b) d > 0;
   In this case we traverse $Gq^{(l)}$ and execute the following operations for every leaf node encountered:
   * If it corresponds to a single array element, modify the value of the node with the higher d bits of the corresponding element in $A^{(t-1)}$, that is, add the value of higher d bits of the element to 2^d times the old value of the node.
   * Otherwise, apply GAGQC to the corresponding quadrant in the current image array $A^{(t-1)}$ by using its higher d bits as grade values. Then replace the visited node with the resulting G-quadtree, and add 2^d times the value of the replaced node to the newly created leaves.

Note that in b), a leaf node depth in the G-quadtree can determine whether or not the leaf node corresponds to a single array element. The quadrant corresponding to a leaf node can be determined by the path to reach that node.

PROCEDURE A is developed especially for the purpose of interactive image processing. Whenever a G-quadtree of more grades than the existing G-quadtree is built, the superior bits of the current image array are released for node value modification. When a G-quadtree of fewer grades is constructed, there are two alternatives to retain information. One way is to create a new tree and preserve the original one. The other alternative is to "return" the compressed portion of the original tree to the image array.

It is obvious that PROCEDURE A requires at most the same time as BAQC to build a G-quadtree of 2^k grades for an arbitrary k; because we only apply GAGQC to some quadrants of the image array, and the time required by BAQC is proportional to the number of the image array elements. The spatial efficiency is better than that of the method presented in (Kunii 1986), because the new procedure does not need the temporary space for storing binary-valued quadtrees.

Figure 4 shows an example of constructing $Gq^{(4)}$ from $A^{(5)}$ via $Gq^{(2)}$ and $A^{(3)}$. A direct application of GAGQC (Case I of PROCEDURE A) to $A^{(5)}$ produces $Gq^{(2)}$, which is further processed (Case II) to yield $Gq^{(4)}$ (leaf node modification).

The general idea behind PROCEDURE A is further explored by the development of the two-way G-quadtree/G-octree conversion procedures which will be presented in Sections 5 and 6.

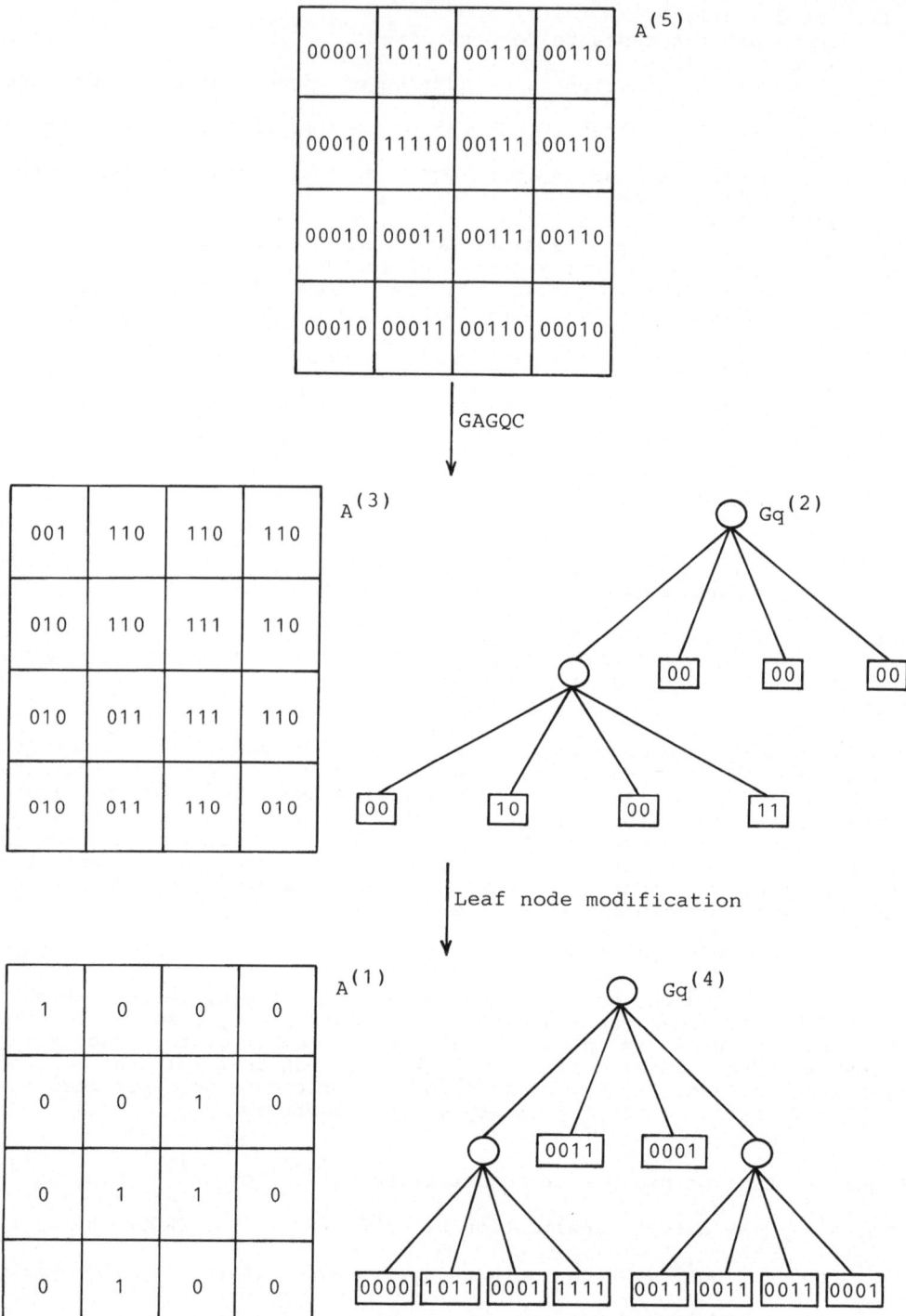

Fig. 4. Construction of $Gq^{(4)}$ from $A^{(5)}$ using PROCEDURE A.

4. G-OCTREE

In a fashion similar to the two dimensional case, a three dimensional gray-scale digital image is given in the form of a 3D array $V^{(t)}$ of size $2^n \times 2^n \times 2^n$. Each element $v_{xyz}^{(t)}$ $(0 \leq x,y,z < 2^n)$ of $V^{(t)}$ is a non-negative integer represented with t bits, that is,

$$v_{xyz}^{(t)} \in [0,2^t) \qquad 0 \leq x,y,z < 2^n.$$

Let $V^{(t)}$ represent a universe cube in the 3D Cartesian space. The cube is composed of subcubes of unit side, which are denoted by $v_{xyz}^{(t)}$ $(0 \leq x,y,z < 2^n)$. Here (x,y,z) denotes the coordinates of the vertex of each subcube that is nearest to the origin $(0,0,0)$ (Fig. 5(a)).

Planes of subcubes orthogonal to X, Y and Z axes are denoted by 2D arrays $V_{dxyz}^{(t)}$, $V_{xdyz}^{(t)}$ and $V_{xydz}^{(t)}$, respectively, where dx, dy, dz are the distances (the number of subcubes) between the planes and the origin. We call such planes cross-sections. Figure 5(b) shows the four cross-sections of $V^{(4)}$ which are orthogonal to the Z axis.

We now assume the gray-level intervals are divided into 2^k grades $(1 \leq k \leq t)$ just like in the case of G-quadtrees. We here give a formal definition of G-octree.

Definition (G-octree)

A set GO(k) of G-octrees of 2^k grades $(1 \leq k \leq t)$ is defined recursively as follows:

(1) integer i in $\{0,1,\ldots,2^k-1\} \in$ GO(k);
(2) $(O_{000}, O_{001}, O_{010}, O_{011}, O_{100}, O_{101}, O_{110}, O_{111}) \in$ GO(k) if $O_{lmn} \in$ GO(k)

   for $l,m,n \in \{0,1\}$;
(3) GO(k) consists of only those elements which are constructed under the rules 1 and 2.

Note that the binary-valued octree is just a special case of G-octree, which belongs to GO(1). Figure 8 shows a G-octree of 2^2 grades (denoted by $Go^{(2)}$) for $V^{(4)}$ in Fig. 5. The numbering of octants is also given in Fig. 8.

5. G-OCTREE RECONSTRUCTION FROM G-QUADTREES

An algorithm to construct a binary-valued octree directly from a 3D binary image array is known (Jackins 1980; Meagher 1982; Yamaguchi 1984a). The algorithm can also be utilized for gray-scale images after the extension of BAQC to GAGQC described in Section 3. We divide $v^{(t)}$ into octants recursively until every octant consists entirely of the elements of the same grade, leading to a G-octree representation.

When a G-quadtree of 2^k grades is constructed, the higher k bits of each element of $v^{(t)}$ are used as grade values. Hereafter we refer to this algorithm as GAGOC (3D Gray-scale image Array to G-Octree Conversion).

This algorithm, however, has a disadvantage. The entire 3D image array $v^{(t)}$ should be loaded into computer memory from the start, and left there throughout a session.

Yau and Srihari (1983) proposed a general approach to construct a 2^d-tree representing a d-dimensional binary image array from the 2^{d-1}-trees representing (d-1)-dimensional cross-sections of the array. The algorithm influences the idea of constructing quadtrees from rasters (Samet 1981) rather than from arrays when the amount of computer memory is limited. This memory restriction is expected to be more common not only for binary images in three or more dimensions, as Yau and Srihari pointed out, but also for gray-scale images of more bits. Fortunately, we already possess a series of G-quadtrees representing cross-sections orthogonal to one coordinate axis. Therefore, we present here a procedure for constructing a G-octree from a series of G-quadtrees.

Before giving the outline of the procedure, we first refer to the quadtree-to-octree conversion algorithm developed by Yau and Srihari (1983). The algorithm is established in such a way that 2^n quadtrees $q_0, q_1, \ldots, q_{2^n-1}$, all of which are generated from the array of side 2^n, are sequentially loaded. Then q_1 is merged to q_0, q_3 to $q_2, \ldots,$ q_{2^n-1} to q_{2^n-2}, to have new 2^{n-1} trees $q'_0, q'_2, \ldots, q'_{2^n-2}$. Repeat such merging steps n times, and we obtain the octree. The only operation at every merging is to copy the subtree whose root is the visited node onto the corresponding node of the other tree while traversing the two trees in parallel. Therefore the algorithm can be used in principle without any changes to construct a G-octree from a series of G-quadtrees of the same number of grades. In this paper, we call this algorithm G-Quadtree to G-Octree Conversion (GQGOC).

A method for the general case is presented below:

PROCEDURE B (G-OCTREE RECONSTRUCTION FROM G-QUADTREES)

    Input: $Gq_0^{(1)}$, $Gq_1^{(1)}, \ldots,$ $Gq_{2^n-1}^{(1)}$: 2^n G-quadtrees of 2^1 grades,

           and

           $A_0^{(t-1)}$, $A_1^{(t-1)}, \ldots, A_{2^n-1}^{(t-1)}$: 2^n $A^{(t-1)}$'s.

    Output: The G-octree of 2^k grades piled up along the Z axis.

Let d = k - 1;

Step 1. Apply GQGOC to the $Gq_0^{(1)}$, $Gq_1^{(1)}$,...,$Gq_{2^n-1}^{(1)}$ to construct a G-octree of the same number of grades, which is denoted as $Go^{(1)}$.

Step 2. This step has three cases:
    a) d = 0;

        $Go^{(1)}$ is the required G-octree in this case;
    b) d < 0;
        We need to construct a G-octree of fewer grades than $Go^{(1)}$. So the required G-octree can be obtained by d-bit right-shifting of the each node's value of $Go^{(1)}$, followed by compaction.

    c) d > 0;
        We treat $A_0^{(t-1)}$, $A_1^{(t-1)}$, ..., $A_{2^n-1}^{(t-1)}$ as $V_{xy0}^{(t-1)}$, $V_{xy1}^{(t-1)}$, ..., $V_{xy2^n-1}^{(t-1)}$ of $V^{(t-1)}$, respectively. For every leaf node of $Go^{(1)}$ do the following:

        * If it corresponds to a single 3D image array element, we modify the node's value with the higher d bits of the corresponding element of $A^{(t-1)}$ in the same way as case II(b) of PROCEDURE A.
        * Otherwise,
            1. Apply GAGOC to the corresponding octant in the current 3D image array $V^{(t-1)}$ by using the higher d bits as the grade value to construct a sub-G-octree of 2^d grades.
            2. Modify every leaf node of the resulting G-octree with the node's value in the same way as in case II(b) of PROCEDURE A.
            3. Replace the leaf node with the modified sub-G-octree.

The Step 2 above performs the leaf node modification on a G-octree, and is a 3D extension of Case II in PROCEDURE A. The same effect can also be attained by the leaf node modification applied on the given set of G-quadtrees followed by GQGOC (Fig. 6).

Figures 7-9 illustrate how PROCEDURE B works. The four G-quadtrees of 2^2 grades and four current image arrays of 2 bits are given (Fig. 7); $Go^{(2)}$ is constructed from the four G-quadtrees by applying Step 1 of PROCEDURE B (Fig. 8); and $Go^{(3)}$ is also obtained using the current image arrays by executing Step 2 of PROCEDURE B (Fig. 9).

In Fig. 10, four parallel projections of the reconstructed G-octree macroautoradiography images (32 x 32 x 32 x 3bits) of a rat brain are shown. The lower hemisphere image shown in Fig. 10(a) is reconstructed from the sixteen lower (farther from the origin) G-quadtrees and sixteen "0"'s representing background planes. For the whole reconstructed brain image in Fig. 10(b), a cut-away view as shown in Fig. 10(c) can be generated. Such an effect is realized by parallel-traversing the reconstructed G-octree and the <u>reference octree</u> which specifies the octants to be displayed. The corresponding reference octree is shown in Fig. 10(d). The idea of reference trees was first implemented for the purpose of average calculation on G-quadtree in (Kunii 1986).

The spatial efficiency of a linearly coded G-octree should be noted. We extend SKF to represent G-octree. The length of SKF is defined as the number of nodes. The SKF for Fig. 10(b) requires 14633x4 bits = 58532 bits, approximately 60% of $32^3 \times 3$ = 98304 bits for the array form. For more details on SKF, refer to (Kunii 1986).

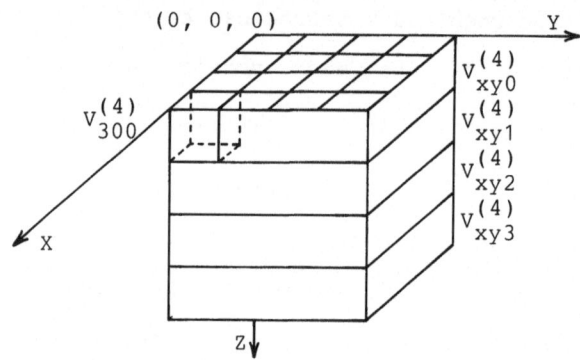

(a) 3D image array $V^{(4)}$.

$V^{(4)}_{xy0}$

0001	0110	0001	0000
0110	1111	0001	0001
0010	0011	0111	0110
0010	0011	0110	0110

$V^{(4)}_{xy2}$

0001	0001	0110	0110
0000	0001	0111	0111
1001	1011	1011	1010
1001	1010	1010	1011

$V^{(4)}_{xy1}$

0010	1001	0000	0000
0110	1110	0001	0001
0010	0011	0111	0111
0010	0011	0111	0110

$V^{(4)}_{xy3}$

0001	0001	0110	0110
0001	0001	0111	0110
1001	1011	1011	1011
1010	1010	1010	1010

(b) Cross-sections orthogonal to the Z axis.

Fig. 5. A 3D image array and its cross sections.

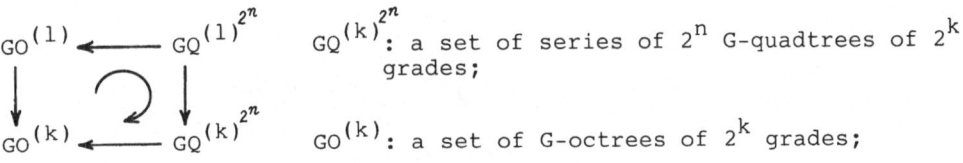

$GQ^{(k)}$: a set of series of 2^n G-quadtrees of 2^k grades;

$GO^{(k)}$: a set of G-octrees of 2^k grades;

Fig. 6. Commutativity in G-octree reconstruction from G-quadtrees.

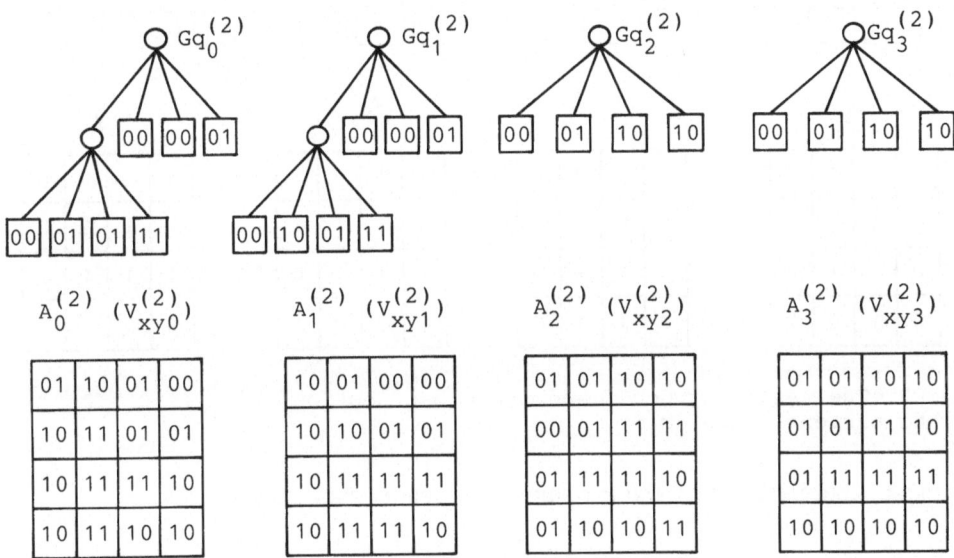

Fig. 7. G-quadtrees of 2^2 grades and current image arrays generated from the cross-sections of Fig. 5(b).

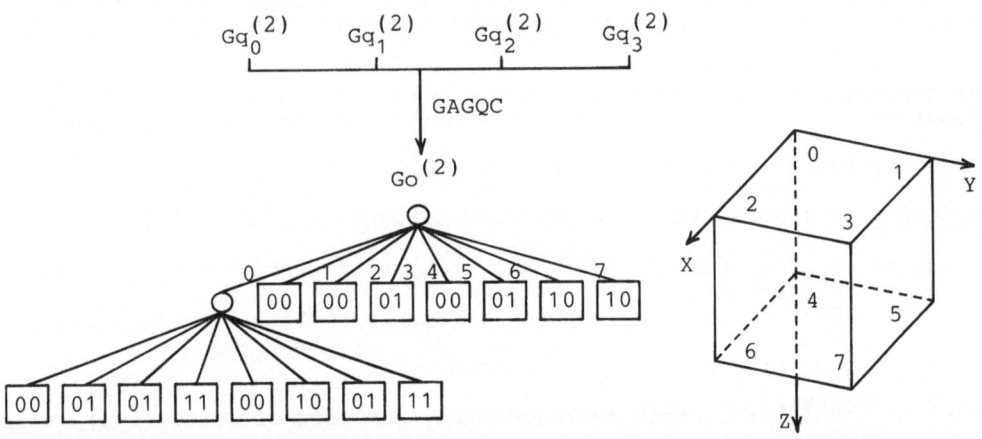

Fig. 8. Reconstruction of G-octree from G-quadtrees of the same number of grades.

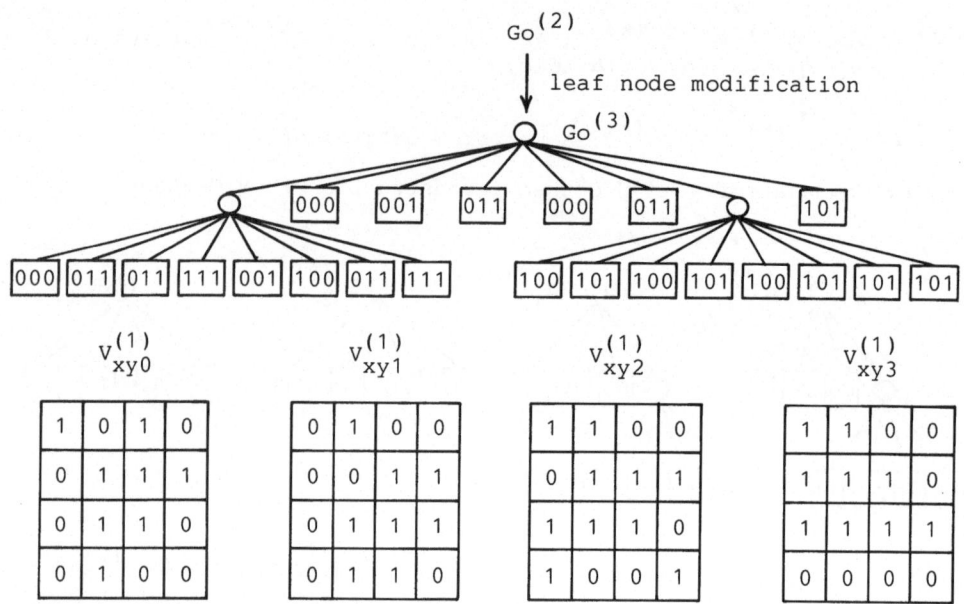

Fig. 9. The resulting Go$^{(3)}$ and the cross-sections $V_{xyi}^{(1)}$ (i=0,1,2,3) of the current image array.

6. CROSS-SECTION G-QUADTREE GENERATION FROM G-OCTREE

Yau (1984) presented an algorithm for generating a binary-valued cross-section quadtree orthogonal to one coordinate axis from a binary valued octree. Since in the algorithm the required quadtree is obtained by selecting adequate branches of the given octree, it can also be used in principle without any changes for getting a G-quadtree from a G-octree of the same number of grades. The algorithm is referred to as G-Octree to G-Quadtree Conversion (GOGQC) in the remainder of the paper.

We present a constructive procedure for extracting a cross-section G-quadtree of any number of grades orthogonal to one coordinate axis from a G-octree of 2^1 grades and the current 3D image array $V^{(t-1)}$.

PROCEDURE C (CROSS-SECTION G-QUADTREE GENERATION FROM G-OCTREE)

    Input: N: the name of the axis to which the cross-section is
            orthogonal;
            dn: the distance between the cross-section and the origin;

            GO$^{(1)}$: G-octree of 2^1 grades;

            $V^{(t-1)}$: current 3D image array composed of lower (t-1) bits

            of $V^{(t)}$.
    Output: G-quadtree of 2^k grades representing the cross-section which
            is dn away from the origin along the N axis.

    Let d = k - 1;

Step 1. Apply GOGQC to the $GO^{(1)}$ to get G-quadtree of 2^1 grades. Note that one of the input parameters, dn is used here.

Step 2. There are two cases to be considered:

    a) d = 0

      We have already obtained the result required at Step 1.

    b) d ≠ 0

      This case reduces to case II of PROCEDURE A where the cross-section of interest out from $V^{(t-1)}$ replaces $A^{(t-1)}$.

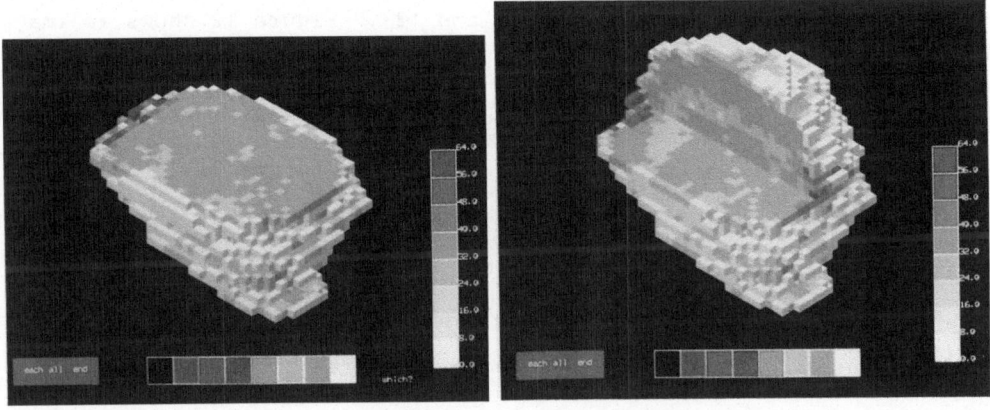

(a) The lower hemisphere.   (b) The whole brain.

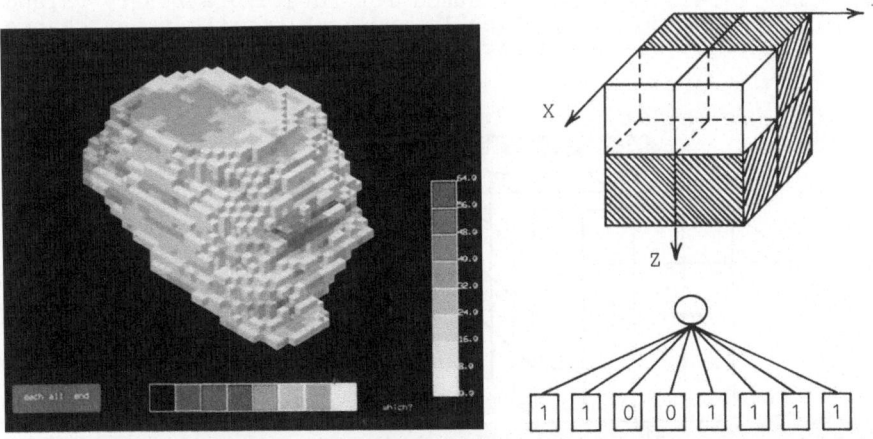

(c) A cut-away view of the whole image.   (d) Reference octree used in (c).

Fig. 10. Parallel projections of the G-octree for a rat brain.

Just as with PROCEDURE B, the same effect as that of PROCEDURE C can be attained by the leaf node modification of a series of G-quadtrees (PROCEDURE A), followed by GOGQC (Fig. 11).

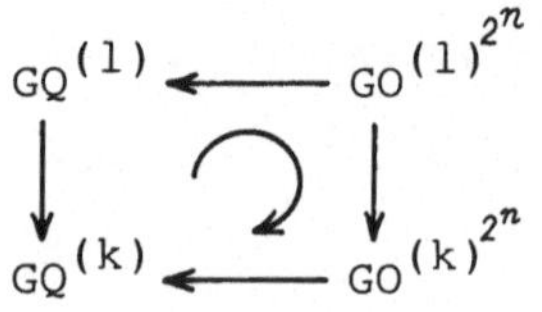

$GQ^{(1)} \longleftarrow GO^{(1)^{2^n}}$ $GQ^{(k)^{2^n}}$: a set of series of 2^n G-quadtrees of 2^k grades;

$GQ^{(k)} \longleftarrow GO^{(k)^{2^n}}$ $GO^{(k)}$: a set of G-octrees of 2^k grades;

Fig. 11. Commutativity in cross-section G-quadtree generation from G-octree.

Let us look at an example (Figs. 12 and 13). Figure 12 shows an image array $V^{(4)}$. This array is same as the one shown in Fig. 5. Suppose that we are given a G-octree of 2^3 grades $Go^{(3)}$ constructed from $V^{(4)}$, and that we are to extract a cross-section G-quadtree $Gq_{0yz}^{(k)}$ orthogonal to the X axis. By applying Step 1, $Gq_{0yz}^{(3)}$ is cut from $Go^{(3)}$ (Fig. 13(a)). Next, $Gq_{0yz}^{(3)}$ can be modified into $Gq_{0yz}^{(2)}$ (Fig. 13(b)) or $Gq_{0yz}^{(4)}$ (Fig. 13(c)) at Step 2 according to users' choice. Figure 14 shows $Gq_{16yz}^{(3)}$ generated from the reconstructed G-octree image in Fig. 10(b).

Although the above algorithm is for generating only those cross-section G-quadtrees which are orthogonal to a certain coordinate axis; a cross-section G-quadtree of an arbitrary direction can also be obtained by rotating the 3D image before applying PROCEDURE C. For example, Meagher (1982) proposed a method for rotating a binary-valued octree about any rotation axis, which is applicable without any change to the cases with gray-scale images.

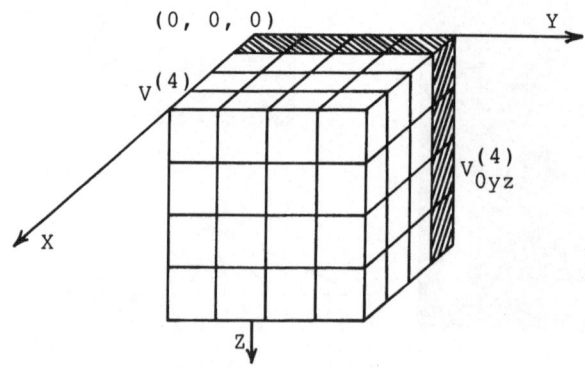

Fig. 12. A cross-section orthogonal to the X axis.

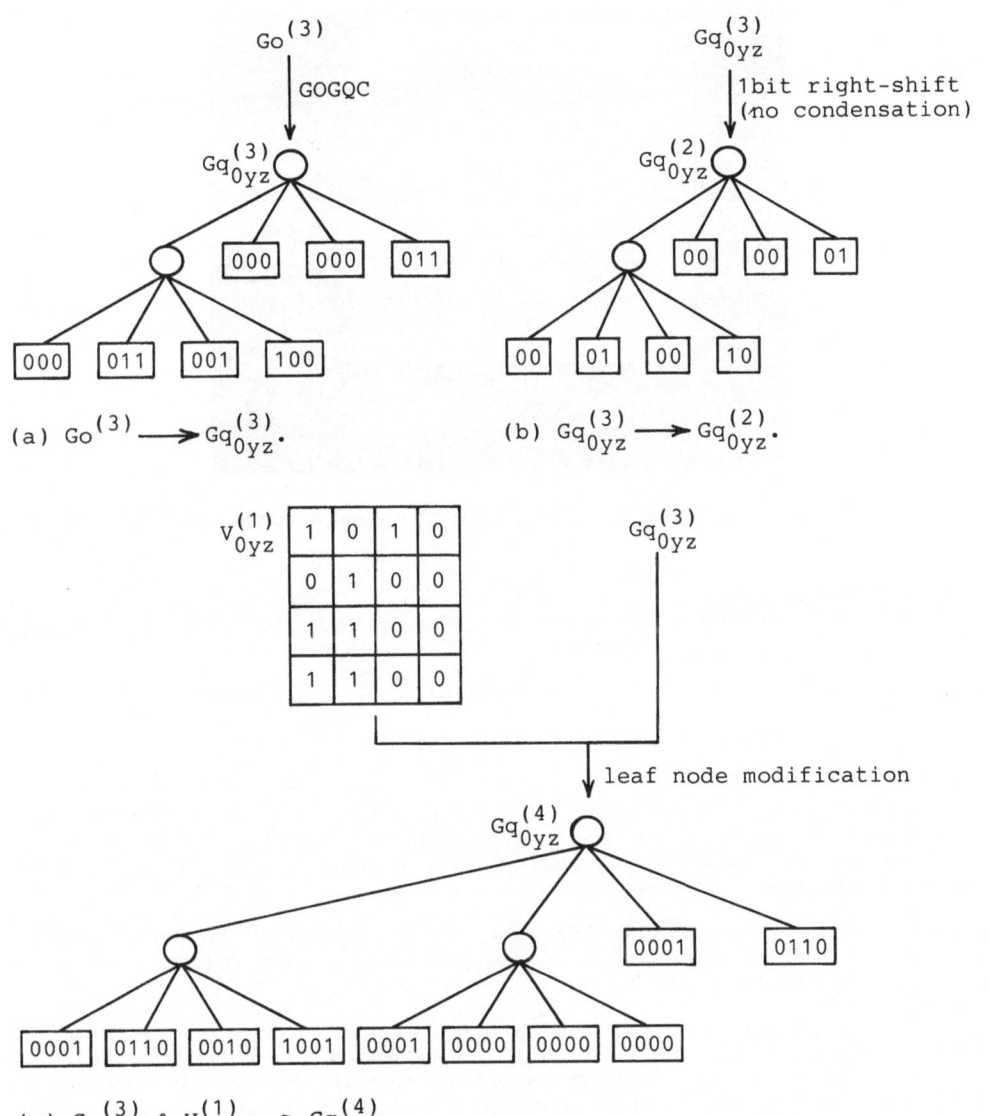

(a) $Go^{(3)} \longrightarrow Gq_{0yz}^{(3)}$.

(b) $Gq_{0yz}^{(3)} \longrightarrow Gq_{0yz}^{(2)}$.

(c) $Go_{0yz}^{(3)} \ \& \ V_{0yz}^{(1)} \longrightarrow Gq_{0yz}^{(4)}$.

Fig. 13. Construction of $Gq_{0yz}^{(4)}$ from $Go^{(3)}$ using PROCEDURE C.

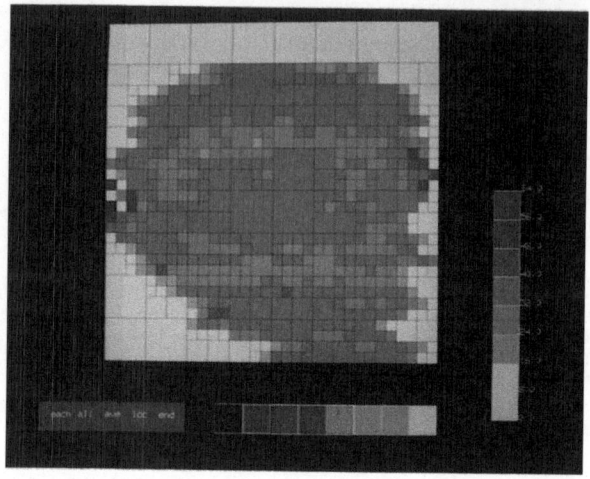

Fig. 14. A cross-section G-quadtree $Gq_{16yz}^{(3)}$ image extracted from $Go^{(3)}$ of Fig. 10(b).

7. CONCLUDING REMARKS

We presented G-octree as an extension of G-quadtree to three dimensional gray-scale images. The two-way G-quadtree/G-octree conversion procedures were designed for providing a desirable environment which enables us to effectively display and analyze the reconstructed 3D images as well as cross-section images in an integrated manner. The basis of these procedures lies in the existing algorithms developed by Yau and Srihari for the binary case. Application to color-coding macroautoradiography images of rat brains demonstrated the advantages of our approach. All the coding has been

done in the programming language C on a VAX11/750 running UNIX[1] 4.2bsd. The photographs used in the paper were taken directly from a JRC NWX-237 graphics display.

In future research, a set of graphics operations on G-quadtrees delineated in Section 2.2 will be extended to G-octrees. To this end, we need to study a method to interactively specify a region of interest in 3D. We intend to adopt the cyclic octree editing scheme (Yamaguchi 1984b). Moreover, to investigate the internal structure of an object more closely, we are now working on the development of semi-transparent display techniques for irregular voxel-based images.

ACKNOWLEDGEMENTS

The authors wish to express their gratitude to Dr. Shozo Ishii and Dr. Akira Shimizu of Juntendo University for offering the image data of macroautoradiography. This work has drawn a great value from extensive comments of Dr. J. R. Woodwark, IBM UK Scientific Centre, Winchester, on G-quadtree. The authors sincerely acknowledge and appreciate his contribution.

---

1 UNIX is a trademark of AT&T.

Special thanks are due to Mr. Yasuto Shirai, Mr. Masaaki Fujisaka, and Mr. Naohiro Oshima of the Kunii Laboratory of Computer Science, the University of Tokyo. Mr. Shirai carefully read the manuscript and the authors have benefited from many valuable and stimulating comments from him. Mr. Fujisaka had a share in the implementation of the system. Mr. Oshima kindly prepared all the photographs used here.

This work is supported by Software Research Center (SRC) of Ricoh Co., Ltd. The authors extend their appreciation to Dr. Hideko S. Kunii, Director of SRC, for her continuous support and encouragement.

REFERENCES

Gargantini I (1982) An Effective Way to Represent Quadtrees. Commun. ACM 25(12):905-910

Goochee C, Rasband W, Sokoloff L (1980) Computerized Densitometry and Color Coding of [^{14}C] Deoxyglucose Autoradiographs. Ann. Neurol 7:359-370

Horowitz SL, Pavlidis T (1976) Picture Segmentation by a Tree Traversal Algorithm. J. ACM 23(2):368-388

Jackins CL, Tanimoto SL (1980) Oct-Trees and Their Use in Representing Three-Dimensional Objects. Comput. Graph. Image Process. 14(3):249-270

Kawaguchi E, Endo T, Matsunaga J (1983) Depth-first Picture Expression Viewed From Digital Picture Processing. IEEE Trans. Pattern Anal. Mach. Intell. PAMI-5(4):373-384

Klinger A, Dyer CR (1976) Experiments on Picture Representation Using Regular Decomposition. Comput. Graph. Image Process. 5(1):68-105

Kunii TL, Fujishiro I, Mao X (1986) G-quadtree: A Hierarchical Representation of Gray-scale Digital Images. Visual Computer 2(4):219-226

Mao X (1987) A Hierarchical Representation of Gray-scale Digital Images. Master's Thesis, Department of Information Science, the University of Tokyo

Meagher D (1982) Geometric Modeling Using Octree Encoding. Comput. Graph. Image Process. 19(2):129-147

Oliver MA, Wiseman NE (1983) Operations on Quadtree Encoded Images. Comput. J. 26(1):83-91

Ranade S (1981a) Use of Quadtrees for Edge Enhancement. IEEE Trans. Syst. Man Cybern. SMC-11(5):370-373

Ranade S, Shneier M (1981b) Using Quadtrees for Smooth Images. IEEE Trans. Syst. Man Cybern. SMC-11(5):373-376

Samet H (1980) Region Representation: Quadtrees from Binary Arrays. Comput. Graph. Image Process. 13(1):88-93

Samet H (1981) An Algorithm for Converting Rasters to Quadtrees. IEEE Trans. Pattern Anal. Mach. Intell. PAMI-3(1):93-95

Samet H (1984) The Quadtree and Related Hierarchical Data Structures. ACM Comput. Surv. 16(2):187-260

Woodwark JR (1984) Compressed Quad Trees. Comput. J. 27(3):225-229

Wu AY, Tsai-Hong, Rosenfeld A (1982) Threshold Selection Using Quadtrees. IEEE Trans. Pattern Anal. Mach. Intell. PAMI-4(1):90-94

Yamaguchi K, Kunii TL, Fujimura K, Toriya H (1984a) Octree-Related Data Structures and Algorithms. IEEE Comput. Graph. Appl. 4(1):53-59

Yamaguchi K, Inamoto N, Kunii HS, Kunii TL (1984b) Three-Dimensional Data Input by Selection of Hierarchically Defined Blocks. In: Proc. Eurographics '84 pp 15-24

Yau M, Srihari SN (1983) A Hierarchical Data Structure for Multidimensional Digital Images. Commun. ACM 27(7):504-515

Yau M (1984) Generating Quadtrees of Cross Sections from Octrees. Comput. Vision Graph. Image Process. 27(2):211-238

480

BIOGRAPHICAL SKETCH

Xiaoyang Mao is currently a doctor course graduate student of information science at the University of Tokyo. Her research interests include image processing, computer graphics and their applications. She received the BSc degree in computer science in 1983 from Fudan University in China, and the MSc in information science in 1987 from the University of Tokyo.

Tosiyasu L. Kunii is currently a Professor and Chairman of Department of Information Science, the University of Tokyo. At the University of Tokyo, he started his work in raster computer graphics in 1968 which was led to the Tokyo Raster Technology Project creating new inventions such as a random access virtual frame buffer in 1972. His research interests cover computer graphics, database systems, software engineering, and systems for science parks and intelligent cities. He authored and edited 27 computer science books, and published 80 refereed academic/technical papers in computer science and applications areas.
Dr. Kunii is the President of the Computer Graphics Society, the Chairman of the Board of the Handheld Computer Society, and on the Editorial Board of IEEE Computer Graphics and Applications magazine. He is on the IFIP Data Base Working Group and the IFIP System Modelling Working Group. He organized and was chairing the Technical Committee on Software Engineering of the Information Processing Society of Japan from 1976 to 1981. He also organized and was the President of the Japan Computer Graphics Association(JCGA) from 1981 to 1983. He served as the General Chairman of the 3rd International Conference on Very Large Data Bases(VLDB) in 1977, the Program Chairman of InterGraphics '83 in 1983, and the Organizing Committee Chairman and the Program Chairman of Computer Graphics Tokyo '84 in 1984, Computer Graphics Tokyo '85 in 1985, and Computer Graphics Tokyo '86 in 1986. He is serving also as the Organizing Committee Chairman and Program Chairman of CG International '87 in 1987, the Program Co-Chairman of IEEE/IPSJ COMPSAC 87 in 1987 and IFIP Working Conference on Visual Database Systems in 1989.
He received the BSc, MSc, and DSc degrees in chemistry all from the University of Tokyo in 1962, 1964, and 1967, respectively.

Issei Fujishiro is currently a research associate of Kunii Laboratory of Computer Science at the University of Tokyo. His research interests include image processing, computer graphics, and database systems. He received the BEng degree and the MEng in Information Sciences and Electronics from University of Tsukuba, in 1983 and 1985, respectively. He is a member of the Computer Graphics Society.

Tsukasa Noma is currently a doctor course graduate student of information science at the University of Tokyo. His research interests include computer aided design and computer animation. He received the BSc degree in mathematics in 1984 from Waseda University, and the MSc degree in information science in 1986 from the University of Tokyo. He is a student member of ACM and a member of the Computer Graphics Society.

Address: Department of Information Science, Faculty of Science, the University of Tokyo, 7-3-1 Hongo, Bunkyo-ku, Tokyo 113, JAPAN.

Keywords Index

The page numbers refer to the page on which term is defined.

CGInternational'87

The 5th International Conference on Computer Graphics in Japan
May 25–28, 1987, Karuizawa, Japan

Organized by
The Computer Graphics Society

In Cooperation with
Association for Computing Machinery
The European Association for Computer Graphics
IEEE Computer Society
Information Processing Society

Hosted by
International Information Science Foundation

Organizing Committee

Chairperson: Tosiyasu L. Kunii
Department of Information Science
Faculty of Science
The University of Tokyo
7-3-1 Hongo, Bunkyo-ku, Tokyo, 113 Japan

Members: Rae A. Earnshaw
University of Leeds
Computing Service
Leeds, LS2 9JT, U.K.

Kansei Iwata
Graphica Ltd.
6-21-6, Nagayama, Tama
Tokyo, 206 Japan

Nadia Magnenat-Thalmann
Hautes Etudes Commerciales
Université de Montréal
5255, av. Décelles, Montréal Q. C.
Canada H3T-1V6

Naomasa Nakajima
Department of Mechanical Engineering
for Production
Faculty of Engineering
The University of Tokyo
7-3-1 Hongo, Bunkyo-ku, Tokyo
113 Japan

Tadao Nakamura
Department of Information Engineering
Faculty of Engineering
Tohoku University
Aza-Aoba, Aramaki, Sendai
Miyagi, 980 Japan

Ikuo Nishioka
Computer Systems Laboratories
Engineering Center
Sharp Corporation
2613-1 Ichinomoto, Tenri
Nara, 632 Japan

Daniel Thalmann
Départment d'Informatique et
Recherche Opérationnelle
Universite de Montréal
C.P. 6128 Succ. "A" Montréal P. Q.
Canada H3C-3J7

Tony C. Woo
Department of Industrial and
Operations Engineering
The University of Michigan
IOE-Building, 1205 Beal Avenue
Ann Arbor, MI 48109, U.S.A.

Michael J. Wozny
Center for Interactive Computer
Graphics
Rensselaer Polytechnic Institute
Troy, NY 12180-3590, U.S.A.

Honorary General Chairpersons:

Nadia Magnenat-Thalmann
Hautes Etudes Commerciales
Université de Montréal
5255, av. Décelles, Montreal Q. C.
Canada H3T-1V6

Daniel Thalmann
Départment d'Informatique et
Recherche Opérationnelle
Université de Montréal
C. P. 6128 Succ. "A" Montréal P. Q.
Canada H3C-3J7

General Chairpersons:

Michael J. Wozny
Center for Interactive Computer
Graphics
Rensselaer Polytechnic Institute
Troy, NY 12180-3590 U.S.A.

Rae A. Earnshaw
University of Leeds, Computing Service
Leeds, LS2 9JT, U.K.

Publicity Chairperson:

Ken Sakamura
Department of Information Science
Faculty of Science
The University of Tokyo
7-3-1 Hongo, Bunkyo-ku, Tokyo
113 Japan

International Coordinator:

Mary Johnson
Manager Corporate Relations
School of Engineering
Center for Interactive Computer Graphics
Rensselaer Polytechnic Institute
Troy, NY 12180-3590, U.S.A.

Treasurer: Issei Fujishiro
Department of Information Science
Faculty of Science
The University of Tokyo
7-3-1 Hongo, Bunkyo-ku, Tokyo
113 Japan

Program Committee

Chairperson: Tosiyasu L. Kunii
Department of Information Science
Faculty of Science
The University of Tokyo
7-3-1 Hongo, Bunkyo-ku, Tokyo, 113 Japan

Members: Hiroaki Chiyokura
Software Research Center
Ricoh Co., Ltd.
Tomin-Nissei-Kasugacho Building
1-1-17 Koishikawa, Bunkyo-ku, Tokyo
112 Japan

Rae A. Earnshaw
University of Leeds, Computing Service
Leeds, LS2 9JT, U.K.

Henry Fuchs
Department of Computer Science
University of North Carolina
New West Hall 035 A
Chapel Hill NC 27514, U.S.A.

Akira Fujimoto
Integra Inc.
2-7-1 Komagome, Toshima-ku, Tokyo
170 Japan

Kansei Iwata
Graphica Ltd.
6-21-6, Nagayama, Tama, Tokyo
206 Japan

Aristair Kilgour
Department of Computing Science
University of Glasgow
17 Lilybank Gardens, Glasgow
G12 8RZ, U.K.

R. J. Lansdown
System Simulation Ltd.
50/51 Russel Square London
WC1B 4JP, U.K.

Nadia Magnenat-Thalmann
Hautes Etudes Commerciales
Université de Montréal
5255, av. Décelles, Montréal Q. C.
Canada H3T-1V6

Martti Mantyla
Helsinki University of Technology
Laboratory of Information
Processing Science
Otakaari 1 A, SF-02150 Espoo 15
Finland

Naomasa Nakajima
Department of Mechanical Engineering
for Production
Faculty of Engineering
The University of Tokyo
7-3-1 Hongo, Bunkyo-ku, Tokyo
113 Japan

Eihachiro Nakamae
Cluster 2, Electrical and Industrial
Engineering
Faculty of Engineering
Hiroshima University
Shitami, Saijo-machi
Higashi-Hiroshima, Hiroshima
724 Japan

Tadao Nakamura
Department of Information Engineering
Faculty of Engineering
Tohoku University
Aza-Aoba, Aramaki, Sendai-shi, Miyagi
980 Japan

Ikuo Nishioka
Computer Systems Laboratories
Engineering Center
Sharp Corporation
2613-1 Ichinomoto, Tenri, Nara
632 Japan

Aristides Requicha
Department of Computer Science
University of Southern California
Los Angeles, CA 90089, U.S.A.

David F. Rogers
Department of the Navy
United States Naval Academy
Annapolis, MD 21402, U.S.A.

Hanan Samet
The University of Maryland
College Park Campus
Center for Automation Research
College Park MD 20742 U.S.A.

Issac D. Scherson
Department of Electrical and Computer
Engineering
University of California, Santa Barbara
Santa Barbara CA 93106 U.S.A.

Daniel Thalmann
Départment d'Informatique et
Recherche Opérationnelle
Université de Montréal
C.P. 6128 Succ. "A" Montréal P. Q.
Canada H3C-3J7

Tony C. Woo
Department of Industrial and
Operations Engineering
The University of Michigan
IOE-Building, 1205 Beal Avenue
Ann Arbor, MI 48109 U.S.A.

Fujio Yamaguchi
School of Science and Engineering
Waseda University
3-4-1 Ohkubo, Shinjuku-ku, Tokyo
160 Japan

Secretariat

Secretary General: Yuji Yamadori

Secretary: Toshio Kaneko

Japan Information Processing Development Center
Kikaishinko Building
3-5-8 Shibakoen, Minato-ku, Tokyo 105
Japan
Phone: 03-432-9381
FAX: 03-432-9389

List of Technical Program Reviewers

Masaki Aono
Yoshinao Arai
Brian A. Barsky
Jack E. Bresenham
Weiguo Cao
Indranil Chakravarty
Hiroaki Chiyokura
Kazuhiro Fuchi
Henry Fuchs
Akira Fujimoto
Issei Fujishiro
Klaus Hiurichs
Atsushi Iizawa
Atsumi Imamiya
Masa Inakage
Naota Inamoto
Kansei Iwata
Katsumi Kanasaki
Satoru Kawai
Alistair Kilgour

Tosiyasu L. Kunii
Kyu Jae Lee
Mamoru Maekawa
Benoit B. Mandelbrot
Martti Mantyla
Shunji Mori
Naomasa Nakajima
Eihachiro Nakamae
Hiroshi Nakamura
Tadao Nakamura
Ikuo Nishioka
Tsukasa Noma
Nobuo Ohbo
Naohiro Oshima
D. Rambaud
Paolo Sabella
Hanan Samet
Isaac D. Scherson
Yasuto Shirai
Yukari Shirota

Yasuzo Suto
Tapio Takala
Kojun Terai
Daniel Thalmann
Nadia Magnenat-Thalmann
Stephen Todd
Robet E. Webber
Carl L. Williams
Tony C. Woo
John. R. Woodwark
Brian Wyvill
Geoff Wyvill
Masakazu Yamada
Fujio Yamaguchi
Kazunori Yamaguchi
Hiroto Yasuura
Hiroyuki Yoshida
Y. Yuan